The Rise of Mass Advertising

The Rise of Mass Advertising

Law, Enchantment, and the Cultural Boundaries of British Modernity

ANAT ROSENBERG

Great Clarendon Street, Oxford, OX2 6DP,
United Kingdom

Oxford University Press is a department of the University of Oxford.
It furthers the University's objective of excellence in research, scholarship,
and education by publishing worldwide. Oxford is a registered trade mark of
Oxford University Press in the UK and in certain other countries

© Anat Rosenberg 2022

The moral rights of the author have been asserted

First Edition published in 2022

Impression: 1

All rights reserved. No part of this publication may be reproduced, stored in
a retrieval system, or transmitted, in any form or by any means, without the
prior permission in writing of Oxford University Press, or as expressly permitted
by law, by licence or under terms agreed with the appropriate reprographics
rights organization. Enquiries concerning reproduction outside the scope of the
above should be sent to the Rights Department, Oxford University Press, at the
address above

You must not circulate this work in any other form
and you must impose this same condition on any acquirer

Published in the United States of America by Oxford University Press
198 Madison Avenue, New York, NY 10016, United States of America

British Library Cataloguing in Publication Data

Data available

Library of Congress Control Number: 2022935027

ISBN 978–0–19–285891–7

DOI: 10.1093/oso/9780192858917.001.0001

Printed and bound by
CPI Group (UK) Ltd, Croydon, CR0 4YY

Links to third party websites are provided by Oxford in good faith and
for information only. Oxford disclaims any responsibility for the materials
contained in any third party website referenced in this work.

To Ariel

Acknowledgements

This book has been a terrific journey. Controversies over advertising are full of humour and creativity in all their variety, yet the long nineteenth century in Britain remains unrivalled on these fronts, as an entire culture sharpened its intellectual and aesthetic wits, and its powers of imagination, over the rise of a new system of capitalism. Travelling through this culture to understand what advertising was, has done, and has been done with, opened up vistas I had not expected.

I had time for the journey with a prolonged stay in Cambridge, as a sabbatical became three years. I am thankful to Reichman University for giving me the time off teaching and duties, and to the University of Cambridge for generously hosting me. I am especially grateful to Peter Mandler, whose hospitality at Cambridge's Faculty of History was matched only by his generous sharing of knowledge and insightful readings of chapters as I worked through them. I am also grateful to Wolfson College, which hosted me for two years, and to Emmanuel College, and particularly my wonderful host Larry Klein, for the last year (minus Covid). At the University of London, the Institute of Advanced Legal Studies hosted me for two years and offered a space for thought during many visits to London archives.

Friends, colleagues, journal editors, and reviewers have read parts or all of this study over the period, agreed to discuss dilemmas, and offered precious advice. Occasionally, the mention of a source, an idea, or even a term were fantastic leads that shaped this work, and I remain grateful for those sparks. Nothing like the history of advertising shows how critically our mind depends on them. I am thankful to Einat Albin, Victoria Barnes, Marija Bartl, Lionel Bently, Leora Bilsky, Michael Birnhack, Stephen Bogle, Eli Cook, Jospeh David, Jennifer Davis, Lindsay Farmer, Joshua Getzler, Ben Griffin, Timothy Hickman, Andrew Hobbs, Mark Hampton, Dirk Hartog, Jason Hill, Amos Israel, Mirthe Jiwa, Mario Keller, Chloë Kennedy, Roy Kreitner, Shelly Kreiczer-Levy, Assaf Likhovski, Sharon Morein-Zamir, Moran Ofir, Frank Palmeri, Daniel Pick, Stav Rosenzweig, Yair Sagi, David Schorr, Galia Schneebaum, Vanessa Ruth Schwartz, Adam Shinar, Chantal Stebbings, Lesley Steinitz, Simon Stern, David Sugarman, Astrid Van den Bossche, James Taylor, Noam Yuran, Sharon Zmigrod, and participants at a number of excellent forums: the Critical Legal Studies conference, Milton Keynes, 2018; the Sexuality and Consumption—18th Century to 21st Century Conference, the University of Vienna, 2018; the American Studies Seminar, Princeton University, 2018; the Institute of Advanced Legal Studies Fellows Seminar, 2018; the Modern Cultural History Seminar, the University of

Cambridge, 2018; the Nineteenth-Century Seminar, the University of Cambridge, 2018; the Interdisciplinary Nineteenth-Century Studies Conference, Roma Tre, 2018; Hagley Museum and Library Conference on Commercial Pictures and the Arts and Technics of Visual Persuasion, 2019; the University of Edinburgh Legal History Seminar, 2019; the Oxford Seminar for Socio-Legal Studies, 2019; the Living with Machines Seminar, the British Library, 2019; the History Seminar at the University of Lancaster, 2019; the Centre for Transformative Private Law Seminar, the University of Amsterdam, 2020; the International Association of Consumer Law Seminar, 2020; the Legal History Seminar on Commercial Morality and Identity, 2020; the Science Abroad group, the University of Cambridge, 2020; the Law Faculty Seminar, Reichman University, 2020; the Israeli History and Law Association Conference, 2020; the American Comparative Literature Association Conference, Seminar on Legal Forms, 2021; –the Interdisciplinary International Conference on Censorship, National Taiwan University, 2022; the Rubin Forum, Department of History, Tel Aviv University, 2022; the Department of English Seminar, University of Haifa, 2022; the Law and History workshop, Tel Aviv University, 2022; the Law Faculty Seminar, Sapir College, 2022; the Law Faculty Seminar, Hebrew University, 2022; the Legal History Seminar, University of Galsgow, 2022; the Law Faculty Seminar, Bar Ilan University, 2022; and the Berg Forum for Research Students in History and Law, 2022. The wonderful group of Israeli women at Cambridge willingly chimed in on definitional conundrums and other stumbling blocks along the way in our joint network, and I remain grateful for their help and curiosity. The Research Network on Enchnatment in the History of Capitalism I established with Astrid Van den Bossche in the last stages of research for this book, has and continues to inform my thinking about enchantment.[1]

In archives I often met staff for whose professional help, not least when the pandemic struck, I am deeply grateful. I thank Heather Jardine, St Bride Foundation; Kathy Young, the Squire Law Library at the University of Cambridge; Alison Zammer, Cambridge University Library; Alistair Moir, the History of Advertising Trust; Julie Anne Lambert, the John Johnson Collection of Ephemera, Bodleian Libraries, Oxford; Jeremy Parrett, Manchester Metropolitan University Special Collections Library; and John Arthur, the National Railway Museum, York. I am also grateful to Aisling Towl, whose help with British Library sources was indispensable for the last phases of this research; to Yael Nesher and Miri Apel Herz, the Marc Rich Library at Reichman University, who assisted me during those challenging phases with material I could not access directly; and to Noya Shelkovitz for bibliographical assistance.

---

[1] https://economic-enchantments.net/

This book is published with the support of the Israel Science Foundation. Research and publication were also supported by the Gerda Henkel Foundation, and by the David Berg Foundation Institute for Law and History at Tel Aviv University. I am grateful to all of them.

Chapters or parts of Chapters 2, 3, 4, and 5 have appeared in articles in the *Law & History Review*, *The Journal of Legal History*, *American Journal of Legal History*, and *Law & Social Inquiry*. An article drawing on Chapter 7 is forthcoming in *Cultural History*.

Last but not least, my family, far and near, supported me with patience and faith. Ariel, Nitzan, Nitai, and Eylon agreed to relocate and join the journey. They have had their share of challenges in consequence, and I hope also of the adventure. They certainly know about advertising more than they ever wished, and I love them for that too. This book is dedicated to Ariel, partner in all.

Anat Rosenberg

August 2022

Contents

List of Illustrations and Credits	xiii
Introduction	1
1. Mass Advertising's Appeals: Market Enchantments	35
2. Advertising and News: The Fetters of the Commercial Press	94
3. Advertising and Art: The Hoarding as Aesthetic Property	136
4. Advertising and Science: The Exaggerations of Quackery	195
5. Puffery: Exaggeration as Doctrine	238
6. Gambling, Indecency, and the Bounded Realms of Enchantment	263
7. The Market Enchanters: Professional Advertisers' Self-Branding	320
Conclusion	359
Bibliography	363
Index	393

List of Illustrations and Credits

Figures

0.1a *Illustrated London News*, advertisement page, 1873. 4
© Illustrated London News Ltd/Mary Evans.

0.1b *Illustrated London News*, advertisement page, 1896. 5
© Illustrated London News Ltd/Mary Evans.

0.2 Top: F.H. Roberts, hoarding at Grangetown. *Advertising News*, 16 December 1904, 28. Bottom: Rotary Illuminated Advertising, *c.*1907. 6
Top: © British Library Board LOU.LON 916 (1904). Bottom: private collection.

0.3 Left: G. Van Volen Hair Merchant & Ornamental human hair manufacturer, trade card, *c.*1876. Right: Singer Manufacturing Company, sewing machine advertisement, 1894. 6
© Bodleian Library, University of Oxford: John Johnson Collection. Left: Beauty Parlour (43) © 2008 Proquest. Right: Sewing Cottons and Sewing Machines (44a) © 2009 Proquest.

0.4a Arthur Norris, sandwichman caricature. *Punch*, 17 January 1912, 43. 8
© British Library Board HIU.LD34A.

0.4b A London boardman. John Thomson and Adolphe Smith, *Victorian London Street Life in Historic Photographs*, vol. 1 (London: Sampson Low, Marston, Searle and Rivington, 1877). 8
LSE Digital Liberary. Creative Commons Attribution-NonCommercial-ShareAlike (CC BY-NC-SA 3.0).

1.1 John O'Connor, *From Pentonville Road Looking West: Evening*, 1884. 43
© Museum of London 52.87.

1.2 George Earl, *Going North*, 1875. 45
Wigan Museum Collections.

1.3 George Earl, *Going North*, 1893, third version. 45
Courtesy of the Art Renewal Center® www.artrenewal.org

1.4 Abraham Solomon, *Second Class—the parting*: 'Thus part we rich in sorrow, parting poor', 1854. 50
Yale Center for British Art, Paul Mellon Collection, B1987.26.4. Public Domain.

1.5 Cox & Co., London, Next-of-Kin advertisement. *Exeter and Plymouth Gazette*, 6 February 1886, 1. 51
© British Library Board. All rights reserved. With thanks to The British Newspaper Archive (www.britishnewspaperarchive.co.uk).

xiv LIST OF ILLUSTRATIONS AND CREDITS

1.6 *Weekly Dispatch,* locations of buried 'treasure'. *Weekly Dispatch,*
    24 January 1904, 5. 53
    © British Library Board MFM.MLD38.

1.7 *Weekly Dispatch,* buried treasure medallion. *Weekly Dispatch,*
    17 January 1904, 5. 53
    © British Library Board MFM.MLD38.

1.8 Frederick Paynter, employment advertisement. *Irish News and Belfast
    Morning News,* 25 May 1905, 2. 55
    © British Library Board. The British Newspaper Archive.

1.9 *Weekly Dispatch,* a clue for Brighton. *Weekly Dispatch,* 17 January 1904, 5. 57
    © British Library Board MFM.MLD38.

1.10 Liebig advertisement. *Bexhill-on-Sea Observer,* 21 July 1900, 3. 58
    © British Library Board. The British Newspaper Archive.

1.11 George Binet, detectives advertisement. *Bath Chronicle,* 15 September 1892, 4. 59
    © British Library Board. The British Newspaper Archive.

1.12 Arthur Pointing, Invisible Elevators advertisement. *Illustrated Chips,*
    3 October 1896, 6. 62
    Cambridge University Library.

1.13 Arthur Pointing, Invisible Elevators illustrated advertisement. *Pick-Me-Up,*
    14 November 1896, 112. 63
    National Library of Scotland (https://creativecommons.org/licenses/by/4.0/).

1.14 Pointing and his customers in court. *Penny Illustrated Paper,* 3 July 1897, 6. 64
    © British Library Board. The British Newspaper Archive.

1.15 Advertisement page, *Bath Chronicle,* 15 September 1892, 4. 67
    © British Library Board. The British Newspaper Archive.

1.16 Tom Browne, *Beauty and the Barge* play advertisement, *c.*1905. 69
    © Victoria and Albert Museum, London, S.541-1996.

1.17 Anonymous album.
    Private collection. 71

1.18 Anonymous album.
    Private collection. 71

1.19 Anonymous album.
    Private collection. 72

1.20 Anonymous album.
    Private collection. 72

1.21 Anonymous Victorian scrapbook. 73
    With kind permission of private owners.

1.22 Scrapbook contributed by the Institute of Advertising Professionals,
    source unknown.
    History of Advertising Trust. 74

1.23 Anonymous scrapbook. 75
    © Sir Harry Page Collection of Scrap Albums and Common Place Books at Manchester
    Met University Special Collections. Scrapbook 103.

LIST OF ILLUSTRATIONS AND CREDITS   xv

1.24 Anonymous scrapbook.
      With kind permission of private owners.   76
1.25 George William Joy, *The Bayswater Omnibus*, 1895.   77
      © Museum of London 29.166.
1.26 *Strand Magazine* advertisement. *Advertisers' Review*, 26 August 1901, 4. 81
      © British Library Board LOU.LON 401 (1901).
1.27 George Halley, prize competition advertisement. *Penny Illustrated
      Paper*, 17 January 1885, 48.   84
      © British Library Board. The British Newspaper Archive.
1.28 Charles Hanford, 'link' bicycle advertisement. *Illustrated Police News*,
      1 December 1900, 10.   85
      © British Library Board.The British Newspaper Archive.
1.29 Anonymous scrapbook.   89
      © Sir Harry Page Collection of Scrap Albums and Common Place Books at
      Manchester Met University Special Collections. Scrapbook 157.
2.1   *Evening News*, front page, 26 July 1881.   94
      Wikimedia Commons.
2.2   Evading the advertisement duty. *Punch*, 11 January 1845, 26.   112
      © British Library Board HIU.LD34A.
2.3   Brinsmead advertisement. *Graphic*, 3 August 1889, 153.   116
      © Illustrated London News Ltd/Mary Evans.
2.4   Brinsmead 'puff paragraph'. *Era*, 14 November 1885, 7.   117
      © British Library Board. The British Newspaper Archive.
2.5   Ridicule of the matinee hat. *Judy*, 31 March 1897, 155.   122
      National Library of Scotland (https://creativecommons.org/licenses/by/4.0/).
2.6   Selfridge combining advertisements and editorials. *Penny Illustrated
      Paper*, 15 March 1913, 11.   128
      © British Library Board.
2.7   The *Times* committing to stricter separations between advertisements
      and news. *Times*, 29 October 1913, 8.   132
      The *Times*/News Licensing.
3.1   An Irish Bill-Posting Station. Clarence Moran, *The Business of
      Advertising* (London: Methuen & Co., 1905).   136
      Cambridge University Library Misc.7.90.1529.
3.2   Bovril Magic Lantern Slides, *c*.1900.   141
      Lesley Steinitz, private collection, by kind permission.
3.3   Sheffield's Ltd, a billposting firm. *Progressive Advertising*, 2 May 1902, 50. 142
      © British Library Board LOU.LON 954 (1902).
3.4   William Henry Fox Talbot, Nelson's Column under construction,
      Trafalgar Square, April 1844.   151
      The Met Museum, 2009.279. Public Domain.

xvi LIST OF ILLUSTRATIONS AND CREDITS

3.5 An old bill-posting station. Clarence Moran, *The Business of Advertising* (London: Methuen & Co., 1905). 152
Cambridge University Library Misc.7.90.1529.

3.6 John Orlando Parry, *A London Street Scene*, 1835. 153
Wikimedia Commons.

3.7 R.T. Powney, Wall-posting as it is and as it should be. William Smith, *Advertise: How? When? Where?* (London: Routledge, Warne and Routledge, 1863). 154

3.8 Keighley hoarding. *Billposter*, April 1897. 156
© British Library Board LOU.LON 983 (1897).

3.9 Horwich hoarding. *Billposter*, July 1897. 157
© British Library Board LOU.LON 983 (1897).

3.10 Hoarding, *Placard*, April 1912. 158
© British Library Board LOU.LON 790 (1912).

3.11 Hoarding, *Placard*, April 1912. 159
© British Library Board LOU.LON 790 (1912).

3.12 Stall at the Advertisers Exhibition, Niagara Hall, London, 1899. *Billposter*, April 1899. 160
© British Library Board LOU.LON 711 (1899).

3.13 Redhill hoarding. *Billposter*, August 1911. 160
© British Library Board LOU.LON 798 (1911).

3.14 East Sheen hoarding. *Billposter*, August 1911. 161
© British Library Board LOU.LON 798 (1911).

3.15 Skipton hoarding. *Billposter*, July 1898. 162
© British Library LOU.LON 933 (1898).

3.16 Hoarding adornment. *Billposter*, June 1912. 163
© British Library Board LOU.LON 790 (1912).

3.17 Nottingham hoarding. *Billposter*, September 1897. 164
© British Library Board LOU.LON 983 (1897).

3.18 Grimsby hoarding. *Billposter*, August 1898. 164
© British Library LOU.LON 933 (1898).

3.19 Frederick Walker, *The Woman in White*, 1871. 166
© Tate, N02080, Creative Commons CC-BY-NC-ND 3.0 (unported) (https://www.tate.org.uk/art/artworks/walker-the-woman-in-white-n02080).

3.20 John Everett Millais, (artist), A. & F. Pears Ltd (publisher), *Bubbles*, c.1888 or 1889. 167
© Victoria and Albert Museum, London, E.224-1942.

3.21 The studio at Benson's advertising agency. S.H. Benson, *Force in Advertising* (1904). 168
Private collection.

3.22 Dudley Hardy, *The Geisha*, Daly's Theatre, 1896, Waterlow & Sons Printers. 169
© Victoria and Albert Museum, London S.965-1995.

3.23 Chadwick Rymer, *Charley's Aunt*, c.1892. 169
© Victoria and Albert Museum, London E.541-1939.

3.24 Map filed by the Borough of Margate, 1908. 176
National Archives HO45/10597.189.790/2.

3.25 Map filed by the Borough of Bromley, 1909. 177
National Archives HO45/10565.173.473/4.

3.26 Home Office official's recommendations on Newark's draft bylaws, 11 January 1913. 178
National Archives HO45/10640.205.460/9.

3.27 Beacon Hill photo submitted by the Council of Newark. 179
National Archives HO45/10640.205.460.

3.28 Evesham hoarding between Bengeworth Church and Bench Hill, 1904. 180
National Archives HO45/10697/233.030/7.

3.29 Evesham hoarding, 1904. 180
National Archives HO45/10697/233.030/7.

3.30 Evesham view, 1904. 181
National Archives HO45/10697/233.030/10.

3.31 The Beggarstaffs, Rowntree advertisement, c.1896. 184
© Victoria and Albert Museum, London E.713-1919.

3.32 Walter Hill & Co., London hoarding. *Billposter*, April 1901. 187
© British Library Board LOU.LON 482 (1901).

3.33 Illegitimate billposting on high-class architecture illustrated. *Billposter*, October 1888. 190
© British Library Board LOU.LON 282.

3.34 Advertising by the Great White Horse Hotel, Ipswich. *Billposter*, January 1913. 191
© British Library Board LOU.LON 743 (1913).

4.1 Russell and Sons., the first British airship, flown as an advertisement for Mellin's Food. *Illustrated Sporting and Dramatic News*, 27 September 1902, 24. 200
© Illustrated London News Ltd/Mary Evans.

4.2 Linley Sambourne, quackery caricature. *Punch*, 11 November 1893, 218. 205
Wellcome Collection: no. 14302i. Attribution 4.0 International (CC BY 4.0).

4.3 Vase presented to the owner of the *Pall Mall Gazette*. *Illustrated London News*, 17 August 1867, 12. 211
© Illustrated London News Ltd/Mary Evans.

4.4 Carbolic Smoke Ball, testimonials in advertisement, 1890. 220
© Bodleian Library, University of Oxford: John Johnson Collection: Patent Medicines 8 (33a) © 2008 Proquest.

4.5 Bile Bean, testimonials in advertisement, 1902. 221
© Bodleian Library, University of Oxford: John Johnson Collection: Patent Medicines 8 (15a) © 2008 Proquest.

xviii   LIST OF ILLUSTRATIONS AND CREDITS

4.6   Mellin's Food, testimonials in advertisement, c.1890–1900.   222
      © Bodleian Library, University of Oxford: John Johnson Collection: Window Bills
      and Advertisements 6 (33) © 2009 Proquest.

4.7   Canning & Co. Lancashire, Beecham, 'worth a guinea a box' advertising
      song sheet, c.1890–1910.   225
      Wellcome Collection: Drug advertising ephemera, box 14. Public Domain Mark.

4.8   Indian Oculitsts, testimonial advertisement. *Freeman's Journal*,
      7 April 1892, 8.   232
      © British Library Board. The British Newspaper Archive.

4.9   Electropathic & Zander Institute by Cornelius Bennett Harness,
      magazine insert advertisement, c.1890.   233
      Wellcome Collection: Clothing ephemera, box 1. Public Domain Mark.

4.10 William Henry Hawkins, guaranteed cure advertisement. *Stonehaven
      Journal*, 28 November 1901, 4.   235
      © British Library Board. The British Newspaper Archive.

5.1   Carbolic Smoke Ball Co., advertisement. *Pall Mall Gazette*,
      13 November 1891, 4.   247
      © British Library Board. The British Newspaper Archive.

5.2   Bile Beans competing labels. *Bile Bean Manufacturing
      Co. v. Davidson* (1906) 22 RPC 553.   249

5.3   Bile Bean Manufacturing Co., pamphlet advertisement, 1900s.   250
      © Bodleian Library, University of Oxford: John Johnson Collection:
      Patent Medicines 8 (24) © 2008 Proquest.

5.4   Bile Bean Manufacturing Co., cure promises, magazine insert
      advertisement, 1902.   253
      Wellcome Collection: Drug advertising ephemera, box 18. Public Domain Mark.

5.5   Bovril and influenza, advertisement cuttings. *Knaresborough Post*,
      12 April 1902; *Speaker*, 26 February 1898, 279; *Judy*, 20 March 1901.   256
      Left: © British Library Board. The British Newspaper Archive. Centre and right:
      Images published with permission of ProQuest. Further reproduction is prohibited
      without permission.

5.6   Mellin's Food, magazine insert advertisement, 1900s.   258
      History of Advertising Trust HAT62/1/62.

6.1   *Pearson's Weekly*'s missing-word competition. *Pearson's Weekly*,
      10 December 1892, 323.   271
      © British Library Board. The British Newspaper Archive.

6.2   *Pearson's Weekly*'s missing word paragraph. *Pearson's Weekly*,
      10 December 1892, 331.   271
      © British Library Board. The British Newspaper Archive.

6.3   *Pick-Me-Up* art competition, 22 October 1892, 55.   272
      National Library of Scotland (https://creativecommons.org/licenses/by/4.0/).

LIST OF ILLUSTRATIONS AND CREDITS xix

6.4 Edward Cook & Co., soap competition advertisement.
Ampthill & District News, 29 July 1905, 3. 275
© British Library Board. The British Newspaper Archive.

6.5 Leeds Laboratory Co., limerick advertisement. *Hull Daily Mail*,
31 January 1908, 8. 278
© British Library Board. The British Newspaper Archive

6.6 Zaeo the 'moral marionette, and the vigilantes on their way to the London
City Council.' *St Stephen's Review* presentation cartoon. 287
Getty Images 90776106.

6.7 Adverts for abortifacients? Top: *Illustrated London News*, 27 November
1886, 596; Bottom: *Jackson's Oxford Journal*, 28 December 1895, 2. 292
Top: © Illustrated London News Ltd/Mary Evans. Bottom: © British Library
Board. The British Newspaper Archive.

6.8 Chrimes brothers, advertisement for miraculous female tabules.
Royal Cornwall Gazette, 7 July 1898, 2. 294
© British Library Board. The British Newspaper Archive.

6.9 Chrimes brothers' blackmail letter. 295
National Archives HO144/562/A67016B.

6.10 Posters wreaking havoc. *Punch*, 3 December 1887, 262. 297
© British Library Board.

6.11 Censored poster, 1902. Maurice Rickards, *Banned Posters*
(London: Evelyn, Adams & Mackay, 1969), 14. 300

6.12 Mosnar Yendis, censored poster. *Poster*, September 1899, 5. 302
Collection ReclameArsenaal (https://ddec1-0-en-ctp.trendmicro.com:443/wis/
clicktime/v1/query?url=www.iaddb.org&umid=8b59687c-aef5-4af1-b676-
827dd8f72163&auth=64470b2ec4c75fdcd3614d4ab3a31bff290a61d3-
2dd7b08af64410292d2bc90030c81d7c19d2783a).

6.13 G. Lackeray, Nestlé poster. 303
© Getty Images 526795484.

6.14 The horrors of the cross. United Billposters' Association, *Posters Condemned
by Censorship Committee of the United Billposters Association* (London:
Burton, c.1904). 304
National Gallery of Canada, NC1807 G7 U63.

6.15 Advertisement for remedy to remove all obstructions and irregularities.
Illustrated Police News, 2 October 1897, 10. 306
© British Library Board. The British Newspaper Archive.

6.16 Frank H. Roberts, hoarding. c.1900s. 312
© Bodleian Library, University of Oxford: John Johnson collection: Publicity box 5.

6.17 Three of 'the least objectionable' posters censored by the Billposters
Censorship Committee according to Cyril Sheldon, *Advertising World*,
September 1909, 386. United Billposters' Association, *Posters Condemned by
Censorship Committee of the United Billposters Association* (London: Burton,
c.1904). 314

National Gallery of Canada, NC1807 G7 U63.

6.18 Censored posters. United Billposters' Association, *Posters Condemned by Censorship Committee of the United Billposters Association* (London: Burton, *c.*1904). 315
National Gallery of Canada, NC1807 G7 U63.

7.1 Pears optical illusion advert. Pears scrapbook, source unknown. 336
History of Advertising Trust.

7.2 Mather & Crowther, advertisement for agency services. *Practical Advertising* (London: Mather & Crowther, 1905–6). 339
History of Advertising Trust.

7.3 T.B. Browne's agency, checking department and newspaper filing room. William Stead, *The Art of Advertising: Its Theory and Practice Fully Described* (London: T.B. Browne, Ltd, 1899), 67, 69. 343

7.4 Mather and Crowther's agency, images of specialized departments. *Practical Advertising*, January 1903, ix. 344
History of Advertising Trust.

7.5 Nestlé's cats advertisement, *c.*1890s. 352
© Bodleian Library, University of Oxford: John Johnson Collection: Food 2 (30)
© 2009 Proquest.

7.6 British Vacuum Cleaner Company booklet of poster adaptations, 1906–9. 355
© Bodleian Library, University of Oxford: John Johnson Collection: Publicity box 1.

Graphs

0.1 Appearance of 'age of advertisement' in British newspapers. BNA data as of January 2021. 7

5.1 Proportion (in decimal fractions) of auction advertisements to advertisements containing the letter 'a' over time. BNA data as of April 2019. 243

5.2 Trends of references in the press to the 'puffing system' and the 'advertising system'. BNA data as of May 2019. 245

5.3 Gale's Topic Finder Tool, October 2017. 251
Gale (https://support.gale.com/doc/galetools-video6).

6.1 Relative change in the occurrence of advertisements with 'female' + 'remedy' compared with advertisements with 'remedy'. BNA data as of June 2019. 310

Introduction

Advertising's Modernity

It is in the skies and on the ground; it swells as the flag in the breeze, and it sets its seal on the pavement; it is on the water, on the steamboat wharf, and under the water in the Thames tunnel; it roosts on the highest chimneys; it sparkles in coloured letters on street lamps; it forms the prologue of all the newspapers, and the epilogue of all the books; it breaks in upon us with the sound of trumpets, and it awes us in the silent sorrow of the Hindoo. There is no escaping from the advertisement, for it travels with you in the omnibuses, in the railway carriages, and on the paddle-boxes of the steamers.

Max Schlesinger, 1853[1]

So felt the German tourist and author Max Schlesinger in his mid-nineteenth-century visit to London. The advertisement, he concluded, is omnipresent. Brits could not agree more, and as the century progressed, not only in London. Theirs, they knew, was the Age of Advertisement, which marked a distinct kind of life form. As one commentator expressed it towards the close of the next decade, 'the real and commercial system of advertising now carried on to an extent that puzzles comprehension...may be looked upon in its universality as one of the most extraordinary proofs of the mighty change which has taken place in the manners, morals, and doings of the civilized world.'[2] The change was certainly mighty. Between the 1840s and 1914, advertising became a mass phenomenon and an immersive experience. Its unprecedented geographical and social penetration in this period, beyond urban centres and below the middle classes, its material enveloping of multiple environments as Schlesinger observed with dismay, and its routinization, all made it a presence that captivated and disturbed observers across social divides.

Many features of advertising circa 1840–1914 were new, and felt new. Manufacturers and service providers became the dominant advertisers, rather

---

[1] Schlesinger, *Saunterings*, 23. The comment on the Hindoo referred to a man who distributed religious tracts. Schlesinger thought that he was better off in his 'primitive nudity among his native palm-forests, adoring the miracles of nature in the Sun'. The reference to religious competition in a commentary on advertising was tuned to questions of enchantment discussed below.

[2] 'Grand Force', 1869, 382.

than wholesalers and retailers whom the previous century would have identified as key. While advertisers' identities changed, so did their audiences, for they could now reach consumers of all classes and places, and regularly, where in earlier decades advertising to lower classes and beyond commercial centres was low in intensity and tended to occur in peaks.[3] Style, size, content, quantities, and media all changed. Contemporaries observed how images expanded in complexity, overall occurrence, and size (in an inverse relationship to the rise in literacy[4]), and how variety in rhetorical and visual style left no cultural association untapped. Variety in content was 'perhaps as astonishing as the number of advertisements...'[5] The march of commodities appeared limitless, and with it the incidence of brands. Advertising tropes, images, and gestures entered the languages of political and social debate, satire and caricature, fiction, poetry, painting, and photography. Comments and rhymes about advertising, and sustained efforts to theorize and historicize it, multiplied.[6]

---

[3] On early modern advertising, see McKendrick et al., *Birth of a Consumer Society*; Styles, 'Manufacturing, Consumption'; Berg and Clifford, 'Selling Consumption'. See also accounts of trends before and after the mid-nineteenth century in Nevett, *Advertising in Britain*; Elliott, *History of English Advertising*; Turner, *Shocking History*; Presbrey, *History and Development of Advertising*; and reviews in Church, 'Advertising Consumer Goods'; Hawkins, 'Marketing History'; Beard, 'History of Advertising'. For a historiographical discussion of change in class reach during the nineteenth century and criticism of the overemphasis on the middle classes in this period, see Kelley, *Soap and Water*, ch. 3. Studies of nineteenth-century advertising are discussed below and throughout this book.

The term 'consumer', which I will often use, was familiar in this era. The *OED* confirms its use from the late seventeenth century in the sense of 'a person who uses up a commodity; a purchaser of goods or services, a customer. Frequently opposed to producer'; see 'consumer', *OED Online*. However, this use did not usually carry the ideological meaning of consumerism, coexisted with and was even overshadowed by other terms like buyer, purchaser, and customer or, in the context of advertisements, reader.

[4] On variations in textual literacy, see Vincent, *Rise of Mass Literacy*.

[5] *Quarterly Review*, June 1855, 222.

[6] Encyclopaedic representations are a case in point. In its seventh edition of 1842, *Encyclopaedia Britannica* carried a single-sentence definition of 'advertisement' that referred to information provided to a party interested in an affair. In the eighth edition, 1853, the definition spanned almost a full column and addressed the commercial contexts of trade and newspapers. It was also engaged in advocacy against the advertisement duty, more on which in Chapter 2. The ninth edition of 1878 was about the same length, celebrated the repeal of the duty, and added etymological references. In the tenth edition, 1902, the category was over ten columns long and added 'advertising' after 'advertisement'. Here we find an origins myth in which advertising is the mode of rational communication underwriting the shift from primitive barter to anonymous markets. The author also divided it into classes by media and reviewed business development, social controversy, and legal regulation. A barrister joined the same author for the eleventh edition of 1910, when a review of foreign laws was also included.

Advertising gradually changed its meaning to what one commentator called a 'limited commercial sense' relating to the sale of goods. Russell, *Commercial Advertising*, 1919, 48 n. 1. Older meanings, relating generally to making something known, lingered, as could be seen for example in the first legal treatise on advertising law, Jones, *Law Relating to Advertisements*; see also Slauter, 'Periodicals', 144.

The 1878 edition of *Encyclopaedia Britannica* included also historical references from 1843 and 1855, which reflected a broader scene of mushrooming of historical narratives for advertising. Sampson, *History of Advertising*, 1874, was a first book-length account, although preceded by the more narrowly defined Larwood and Hotten, *History of Signboards*, 1866. Books were surrounded by shorter narratives that placed advertising in time. The prevalent narrative, promoted primarily but not exclusively by industry actors, neutralized advertising as a universal and irrepressible human instinct, a protean force. Advertising was therefore found in all historical periods. Commentators found adverts in antiquity and brought evidence from around the world. This flourish was set up against the prevalent sense that advertising was new and wild. While many narratives acknowledged that the forms, scale,

Archives accumulated.[7] Advertising emerged as a field as well as a profession, with training options, dedicated publications, an internal division of labour, trade associations, social clubs, and expanding international networks.

The rise of advertising was concurrent with mass consumption, evinced in a spike in both demand and supply. In the second half of the nineteenth century, growth in the supply of goods kept pace with population growth, which had doubled, and from the end of the century supply outstripped it. Asset ownership became more common, real income per head doubled and doubled again in the first half of the twentieth century. Mass production in the wake of the industrial revolution—which drove a need to differentiate standardized products, retail growth, the commercialization of leisure, and the geographical and social expansion of consumer credit—were all part of this transformation. All this was also tied with the broad picture of the British Empire. Trade policies opened up colonial and overseas markets for British manufactures, in the shaping of which advertising played a critical role. Concurrently, the expanding offer of goods in the domestic market was itself enabled by colonial control, and traded on the images of empire and its exoticism popularized by advertising.[8]

Mass advertising drew on advances in commercial print, which attained huge heterogeneous audiences from the mid-nineteenth century, rendering texts and images potentially more influential than ever before—a mediamorphosis.[9] Its main forms were press adverts[10] (Figures 0.1a, 0.1b), outdoor posters (Figure 0.2), and printed ephemera (Figure 0.3): brochures, pamphlets, and cards distributed in shops, on streets, as inserts in press publications, door-to-door, and through the post that was itself revolutionized in the same years. However, print was also set in a context of more expansive promotional efforts. Advertisers distributed all kinds of brand-name carriers. Alongside print carriers like musical sheets, stamps, or year books were hosts of things, from town clocks through toys and coins to suits, to say nothing of model villages like Bourneville and Port Sunlight that experimented with

---

and systemic qualities of their era were new, they characterized critical commentary as reactionary, coming from social classes who had historically enjoyed exclusive access to marks of distinction. For example, Stead, *Art of Advertising*, 1899.

[7] For example, in the British Museum. *Advertisers' Review*, 1 October 1900, 5.

[8] See generally, Benson, *Rise of Consumer Society*, chs 1–2; Gurney, *Making of Consumer Culture*. The periodization and causes of consumption, and particularly the idea of a consumer revolution, are contested. However, the drama of the second half of the nineteenth century for the concept of mass consumption is generally conceded. For a review of the historiographical debate, see Trentmann, *Empire of Things*. On the low participation of working classes in expansions of consumption until the mid-nineteenth century, see generally Horrell, 'Consumption, 1700–1870'. As Erika Rappaport demonstrates regarding the role of advertising, its history needs to move from the periphery to the centre of commodity studies and world history. Rappaport, *Thirst for Empire*.

[9] Nead, *Victorian Babylon*, 154; Plunkett and King, *Victorian Print Media*, 1. The term 'mediamorphosis' is Roger Fidler's.

[10] Throughout this book I use 'advert/s' alongside 'advertisement/s'. 'Advert' and 'ad' were familiar in the period discussed, and the dignity of colloquialism was contested, as it still is. For example, '"Ads" or "Advertisements"', *Advertisers' Review*, 8 November 1902, 10.

Figure 0.1a *Illustrated London News*, advertisement page, 1873.

Figure 0.1b *Illustrated London News*, advertisement page, 1896. Images became more frequent and dominating.

Figure 0.2 Poster advertising created immersive environments. Top: F.H. Roberts, hoarding at Grangetown. *Advertising News*, 16 December 1904, 28. Bottom: Rotary Illuminated Advertising, *c*.1907.

Figure 0.3 Printed ephemera circulated in large numbers. Left: G. Van Volen Hair Merchant & Ornamental human hair manufacturer, trade card, *c*.1876. Right: Singer Manufacturing Company, sewing machine advertisement, 1894. Additional text would appear on the other side or pages.

the implications of brands.¹¹ Advertisers provided entertainment, organized games and distributed dream prizes. They transformed structures, bodies, and environments as they tested their potential as media: drop-curtains, street lamps, statues, pavements, bridges, boats, buses, trains, carriages, balloons, airships, animals, and humans. The historical sandwichman, as he was colloquially known, was an icon of misery (Figure 0.4a, 0.4b), but people were also enlisted in more exciting ways to advertising performance, for example in games, theatrical performance, and rides on land, water, and in the air.

Far from a 'transparent background that had always been taken for granted', as the art critic Clement Greenberg once argued, the rise of mass advertising was experienced like a cultural earthquake.¹² It disrupted basic perceptions, which have since become paradigms of modernity. One was the idea that culture was organized according to distinct and identifiable fields of knowledge, experience, and authority. Advertising trod and traded on the claims of some the era's most celebrated fields: news, art, science, and religiously

---

¹¹ On the complexity of company towns and their fusion of production and consumption, see Trentmann, *Empire of Things*, ch. 12. See also Outka, *Consuming Traditions*, ch. 2.

¹² Greenberg discussed kitsch, in which he included advertising. Greenberg, 'Avant-Garde and Kitsch', 9.

Graph 0.1 shows search results for the term 'age of advertisement' in the British Newspaper Archive database. Its high incidence is one of many indications of the cultural attention to advertising as a novel phenomenon. The data should be treated with caution. Consistency in the database's representation of newspapers over time is unknown, therefore apparent change may reflect the scope of newspapers scanned for each decade, although clearly the absolute rise in newspaper numbers after the mid-nineteenth century means that there was a rise in term use too (for data on newspapers, see Chapter 2). Another weakness concerning change over time is that a search for a particular term is insensitive to linguistic change. As we will see in Chapter 5, a change from 'puffery' to 'advertising' typified the nineteenth century. Lastly, results include false positives and negatives, hence numbers are inaccurate. With these caveats, the high numbers for the period examined in this book, in the hundreds of thousands, do capture at least a discursive tendency. It is confirmed by Google Ngram, although the peak there begins in the 1880s, which might be expected given the lag between newspapers and books (the Google Ngram corpus).

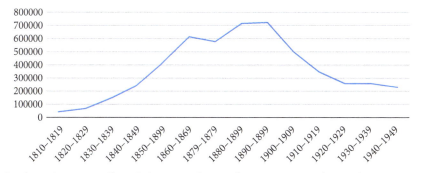

Graph 0.1 Appearance of 'age of advertisement' in British newspapers. BNA data as of January 2021.

Figure 0.4a Arthur Norris, sandwichman caricature. A sandwichman who had lost touch with his body asks a policeman to help him. *Punch*, 17 January 1912, 43.

Figure 0.4b A London boardman. John Thomson and Adolphe Smith, *Victorian London Street Life in Historic Photographs*, vol. 1 (London: Sampson Low, Marston, Searle and Rivington, 1877). Smith, a radical journalist, and Thomson, a photographer, described the job as a state of misery.

inflected morality, cast doubt on their cultural authority and undermined cultural boundaries. As advertising expanded, Brits debated problems of cultural organization. Where did advertising stop and art begin? What made news distinct from adverts? In what sense did scientists' knowledge of natural phenomena, particularly of the human body, differ from advertisers'? Could moralists concerned about gambling and indecency really tell where and when rational self-control failed?

In efforts to come to terms with the disruptive impact, contemporaries turned to the legal means and powers available to them. The central chapters of this book map debates concerned with the boundaries of advertising with news production, artistic creation, scientific exploration, and common morality, and examine how diverse actors mobilized law to assert their viewpoints and formalize them. These efforts implicated a wide variety of legal loci. They included courts, where a stream of cases addressed advertising. In criminal law, advertising was considered in a number of routes: in fraud cases, as consumers complained to state authorities and pressed charges against advertisers who had misrepresented wares and services, or did not deliver as they promised; in cases of damage to property and trespass, advertisers sought to create and protect new property rights in adverts and advertising spaces; and under criminal legislation against gambling and indecency, adverts were examined for violations of their prohibitions, often at the behest of civil-society organizations. In civil (or private) law, advertising occupied courts in breach of contract cases of two main types: suits by consumers against breaching advertisers, and suits between contracting actors along the advertising chain, such as advertising agents and media owners. Also in civil law, courts examined advertising under a number of tort law categories: in passing off suits, advertisers challenged the use of their identifying marks and words by competitors; in trade libel cases, competitors sought remedies for disparaging statements in comparative adverts; in defamation suits, advertisers tried to protect their reputations against disparaging comments by critics; under trespass, they attempted to create and protect property in advertisements and advertising spaces.[13] Alongside courts and in dialogue with them were additional loci of law that fed into public debates. During the era, the British parliament passed legislative reforms concerned with advertising in taxation, licensing, and specific market sectors such as sex-related medical adverts. Municipal authorities exercised administrative legal powers of town planning and business licensing to

---

[13] The cases studied in this book include some known High Court decisions, but also many that have not been addressed by advertising scholars, and occasionally, to the best of my knowledge, have not been addressed in any scholarship. Many cases were not formally reported and are therefore studied through informal press, trade, and private reports.

regulate advertising and respond to local demands about it. Meanwhile, industry and professional self-regulation involved censorship and ethical codes concerned with advertising. Industrial legal measures also involved trade-wide standardizations of legal policies concerning advertising contracts and standards of work by media owners and by advertisers. Such modes of legality interacted with adjudicative, legislative, and administrative legal power. This dizzying array of legal contexts is held together and examined in this book within the questions of field boundaries that occupied British culture.

Law, understood as a dynamic part of cultural negotiation rather than a predefined profession, discipline or institutional setting, became implicated in directing the system of advertising in the different media, defining approaches for analysing and understanding it, and determining its boundaries. Ultimately, by performing boundary work law shaped the status of advertising, which this book shows to have emerged as deeply conflicted: legal means constituted advertising as a legitimate and indeed indispensable system of modern life, but also as a disparaged, ridiculed and criticized one, considered suspect in epistemological and aesthetic terms.[14] Advertising was mainstreamed with legal means, but with the critical edge that guarded field boundaries.

While advertising generated a seemingly endless chain of challenges to cultural organization, it also revealed that enchantment was rampant in commercialized Britain. An array of experiences based in non-rational ontologies and a play of mystery, involving possibilities for metamorphoses, magical efficacy, animated environments, affective connections between humans and things, imaginary worlds and fantasies informing mundane life, multiplied. Advertising imbued everyday realities with qualities that might have been readily associated with supernatural powers in earlier periods, and therefore challenged the assumption that the world was becoming progressively disenchanted. This has since become another governing paradigm of modernity. Max Weber's influential theorization of modernity-as-disenchantment, offered just a few years after the period examined here, was intimately linked with a theory of the modern separation of fields, which described the emergence of distinct field-identities and rationalities. The history of advertising clarifies how closely concerns about enchantment and boundary problems cohered, as these themes revolved around advertising's relationship to rationalist values. The trouble was, and remains, that advertising was Janus faced. On the one hand, it was a proxy of the era's rationality. This book shows how it was theorized and justified as a means of disseminating information about the array of goods, services and

---

[14] The concept of 'boundary work' originates in the sociology of science, where Thomas Gieryn coined it to describe processes of demarcation of fields and meaning-making through differentiation. See Gieryn, *Cultural Boundaries*; and originally, Gieryn, 'Boundary-Work'.

opportunities on offer; as rationally assessed and technologically applied aesthetics that educated tastes and enhanced skills; and as a marketing tool that brought the benefits of applied science to the masses. On the other hand, advertising was also an agent of enchantment that fuelled imaginations, newly sensualized experience, and animated daily lives. As the opening chapter of *The Rise of Mass Advertising* shows, the expansion of advertising circa 1840–1914 involved enchanted experiences that challenged contemporaries' sense of reason and realism.

In these conditions, understandings of modernity generally and economic life specifically in terms of disenchantment required an active preservation, in which law had a crucial role to play. Legal treatments of advertising shared a persistent focus on its rationalizing elements, with questions of information, knowledge, education, and morality at the forefront of boundary work. The focus came necessarily with criticisms, because as a rationalizing force advertising was indeed limited. Meanwhile, a conceptualization of advertising's powers of enchantment was avoided. This historical pattern, found in multiple cultural legal loci, can be described as a legally supported disavowal of enchantment. While this was not a necessary feature of law as I explain below, it became a feature of its many uses in historical responses to advertising. This history suggests that disenchantment was not an inexorable process of the modern iron cage, but was also not, alternatively, just a wavering ideology. It was a historical struggle conducted with legal means. At stake was an active and wide-ranging normative enterprise in which legal powers and ideas sustained and disseminated the view of modernity-as-disenchantment despite—or because of—the prevalence of enchantment that advertising brought forth.

The Rise of Mass Advertising thus addresses the formative decades of mass advertising, and provides a first cultural legal study of its history, which operates on two dependent registers. One is the history of boundary work, in which advertising's cultural meanings and its organization were shaped dialectically vis-à-vis other cultural fields. In this process, the modern sense of field distinctions was preserved, while inferiorization and ridicule were encoded into an expanding capitalist culture. Each chapter tells a differently situated story, in which boundary work was performed within uniquely contextualized value systems, conceptual languages, material environments, and perceived stakes, involved a distinct set of actors, and relied on a distinct set of legal means. Therefore, each story can be read and in some cases has been, within other narratives, for example of urbanity, liberal governance, or scientific progress. Yet, to understand the history of advertising requires reading the concurrent performances together. They reveal how the problem of cultural boundaries became an urgent concern, how advertising was imagined through differentiation, and how in the process it attained a conflicted status as a legitimate and yet despised system of capitalist modernity.

A second register is the (hi)story of modern disenchantment. Here, the story addresses the legally supported disavowal of enchantment, manifest in the focus of boundary work on the rationalizing implications of advertising, and in repeated failures to conceptualize its enchanting ones. Again, it is the accumulation of debates despite different contexts that reveals the cultural drama. The closing chapter of this book brings the story, with its two registers, to its ironic close. Repeated criticisms of the rationalizing potential of advertising, coupled with the disavowal of its enchantments, meant that rationalizing claims by advertisers were closely policed while enchantment was left free from direct legal attention. The effect was to encourage advertising's enchantments. Uses of law, thus, were not ultimately disenchanting if we take the term to mean the actual disappearance of enchantment from social life. Critical views unwittingly liberated advertising from the strictures of rationalism, while disavowal implied an absence of conceptual language to address enchantment, and so advertising was left to its own magical devices. This dynamic finally encouraged professional advertisers to claim enchantment as their peculiar expertise. Toward the turn of the twentieth century, they began to self-brand as market enchanters capable of mastering consumer minds, a myth that has held incredible sway.

The two registers of *The Rise of Mass Advertising* together offer a new understanding of advertising history in terms of definitive problems of modernity, and of the central role of law in negotiating them. This book shows how, with the aid of law, advertising was organized, shaped, given meaning, and embedded in modernity, and as a system *of* modernity—a gruelling idea. It suggests that law was constitutive of advertising's modernity—by which I mean the formative period of advertising itself, and the modernity that advertising marked. The following discussion introduces the findings and arguments in more detail. I begin with modernity-as-disenchantment, within which questions of cultural boundaries unfolded. In conclusion I address this book's legal theory, methodology, and sources, and end with brief comments on choices of place and time.

Advertising and Disenchantment

Weber, Enchantment, and Advertising Scholarship

In his influential 1917 lecture in Munich, Weber described the modern ontological outlook of his time as one that rejected ideas of incalculable forces operative in daily life, and assumed the mastery of reason and a rational knowability of the conditions under which one lived. Unlike the savage, he argued, the modern did not need recourse to magical means. Mysterious powers had been replaced by technical means and calculations.¹⁵ Capitalism was crucial to Weber's tale as the primary culprit in the eclipse of the sacred, as Eugene McCarraher puts it. While he established affinities between protestant theology and the capitalist economy in *The Protestant Ethic and the Spirit of Capitalism*, the thesis saw capitalism as a disenchanting force that severed historical associations of commerce with magic, religion, and sacralized relationships.¹⁶ Enchantment's presence in the nineteenth century and later has ever since been a fact to be reckoned with. States of wonder, magical thinking, a dwelling in mysteries, searches for transfiguration, vital matter, subliminal communication, and powerful fantasy are part a broad array of experiences that historians have been documenting and rewriting into narratives of modernity. Revisionist efforts have picked up from the late twentieth century, challenging the Weberian account in historical scholarship on science, technology, art, philosophy, fringe religion, spiritualist movements, popular culture, and capitalism.

It is easy to place advertising scholarship within these frameworks. In one sense, advertising belongs to all of them because it cut across fields of culture as it drew on the authority of science as well as art, became a popular culture and prevalent reading matter, but was of course a commercial system hinging on new technologies, which occupied the critical juncture between production and consumption and came to seem as the *sine qua non* of the national and global economy of its time.¹⁷ And whether or not advertising scholarship has been geared to revise the narrative of disenchantment, it has long argued that advertising enchants us. To clarify the contributions of this book, it is worth first getting a sense of the ongoing flow of arguments.

We might begin with Raymond Williams's *Advertising: The Magic System*, 1961, which famously argued that advertising works not because society is too materialist but because it is not materialist enough, and therefore attaches symbolic meanings to objects. Williams recognized what Frank Trentmann describes as the renaissance of the material self from the late nineteenth century—a renewed appreciation of the role of things in the development of identities, albeit in a critical vein that doubted the potential of the capitalist form. The pattern Williams

---

¹⁵ Weber, *From Max Weber* (Science as a Vocation). This 1917 lecture was preceded by earlier work that already included Weber's diagnosis of disenchantment. Wohlrab-Sahr, 'Disenchantment and Secularization'.

There was an earlier intellectual articulation in Britain that originated not in sociology but in folklore—a discipline usually invested in showing the persistence of magical thinking. As Jason Josephson-Storm shows, the Scottish folklorist and classicist James George Frazer penned a disenchantment thesis in the 1890s. Josephson-Storm argues that Weber read Frazer and fashioned a streamlined version of the disenchantment thesis from his work, yet stripped of complexities that suggested the survival or reemergence of magic. Josephson-Storm, *Myth of Disenchantment*.

¹⁶ McCarraher, *Enchantments of Mammon*.

¹⁷ The history of advertising thus overcomes the false choice between producerist and consumerist perspectives on capitalism. For a discussion of this divide, see Kriegel, *Grand Designs*, introduction.

analysed in advertising was of magical inducements and satisfactions, functionally similar to magical systems of simpler societies but, as he put it, strangely coexistent with a highly developed scientific technology. Enchantment was only strange, of course, when viewed through Weberian lenses, and anyway, as Williams observed, there it was. Colin Campbell accordingly conceived his now canonical work, *The Romantic Ethic and the Spirit of Modern Consumerism*, 1987, as the missing half of Weber's story of capitalism. On Campbell's argument, Weber overemphasized the rationalism of production, and failed to account for the spirit of consumerism, characterized by hedonic investments in worlds of imagination and fantasy. Advertising, he remarked in introducing the work, is a modern phenomenon that links the romantic with consumption and undermines the contrast between the definition of 'romantic' as visionary, imaginative, and remote from experience, and the seemingly dull matters of everyday purchases of goods and services. Modern individuals inhabit not just the iron cage of economic necessity, but a castle of romantic dreams, striving through their conduct to turn the one into the other. Campbell saw the strain between dream and reality, pleasure and utility, as a source of restless energy.[18]

Williams and Campbell shared an interest in enchantment, but are approximately representative of alternative positions in the political debate about its implications. Williams ranks with thinkers who have studied enchantment within critical perspectives on capitalism and approached it with apprehension. The spectrum here is broad, engaging diverse intellectual traditions from the 1930s into the twenty-first century. For example, F.R. Leavis and Denys Thompson (1933) recommended rational education against the enchanting powers of advertising, and repeated the words of the American critic Edgar Mowrer: 'When the acquiring of things is a religion, the offering of them is sacerdotal. There is a theology of advertising.' They put their faith in critical awareness and the mastery of reason. In the next decade Max Horkheimer and Theodor Adorno were unforgiving about the flight from the everyday world that the culture industry—advertising included—promised. On their account, the everyday was held out as paradise, only to deny consumers who imitate compulsively what they know to be false. Within a few years Roland Barthes applied to adverts the concept of the myth—not a lie but a distortion that transforms history into nature. Adverts substitute the banal invitation to buy a product with a spectacle of a world in which it is natural to buy it. Commercial motivation is doubled by a broader representation of great human themes, and thus the dream is reintroduced into the humanity of purchasers, adding the truth of poetry to the alienation of competition, and transforming simple use into an experience of the mind. Guy

---

[18] Williams, 'Advertising'; Trentmann, *Empire of Things*, ch. 5; Campbell, *Romantic Ethic*, introduction to the first edition.

Debord (1967) analysed advertising as part of the modern spectacle in which social relations are mediated by images. Debord reworked Karl Marx's commodity fetishism, which relied on the religious concept of the fetish to account for the mysteries of the commodity, abounding, as Marx put it, in metaphysical subtleties and theological niceties. Marx did not address advertising, which Debord took up to theorize its role in alienation. In his view, spectacle was unique to late capitalism. Images become autonomous and overtake reality, so that 'the commodity contemplates itself in a world it has created.' This organization was fundamentally similar to religion in its displacement of human power. In the early 1970s Wolfgang Fritz Haug theorized the power of commodity aesthetics, which, on his argument, countered religion, education, and art, and became the dominant force in the collective imagination of millions. Advertising was part of the production of an aesthetic illusion—a technically produced sensual appearance of the use value of commodities. The result is a fascinated public, dominated by its own senses, engrossed in a hall of mirrors showing it its own yearnings. Haug found these phenomena in the history of cults and saw capitalism expanding their reach beyond holy places. Meanwhile, Jean Baudrillard argued that adverts are self-fulfilling prophecies: what is true is what they say is true. Like all myths and magic formulas, there is no referential dimension against which veracity can be tested. Advertising is a prophetic language, he wrote, which does not promote understanding or learning, but hope.[19]

Across the Atlantic too critical commentary on enchantment multiplied. Vance Packard (1957) warned against the 'hidden persuaders' who approached people not as flowers of the Enlightenment but as 'bundles of daydreams, misty hidden yearnings, guilt complexes, irrational emotional blockages.' Concurrently, Ken Galbraith found individuals who did not know themselves. Their wants were products of a powerful industry that synthesizes desires for the purpose of supplying them. As he put it, '[e]very corner of the public psyche is canvassed by some of the nation's most talented citizens to see if the desire for some merchantable product can be cultivated.' Stuart Ewen (1976) saw captains of consciousness, a modern advertising industry orchestrating a psychic economy to appease the masses in the service of a secular religion of capitalism. Judith Williamson's semiotics (1978) began with Freud's dream work that she analogized to 'advertising-work'. She theorized advertising as a system of meaning-making that hollows historical, social, natural, and human meanings, and replaces them all with a system of signs in which a mythological world is constructed. That world seems more real than reality because it is a shared system, a key part of

---

[19] Leavis and Thompson, *Culture and Environment*, 26; Horkheimer and Adorno, 'Culture Industry'; Barthes, *Mythologies*; Barthes, 'The Advertising Message'; Debord, *Society of the Spectacle*, 53; Marx, *Capital* vol. 1, 101; Haug, *Critique of Commodity Aesthetics*; Baudrillard, *Consumer Society*, 53.

which is promising instant results with little effort, turning magic into an element of modern everyday life. Franco Moretti (1996) theorizes advertising as enchanted mist composed solely of images. With no things left, desire expands freely without the constraints of true or false, and consciousness becomes fragmented. George Ritzer's thesis of consumer enchantment (1999 and later) addresses advertising together with new loci of the late twentieth and twenty-first centuries, which he theorizes as cathedrals of consumption. On his account, these quasi-religious institutions attract and exploit consumers.[20]

The critical line of writing has been supplemented by studies that do not view advertising's enchantments as manipulative, distortive, or inherently troubling, and take more interest in their relationship to agency. Campbell tended in this direction, which has gathered momentum in recent years across disciplines. For example, political theorist of new materialism Jane Bennett argues for the positive political potential of advertising enchantments, because of the affective states involved. On her analysis, enchantment can be both a way of eluding power and control, and a source of energy needed to challenge and change existing social structures. Anthropologist William Mazzarella criticizes the false choice between a totalizing ideology critique and a celebration of popular pleasures, and proposes a theory of the magic of mass publicity in which vital objects and choosing and interpreting subjects are co-constitutive. Art historian David Morgan argues that in emphasizing rationality as the basis for consciousness, a negative view of enchantment results as false consciousness, self-delusion, magical thinking, faulty reason, or superstition. The approach fails to account for the pragmatic value of enchantment in all theatres of human experience. In Morgan's view, enchantment secures a sense of belonging even as it also entails the risk of domination. Literature and philosophy scholars Joshua Landy and Michael Saler propose a taxonomy of approaches to enchantment, and reject either/or understandings of its relationship to reason in favour of an antinomial account in which fruitful tensions typify modernity, and enchantment delights but does not delude; it is voluntary, compatible with rationality, multiple, and prevents the impoverishments of disenchantment. Economic sociologist Jens Beckert sees the imaginative values invested in consumer goods by the marketing industry as a productive force with a manipulative but also utopian element. While remaining sceptical about the emancipating potential of creativity harnessed to capitalist gain, Beckert also challenges the structuralist account of the iron cage of rationality by arguing that capitalism is animated by expressions of agency that are non-rational. Extra-technical and non-calculative expressions generate imaginaries of counter-factual futures, creating a secular enchantment of the world. Historian of magic Owen

---

[20] Packard, *Hidden Persuaders*, 34; Galbraith, *Affluent Society*, 170; Ewen, *Captains of Consciousness*; Moretti, *Modern Epic*, ch. 6; Ritzer, *Enchanting a Disenchanted World*.

Davies concludes: 'If we did not still live in a magical world, the advertising industry would not exist as we know it.'[21]

Walter Benjamin's *Arcades Project* (1927–40) has repeatedly informed studies of advertising. He usually features on the critical side, but I hesitate about placing him. His theological perspective and style of critique, which refused to speak from the outside of capitalist phenomena, did not stake a clear position in the debate about political agency. Benjamin's investigation of the *flâneur* strolling the artificial world of high capitalism was filled with forebodings mixed with fascination. The important point for now is that he centralized enchantment. In one of his enigmatic one-liners, he described the advertisement as 'the ruse by which the dream forces itself on industry,' and he narrated encounters with advertising in mystical terms.

Historians have drawn on Benjamin as well as the host of conceptual approaches developed in scholarship. As even the limited and brief review here suggests, and as McCarraher observes, there is an embarrassment of riches by this point. However, its variety at least confirms the centrality of enchantment. He thus argues, '[w]hether they see consumer culture as a form of bondage or as a prophecy of impending jubilee, historians agree that it draws its power from the deepest recesses of desire.'[22] With this rich literature, the question becomes, what do we actually know about enchantment in the first era of mass advertising?

Enchantment and British Advertising c.1840–1914

Despite the focus on enchantment in the many studies of advertising and modernity, historians of British advertising have had little to say about this theme circa 1840–1914, for conceptual and methodological reasons. Conceptually, while historians of the eighteenth and nineteenth centuries find psychologically sophisticated advertising and symbolic contents that might speak to enchanting appeals, the relationship of enchantment to advertising as a distinct conceptual problem has simply been peripheral in British histories.[23] Thomas Richards's application of

---

[21] Bennett, *Enchantment of Modern Life*; Mazzarella, *Mana of Mass Society*; Morgan, *Images at Work*; Landy and Saler, *Re-Enchantment of the World*, introduction. Landy and Saler do not discuss advertising, yet some of their authors observe consumerist magic; see also Saler, 'Modernity and Enchantment'; Beckert, *Imagined Futures*; Davies, *Magic*, ch. 6. For an additional review, see Crawford, 'Trouble with Re-enchantment'.
[22] Benjamin, *Arcades Project*, G1, 1; McCarraher, *Enchantments of Mammon*, 225–6.
[23] Eighteenth-century studies of sophisticated appeal include, for example, Berg and Clifford, 'Selling Consumption'; McKendrick et al., *Birth of a Consumer Society*. Nineteenth-century studies have had a more expansive field to address in terms of symbolic content. Especially salient are studies of identity categories like race, gender, nationality, and selfhood (see note 27).

Debord's spectacle to late Victorian adverts is probably the closest exception.[24] Scholarship interested in advertising and enchantment has been mostly philosophical and theoretical, or grounded in later decades or other places, particularly the USA. Jackson Lears's *Fables of Abundance* provides one of the most penetrating accounts of American advertising and enchantment, for roughly the same period studied in this book. His argument about enchantment's decline with the rise of corporate managerialism has been challenged by McCarraher, who views the country's capitalism as a religion and advertising as a provider of icons, chants, and commandments.[25] As I explain further in Chapter 1, the peripherality of this theme in British advertising historiography of the long nineteenth century, coupled with extensive commentary on enchanting power in later periods, has contributed to a narrative that marginalizes enchantment. This in turn also undermines conversations with work on contemporary advertising and consumer culture, in which the frameworks of enchantment are rapidly becoming a fully fledged paradigm. Ritzer has been an influential figure, but he is not alone. There is a growing body of work in marketing and business, particularly business anthropology, which explores enchantment. Brian Moeran and Timothy de Waal Malefyt, for example, each analyses the tripartite anthropological account of magical systems: magicians, rites, and formulae, in the advertising industry.[26]

On the level of methodology, what we do know about enchanting appeals in this era comes mainly from interpretations of adverts, and histories of advertising agencies or specific advertisers. These interpretations privilege the producer-end of adverts. Because producers have generated archives in abundance, while reception is much more challenging to recover, the producer-bias has been overwhelming. The same interpretations also typically work from individual specimens (discrete adverts and campaigns) to advertising accumulation, rather than vice versa.[27] Consequently, enchantment can be mischaracterized as a unilateral force

---

[24] Richards, *Commodity Culture*. The thesis is limited by its interpretive basis in adverts, which is a broader problem as I explain in a moment. The interpretive basis leads Richards to a leap in periodization, so that he does not account for enchantment in the period between the Great Exhibition and the late 1880s. The argument is also overly focused on the middle classes.

[25] Lears, *Fables of Abundance*; McCarraher, *Enchantments of Mammon*.

[26] Moeran, 'Business, Anthropology'; Timothy de Waal Malefyt, 'Magic of Paradox'. See also Beckert, *Imagined Futures*. I draw on this and additional scholarship in Chapter 1.

[27] Individual adverts and campaigns have been categorized in the contexts of specific commodities, businesses, the advertising industry, marketing strategies, print culture, and consumer culture; literary and art histories, where textual and visual styles are examined in relation to broader generic contexts and reading practices; and histories of social and political categories, including gender, race, class, nationalism, imperialism, and modern subjectivity. For example, Rappaport, *Thirst for Empire*; Lewis, *So Clean*; Leiss et al., *Social Communication*; Richards, *Commodity Culture*; Wicke, *Advertising Fictions*; Iskin, *Poster*; Jobling, *Man Appeal*; Loeb, *Consuming Angels*; Strachan and Nally, *Advertising, Literature*; Ramamurthy, *Imperial Persuaders*; Thornton, *Advertising, Subjectivity*. For an overview and critique of the dominance of content analysis, see Schwarzkopf, 'Subsiding Sizzle'.

controlled by individual advertisers, which is misaligned with historiographies of print, where readerly experience has been central.

This book responds to limitations in conceptualization and methodology with a reception-based analysis of the first decades of mass advertising, which demonstrates that enchantment was significant before the twentieth century, and explores its historically situated characteristics. In the opening Chapter 1 I show how advertising immersed a mass readership in the multiple meanings that markets could have for everyday life, and gave rise to new types of enchanted experience. Readers experienced advertising as a revelation of invisible planes of existence. Adverts offered imaginative contact with unknown persons, things, activities, logics, and lives that exceeded readers' sensual surroundings, invited renewed engagements with hidden potentialities of familiar environments, and enlivened daily realties. Mundane communication and purchasing decisions were at the same time explorations of alternative ways of seeing, relating, and being; haphazard ventures into fantasized life stories and mysterious worlds; leaps of faith into adventures in search of magical transformations that might break with any sense of incrementalism or the drudgery of labour and of competition, and with expectations of the ordinary difficulty of action. Searches for new sensations and feelings, for affective immersion in one's surroundings, and for unexpected revelations, were widespread.

While enchantment was pervasive, it was not a unidirectional force controlled or even acknowledged by advertisers. The story of powerful enchanters who could master consumers through discrete adverts was a myth that professional advertisers began to create towards the turn of the twentieth century. Rather than a mode of control, enchantment was a product of mass culture, a function of advertising as a system and an environment, which did not depend only on specific contents nor on the goals of content creators. Put simply, the accumulation of adverts was a historical form in its own right. By shifting the analytic emphasis from designed spectacle to the numerous and the banal, we can also move beyond the vitality of the commodity as a mode of enchantment, which has received the bulk of intellectual attention, to other elements such as labour advertising, or the material encounter with mass print.

Enchantment depended on an active involvement of advert readers who revealed what I call a *will to enchantment*. Importantly, readers' sense of realism and reason was not forsaken but rather deployed to support enchanted viewpoints. Contrary to the Weberian account of disenchantment as a critical awareness of the power of reason to know how the world works, claims to reason were often invoked to fence off such knowledge. By not knowing too much, readers protected a magical vision of the world that was central to their experience of advertising, and that rationalism threatened to destroy. Chapter 1 highlights this phenomenon without promoting a particular position in the debate between bondage and freedom. The will to enchantment was a form of agency, but agency is not yet freedom; that is a separate question.[28] Speakers to both sides in the debate will find material to their taste and distaste in the everyday world that readers of adverts inhabited.

Evidence of enchantment supports revisions to Weber-inspired theses. However, my main interest is in moving beyond revision to explain disenchantment as a historical struggle, and demonstrate how law was mobilized to keep views of modernity-as-disenchantment alive under conditions of rampant enchantment. Chapter 1 therefore sets the scene for the cultural legal history of advertising examined in Chapters 2–6, which speaks to this question while looking closely at problems of cultural boundaries.

Advertising and Cultural Boundaries

Boundary Anxieties c.1840–1914

Each of the central chapters of *The Rise of Mass Advertising* is a synchronic study that covers one facet of the history of advertising in terms of a boundary problem debated and precariously settled with the aid of law. As advertising encroached on the authority of news, art, science, and religiously inflected morality, questions about the boundaries between advertising and each of those fields became momentous and gained serious attention. In each case, conceptual and legal frameworks affecting advertising and adjacent fields began to consolidate around the mid-nineteenth century and developed over the next decades, with the most intensive cultural legal action taking place in the closing decades and the early twentieth century. Intensifying processes of commercialization, professionalization, and expansion in each field, advertising included, reached pitches in those decades that manifested in frenzied boundary work, which renegotiated earlier frameworks in efforts to settle advertising's place and meanings at the height of its challenge to perceptions of modernity.

Needless to say, these were not the only boundaries that troubled British culture. One question that this book does not address independently is advertising's relationship to literature, which arose already in the eighteenth century and even earlier. I have occasionally drawn on literary and print histories that examine this juncture, particularly in terms of problems of reading.[29] The question of

---

[28] On the distinction between agency and freedom, see Appadurai, *Modernity at Large*, 7.
[29] Jennifer Wicke argues that advertising and literature were originally inseparable. Wicke, *Advertising Fictions*, introduction. I discuss reading practices in Chapter 1, and the overlap of news and advertising in Chapter 2. Megan Richardson and Julian Thomas examine some legal angles of the literature/advertising relationality in terms of advertisers' impact on copyright and trademark law, albeit within an interest in legal change rather than the impact of legal change on the cultural meanings of advertising. Richardson and Thomas, *Fashioning Intellectual Property*.

advertising's relationship to politics could be glimpsed at the other end of the period and would become salient during and after the First World War with organized state and imperial propaganda. This boundary question was differently situated because the prospect of commercialization did not affect political institutions in the same way as the fields examined in this book. Nonetheless, pressures did materialize and boundary anxieties plagued politics too, particularly when political argument seemed indistinguishable from marketing. Again, resonances will appear, and where relevant I draw on scholarship interested in these questions. In the middle, the threat of advertising to legal institutions, particularly to courts, occasionally arose. Courts were discussed as advertising media, or as one commentator put it, the theme was the 'advertising value of the Law Courts'.[30] This was not a fully fledged cultural theme, but I will discuss some of its implications.[31] Thus, the boundary debates examined in *The Rise of Mass Advertising* are not exhaustive. Instead, they represent concerns that contemporaries recognized as pervasive and urgent, and that cumulatively provide a broad picture.

In terms of industry coverage, the debates studied in this book addressed the varieties of print advertising and occasionally non-print publicity measures, including performances and gifts. In terms of market offerings, two debates (news, art) were media oriented rather than product-specific, while two more (science, morality) allow a closer look at sector advertising, namely, medical products, gambling, and entertainment. In terms of advertising style, the debates addressed both texts and images, the latter especially dominant in the debates about art and about indecency. Issues of size, presentation and material were also involved in those cases. In terms of social participants, the history told here was polyphonic. It involved political institutions, legal professionals, trade and professional organizations, civil society organizations, advertising practitioners, traders, social critics, and consumers. In each case, a constellation of historical circumstances led some actors to see advertising as a threat to a cultural field and its associated set of values, and set boundary work in motion. To avoid misconception, boundary work was the effect of accumulating legal investments, not all of which were so intended. Actors were often merely pursuing local concerns, for example protecting their private property or good name. Nonetheless, these investments partook in widespread anxieties about cultural differentiation, and their cumulative effect was to establish the boundaries that defined advertising.

Chapter 2 is dedicated to the dilemma of differentiating adverts from news. It begins in 1848 with the successful campaign to free the press from the so-called taxes on knowledge, one of which was the advertisement duty. The campaign

---

[30] Select Committee on Patent Medicines, 1914, q. 6354.
[31] Arguments that traders abused legal proceedings for publicity were standard. Some instances informed precedential decisions, as we will see in Chapters 2 (*Dann* (1911)) and 5 (*White* [1895]).

relied on a theory of advertising as essential information, which undergirded a liberal-individualist account of the market. However, newspaper owners, who became free to print adverts without tax inhibitions, quickly realized that advertisers were threatening their control of the medium. It was not clear how adverts differed from news when both were described in terms of information, and both were produced in a fully commercialized environment. Newspapers therefore engaged in boundary work through standardized legal practices. While their practices treated advertising as an informational category, they also conceptualized it as inherently biased and therefore inferior to news.

The persistent informational focus of this debate celebrated news as the main public service of the press and elevated it over advertising, which appeared compromised. However, the same focus legitimized advertising within the terms of a disenchanted modernity. Legitimation and degradation were both necessary for newspapers to operate on a commercial model based on advertising revenues. The informational hierarchy had little to hang on in theory and in practice, as Chapter 2 shows, yet it assumed the status of common sense. Meanwhile, it marginalized the possibility that information was simply an incomplete framework for assessing advertising. Magic, dream, and imagination, irreducible to biased information, were almost entirely absent from the discussion. The normative universe of the press thus offered scant language and conceptual tools that could make sense of enchantment, which only appeared negatively, in terms of the shame of relying on an inferior type of information.

Chapter 3 moves from newspapers to the hoarding, that is, the outdoor advertising surface for posters. Beginning piecemeal in the 1840s and gaining momentum in the 1870s, billposting companies relied on contracts and courts to establish a previously unfamiliar legal regime of property in advertising spaces. The expanding exhibition of images in the public sphere provoked a heated debate about art in advertising, and advertisers soon found their rights caught up in anxieties about aesthetic education and social access to beauty. In efforts to settle the aesthetic meaning of the hoarding, the billposting industry resorted to private law practices. It relied on contracts and property to monopolize spaces while claiming to introduce rational aesthetics to the public sphere, in support of the nation's aesthetic education. Ironically, the industry's success only accentuated the sense of threat that advertising posed to the domain of art and energized critics, who promoted licensing regimes through public laws. Those gained momentum when the industry's private-law efforts reached a cultural height in the 1890s. Building on earlier achievements of the industry itself, public laws privileged the hoarding over competing forms of outdoor advertising. However, they also introduced an aesthetic hierarchy that established the hoarding as inferior in relation to legislated ideals of beauty, which were characterized by being detached from commerce.

The aesthetic hierarchy that emerged over the period was driven by anxieties about the power of images. Yet, it adopted a rationalist approach that did not conceptualize images' enchanting powers, nor even the more limited question of visual persuasion. The aesthetic evaluation of hoardings and posters was detached from their effects as persuasive devices, which were marginalized while other concerns, particularly the role of beauty in the nation's education, remained forefront and justified advertising's inferior status.

Chapter 4 turns to the relationship between advertising and science. Unlike the debates about news and art, this one focused on a particularly dominant sector, namely, medical commodities and services, often decried as quackery. It also cut across advertising media, albeit with important uses of pamphlets sent through the post. Yet, like the two previous chapters, Chapter 4 addresses a question of cultural boundaries and historicizes the legal consolidation of a view of advertising that has become axiomatic—in this case, advertising as a field of acceptable exaggeration.

Tensions over quackery were addressed by a legally supported cultural division of labour between the market and science, which we can find in medical ethical codes as well as libel and fraud litigation. In this conceptual division, science was defined by ideals of restraint that typified scientific method, logic, and subjectivity, while their negation—leading to exaggeration—defined advertising and the consumer market. The analysis shows how advertisers' claims to scientific value lost in seriousness as advertising was associated with exaggeration by courts. Quack adverts were construed less as frauds than jokes, the medicines they marketed less dangerous than useless, and the medical choices they encouraged more embarrassing to consumers than interesting for scientific knowledge. Advertising was explicitly disparaged in the ongoing comparison with science, and the consumer market was rendered epistemologically inferior. However, the markdown in cultural capital was also a form of license, for it implied liberation from rationalist restraints.

Views of advertising as exaggeration joined views of advertising as biased information (Chapter 2) and low aesthetics (Chapter 3) in their rationalist perspective, which implicitly dismissed the seriousness of advertising's enchanting appeals, even as they liberated it from the strictures of rationalism. As historians have shown repeatedly, health consumerism was driven by fantasies of well-being and a search for magical efficacy that had deep cultural roots. However, within a rationalist contrast between scientific restraint and market exaggeration, a legal conceptualization of enchantment was relinquished.

The dual logic of legitimation and critique attained a dedicated legal doctrine that applied in multiple fields of law, known as the doctrine of puffery, which is the subject of Chapter 5. Puffery, familiar beyond legal circles from the 1892 case of *Carlill v Carbolic Smoke Ball*, was and still is usually invoked as a defence argument by a speaker claiming that their speech was just a puff, for which they cannot be sued. In part, my study of the doctrine continues Chapter 4, because its elaborate examples come from the history of quackery, which produced important decisions about puffery as a formal legal concept. In part, however, Chapter 5 takes a step back from the concreteness of historical debates, and approaches the history of advertising in terms of a legal doctrine. I do so because it was a construct that epitomized approaches to advertising found elsewhere.

The chapter examines the doctrine of puffery's role as a legal mode of ridicule, challenging its traditional view as an instance of *caveat emptor*. In effect, language intended to promote a sale was construed as legally meaningless, on the normative assumption that it was anyway futile and ineffective in the market. The implication was a markdown in the cultural capital of advertisers. By licensing advertising and yet treating it as unserious, the doctrine of puffery joined other realms of law in a disavowal of enchantment. Yet, telling consumers that they lacked common sense, or assuming that they were irrational, ignorant, or weak when they responded to adverts, was simply beside the point for those actively seeking transformative miracles in the market and inhabiting imaginary worlds as a matter of course.

In Chapter 6, I return to thematic historical controversies about advertising, to examine boundary work on the lines between advertising and so-called moral questions in the debates about gambling and indecency. These were the two areas in which uses of law came closest to conceptualizing advertising's enchantments. The theory of gambling that informed legislation and case law highlighted gamblers' defiance of reason and failure to follow rationalist approaches to time, money and labour, all replaced with quasi-mystical views and ecstatic behaviours. The theory of indecency placed primacy on concepts of influence, famously articulated in the 1868 case of *R. v Hicklin*. The theory considered the power of print to interact with receptive minds, ignite desires, and draw affective responses beyond reason's control. In both theories, the unstable boundary between popular culture and enchantment was crossed. They provided conceptual languages that could potentially open up a broader debate about enchanting appeals. However, this conceptual possibility was curbed as legal logic and practice shielded advertising from a developed discussion of the role of enchantment.

Chapter 6 explores select contexts: prize competition adverts scrutinized under anti-gambling law, poster censorship managed by the billposting industry, and the medico-legal campaign against adverts for abortion medicines. From differing directions and with no unified perspective, these all demonstrate how even with theories of enchantment at hand, and legal operations intended to apply them, the role of enchantment in advertising remained only minimally acknowledged, while advertising was once again theorized as an inferior part of a disenchanted culture—at that culture's margins yet within its bounds.

Advertising, Law, and Boundary Work

Let us take stock of boundary work before saying more on enchantment. Over the period, advertising was normalized with legal means as a necessary system of commercial modernity, explained and justified by the logic, needs, and products of its advancing rationality. It was theorized within rationalist perspectives concerned with economic information, aesthetic experience, and scientific knowledge. At the same time, legal framings also criticized the limitations of advertising as a rationalizing force, and thus unwittingly freed it from rationalist restraints. Advertising was viewed as an inferior simulation of the values of a progressive modernity, exhibiting epistemological shortfalls and aesthetic compromises. It deserved, therefore, to be treated ironically, disparagingly, even contemptuously. Consumer responsiveness was correspondingly seen as sign of incompetence and cause for embarrassment. It was often described as misdirected, superficial, or poorly informed, a problem of unsophistication, ignorance, weakness, lax morals, or just bad taste. By the cumulative force of these processes across British culture, advertising appeared legitimate but inadequate, and so attained a conflicted status still familiar today. Take, for example, economic historian Joel Mokyr's *Enlightened Economy*. Mokyr tries to include advertising in his account of the Enlightenment-based economic growth of Britain, and finds it revealingly challenging: 'Advertising may seem far removed from ideas of Enlightenment, but free competition, ingenuity, and the dissemination of information, all core values of the Industrial Enlightenment, were what advertising were all about. So, of course, were dissimulation and consumer manipulation.'[32] The analysis is committed to the logic of disenchantment and so necessarily shifts from rationalist ideals to a criticism of their limits, with little space in between to account for enchantment, which was not a failure but rather an alternative outlook. The same conflicted approach implicates popular views of advertising, as commentators often observe.[33]

The impact of boundary work not only on advertising but dialectally also on other fields, deserves emphasis. Historians take for granted that cultural categories gain their meaning through processes of differentiation. However, the historical centrality of advertising for defining the fields of news, science, and art, and even for setting limits to the moral breaches of gambling and indecency, has not been adequately acknowledged. Advertising is more often described on the one hand as the financial engine of other fields, and on the other hand as a disturbance, when it was in fact a productive cultural power for fields by which Britain defined itself as

---

[32] Mokyr, *Enlightened Economy*, 201.
[33] Observations of popular scepticism abound; for example, Tungate, *Adland*, 4.

progressive, knowledgeable, and moral. Advertising functioned as a scapegoat that salvaged forms of knowledge, aesthetic experience, and ethical being in capitalism by assuming the role of their dark alter ego. As scholars have observed before, attacks on advertising ward off social anxieties.[34] No field was free from the pressures of commercialization at this historical point, no consciousness could escape the challenges of capitalist existence. In attributing the dangers of the profit motive to advertisers, who were associated with concepts of bias, vulgarity, or exaggeration, other fields appeared less contaminated. By mobilizing legal powers, Britain projected to advertising fears about commercial degeneration in a process that helped it live with its capitalism. Of course, dealing with categories in this manner only deflected attention from fundamental questions about the terms on which cultural fields placed under the pressures of the profit motive could be expected to promote the values and aspirations they stood for.

Curiously, some critics conclude that the most prevalent criticisms of advertising are part of its highly sophisticated logic. For example, Northrop Frye argued that advertising stuns the critical consciousness with statements too absurd or extreme to be dealt with seriously, but this stunned consciousness becomes dependent on the version of reality that adverts offer. Because advertising behaves like an ironic game, not entirely serious about itself, readers experience detachment and moral superiority even when its extortions are obeyed.[35] Advertisers tried and still try to put irony and scepticism to good use, but as a theoretical account this explanation assumes too much ideological perfection, and overlooks the historical struggles that gave rise to ironic views of adverts as well as perceptions of adverts as incredibly powerful. While Frye captured the paradox of a system that became omnipresent to the same extent that it was scorned, in evaluating it he replicated the historical oscillation between two perspectives. One perspective disavowed enchanted viewpoints, and therefore treated adverts as not serious, indeed absurd. This was the common response in cultural legal debates discussed so far. The other perspective saw enchantment as a rationally planned unilateral force that vacates reason and agency. It had its roots in historical theories of advertisers who despaired of attaining a cultural standing by speaking only about rationalist values. The next section discusses the move between these perspectives.

---

[34] Stephen Fox explains advertising as a convenient target for critics who fail to address deeper cultural tendencies; Mica Nava see attacks as a protective ritual and voyeuristic pleasure; and John Sherryl as a surrogate target for concerns about the excesses of market capitalism. Fox, *Mirror Makers*, 7; Nava, 'Framing Advertising'; Sherryl, 'Foreword', xi.

[35] Frye, *Modern Century*, ch. 1. Michael Schudson follows Frye in this respect. Schudson, *Advertising, the Uneasy Persuasion*. That consumers both recognize falsity and continue in imitation was defined by Horkheimer and Adorno as the 'triumph' of advertising. Horkheimer and Adorno, 'Culture Industry', 136.

Enchantment Disavowal as a Normative Enterprise

Law and Disavowal

Weber himself did not argue that people lost their capacity for enchantment but rather that sublime values 'retreated from public life either into the transcendental realm of mystic life or into the brotherliness of direct and personal human relations'.[36] As Karl Mannheim observed regarding the capitalist order, the point was never that people had somehow lost their ability to experience the world non-rationally, but that the social aims of the propagators of capitalism made rationalism overwhelm all other tendencies.[37] Put otherwise, the point about disenchantment was that it shaped the social order, whatever happened in private experience. Yet the system of mass advertising revealed that other tendencies were not overwhelmed but to the contrary, encouraged, and enchantment therefore did not retreat from public life and the social order, but instead occupied their centre. The rise of mass advertising thus shone light on the problematic relationship of capitalist systems to interpretations of modernity as disenchantment.

Scholarship on disenchantment confirms that it was never an established reality. Historian of religions Egil Asprem, for example, argues that disenchantment should be viewed as a set of problems faced by historical actors. In a recent contribution to revisionist work, historian and philosopher of the human sciences Jason Josephson-Storm interprets Weber's argument as an account of an aspiration—not an accomplished state of affairs but a process and programme that set out to embattle and contain magic. Disenchantment was thus an ideology, or as Josephson-Storm puts it, a regulative ideal. The programme involved an occult disavowal that embraced magic privately but rejected it publicly.[38] The normative language that Josephson-Storm uses points us in the right direction. Whether or not this was Weber's view, disenchantment certainly materialized as an aspirational normative project in the history of advertising. If we understand disenchantment as a regulative ideal, the legal disavowals that characterized that history become clearer.

In the conditions created by mass advertising, the disenchanted mentality that Weber described as the fate of his times was actually an uneasy one that required constant effort. Uses of law across the variety of historical debates suggest that commercial Britain refused to acknowledge that it was thriving on enchantment. Languages of reason and its failure, which typified legally informed responses, could not account for enchantment nor explain consumer experience, and thus

---

[36] Weber, *From Max Weber*, 155.
[37] Mannheim, *From Karl Mannheim*, 145. Of course, the idea that economic interest was a rationalizing force and not a dangerous passion was never stable. Hirschman, *The Passions and the Interests*; Hirschman, *Essential Hirschman*, pt 2.
[38] Asprem, *Problem of Disenchantment*; Josephson-Storm, *Myth of Disenchantment*.

highlighted the fact that enchantment was being actively disavowed. It was the elephant in the room that no one wanted to address. Whether or not Brits could stomach enchantment in realms of entertainment, leisure, religious practice, or avant-garde experimentalism (and there too they often tried to subject it to rational analysis[39]), they did not want to conceptualize its role in the structures of mundane and practical lives and in economic relationships. Instead, they relied on law to mainstream advertising while policing it within the vocabularies of rationality, producing a stream of criticisms cast in disenchanted terms.

The legal disavowal of enchantment was, of course, a mode of ordering. From this perspective, the binarist view that Saler and Landy reject, in which enchantment is construed as the residual, subordinate 'other' of modernity's rational, secular, and progressive tenets, is not entirely misleading because it was forged historically with the aid of law. The role of law in disavowal explains how common perceptions of modernity-as-disenchantment retained force in late capitalism, and specifically how they were kept alive in the world that incorporated advertising into its fabric. It is important in this context that we do not limit 'law' to a state or elite apparatus, but understand it as a culturally dispersed power and practice, as I explain further in the discussion of method below. This perspective clarifies how law informed a popular mentality, beyond the circles of scientists and intellectuals on which both Josephson-Storm and Asprem focus. Formal legal powers and practices gave modernity-as-disenchantment endurance and embedded its logic within state structures, local governance, and daily routines. Attention to law therefore offers a new angle on this longstanding debate in the history of modernity. It proposes that while disenchantment was not a historical reality, it was also not just an ideology or aspiration, but a formally normative enterprise that carried practical outcomes.

The aftermath was an ironic turn of events, which I explore in this book's final chapter, Chapter 7. The manifold legal powers that were being mobilized to deal with advertising disavowed its enchantments to such an extent that enchantment became an attractive field of action for advertisers, free from direct legal attention. In this way, fears of enchantment finally encouraged professional advertisers to claim it as their peculiar expertise.

Enchantment as Professional Brand

By the close of the nineteenth century, advertising professionals—a growing rank of agents, consultants, contractors, and others who defined their work in terms of

---

[39] As Daniel Pick observes regarding efforts to scientize fascination. Pick, *Svengali's Web*, ch. 3. Uses of fetishism as a failure of Enlightenment and culture likewise reveal the era's discomfort. For example, Pietz, 'Fetishism and Materialism'; Logan, *Victorian Fetishism*.

advertising expertise—faced a formidable challenge of self-definition. They wanted to extend their services in the growing market for advertising, but confronted the weight of criticisms that were attaining legalized forms. Criticisms denied professionals the comfort of a seamless integration with fields of knowledge, information, aesthetics, or common morality, and left the meaning of expertise in advertising in a conceptual vacuum. They were looking for a different ground for cultural authority, and found it in the idea of expertise in the human mind. Drawing on psychological languages, professionals self-branded as experts who could create adverts that worked magic across the distance between producers and consumers, capturing consumers' attention and altering their desires.

Advertising historians have mostly concentrated on the uses of psychology in advertising after the First World War, but their roots were earlier. The branding process of advertising expertise occurred in a peculiar genre of advertising literature that emerged in the mid-1880s, and included books, essays, pamphlets, courses, and periodical publications. This new genre facilitated processes of professionalization, but more critically and less well appreciated, it was a form of advertising intended for potential clients, which reveals the cultivation of a new industry image. Professionals claimed mastery over the scene of enchantment left unaddressed by law, in terms of the non-rational mind. The psychological version was attractive not simply because it suited advertisers' natural proclivities, or because competitive market conditions mandated psychological control, but against the longer-term history examined in this book, which sent advertisers searching for a role that would not end in a backlash. A profession without a cultural home finally found a mediating language with which to domesticate the already widespread phenomenon of market enchantment, which lacked a conceptual home.

Professionals assumed the mythical role of the creators of enchantment, and presumed to be its rational tamers: to design and control the non-rational mind. There was paradox in the very definition of this goal, which remains elusive. Nonetheless, viewed in retrospect, the myth of advertisers as the sorcerers of capitalism succeeded beyond their wildest dreams.

Law, Method, and Sources

One advertising journal argued in 1903, 'the mere fact that advertising is making itself felt in the legal atmosphere must surely be regarded as a sign of the times.'[40] It surely was, and yet law has been marginal in the historiography of advertising

---

[40] *Progressive Advertising*, December 1903, 13.

despite its dominance in historical developments, and the widespread faith contemporaries showed in its power to settle contentious questions. Recent decades have seen rich scholarship on the role of law in the history of capitalism, which make this marginality even stranger. *The Rise of Mass Advertising* takes a step towards closing the gap. As should be clear by now, 'law' in this book does not denote a discipline, a profession, or institution, but a diffuse mode of activity. I rely on a cultural theory of law that sees it as a set of endeavours to formulate social meanings, resolve cultural dilemmas, and frame normativity with the backing of legitimate coercive power. Such endeavours involve not only the state legislature and courts, with their products of legislation and doctrine, and not only trained legal professionals but also local organizations, practices, and material environments that are part of daily pursuits, market relationships, and substate structures. Multiple actors create, adapt, and perform normativity in these environments, and attempt to formalize it within distinct constraints and opportunities. From this perspective, law is emergent and dispersed rather than predetermined and unified.

That law is not a unified concept in this book is significant for the arguments made, but also for those not made about the role of law in boundary work and in disenchantment. Regarding boundary work, this is not a story about law adjudicating the claims of all other fields and agents from above. Such a theoretical privileging of law is not supported by the methodology, and would be unconvincing. Law was dispersed and mobilized by actors as a compound element of cultural dynamics. It needs to be identified and appreciated within those dynamics, but not separated from them.

Regarding law's relationship to disenchantment, this book does not argue that the disavowal of enchantment was a necessary feature of law. Methodologically, the analysis is organized by cultural debates and explains how law functioned in them, rather than approach the question with an a priori about law. Of course, that fact that myriad actors concurrently mobilized legal means to preserve modernity-as-disenchantment suggests that they perceived law as a disenchanting force. Moreover, the accumulation of responses reveals the actual functioning of law, which amounted to a normative project of disenchantment. However, this does not rule out the possibility that in other contexts enchantment *was* conceptualized and underwritten by law, nor does it say anything about the mystifications of legal theory and legal reason itself.[41] Finally, it bears repeating that law unwittingly encouraged enchantment by advertising. Disavowal can therefore be viewed as enabling no less than disabling. If we were to generalize about law and dis/enchantment from this history, the generalization would not fall clearly on one side.

---

[41] Aspects of legal discourse, theory, and institutions, and the centrality of reason can and have been theorized as mystified and mystifying. An early discussion is Boorstin, *Mysterious Science*. See also, for example, Schlag, *Enchantment of Reason*. Recent years have seen an avalanche of work on re-enchantment, in which legal scholarship partakes; for example, Blank, 'The Reenchantment of Law'.

The types and uses of law and legality examined in this book are determined by problems of advertising's modernity, rather than fields of law.[42] Consequently, the legal angles I address are expansive but do not exhaust the legal developments that affected advertising. A legal textbook on the subject will include areas of law that are marginal or missing here, because I am interested in areas that historical actors identified as important or useful for their goals in contexts of specific cultural anxieties. The sources required to apply this approach include traditional legal ones for case law—both high and low courts, both formally reported and unreported, and legislation, as well as sources for administrative law and for everyday legal practices and standards of private actors. All of them are read with an expansive cultural archive. *The Rise of Mass Advertising* relies on parliamentary records, Home Office records, legal treatises, formal and informal case reports, trade journals, civil society journals, newspapers, periodicals, ephemera, professional literature of the advertising industry, works of fiction and drama, works of art, scrapbooks, albums, memoirs, and autobiographies. Many of these sources have not been attended by historians of advertising. Those that have, have been treated in isolation or in contexts that obscure their place as part of a wide-ranging cultural legal effort to stabilize advertising's modernity. My treatment of these archives draws on methods of cultural analysis as I read for significant patterns of thought, modes of experience, and structures of meaning across the lived environments that advertising implicated.

The broad treatment of law contributes to historiographical re-evaluations of traditional categories of analysis in British legal modernity, three of which deserve emphasis: the distinction between state and market; the prominence of class and gender; and the emphasis on ideas over matter. I briefly explain each.

The Rise of Mass Advertising veers away from free-market assumptions by showing that advertising was underwritten by law. Attention to private and public legal settings challenges understandings of law in terms of state intervention in market dynamics, which still inform some advertising histories. If law is not reduced to interventionism, it is easier to appreciate its effects not only as a limiting force vis-à-vis advertising but also as a key to advertising's legitimation. Capital and state were in fact interwoven in this history. I therefore examine the dynamics of legal cooperation among actors who pursued divergent approaches. A related division is between critics and supporters of advertising, often associated with non-commercial and commercial actors, respectively. As we will see, support came from public authorities on local and state levels as well as from citizens, no less than from commercial actors. Meanwhile, criticisms also came from commercial actors. For example, Chapter 2 shows how commercial newspapers

---

[42] The theory of legality was originally developed in Ewick and Silbey, *Common Place of Law*, to refer to meanings, sources of authority, and cultural practices that are recognized as legal, whether or not they are acknowledged or approved by formal legal institutions.

denigrated advertising in efforts to undermine support that came from radical politics as much as from commerce. The history of advertising was not that of market versus state, nor commercial versus non-commercial interests, but of a cultural negotiation of modern capitalist life, in which all actors were implicated, and towards which many of them exhibited a profoundly conflicted attitude.

Conflicted attitudes received legal forms. *The Rise of Mass Advertising* is attentive to their presence in the legal structures and practices that mainstreamed advertising, showing the implication of law in advertising's associations of with ideas like bias, vulgarity, and exaggeration. These associations have been not been examined as legally constructed, or indeed as constructed at all; they are too often treated axiomatically. This book explains their otherwise elusive history. In the context of state/market distinctions, ridicule and critique are reminders that while law was implicated with the spread of advertising, it cannot be reduced to a handmaiden of capital without a crude simplification.[43]

Another analytic category re-evaluated in this book is the impact of gender and class. Denigrations of advertising often represented the lower classes, the 'multitudes', or women as more susceptible to advertising's supposedly inferior appeals. *The Rise of Mass Advertising* acknowledges and observes classed and gendered languages, but its approach to law demonstrates that derogative views of advertising could not be mapped onto a high/low classed regimentation, nor onto a gendered one. Gender and class carry only partial explanatory power for the history examined in this book, because mass advertising was a reminder that everyone was a consumer, and no gender or class was immune to its appeals. Everyone was also an advertiser or stood to profit from advertising, at least in potential. The bite of critical views of consumers and of advertisers was not rooted in differences between them and their critics, but in a growing consciousness of similarities. For example, medical advertising, examined in Chapter 4, revealed a cross-class and cross-gender picture of health consumers and market providers. Legally embedded debasements of advertising were therefore irreducible to a class or gender divide despite the appearance of such tropes in the debate. Instead, they were organized by a different conceptual division, between market and science, which only partially corresponded to traditional social hierarchies. In Chapter 7, we see how advertising professionals, who embraced enchantment in response to attacks on their field, struggled to overcome the feminine connotations of the non-

---

[43] The complexity in which critique attended legitimation suggests another angle on the so-called decline controversy. Martin Wiener famously argued that cultural aversion to commerce was an aristocratic norm that penetrated the middle classes and led to Britain's economic decline. Wiener, *English Culture*. Both decline and aversion have since been disputed. In any case, it is worth questioning Wiener's assumption that aversion translated into inhibitions in practice. In the history of advertising aversion went hand in hand with legitimating legal frameworks, and was actually an indication of expansion. This picture cannot be read as obviously inhibiting.

rational. Legal criticisms thus unwittingly confused gendered divisions on both practical and symbolic levels.

Lastly, the traditional treatment of law in terms of discourse and text is complicated by the prominence of materiality in this history. Advertising environments had inescapable material dimensions, and enchantment was inescapably tied with matter and with sensual bodies, not only meaning and minds. The legal means that shaped advertising and negotiated its implications consequently involved material dimensions that were central to their operation. For example, in Chapter 3, I examine the art/advertising boundary. While a question of cultural meaning, the analysis shows how legal efforts to settle the boundary operated by addressing matter: wood, paper, colour, size, space, frame, background, and more. Matter was in this instance itself a normative component and not only an abstract concept. The status of the hoarding as a recognized legal environment depended on material practices, for example of cleanliness and symmetry in poster organization. Even the legal doctrine of puffery discussed in Chapter 5, which was abstract and theorized speech, typically depended on material encounters, for example with stickers, visuals, and commodities, to explain the concept of exaggeration. These were the grounds of doctrine, not incidental applications.[44] The history of advertising thus demonstrates the entanglements of thought and matter.

Overall, the legal theory and methodology of this book provides the basis for a cultural legal history of advertising that rethinks accepted categories of analysis, in an effort to do intellectual justice to the challenges that this capitalist system brought forth, and to the modernity that it shaped.

Place and Time

The focus of *The Rise of Mass Advertising* on Britain raises questions of comparative and global history. Advertising has not been consistently examined in terms of cultural legal history in any industrializing state as far as I have been able to discover, many of which saw similar developments. American, French, and German advertising, for example, have been compared with British history, while from the perspective of print history, global connections rendered print matter uncontainable within national lines.[45] Furthermore, Britain was ruling an empire and large advertisers operated in colonies and in Britain alike. The stakes addressed here, especially the story of modern disenchantment and law's role in its sustenance, had obvious implications for imperial rule that depended on this self-image of Britain. Therefore, a cross-border account could be easily imagined.

---

[44] For a review of law and materiality, see, for example, Kang and Kendall, 'Legal Materiality'; Johnson, 'Legal History and the Material Turn'; Faulkner et al., 'Introduction'.
[45] Zieger, *Mediated Mind*.

While it remains beyond the scope of this book, the methodology of cultural legal history and the multidisciplinary approach to advertising are offered here in the open mode of starting these conversations.

Like the focus on Britain, the endpoint in 1914 is only provisionally justifiable, for if mass advertising emerged in the second half of the nineteenth century, it did not end there. *The Rise of Mass Advertising* covers key developments and traces conceptual structures in advertising's modernity that attained a robust presence by that point. The duality of legitimation and suspicion remained robust thereafter. The shift in the image of advertisers was already in view. This pre-First World War history set the stage for the later twentieth- and twenty-first-century debates and anxieties, which already responded to the myth that advertisers were masterfully pulling our unconscious strings, enchanting us away. With key moves and responses set in place, this book ends, but as nineteenth-century Brits knew only too well, you offer final prognoses on advertising at your peril.

1
Mass Advertising's Appeals
Market Enchantments

Mysterious Manx Mannikin
The greatest scientific men of the day have decided that they are really alive, for if pricked with a needle blood flows instantly and pain is visibly suffered. The heads (male and female) are equal in size to those of small babies and their intelligence is marvellous. They have no objectionable smell like guinea pigs or monkeys, for they eat no solid food, but they enjoy a bath once or twice a day. Some have wizened faces and rough hairy skins, which render them grotesque or hideous, while others have lovely white skins, and are really beautiful. All are guaranteed to be equally affectionate and attached to their owners, and ladies in the Isle of Man carry them about, and a boy, although poor, has refused to part with one for £10. Professor Huxley, who has two fine specimens, has expressed the opinion that their origin dates from the Garden of Eden, they are thus coeval with man.[1]

This 1895 advertisement led upper-class consumers to spend their money. The advertiser, Walter O'Reilly, clearly had a taste for mystery and was also selling 'Demon Cameras'. The aftermath was something between a joke and a disappointment that ended up in court, for O'Reilly was selling hand-puppets, and failed to supply even those. This chapter investigates the cultural conditions of responsiveness to advertisements that ranged from O'Reilly's venture to the most banal adverts for employment, commodities, and services. Drawing on reception evidence for approximately 1840–1914, it shows that mass advertising brought forth a range of experiences based in non-rational ontologies and a sense of mystery, which motivated contemporaries to respond to its appeals: mundane miracles, animated environments, a consciousness of a greater design, possibilities of transformation, even redemption, a surplus of meaning in things, a wide scope for imagination, dream, fantasy, play, surprise, and adventure. These were elements of commercially driven enchantment, which became a prevalent cultural condition, indeed a way of being. This prevalence did not rule out a sense of reason and realism, all the less agency. To the contrary, consumers, including the

---

[1] *St James's Gazette*, 12 July 1895, 6.

buyers of the mysterious Manx mannikin, revealed what we might call a *will to enchantment* as they actively pursued it. Enchanted experiences also did not imply a unified belief system, nor uniform emotive or cognitive stances. As we will see, when different buyers were disappointed with the mysterious creature, they reacted differently. In interactions with mass advertising, fear mixed with pleasure, frustration with humour, recoil with fascination, fragmentation with holism, new confusions with new comprehensions. While advertising caused a 'migration of the holy' to putatively secular objects of reverence, the experience was varied and patchy. These qualities of enchantment by advertising gave it its distinctly modern character.[2]

The role of enchantment in the first decades of mass advertising has not been established in British advertising historiography even as some findings support it, as does scholarship on mass print more broadly. The reception analysis that follows aims to establish the presence and significance of enchantment, and characterize it in historical terms. Simon Eliot, founder of the Reading Experience Database, observes that advertising was, alongside newspapers, the most important and least recorded reading matter for the period considered here:

> The most common reading experience, by the mid-nineteenth century at latest, would most likely be the advertising poster, all the tickets, handbills and forms generated by an industrial society, and the daily or weekly paper. Most of this reading was, of course, never recorded or commented upon for it was too much a part of the fabric of everyday life to be noticed.[3]

Reception evidence is certainly sparse, but it is not absent. I examine a variety of sources to gather insight: testimonies of consumers in fraud cases against advertisers, comments in the press, autobiographies and diaries, fiction, works of art, albums and scrapbooks. These contain implicit and explicit reflections on advertising, recollections of reading and viewing, and accounts of responses to adverts by individuals and crowds. They come in different forms: narrative and visual, report and imaginative response, self- and other-oriented, and are set in diverse institutional and social contexts. The analysis does not attempt to harmonize them but rather to explore symptomatic recurrences within a variety.

The use of fraud cases as reception sources merits explanation. I have examined informal reports in the press as well as a few hundred records of the Old Bailey—the central criminal court for the City of London and the County of Middlesex, which adjudicated crimes in the London area north of the Thames. Its reports

---

[2] Eugene McCarraher draws on William Cavanaugh's concept to describe capitalism as a migration of the holy. McCarraher, *Enchantments of Mammon*. Variation in experience was arguably true of premodern society as well, which should not be reduced to a homogenous fabric, but patchiness and inconsistency as a regular *individual* experience were dramatic with advertising's enchantments.

[3] Eliot, 'Reading Experience Database'.

were often limited in terms of legal argument, while testimonies were richly reported—which does not imply full and accurate reports, but, relatively, the most valuable ones we have. Consumer-witnesses came from across Britain as it was enough that the advertiser operated within the court's jurisdiction. Despite the richness of these sources, there remains a selection problem in considering adverts that became the subject of criminal charges, and comments elicited in a context of legal evidence. Aware of this bias, I draw on testimonies alongside other sources. I read them for what they tell us about how people reacted and expressed themselves about adverts, and focus on material dealing with commonplace advertising strategies and encounters, rather than the idiosyncratic circumstances that led to a criminal charge. On these terms, testimonies prove valuable.[4]

Reception evidence supports a number of insights about enchantment. First, it was a product of accumulation no less than single adverts. Methodologies that build their analyses from individual adverts need complementing by attention to the level of wholes, and from the reception end that places readers within the advertising environment and observes their experience. Enchantment did not hinge only on the content of particular adverts, campaigns, or sub-sets, particularly not modern branding and uses of imagery that emerged only gradually and anyway did not transform the bulk of adverts. Rather, enchantment depended on encounters with a new mass culture and on the materiality of accumulating print. Accumulation, in other words, became a distinct historical form.[5] It was at the forefront of cultural consciousness as all media were characterized by unprecedented advertising concentration. The first section shows how readers inhabited the mass of adverts, which was experienced as a revelation of invisible planes of existence.

Second, as we move beyond leading advertisers and spectacular campaigns, towards the numerous and trivial, we can also move beyond the animation of the commodity, which is the most theoretically developed aspect of consumer enchantment. As we will see, work on commodities examines advertising's role in turning objects into meaning, rendering matter vital, and endowing things with magical powers and sacral functions. Closely aligned with this perspective is scholarship on branding. For all its importance, a focus on commodities and brands risks missing the mark because a notable characteristic of advertising in the long nineteenth century was that it advertised the market, or more precisely life as a market. Large corporate manufacturers featured alongside a huge circulation of smaller as well as non-business advertisers. Commodities and second-hand goods circulated alongside entertainments, services, financial and labour opportunities, and with less separation than we find in later periods. Personal 'advertisements',

---

[4] For a discussion of the reports, see https://www.oldbaileyonline.org/static/Value.jsp.
[5] As Jennifer Wicke argues, the 'huge archive of advertisements' was more influential than individual specimens. Wicke, *Advertising Fictions*, 13.

for example, those seeking lost persons or things, airing disputes, or communicating coded messages via a newspaper, were also part of the scene, as were political adverts.[6] Such hefty mixtures, which gave shape, feeling, and meaning to abstract ideas about market society, were the contextual and atmospheric backdrop for engagements with individual adverts. (Incidentally, this also suggests an important difference between dedicated forms of commodity display like department stores and shop windows, and advertising, which was systematically more expansive in the imagined worlds it opened up.) While reading was becoming more private with the cheap mass press, the search for economic opportunity also socialized advert-reading as a standardized practice outdoors and in shared spaces that offered access to newspapers, thus providing another level of mixture between commodity consumption and other market activities.[7] Because the animation of commodities and the rise of branding are familiar themes, I invest more effort in other elements of enchantment. The second section explores the kinds of magic that advert readers were seeking, from the all-important fantasy of reconfiguring social relationships, often built on miraculous windfalls, through animating everyday life with mysteries, discovering deep meanings and forces in mundane environments, to reconstituting the self. Advertising encouraged the view that endless transformative experiences were lying within easy reach, and readers became busy with possibilities.

Third, reading modes provide a vital viewpoint on enchantment as fascinated travel. Ways of reading have been a recurrent concern of advertising theorists and cultural historians of modernity, as they reveal the experience of encountering adverts and strategies of interaction with mass print, or more generally modes of navigating modern environments. The third section examines evidence for two opposite reading modes: inattentive browsing, and collecting, to highlight their relationship to enchantment. Both modes reveal readers' fascination and shed light on elements of enchantment that previous sections introduced, particularly the role of irregular time, the dominance of surprises, and a sense of the mutually constitutive agency of humans and adverts. As we will see, such perspectives came in more and less critical garbs.

A final finding of this chapter concerns the central role of realism and reason in advertising's enchantments, discussed in the fourth section. Readers repeatedly invoked rationalist anchors, a phenomenon also found by historians in other contexts of modern enchantment. At first glance, readers' accounts appeared to adopt disenchanted ontological viewpoints. However, contrary to the Weberian theory of disenchantment, which saw reason and realism as alternatives to enchanted ontologies, in many cases readers invoked reason in order to protect

---

[6] Henry Sampson's *History of Advertising*, 1874, was instructive: it covered multiple categories, among which 'trade' was but a small part.

[7] *All the Year Round* 35 (1892): 305–309, in Plunkett and King, *Victorian Print Media*, 281–284.

a magical vision of the world that was central to their experience of advertising, and that rationalism threatened to destroy. The fourth section therefore reinforces an implication of previous sections, namely, that enchantment was often a willed condition. Mass advertising enabled and encouraged enchantment, but readers nurtured it and actively structured positions within it.

Overall, this chapter demonstrates the centrality of enchantment in experiences of advertising circa 1840–1914, with two goals in mind. First, while the argument treads familiar *conceptual* ground—indeed the prevalence of enchantment is almost too familiar a claim as we saw in the Introduction, the methodology examines unattended aspects of enchantment and corrects historiographical biases, so as to establish the role of enchantment in this period. Few historians explicitly deny its prevalence, partly because of the peripherality of this theme in scholarship on the era's advertising. However, lack of commentary, coupled with extensive commentary on the later twentieth century, risks an implicit denial, as does a narrative that focuses on post-First World War psychological techniques, which suggests that enchantment only became central to advertising after the war. As Liz McFall observes, there is an epochal bias that sees the twentieth century as unprecedented in terms of the fetishizing powers of advertising. Some historians have been explicit. For example, Raymond Williams argued that 'true "psychological" advertising was very little in evidence before the First War'. Only then, he thought, did advertising become a 'magic system'. In *Social Communication in Advertising*, William Leiss and his co-authors present a periodization of marketing and advertising strategies, which describe the period before 1920 as rational and focused on utility, not yet transitioning from an industrial to a consumer society. Implicitly, there was little to enchant consumers in this period. As a matter of content-analysis, many contemporaries would disagree, for example an 1862 author convinced that advertising had become sensational following the rise of sensational fiction.[8] Meanwhile, studies of persuasive and symbolic advertising, which potentially imply enchantment, often draw on campaigns of outstanding innovators who led developments in branding and visual work. The approach implies that the mass of adverts was but the prehistory or discarded past of modern enchantment. This chapter demonstrates that enchantment did not depend only on innovations, professionalization, large advertisers, or discrete contents, and was prevalent before 1914.

Admittedly, working with reception sources for advertising is a humbling task, for they bring enchantment down to earth as it were, concretize the more

---

[8] McFall, *Advertising*; see also Schwarzkopf, 'Subsiding Sizzle'; Williams, 'Advertising', 330; Leiss et al., *Social Communication*. Separations between information and persuasion in advertising content have been repeatedly criticized; see, for example, Church, 'Advertising Consumer Goods'. 'Sensational Advertising', 1862.

philosophical and interpretive scholarship out there, and check the flight to the symbolic. Nonetheless, the analysis corrects the producer bias in scholarship on advertising, which can too easily lose sight of enchantment's basis in advertising accumulation and diversity, and risks over-attributing power to advertisers by treating advertising simply as a means of control by capital. Advertisers were participants in a cultural dynamic they did not plan nor control. There were interesting forms of consumer agency undergirding enchantment, as well as a mixed class and gender presence that can be more easily appreciated from the reception end.[9] Yet the records show—and that is the first goal of this chapter—in what senses arguments about enchantment by advertising *have* been deeply perceptive.

A second goal speaks to this book's broader analysis. I recover enchantment in order to reflect in the chapters that follow on its disavowal in legally inflected debates. Unlike all the following chapters, this one does not relate a historical narrative but rather attempts to capture an atmosphere that was the backdrop for developments examined in the rest of this book, yet remained little acknowledged within them.

Strange New World

With mass advertising, life occurred on more than one plane. Adverts were experienced as openings into invisible worlds of unknown persons, things, activities, logics, and lives, and pulled readers into expansive scenes beyond their sensual surroundings. With Britain's population surge, urbanization, and systems of transportation built between 1830 and 1880, contemporaries were learning to live among strangers, as James Vernon observes, yet advertising extended and shaped this modern experience in distinct ways.[10] Vernon emphasizes print culture's functions of standardization and trust-creation, yet advertising, which he does not address, was not a system serving rationally to abstract and disseminate information over social and geographical distance. Rather, it facilitated imaginative living as a matter of daily practicalities. Advertising was giving images, colours, rhythms, styles, and contents to unknown worlds so as to facilitate a strange familiarity as it were, with things one encountered sensually only in adverts. In Walter Benjamin's terms, adverts were thresholds, supplying transitory experiences between different states of being. The important implication did not come from single advertisements but rather their accumulation.

---

[9] On reception evidence and agency, see Kelley, *Soap and Water*, ch. 3. On classed and gendered biases in accounts of advertising as a persuasive power overtaking cultural consciousness, see Schudson, *Advertising, the Uneasy Persuasion*; Nava, 'Framing Advertising'; McFall, *Advertising*; Rose, *Intellectual Life*.

[10] Vernon, *Distant Strangers*.

On this level, the key construct was the abstraction of the social world, which could be regional, national, or global, a 'reflex' of the life of the people as one commentator put it.[11] A widely discussed 1843 article in the *Edinburgh Review* recounted opening the *Times* and having a lively performance unfold:

> Here, within the compass of a single newspaper, are above five hundred announcements... remedies for all sorts of ailments – candidates for all sorts of situations – conveyances for those who wish to travel, establishments for those who wish to stay at home – investments for him who has made his fortune, and modes of growing rich for him who has that pleasure yet to come – elixirs to make us beautiful, and balsams to preserve us from decay – new theatres for the ideal, new chapels for the serious, new cemeteries in pleasant situations for the dead – carriages, horses, dogs, man-servants, maid-servants, East-India Directors, and Governesses – how is all this to be disregarded or disbelieved, without wilfully shutting our eyes to the progress of society; or living in an habitual state of apprehension...?[12]

In this account, the world was expanding as rapidly as it was fragmenting and the sense of the real became fraught. At the other end of the period examined in this book, Oliver Onions, whose career began in commercial illustration and poster art, published *Good Boy Seldom: A Romance of Advertisement*, 1911. The novel, brimming with insight as well as references to historical advertising events, has been oddly neglected by advertising historians. Onions too pointed to accumulation as the source of ontological doubt:

> Its posters, bills, columns of newspaper display; its free booklets, bonuses, coupons, gratuities to advertisers, rebates to purchasers; its competitions, incentives to canvassing, railway-fares refunded, cab-fares paid; its Missing Ladies, Ten Pound Notes, Buried Treasure, Limericks, Fifty Pounds a Year for Life; its gifts of gold watches to buyers of watch-chains, its free photographs for purchasers of the frame; its flags, hoops, kites, toy-balloons; its rippling, ceaseless eye-fatiguing Writing on the Wall high overhead at night; its processions of masquerading sandwichmen; its illuminated screens, its theatre-curtains, its transparencies; its toys, trinkets, novelties, budges, diaries, calendars, dummy diplomas, drafts on the Bank of Enjoyment; its this, its that, its heaven knows what not – these might have unseated the reason of twenty metaphysicians. Greater the tension could hardly become; less it dared not.[13]

---

[11] *Chamber's Journal*, 13 May 1895, 311–14. [12] 'Advertising System', 1843.
[13] Onions, *Good Boy Seldom*, 207–8.

Like the 1843 commentator, Onions saw accumulation as a challenge to reason. However, it was a dynamic that propelled itself, a point we will see often iterated. His novel examined the new imaginaries of this immersive world.

Between an urge to disbelieve and the dawning of a new consciousness that commentators expressed, we see the shock of losing what Marshall McLuhan called a provincial outlook. Thus Dorothy Wallis, who worked in wrapper writing—the female occupation of the Age of Advertisement (which she hated) recalled how the women in the office gained a sense of 'a wide acquaintance with the entire dominion of Great Britain'. She explained: 'One gets a kind of idea of the roads and streets, and speaks of them as if one had been there ... One gets to know that the Scotch are fond of railways and the Irish of mines. Gas shares will be well taken up in certain districts, and iron in others.' Similarly, a girl 'living in the depths of Devonshire' remarked that newspaper adverts were her 'walk down Bond Street'. As these comments suggested, adverts could transport persons to invisible places. The print form was capable of magically becoming an environment made of other materials altogether, participating in what Susan Zieger calls a literary idiom of enchanted transport.[14]

George Gissing's *In the Year of Jubilee*, 1894, described adverts in the public sphere as a revelation of a new plane of existence: 'High and low, on every available yard of wall, advertisements clamoured to the eye: theatres, journals, soaps, medicines, concerts, furniture, wines, prayer-meetings—all the produce and refuse of civilisation ... a symbol to the gaze of that relentless warfare which ceases not, night and day, in the world above.' 'World above' was a precise choice of term, which spoke to a field of force that the nineteenth century was learning to see, feel, and act with. A religious thinker like Thomas Carlyle perceived it as a source of enchantment competing with the highest powers of traditional religion. Moved to comment on an advertising extravaganza of a perambulating hat, Carlyle bemoaned the phantasms that 'walk the Earth at noonday'.[15] Over forty years later, John O'Connor's painting, *From Pentonville Road Looking West: Evening*, 1884 (Figure 1.1) provided a dramatic representation of this competition, in which traditional forms of transcendence give way to advertising. The romantic skies occupy roughly the top half of the painting, yet their power is receding, and engulfs the gothic St Pancras like an enchanted castle fading away. Most churches are fading, while the concentration of advertising posters, next in height, is in clear view. The adverts literally compete with the architecture of power for domination in the painting's formal arrangement. Despite being on the left rather than centre, the painting's perspective and the sky movement draw leftward, to the adverts.

---

[14] McLuhan, *Mechanical Bride*, 3; Besant and Wallis, *Dorothy Wallis*, 1892, 75–6; Evelyn March-Phillipps, 'Women's Newspapers', *Fortnightly Review*, vol. 56, 1 November 1894, 664; Zieger, *Mediated Mind*, 81.

[15] Gissing, *In the Year of Jubilee*, 37 (pt v ch. 2); Carlyle, *Past and Present*, 1843, bk 3 ch. 1.

Figure 1.1 John O'Connor, *From Pentonville Road Looking West: Evening*, 1884.

The receding power in the sky is just above them, while the adverts—a colour patch above the world on the street, at the intersection of commercial and residential life, demand attention and draw the eye as they compete in brightness with that power. They condition the viewer to search and find many more adverts on the street.

The competition with traditional enchantment was a recurrent theme. In Onions's novel, the narrative revolved around the relationship between religion and popular culture. It told the story of James Enderby Wace, nicknamed Good Boy Seldom by a grandmother who sees his transgressive bent. Wace is attracted to advertising from youth, when he watches the local reverend of Ford using it to overcome a dwindling attendance in church. At the novel's opening, he observes the hanging of a poster that insinuates itself into the place of religion: 'it appeared to be a sort of secular confirmation of things he heard...at the Congregational Chapel.' While the reverend hopes to retain a congregation by harnessing 'the forces of the New', the narrative posits a competition between religion and capitalist experience as alternative sources of spirituality. Wace soon abandons Christian commitments to become a phenomenally successful advertising agent and moves to London, which he sees as less lacking in 'commercial faith which is the evidence of things unseen'. At one point he too creates a perambulating extravaganza, in this case a shoe, on which the narrator comments:

> what did the eye see in that [shoe]? Ah, what? The poor bodily eye perhaps saw only a painted and varnished 'property'...but the eye of the spirit saw more, far more...[The advertiser] left the Shoe behind her, lest men should forget her and turn to other gods.[16]

Onions explicitly juxtaposed religion and commerce as congregations of faith that required spiritual scenes from above.

A different view of the 'world above' appeared in George Earl's painting, *Going North*, which featured travellers in Kings Cross station. Together with a second painting, *Coming South*, it told the story of aristocrats travelling to Scotland for the shooting season. The first version was painted in 1875, and contained no adverts (Figure 1.2). In the second and third ones, 1893, adverts appear above the crowd (Figure 1.3). They are hazy, yet invite a reflection on their recent emergence. This is reinforced by the man fixing the gas lighting before the adverts, who calls attention to an industrial level of existence undominated by the aristocracy.[17] Enigmatically, the 1875 version showed two blocked arches, while the 1893 version showed three. In fact, only two exist; the later version actually breached

---

[16] Onions, *Good Boy Seldom*, 1, 74, 131, 226.
[17] For the historical relationship of gas lighting and the rise of the self-governing liberal subject, see Otter, *Victorian Eye*. Otter discusses the interdependence of light and darkness, clarity and confusion, also evident in Earl's painting.

MASS ADVERTISING'S APPEALS   45

Figure 1.2 George Earl, *Going North*, 1875.

Figure 1.3 George Earl, *Going North*, 1893, third version.

realism as it gave more prominence to the upper scene. The middle arch does not carry an advert and so functions as a strange void, inviting a sense of absence or anticipation of more.

Benedict Anderson's theory of nations as imagined communities based on print consumption, can be a starting point in examining how mass advertising gave new force to enchantment in social life. As Arjun Appadurai argues in extending Anderson's theory, 'mass media...present a rich, ever-changing store of possible lives, some of which enter the lived imaginations of ordinary people...' The point is not just imagination, because all social life is in one sense imagined.[18] Rather, the imaginative experiences at stake imbued the quotidian with qualities that earlier times associated with supernatural powers. Anderson's point was the proximity to religious imagining, which responded to the mysteries of existence and to human limitation. Mass advertising functioned in ways analogous to the role newspapers had in Anderson's theory, albeit with important specificities. Significantly, the imagined worlds of mass advertising appeared held together by economic relationships. Advertising implied a constitutive link between the structures of exchange and labour, and virtually every other order of meaning. As we will see, that link was often experienced as a miraculous point of transformation, by which dreams could come true. In the accumulation of adverts, the utilitarian value of things was not rejected in favour of a sacral function, as might happen in collections that turn things into objects of worship by *removing* them from economic circulation.[19] Instead, advert collections collapsed the sacral and the functional together so that economic circulation *was* the locus of enchantment. The centrality of economic relationships to enchantment suggests that the ethos advertising encouraged was not a harkening to past traditions of animism on their way to disappear, as Jackson Lears describes it in the USA, but rather a deepening engagement with the still new and, for many, futuristic meaning of a distinctly modern market culture.[20]

Advertising gestured at a greater order based on economy, but beyond that starting point there was no key to its meaning. It was left to readers to navigate the mass imaginatively. There was a sense of a party going on that anyone could join, which induced readers to try at least some things, sometimes. In the following sections I highlight fascination, excitement, and will to enchantment. These experiences did not preclude anxiety and perplexity. While some readers embraced the vistas opened by advertising, for example the author Thomas Burke who as a child saw the *Bookman's* adverts as part of his 'Magic Lantern', many others revealed a sense of wilderness. As Peter Fritzsche observed, the messy debris of print culture put into question fantasies of disorder but also delusions of order[21]; readers of adverts indeed spoke to both. Anderson's theory explained how disorder and order came together. He posited that the arbitrariness in juxtaposition of newspaper stories was overcome by an imaginary linkage,

---

[18] Appadurai, *Modernity at Large*, 53–4. As Cornelius Castoriadis argues, reason itself is but a new imaginary. Castoriadis, *Imaginary Institution*.
[19] On the characteristics of collections, see Pomian, *Collectors*, ch. 1.
[20] Lears, *Fables of Abundance*.
[21] Waller, *Writers, Readers*, 114; Fritzsche, *Reading Berlin 1900*, introduction and ch. 7.

based on two anchors: calendrical coincidence, hence the supreme significance of the date; and the ability of the newspaper to create a mass ceremony—which Hegel saw as a modern substitute for morning prayers—of almost precisely simultaneous consumption of the newspaper as fiction, that is, a meaning created by literary convention. But here we come to another specificity of mass advertising, which complicated both anchors. To expand beyond newspapers to other media was a daily occurrence in which the conventional form was lost, and date markers disappeared. Adverts were formally unbound, and out of time. This was a radicalization of permanence, whereby advertising was always already there, having no frames that make it obsolete, and equally a radicalization of ephemerality. That is how mass advertising expressed novelty as a perpetual condition. Social theory has long viewed this feature as definitive of consumer modernity, yet we should note how these conditions related to enchantment. Disenchantment confined all action to profane time. By contrast, as Jane Bennett explains, one of the distinctions of a state of wonder is the temporary suspension of chronological time while sensory activity becomes acute.[22] Readers indeed engaged with adverts as wondrous explorations that were out of standardized time and lacked standardized form. These conditions involved a sense of being lost, as readers were transported to a strange environment.

Readers expressed estrangement by repeatedly saying that they did not know something or someone well, because they only knew them through an advertisement. The Earl of Clancarty described the dazzle and difficulty of comprehension of mass advertising: 'one is lost in a labyrinth of advertisements about trunks, hats, surgical instruments, hosiery, &c.'[23] The carnivalesque atmosphere was also a legal condition: advertisers could legally multiply identities by adopting tradenames, some of which were corporate, such as the Oriental Toilet Company or the Carbolic Smokeball Company, discussed below. Other advertisers liberally used natural names. As one frankly explained, 'it is the custom if you have been unsuccessful, say, as Smith and Co., when you start again...not to take up the name under which you have been unsuccessful...I cannot tell how many names I have traded under.'[24] In the same years, limited liability legislation created companies as distinct entities from the natural persons who established them. This development, alongside the emergent category of trademark in law and the professional creation of brands, produced an artificial space filled by conjured identities. Efforts to fix identities by state registration were repeatedly one step

---

[22] On profane time, see Taylor, *Modern Social Imaginaries*, ch. 13; Bennett, *Enchantment of Modern Life*, ch. 1.
[23] Lords Sitting, 28 July 1853. The statement had a political purpose: Clancarty feared a tax on successions that would replace the lost revenues from the repeal of the advertisement duty, a debate I examine in Chapter 2.
[24] *Humphries* (1884).

behind their creative appearances.²⁵ These entities were strange in many senses: their basis could be formally legal or only practical, their sources could be criminal or commercial, and most deeply, they gestured at human, nonhuman, and interactive realities that were uncertain.

In consequence, advertising was widely considered opaque. This view did not usually stunt interaction with adverts, but it did colour it, occasionally even as an imminent threat. A familiar trope of danger was gendered: stories about young women pursuing the unknown by responding to adverts and ending in prostitution circulated. Yet danger lurked everywhere, as William Thackeray suggested when he commented on investment and loan adverts: 'There is no greater mistake than to suppose that fairies, champions, distressed damsels, and by consequence ogres, have ceased to exist . . . in a certain newspaper there used to be lately a whole column of advertisements from ogres who would put on the most plausible, nay, piteous appearance, in order to inveigle their victims.'²⁶ Readers found themselves in a strange new world that was not all pleasurable charm, but was enlivening and set them on their edges, ready to be surprised.

Economic Magic

More than a window view on otherwise invisible worlds, advertising presented doors into them, and readers became absorbed trying the openings. Commentators often felt that their culture was following the notes of a modern magical pipe, spellbound. One journalist described an 1899 scene in Birmingham reminiscent of the Pied Piper of Hamelin. An advert called for one hundred children for a Christmas sketch at the Gaiety Music Hall. Between three and four thousand arrived: 'Children swarmed everywhere, in the passages, on the stairs, in the galleries, on the stage, in the side wings . . .' When told to go away after one hundred had been selected, 'they howled and yelled till they were hoarse . . .'²⁷ As we will see, this was far from a childish scene. The vivid rendering revealed the enchanted atmosphere in responses to adverts, and the affective investment in the small opportunities that they offered, which could reach ecstatic pitch and recreate the emotional aura of the supernatural.²⁸ 'Who shall say,' mused the manager of the Adelphi Theatre in an early book on advertising, 'that the so-called birch-brooms that witches are supposed to carry, may not be more properly regarded as billstickers' brushes, while the mysterious ceremonies around the witches' caldron . . . may

---

[25] For example, as legal trademark registration emerged, the broader and non-legal development of brands was already reaching beyond it. Bently, 'Making of Modern Trade Mark Law'. I discuss these developments in Chapter 7.
[26] Thackeray, 'Ogres', 1861.
[27] *Billposter*, January 1890, 111. See also *Birmingham Daily Post*, 10 December 1889, 7.
[28] As Castle argues about magic lanterns. Castle, 'Phantasmagoria', 52.

not be... connected with the process of mixing the paste?' One commentator explained the affective charge: 'the... reader... has discovered that the [advertising] department... [has] something to open his mind, to excite his imagination, to soften his heart... and his soul expands...' This state of things, still relevant today, has led Bennett to challenge Horkheimer and Adorno for failing to see that affective engagement precludes total control by the culture industry. As she puts it, 'if the industry operates upon us by means of our affective participation in it, this means that its control over us is simultaneously deep and unpredictable. And that is because affect itself is both deep and never entirely predictable in its movements.' Unpredictability means that commercial things can enchant and not just mystify. As the Birmingham scene suggested, some energies unleashed by advertisers were unpredictable, uncontainable, and unwelcome to them. Like readers, they were participants in a dynamic that exceeded them.[29]

What were readers after? In responding to adverts, they explored opportunities for metamorphosis, which is, as David Morgan argues, what enchantment consists of.[30] There were multiple kinds in the advertising store, tapping desires for social, personal, and environmental transformations. Traversing class structures was one, which still informs views of consumer culture as a democratizing force. To begin exploring it we might look at Abraham Solomon's popular painting, *Second Class*, 1854 (Figure 1.4). Solomon painted a mother parting from a son emigrating to Australia. Adverts cover the carriage wall. No passenger is looking at them, they communicate directly with the viewer to clarify the scene as they market the passage to Australia, outfits for emigrants, and gold-digging tools. These adverts assume the symbolic role of a route to gold at the time of the Australian gold rush. As James Burn wrote in his *Language of the Walls* in 1855, advertisements 'remind us of other lands, and hold out many inducements for the unfortunate and the discontented to fly from home'.[31] Dreams of gold were dreams of a passage out of the lower-class carriage. Looking away from the adverts made perfect sense, for it already transported passengers into the next carriage. Solomon's counterpart for this painting, *First Class*, accordingly contained no adverts.

Charlotte Brontë's *Jane Eyre*, 1847, drew on the magical power of advertising to propel individuals into and up the social structure. Like the departing boy in Solomon's painting, Jane wants to leave her known world. She wonders how she might learn about options when she has no friends. No ideas come; her feverish despair reveals the isolation of someone left outside a tightly knit social fabric.

---

[29] Smith, *Advertise*, 1863, 7–8; *Chambers' Edinburgh Journal*, 25 January 1851, 55; Bennett, *Enchantment of Modern Life*, 125. See also Mazzarella's discussion of Adorno's failure to live up to his own dialectical commitments, which would suggest that the lure of culture industry is not totally rationalized. Mazzarella, *Mana of Mass Society*, ch. 3. On the inability to contain consumer longings, see Lears, *Fables of Abundance*, 9.

[30] Morgan therefore also concludes that consumerism is premised on enchantment. Morgan, *Images at Work*, 11, 17.

[31] Burn, *Language of the Walls*, 1855, 6.

Figure 1.4 Abraham Solomon, *Second Class—the parting: 'Thus part we rich in sorrow, parting poor'*, 1854.

The option of advertising crosses her mind like magic, as if '[a] kind fairy...had surely dropped the required suggestion on my pillow'. Jane perceives advertising as a social opening, makes the gesture and finds Rochester. As Morgan argues about small gestures involved in modern enchantment, they place individuals into a network of human and nonhuman actors that link them to greater powers.[32] Jane's humble dreams are finally subsumed by a more dramatic metamorphosis, when it turns out that she is an heiress. Advertising is the route to this stage too: the searchers advertise in the press for Jane, a plot element that reflected a prevalent practice.

Adverts for claimants of riches circulated fantasies that large sums of money awaited alert readers. Institutions like the Court of Chancery, government stocks, or assets in bankruptcies were modern treasure troves. The adverts encouraged a temporal experience in which readers inhabited in a fleeting moment a lost and mythical place and time and a potentially utopian future.[33] The power of this fantasy was evident when Charles Howard published the following advert:

---

[32] Brontë, *Jane Eyre*, 92; Morgan, *Images at Work*, 18.
[33] 'Next-of-Kin Agencies', 1885. On connecting past, present and future see Belk, Weijo and Kozinets, 'Enchantment and Perpetual Desire.' See also text by note cue 22.

> *Mr. James Hall Cooper Clark, who died in South America in March last, had left 3,000l. each to the first 35 persons who could prove by parish certificates that their ancestors for seven generations had held that name.*

Some 17,000 readers responded. They were asked to pay handling fees, from 50*s.* for a copy of the will, to a few pounds (today, a few hundred pounds). They spent time and resources to establish genealogies, but never saw the will nor the inheritance. One of them seemed still dreaming in the midst of prosecution: 'I have not had the 3,000*l.* yet.'[34] These fantasies had dedicated businesses known as Next-of-Kin agencies, which regularly advertised for people to claim fortunes (Figure 1.5).

Next-of-Kin agencies created name registers from newspaper adverts that searched for relatives or announced unclaimed funds, and charged customers for viewing them. Their adverts essentially amplified mass advertising, and

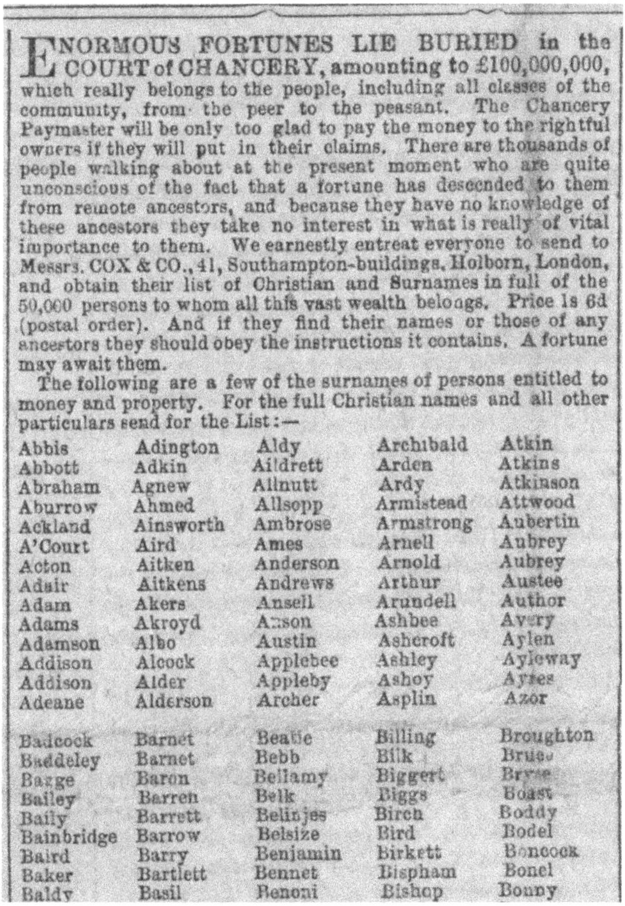

ENORMOUS FORTUNES LIE BURIED in the COURT of CHANCERY, amounting to £100,000,000, which really belongs to the people, including all classes of the community, from the peer to the peasant. The Chancery Paymaster will be only too glad to pay the money to the rightful owners if they will put in their claims. There are thousands of people walking about at the present moment who are quite unconscious of the fact that a fortune has descended to them from remote ancestors, and because they have no knowledge of these ancestors they take no interest in what is really of vital importance to them. We earnestly entreat everyone to send to Messrs. COX & CO., 41, Southampton-buildings, Holborn, London, and obtain their list of Christian and Surnames in full of the 50,000 persons to whom all this vast wealth belongs. Price 1s 6d (postal order). And if they find their names or those of any ancestors they should obey the instructions it contains. A fortune may await them.

The following are a few of the surnames of persons entitled to money and property. For the full Christian names and all other particulars send for the List:—

Abbis	Adington	Aldy	Archibald	Atkin
Abbott	Adkin	Aildrett	Arden	Atkins
Abraham	Agnew	Allnutt	Ardy	Atkinson
Aburrow	Ahmed	Allsopp	Armistead	Attwood
Ackland	Ainsworth	Ambrose	Armstrong	Aubertin
A'Court	Aird	Ames	Arnell	Aubrey
Acton	Aitken	Anderson	Arnold	Aubrey
Adair	Aitkens	Andrews	Arthur	Austee
Adam	Akers	Ansell	Arundell	Author
Adams	Akroyd	Anson	Ashbee	Avery
Adamson	Albo	Austin	Ashcroft	Aylen
Addison	Alcock	Applebee	Ashley	Ayleway
Addison	Alder	Appleby	Ashoy	Ayres
Adeane	Alderson	Archer	Asplin	Azor
Badcock	Barnet	Beatie	Billing	Broughton
Baddeley	Barnet	Bebb	Bilk	Bruce
Barge	Baron	Bellamy	Biggert	Bryce
Bailey	Barren	Belk	Biggs	Boast
Baily	Barrett	Belinjes	Birch	Boddy
Bainbridge	Barrow	Belsize	Bird	Bodel
Baird	Barry	Benjamin	Birkett	Boncock
Baker	Bartlett	Bennet	Bispham	Bonel
Baldy	Basil	Benoni	Bishop	Bouny

Figure 1.5 Cox & Co., London, Next-of-Kin advertisement. Fortunes to all classes, 'from the peer to the peasant'. Advertisement cutting—surnames ran from A to Z. *Exeter and Plymouth Gazette*, 6 February 1886, 1.

[34] *Derby Mercury*, 6 December 1893, 8; *Howard* (1885).

disseminated the idea of treasures to be had. Readers were willing dreamers, ready to discover that they were on their way upward: 'I hoped my husband's nephew had left some property – I saw several Sheppards spelt the same as our name...I believe there is money in the family, but whether in land or other property I do not know...' And another: 'I believed money was left which was unclaimed, and I paid my guinea to find out.'[35] A commentator reflected on the enchanting experience:

> To mount the dingy stairs and hold speech in the dark office of an advertising-agent for next of kin is, figuratively, to grope and talk in the dismal dungeon scene that in the pantomime precedes the brilliant and dazzling transformation...the depression and the gloom are dissipated when...the curtain rises on the entrancing scene of *The Home of Untold Millions*...the senses are stupefied by visions of wealth beyond the power of an imaginative penury to conceive or long for.

The experience of search itself was entrancing, a stand-still moment in which imagination coloured the banality of advertised detail with exoticism:

> For twenty minutes you are raging through temples and plucking jewels from the ears and eyes and noses of idols;...sacking palaces and carrying off bangles, necklaces, strings of pearls, elephant trappings, and uncut emeralds;...weighting your cummerbund with Venetian coins, Calcutta mohurs, promissory notes, and bars and bricks of gold; and in twenty minutes you are back again in the bald light of Bedford Row, with your hair ruffled...[36]

The material means by which wealth was conjured—with a technique defying conventional explanations of practical reason, and the ethical language that placed no inhibitions on access to dream riches, match the theory of occult economies.[37]

Advertisers repeatedly fired imaginations with treasures. In 1842, for example, a letter to the editor of the *Times* worried that others (not the writer, to be sure), would be tempted to invest in a company advertising that it was going to recover the treasures of the *Le Télémaque*, the drowned ship on which French elites allegedly tried to smuggle their riches away from the revolutionary masses.[38] A treasure-hunt advertising campaign by the *Weekly Dispatch* turned the enchantments of riches into mass action. Alfred and Harold Harmsworth bought the newspaper in 1903, and wanted to boost a dwindling circulation.[39] Medallions of £10 to £50 were hidden across Britain, the total and number of localities

---

[35] Woodman (1899).   [36] 'Next-of-Kin Agencies', 1885, 632.
[37] The theory was developed in the context of the neoliberal era. Comaroff and Comaroff, 'Occult Economies;' Comaroff and Comaroff, 'Millennial Capitalism.'
[38] *Times*, 20 August 1842, 4.
[39] Circulation was at a few thousands. McEwen, 'The National Press'. At the height of the campaign, it reached 500,000 a week. *Advertising News*, 26 August 1904, 8. The advertising consultant Charles A. Barrett claimed that he originated treasure-hunt advertising campaigns. *Progressive Advertising*, February 1904, 25–6.

London	»	£1,000	Chatham	» »	£40
Manchester	»	500	Luton	» »	20
Liverpool »	»	500	Reading	» »	50
Leeds, Bradford, Halifax, and Huddersfield »	»	150	Brighton	» »	20
			Birmingham and District	»	100
Dublin »	»	100	Ramsgate »	»	20
Belfast »	»	100	Margate »	»	20
Swindon »	»	20	Cardiff »	»	70
Colchester »	»	20	Newport »	»	40
Enfield »	»	20	Coventry »	»	30
Wimbledon »	»	20	Nottingham »	»	50
Croydon »	»	20	Exeter »	»	30
Gravesend »	»	20			
Bristol »	»	40	Total	»	£3,000

Figure 1.6 Locations of buried 'treasure'. *Weekly Dispatch*, 24 January 1904, 5.

Figure 1.7 Buried treasure medallion. *Weekly Dispatch*, 17 January 1904, 5.

increased from week to week (Figures 1.6, 1.7). £3,000 would be roughly equivalent to £370,000 in 2020. The newspaper committed to exchange medallions for cash and published clues in its weekly issues.

At the fingertips of anyone, the adverts promised, 'the treasure has been purposely placed in conspicuous positions where people may be walking over it every day.' Finding was so simple that 'it seemed impossible' that it was right.[40] Marvels were just beneath the surface.

---

[40] *Weekly Dispatch*, 17 January 1904, 5.

54   THE RISE OF MASS ADVERTISING

The stories of finders were cast as stories of salvation through mundane action. For example, Ernest Welsford was a mason's labourer from Bristol, who was unwell on the fateful day of his find. He nonetheless went to work, 'feeling the need of earning all the money possible'. He was uprooting a tree 'which stood in the way of progress', and lo and behold, 'the disc upon which were the magic words' was in the first shovelfuls. He had found £20. The annual nominal earnings for full time jobs in building (where some level of casualization was typical) would have been between £68 and £74 2s. Another finder, Joseph Markham, almost collided with a horse while daydreaming about medallions. He narrowly escaped, fell to his knees on the roadside, and there and then found the treasure. It was hard to miss the imagery of worship and the life-giving power of the advert-containing earth. Children too were involved. Six-year-old Charlie Daley, the son of an unemployed stevedore, searched with his mother. They followed a route that she had seen in a dream, charted by a fairy holding 'the medallion – shining and glistening like a diamond studded ball of gold' (the *Weekly Dispatch* clearly saw no need to choose between images of wealth and crammed many in, giving narrative form to the excitements of hunters). Charlie found a medallion, causing his mother to faint.[41]

Hundreds of people joined the hunt every week, revealing the appeal of treasure fantasies. The publishing office in London was besieged, its fourteen windows broken and its side door burst as people struggled to get first copies. Lines stretched down surrounding streets. Distribution to newsagents, wholesalers, and railway stations was blocked. A secondary market in papers developed rapidly. Hunters spared no effort in their search for medallions: they removed paving stones, examined chinks of walls, fell into rivers, trampled flower beds, raided a hospital, clamoured near a prison where ten constables were called to clear the road. A host of things were enlisted to aid humans: spades, pickaxes, knives, screwdrivers, shovels, sticks, brooms, iron bars, even an invention of an 'electric fork' to pull medallions—a modernized version of occult paraphernalia for treasure hunting found in older traditions.[42] Night searches came with candles, tapers, and lanterns. Unemployment was 'temporarily solved' and disability overcome as blind and injured persons joined in. Classes and genders mixed in a reshuffling of social relationships. The 'poorer classes' were reportedly the most active, but 'well-dressed young men,' who were clearly acquainted with Sherlock Holmes (more on which later) were also on the hunt, as were women. 'Idlers' were daytime seekers; clerks and shop assistants, with their 'sisters and sweethearts', took to the night. Some claimed they had only come to look on, but 'prodded the

---

[41] Boyer, 'Living Standards', table 11.3; *Weekly Dispatch*, 31 January 1904, 6; *Weekly Dispatch*, 24 January 1904, 6.
[42] *Weekly Dispatch*, 24 January 1904, 6. On treasure seeking through occult means, see Lears, *Fables of Abundance*, 44.

ground with their sticks'. 'Unbelievers' were reportedly converted to faith in the transformative potential of the hunt. The romantic non-rationalism was obvious to contemporaries. In 1911 Onions fictionalized the events and explored the enchanting force of assemblages of people, technologies, and the natural and artificial surroundings brought together by adverts. A fictional hunter who was a 'virgin to Romance' was shown in ecstasy as 'the limpid blue pools of [his] eyes danced with the glamour of it, and, equipping himself with dark lantern and scarp knife... went forth... into fields and lanes, there to scrabble in the mire with a hundred others...'[43]

The logic of treasure hunting appeared in contexts that might seem remote. One example was employment adverts that promised easy money. Frederick Paynter published the advertisement in Figure 1.8.

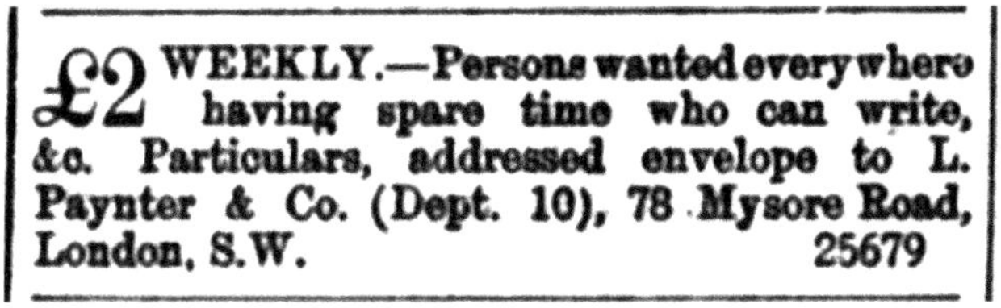

£2 WEEKLY.—Persons wanted everywhere having spare time who can write, &c. Particulars, addressed envelope to L. Paynter & Co. (Dept. 10), 78 Mysore Road, London, S.W. 25679

Figure 1.8 Frederick Paynter, employment advertisement. *Irish News and Belfast Morning News*, 25 May 1905, 2.

The job was addressing circulars. Paynter demanded 2s. (approximately £12 in 2020) from every applicant. In twelve months, 8,230 letters with money arrived. A similar offer from another advertiser, who asked his candidates to buy pens and then also pay for the envelopes that they had to address, received five hundred to one thousand letters every day. Henry Sampson argued in his history of British advertising, 1874, that home employment adverts were a major category of 'swindles'.[44] However, their persistence was rooted in a cultural logic that kept surfacing: they pointed literally and symbolically to gold that existed right where people already were, hinting at treasures at the tips of one's fingers. People just had to choose the right key to miraculously transform their lives.

George Bernard Shaw's *Pygmalion*, 1912, investigated this cultural scene. The play charts fantasies of metamorphosis in the change of a flower girl to duchess. Shaw drew on the classical myth of Pygmalion, in which a supernatural vivification brings an ivory statute to life. In his rendering, however, Eliza does not marry her maker, the phonetics professor Henry Higgins—she revolts against him. In her moment of liberation, she threatens to advertise and so sell the same magic to an entire society and finally erase classes:

---

[43] Onions, *Good Boy Seldom*, 1911, 206.
[44] Paynter (1908); Edgar (1910); Sampson, *History of Advertising*, ch. 12.

I'll advertise it in the papers that your duchess is only a flower girl that you taught, and that she'll teach anybody to be a duchess just the same in six months for a thousand guineas. Oh, when I think of myself crawling under your feet... when all the time I had only to lift up my finger to be as good as you, I could just kick myself.[45]

The erasure of class demystifies it, as class markers like accent prove arbitrary and mutable. I concur with Lili Porten that Shaw was not celebrating the magical power of education, for his plot was a levelling down of privilege shown to be empty, rather than a substantive levelling up of the underprivileged. But he *was* showing the magical potential of commodification. We see the idea of extraordinary ease: only lift up a finger, and a radical transformation can be achieved by advertisement.[46]

Erasing class was just one fantasy. Mass advertising presented multiple options that were not 'ministering directly to [a] narrative at all' as H.G. Wells had it, but had the potential of effecting an unpredictable change by an 'unusual transverse force'.[47] This allied and fed diverse desires. In the *Weekly Dispatch*'s treasure hunt, hunters were also after adventure. The adverts invited them to see environments that had grown overfamiliar anew, reanimated. Figure 1.9, for example, was the clue a Brighton medallion. It linked the travel through city streets with cultural symbols: the War of the Roses, the Hub of the Universe, nobility, and institutions of modern public life, and so deepened a sense of meaning in immediate surroundings.

The locations of ad-clues were similarly embedded in expansive cultural contexts. Some appeared within the newspaper's serial story, while others were outside the newspaper altogether: pantomime comedians in *Forty Thieves and a Half* gave clues during performances. Clues were also interspersed with the stories and portraits of finders, who were themselves continually in the public eye through the dailies of the Harmsworth empire, the *Daily Mail* and *Evening News*. Readers accepted these invitations to treat treasure hunting not as a game away from life but as a deeper engagement with it, which could elevate the trivial. As Bennett explains, the sense of a world inspiring deep powerful attachments is key to enchantment.[48]

Joining enchanted adventures was not without hesitation for some readers, as a commentary on a Liebig advertising campaign demonstrated. Liebig sent consumers searching the English coasts for bottles with the Lemco brand, which contained prize notes (Figure 1.10). One reader reported a crowd of military volunteers in Yarmouth oblivious to immediate realities, 'their heads fixed at an angle of 45 degrees seaward, and with eyes rivetted on the wild and stormy waters'. He returned the next day, entertaining 'a wee small hope of, casually

---

[45] Shaw, *Pygmalion*, 1912, act V. [46] Porten, 'Metamorphosis of Commodities'.
[47] Wells, *Tono-Bungay*, 1.
[48] *Weekly Dispatch*, 24 January 1904, 6; Bennett, *Enchantment of Modern Life*, ch. 1.

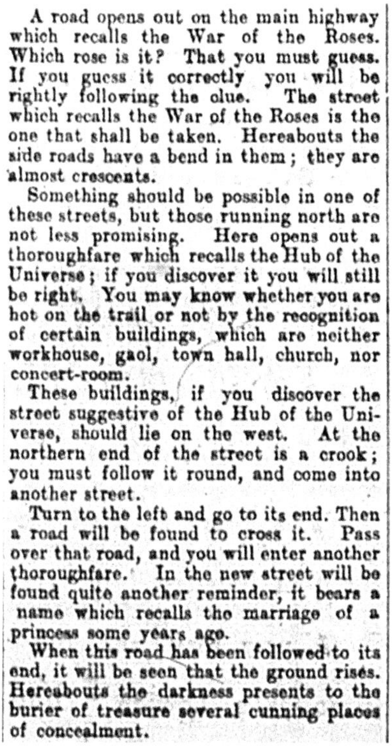

MASS ADVERTISING'S APPEALS 57

> A road opens out on the main highway which recalls the War of the Roses. Which rose is it? That you must guess. If you guess it correctly you will be rightly following the clue. The street which recalls the War of the Roses is the one that shall be taken. Hereabouts the side roads have a bend in them; they are almost crescents.
> Something should be possible in one of these streets, but those running north are not less promising. Here opens out a thoroughfare which recalls the Hub of the Universe; if you discover it you will still be right. You may know whether you are hot on the trail or not by the recognition of certain buildings, which are neither workhouse, gaol, town hall, church, nor concert-room.
> These buildings, if you discover the street suggestive of the Hub of the Universe, should lie on the west. At the northern end of the street is a crook; you must follow it round, and come into another street.
> Turn to the left and go to its end. Then a road will be found to cross it. Pass over that road, and you will enter another thoroughfare. In the new street will be found quite another reminder, it bears a name which recalls the marriage of a princess some years ago.
> When this road has been followed to its end, it will be seen that the ground rises. Hereabouts the darkness presents to the burier of treasure several cunning places of concealment.

Figure 1.9 A clue for Brighton. *Weekly Dispatch*, 17 January 1904, 5.

like, coming across one... with a free holiday coupon'. As it turned out, hosts of men from an encamped regiment were doubling again on their duties with an active search. A conversation with another seeker revealed the guilt each experienced about 'looking for two things at once', mixing the mythical pull of a message in a bottle with the duties of rational and even military masculinity. However, neither was willing to give up the adventure.[49]

The taste for excitement could be seen in responses to George Binet's advert for detectives (Figure 1.11). It invited readers to assume secret identities and dive into mysteries, implying a hidden layer of meaning as well as income that could be easily accessed. All a reader had to do was wish it, without any other change of terms: their own locality, within their 'rank', appropriate for their sex and age. The idea was to add adventure to routines; therefore a letter sent to thousands of respondents recommended that they keep their regular jobs. The best candidates were employed persons who would not be suspected as detectives. We see here the culture of 'as if' as Michael Saler calls it, moving beyond fiction to give real life a fantastic dimension, becoming, in his terms, 'just so'. Respondents were diverse: a

---

[49] *Modern Advertising*, August 1900, 4. Charles A. Barrett claimed that he originated this campaign too. *Progressive Advertising*, December 1903, 26–7.

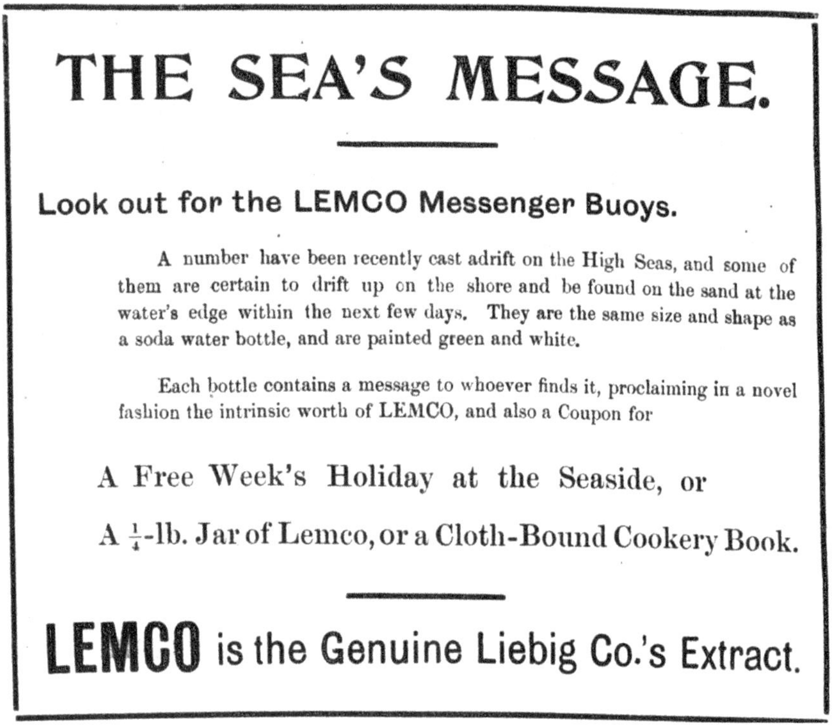

> # THE SEA'S MESSAGE.
>
> **Look out for the LEMCO Messenger Buoys.**
>
> A number have been recently cast adrift on the High Seas, and some of them are certain to drift up on the shore and be found on the sand at the water's edge within the next few days. They are the same size and shape as a soda water bottle, and are painted green and white.
>
> Each bottle contains a message to whoever finds it, proclaiming in a novel fashion the intrinsic worth of LEMCO, and also a Coupon for
>
> A Free Week's Holiday at the Seaside, or
>
> A ¼-lb. Jar of Lemco, or a Cloth-Bound Cookery Book.
>
> **LEMCO** is the Genuine Liebig Co.'s Extract.

Figure 1.10 Liebig advertisement, myths of message in a bottle. *Bexhill-on-Sea Observer*, 21 July 1900, 3.

grocer with experience in detective work; a labourer's wife; a blacksmiths' striker; a sewing machines agent; a boot clicker; a man 'of no occupation'. A few hundred people paid 10s. 6d. each (about £65 in 2020), and were appointed private detectives by correspondence. One was asked to recruit understaff over whom he was appointed as superintendent. Another was assessed by the agency as 'a very shrewd woman' and promised that she 'would have all the tit-bits of scandal to investigate'. They all revealed a drive to enliven the mundane, readily accepting that there was more to it than met the eye.[50]

The Manx mannikin incident—the advert quoted at the opening of this chapter, drew on the taste for mystery in upper classes. A few hundred people sent money to buy the creature. Reportedly, Lady Randolph Churchill bought a dozen. The advertiser, O'Reilly, was charged with fraud because he failed to meet orders, on his account because they overwhelmed him. The creature was unveiled in court. A police detective opened a box that contained wax ears, eyes, nose and

---

[50] *Bristol Mercury*, 20 May 1893, 6; Saler, *As If*; *Sheffield Evening Telegraph*, 5 May 1893, 3; *Binet* (1893).

> **DETECTIVES.**
>
> WANTED, in every locality, intelligent Men and Women in every rank of Society to act as PRIVATE DETECTIVES under our instructions ; age no object ; previous experience unnecessary, and no hindrance to present occupation ; good pay.—Send photo and stamped directed envelope for particulars to The National Detective Agency, New Inn Chambers, Strand, London.
>
> MANAGER—G. J. BINET (ex-Chief of Police).

Figure 1.11 George Binet, detectives advertisement. *Bath Chronicle*, 15 September 1892, 4.

tongue, a wig, and two white handkerchiefs. Placing them between his fingers, he produced 'grotesque faces... and the court laughed heartily'. For all the laughter, press attention to the story confirmed that of the hundreds of respondents, not all and perhaps not many were ordering puppets. Rather, they pursued mysteries in the unknown expanses between myth and science. As Mark Schneider argues, enchantment occurs in confrontations with circumstances beyond one's present understanding, which have the potential of transforming her image of how the world operates. It is facing something both real and mysterious, uncanny, or awesome.[51] The mood of Manx mannikin buyers was engaged, just like the treasure hunt, and readers showed an appetite for surprise. Behind this appetite were diverse attitudes that came to light when disappointment struck: some consumers were frustrated while others were ready to let go with a disenchanted laughter.[52] This latter group, of laughing consumers, was itself diverse. As we will see in Chapter 4, the meaning of laughter in courts was complex for it revealed not only rationalist mockery but also the embarrassment of identification. Either way, laughter signalled the breaking of a spell, if only momentarily.

The move to laughter speaks to a contentious point in consumer history, namely, the extent to which enchantment was a matter of the individual psyche, independent of external realities and especially of the actual experience of commodities. Colin Campbell argues that enchantment occurs as isolated individual daydreaming, and that realization of consumer fantasies is bound to disappoint and therefore underwrite the dynamic of renewed desires. I will later suggest that enchantment actually depended on action and that Campbell argues too strongly for a separation from reality, but we can also read Campbell as suggesting, more basically and profoundly, that imagination, fantasy, and dreaming had a value

---

[51] *Henley Advertiser*, 27 July 1895, 3; *Lloyd's Weekly*, 21 July 1895, 3; Schneider, *Culture and Enchantment*, 3.

[52] For a theoretical analysis shedding light on this phenomenon in terms of seduction in which consumers are complicit, see Deighton and Grayson, 'Marketing and Seduction'.

independent of their realization. The laughter in court confirms this point. As this and other events suggest, readers were aware that realization could disappoint, and were interested in the search nonetheless. There was a sense of empowerment in attempts to disrupt life courses and familiar ontologies by responding to adverts, but many were dead-ends. Readers were therefore willing to let go when fantasies became overstrained, move on to the next search, and reorient their desires.[53]

The independent value of imagination receives its most important support from the general dynamics revealed by fraud cases. Fraud suits usually featured complainants who were a small proportion of the tens, hundreds, thousands, and sometimes tens to hundreds of thousands who responded to the advertiser. We could explain this away by assuming that consumers did not find it worthwhile to complain and testify. However, an additional explanation, which takes seriously the sparsity of complaints as a cultural phenomenon, is that most people acknowledged an element of enchantment at work and did not intuitively recognize themselves within the terms of fraud that saw them as victims, often ignorant victims. Consumers' sense of agency was grounded in their ability to negotiate imagination and realism as I explain in the next section, and fraud cases put difficult pressure on that subtle movement. Most consumers therefore would not complain nor otherwise sue for civil remedies. This point was famously at issue in *Carlill v Carbolic Smoke Ball Company* in 1892, which started when the company refused to pay an advertised reward. The adverts said that consumers who used the smoke ball medicine and nonetheless caught influenza would receive £100. I will discuss the case in detail in Chapter 5, but here I would like to note the question of consumer complaints. In court, the company's counsel warned against a judgement that would open a flood of demands: 'At the present moment there might be 10,000 people watching for the result of this appeal.' The court did not heed the warning and decided against the company, yet as Brian Simpson noted in his study of the case, there was no flood. The company even turned the fact that it only received three demands into a new advert for the medicine.[54] Perhaps no one else caught influenza, but perhaps those who did appreciated that they were treading the lines of fantasy, and did not subscribe to reductions that crushed it. From this perspective, J.R.R. Tolkien was more legalistic than he intended when he wrote, 'Fantasy remains a human right'. Implicitly, he suggested that legal structures that did not recognize fantasy were lacking.[55]

I have been highlighting enchantments beyond commodity advertising, but *Carlill* already takes us into this area. Of course, with commodities an array of

---

[53] Campbell, *Romantic Ethic*. And see Beckert, *Imagined Futures*, ch. 8, for a discussion of the disillusionment entailed in appropriating commodities, when the imaginative value of transcendence is lost. On possibility itself as an ideology and survival mechanism, see Moretti, *Modern Epic*, ch. 6. On desire for desire see Belk, Weijo, and Kozinets, 'Enchantment and Perpetual Desire'.

[54] *Chemist and Druggist*, 10 December 1892, 841; Simpson, 'Quackery and Contract Law'.

[55] Tolkien, *On Fairy Stories*, 66.

imaginative metamorphoses opened up. As a commentator explained in 1869, adverts for commodities were '[m]agical and cabalistic, compelling mere words to alter, confuse and confound the realities of things, or to endow them with ideal properties, qualities, and perfections beyond the belief of credulity itself.' The phrasing seemed to waver between alternative interpretations of commodity animation: a real and dangerous animation, a false one, or possibly neutral fact of his historical moment, in which things are alive with people. All these positions are today familiar in scholarship. Raymond Williams's analysis of the 'Magic System' argued that the material object must be validated, if only in fantasy, by association with social and personal meanings without which most advertising would be insanely irrelevant. Williams drew on historical materialism, which following Marx's commodity fetishism has viewed the animation of things in capitalism as powerful and dangerous. Later critical views have drawn on post-structuralist traditions that interrogate animated things as reified meanings, which function as vehicles of power and domination. Meanwhile, the deep entanglements of matter and meaning in modernity have also been confirmed by alternative theories set in explicit opposition to critique. Thus, Mary Douglas and Baron Isherwood argued against the Cartesian dichotomy between physical and psychic experience that can only explain attachment to goods by sinister advertising and gullible consumers. Bruno Latour, the father of the ontological turn in the human sciences, has collapsed dichotomies between human and nonhuman: 'Humans are not the ones who arbitrarily add the "symbolic dimension" to pure material forces. These forces are as transcendent, active, agitated, spiritual, as we are.' Disenchantment is impossible on this theory, and advertising's animations inescapable. Where Williams argued that society was not materialist enough, Bennett posits an enchanted materialism in which commodities reveal a playful and surprising will. On her argument, the theory of commodity fetishism is not capacious enough to account for the fascination with commercial goods. She locates the enchantment effect primarily in the aesthetic or theatrical dimension of commodities, and in their function as tangible and public elaborations of identities. In short, the 'magical and cabalistic' power of commodity adverts is now accepted across disciplines and intellectual traditions, which have provided alternative interpretations of its implications for modernity.[56]

The 1897 story of Arthur Lewis Pointing reveals how the power of commodity advertising played out in the lives of ordinary people, and shows some of the complexities of mundane experience that invited, as they still do, competing interpretations. Described as a druggist's sundryman, Pointing was in fact

---

[56] 'Grand Force', 1869, 380; Williams, 'Advertising'; Douglas and Isherwood, *World of Goods*, 49; Latour, *We Have Never Been Modern*, 128. See also Latour, *On the Modern Cult*, ch. 1. For an application of Latourian sociology to contemporary advertising as magic, see Malefyt, 'Magic of Paradox'. Bennett, *Enchantment of Modern Life*.

something of a chameleon: like other dodgy tradesmen of his time, he multiplied himself with changing names, addresses, genders, and legal forms. He was the man behind the Oriental Toilet Company, which offered what the *Daily News* mockingly called the elevation of mankind.[57] The adverts urged short people to buy elevators. The capitalized LITTLE, performed the fantasy of amplification (Figure 1.12).

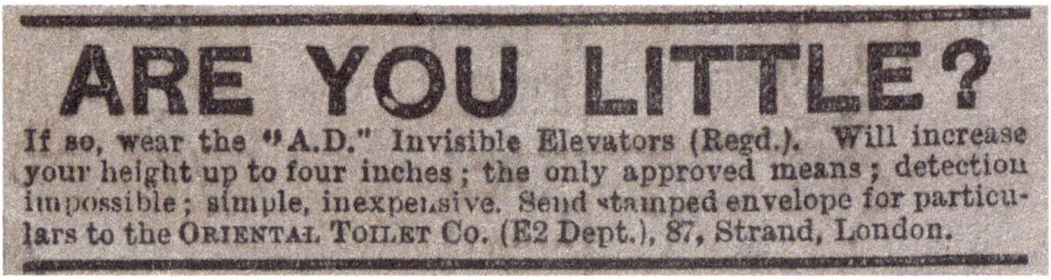

ARE YOU LITTLE?
If so, wear the "A.D." Invisible Elevators (Regd.). Will increase your height up to four inches; the only approved means; detection impossible; simple, inexpensive. Send stamped envelope for particulars to the ORIENTAL TOILET Co. (E2 Dept.), 87, Strand, London.

Figure 1.12 Arthur Pointing, Invisible Elevators advertisement. *Illustrated Chips*, 3 October 1896, 6.

Like Alice's bottle in wonderland, the advert offered a magical transfiguration. Those who responded received a circular stressing the urgency of Pointing's invention in a rapid move from flattery to insult:

> 'Little and good' had long been an accepted axiom... That little people are fully as capable, as brave, as good, and as intellectual as their bigger brethren, history has exemplified... Unluckily the world is hard to please... Hence the unquestionable advantage of a tall imposing figure. Many will... praise... little women, but few little men. Little women... can be... very attractive; but when [they]... get past their fresh beauty and become fat or thin their trials begin. We all know how ridiculous it is to see a little fat woman waddling along like some motherly old duck... a small, thin woman... most often succeeds in looking vulgar... Even her Gracious Majesty is aware of the added dignity a tall figure gives, for it is a well-known fact that she stands on a footstool at her receptions...[58]

Adverts also offered illustrated instruction (Figure 1.13).

Despite the designation 'regd.', there was no registered patent or trademark; Pointing was selling pieces of cork to place inside shoes. On offer were elevators to raise a person from 1 to 4½ inches, in two qualities. Going rates were 2*s.* 6*d.* and 5*s.* 6*d.*, but the company regularly wrote to consumers that the cheaper version was out of stock, and prompted them to buy the expensive one (approximately £35 in 2020), in fact identical. Pointing's business was no empire, but he employed thirteen girls to open his letters, two thousand of which were seized in a police

---

[57] The list appeared in the *Morning Post*, 27 May 1897, 8; *Daily News*, 18 June 1897, 9.
[58] *Standard*, 3 June 1897, 3.

Figure 1.13 Arthur Pointing, Invisible Elevators illustrated advertisement. *Pick-Me-Up*, 14 November 1896, 112.

search in his fourteen addresses. Within a year and a half, he had sold 4,150 pairs of elevators. The trouble was that not all consumers got high; the elevators were too small, or too painful, or both. Frederick Day, for example, an amateur actor who wanted to look taller on stage, only gained one-eighth of an inch, with back pain and cramped toes. The company was not responsive and so some consumers went to the police.

At the Bow Street Police Court, witnesses of 'short or...medium height' came to testify (Figure 1.14).[59] The testimonies revealed the extent of imagination in the reception of adverts, which continued even after the pieces of cork had arrived, when dreams of transformative science met with the simplicity of conception and with the actual smallness of size. The banality of the commodity did not preclude fantasy. A domestic servant, for example, said she did not use mirrors and did not know whether she looked taller with the elevators. A shop assistant measured himself against a wall and was disappointed that a miraculous metamorphosis never occurred: he gained only an inch. He was also surprised that the elevators were uncomfortable when science was so advanced. The testimony of Stephen Gent, a plumber from Lancashire, showed how dreams could shift from one commodity to the next. Having found the elevators so painful that he had to remove them in the middle of the street in a literal subversion of his secret elevation, Gent wanted his money back, but the company proposed an exchange.

[59] *Illustrated Police News*, 12 June 1897, 7.

Figure 1.14 Pointing and his customers in court. *Penny Illustrated Paper*, 3 July 1897, 6.

He decided to ask for a hand-glass, but got a box of liver pills (a quack remedy associated with a variety of cures) with a letter hoping they would satisfy as the company was out of hand-glasses. Fantasy could circulate, Pointing knew: he always kept letters offering exchanges. Gent was not satisfied, thinking that 'a good dose of Epsom salts' would have been better. Horace Avory, the prominent criminal lawyer, Treasury Counsel, and judge-to-be who represented Pointing, asked Gent how many pills he took, a question that implied that Gent was not really dissatisfied, and forced the image of moving desire to keep moving. Gent said he only took two, but gave four to his daughter. Transforming oneself was an imaginative search, not a conclusion. Gent was a consumer willing hold to the magical power of commodities to significant lengths, while others were quicker to become disenchanted and frustrated. We also hear again laughter in court, as still others let go on enchantment with light hearts. The range of reactions revealed a range of views on commodity power.[60]

Pointing's elevators were also a reminder of the complex background of advertising magic, which is sometimes lost in accounts of hedonistic consumerism. Magic was often pursued in desperation. Imaginative escape from pain is formally hedonic, yet it bears emphasis that in these instances readers were conscious of difficulties rather than pleasures. In responding to adverts, they chased miracles to overcome struggles of economy, malfunctioning bodies, painful emotions, and a sense of failure. As theories of magic drawing on Bronislaw Malinowski argue, it is a cultural resource for assuaging anxiety, facing uncertainty, and overcoming powerlessness. We might listen to 'Mr A', a witness before the Select Committee on Patent Medicines, who explained in 1912 why he responded to a market advertiser of medicine for tuberculosis: 'You must understand that we poor mortals who happen to have this disease are anxious

---

[60] *Reynolds's Newspaper*, 13 June 1897, 1; *Illustrated Police News*, 19 June 1897, 8.

to try everything... and if we do find a man who tells us these things, we hang on to it... to see if there is any chance whatever.' In despair, faith kicked in. Similarly, Jane Eyre keeps 'involuntarily framing advertisements' when miserable. As Mr A implied, despair was an existential condition of mortal beings, and faith was their way of allaying it.[61]

Accounts of and by readers reveal them active in searches for metamorphoses. With different moods: playful, adventurous, excited, desperate, bewildered, pragmatic, and with different levels of engagement, they explored possibilities for transforming their social and private selves, and recasting lived meanings by tapping into the economically held worlds of mass advertising. The next section shows how evidence of reading modes can deepen our understanding of these enchantments.

Fascinated Travels

Reading modes reveal how mass advertising was navigated as an enchanted environment. Evidence suggests that the typical reading mode involved a dual condition: on the one hand, a drifting amid adverts in a mode of superficial attention. On the other hand, a willingness to sharply focus attention and be dragged in by a particular advert. This mode reflected the broader phenomenon of a teeming sensory environment explored by theorists of modernity. Georg Simmel argued in 1903 that the overstimulation of cities led people to apply 'an extremely varied hierarchy of sympathies, indifferences and aversions', precisely as readers were doing with adverts. As Jonathan Crary observes, Simmel was theorizing a problem of attention. Capacities were overburdened by capitalism's demand for a rapid switching from one thing to another, as novelty and distraction became constituents of perceptual experience. Already in mid-century, a commentator observed that adverts revealed 'a public which had not time to inquire, nor the habit... of reflection'.[62] The overload was such, argues Crary, that by the 1870s thinkers in Western culture became concerned with the malfunction of capacities for synthesis. Focusing attention, that is, isolating certain contents of a sensory field at the expense of others, emerged as a social, economic, psychological, and philosophical theme, and as a normative requirement central to accounts of subjectivity. In reading mass advertising, superficial attention spoke to a quantity and variety that eluded a comprehensive grasp and left no choice but to wander. The overload was a given for readers, but with benefits: it enabled an enjoyable aimless

---

[61] Select Committee on Patent Medicines, 1914, q. 4158; Brontë, *Jane Eyre*, 1847, 170. For an analysis of Jane's (alienating) metamorphosis through advertisement, see Marcus, 'Profession of the Author'.
[62] Simmel, 'The Metropolis and Mental Life', 53; 'Age of Veneer', 1852.

browsing that was only just becoming acceptable in large department stores, encouraged fascination with strangeness, playfulness, and a taste for surprise.[63]

The reading mode of mass advertising manifested in the prevalent use of the verb *to see*, despite the fact that readers were usually referring to textual matter: 'I saw an advertisement in the *Times* of that day'; 'I had seen the advertisements'; 'in May last my wife saw in the *Bazaar and Mart* an advertisement'. The sensory experience of sight was privileged over the intellectual experience of reading, speaking to Bennett's account enchanting power: 'to be enchanted...is to participate in a momentarily immobilizing encounter; it is to be transfixed, spellbound.' As Morgan explains, visualization is a staple feature of advertising, and that is how enchantment begins: in the simple act of training one's attention on the object of desire, usually as mediated by the image or representation of it.[64]

The terminology of seeing also communicated a discontinuous experience with a spontaneous undertone, in which an advert suddenly, without previous plan, entered a person's perceptual field and consciousness. Some readers felt that their browsing was becoming a new visual technology: 'his experienced eye, ranging from column to column, can pick out all that is peculiar and interesting...as readily as a deer-stalker can detect a royal hart upon a distant hill-side, or an alderman the tid-bits of turtle in the wide turee.' Many opted for the passive voice, which expressed their sense of being transfixed by attributing agency to adverts. Lacking authors and acting of themselves, adverts seemed to reach out and stop people in their tracks: 'my attention was attracted to this advertisement'; 'my attention was first drawn to this sale, by an advertisement in the *Morning Post*.' Harriet Martineau recalled an 1827 advertisement that she described fifty years later in active terms: 'a spirited advertisement...met my eye...I could not resist sending a practical reply...' Although readers sometimes described an active intention to find adverts, for example for a particular job or product, more often they were not engaged in a methodical search, a linear accumulation of knowledge, or a rational comparison. They were in for the unknown.[65]

If we return to the detectives' advert discussed earlier (Figure 1.11), we might consider again the encounter with it. Figure 1.15 shows the full page on which it appeared.

---

[63] Crary, *Suspensions of Perception*. On aimless browsing and new open-entry shops, see Bowlby, *Just Looking*. For a study of the reading experience in the Dickens Advertiser as 'floating attention', see Thornton, *Advertising, Subjectivity*. For a study of magazine experience as 'tessellating reading' in which readers create meaning across fiction and adverts, see Lanning, 'Tessellating Texts'. For an analysis of absentmindedness, see Moretti, *Modern Epic*, ch. 6.

[64] Ward (1844); Leverson (1868); Walker and Carter (1879); Bennett, *Enchantment of Modern Life*, 5; Morgan, *Images at Work*, 18.

[65] *Chambers' Edinburgh Journal*, 25 January 1851, 55; Bays and others (1862); Milson (1851); Salmon (1886); Martineau, *Harriet Martineau's Autobiography*, 1877, 106.

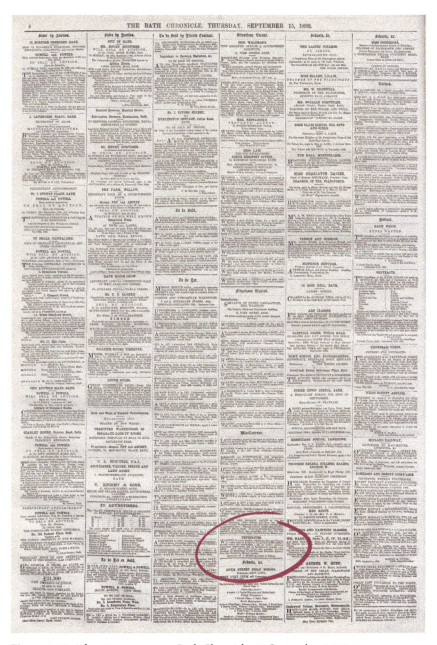

Figure 1.15 Advertisement page, *Bath Chronicle*, 15 September 1892, 4.

Placed under a 'miscellaneous' category, the advert stood out with its bold 'Detectives' title, but required a searching mode that scanned the page. As the variety of respondents revealed, becoming detectives was an afterthought of the encounter, not a pre-planned search. Indeed, the arrest of attention *in medias res* was a common way to begin a story about advertising. Even a person prone to search, like Olive Malvery on an investigative journalistic mission, described inattentive browsing suddenly broken by an advert. She bought a local Brixton paper casually, because she was waiting at a station: 'glancing through the advertisements, I was struck by one which gave the address of the same house that I had lately passed...'.[66] The sense of small shock, the halt of regularity, was central to accounts of reading mass advertising.

A different example comes from a bus ride in London, where passengers passed through streams of posters. A bus driver recounted a group from Blackwall who asked his advice on 'the best "bit" to see' as they rode to Piccadilly Circus. While he was offering his experience, they saw a poster, which was in all likelihood the same one found in Oxford, shown in Figure 1.16. The advert 'pleased them very much, as the old boys were seafaring chaps', and the play became their destination. The unexpected encounter with the advertised image offered these East Enders an entry point into the other side of town, a basis for imaginatively relocating their selves and affectively relating to the unfamiliar scene.[67]

Usually, a methodical reading of masses of adverts was a vocational practice. Some business models, such as Next-of-Kin agencies, were based on intermediary capacities of systematically reading and collecting adverts, which contrasted with the way individual readers browsed, regularly skipping, failing to notice, and forgetting.[68] However, lay readers could also turn vocational in their capacity as collectors of adverts in albums and scrapbooks. Scrapbooking involved the selection and arrangement of print cuttings in ways that repurposed them, slowed down, and deepened engagements. Collectors created, as Alexis Easley argues, a permanent record that overcame ephemerality, and imbued adverts with personal and cultural value by appropriating and recontextualizing them.[69] Scrapbooking motivations were sometimes professional, for example when used by advertisers to study or present copy designs, but a dominant use was domestic, a female art form and culture responsive to the availability of mechanically reproduced images. These revealed a more dispersed fascination.

Historians of popular culture have studied scrapbooks to learn about reception and particularly about agency and resistance to dominant gender and consumerist imperatives. Resistance would appear to imply a disenchanted distance from adverts, and occasionally was. However, subversive challenges to

---

[66] This led to her investigation of working conditions at a dressmaker's shop. Malvery, *Soul Market*, 1907, 182–3.

[67] *AW*, March 1905, 358.   [68] Another example was car trading.

[69] For a discussion of the interrelations between distracted attention and collecting, see Jervis, *Sensational Subjects*, ch. 5. On the coexistence of models of volitional and desensitized observers, see Otter, *Victorian Eye*. Easley, 'Resistant Consumer'.

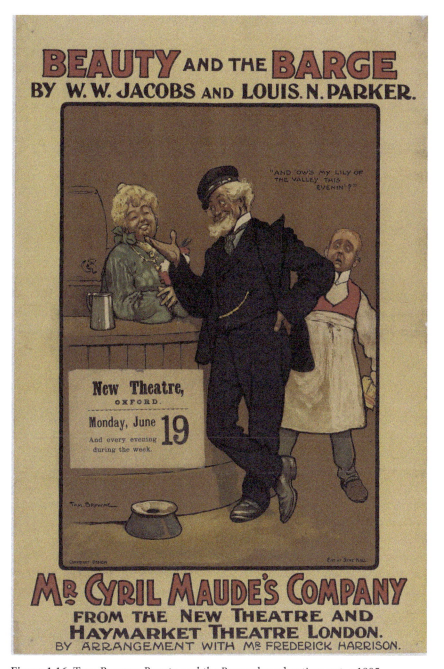

Figure 1.16 Tom Browne, *Beauty and the Barge* play advertisement, c.1905.

commercial culture were unusual, while scrapbooking often sanctioned advertising. Moreover, even where satire and ideological subversion appeared, scrapbooking foregrounded fantasy, desire, play, and tactility, fired the imagination and inspired attachments. A creator could ignore or resist, for example, the marketing imperative of an advert, and yet be engrossed in its enchanting images, as Walter Benjamin was with a poster to which I turn later. Enchantment was not the same as functional persuasion and was not bound to any advertiser's goals, but that did not mean a consumer somehow wriggled out of the worlds of advertising altogether. As Craig Thompson argues in a contemporary context of consumer myths, all identity positions, including resistance, occur within the marketplace and draw on its resources.[70]

An anonymous album from the late nineteenth or early twentieth century reveals how enchantment occurred beyond the goals of advertisers. The creator meticulously cut images from adverts, separated colour from black and white, and arranged cuttings by what appear to be commodity clusters of food and hygiene products, although not all images are locatable. Brand names were preserved where they were part of the image, but not otherwise. For this creator, adverts came together to reveal fanciful relationships. She (most likely) was rearranging their iconography to present imagined communities of humans and nonhumans in print material. The arrangements were absorbed in alternative animations of commodities to those purportedly intended by the advertisers, and foregrounded flows of meaning through and among advertising images (Figures 1.17–1.20).

Advertising images often appeared to enter unproblematically into a broader visual imagination, as in the example in Figure 1.21, where the racist Pears soap image at the centre blended with the compiler's revelling in the stimulation of image crowding.

Even in an album apparently compiled by an advertising professional (Figure 1.22), the creator was fascinated by the interaction of adverts, and engaged in combinations that suggested animated conversations rather than a hard-nosed organization of designs, which was presumably the practical goal. These talking hands foregrounded the supernatural undercurrents of advertising. Hands detached from bodies or indeed human consciousness were entering communities of their making. The pages invited a rethinking of the nature of things, for instance when a bicycle was miniatured, or an intangible reputation visualized. It showed unexpected yet apparently easy interactions between different orders of meaning: the violence of a pistol, the promise of a medicine, the cleanliness of a soap, the claim of a newspaper to integrity, all coming together,

---

[70] Easley, 'Resistant Consumer'; Damkjær, *Time, Domesticity*; Garvey, *Adman in the Parlor*; Di Bello, *Women's Albums*; Zieger, *Mediated Mind*, introduction; Thompson, 'Marketplace Mythology'.

Figure 1.17 Anonymous album. The human and nonhuman brought together in a set of masculine images, each throwing into relief as well as radically questioning the others. How can the smoking dog, for example, appear supreme to the contained colonial producer of cocoa? If he is contained, why is he walking when Quaker Oats says 'stop'? Who is the ass in the composition?

Figure 1.18 Anonymous album. Women's sexualized images placed so as to conform to the caricatured policeman's gesture. A unidirectional hand-gesture appears to be compulsively repeated.

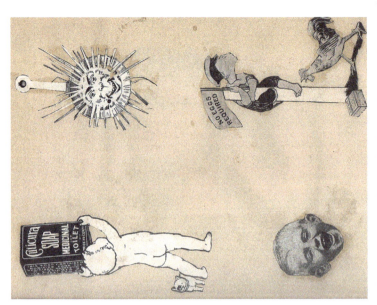

Figure 1.19 Anonymous album. The advertisement hailing the reader to look over also performs the task itself by looking over the other images. The same is performed by the bull and child in those images. The structure presented an animistic world of unseen connections.

Figure 1.20 Anonymous album. The diagonal juxtapositions of faces and children in inverted sizes highlighted the surreal in advertising. Does fear strike as much as amusement with unseen similarities between the baby and the monkey sun?

Figure 1.21 Anonymous Victorian scrapbook. Image crowding; the round Pears image curiously invites a sense of circulation in the encounter with the page.

Figure 1.22 Scrapbook contributed by the Institute of Advertising Professionals, source unknown. Hands in imaginative dialogue.

MASS ADVERTISING'S APPEALS   75

undermining or complicating one another in what at first glance seems too obvious because of the common theme of hands, the common matter of print, and the common system of advertising.

An 1870s–80s scrapbook dominated by personal and religious themes, with reflections on the connections between nature and faith, featured a single advert (Figure 1.23). Speculatively, we might read the implied statement about competing sources of enchantment, along the same lines we saw in O'Connor's painting (Figure 1.1), Onions's novel, or Carlyle.

Figure 1.23 Anonymous scrapbook. A single advert in a religiously inflected scrapbook composition.

A similar speculation is invited by the mixtures in the scrapbook in Figure 1.24. The centre image on the left page is an advert for puppy biscuits marketed

76   THE RISE OF MASS ADVERTISING

Figure 1.24 Anonymous scrapbook. Est. late 1890s or early 1900s.

with children as 'the beauty of innocence'. Meanwhile, in the equivalent centre on the right we find a religious narrative of children being blessed. The creator seemed attentive to competing demands for higher meaning, on the one hand those of traditional sources of enchantment and, on the other, advertised images.

George William Joy's 1895 painting, *The Bayswater Omnibus* (Figure 1.25) was a sophisticated comment on advert-reading as enchanted travel. Sitting below a line of posters, the characters do not look at them, which, Ruth Iskin argues, reflects the common experience of outdoor advertising as an unintended viewing taken in passing. She also notes that the adverts were probably the actual posters on that particular bus, because Joy convinced the London General Bus Company to lend him a vehicle.[71] However, these comments have each, and together, a complementary side. As with Solomon's painting discussed earlier (Figure 1.4), the adverts communicate with the viewer, who *is* contemplating them, and the sitters' composition was Joy's artistic choice even if the adverts were given. There is therefore good reason to consider the painting as a visual comment on reading advertising. Joy's construction invited the viewer to speculate on the characters' and adverts' mutual animation. For example, the nurse on the right assumes the same wondering look of the child in the Pears soap advert created from John Everett Millais's painting ('*Bubbles*', which also appeared in Earl's painting (see Figure 1.3), more about it in Chapter 3). At the same time, in terms of colour, the *Bubbles* child blends with the gentleman passenger underneath him, who matches the child's sitting angle yet contrasts him exactly by looking down and to the right, rather than up and left. The gentleman with newspaper is also in dialogue with the second Pears soap advert, in which a woman bursts through a paper. Nixey's Black Lead

---

[71] Iskin, *Poster*, ch. 5.

Figure 1.25 George William Joy, *The Bayswater Omnibus*, 1895.

advert with a box is echoed in the milliner with the box entering the omnibus, while the colourful Roussillon advert is echoed in the fashionable woman underneath it, down to the bright orange patch tending left. The advert above the poor anxious mother, as Joy described her, appears to depict some kind of glow, but it is faded and cannot be made out although there is nothing in the viewing angle to justify the stark difference from other adverts, just as the mother's expression is the least clear to the viewer and intentionally shrouded in the black background.[72] The invitation to consider these relationships of mutual constitution spoke to the entanglements of identities with adverts that the viewer was bound to contemplate. Here again, the search was more important than any specific conclusion.

Ways of reading adverts, both browsing and collecting, demonstrate the experiences of enchantment in which time was irregular, surprise dominated over predictability, and meanings flowed from things to humans and in imaginative in between spaces, so as to recast natural properties, reveal unexpected relationships, and reanimate familiar environments. In the next section I examine the central role of reason and realism in these experiences.

Reasoned Enchantments

In 1908 H.G. Wells published *Tono-Bungay*, which narrated the rise and fall of an advertising-propelled brand of health commodities. The narrator, George Ponderevo, is consumed with guilt over his part in the business, which he

---

[72] On Joy's description, see Galinou and Hayes, *London in Paint*, 333.

sees as a fraud. His uncle Edward takes a different view: 'Romance. 'Magination, See?...There's no fraud in this affair...' In staging this conflict, Wells interrogated the basis of the economy. According to Edward, advertising appealed to a romantic spirit and was therefore impervious to epistemological verification. According to George, it was referential and therefore either true or false. Wells was an acute philosopher of advertising and realized, to his socialist frustration, that lived experience was in the muddy water between these idealizations. After all, Wells himself was in the business of "magination' as Michael Ross notes. A contemporary advertising professional commented that Wells could have been a genius advertiser.[73] With the character of Ewart, George's artist friend called to design adverts for *Tono-Bungay*, Wells explained the co-dependence between enchantment and realism that undergirded the business success:

> Think of the little clerks and jaded women and overworked people. People overstrained with wanting to do, people overstrained with wanting to be... None of us want to be what we are, or to do what we do. Except as a sort of basis. What do we want? *You* know. *I* know. Nobody confesses. What we all want to be is something perpetually young and beautiful...pursuing coy half-willing nymphs through everlasting forests...[74]

Ewart knew that advertising tapped existential desires but required grounding in a 'sort of basis' of realism. His insight resonated with the treasure-hunt adverts, which invited consumers to ground their participation in reason, as consumers indeed claimed to be doing. They had to be careful readers, have conventional historical knowledge, be embedded in the locality and its daily doings, and prove observant. As one of them explained his success, 'I worked on a system...with good results.' A rational actor, he was efficient and methodical rather than feverish in his search for treasures: set for breakfast, read carefully, and made a plan. Another hunter worked 'thoroughly, measuring the distances'. These ideal rational beings applied their faculties of reason to dreams of life-changing treasures in affectively charged ways, liberated their desires for adventure and play, and imagined their worlds anew. Along similar lines, Kelley argues that consumers who responded to prize soap adverts engaged in rational thrifty behaviours, and in this way tapped into the pleasures of advertised luxuries and staged spectacle.[75]

This section explores more closely the central place of reason and realism in enchantment, which challenges a basic premise of the thesis of disenchantment. In a disenchanted culture as described by Max Weber, enchantment would make no

---

[73] Wells, *Tono-Bungay*, 136; Ross, *Designing Fictions*, ch. 2; *AW*, December 1911, 714. In Chapter 4, I examine *Tono-Bungay*'s complex position on the tension between advertising and science.
[74] Wells, *Tono-Bungay*, 158.
[75] *Weekly Dispatch*, 17 January 1904, 5; Kelley, *Soap and Water*, 157–62.

claims to realism and would forsake empirical evidence and reason.[76] Yet historians of enchantment repeatedly find that this was not the case in the late nineteenth and early twentieth centuries. For example, Alex Owen's study of British occultism in the *fin de siècle* suggests that modern enchantment was committed to the guiding principle of reason and played to a formalized concept of rationality even as it contested rationalism. Terry Castle observes that the fascination with magic lanterns celebrated rationalist explanations yet mixed them up with imagination. Eugene McCarraher finds mixtures of realism and enchantment in poetic Romanticism: 'In the Romantic sensibility, imagination was not a talent for inspiring fantasy, but the most perspicuous form of vision – the ability to see what is really there...' This view saw no fundamental contradiction between reason and re-enchantment. Saler shows rationalist modes of thought applied to enchantment in New Romance fiction that combined the objective style of realism with the fantastic content of romance. As he argues, in the second half of the nineteenth century imagination was liberated from historical shackles, and unlike historical romanticism it could be contingent and artificial rather than metaphysical, and endorse the artifices of mass culture rather than stress sincerity and authenticity.[77]

With readers of adverts, the role of reason and realism manifested in less rigorous terms than self-conscious theories of spiritualism, carefully authored fiction, orchestrated performances, political philosophy, or scientific theory. We are dealing with the everyday of ordinary people from all classes deciding where and how to obtain things, services, work, amusement. Yet the traces they left reveal hybridizations of enchanted and disenchanted worlds.[78] As the following discussion demonstrates, hybridizations occurred in two directions. In some cases, readers treated adverts as providing a rational basis for pursuing fantasies. In other cases, they treated adverts as the stuff of dreams, which they were adjusting to realism through their own knowledge and experience of the world, supposedly more sober. Adverts appeared to assume contradictory roles in these cases, but the contradiction was superficial. In both directions, advertising required weaving together enchantment and reason. In both directions, readers did so by moving back and forth between individual adverts and the broader world of mass advertising. A number of characteristics of the mass facilitated enchantment but also made it seem reasonable or realistic: scantiness of information, which required a reasoning from clues and resort to background knowledges; the presence of

---

[76] As Egil Asprem puts it, 'Forsaking reason and the pursuit of empirical evidence is the only way in which religion exists for a disenchanted view.' Asprem, *Problem of Disenchantment*, 80.
[77] Owen, *Place of Enchantment*; Castle, 'Phantasmagoria'; McCarraher, *Enchantments of Mammon*, ch. 3; Saler, *As If*. The role of reason is also central to contemporary studies of enchantment. For the debate about rationalization in consumer enchantment in the late twentieth and twenty first centuries, see, for example, Ostergaard, Fitchett, and Jantzen, 'Critique'.
[78] On hybrids in scientific thought, see Asprem, *Problem of Disenchantment*.

addresses, which grounded adverts and created a sense of place; and repetition, the *sine qua non* of advertising that gave reality to ephemeral and imaginative presences. Critically, the role of reason in all cases was to allow enchantments to proliferate. I explore some examples before discussing the implications.

Charles Wells advertised for investors to tap into the symbols of industrial progress by financing his inventions of steam engine and arc-light improvements. He raised almost £30,000 in investments and loans (close to £4 million in 2020), most of which, as it turned out, he gambled away in Monte Carlo. Catherine Phillimore, sister of Judge Walter Phillimore, advanced more than half of the money in the hope of benefiting humankind. She reflected on her reading of the advert: 'the letters "C. E." [civil engineer] influenced me to a certain extent.' This apparently simple comment reveals a prevalent cultural condition in reading adverts: scanty in information, they functioned like clues released into circulation. Every advert invited an active imagination to develop its implications. Saler argues that Sherlock Holmes's iconic status lay in his animistic reason that moved between the observation of discrete facts and a lively imagination, demonstrating how profane reality was as mysterious and alluring as the supernatural.[79] Advertising revealed how moves from minuscule and isolated facts to encompassing meanings infused everyday life. *Fin de siècle* culture encouraged them, but was not a unique moment so much as an evident pitch of an earlier proliferation. As Carlo Ginzburg suggests in 'Clues and the Scientific Method', the late nineteenth century saw the rise of conjectural knowledge to respectability in the human sciences. The conjectural paradigm, however, had old roots in the ancient practice of divination. Sherlock Holmes was one example of its late Victorian success (and fittingly, advertisements figured prominently in his mystery-solving methods). Conjecture moved from clues to knowledge and so breached the sterile contrast, as Ginzburg calls it, between rational and irrational, and sustained a sense of comprehension by drawing on factors that could not be measured.[80] Compelled to create knowledge in the environment of mass advertising suffused with minute clues, readers practised this form of knowledge regularly. The *Strand Magazine*, which featured Sherlock Holmes chapters, shrewdly invited advertisers to take advantage of the combination (Figure 1.26).

Like Phillimore, many readers anchored their imaginative projections in rational indications found in adverts. For example, Charlotte Tidy participated in a puzzle-solving competition that required her to first buy a bottle of the advertiser's ink. She discovered that the solutions were tricky and the ink useless. What made her pay in the first place? Tidy explained: 'seeing the name of "Deacon" on them [adverts], I thought they were the bankers.' She had in mind

---

[79] *Mansfield Reporter*, 27 January 1893, 3; Wells (1893); Saler, *As If*, 108–9.
[80] Ginzburg, 'Clues and Scientific Method'.

Figure 1.26 *Strand Magazine* advertisement. *Advertisers' Review*, 26 August 1901, 4.

Williams, Deacon, and Co.[81] That a banker should be behind an ink advertisement, and with a partial name, required a fantastic jump that clearly made the world seem more holistic and familiar than it was. Or we might listen to some of the 18,966 persons who invested in a losing concern described as a bank that offered safe, high-yielding investments. They explained how they imaginatively drew on adverts. The words 'Established 1870', and a statement about forty branches, for example, gave reality to an unknown business, as did references to colonial investments. Respondents admittedly did not want full knowledge and opted for imagination instead. As one explained, 'there was an intimation that "any additional information required" could be had from the bank; I never asked for any further information.' These people were not interested in demystifying economic gain or economic entities, they preferred to live with dreams of windfalls and retain room for incalculable powers in their lives. To preserve such powers, elements of inscrutability had to be in place, and those often required an active avoidance of full knowledge. The *potential* of verifiability was reassuring, but actually verifying things

[81] *Gabriel and others* (1899).

could ruin imaginations and take away the small enchantments that adverts offered.[82]

The carefully orchestrated distance that readers maintained from full knowledge manifested in the most commonplace instances. For example, in 1891 Griffiths Jones advertised coal described as 'the talk of London', and the 'best burning coals the world produces'. Coals were sold at 18s. per ton when the market price for high-quality coals was 26s. The coal disappointed. Women whose Sunday dinner did not cook, whose houses remained cold, whose water would not boil, testified against Jones. One of them, the wife of a commercial traveller, explained: 'I do not know the price...I expected to get the best coal for 18s.'[83] As household manageress she was generally aware that the price was attractive, and she expected the unusual, hence her denial of exact knowledge. We see here the constitutive tension between the doubting attitude that reason demanded, and the tendency towards intuitive certainty and fantasy against reason. A retired tradesman who lost money by responding to a stockbroking advert in the 1870s, revealed a fully contradictory consciousness between rational doubt and dreaming belief:

> I entrusted 50*l*. to people whom I had never seen, to do something, I don't know what. I could not tell whether I should lose or win I did not expect to lose; I did not think I could lose. I expected to get some return on the investment. I thought I should make money – I did not think I was going in for a fortune – I read the pamphlet carefully through.[84]

The man represented himself as careful even as he admitted to not knowing what he was investing in, and with whom. He denied having wild expectations while also denying the rational option of losing. His contradictory statements demonstrated how uneasy the negotiation of reason and imagination could become.

The role of addresses in advertising played to the same tension. Most adverts contained an address, which represented market activity as physically locatable in years in which shopping outlets were not yet standardized. In its most abstract form, modern branding required consumers to know where to find the product. Only then could they forge a direct relationship with the branded commodity, without additional details. This was not yet available for many commodities, nor for many services, investments, and labour. Searching for a business in trade directories would have been cumbersome if not inaccessible, therefore an address was necessary. Even when abstract brand advertising was present, it depended on the sense of place that the rest of advertising provided. As the *Advertising World* explained, the 'artillery' of posters often did not contain addresses and therefore depended on the press:

---

[82] *Carpenter* (1911); *Manchester Courier*, 7 December 1911, 9; *Dundee Evening Telegraph*, 26 January 1911, 1. On instructibles in occult economies see Comaroff and Comaroff, 'Occult Economies;' Comaroff and Comaroff, 'Millennial Capitalism'. *Times*, August 20, 1842, 4.

[83] *Jones* (1891); *Standard*, 25 November 1891, 3.   [84] *Riches* (1877).

My picture gallery is, after all, the artillery of advertising, and the infantry must be brought into use by means of the press and other mediums. Well, when artillery fire, they do not bother to leave their name and address. They simply bang away, so as to advise their friends and foes alike that they have arrived.[85]

However, the use of addresses by readers was complex, as they often kept their distance. Many did not know what the address represented, and more importantly, did not want to know. They wanted the knowledge to be available in principle, while in practice they conducted transactions by post. Actual verification usually occurred only when things went wrong. Then, stories about premises that were vacant, tiny, or only mailing addresses revealed the emptiness of what should have been a lively business, and were told in damning terms. Finding a vacuum violated the belief fostered by addresses that there was a 'genuine' business, as it was often put, and undermined the towers of dreams built on that basis.[86]

Repetition was another rationalist anchor that readers invoked. A woman asked why she had given her baby a medicine suspected to have killed him, explained: 'It is advertised in a great many papers.' Another reader explained, 'I believed the statements contained in that advertisement for the reason that I saw it, or a similar advertisement, a number of times.' Part of the effect for consumers was the reality that repetition gave to the obscure being or thing gestured by the advert. It signalled persistence in time and space that withstood competitive trials in the market, and therefore rationally justified trust. At the same time, repetition was closely tied with enchantment. It indicated the mysteries of economic abundance, as Burn commented in 1855: 'We cannot help thinking, that their [advertisers'] stock is like the magic bottle, the more it decreases the larger it grows!'[87] There was an element of ritualism that countered the sense of wilderness and encouraged comfort with ephemeral and often strange presences. As we will see in Chapter 7, professional advertisers indeed viewed repetition as a way to bypass reason. Horkheimer and Adorno picked it up in the interwar era when they wrote about repetition as sorcery.[88]

I have so far looked at readers reasoning from the adverts they encountered to rationalize their trust. In some cases, readers reasoned in the other direction, by explaining that they *did* doubt adverts but then applied external knowledge that justified their decision to respond. As already noted, the difference was ultimsately unimportant, because in both directions imagination and reason were interwoven, and in both readers resorted to characteristics of mass advertising to stabilize their viewpoints.

An example of doubting readers could be seen in responses to the 1885 advertisement in Figure 1.27, a prize competition for newspaper subscribers.

---

[85] *AW*, June 1902, 27.   [86] See, for example, *Reeves* (1880).
[87] *Times*, 23 August 1902, 10; *Symons and others* (1907); Burn, *Language of the Walls*, 1855, 6.
[88] Horkheimer and Adorno, 'Culture Industry', 134.

84   THE RISE OF MASS ADVERTISING

Figure 1.27 George Halley, prize competition advertisement. *Penny Illustrated Paper*, 17 January 1885, 48.

Every morning George Halley, the advertiser, received some one hundred letters with remittances from readers who obtained subscriptions for his magazine, allegedly amounting to £70,000 (over £9 million in 2020). Readers were disappointed to receive cheap gifts. A tailor from Caterham who had convinced fifty of his clients to subscribe, described his expectations: 'I did not think it was likely I should get the 1,000*l*. prize, but I thought I should something worth more than the picture.' The man's logic was shared by others. A private in the Coldstream Guards similarly did not expect the maximum. He would have been satisfied with a 'locket or with a good watch'. He 'expected something worth having in consequence of the advertisement'. A woman confirmed: 'If I had had a shilling present I should have been satisfied.' These readers saw the large prizes as beyond rational expectations, yet justified their responsiveness to the advert by bringing their own rationalist ideas into dialogue with it. Put otherwise, perceptions of reality were anchored by dreams, which were explicitly understood to be beyond reason. In another case, a business manager lost his money after he responded to an advert that promised 25s. a week on every £10 invested, 'with the capital under your own control. No stocks or gambling transactions...' He recalled: 'Radcliff said there was no risk – I thought there was a "part risk" – I do not believe everything I am told – I take it with considerable discount as a business man.' We see a discounting of advertising promises at work, yet the fantasy that amid piles of adverts an unusual opportunity had been discovered palpitated.[89]

In 1900, hundreds of people sent money in response to the advert in Figure 1.28.

Figure 1.28 Charles Hanford, 'link' bicycle advertisement. *Illustrated Police News*, 1 December 1900, 10.

---

[89] *Shields Daily Gazette*, 5 August 1885, 4; Halley (1886). For another example, see *Davenport and Moyle*, 1906: 'my reason for investing was that I thought there would be a fair interest and some bonus; I did not expect such a large bonus as they promised; I expected that some months it would be less and some more.'

Consumers expected a 'link' bicycle for 1s. 6d., but got a pair of links worth 2d. Charles Hanford, the man behind the scheme, received weekly amounts of £16–17 (over £2,000 in 2020). After his arrest the police seized 1,200 letters, which contained £83. Hanford protested: 'People must be fools to expect a bicycle for 1s. 6d.'[90] One of the witnesses, Herbert Cole, was asked whether he really expected it. A dialogue with the defence counsel ensued:

> Read the advertisement a little further on, and you will see the words, 'If all the bicycles are given away the 1s. 6d. will be returned'...I expected what they promised in their advertisement.
>
> Do you mean to say that you as a plumber, and therefore an intelligent man, thought it meant a link in a bicycle?
>
> You cannot say. There are such funny ways of putting advertisements together.[91]

Cole represented himself as a careful reader of the advertised text, but when pushed on the rationality of his expectations, he shifted to his experience and showed himself a careful reader of genre. Aware that the advert seemed fantastic, he pointed to an environment that regularly produced surprises and therefore rationally justified imaginative leaps. Being an 'intelligent man' did not, in his view, contradict embracing small mysteries but to the contrary, explained it.

Weber argued that rationalization and intellectualization did not mean general knowledge of the conditions under which one lived, but rather a belief that if one wished one *could* know. Disenchantment lay in that distinctly modern ontological outlook, in which recourse to magical means was unnecessary. Readers of adverts repeatedly ask us to turn this account on its head. Superficially, they expressed the view that things were knowable, and that they evaluated adverts realistically and reasonably. However, they often evaded knowing and acted with the enthusiasm of conversion to faith, with passionate wanting, dreaming, and bathing in imaginary constructs that overwhelmed rational doubt. Ultimately, readers invoked tropes of reason and realism in order to actually protect a magical vision of the world from the reductions of rational explanation, where little transformative meaning would remain, and from the possibility that there was no greater design that *could* be known, and that the wilderness was just that. They preferred intuitive certainty to the doubting attitude that reason demanded. What might appear from a disenchanted perspective like 'broken knowledge', was a wilful alternative approach to experience.[92]

Benjamin quoted a 1906 reflection on the superstitious spirit that resulted from the complexity of economic processes: 'Modern economic development...tends... to transform capitalist society into a giant international gambling house... Successes and failures...are unanticipated, generally unintelligible...predispose

---

[90] *NSC*, January 1901, 10; *Long Eaton Advertiser*, 28 December 1900, 2.
[91] *Leicester Chronicle*, 8 December 1900, 4.
[92] Weber, *From Max Weber*, 139; Jenkins, 'Disenchantment, Enchantment', 12; Nightingale, 'Broken Knowledge'.

the bourgeois to the gambler's frame of mind...The gambler...is a supremely superstitious being.' However, readers' accounts suggest that they repeatedly endorsed a *willed* ignorance that protected dreaming. Stefan Schwarzkopf argues in a contemporary organizational context that theorizing ignorance in terms of an absence of knowledge misses the ontology of presence that it reveals. His argument is also relevant for period examined here, as it points us away from negative accounts of enchantment as failures of rationality. However, Schwarzkopf defines the ontology of presence as information itself, specifically too much information that becomes sacralized. Historical readers' comments suggest that we should also move beyond the narrative of overload as presence, to the contents of the imaginative worlds that it produced. These worlds were threatened by informational detail, therefore readers kept away from it.[93]

Some readers did argue that their rational faculties were overwhelmed by adverts. George Smith, owner of the *Cornhill Magazine* and *Pall Mall Gazette*, recalled a poster on a tree, which influenced him inexplicably:

a flaming placard, announcing some trumpery penny publication. The placard depicted a young woman, with long black hair, thrusting a dagger into the heart of a ruffianly looking man, with the blood spurting all over the neighbourhood. When I first saw the placard my eyes scarcely dwelt for a moment on it. It awakened no curiosity. But after seeing it twice a week for six weeks, that girl's figure had so 'soaked in' that I felt impelled to go and buy the publication.[94]

Smith's account anticipated Benjamin's famous discussion of a Bullrich salt poster, where he described an impression so deep that it caused a violent shock and remained irrecoverable to his consciousness. Smith's terminological choices—flaming, thrusting, spurting—spoke to the same sense of drama. For Benjamin, the poster, a parable for things 'no one in this mortal life has yet experienced', resurfaced when he saw the brand name again. Smith was not interested in the surreal in posters as Benjamin was, yet like him he experienced a powerful grip in a repeat encounter. A woman who read a medical advert spoke to that grip as an affective response that contradicted known facts: 'Those advertisements...positively frighten me. If I read one of them through and happen to be suffering from a headache, or some slight ailment like that, I absolutely get to feel that I must be on the verge of a serious illness, from which the only escape is by taking the remedy I have been reading about.' Another reader worried about the loss of free will that 'cunningly devised pictures' entailed. You find yourself, he complained 'invariably purchasing the goods most advertised against your will'. Comments of this kind, which complained about adverts crushing their volition, were efforts to acknowledge enchantment while also

---

[93] Benjamin, *Arcades Project*, O4, 1; Schwarzkopf, 'Sacred Excess'.
[94] Smith, *George Smith*, 1902, 119.

reflecting on it from the outside, as it were. They reverberated with broader concerns of the era about the enchantments of mass culture, and finally informed professional advertisers' own version of enchantment, which we will see in Chapter 7. The point here is that these approaches suggested yet another mode of hybridizing reason and enchantment. In this mode, enchantment was inescapable, but it was explicable as a technology.[95]

The insight that critical reason did not escape enchantment informed a remarkable scrapbook from the 1870s or 1880s, which presented four graphic stories elaborately created from press and advertisement cuttings. Easley's case study of this scrapbook observes its satiric commentary on middle-class commodity culture, and highlights resistance. Yet, this critically minded creator was addressing not only commodity culture but her own performance. Her elaborate book revelled in adverts, which she collected and studied with more attention and labour than most readers. She allowed adverts to enter her linguistic and visual choices and presented a world literally constituted in their image, in which resistance itself depended on them. The third narrative, titled 'The opinions of James and Sarah Black and those of Edwin and Angelina Grey', developed this insight. It contrasted views of advertising—the Blacks were prudently critical, the Greys ridiculously enthusiastic. Yet, the overarching insight was not a choice between them, but rather the fact that both depended on a single environment— as image arrangements juxtaposing them on two pages (Figure 1.29) made abundantly clear: the visual environment is continuous, while attitudes contrast. From this perspective, reasoned resistance was itself a form of immersion.

The weaving of reason and realism into advertising's enchantments suggests that enchantment was not passive. This leads to a more general point about agency. Unlike other print content, adverts were not there merely to be absorbed, and readers were more than audiences, even in the most complex rendering of that role.[96] Adverts were there to respond to. In responding, readers conceived themselves as agents and were not withdrawing from practical action to a secluded fantasy. As Morgan argues, enchantment-as-escapism implies leaving the ordinary world, but enchantment is pervasive in everyday life.[97] To grasp the power of advertising, theories of manipulation and passivity like Horkheimer's and Adorno's, which argue that mass culture creates a passive audience, must be reformulated to account for historical participation, which scholarship often recognizes in contemporary contexts. This does not necessarily imply freedom in

---

[95] Benjamin, *Arcades Project*, G1a 4; Iskin, *Poster*, ch. 6; *AW*, June 1902, 8; *Western Mail*, 26 February 1892, 6.

[96] On audiences as imagined communities and efforts to construct them in adverts, see Loeb, *Consuming Angels*, 143–5. On different types of audiences and a study of their representation in nineteenth-century France, particularly the badauds rather than flâneur, see Alsdorf, *Gawkers*. On theories of audience response to sensational print see Chapter 6.

[97] Morgan, *Images at Work*, 10.

MASS ADVERTISING'S APPEALS 89

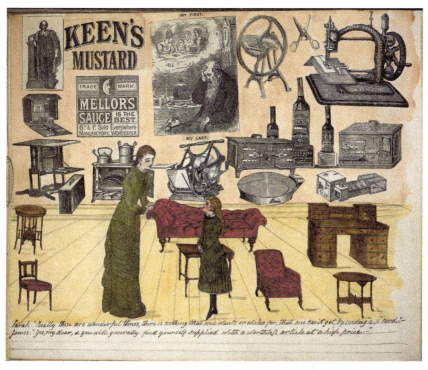

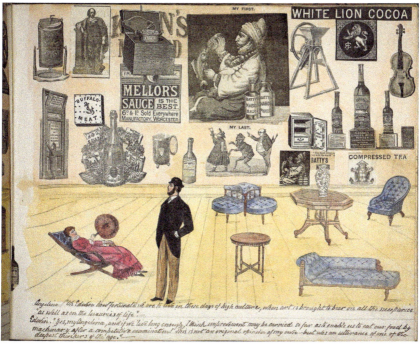

Figure 1.29 Anonymous scrapbook. Contrasting attitudes to advertising saturation.

the last account, but it does imply a mode of being that the concept of mass deception does not explain. Responding to adverts was in fact a form of work, with readers projecting themselves, by their own power and will to adventure, into enchanted realities, infusing them with value and adding layers of meaning of their own.[98]

If we again consider the treasure hunt, we can see how labour, consumption, and dreams of metamorphosis came together. Labour was perhaps the most prominent part of this experience: consumers had to be up before sunrise to get a newspaper copy, use intellectual skills of analysis, social skills of cooperation, and manual skills with tools. That they consumed the newspaper in the process, as intended, was only part of the picture. They were joining an exciting world beyond print which, it should be clear, was not just of the *Weekly Dispatch*'s hunt. Just like the hunt, every advert required labour, because advertising remains incomplete without consumer response. The *Weekly Dispatch* was not the only newspaper that advertised in this way, treasure hunts were not the only games played, and games were not the only activities offered to advert readers. Judith Williamson argues that adverts compensate for the inactivity of consumption, in which everything is ready-made, with their romantic emphases on adventure and excitement. Because all consumers can do is buy, adverts involve a magical element whereby the small action of buying leads to transformative meanings with material effects. Consumption is therefore misrepresented as production.[99] However, to argue for misrepresentation is to dismiss the will to enchantment. As Campbell argues, consumers were active in demanding romanticism. His argument too is qualified in light of reception evidence, because enchantment was not confined to the inner self but rather translated to activity. Far from a retreat to individual fantasy, advertising's enchantments prompted an expanding consciousness of the outer world, a desire to engage with it, and a search for validation that was not bound to always disappoint as Campbell suggests, although it sometimes did. As noted earlier, Campbell's point may be simply the independent value of imagination. Moreover, as scholarship shows in historical and contemporary contexts, a host of processes, including post-sale communication, consumer creativity, and collective effervescence reduce disappointment by reconfirming the transcendental qualities of commodities and sustaining enchantment. We might expand this point beyond commodity-specific efforts, to the effects of advertising accumulation that created affordances for active imaginations. If the pixie dust of specific adverts necessarily settled, the important effect was on the level of wholes, where conditions of enchantment were ever present.[100]

---

[98] See, for example, Litman's analysis of consumer collaboration in advertising mystique and its normative implications, Litman, 'Breakfast with Batman'. On imagination as work, see Appadurai, *Modernity at Large*. Appadurai attributes this work to the age of electronic media, but the history of mass advertising challenges the late periodization.

[99] Williamson, *Decoding Advertisements*, ch. 6.

[100] Campbell, *Romantic Ethic*; Beckert, *Imagined Futures*, ch. 8; Belk, Weijo and Kozinets, 'Enchantment and Perpetual Desire.' On affective labour and the erosion of work and play in media habits see Zieger, *Mediated Mind*, introduction; and see Crary, *24/7*, ch. 2, for a critique of the activation of consumers of contemporary media, which produces repetitive temporal patterns.

The significance of small actions becomes clearer when viewed within the more thorough blurring of lines of economic action by advertising. As noted at the beginning of this chapter, histories tend to marginalize the fact that advertising did not market only object-commodities. This fact does not sit well in a history of *consumer* culture, especially as understood in terms of the sociopolitical role of the commodity. Yet, if we do not overlook the co-presence of labour and investment adverts alongside commodities and services, and the fact that advertisers were not all professional traders, we can see how the mass was encountered as a market in which production and consumption mixed. It could be argued, correctly, that mixtures meant that everything was now a commodity, including labour. However, the important point from the perspective of consumers was that commodification was not distinct from the forces of production—both labour and capital.[101]

In this atmosphere, it is unsurprising to find that consumers often became advertisers. One way to do so was by responding to invitations to design copy. For example, the *Daily Mail* offered a £25 prize to the winning poster design for its Ideal Home exhibition and received hundreds of replies.[102] The Hovis Bread Company offered a prize for a new tradename. 'Hovis' was the winning idea of a Cambridge undergraduate.[103] Consumers were also invited to find more customers for advertisers as we saw in newspaper subscription competitions, and so became themselves advertisers. Some consumers actively participated in campaigns. For example, Rowntree gave two hundred thousand tins of cocoa to women who rode on London buses that carried Rowntree adverts. Another participatory form was testimonials, which were a dominant advertising strategy. As we will see in Chapter 4, testimonials implied a bidirectional flow of knowledge between consumers and advertisers. They arguably engendered trust, but their deeper significance was in acculturating consumers into invisible and strange worlds by making them active in them. Enthusiastic readers also sent unsolicited ideas to advertisers. The advertising manager of Lemco & Oxo attributed their best adverts to 'unknown friends' from the public. Most significantly, adverts and advertising characters assumed lives of their own in the hands of consumers, political commentators, and communities.[104]

The atmosphere of blurred lines might seem like a pre-professionalized advertising world, and formally it was. However, we should resist the trap of conceptualizing it as a messy transition. This was the fertile ground of enchantment, which made imaginative projections part of daily realities. As Karl Bell finds in his study of the magical imagination in modernity, it had rationalizing and pragmatic

---

[101] The historical drama of the process of commodification was famously theorized by Polanyi, *Great Transformation*.
[102] See also the design competitions of the *Advertising World*, *AW*, June 1902, 26; *AW*, November 1902, 347.
[103] Morton 'How the Manufacturer Advertises', 1908. Morton was the company's director.
[104] Fitzgerald, *Rowntree*, 93; on trust, see Barker, 'Medical Advertising'; Maltwood, 'How Advertising Grows', 1908. Some examples of animated advertising characters are discussed in Chapter 7.

components. From this perspective, the distinction that Tolkien made between magic as an attempt to exert power on things and wills in the primary world, and enchantment or fantasy as an artistic endeavour creating a secondary world without tension with reason, does not hold: both dreams and attempts to alter realities were at work in advertising's enchantments, with the aid of reason.[105] Advertising professionals recognized this condition and would gradually try to own it as a matter of expertise. Meanwhile, readers who laboured to weave enchantment and reason repeatedly described their responses to adverts by saying: *I believed*. This standard linguistic gesture, which covered the distance between an advert and the reader's projection, seemed precise because of its indeterminate status between knowledge as justified belief—and faith. Engaging the invisible worlds of mass advertising depended on being able to draw on the powers of reason as well as enchantment, which readers did in sophisticated if little articulated ways.

Conclusion

Advertising enlivened capitalist life with some experiences that supernatural entities had once supplied. It assumed a vital cultural role, taking the place of the 'ghost in the machine of capitalism'.[106] The effects, however, also caused considerable anxiety. They confused the real and imagined and raised the spectre of an economy thriving systemically on enchantments. This was a challenge that could not be easily answered by theological frameworks that otherwise justified capitalism, because such theologies were not perceived as themselves a product of capitalism. By contrast, advertising's enchantments were generated by a new system of the mass market, that is, by economic activity itself.[107] We can see the anxiety in minuscule form if we revisit the treasure hunt one last time. Responses revealed the discomfort that advertising's enchantments caused when their ecstasies raged too fiercely, and the clash of their tempo with routines became too obvious. The hunt's fortunes also demonstrate that when legal powers were mobilized, they disavowed enchantment.

The hunt ended abruptly after six weeks, when only £2,935 out of hidden treasures of £3,790 had been found. Its excitements became disturbing, for

---

[105] Bell, *Magical Imagination*, 7; Tolkien, *On Fairy Stories*. Tolkien acknowledged that shared fantasy also intended real effects, namely, the realization of imagined wonder independent of the creating mind. Ibid, 35.

[106] Appadurai, foreword, v. Appadurai of course references Weber's thesis about the spirit of capitalism. His comment summons a debate which is beyond the scope of this chapter, namely, whether advertising is closer to magic or to religion. See, for example, McCreery, 'Malinowski'.

[107] Historians have traced theological roots for both producer and consumer drives, and have demonstrated ongoing efforts in Britain to reconcile capitalism with religious world views. On theological roots, and particularly the decline of evangelical influence on economic thought after mid-century, see Hilton, *Age of Atonement*. On differing Christian approaches to capitalism and efforts to reconcile it with religion also after mid-century, see Searle, *Morality and the Market*. On consumerism and theology, see Cohen, *Household Gods*; Campbell, *Romantic Ethic*.

example in Luton, where the Men's and Women's Sunday Afternoon Society fumed about the desecration of the Sabbath and demanded a stop to scenes of the 'hidden gold nuisance'. At a council meeting the mayor described people tearing clues from newspapers as they arrived by train. Sunday school children were excited and could not settle down to bible reading. Damage to fences, grounds and other structures needed repair.[108] Authorities began to prosecute hunters. In Norwich Guildhall the mayor adjudicated damage to Newmarket Road and imposed a fine on a hunter; a judge in Liverpool threatened them with imprisonment; and at the Lambeth Police Court a 'batch of treasure seekers' was charged with wilfully injuring public highways. The judge asked whether 'half London has gone mad', and fined the accused while threatening to escalate punishments. In Woolwich, six men were prosecuted and fined for damage to the Woolwich Common, which was closed by the military. The magistrate could not imagine a 'more idiotic craze'. As these judicial comments suggest, judges did not acknowledge enchantment, and instead criticized consumers in rationalist terms. They implied radical cognitive failures. As one commentator put it, 'the...magistrates...do not seem to have realised...what is the inner meaning...It is not lunacy or idiocy which drives these thousands of poor people...It is human nature.'[109]

The Luton Council was frustrated that it did not have a legal cause against the newspaper owners, and the London County Council too wanted to get at the 'prime authors of the mischief'. The *Law Times* advised about civil and criminal options. It thought that the prospect of liability was not enough to deter consumers themselves when 'set against the pleasures of the hunt and the anticipations of success'. This comment gently acknowledged the force of enchantment, but in consequence suggested that legal means were unhelpful, and turned from consumers to a disenchanted consideration of the advertisers' liability. A few days later, a police superintendent announced in a Manchester court that they were after the owners, who were eventually fined. The Director of Public Prosecutions warned that he would initiate proceedings against them unless they stopped advertising, and so they did.[110]

The treasure hunt breached the implicit expectation that challenges to rationalism should remain at low key, as they usually did even as they transformed modern life beyond recognition. Responses to this breach, which led to the hunt's sudden end, revealed the anxieties summoned by advertising's enchantments, as well as their disavowals in legal contexts that applied rationalist perspectives. The rest of this book explores these cultural dynamics on a broader scale.

---

[108] *Weekly Dispatch*, 14 February 1904, 9; *Luton Times and Advertiser*, 29 January 1904, 8.
[109] *Coventry Herald*, 29 January 1904, 6; *Norfolk News*, 6 February 1904, 12; *Advertising News*, 5 February 1904, 4, quoting the *Spectator*.
[110] *Luton Times and Advertiser*, 29 January 1904, 8; *Coventry Herald*, 29 January 1904, 6; 116 *Law Times* 290 (1904); *Western Daily Press*, 5 February 1904, 5. The DPP's warning was reprinted in *Advertising News*, 5 February 1904, 4.

2
Advertising and News
The Fetters of the Commercial Press

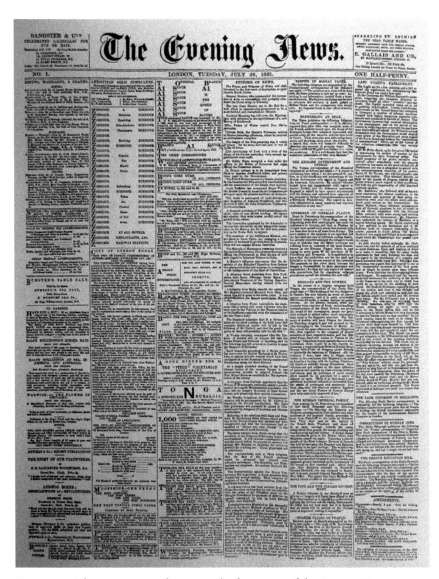

Figure 2.1 Advertisements and news on the front page of the *Evening News*, 26 July 1881.

In October 1883, a number of British newspapers reported a case of patent medicine forgery:

> PROSECUTION BY THE SUSSEX DRUG COMPANY. At the West Ham Police-court, Frederick William-Stubbs...was charged on a warrant for that he, with intent to defraud the Sussex Drug Company, did unlawfully and falsely apply a certain trade mark to a bottle in which Cobden pills were intended to be sold.—Mr. Charles Lamb, of Brighton, prosecuted...Mr. Lamb said his clients resided at Brighton, and carried out business as the Sussex Drug Company. One of their leading articles was a pill invented by Mr. R. Cobden Cox, called 'Cobden's Quinine and Phosphorus Pills,' on which £10,000 had been expended in advertising and establishing the proprietary rights, so that it was very important that the article should be protected. In June last, the prisoner went to Mr. Little, carrying on business at Stratford, and, producing a copper plate relating to Cobden pills, he asked for a number of labels to be struck off. He...stated that he was one of Mr. Cobden's agents. The labels were printed...When prisoner was arrested he had...bottles on which the trade mark of Cobden's pills was forged...as the prisoner...had offered to hand over all...blocks, plates, and moulds...the Company were willing to withdraw the prosecution...[1]

In a following circular of the Newspaper Society, intended for newspaper owners and editors, a warning appeared that the report was not news, but an advertisement.[2] Was it? How could you tell the difference? What marked a publication as an advert rather than news? These questions became urgent in the years of press commercialization, after mid-century. This chapter traces the rise of the dilemma of differentiating adverts from news, and the answers provided by participants, who wielded legal powers to back their positions in public and private contexts. It begins in 1848, when the campaign to repeal taxes on newspapers, one of which was the advertisement duty, gained momentum. The campaign, examined in the first section, consciously framed advertising as a communication of essential information, a rationalist paradigm. Its successful end gave full reign to advertising in the newspaper press, but also triggered a dialectical movement to readjust the framing. Newspaper owners soon faced advertisers' threat to their effective control of the medium. Their proprietary power to differentiate advertisements from their self-proclaimed business—news—and thus limit advertisers, was put to the test. They proceeded by developing conceptualizations of advertising that worked within the mid-century paradigm, but implied a hierarchic distinction between

---

[1] *Bury and Norwich Post, and Suffolk Herald*, 9 October 1883, 3. Also *Hull Packet*, 12 October 1883, 8; *Leeds Mercury*, 10 October 1883, 5; *Royal Cornwall Gazette*, 12 October 1883, 6.

[2] *NSC*, December 1883. On the society, see 'Advertisements versus News' below.

news and adverts. The power struggle, at its zenith between the 1880s and the First World War, is examined in the second section.

The overall process examined in this chapter framed advertising as an informational category, but of a lesser order, different from and inferior to—because more biased than—news. The framing reflected contradictory pulls. On the one hand, the persistent informational focus legitimized advertising, which was necessary to sustain newspapers without political patronage. On the other hand, the same focus elevated news over advertising, and kept news as the press's main public service. The informational hierarchy assumed the status of common sense, yet had little to hang on in theory and in practice. At once powerful and precarious, this framing has given rise to challenges that still trouble debates about communication media.

This history has been overlooked in the literature on the relationship between advertising and the press. Scholarship has tended to consider that relationship from the perspective of the latter, privileged as a democratic institution—at least in potential, and to examine how it changed with the rise of advertising. An ongoing debate examines advertising's role in turning the press from a potentially critical power in democracies, to a docile one. Jürgen Habermas memorably turned his fall-of-the-public-sphere narrative on the role of advertising in the press's financial structure. Contra affirmative interpretations of newspapers' liberation from political control, a line of critical inquiry has shown that the radical press in Britain was brought to a halt with the rising power of advertisers, and has argued for the depoliticization of newspapers after mid-century. The effect was a pull towards the middle class; thus James Curran and Jean Seaton describe advertising as a new licensing system that replaced traditional political control.[3] This chapter examines how newspapers struggled with advertisers' power, while attending a second question: what happened to the status of advertising under the pressure of newspapers' responses? Just as advertising did not simply enable the growth of newspapers but also curbed their political edge, so newspapers did not simply provide an expansive medium for advertisements but also undermined advertisers' claims to serious attention. By the end of the period, press advertising had been mainstreamed, but it had also been inferiorized. The inferiorization of advertising as biased information has not been examined as a historical

---

[3] Habermas, *Structural Transformation*; Curran and Seaton, *Power Without Responsibility*; Hampton, *Visions of the Press*; Chalaby, *Invention of Journalism*. Depoliticization refers to a reduction in political content and to a depoliticized approach to political news, which emphasizes personal aspects of political figures. Chalaby, *Invention of Journalism*, 76–8. See also the discussion of the commercialization and professionalization of the press below, note 36. Curran has continued to examine the disproportional advertising revenue and hence success of conservative newspapers, and a general pull towards the young middle class in journalism. Curran, 'Impact of Advertising'.

occurrence; instead, is has been treated as axiomatic, an inherent characterization. This chapter recovers the history of this view.

Both stages of the historical process—advertising's elevation with the repeal of taxes, and a readjustment of its status when newspapers were threatened—depended on legal powers mobilized to give practical implications and cultural prevalence to specific interpretations. The legislative process that abolished the advertisement duty was attended by a theory of advertising as essential information, which it endorsed, and which became the prevalent justification for advertising's uninhibited expansion. In the years following, newspaper owners did not mobilize legislation but they did use their proprietary powers to readjust that prevalent view. They created a normative universe consisting of recommended policies for the industry, articulations of the roles of journalists, editors and departments, flaggings of violations, and examinations and channelling of everyday contractual relations with advertisers and agencies, often in dialogue with court cases. This universe bespoke the superiority of news over advertising. While this chapter shows that the hierarchy was deeply troubled for both conceptual and structural reasons, it was still the case that legal categories mattered. Legal ownership of a newspaper and the attendant ability of owners to claim that news, but not adverts, were their core service, and to give that claim practical meaning, were significant enough to retain in cultural understandings the separation between advertising and news, and to establish a hierarchy.

The informational hierarchy was not in conversation with advertising's enchantments and did not conceptualize its imaginative appeals, as will become apparent.

Advertising Unleashed

The Taxes on Knowledge

When newspapers had become fully commercialized, their pages included a variety of material that was all, in one sense or another, commercial (Figure 2.1). What defined advertising in that environment? And how did its definition reflect back on news? The campaign against the 'taxes on knowledge', which opened up the race of commercialization, was a central legal arena in which these questions were addressed. Its terms of art set the stage for the struggle of capitalist owners themselves with the problematic of advertising's boundaries.

The 'taxes on knowledge' were the newspaper stamp duty, paper duty, and advertisement duty. The banner was a radical cry against keeping potential readers in the dark by making newspapers too expensive, thus securing an anti-democratic political status quo. The campaign against the taxes saw one peak in the 1830s and a second in mid-century; they were finally repealed between 1853 and 1861.[4] Accounts of the campaign straddle the history of the newspaper press, and that of politics and fiscal policy. In the history of British advertising, the repeal of the advertisement duty is typically noted together with the other taxes as a functional turning point that opened up competition in the newspaper market, and led to a sharp rise in newspaper advertising and an increasingly powerful stand of advertisers. This section changes perspective to examine the cultural significance of the campaign for conceptualizing advertising. To do so, it is worth recounting the background in order to contextualize the campaign and clarify the concerns that have attracted the attention of historians, and deflected it from the conceptualization of advertising.[5]

The taxes were legislated in the Stamp Act of 1712. The act was a source of revenue but also, according to a common Victorian interpretation, another means of political control of the press less than twenty years after prepublication censorship ended.[6] Efforts to remove the taxes animated the early Victorian era; best known are the violent unstamped papers campaigns of the 1830s. The government reformed the tax regime in 1836 in a manner that Martin Hewitt describes as partly responsive to moderate radicalism, yet retaining controls on the popular press. The advertisement duty was reduced from 3s. 6d. to 1s. 6d. per advertisement (a few pounds in 2020), and remained at that level until mid-century.[7]

The campaign was rekindled in 1848. The year had seen the European revolutions that sparked fears in Britain about Chartist violence. Hysteria receded when Britain remained stable, but the consciousness of danger encouraged a reformist agenda both outside and in government. From outside, a radical revival was pressing for financial and electoral reform, and was viewed as a more palatable alternative to the Chartist threat to social order. From within, the Whig Prime

---

[4] The advertisement duty in 1853, the stamp duty on newspapers in 1855, the paper duty in 1861.

[5] On the campaign see, for example, Hewitt, *Dawn of the Cheap Press*; Oats, 'Abolition.' See additional examples in Hewitt, 1–2. The reading of taxes in functional terms has typified histories coming from different schools and methodologies; see, for example, Nevett, *Advertising in Britain*, 67; Thornton, *Advertising, Subjectivity*, 4.

[6] For the interpretation of taxes as political inhibitions among Victorian constitutional historians, see, for example, May, *Constitutional History*, 1865; Smith, *History of the English Institutions*, 1874. For debates in current historiography between politics and finance as the driving motivation, see Oats, 'Abolition'. The 1830s campaign was rooted in seventeenth- and eighteenth-century traditions that associated civil liberties with freedom of the press from direct state control. Jones, *Powers of the Press*, 12.

[7] Hewitt, *Dawn of the Cheap Press*, ch. 1. Collet Dobson Collet, one of the campaign's leaders, explained the quiet after 1836 as an effect of the consolidation of the press industry under the supervision of the Commissioners of Stamps, which protected a monopolist trade. Collet, *History of the Taxes on Knowledge*, 1899, 62–3. Even after reduction, the taxes functioned as anti-competitive entry barriers; the advertisement duty was not imposed at the source but on newspapers, and therefore burdened those strained for cash. The 1836 reform also made entry difficult in other ways, such as greater powers of confiscation of printing presses and augmented securities. Meanwhile, stamp-paying papers enjoyed postal privileges. The greatest benefactor was the *Times*; as Hewitt observes, much of the hostility that fuelled the mid-century campaign was against its monopolist power.

Minister John Russell, who was then premiering a weak government, endorsed the view that reforms responsive to social demands were necessary, indeed the historical reason for Britain's escape from revolution and the only guarantees against the dangers of a full democracy.[8] In that context, Hewitt describes the encouragement that campaigners found in recent reforms, particularly the 1846 repeal of the Corn Laws and removal of duty on glass. Campaigners also built on the invocation of 'taxes on knowledge' as a cross-class political agenda after the fragmentation of Chartism. The campaign involved a number of organizations, including the Newspaper Stamp Abolition Committee (NSAC), a reorganization of dismantled Chartist movements headed by metropolitan radicals who had been involved in the 1830s campaigns. NSAC created a national agitation and was supported significantly by the *Daily News* and a few radical provincial papers. In parliament, Anti Corn Law League veterans John Bright, Thomas Milner Gibson, and Richard Cobden headed the campaign, supported by a diverse group in the Commons. The London Committee for Obtaining the Repeal of the Advertisement Duty, supported by a number of newspaper editors and owners, joined NSAC.[9]

The historical background that encouraged campaigners also explains the challenges they faced. The shift to free trade left the government dependent on taxes for revenue while the protectionist threat to prove free trade a mistake and reinstate the Corn Laws was still looming. The government was guarding against deficit in the face of what Jonathan Parry describes as an unofficial radical-protectionist combination against fiscal policy. Doing so while also responding to agitation was difficult.[10] The campaign not only drew on key concerns of its time—both democratic consciousness and fiscal reform politics—but also was undermined by their broader scope and real politics. As Hewitt shows, motions in 1850 failed and the campaign fragmented; the radicalism of NASC and its insistence on tying the three taxes together alienated more conservative voices. To overcome fragmentation, the campaign was reorganized in 1851 and NSAC was subsumed under the Association for the Promotion of the Repeal of the Taxes on Knowledge (APRTOK). APRTOK mobilized a diverse set of interest groups to petition parliament, and attacked the inconsistencies in implementation by the Board of Inland Revenue ('the Revenue'). The pressure led to the establishment of a select committee headed by Gibson in 1851, which issued a critical report calling for repeal.

---

[8] Saunders, *Democracy and the Vote*. On the prevalence of political lobbying aimed at extracting social legislation from government, see Mandler, *Aristocratic Government*, ch. 1.
[9] Hewitt, *Dawn of the Cheap Press*, ch. 2.
[10] Russell's cabinet was also not as enthusiastic about reforms as he was; he was facing complaints about unprincipled responsiveness to factional criticism. Parry, *Rise and Fall*, ch. 8.

Agitation continued as governments changed. In 1853, Lord Aberdeen was prime minister of a Whig–Peelite (anti-Tory) coalition, and William Gladstone was Chancellor of the Exchequer. The divisive issue of fiscal policy was the use of taxes for redistribution while avoiding debt. Gladstone viewed indirect taxes, including the advertisement duty, as part of a needed package within a broader goal of balancing the budget to retain political stability. In his 1853 budget, he opted for a reduced advertisement duty over repeal. Thus, the prospect of repeal was once again drowned within broader political stakes. However, the government was defeated in a night of parliamentary manoeuvres, and the advertisement duty became the first of the three taxes to be repealed.[11]

As this brief review clarifies, the advertisement duty was just one and in retrospect the easiest goal in the campaign. It was not consistently viewed as a separate theme but rather as part of tax inhibitions on newspapers, the ultimate focus being democratic consciousness. Nevertheless, the real political need to discuss each tax in itself led to devoted attention to the duty. Even then, some of the attention addressed issues that exceeded the meaning of advertising, particularly questions of tax policy. The inconsistency of the tax, which applied to newspapers but not to other advertising media like handbills or posters, and its regressive character—a flat tax, more prohibitive for small advertisers, small advertisements, and newspapers with small circulations that could not attract advertisers, were all arguments mobilized in the process.[12] At the same time, the highly active and publicly visible campaign pushed participants to debate the category of advertisement and its significance. The most interesting and successful element of these efforts turned on the social benefits of advertising, which I now turn to examine.

The Communication of Wants

Two celebrations of adverts, one early in the campaign and another summing it up, offer succinct versions of the theme that won the day: the communication of wants.

> Language (the power of communicating his thoughts, the expression of his wants) constitutes the great distinction between man and the brute creation...

---

[11] Repeal of Certain Stamp Duties Act, 1853. The decision passed when government supporters left after voting for Gladstone's budget. It involved significant conservative support, including Lord Derby and Disraeli. On the drama of the night's votes, see Hewitt, *Dawn of the Cheap Press*, ch. 2; Collet, *History of the Taxes on Knowledge*. The government finally accepted the result. On the budget see, for example, Matthew, 'Disraeli, Gladstone', ch. 8; and see Hewitt's account of Gladstone's indecisiveness between repeal and reduction.

[12] The fact that the duty applied only to newspaper advertisements, and was a minor source of government revenue, rightly raised suspicions that its real target was the political control of newspapers. For example, *Leader and Saturday Analyst*, 29 March 1851, 290. On tax policy arguments see, for example, *Illustrated London News*, 22 March 1851, 418 (deputation to Russell).

Any thing, then, which, in any degree, deprives man of the power of expressing his wants, has a tendency to bring him nearer a lower species of being... The expression of thought, speech, is... intangible and impalpable, but there is a mode of fixing it by the printing press, and immediately it is taxed![13]

The alternation in the advertisement duty, by removing restrictions upon communication between parties desirous of meeting each other... will produce... vast moral revolution... The inevitable increase in the number of advertisers will necessitate changes that will bring the people who issue advertisements more directly in contact with the people who read those always useful, often amusing, and frequently important announcements.[14]

As these examples suggest, adverts were framed at once practically and ideationally. They were a practical exchange of individualized information among persons whose market-oriented 'wants' were givens, but who were barred from revealing and so realizing them. At the same time, the exchange was elevated speech, humanity's expressive capacities beyond its physical needs. Wants-communication had old roots, which were now tailored to mid-century ideas.[15]

The communication of wants was elaborated with the pressure to separate the three taxes on knowledge. Early campaigners often rested their position on 'the dignity of a public principle' of knowledge and education for the people. Gibson continually maintained that the taxes were connected, as the governmental history of handling them together proved. However, difficulties in parliament led him to accept a separation and to encourage members to vote without feeling committed to the full length of his campaign.[16] When pressed to discuss the advertisement duty on its own, the dominant view was that it was only indirectly a tax on knowledge in the political sense.

If advertising was not knowledge like other newspaper content, that was not because it was merely a funding source for newspapers, of a lesser order than political knowledge. On the contrary, advertising was conceptualized as a special kind of knowledge, less abstract and more directly involved in social interaction. The tax on advertising was 'more generally onerous than taxes upon knowledge, since it taxed commerce, agriculture, literature, and the social wants of the community. It taxed opinions, and the transactions between man and man. It went further; it taxed the arts, and even religious communication.' The *Lady's Newspaper and Pictorial Times* explained the conflation of knowledge with what

---

[13] *Liverpool Mercury*, 8 May 1849, 8. [14] *Daily News*, 16 September 1853, 7.
[15] On efforts to create a 'public register of wants', beginning with Michel de Montaigne in 1594, see Presbrey, *History and Development of Advertising*, ch. 5.
[16] Collet, *History of the Taxes on Knowledge*, 128, referring to a speech by George Holyoake in a meeting of the Association for the Abolition of the Duty on Paper, January 1851. See also *Bradford Observer*, 3 January 1850, 4, describing the taxes as 'spiritual window duties, which exclude the light of truth from the soul'. Commons Sitting, 14 April 1853.

'would be a better word' in discussing advertisements—information: 'To the servant or youth who wants a place, all "knowledge" converges to the centre of his particular need.' While 'knowledge' remained the effective header of the campaign, the emphasis regarding adverts was akin to information, a realm of factuality and transparent communication ideally freed from contextual complexity.[17]

Gibson, whose oratory skills did much for the campaign in parliament, wedded the practical communication of wants with higher ideals when he described the tax as a ban on free speech: 'A tax on advertisements! A tax providing that no man may say what he wishes, or tell what he wants, in the way of business transactions, without being fined eighteenpence every time he speaks through the only channel by means of which he can make himself generally heard.' He continued: 'There is nothing a man has to sell which some other man does not want to purchase, if they could only be brought together.' Trade, like citizens, required freedom of speech. How can trade be free, asked the *Bradford Observer*, 'if the merchant may not tell the world that he has goods to dispose of?' The tax on free speech in trade, it was argued, was worse than limiting political free speech because 'the stamp and advertising duties are fines, not on opinions, but on facts.'[18]

Punch saw the amusing side of these formulations; early in the campaign it printed an ironic rendering of an 'enormous meeting of Advertisers of all dominations' who agitate against the advertisement duty. The comic characters attack the duty as a 'blow at *habeas corpus*', one that 'if the Queen only knew it' would not be allowed. Still, the association of adverts with freedoms to communicate foundational information was effective. APRTOK argued that the denial of 'means of communication' prevented revenues that would enrich the state. Worse still, the tax actually destroyed value because '[t]housands misemploy their time from mere ignorance of the wants of others.' The tax was a veil of darkness, a structure of miscommunication.[19] By the time of repeal, the synonymity between advertising and the communication of wants resonated widely. The *Era* summarized the campaign's achievement:

> A tax injurious to the spread of information... is on the point of extermination. The revolution which the abolition of the long obnoxious eighteenpence will

---

[17] William Ewart in the House of Commons, *Times*, 8 May 1850, 4; see also *Examiner*, 4 January 1851, 3; *Athenaeum*, 12 January 1850, 33 (proceedings of the London Committee for the Repeal of the Advertisement Duty, founded by the *Athenaeum's* publisher, John Francis); *Lady's Newspaper & Pictorial Times*, 23 July 1853, 3. The second section of this chapter discusses the shift in the role of newspapers themselves from more complex 'views' to 'news', which gestured at a neutral communication of information. On the informational emphasis, see also Mussell, 'Elemental Forms'.

[18] Commons Sitting, 22 April 1852; *Bradford Observer*, 17 January 1850, 4; *Athenaeum*, 4 December 1852 (Cobden).

[19] *Punch*, 27 April 1850, 167; *Leader and Saturday Analyst*, 29 March 1851, 290.

cause in the newspaper world will probably be very great, and a vast impetus will be communicated to the extension of business of all kinds... Common sense, the principles of common justice and reason, and the at length received conviction that the advertisement duty was a clog upon intercommunications of mutual wants... were the allies by whose help the victory has been achieved.'[20]

The communication of wants was a market paradigm that captured not only commodity selling but also wage labour. Opening up the job market was an important element in advertising as we saw in Chapter 1, not yet consistently separated to a classified section, and it was useful in the campaign. George J. Holyoake's the *Reasoner*, for example, relied on the poor governess trope to attack the regressive tax, which required her to pay as much as 'a wealthy insurance Company or a prosperous mercantile establishment'. The *Newcastle Guardian* was happy to take it to the extreme: 'If a poor orphan lad thinks he could get a job... or a girl on the verge of prostitution or beggary fancies she might hear of a situation, by putting an advertisement in the paper, the Government steps in... and... swells the long catalogue of crime'. The downward trajectory could come to an even bleaker end, as the *Liverpool Mercury* darkly reflected: 'How many have sunk into a premature grave from the... cause[?]'[21]

The poor employee trope was ambitious. Some mistook it to imply that only adverts for lower-class employment should be exempted from the tax. However, its role in the campaign was to construe all adverts as carriers of speech in the market, 'a medium of universal communication' extending the mythological face-to-face interaction of the market square to a national level. In the parliamentary debate that finally led to repeal, Gladstone argued that the tax was on trade and, to a lesser extent, labour, but Cobden resisted. No, he said, it was a 'tax on the intercommunication of wants and wishes, which, in a commercial community, strikes at the foundation of all transactions'. What would be said, he continued, 'if it were sought to lay a tax on every bargain made, or attempted to be made, on the Exchange, between merchants who meet there at four o'clock, if asking the rate of exchange between London and Hamburg were to render the broker seeking the information liable to a tax? Yet that is what you do under the advertisement duty.'[22]

---

[20] *Era*, 24 July 1853, 9.
[21] *Reasoner*, 1850, vol. vii, no. 171, 155–6 (citing with admiration the *Dublin Commercial Journal*). See *Observer*, 3 February 1851, 3, for a report of the same argument in a deputation to Chancellor of the Exchequer Charles Wood. *Newcastle Guardian*, 6 October 1849, 5. See also *Bradford Observer*, 17 January 1850, 4: 'This is something more than a tax upon labour; it is a fine levied upon the attempt to seek for it!'; *Liverpool Mercury*, 8 May 1849, 8; *Aberdeen Journal*, 20 April 1853, 8.
[22] For example, *Examiner*, 25 October 1851; *Standard*, 13 May 1852, 2; *Morning Post*, 14 January 1850, 6; Commons Sitting, 1 July 1853.

America was the counterexample, the land of free communication of wants. The radical MP Joseph Hume was envious of the tax-free American system: 'He held in his hand an American paper which was sold for a cent, and contained a thousand advertisements, making known all the wants of the community.' Charles Dickens, who did not support repeal, ridiculed the lust for America. His main concern was not adverts but that reform would unleash 'blackguard' newspapers. Nonetheless, after the repeal he published an ironic rendering of *Cinderella* for the age of platform professionals. In Dickens's *Cinderella*, the prince advertised for the women of the kingdom to try on the glass shoe. Recalling the campaign's references to America, the narrative voice soaked in irony: 'for, the advertisement duty, an impost most unjust in principle and most unfair in operation, did not exist in that country; neither was the stamp on newspapers known in that land—which had as many newspapers as the United States, and got as much good out of them.'[23]

The communication-of-wants construction emphasized a number of elements, all speaking to the disenchanted side of advertising: discrete communication over meanings embedded in advertising en masse; information over persuasion; and crucially, strict factuality over imagination. It thus limited the discussion of advertising's cultural implications. In doing so, the communication of wants soothed the radical edge of the campaign with market individualism and offered an appealingly rational vision of national life.

The radical motivation, to reiterate, was feared. Withdrawing governmental limitations on newspapers therefore had to be seen as a pacifying mechanism. Knowledge had to be explained as non-revolutionary, an appeal that resonated in the aftermath of 1848, but was also true in the 1830s, when some radicals argued that all unrest would cease if only the newspaper press was not taxed. Supporters of the campaign argued that '[p]ower, as was shown on all hands, was rapidly passing into the possession of the multitude; and it could only be made safe by the accompaniment of knowledge.' The communication of wants described economically rational individuals, separately seeking to sell, buy, and work according to their separately predefined wishes; set against fears of the multitude, it was particularly unthreatening. It simultaneously legitimized advertising for the masses, and more broadly their consumer agency, and delimited the implications to a thinly formal market paradigm.[24]

Alongside the soothing individualism, national life emerged as a peacefully rational coordination through free speech, cutting across political discord and providing a clear and agreed-on picture of progressive realities. In an 1852

---

[23] Commons Sitting, 1 July 1853; Dickens, Letter to W.C. Macready, 1852. The alternative view was that the removal of taxes would allow real news to replace 'trashy tales'. Select Committee on Newspaper Stamps, 1851, q. 679. For *Cinderella* see *Household Words*, 1 October 1853, 8.

[24] Jones, *Powers of the Press*, ch. 1; *Daily News*, 17 April 1850, 4, reporting a debate in parliament (John Roebuck).

parliamentary debate, the Liberal MP William Clay glorified the information provided by adverts over that of news:

> No one could doubt the great ability manifest in the leading articles in the *Times*, or its admirable arrangements for the collection and prompt diffusion of news from all parts of the world; but if you went into the shops and warehouses and counting-houses of men of all shades of political opinion, and asked them why they took the *Times*, you would find them all concur in one reason...it was indispensable to them to take in a paper in which they found such a vast amount of information as was supplied in its advertisements...[25]

The information, it was repeatedly argued, allowed an understanding of the progress and character of the country. The community that advertising brought into being was not an imaginative construct of the kind I examined in Chapter 1, which different readers construed in different terms, but rather a simple truth—previously hidden, now revealed. Some commentators argued that adverts revealed not only the progressive condition of national life but also local culture; they allowed people to be part of their immediate surroundings, beyond the pale of London. William Ewart explained during sessions of the select committee that adverts allowed local communities 'to know what they are about, and what is doing around them'. In these versions, advertising was a rational democratic representation and form of inclusion.[26]

The success of the communication of wants was born out by the failure of opposition to articulate an alternative conceptualization of advertising. Most of those who did not support the repeal, nonetheless accepted the substantive arguments of the campaign and explained their choices by resorting to overriding considerations, typically political loyalties or the financial needs of the government. The only resounding argument came from landed paternalists who drew on little more than traditional suspicions of puffery. Here was Henry Drummond: 'And what do you want? Why, you want the advertisement duty to be taken off; you want to be puffed off in the newspapers.' Let the labourer have his beer in the evening if you care for him, he argued, not a newspaper. Even less persuasive was the Earl of Clancarty, who appealed to advertisers' interests: 'the practice of advertising certainly requires no encouragement; its very excess defeats in a great measure the interests of advertisers...' With such limited alternatives, the conceptual account won the day. The first edition of *Encyclopaedia Britannica*

---

[25] Commons Sitting, 12 May 1852.
[26] Select Committee on Newspaper Stamps, 1851, qq. 650, 669. See also q. 2356. Provincial newspapers, which expanded after the repeal, indeed exhibited local contents, adverts included. Hobbs, *A Fleet Street in Every Town*.

after the repeal, in 1878, could confidently assert that repeal was '[i]n compliance with all but unanimous voice of the public'.[27]

The picture of mid-century bears emphasis. Advertising—a cornerstone of capitalist expansion—received some of the most enthusiastic support in its history, and some of its most elaborate justifications, which exceeded its practical function in releasing newspapers from political control, through a campaign rooted in radical politics. Explicit support was obvious in radical attacks on the advertisement duty that saw advertising as a communicative means for gaining employment, and the duty as an unequal burden on the most disadvantaged. Implicit support was just as crucial: within the campaign's dynamics, the communication-of-wants paradigm did not meet with sustained radical challenges.[28] The support reflected the sway of free-trade radicalism, but it was not limited to it. While historians have repeatedly associated the victory of capitalism with the commercial press, they have too often dismissed the ironic fact that radical politics themselves were implicated in the process.[29] Meanwhile, the implication of radical politics in justifying advertising specifically has been entirely overlooked.

After the repeal of the taxes the newspaper industry grew rapidly, from 563 newspapers in 1851 to 2,421 by 1916.[30] Provincial newspapers attained a new dominance relative to London ones.[31] Circulations jumped. Figures are contested given the limitations of sources, but rough indications reveal the dramatic change: annual sales rose from approximately eighty-five million copies in 1851, to more than 5,600 million in 1920; the number of newspapers purchased per year per capita over the age of 14 rose from six copies in 1850, to 182 in 1920; even allowing for a reduction in the number of readers per copy due to the decline in collective

---

[27] Commons Sitting, 19 February 1850; Lords Sitting, 28 July 1853; 'Advertisement', in *Encyclopaedia Britannica*, 1878, 178.

[28] The irony is manifest when we look, for example, at Sidney Webb's socialist ideas about advertising. He argued that an informational ideal of the kind promoted in the campaign would only apply to advertising in a socialist cooperative commonwealth, whereas capitalist advertising is 'decided by irresponsible individuals...and not even pretending that their statements are either true or for the common good'. Webb, Introduction in Goodall, *Advertising*, 1914, xvi–xvii. Charles Kingsley put these ideas in mid-century in the mouth of his Alton Locke, who explodes at an editor:

> Look at those advertisements, and deny it if you can. Crying out for education, and helping to debauch the public mind...shrieking about slavery of labour to capital, and inserting Moses and Son's doggerel—ranting about...the march of knowledge, and concealing every fact which cannot be made to pander to the passions of your dupes...
>
> (Kingsley, *Alton Lock*, 1850, ch. 23)

[29] Hewitt, however, argues against reductions of the campaign to Manchester free-trade radicalism. Hewitt, *Dawn of the Cheap Press*, ch. 1.

[30] It had doubled, to 1,271 by 1865; in 1880 it was 1,835, in 1900 the number was at its highest, with 2,491 titles. British Library data, based on figures taken from Mitchell's Newspaper Press Directories. A count based on the British Library catalogue confirms roughly the same figures.

[31] Slauter, *Who Owns the News*, ch. 5.

newspaper consumption, the readership increased sharply.[32] Adverts became newspapers' main source of stability. At the close of the century William Stead Jr. argued, 'Were advertising to cease, not one in a hundred papers and periodicals would outlive the year.'[33]

The idea, boldly put in 1881 by the then Liberal MP and owner of *Truth*, Henry Labouchere, that in present conditions the advertisement department was the most important one in a newspaper, was hard to swallow for the heads of the Fourth Estate. Edward L. Lawson, owner of the *Daily Telegraph*, tried to refute it only to actually confirm: 'I should say that the literary department was the most important, because if that were not efficiently conducted you could not make a good position for the paper, and attract advertisements.'[34] The next section examines the pressures that newspapers faced, and their responses.

Advertisements versus News

Fetters of the Free Press

With the rapid expansion of advertising, the limits of the campaign's victory came into view. The financial interests and political aspirations of newspaper owners required that adverts be recognized as a distinct type of publication, separately paid for, and subordinated to their control of the medium. However, advertisers were resistant. An advertiser might have wanted a piece published for free; a publication originating from an advertiser could be offered to a newspaper through other sources; an advertiser could be willing to pay but demanded a say about the placement of the publication, in news or editorial columns, or without conventional marks of adverts; or he might condition a contract for paid adverts on a newspaper's willingness to include additional material offered.[35] If, as the mid-century legislation confirmed, adverts were part of free speech and an

---

[32] Curran and Seaton, *Power Without Responsibility*. See discussion and more data in Wadsworth, 'Newspaper Circulations'; Altick, *English Common Reader*, Appendix C. Generally, circulations of individual newspapers were typically in the thousands until mid-century, with some unusual figures in the tens of thousands; hundreds of thousands appeared in the 1860s and 1870s, and million figures appeared towards the close of the century.

[33] Alan Lee estimates that in the 1860s and 1870s smaller provincial papers' revenue was one half to two thirds from advertising. For Sunday papers, 30–40 per cent of the revenue came from advertisements. Lee, *Origins of the Popular Press*. The space devoted to adverts increased, as did their total numbers. See also Hampton, *Visions of the Press*, for an account of the rising importance of advertising revenue. Stead, *Art of Advertising*, 1899, 128. See further details below, note 36.

[34] Labouchere (1881).

[35] Formal indications of adverts within newspapers varied, yet most newspapers printed the bulk of their adverts in running columns that occupied the front and back pages. In addition to placement, indications often included separations by whole single lines within columns, and fonts smaller than news after the first line. For a discussion of newspaper forms see, for example, Mussell, 'Elemental Forms'.

informational realm of the first order, then resisting distinctions between adverts and news made sense. Newspapers had to develop responses that pushed back against the communication-of-wants paradigm. The victory of the campaign thus initiated a dialectic: as newspapers' business models moved from political paternalism to advertising, the need to distinguish news from adverts asserted itself and required a readjustment of the meaning of advertising. The power of the campaign was in forcing a dialogue with the informational ideal that it posited.

The following analysis traces the shifts in the conceptualization of advertising brought about by newspapers. It focuses on the 1880s and onwards, years that capture the height of the challenge, after two and a half decades of press expansion. These years have been identified by media historians as distinctive in two senses: commercialization—with advertising as newspapers' financial engine— and professionalization of the British press.[36] As these processes advanced, newspapers' battle with advertisers over the substantive control of the medium became

---

[36] Whether the period was revolutionary or continuous with earlier trends is contested. Scholarship on the press's commercialization and professionalization observes a number of points. Generally, the tax reform marked one stage in shifting newspapers' financial basis to the market. The fall in newspaper prices (halved for popular papers in the 1850s, and again in the 1860s), and rising capital requirements, led to dependence on advertising for profitability. Market structures, however, did not imply the end of political patronage. They were an opportunity to divert newspapers to political ends anew, particularly by Liberal elites who saw the market as an agent of diversity and wanted to displace practices of intimacy between editors and government ministers. Limited-liability legislation allowed subscribers to become shareholders to whom editors were directly answerable. Both ownership and the selling of space served political control.

The next stage followed the 1883 Corrupt and Illegal Practices Act, when political candidates could no longer buy newspapers. Direct political finance had to go underground (it finally disappeared in the interwar period). Newspaper owners had, of course, identified political allegiances, and advertisers could also exercise political discrimination; for example, a boycott by some on the *Daily News* in 1886 when it campaigned for Home Rule. The government was itself an advertiser, and worked on a partisan basis. The more common discrimination in financial support, however, was economic; its political edge was rooted in advertisers' perceptions of the relationship between the politics of a newspaper and its economic readership.

Newspaper prices continued to fall while newspapers became larger industrial organizations requiring significant capital, and advertising expenditure continued to rise. The same period saw further rapid growth in numbers and circulations. It also saw incorporation and concentration of ownership, ushering the era of the so-called Press Barons. By 1913, 90 per cent of leading daily and evening newspapers had become limited-liability companies, replacing the historical structure of individual ownership that still dominated twenty years earlier; from the 1890s, major newspapers were listed on the London Stock Exchange, while small ones closed.

The professionalization of news involved structural reorganization and attempts to delineate a professional ethics and ideology. News reporting, and the newspaper itself, emerged as a particular calling, distinct from literature, part of a mass communication that would later expand to include new kinds of media. Discussions of the interrelations between commercialization and professionalization intensified with the New Journalism, characterized by shorter and speedy news coverage, more 'human interest' stories, a more informal literary style, visual matter, and typographical boldness. See also the discussion of professionalization in the text surrounding note cues 77–84.

See, generally, Jones, *Powers of the Press*; Curran and Seaton, *Power Without Responsibility*; Lee, *Origins of the Popular Press*, ch. 4; Wiener, *Americanization of the British Press*; Conboy, *Press and Popular Culture*. On controversies about the newness of New Journalism, see Hampton, 'Newspapers'. On the process of incorporation, see Taylor, *Robert Donald*, 266 (address by Robert Donald, 1913).

salient. Pressures were mounting on advertising prices and terms of contracts (commissions, credit, periods of commitment, exclusivity, and more[37]), on payments for inclusion in press directories published by advertising agencies, on circulation data that advertisers wanted, and most crucially on the content and form of newspapers that advertisers tried to influence. Newspapers were defending themselves against allegations that they were in the service of advertisers.[38]

The Newspaper Society had a key role in orchestrating newspapers' responses to pressures. The society was established in 1836. Initially it represented the provincial newspapers, until they merged with London in 1889. Its membership rose steadily until, by 1908, it had 357 members who represented over one thousand papers, and could 'speak with authority on behalf of practically the whole press of the land'. The declared purposes of the society included 'careful supervision over Advertising Contractors and Agents, some of whom seek to impose upon and defraud Newspaper Proprietors'. It issued monthly circulars prepared by its secretary, Henry Whorlow, the functionary who 'watches over, and obtains information about, Advertisers and Advertising Agents' and passes it on to society members. Whorlow also advised newspapers individually, obtaining legal advice as needed. He estimated that between 1881 and 1903 approximately twenty-three thousand letters were written in response to individual inquiries, most relating to advertising. A central problematic in the monthly circular was the categorization of publications. It ran a regular section, 'Advertisements Disguised as News', in which it articulated the boundaries between these categories. It also carefully followed litigation with advertisers in local and national courts. The circular thus filled a double function as a detailed descriptive record, and a normative source for an un-unionized industry. It collected information from members revealing how various newspapers dealt with advertisers, and disseminated the information with policy recommendations.[39]

---

[37] There was no single contractual format for newspapers' relationships with advertisers. Much of the discussion concerned advertising agents. By the late nineteenth century, most papers would not sell space to an agent (or the so called 'advertising contractor') without a specified client, but rather worked with orders. Agents were usually paid commissions of 10–15 per cent by newspapers, rather than directly by the business client; some rebated clients, thus lowering the cost of advertising for them; many others proposed to leverage their position with newspapers. The newspaper charge was paid by the client in some cases, and by agents in others. Agents provided varying services: the largest agencies handled full campaigns, including the writing of copy, whereas smaller ones just placed adverts. On the significance of diversity of institutional arrangements, see McFall, *Advertising*, ch. 4.

[38] For example, Gilzean-Reid, 'Mr. Harold Cox', 1910.

[39] *NSC*, June 1908, 18; *NSC*, June 1885, 2; *NSC*, June 1903, 3. The explicit goal of supervising advertisers was submerged in 1889 under 'all topics having a practical interest for Newspaper Proprietors', *NSC*, August 1889, 1, but the interest in advertising continued as a persistent preoccupation. The 'supervision' over advertisers was a tricky business, not least because doing so in a circular

Two Views of Advertising

Newspapers' responses to pressures from advertisers involved two dominant views on the categorization of publications. According to one, the profit motive of the advertiser was the determining question. If an item contributed to a business's profit or could even save it money, it was an advert. Any mention of a business name therefore gravitated towards the 'advertisement' pole. To return to the report at the introduction of this chapter on a legal case of forgery, in categorizing it as an advert the circular did not note unusual content—neither in the complimenting description nor in the apparent redundancy of the legal proceedings. It noted the number of 'allusions to Cobden's Pills and the Drug Company'. The circular customarily flagged mentions of business names; all of them reflected business profit interests. We might think about this as the *pecuniary view*.[40]

A second view centred on the discretionary independence of newspaper professionals, regardless of the advertiser's motive. The important point, elaborated in the *Nineteenth Century* by H. James Palmer, editor of the *Yorkshire Post*, was not that a business was mentioned, even in commendatory terms; it was instead that the editor was indifferent to the advertisers' interests and could equally publish criticism. This was the *professionalist view*.[41]

The two views spoke to the dual and co-dependent processes of commercialization and professionalization of the newspaper press. The professionalist view often compensated for the limits of the pecuniary one, but shared much with it. Both views assumed that the profit interests of advertisers made their publications epistemologically suspect. The suspicion was accompanied by rhetorical insistences on the difference between adverts and news, which were hard to support in practice. The consequence was a second commonality: a tendency to treat formal separations—in the location and marking of adverts in newspapers and in divisions of functions, departments, and sourcing in agencies and newspapers—as indications of difference, when they were in fact the main support for it, and often breached. The effort in both views was to negotiate fine lines between observance and violation of an asserted difference between news and adverts, which ultimately brought about a reconceptualization of advertising. The following sections examine them in turn.

---

issued in a few hundred copies every month ran a risk of libel suits, and of jeopardized business. Amusingly, the circular was issued as confidential, and Whorlow was repeatedly disappointed to learn that it landed in the wrong hands.

The disguised advertisements section morphed in the 1900s into a generalized 'Advertisement Department', reflecting an expanding array of issues, but also the incoherence of the conceptual boundaries that marked adverts apart from news.

[40] *NSC*, December 1883, 14.   [41] Palmer, 'March of the Advertiser', 1897.

In Search of the Profit Motive

The Newspaper Society prided itself on its 'prominent part in the movement for the abolition of the "taxes on knowledge"'.[42] However, the pecuniary view it supported was ironically an adaptation of a state practice developed for the collection of the advertisement duty, which the press decried for decades. To understand the pecuniary view, we can start with that state practice.

In 1851 the Revenue decided to apply the advertisement duty to announcements of 'arrivals at hotels', a Victorian celebrity-gossip favourite. Each hotel name would give rise to a charge as a separate advert. The *York Herald* thundered: 'To officially forbid this trifling gratification to the public... through fear that the Innkeepers may derive a little advantage from this mode of publicity, is one of the most contemptible movements ever made by officials of a *liberal* Government in an *enlightened* nation...' It hoped that reports of the Queen's whereabouts would be forbidden, to drive home the absurdity of the Revenue's interpretation. The *Daily News* decided to launch a local revolt, and published a list of arrivals that it brought to the Revenue's attention. The Revenue, at this high point of the campaign against taxes on knowledge, withdrew. The clash was nothing out of the ordinary. To collect the advertisement duty, the stamp authorities got copies of every issue, counted adverts, and calculated the charge; they were therefore in repeated clashes with newspapers. Like the Newspaper Society in the second half of the century, the Revenue was seeking a rule of thumb that would maximize payments and answer to a defensible logic. The profit motive was its solution.[43]

Newspapers complained about the Revenue's 'excessive strictness'. They rallied against what they saw as an overpowering suspicion of private profit. The *Era* accused it of prohibiting reports in which there was public interest just because it begrudged gratification to individuals. The cause in this instant was horse racing reports, but the Revenue's principle was encompassing. A book review would become an advert if it mentioned a price, or if it commended the book; an article about a fair, a mention of a musical society, or a report about boat races, were all charged as adverts. Newspapers summarized the principle: 'paragraphs referring to events to take place... when there is a pecuniary interest in them'. To avoid liability, they omitted names and dates. They complained that they were being pushed to be 'somewhat niggardly and stingy in our insertion of complimentary

---

[42] *NSC*, June 1903, 4; *NSC*, January 1904, 10–11. The history of its support may have been less straightforward: there are indications that a significant number of its members were apprehensive about repeal. Hewitt, *Dawn of the Cheap Press*, ch. 2. The later consciousness, however, is the important point here.

[43] *Bristol Mercury*, 17 May 1851, 8; *Daily News*, 24 September 1851, 5; *York Herald*, 13 September 1851, 5; *Daily News*, 24 September 1851, 5. On difficulties of differentiation by tax authorities and support for the pecuniary view, see *Mitchell's Newspaper Press Directory*, 1851, 91.

paragraphs'.⁴⁴ Perhaps pantomimes would be the venue for untaxed exuberance, as *Punch* had it (Figure 2.2).

IMPORTANT TO TAILORS, PILL-MERCHANTS, &c.

ADVERTISING in pantomimes is rapidly rising into popular favour, and is an ingenious method of evading the advertisement duty. We have drawn up the following SCALE OF PRICES FOR PANTOMIME ADVERTISEMENTS for those puffing tradesmen who are anxious to get their goods off by the help of harlequin, clown, and pantaloon :—

	£	s.	d.
A trick, with complete change	0	5	0
A very good ditto, with blue-fire, or gunpowder	0	7	6
A joke, by clown, (per scene)	0	10	0
Something beyond a joke	0	15	0
Half a scene, with correct view of the shop, or nostrum	2	10	0
The entire stage, with flats, real doors, a leap through the window, appropriate music, and a red-hot poker	5	0	0

Figure 2.2 Evading the advertisement duty. *Punch*, 11 January 1845, 26.

Frustrated newspapers argued for a straight line leading from the Queen's whereabouts to the sale of commodities: 'Who shall say that...all news or information is not taxable?' Alexander Sinclair of the *Glasgow Herald* reflected that publications 'which newspapers have been accustomed to insert merely as pieces of news and as likely to interest their readers, have been suddenly discovered to be advertisements...'⁴⁵

And yet, when the state no longer managed the distinction between adverts and other content, and the interest in advertising revenue fell to newspapers themselves, they applied the Revenue's logic to the dot. We can find an analogous recommendation by the Newspaper Society for virtually every Revenue position that frustrated newspapers. If hotel names were suspect for the tax authorities, so were the attractions of a town suspect for newspapers. The circular even warned that weather reports, which had become standard in dailies, were suspected adverts, with 'a tendency to see only the bright side of the barometer'. Fashionable 'literary notes' were flagged as adverts for books, just as the Revenue flagged reviews; if the Revenue taxed musical society notices, Whorlow remonstrated against attempts to get free notices of Brinsmead's concerts, more on which below; a billiard competition notice organized by a billiard table manufacturer attracted the circular's scrutiny, just as sporting events did the

---

⁴⁴ *Times*, 8 May 1950, 2; *Era*, 19 March 1848, 9; *Athenaeum*, 22 August 1835, 652; *Age*, 16 November 1828, 364; *York Herald*, 16 April 1831, 3; *York Herald*, 4 May 1833, 3; *Liverpool Mercury*, 28 September 1827, 6; *Leeds Mercury*, 23 December 1848, 5; *Newcastle Guardian*, 6 October 1849, 5.

⁴⁵ *Era*, 19 March 1848, 9; *Glasgow Herald* as quoted in Goodall, *Advertising*, 10.

Revenue's. The circular routinely advised that reports of exhibitions mentioning specific products should be treated as adverts, and exhibitions themselves, which profited the organizers, were matters of debate as fairs were for the Revenue. The pursuit of business names that stood for the profit interest was no trivial effort. Even death was not beyond suspicion: obituary notices and debates about burial methods might mention a business that stood to profit from publicity. Thomas Russell, who had been the advertising manager of the *Times* and founder of the Incorporated Society of Advertisement Consultants (1910), taught a course on advertising at the London School of Economics in 1919, where he complained that if an advertised product happened to enter into the news, 'the papers will go ever so far round to avoid naming it'.[46]

Business name-dropping was flagged by newspapers as advertising and the society advised to avoid free mentions. More generally, the circular advocated an ironic view of advertisers' appeals to the public interest given their private pecuniary one. Newspapers' stakes were higher than the Revenue's had been: the advertisement duty was a small budget item and only one part of press control, but the news/advertisements distinction was a matter of survival, of power—economic and political—and of self-definition for commercial newspapers. Set against the sharp increase in advertising volume, more systematic approaches of professional advertisers than either the Revenue or earlier newspapers had encountered, and the established framing of advertising as essential information following the tax reform, the pecuniary view was advocated and tested across a dizzying array of challenges, which revealed its limitations.

Advertisers argued that there was a direct and general public interest in their commodities, be they survey maps of which the public was ignorant, bicycles with which it was ecstatic, new inventions like safe paraffin lamps, cures for cancer, and anything in between. Styles of proposed publications varied: hard-nosed reports, lectures, historical accounts of the business or the commodity, and pieces with promotional and sensational tones. When a newspaper was recalcitrant, advertisers could be explicit: 'Will you allow me to point out that...it is an advertisement not for the benefit, or only very indirectly for the benefit of the college, but very directly for the benefit of persons living in the locality...' Advertisers also argued that they were the only professional sources on the technical details of their products.[47] These positions endorsed the logic of the campaign against the advertisement duty. They were developed further in advertising literature, importantly in the new genre of press directories. Henry Sell, for example, argued that 'to the trading community, the markets and the advertising columns...are not only

---

[46] *NSC*, February 1894, 7; *NSC*, August 1902, 7; *NSC*, July 1903, 3; *NSC*, 13 April 1882, 11; *NSC*, March 1892, 7–8; *NSC*, March 1888, 16; *NSC*, September 1883, 12; *NSC*, April 1903, 10; *NSC*, December 1903, 10; Russell, *Commercial Advertising*, 24–5.

[47] *NSC*, January 1887, 17; *NSC*, August 1896, 7; *NSC*, December 1897, 7; *NSC*, January 1896, 7; *NSC*, September 1907, 11; *NSC*, December 1896, 8; *NSC*, May 1904, 11.

significant, but indispensable.' Press directories expressed the same view structurally, by reversing the roles of publisher and advertiser: advertisers compelled newspapers to advertise in directories, published essays on key themes of the press, and most crucially assumed the position of the only reliable suppliers of newspaper data, represented as information in the public interest that newspapers tried to hide.[48] If all that was not enough, the public interest argument for adverts had to be resisted in years in which the concept of 'public interest' was increasingly associated with what the public wanted, rather than what was paternalistically considered good for it.[49] The task was daunting.

The argument for a public interest in commodities was just one challenge; a branded commodity or service could be part of a broader story of interest to the public. For example, a report about a new theatre mentioned the decorators, a report about a ship accident noted the brand of soaps floating on the water, and a 'Ladies Column' on daily gossip discussed household brands. The issue would be familiar today as 'product placement', but the banner already assumes what historically needed proving, namely, that there was a way of disentangling adverts from news.[50]

Legal case reports involved businesses, as we have seen. While suspicious, the precise crossing of the line from news reporting to advertising was open to creative interpretation. On one suggestion, it only occurred with the reproduction of the case report after it had first appeared in a newspaper.[51] No less challenging was business involvement in patriotic and imperial concerns. For example, during the Boer War, the Eiffel Tower Factory asked for a publication of its contribution of one thousand bottles of Eiffel Tower Lemonade in response to the outcry of soldiers, as it reported, to improve the bad water in South Africa. The company also offered discounted concentration to soldiers' families and tried to enlist the newspapers, which the circular described as an abuse of public patriotic sentiment. A shoe factory fared no better when it played on the same sentiments as the First World War broke. Schweppes's advertising agents asked for a publication of the purchase of a soda bottle received from the wreck of the Royal George, but at least one newspaper refused; the Khedive of Egypt purchased a Merryweather steam fire engine, but the circular resisted the publication; the Princess of Denmark received a photography book by F. and R. Speaight at Buckingham, yet a society member forwarded the piece to Whorlow rather than publish it; towards the coronation of George V, the 'pyrotechnists' Pain and Sons argued that the historic event justified an article on their expertise, to Whorlow's frustration; when

---

[48] Sell, *Sell's Dictionary*, 1887, 12; Moran, *Business of Advertising*, 1905, 3; Williams, 'Early History', 1907; Stead, *Art of Advertising*, 1899, 16.

[49] This was one major implication of the rise of the New Journalism. On changing considerations in news selection, see, for example, Chalaby, *Invention of Journalism*, 81–4.

[50] *NSC*, December 1881 17; *NSC*, December 1903, 9; *NSC*, December 1884, 10.

[51] *NSC*, January 1906, 12 (suggestion by a member, regarding a dispute of the London General Omnibus Company reported in the *Times*).

Mellin's Food financed the first British airship, which carried their advert, newspapers could not ignore the news value but did their best not to mention Mellin, ignoring, as the *Advertising World* complained, 'their best friends'. Businesses were involved in philanthropic activity and expected newspaper reports, but the circular resisted; one corporate group attracted the wrath of the active secretary when it sought to publish pieces about a 'novel combination of charitable effort and commercial enterprise,' an advocacy book for the Chelsea Hospital for Women that happened to include adverts for the group; a similar fate met the Lever Brothers, who wanted to publish their contribution of a ton of soap to the poor of Marylebone.[52]

Finally, adverts were often themselves a public issue. When the London Aquarium advertised the athletic performances of Zaeo in a controversial poster that enraged the National Vigilance Association, a heated debate ensued. The Aquarium only drew more profits, and the *Star* repeated the wisdom of the circular's advocacy: 'And here again the Aquarium has got two and a quarter column advertisement in the *Times* and a corresponding measure in all the other papers free—gratis.'[53]

The advocacy against free adverts did not mean that advertisers were unsuccessful. On the contrary, numerous examples revealed that they successfully challenged the boundaries between adverts and news. Publishing 'gratuitous advertisements' and 'free puffs' as the circular called them, was standard.[54] Articulations of the problem only made more glaring the discrepancy between the principle of singling out adverts for pecuniary motives, and the inability to maintain separations in practice. Two main reasons explain it. Practically, it was impossible to identify the profit motive for isolated publications. Then again, the substantive logic was unstable: there was, as advertisers argued, a public interest side to advertising, and there was also a pecuniary side to news. These made it difficult to use the profit motive as a guide to distinction.

The difficulty of isolating the profit interest could be seen in the 1892 case of *Morris v Brinsmead*. Brinsmead were piano-makers who appreciated the benefits of advertising (Figure 2.3). In the mid-1880s Morris was their advertising agent. He published not only regular adverts but also news paragraphs. When not paid for the latter, he sued. In opening the case, Morris's lawyer argued that the contractual arrangement was 'to supply notices to the press in the shape of ordinary news, but were really "puffs"'. In a letter to Brinsmead, Morris asserted:

---

[52] *NSC*, April 1900, 12; *NSC*, September 1914, 13; *NSC*, April 1903, 11; *NSC*, February 1894, 7; *NSC*, December 1903, 10; *NSC*, May 1911, 17; *AW*, October 1902, 262; *NSC*, December 1885 13; *NSC*, February 1894, 7. More on the airship in Chapter 4.

[53] *Billposter*, November 1890, 279. More on Zaeo in Chapter 6.

[54] The same was true for magazines and trade journals. On women's journals, see, for example, Malvery, *Soul Market*, 1907, 170–1; on trade journals, see 'Puffing System', 1894. On this phenomenon in France, see Hahn, *Scenes of Parisian Modernity*. The notoriety of women's magazines in particular was one way to deflect attention from the pervasiveness of the same practices in the rest of the press. The gendering of advertising's failures nurtured anxieties that I examine in Chapter 7.

116 THE RISE OF MASS ADVERTISING

Figure 2.3 A Brinsmead advertisement. *Graphic*, 3 August 1889, 153.

'As you are aware, the successful results of my unwavering efforts have...been most beneficial...in securing unusual publicity...portraits, memoirs, articles, notices, and flattering paragraphs in every conceivable form...'[55] Figure 2.4 shows an excerpt from one publication of the kind discussed in the trial.

[55] Morris (1892).

BRINSMEAD SYMPHONY CONCERTS.

On Saturday evening last the first of a series of orchestral concerts projected by Messrs John Brinsmead and Sons took place at the St. James's Hall. For some undefined reason the performance in London of orchestral music of a high character has been restricted to the earlier portion of the year, extending over a space of five or six months. At all other times orchestral concerts of a nature consonant with the value of the works performed have been few and far between. Except during the summer, indeed, until quite lately, London had no regular series of orchestral concerts. Believing that the numerous advances which have been made in musical knowledge and education warranted such an enterprise, Messrs Brinsmead organised the Symphony Concerts, of which the first took place on Saturday evening. We need hardly say that any effort in this direction has our heartiest sympathy, which is also deserved by the practical manner in which Messrs Brinsmead have carried out their idea, as regards the comparative lowness of the prices of admission, and the abolition of the usual charges for books of words, annotated programmes, and cloak-room attendance. The result partly of these judicious alterations was the attraction of an audience composed principally of real lovers of music, whose reception of the items in the varied programme was both appreciative and enthusiastic. The programme was well chosen, and excellently adapted to the differing tastes of an average musical audience. It takes amateurs of all shades to fill the St. James's Hall, and, whilst lovers of the classical were not neglected, there was enough and to spare for those who preferred something less severe in style. Beethoven's Fifth Pianoforte Concerto, a work in which, as Sir George Grove says, the composer "reached the very summit of his art, and on which there is only one universal verdict of applause," and Mendelssohn's beautiful overture to *Melusina* were instances of successful catering for the former class; and the procession movement in Moszkowski's symphonic poem "Joan of Arc," and Liszt's First Hungarian Rhapsody were well calculated to delight admirers of modern music. The work the production of which on Saturday evening excited most interest and evoked most enthusiasm was Mr Ebenezer Prout's Symphony in F major, composed for the late Birmingham Festival, and now gradually becoming popular all over the country. This is the third work of the same class which Mr Prout has already produced. It is laid out on an appropriately broad scale, but without unnecessary diffuseness. In its marked, but not servile, imitation of classical models, in the clearness with which the ideas are expressed, and in the copious variety and poignancy of its thoughts, we have fresh proofs of Mr Prout's musical genius. Mr Prout has shown that it is possible to adopt the restrictions of form without being formal, and that a deep reverence for the best models is not incompatible with the exercise of fertile melodious invention. The symphony was conducted by the composer, and achieved an extraordinary success. Every movement was warmly received, and at the close of the symphony Mr Prout was twice called to the platform to receive the excited plaudits of an earnest and enthusiastic audience.

With reference to the performance of the various selections we have only slightly to qualify our warmest commendation. The band, which is made up of English artists drawn from the ranks of the Philharmonic orchestra, and is conducted by Mr George Mount, is a splendid one, and only needs a little further familiarity between conductor and performers to render its execution perfectly smooth and precise. Herr Emil Bach played Beethoven's Concerto in a style that somewhat lacked dignity; but his rendering of the slow movement was very sympathetic. His performance displayed great talent and elicited loud applause. The vocal selections —Mozart's "Dalla sua pace," and the tenor air from Gounod's *La Reine de Saba*—were sung by Mr Maas with that perfection which we always expect from this artist, whose fine voice and excellent training enabled him to do full justice to both *morceaux*, though he was particularly happy in his rendering of the former.

Figure 2.4 A Brinsmead 'puff paragraph'. *Era*, 14 November 1885, 7.

Items like this were published without charge in some papers, particularly London dailies like the *Graphic* and *Illustrated London News*. Press reports on the case revealed newspapers' discomfort. Thus, the *Pall Mall Gazette*, itself implicated in publications, called the case 'The Paragraphist and the Piano Makers', *Lloyd's Weekly* called it 'The Puff Paragraph Case', and the *John Bull* denied a connection with Morris. As reports multiplied, and laughter in the court became laughter beyond it, the *Billposter*, a periodical for outdoor advertisers, enjoyed seeing a competing advertising medium in embarrassment.[56]

Things became complicated when Brinsmead, who refused to pay, argued that matters of public interest were customarily published for free, as a complementary aspect of paid advertising. They brought to the stand the cashier of the *Morning Post* who confirmed as much, and were about to call witnesses from the *Times* and the *Daily News* when the judge ruled that the evidence was inadmissible. The reason was not clear; an explanation in the *Morning Post*, which obscured its own employee's testimony, suggested that these were not expert witnesses but rather 'men speaking with a respect to a particular office'. Whether that was the judicial reasoning or an interested interpretation remains in question.[57]

There was no legal principle that made 'puff paragraphs' illegal, as the judge explained to the jury, hence all depended on the contract between Morris and Brinsmead. Morris won the case, and Whorlow gloated in the circular that they finally had a clear confirmation of the hidden profit: the money did not reach the newspapers, which were asked to acknowledge the public interest in the publications, but it passed between the trader and the agent, revealing the real category of the publication—an advertisement. However, the case only showed how difficult it was to put a finger on the profit motive for specific material. The evidence showed that the terms of payment between Morris and Brinsmead were never clear, the jury had a hard time reaching a decision, and in any case, Morris won less than 25 per cent of his demand (£150 of £637). Whorlow was simplifying a complex picture to suit the circular's standard warnings against free adverts.[58]

Morris v Brinsmead revealed the tip of the iceberg in the relationships among businesses, agencies, and newspapers, which were too complex for the attempt to nail down a profit element that would set adverts apart. One could see the profit motive nowhere and everywhere: relationships involved implicit and explicit

---

[56] *Pall Mall Gazette*, 3 February 1892, 4; *Lloyd's Weekly*, 7 February 1892, 4; *Times*, 4 February 1892, 12; *Standard*, 4 February 1892, 3; *Billposter*, March 1892, 141.

[57] *Morris* (1892); *Morning Post*, 3 February 1892, 8.

[58] *Morning Post*, 3 February 1892, 8; *NSC*, March 1892, 7–8. A similar position, which gave primacy to the parties' agreement, was reported in a case at the Belfast Quarter Sessions, *Northern Whig* (1904). In that case the defendants argued that the material for publication was supplied as a news item, but the judge found that they had ordered the publication of an advertisement.

conditionings of advertising on news publications, for example, when Kodak suggested that if their 'camera notes' were published, a large advert would also appear alongside. More generally, newspapers understood that future business depended on these expectations, and were also involved in a signalling game vis-à-vis other advertisers. These demands were bidirectional, coming from newspapers no less than advertisers, in recognition of the fuzzy boundary line between news and adverts. The *Times*, for example, suggested that colonial news would be more forthcoming with colonial adverts. Relationships also involved occasional barters in which adverts were exchanged for commodities. One society member, who had published a report mentioning the brand of champagne used at the Lord Mayor's banquet, did so only after he received a bottle: 'I never expected it...I didn't know what to do with it. I like champagne...I inserted a two-line paragraph...' Other barter exchanges were less amused and more systematic. Newspapers were also willing to accept payments in kind for elements in a contract like timing and position, as in this order: 'Mr. Cook will give you a first-class ticket to Paris if you will insert enclosed as a well-displayed advertisement at once.' The relationships also included conditional payments that depended on sales generated by the advert. Most significantly, there were long-term credit arrangements with both end-advertisers and advertising agencies, which, as Morris admitted in court, 'certainly has not lessened' his influence with newspapers. As the *Builder* observed, advertisers got newspaper 'notices' which they themselves wrote 'by paying a man who is not officially on the staff of the paper, but who has credit with them...'[59]

Isolating the profit motive was not only hopeless in these realities, it was also counterproductive for business. For this reason, the prediction of the *Saturday Review* after *Morris*, that 'tricks...cease to be useful when they become public property' was naïve. Unsurprisingly, a consistent position of the Newspaper Society was that 'they were not a trades union'; the society's function was to disseminate information and give advice, not enforce a uniform practice that did

---

[59] *NSC*, July 1904, 11. The 'supply' or promise of 'paragraphs' with adverts was widely familiar. The practice created an unstable distinction between binding promises and non-binding expectations. For a criticism of the practice in a City of London Court, see *Illife, Sona and Strumey Ltd.* (1900). On signaling see, for example, *NSC*, October 1904, 8. On the practice of inserting 'dummy' adverts copied from other newspapers in order to attract advertisers, see *Fryer* (1892). On colonial news, see Potter, *News*, 122 (letter from C.F. Moberly Bell, manager of the *Times*). On barter, see *NSC*, August 1905, 7. One company liquidator found that it had issued 4,387 shares to 297 shareholders who were newspaper proprietors, in consideration of advertisements. *Stanley* (1882). Presents to journalists and editors were also common practice. See, for example, March-Phillipps, 'Women's Newspapers', 1894. *Lloyd's Weekly*, 7 February 1892, 4; *Builder*, 6 February 1892, in *Billposter*, March 1892, 145.

The Paris exchange appeared in an order to the publisher of the *Bradford Chronicle and Mail*; the newspaper applied in addition the regular scale of charges, and added another paragraph to boost sales of travel tickets. After publication, it turned out that the order was fraudulent. *Thompson* (1878).

Conditional payments also occurred in the relationships between traders and agents. For example, *NSC*, March 1906, 15.

not fit the competitive newspaper market. The circular thus advocated ideals breached by consent.[60]

Alongside the realities of business that complicated the pecuniary view, the logic of this view was unstable: there was a public interest side to advertisements, and there was a pecuniary side to news. The substantive argument of advertisers was not without merit. Public life hinged on economic life, and there was no obvious way to explain how it could *not* bleed into news. As one London magistrate frankly said about the categorization of horse racing publications, 'I do not know how you would draw the line.'[61] Some publications seemed to gradually move from one category to another. For example, reports about the business and financial condition of companies increasingly shifted from paid advertising to news, a process some commentators were amazed to see accepted complacently. Companies, expectedly, argued that their business information was 'for the benefit of... readers'. Sports items were also contested, with some papers treating them as adverts, and many others as news. Political and economic concerns were hopelessly mixed in government advertising which preoccupied the society. Governmental departments required official and unofficial material to be published but were not happy to pay, claiming a public interest. In discussing the question at the annual conference of 1888, the society's then president, Francis Hewitt of the *Leicester Daily Post*, admitted: 'Between what is undoubtedly news and what are undoubtedly advertisements there is a very wide field of public information, where newspaper proprietors interpret their duties according to their interests.' Newspapers were also willing to allow colonial governmental advertisers a say about news columns that dealt with their colonies, as Simon Potter observes.[62]

Whorlow tried to formulate more complex indications that were amusingly tautological. He assumed the naturalness of the distinction between adverts and news and finally reverted to the search for profit as the ultimate guide:

> it is not sufficient, in endeavouring to guard against the advertisement pirate, merely to keep a sharp look out for personal allusions, but a distinction must be drawn between those allusions which come naturally where news is inserted upon its merits, and those which are artfully contrived for the purpose of

---

[60] *Saturday Review*, in *Billposter*, March 1892, 145; Douglas Straight, of the *Pall Mall Gazette* and the society's president, the society's annual trade conference, NSC, June 1904, 10.

[61] Select Committee of the House of Lords on Betting, 1902, q. 605.

[62] NSC, December 1901, 8; NSC, March 1905, 11. On the practices of companies paying for both reports and adverts in financial newspapers, see testimony of the liquidator of the *Financial World* in *Cooke and others* (1895); testimony of staff member of the *Financier and Bullionist*, *Hooley and Lawson* (1904). On sport see for example the complaint of a local paper that refused to print details of a high-profile golf tournament as news, only to find that most dailies and weeklies published them. NSC, November 1907, 10. NSC, June 1888, 6. See also NSC, August 1888, 27–8, for the society's failed efforts to pass legislation that would compel local governments to advertise in local newspapers. Potter, *News*, ch. 5.

hoodwinking the unwary editor. A good serviceable test to apply in all doubtful cases would be to consider whether the suspected matter was calculated, either directly or indirectly, to prevent or diminish legitimate paid for advertising.[63]

Whorlow seemed oblivious to the way his guidance showed the profit motive to be equally that of the newspaper, and therefore offered not substantive insight but rather a raw economic struggle.

The dangers of 'suspected matter' assumed radical proportions in cases that would today be classified as fake news. Thefts and fires were invented to advertise safes; a murder was made up to advertise milk; a report of a drowned body in the Thames turned out to be an invention of the advertisers of the watch allegedly found on the body; and an accident of the Lord Mayor's carriage was fictionalized just outside an aspiring silver shop. The Edward Cook Company, a large soap manufacturer, kept the public in suspense for months in 1905, with a run of announcements published in leading newspapers about a pirate making his way to an English coast. Aboard the invented ship 'The Flying Dutchman', peasant girls were supposedly entrapped and showered with gems. The pirate on board accepted a challenge to meet the owner of another ship on Clarence Pier, Southsea. The residents were at 'fever heat' as bloodshed seemed imminent. 'Here there are all the ingredients of a dual', one paper speculated. '[W]onder and mystification' dominated as crowds gathered in expectation. Finally, a smoking pirate with a green parrot resting on his wrist appeared on a yacht that fired black sails carrying the advert: 'Throne, the Royal Toilet Soap, is Luxury's Necessity'. Far from disappointed, the crowds moved easily into consumerist joy. The actors distributed soap 'amid scenes of wild enthusiasm'.[64]

Enchanting events of this type leaned towards what we might call manufactured news, which confused any sense of reality. Theatres, which by definition operated in these liminal zones, led the way. In 1910, Frank Curzon, manager of the Prince of Wales theatre, was responsible for one event that ended up in court. In the so-called 'matinee hat incident', Blanche Eardley and a friend came to a matinee performance wearing large hats. Matinee hats in theatres attracted hostility, particularly vocal in the 1890s when the debate became something of a gender war.[65] They were widely caricatured, as in the example in Figure 2.5.

Eardley said that they intended to take off the hats, but before they sat down a man behind them cried 'Take off those ridiculous hats.' Eardley refused and the man soon continued, 'Are you going to take off those absurd hats?' The audience

---

[63] *NSC*, January 1893, 10; see also *NSC*, October 1895, 7.
[64] *NSC*, January 1883, 8; *NSC*, January 1889, 2–3; *NSC*, August 1889, 23; *NSC*, January 1892, 34; *Bedfordshire Times and Independent*, 25 August 1905, 7; *Manchester Courier*, 17 August 1905, 10.
[65] For example, *Morning Post*, 19 November 1897, 2; *Era*, 15 December 1900, 11; *Funny Folks*, 28 May 1892, 171; *Dart*, 31 March 1899, 11; *Punch*, 15 February 1896, 76. On the context of the matinee, see Barstow, '"Hedda Is All of Us"'.

Figure 2.5
Ridicule of the matinee hat. *Judy*, 31 March 1897, 155.

A PLEA FOR THE MATINEE HAT.

"*Those people in the stalls behind us were growling awfully 'cause they could'nt see the stage for your hat, Dollie.*"
"*Stupid things! There was nothing on the stage half so much worth looking at.*"

grew excited; Eardley responded that she would not because the man was rude. The man called Curzon, who asked Eardley to remove the hat. She refused and, after an argument, Curzon would not let her return to the stalls. She published a letter about her right as a woman to keep her head covered, Curzon responded that he would not allow the vindication of rights of women at the expense of the peace and comfort of his audience, and Eardley soon sued him for assault, claiming that he had physically held her back. The *Times* reported the proceedings with theatrical detail. Witnesses disagreed about the assault. The magistrate eventually acquitted Curzon: 'It was obviously impossible for any one to get a view who sat behind the hat she was wearing. People who went to the theatre must behave reasonably.' The decision was received with applause in the court.[66]

The episode was notorious. Strangely, it was often memorialized as if it had ended there, when in fact it had not. A few months later, one Thomas Lumley

---

[66] *Times*, 16 April 1910, 6.

Dann and his wife Ethele sued Curzon for failing to pay them for 'carrying out the adventure'. It turned out that the incident was an advertisement: 'Nobody knew how amusing the matinee hat case was until Mr. Curzon explained that the hat, and the lady, and the lady's husband were all actors in a "put-up job."' The interaction, including the assault charges, were orchestrated by Dann as 'an excellent advertisement both for the theatre and for the defendant himself as manager'. Ethele Dann acted as Eardley's friend. An advertiser had finally confirmed suspicions that courts were being used as advertising media.[67]

Curzon admitted the set-up, but denied the promise to pay. The courts were offended. The Westminster County Court, in which Dann's suit was first litigated, would not enforce the contract yet made Curzon pay his own costs in critique of his conduct. The *Saturday Review* was curious about the next round: 'How far you can carry a joke has never yet been decided by a superior court'. Not very far: Curzon and Dann both appealed to the High Court and lost in what became a contract casebook reference. A contract to bring a case into court merely for advertisement was against public policy, and therefore unenforceable. The court essentially defined the event as unreal: whether Curzon had or had not touched Blanche, there was no assault because it was done with the ladies' consent. The Criminal Court was therefore asked to adjudicate something which 'to the knowledge of the parties had not happened'.[68]

Something had happened, of course. At first sight, the entire episode would seem an extreme example of the dangers of advertisers. However, as the *Penny Illustrated Paper* suggested, it could lead to a questioning of the status of news per se. A comic piece explored the 'wonderful possibilities' that Curzon's publicity stunt suggested. The piece featured interviews with a list of characters, among them an 'Amy Shortcash' who argues that the £1,500 worth of jewellery pieces on her were an advertising scheme; and a 'D S Windell', who tells the reporter that his fraudulent banking was an advert treated ungenerously. The implication was that just as adverts could make news, news events could dissolve into adverts, especially if they were motivated by an interest in money.[69] This option was no less troubling; the omnipresent profit motive was a cause of confusion rather than distinction. This was a problem embedded, as we have seen, in the business structures of the commercial press. New Journalism was particularly adept at working with incoherent boundaries, especially when newspapers advertised themselves. The treasure hunt of the *Weekly Dispatch* examined in Chapter 1, for example, was an advertising scheme for the newspaper that became, as the newspaper intended, a news item.

---

[67] Dann (1910), 67; *Saturday Review*, 29 October 1910, 535; *Times*, 25 October 1910, 4.
[68] *Times*, 25 October 1910, 4; *Dann* (1911), 164; 55 Solic. J. & Wkly. Rep. 189; 104 LT (1910), 66, 68 (Justice Phillimore); *Times*, 21 December 1910, 3.
[69] *Penny Illustrated Paper*, 29 October 1910, 554.

Confusion received cultural expression in no lesser a figure than Jack the Ripper, the mysterious perpetrator of murders and body mutilations of London East End women in prostitution between August and November 1888. His pseudonym was coined in a letter known as 'Dear Boss', which the Central News Agency received on 27 September 1888, and handed to the Scotland Yard. The letter was the second alleged communication; it would usher a flood of letters eventually numbering over two hundred from all over Britain, which made the Ripper's mythology. Published by the police as part of the investigation, 'Dear Boss' was exciting news. The writer taunted the investigators for failing to catch him; he claimed that he was 'down on whores and...shan't quit ripping them' until caught; he used red ink because the 'proper red stuff' (blood) he collected 'went thick like glue'; and he promised to 'clip the lady's ears off' on his next 'job'. Another communication shortly sent to the Central News Agency referred to a 'double event' and was also published. Earlobe mutilation (of Catherine Eddowes) and double murder (Eddowes and Elizabeth Stride) had just materialized, giving possible credence to the two letters. However, some police officials and journalists theorized that the letters were written by a journalist seeking to increase newspaper sales. Because news were fully commodified market products, journalists could be described as advertisers. On this understanding, the categorization of any publication would defy an either/or choice between news and advertising.[70]

If newspapers were to resist the conclusion that saw them as fully contaminated by profit, a theory of substantive difference had to complement the inherent suspicion of advertisers. The professionalist view, examined in the next section, assumed the role.

In Search of a Professional Ideal

The professionalist view was necessary not only at the margins of advertising ingenuity that led to fake news but also at the centre: as often as advertisers wanted free publications of items that they argued were news, they were happy to pay for them, and essentially sought to leverage their position to have a say about newspaper content. It was in fact easy to complain about advertisers who refused to pay for valuable publications or fabricated stories, but things were more challenging when they did not, because newspaper owners were experiencing loss of control over their properties, and propertied power. Here there was no

---

[70] The list of victims, and earlier and later possibilities, has never been settled. For a review of sources, see Begg, *Jack the Ripper*. The so-called 'enterprising journalist' theory lives on. A recent forensic-linguistics analysis provides new support for it, and has received media coverage under the banner of Victorian fake news, amusing in its sensationalist tones given the history of this phenomenon. Nini, 'An Authorship Analysis'. The 'enterprising' terminology originates in the memoirs of Robert Anderson, Assistant Commissioner of the Scotland Yard. Anderson, *Lighter Side*, 1910, 138.

need to uncover the profit motive: it was plainly admitted by willingness to pay, and newspapers were getting their share. Because the profit motive cut both ways, when newspapers resisted, they had to articulate alternative ideals.

The professionalist view suggested that advertisers should not influence news and editorial content—formal presentation and arrangement included, because news involved a unique knowledge created by professionals in journalism. The view adopted an informational ideal of veracity and saw news as ideally unbiased, unlike adverts. This position elevated news while retaining advertising as an unredeemed category in the muddy water of profit seeking.

Ideals of journalism, it should be clarified, were being debated in a broader context. The shift in emphasis from 'views' to 'news' and the emerging cult, as Mark Hampton calls it, of facts and impartiality, arose in the context of newspapers' role in an expanding democracy, as well as the intensifying competition between newspapers.[71] What follows examines how ideals of professionalism were used to meet the challenges of advertising. The conceptual language developed in debates concerned with political consciousness and press freedom from state control, could only be shifted to these challenges with some conscious deliberation. At the very least, the meaning of bias and of independence in each context needed examination—yet that was missing. The substantive assumption of difference that animated the professionalist view was typically asserted rather than shown. Contradicted by the practices of the press, its power—which is not to be underestimated—was largely rhetorical. Formal indications of adverts within newspapers, and separations in functions, were stand-ins for the asserted substantive difference between news and advertising. However, the difficulties of maintaining them cast doubt on the hierarchy of publication types.

Concerns for the independence of newspapers were a regular feature of the Newspaper Society's circular due to advertisers' demands. For one, advertisers sent orders for paid material that explicitly dictated avoiding distinction. Here, for example, was an instruction from Sell's advertising agency:

> *To be set in reading matter type. Position to be immediately following and alongside of, or amongst, pure reading matter; and no word advertisement, or any contraction thereof, must be added to it.*[72]

This was usual. *Advertising*, a transatlantic journal edited by J.H. Osborne who managed Thomas Smith's advertising agency, gave expert advice that

---

[71] Hampton, *Visions of the Press*, 81. See also Chalaby, *Invention of Journalism*, 79–80 on the rise of information as the press's main business; Slauter, *Who Owns the News*, ch. 5 on the rising emphasis on news for education. And see Kennedy Jones's proximately contemporary assessments of the press's claims to independence. Jones, *Fleet Street*, 1920.

[72] NSC, April 1887, 27.

'[a] carefully worded "next-to, or amongst reading matter" announcement is always effective'. The *Advertising World* explained, 'a notice amongst reading matter tends to increase the number of inquiries received by the advertiser' and should be given as a function of the 'magnitude of the order'. Newspapers often complied. They needed advertisers, and anyway 'near reading matter' adverts usually paid better. Advertising agencies were careful to deduct payments for failure to comply with orders. The contracts were enforced when they reached the courts, as they occasionally did. However, enforcement could face the same challenges of differentiating advertising from news. In one case, a baffled judge in the City of London Court had to decide if an advert printed next to 'answers to correspondence' could be considered as next to news, as the order required. He saw correspondence as a form of advertising: 'Correspondents are answered to sell the papers', and refused enforcement.[73]

Judicial tolerance was at its limits when readers were deceived. 'If you had sat here and heard the statements of widows who have parted with their money entirely on the strength of these paragraphs, your heart would have guided you as to what was right to do in the future'. This was Alderman Green at the Guildhall Police Court, losing his patience with a witness from the advertising agency of Gibbs, Smith and Co. in a litigation that became known as the 'Press Opinions' case. Thomas Tarrant was a fraudulent stockbroker who expanded his business with the aid of editorials that congratulated the company for 'good profits' under titles like 'Knowledge Is Power'. They were paid publications, charged by the agency at 25 per cent more than regular adverts. Unlike cases that implicated only traders and their advertising agents, here the judges were troubled by the march of defrauded readers. By the time the case reached the Old Bailey, the practice of paid editorials was described as a scandal. Judicial warnings fed into the professionalist view.[74]

Fraud cases like *Tarrant* called attention to the basis of belief. Whorlow warned newspapers that the journalistic voice could induce readers to risk money. Accepting editorials from an advertiser required 'knowledge which justifies the endorsement of their contents'. In the *Tarrant* case one editor testified: 'It never struck me that the object was to represent that it was our independent opinion.' Another, however, admitted that the item was 'full of the editorial "we"'. Such

---

[73] *Advertising*, May 1893, 460 (the author preferred that the reader should be given some indication that the matter was an advert, but admitted that the question was controversial); *AW*, July 1902, 8; testimony of the advertisement manager of the *English Illustrated Magazine*, *Nicholson and Richards* (1901); testimony of a clerk at the *Sportsman*, *Goudie and Burge* (1902); Stead, *Art of Advertising*, 1899, 66; *Walter Judd, Ltd.* (1904); *Charles Pool & Co* (1914).

[74] *Daily News*, 22 October 1897, 3; *NSC*, October 1897, 9; *NSC*, December 1897, 6–7; *Tarrant and Fry* (1897); *Morning Post*, 5 November 1897, 7; *Standard*, 28 September 1897, 6. For another example of judicial commentary on the danger of defrauding readers who mistake adverts for editorials, see *NSC*, February 1907, 15 (a stockbroker case). And see the embarrassment in court by the evidence of the assistant editor of the *Financial Times*, which published paid reports about a fictional company, provided through an advertising agent. *Lupton and others* (1898).

practices were rampant, as were criticisms.[75] Interestingly, in the days of the advertisement duty the Revenue wanted to tax editorials that endorsed brands. The society was resistant; yet, acknowledging the presence of the profit motive in newspapers' own practices, the circular also wondered if in that case taxation did not serve as 'protection against ourselves'.[76]

References to 'independence' and the different kind of knowledge guaranteed by journalism were treated as self-explanatory. '[T]hat independence which is the proud characteristic of English journalism' was a self-congratulating account that started with an obviousness that had little to do with advertising, and then turned to face it. Advertisers' interests were simply assumed to be an inherent taint. One editor received an order from International Plasmon (food sellers) that required an advert to be 'preceded by at least five inches of unpaid reading matter, and not divided from news...Market and Sporting Items...are not regarded as reading matter within the meaning of our order.' The editor wrote to the society about the 'unblushing impudence'; he considered placing the order in the wastepaper basket—the ultimate insult with which newspapers' personnel could treat advertising orders—but first answered the advertiser 'Your order...we consider an insult to any self-respecting newspaper...' Why that was so was too obvious to merit an explanation. Newspapers' insistence on independence was often discussed in the language of a natural order: 'a singular reversal of the order of things is brought about, and newspaper proprietors, and editors, abrogate their proper functions in favour of the advertising agents.'[77]

Advertisers were adept at internalizing critique and could turn the problem itself to use, as a piece titled 'Crooked Ways of Advertising' demonstrated. It featured a complaint about misleading editorials only to end as an ingenious advert for Waterbury watches.[78] There was no end to creativity. Advertisers like Gordon Selfridge combined editorials and adverts in new ways, as demonstrated in Figure 2.6.

The circular hesitated in the face of sophisticated forces: The 'new system of combining advertisements with editorial matter...although...may be harmless

---

[75] *NSC*, April 1899, 8; *Tarrant and Fry* (1897). Another example is the debates about proprietary-medicine advertising through editorial endorsements in the professional (medical) as well as the popular press. Select Committee on Patent Medicines, 1914.

[76] *NSC* of 1847, referring to editorial endorsements of Holloway Pills, quoted in *NSC*, December 1913, 17.

[77] *NSC*, January 1893, 13; *NSC*, July 1906, 10; *NSC*, January 1904, 11 (in this case, a 'Special Inquiry' into Wills's advertising agency management of advertisements of the Great Western Railway. The hundreds of replies from newspapers to the inquiry spoke to the sense of increasing pressure, yet owners were reluctant to take concerted action. *NSC*, February 1904, 8–10). For a parade of society members boasting their use of the wastepaper basket against seekers of free adverts, see *NSC*, June 1909, 2–3.

[78] *Billposter*, October 1890, 250.

128   THE RISE OF MASS ADVERTISING

Figure 2.6 Selfridge combining advertisements and editorials. *Penny Illustrated Paper*, 15 March 1913, 11.

within reasonable bounds...a line ought to be drawn'.[79] Short of obvious fraud, the way to draw the line remained unspecified. The co-dependencies of newspapers and advertisers were such that all had an interest in rhetorically arguing for separations without ever elaborating implications too sharply. Even the higher charges for paid paragraphs in news and editorial columns could be represented by newspapers not as an interested position, but as an attempt to limit the practice.[80]

That said, paid material in news and editorial columns were the least of challenges for the professionalist view. Functions themselves were mixed.

---

[79] *NSC*, December 1911, 14. The challenge was part of Selfridge's broader strategy, which, as Elizabeth Outka shows, sought to elevate the meaning of commerce and consumption. Outka, *Consuming Traditions*, ch. 4.

[80] Letter from Samson Clark and Co. (advertising agents) Dr H.S. Lunn (client), 16 December 1897, re 'paragraphs' in the *Times*, *Morning Post*, and *Standard*. The former refused to discount prices on the pretext that the editor objected to paragraphs and therefore charged prohibitive rates.

Within newspapers, a single person could be both a reporter and an advertisement canvasser. This was unsurprising given patterns of employment that, below the editor and possibly sub-editor, were often precarious—casual or freelance—and given the absence of professional entry requirements.[81] In small newspapers, owners covered multiple functions. The diaries of Anthony Hewitson, who had been the owner of the *Preston Chronicle* and later the *Wakefield Herald*, include entries like this one, from 1872: 'Was out nearly all day getting advertisements for paper. Sub-editing at night till 10.' Alfred Borthwick Emanuel described himself as a journalist yet testified in court in 1897 to inserting stockbroker adverts in the news paragraphs of a provincial paper. One judge complained in 1900: 'It was to be deplored that the proprietors of some journals did not distinguish between the functions [of] their advertisement canvassers and their editors as sharply as they should.'[82]

Functions were also unstable, with new ones developing rapidly. The 'press agent', as Dann (from the matinee hat affair) was called, was one of 'these enterprising intermediaries' who puzzled the society. If only 'the Press rigidly held aloof from all such discreditable schemes, the "publicity agent" would soon die of inanition', Whorlow fantasized after Dann's next attempt at news making, this time with an invented poor boy-protégé and a violinist as client.[83] The professional journalist would not cause such confusions. These positions were ironic, because newspaper owners were largely responsible for the ever-receding liberal ideals of professionalism, which required conditions that secured independence from managerial and owner control (choice, remuneration, job security, status). The circular was essentially redirecting criticism levelled at newspapers themselves for failing to meet these ideals. And even if the professional definition of journalists had been better circumscribed, expanding work with advertising agencies complicated matters, because they too combined operations, and offered news with adverts. As Terry Nevett noted, news and advert supplies were closely interrelated.[84]

In December 1896, the circular reported a new 'per contra' system. An advertising agent offered newspapers a service of news at fixed rates for fixed periods, and guaranteed a quantity of adverts to offset the cost of news. Newspapers who

---

[81] Lee, *Origins of the Popular Press*, 104–17. Journalists' labour organizations began slowly in 1900, with the first national union founded in 1907. Training began in the 1880s, but was both limited and discouraged by low wage levels. For the role of non-journalist personnel, such as correspondents, see Hobbs, *A Fleet Street in Every Town*.

[82] Diary of Anthony Hewitson, 21 March 1872. On 21 November 1872, he wrote: 'Office work in morning; in afternoon out collecting advertisements; in evening writing for Chronicle till 10.30'. I am grateful to Andrew Hobbs for sharing these extracts. *Kahn and others* (1897); *Coventry Evening Telegraph*, 10 August 1900, 3.

[83] *NSC*, January 1911, 15; *NSC*, August 1912, 16. Nevett noted a new type of agent in the early twentieth century who streamlined 'editorial puffs' under the euphemistic title of 'reading-notices'. Nevett, 'Advertising and Editorial Integrity', 161.

[84] Lee, *Origins of the Popular Press*, ch. 4; Hampton, 'Defining Journalists'; Hampton, 'Journalists'; Nevett, 'Advertising and Editorial Integrity', 160–1.

refused to take the news were denied the adverts, and some succumbed to the pressure. Whorlow warned against the loss of independence, which he saw as a forgone conclusion in France. The appetites of advertisers, Palmer was warning, only grew. Palmer argued in 1897 that encroachments on news and editorial columns were comparatively new, apparently not having read the circular of the last decade and a half too attentively, but Whorlow agreed that the problem grew more daunting. The society convened a meeting of the provincial dailies to discuss 'per contra' offers, realizing in retrospect that this was too narrow a group: London papers too faced the heat. The meeting condemned the system and highlighted the risk to independence, the unfair basis for placing adverts, and the danger of mixing news with 'puffs'. However, as in other cases, the society declined to take concerted action. Episodes kept arising.[85]

An additional problem, which vocal spokesmen of newspapers were not as keen to flag, was that news suppliers likewise played on the opacity of distinctions. The rise of New Journalism itself reflected an appeal to styles associated with advertising as a mode of news reporting, and to contents that took a broad account of popular interest, so that claims about the greater vulgarity of the advertiser that Palmer was making with many others, were something of a misnomer. As an early commentator observed, sensationalism cut across news and adverts.[86] Burgeoning news agencies were quick to realize that the profits of blurred boundaries could flow their way. In September 1913, a manager at Reuters's advertising department approached advertisers with an offer: if they shifted their business to Reuters, 'it would enable [Reuters] to make representations to the newspapers for extended editorial reference to [the advertiser's] interests'—which would be a better use of money in both Britain and Australia. Reuters was in a position to persuade newspapers to 'open their columns more readily' and offer advertisers more free publicity, he promised enticingly.

The offer was nothing new, but it was blunt enough, and economically significant enough to cause a commotion. Advertising agencies, chief among them Street and Co. who had been flagged for years in the circular for 'disguised' adverts, jumped to protect the inviolability of newspapers.[87] They immediately notified the Newspaper Society, passed resolutions against the injury to the 'prestige... of the Press', and called on newspapers to limit the activities of news agencies to news. If

---

[85] On Palmer see note 41 and text. *NSC*, December 1896, 3; *NSC*, January 1897, 3–4; *NSC*, February 1897, 7.

[86] 'Sensational Advertising', 1862.

[87] Here was one criticism of Street in the circular: 'Street and Co., Ltd. – This name as associated with the whole art of exploiting the free editorial puff... continue year after year – decade after decade...' *NSC*, February 1907, 15. For a similar tension with Central News, see *NSC*, April 1908, 11; *NSC*, May 1908, 12. See also *NSC*, August 1909, 12, for another complaint, recalling the decision against the per contra system.

the method continued, agents warned as if they had not invented it, 'the impartiality and authenticity of the columns of the newspapers no longer exist.' The *Times* protested that newspapers could not be influenced in any case, but called on Reuters for an explanation. Baron de Reuter had to minimize damages. He assured the society that his 'News Agency is... wholly dissevered from and independent of all financial undertakings or influences whatever'. The manager who wrote the letter may have been 'a little exuberant in some passages' but ultimately the meaning was distorted. It was an 'unfortunate phraseology', de Reuter wrote, and no future confusion would arise.[88]

Nothing could have spoken to the difficulties of differentiating news from adverts more clearly than the fluidity of all roles: a news agency offering advertising as news; advertising agencies that often challenged the distinctions shocked at the affront to newspapers' integrity; a newspaper denying that anything of the kind could happen despite its own practices, and after years of reporting these realities in the circular; and finally two figures: an advertiser (in Reuters) who wrote plainly, and a self-appointed news agent (de Reuter himself) who fudged the meaning of words.

The *Times* was unimpressed with the interpretive turn that de Reuter took, which did not 'show any appreciation of the real *gravamen* of the charge'. Letters flowed in from agencies and newspapers, speaking to the rampant practices of mixing adverts and news. The *Times* concluded that it was time to escalate its position and announced that 'no advertisements will be accepted from agencies which supply news, or vice versa. We shall regard every agency as fulfilling one function or the other, but not both.' The heading was emphatic (Figure 2.7). It soon declared that it would also refuse requests for editorial notices from advertising agents. Traders and companies who wanted to have their announcements considered had to contact the City Editor directly. A newspaper thus framed itself as a reliable guardian of separations by treating all other actors in the chain of commercial press supply as more problematic.[89]

The strategy of the *Times* was in line with a general trend to assert separations between news and adverts by relying on formal rather than substantive grounds, while taking the substantive assumption of difference for granted. It was actually similar to de Reuter's justification, which relied on functional separations within his agency. The assumption that divisions of labour could guard the hierarchy of publications from within organizations—both newspapers and agencies—was repeatedly iterated. For example, the press magnate Alfred Harmsworth

---

[88] *Times*, 25 October 1913, 9; *NSC*, November 1913, 10. Some advertising agencies responded in a similar fashion to the 'per contra' system. *NSC*, January 1897, 3–4; *NSC*, February 1897, 7. However, industry actors were not oblivious to the fact that their practices too injured newspapers. *Advertiser's Weekly*, 19 April 1913, 5–6.

[89] *Times*, 12 November 1913, 15. The *Times* would start using Reuters's services much later, in 1958.

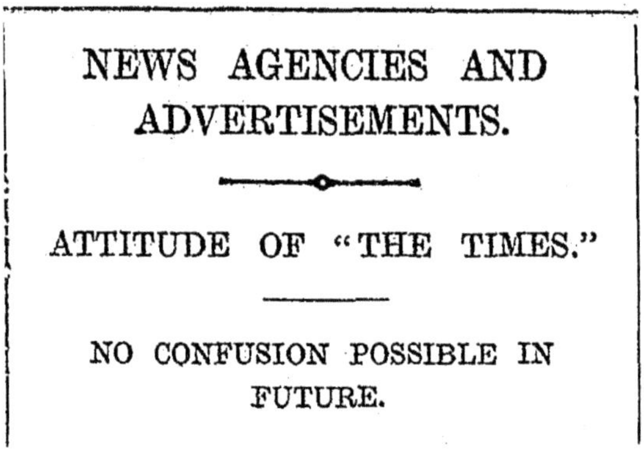

> NEWS AGENCIES AND
> ADVERTISEMENTS.
>
> ———◆———
>
> ATTITUDE OF "THE TIMES."
>
> ———
>
> NO CONFUSION POSSIBLE IN
> FUTURE.

Figure 2.7 The *Times* committing to stricter separations between advertisements and news. *Times*, 29 October 1913, 8.

encouraged his editor at the *Daily Mail* to occasionally remove adverts as an assertion of power, so that the hierarchy of publications be kept clear. He wanted adverts but claimed to refuse to 'perform Byzantine genuflexions' before advertisers, and chided his advertisement manager: 'You are killing the news.' Of course, this was the same persona responsible for the treasure hunt advertising-as-news scheme.[90]

Formal separations had another merit. The process of depreciating adverts was risky, for newspapers could not delegitimize advertising completely without undermining their own financial viability. If they were not careful, they would have to stop publishing adverts, or assume responsibility to screen contents, neither of which they could afford. One way to have the cake and eat it too was to rely on the respectability of the advertising agent. The implication was a division of labour: if advertisers kept to their sections, the assumption was that a serious agent provided some guarantee that the adverts were, within the limits of their genre, legitimate. Processes of professionalization in advertising supported legitimation by distinguishing between competent and incompetent advertising, and between respectable and unrespectable agents.[91]

In some instances, reliance on agencies was not enough. When *Judy*'s editor was convicted in 1907 for knowingly publishing an indecent advertisement, the *Tribune* announced that it was 'as anxious to ensure the clean, bona-fide nature of its advertisements as it is anxious to ensure the accuracy of its news' and would

---

[90] Clarke, *My Northcliffe Diary*, 1931, 37.
[91] I return to these processes in Chapter 7. The Newspaper Society was following them closely. It was not happy with the concentration of the industry but endorsed the broader vision of functional separations.

apply screening processes to exclude fraudulent or offensive adverts. Whorlow worried: 'when it comes to enquiring into the motives of advertisers, where is it possible to draw a line?' The general rule, he assured members in the following year, 'is to assume their [advertisers] genuineness unless the announcements bear upon the face of them unmistakable evidence of fraud or illegality'. The reason was the standard suspicion of advertisers embedded in the self-definition of the newspaper press: 'The whole system of trade advertising is to a large extent made up of exaggeration and puffery, and it has never been looked upon as the duty of the newspapers to act as advertisement censors in regard to taste or strict veracity.' A division of labour reliant on the 'creditable firm' could affirm advertising's inferiority, and yet keep it within the bounds of legitimacy.[92]

Assertions of formal boundaries unified newspapers' responses to the challenge of differentiating news from adverts, because they masked the difficulty of showing a substantive difference. Divisions of labour between advertising and journalism, and a flagging of the difference to readers through formal marks of type, heading, and location in newspapers, were necessary to assert the superiority of news. However, the *levels* of separation varied. For many, the new policies of the *Times* were too much. The executive committee of the society convened to discuss the Reuters affair. It published a detailed report in the (supposedly confidential[93]) circular, intended to calm things down and retain a messiness that the *Times* presumed to clear up. On the committee's analysis, editorial notices and puffs were 'part of the stock-in-trade' of advertising agents. The 'obvious meaning' of the unfortunate Reuters manager was that he could obtain editorial notices, not the contamination of news. While editorial endorsements were also problematic, they still had 'nothing whatever to do with blending advertisements with...news services'. Reuters 'happily stands acquitted'. In distinguishing between news and editorial columns, the committee relied on a longstanding debate about the relative place of values and facts in journalism, and brought it to bear on the problem of advertising with no discussion of a basic question: did editorial opinion, when applied to market products rather than political questions, raise different issues from news columns about the same products? The distinction did not explain the superiority of news in this context, nor addressed the structural porousness at Reuters, nor resolved the 'unsatisfactory' ambiguity of editorial opinion. Thomas Russell was familiar enough with the ironies of the system to point this out.[94] After years of dancing around these questions, the representative body of the Newspaper Society knew that an unstable balance of power hinged on tinkering, gently and confidentially, with fine lines. Bombastic commitments to

---

[92] *NSC*, January 1907, 10–11; *NSC*, September 1908, 9; see also *NSC*, July 1914, 10 ('censorship of "honest advertisers" is an alarming eventuality'); *NSC*, January 1907, 10–11.
[93] On confidentiality, see note 39.
[94] *NSC*, December 1913, 7; *Advertiser's Weekly*, 1 November 1913, 132.

clear distinctions could remain advertisements—or headlines—for the rest of the newspaper press.

Conclusion

Newspapers' renegotiation of the terms imposed by the mid-century tax reform involved a host of normative investments in policies, organizational structures, employment, and contractual relations. Debates about recommendations and divergences from them were shared within the newspaper industry and beyond it. While the ideals embedded in these investments were often honoured in the breach, their power should not be underestimated. They spawned a particular vision of advertising as an informational category, but of a lesser order than news. The process that started with the tax campaign in 1848, first organized the evaluation of advertising in terms of information, and so supported advertising's expansion with the free-market press. Then, as doubts arose about the meaning of news in a commercialized press, advertising was labelled inferior and biased in relation to news. Advertising thus carried the main burden of fears about the corrupting potential of the profit motive, and by implication rescued the press. By 1914 the vision was familiar enough to resonate as common sense. The varied modes of defying distinctions between adverts and news, and responding to defiance, all articulated the inferiority of advertising vis-à-vis news, and on those terms maintained a system of publication that drew profit and enjoyed social legitimacy.[95]

The assumption encouraged in the dialectics between newspapers and advertisers was that news deserved, and commanded, a greater epistemic authority, hence both the efforts to publish 'disguised' adverts, and the idealized professional responsibility to push back. In this debate, advertisers themselves subscribed to the assumption that cultural legitimacy depended on securing a place for advertising within the rationalist paradigm of information. Chapter 7 will demonstrate the emergence of alternative ideas in professional advertisers' theories, who were beginning to advocate against mixing advertising with news, while articulating an expertise in the human mind that had more scope for enchantment. They saw the *creation* of desires as essential to their role, indeed no less than the communication of wants that animated the debate examined in this chapter. However, these concepts did not receive expression in the normative structures of newspapers. As this chapter has demonstrated, the normative universe of the press offered scant

---

[95] A recent if prosaic illustration of the incredible success of this process is the absence of 'advertising' as an independent entry in Princeton's historical companion to information. Advertising is discussed in other entries but is not addressed as a distinct theme, while multiple other genres and concepts are. Blair et al., *Information*.

language and conceptual tools that could make sense of enchantment, beyond the shame of being drawn in by an inferior kind of information. If bad information was the whole story, you could only wonder what consumers saw in adverts. The rationalist focus on information reveals a disavowal of enchantment that will become clearer in the next chapters.

3
Advertising and Art
The Hoarding as Aesthetic Property

Figure 3.1 An Irish Bill-Posting Station. Clarence Moran, *The Business of Advertising* (London: Methuen & Co., 1905).

'Every art-loving inhabitant of this Metropolis must wish that some sort of censorship could be established to which such outrages upon form and colour should be...submitted.'[1] This 1888 *Daily Telegraph* writer was incensed by poster adverts, which had by that point become a ubiquitous scenery not only for Londoners but across Britain, as across other industrialized states (Figure 3.1). The mass exhibition of images in the public sphere sparked a heated debate about aesthetic experience, and calls for legal oversight, drawing a polyphony of voices.

---

[1] *Daily Telegraph*, 21 January 1888, 5.

The meaning of these new visual environments hinged on questions about the boundaries between economic and aesthetic categories: advertising and art, capital and beauty, commerce and culture. Social groups and individuals involved in the debate, among them the organized billposting trade, the National Society for Checking the Abuses of Public Advertising (SCAPA)—a civil society organization that led the aesthetic charge against outdoor advertising, state and local lawmakers, and a variety of citizens, mobilized a range of legal powers and concepts to perform the work of cultural demarcation, They demonstrate another facet of the role of law in historical boundary work, which Chapter 2 explored in the context of the newspaper press. This chapter tells the story of the hoarding—the outdoor advertising surface for posters (better known beyond Britain as billboard), which stood at the practical and symbolic centre of developments. Its history reveals how the aesthetic experience of advertising was contested and stabilized in its formative decades.[2]

The hoarding's history began towards mid-century, when emergent billposting companies started to create new property rights in space by renting or buying display surfaces. This development, which assumed pace roughly alongside the rise of image-centred colour posters, changed the meaning of advertising spaces. Historically they were boundless and lawless, potentially coterminous with any and all surfaces on which bills could be physically posted. Now, spaces were reimagined as a distinct value: fit for capture, divisible, tradable. The creation of new property rights might seem an unremarkable part of the rise of the mass market and the industry's professionalization. However, in this instance it was unusual due to its constitutive entanglement with aesthetics. As advertisers quickly realized, to redefine visible spaces as property regimes with stable conceptual and material boundaries required not only an economic but an aesthetic justification, and not only formal rights but a resonant cultural construction that recognized space as a visual matter and environment. Effectively, rights depended on aesthetics in the process of definition.[3]

To explore this history, the first section begins with the new legal regimes created in advertising spaces, and the aesthetic criticism they attracted. The next sections turn to the processes that shaped the hoarding's aesthetic meaning, which relied on creative uses of law. The advertising industry resorted to private law practices: it managed its properties as exhibitions inspired by the public museum movement, and enlisted artists through contractual commissions and copyrights

---

[2] The hoarding's function as an advertising medium is periodized in the *Oxford English Dictionary* to the nineteenth century: 'a temporary fence made of boards enclosing a building while in course of erection or repair; often used for posting bills and advertisements; hence, any boarding on which bills are posted.' 'Hoarding, n.' *OED Online*. I address older meanings below, note 67.

[3] The more familiar legal approach to aesthetics sees it as a secondary limitation or secondary interest associated with an already existing property right. Unusual in this sense is Maureen Brady's examination of the American history of light projections on property with attention to aesthetic meaning. Brady, 'Property and Projection'.

purchases. These practices, examined in the second section, secured a competitive edge for billposting companies by concurrently monopolizing advertising spaces and transforming their aesthetic meaning. Specifically, the billposting trade argued that it was introducing a rational aesthetic in support of the progressive education of the nation. This move gained a hearing, yet also accentuated the sense of threat that advertising posed to the domain of art. Therefore, criticism pitched in parallel with the hoarding's success. Critics of advertising pursued a route of public laws—state and municipal legislation, which gained momentum when the industry's efforts reached a cultural height in the 1890s, known in art history as the Age of the Poster. Public laws, examined in the third section, focused on the hoarding's locations in landscape, and created a licensing regime. Building on earlier achievements of the trade itself, these laws privileged the hoarding over competing advertising forms, and rendered it especially suitable for urban environments. In this way, laws actively shaped urbanity (and its countryside alternative), as well as advertising. However, public laws mainstreamed the hoarding by creating an aesthetic hierarchy based on legislated ideals of beauty, which construed the hoarding as aesthetically compromised.[4] The overall process reveals a successful capture of space by advertisers, but one that came with a markdown in cultural capital. Laws assisted in mainstreaming the hoarding as obviously appropriate in modern outdoor life, and yet obviously compromised in aesthetic terms. While aesthetically better than some other advertising forms, poster advertising was construed by local and state legislation, as well as by other legal mobilizations as inferior to art, and aesthetically unsatisfying. This way of seeing advertising remained influential long after the hoarding lost its primacy as a strictly material advertising medium.[5]

This chapter's study of the hoarding places law at the heart of visual commercial culture, and asserts its historical significance as a cultural force that shaped ways of seeing advertising and set the terms on which it became a common visual experience. By bringing sources of public and private law together, the analysis shows that daily legalities such as contractual practices, soft recommendations to property holders, and the legal consciousness expressed by advertisers and citizens in encounters with hoardings and posters, were consequential for the emergent legal-aesthetic regime of advertising. Capital, state, and civil society were interwoven, with aesthetic evaluations negotiated by public and private actors. One implication concerns our understanding of the legislative reform that emerged after the turn of the twentieth century to regulate advertising. Contra a common

---

[4] To avoid misconception, the private/public banners indicate formal distinctions between areas of law rather than a market/state separation, as explained below.

[5] I have now invoked more than once John Berger's *Ways of Seeing*, to gesture at ideas of seeing as historically constructed experiences. However, I do not apply these ideas to advertising as something that needs to be seen through, as Berger might have done, but rather to a historical process that conditioned ways of seeing advertising itself.

view of this type of legislation as interventionist, this chapter shows that it was a legal-aesthetic organization of the hoarding that entered a dialogue with an existing aesthetic regime based in private and municipal legal power. Legislation drew on conceptual structures already in place, rather than imposed a novel aesthetic regime on a spontaneous market eruption. Ultimately, it also placed fewer aesthetic pressures on advertisers than had earlier legal developments because, as we will see, it entrenched a previously unstable conceptual opposition between commerce and beauty.[6]

Attention to law also offers more local methodological and conceptual contributions to the historiography of advertising aesthetics. In particular, the analysis highlights the co-dependencies between individual works (posters) and the display strategies of collections. These questions of visual culture draw on two scholarly areas: art and design histories—where most work on poster aesthetics has been written, and histories of exhibitions—where the exhibition of adverts has been a neglected question. The history told here foregrounds the aesthetics of exhibition on the hoarding structure, and within a broader understanding of national spaces, and demonstrates its practical and conceptual ties with the development of poster art. Ultimately, the history of outdoor advertising requires a joint perspective on these questions.

Lastly, the legal perspective also implies a change in the periodization of poster history, which in most accounts begins in the late 1880s. Viewed through the lens proposed in this chapter, the systematic industrial creation of rights in advertising spaces and the emergence of a specifically aesthetic understanding of the implications, a gradual process with roots in the 1840s and clear presence from the 1870s, were the critical starting point for the modern history of poster aesthetics.

Outdoor Advertising and the Legal Transformation of Space

Billposting versus Flyposting

In the second half of the nineteenth century, billposting companies began to mushroom, taking advantage of expansions in advertising spaces with the rapid

---

[6] Distinctions between state and market are challenged in other ways too. Private law routes, it will be seen, depended on the active engagement of courts and background legislation, while public ones were the work of the advertising industry no less than political and civil society actors. On a theoretical level, the hoarding's history concerns the public meanings of private property. This perspective has long challenged market/state distinctions in scholarship, although the role of aesthetics as a specific area of public meaning has received limited attention.
For an analysis of state and municipal legislation in terms of growing interventionism in an otherwise wild spread of advertising, see, for example, Greenhalgh, *Injurious Vistas*. Despite his emphasis, Greenhalgh often acknowledges the role of law in entrenching the acceptability of advertising. See also the discussion of urbanity in later in this chapter.

building in cities. These organizations replaced the so-called billstickers, fated for rebranding as 'flyposters':[7] men, sometimes boys, often on casual hire, whose means of production were a stick, paste-bucket—frequently containing self-made paste—and brush. Their title implied that they pasted bills 'on the fly', on any physically accessible surface. Formally, posting on private properties was forbidden under the Metropolitan Police Act of 1839, s. 54(10), and some other surfaces were also protected. Yet, little was off limits in practice; 'even the doors of homes were not inviolable.'[8] The key feature of commercial billposting, which defined it in contrast to flyposting, was the legal formalization of posting sites. Companies acquired or rented the advertising space from the rights holder in the property. They would typically rent an entire 'station', construct the display structure, and manage it, all of which required capital investment. By contrast, a flyposter was 'a chap as posts his bills wherever he gits a chance'.[9]

The flyposter was a familiar cultural figure, 'a personage of no small importance,' as printer Charles Manby Smith described him in 1857. For him, everything was a hoarding; as an 1830 anonymous ballad put it, 'All the world is puffing, So I paste! paste! paste!!' In 1851, Dickens immortalized him when a meeting with 'The King of the Bill-Stickers' appeared in *Household Words*. The account began with the impression of a plastered London: 'The forlorn dregs of old posters so encumbered this wreck [a house wall], that there was no hold for new posters...' It then described the violent world of illegality of the billsticker who, the King said, 'ought to know how to handle his fists a bit'.[10] Advertisers capitalized on the mythology of rivalry, as the series of Bovril magic lantern adverts in Figure 3.2 demonstrates.

Until the era of capitalist billposting companies, locations of posting were neither bordered nor organized, even as some emerged as 'stations' by mere concentration. Some private owners began to rent space to billstickers, but it awaited corporate economic interests for rent to become an enforced norm.[11]

Commercial companies absorbed many flyposters.[12] Their image as large-scale sophisticated organizations, whose expensive apparatus replaced the bucket and

---

[7] Searches in Google Ngram, the British Newspaper Archive, and the *OED* suggest that 'fly-posting' came into common usage in the 1890s or turn of the century; first appearances can be found in the 1860s.

[8] Lamp posts were protected by the Metropolis Management Amendment Act, 1862, s. 90. See also Greenhalgh, *Injurious Vistas*, ch. 1; Presbrey, *History and Development of Advertising*, 1929, 91.

[9] The annual rent of a hoarding in London could exceed £60,000 (close to £7 million in 2020). Thomson and Smith, *Victorian London Street Life*, 1877. Maintenance repairs in a large town could reach £1,000 a year (about £120,000 in 2020). Sheldon, *Billposting*, 1910, 92. *Walter Hill & Co.* (1903).

[10] Smith, *Curiosities of London*, 1857, 117; Sammy Slap the Bill Sticker', 1830. See also Sampson, *History of Advertising*, 1874, 26; Strachan, *Advertising and Satirical Culture*, 99; Dickens, 'Bill-Sticking', 1851, 604.

[11] On rent to billstickers, see Smith, *Curiosities of London*, 1857, 123.

[12] A large firm in the early twentieth century employed 50–60 billstickers. *Billposter*, January 1904, 63.

Figure 3.2 Bovril Magic Lantern Slides, c.1900.

brush, can be seen in the photo in Figure 3.3. Yet, the transition was gradual. On the side of labour, casualization meant that many men not only worked for billposting companies but also took flyposting jobs. On the side of capital, at least until the late 1870s some companies engaged in both billposting and

142 THE RISE OF MASS ADVERTISING

Figure 3.3 Sheffield's Ltd, a billposting firm. *Progressive Advertising*, 2 May 1902, 50. These images circulated in the firm's adverts from the 1890s.

flyposting.[13] This was part of a broader picture of an advertising industry only just beginning to professionalize. Divisions of labour were murky on other fronts too. Throughout the late decades of the long nineteenth century, some

---

[13] Purcell, 'Billposters and Posters', 1900, 207; Allen, *David Allen's*, 1957, ch. 6. Adolphe Smith reported in 1877 that experienced men earned £1 to £1 5s. per week for a 12-hour day work in billposting. Men 'picked out from the common lodgings houses... the Seven Dials, or even disinterred

billposting companies were also printers, and offered poster production as well as posting. Services also had parallels with advertising agencies, as leading companies advised on campaign planning and management.

The billposting trade was organized from the early 1860s; and consolidated in the national United Billposters Association in 1890, with over six hundred members by 1900. The *Billposter*, a journal published from 1886, became the official organ of the association, reported on legal battles vis-à-vis critics, municipal, and state authorities, and debated and imposed trade-wide legal policies. The association controlled competition by limiting entry, dividing areas of service, and unifying contractual terms. It also centralized the protection of the trade's interests with effective lobbying and legal counselling, and managed an annual directory of 'bona fide Billposters' that consolidated its influence. The trade was the active power and public voice for outdoor advertising. It enjoyed diverse cooperation and support that exceeded its formal organization due to interests in income from billposting.[14]

The same years saw the rise of lithographic, image-centred posters. Until the late nineteenth century, typographic posters with no images, or limited wood-carved ones in circumscribed vignettes surrounded by profuse text were standard; as late as the mid-1870s text still dominated. Improvements in lithographic techniques and high-speed commercial printing enabled large, colourful posters, in which images dominated, and text was minimal and integrated with image. Those started in the 1860s, and became increasingly dominant over the next decades, even as text continued to appear, particularly in smaller bills.[15]

---

from the workhouses' earned 16*s*. to 18*s*. per week. Some contractors paid by the hour, and refused to pay on rainy days, to deter billstickers from pasting wet bills. Flyposters, meanwhile, earned 4*s*. per day. Thomson and Smith, *Victorian London Street Life*, 1877.

[14] The London Billposters Protection Association and district-specific associations cooperated with it. Allen, *David Allen's*, 1957, ch. 6; Purcell, 'Billposters and Posters', 1900, 206; Greenhalgh notes a growing post-war consolidation. Greenhalgh, *Injurious Vistas*, ch. 1.

Income flowed not only to other stakeholders in advertising, like agents and printers with whom billposting companies cooperated, but also to property holders—land owners and tenants—who let surfaces on their properties for advertising. Municipalities were both property holders and tax recipients. The Advertising Stations (Rating) Act, 1889, treated advertising as improvement of land subject to rates, and authorized local governments in some cases to apply fees to hoardings over highways and on public land. On the act's history, see Jones, *Law Relating to Advertisements*, 1906, ch. 4; Greenhalgh, *Injurious Vistas*, ch. 2. The act was not all bad news for the trade, because it reduced local authorities' incentives to resist leases of hoardings to advertisers. Moran, *Business of Advertising*, 1905, 155; *BW*, May 1903, 36.

[15] Earlier uses of images in advertising were on a smaller scale: the broadsides, used mostly for special events and spectacles, and trade cards. McKendrick et al., *Birth of a Consumer Society*, chs 2–4, 8; McFall, *Advertising*, ch. 6; Berg and Clifford, 'Selling Consumption'.

Lithography was invented by Alois Senefelder in the late eighteenth century but only gradually became a widespread technique in commercial print. Chromolithography (colour printing) was available from the 1830s, but was still just beginning as late as 1841. It was a colour revolution that had changed perceptions of the world by the end of the century. Twyman, *History of Chromolithography*; Ryan, 'Images and Impressions'. Photography was rare in poster advertising before 1914, although some lithographs were illustrations based on photographs.

In the visual and legal landscape in which commercial firms intervened, unauthorized posting was standard. Cyril Sheldon claimed that his billposting company inaugurated the system of rent. The story had it that the wife of Edward Sheldon, who established the firm, proposed rent in the 1860s after her husband got involved in a dangerous fight over a site in Leeds to which neither side had exclusive rights. Sheldon did not shy from claiming that it was 'one of the rare instances on record of a wife's solicitude and common sense revolutionising her husband's business'. As James Greenhalgh shows, rent and ownership of stations were in fact familiar from at least the 1840s. The transition assumed pace gradually, with growing trade organization. Over the next decades, billposting companies created the hoarding by turning new rights into mundane experience. Contemporaries had to learn to *see* publicly shared elements in their environments as untouchable, and posting as a violation. This was a late reminder that private property depended on a non-intuitive process of acculturation. One judge observed: 'Of course, the origin of all posting, I understand, was fly-posting. That there was any valuable property and the right to post bills never occurred to people originally...but with civilisation, billposting became a valuable property, and we find companies dealing with it by having special stations.' Lawyers saw that a new legal environment developed with the 'increase in recent years of advertisement hoardings as a distinct form of "lettable interest..."'[16]

To turn its rights into a lived reality, the trade took multiple steps. It established lists of recognized billposters and brought them to the knowledge of advertisers, who increasingly refused to deal with unrecognized ones. It educated billposting companies on the law, explaining how to enforce and protect their rights. It asked members to approach vestry clerks and encourage them to end flyposting, and where private owners allowed posting on their premises, to calculate the rates and impose them so that private interests would align with trade interests. Companies protected their rights in courts, and encouraged private owners to do the same through criminal and civil proceedings, so that both flyposters and those who advertised with them internalized the new order. Civil cases relied on contracts and torts, and sought both damages and injunctions. They included, for example, suits for breach of rent contracts, quasi-contractual demands to pay fees for posting on walls, suits for damage to property—both hoardings and bills—and for trespass on property, and injunctions to prevent access to property. Criminal cases involved prosecutions of flyposters for illegal posting that led to fines and imprisonment. Late in the century, courts saw that the order was still in the

---

[16] Sheldon, *History of Poster Advertising*, 1937, 2; Greenhalgh, *Injurious Vistas*, ch. 1; *Manchester Billposting Co.* (1909); J.H. Redman, *Billposter*, November 1909, 56.

making, and treated cases as exemplary.[17] The process was fraught. Among contested questions were such issues as the forms of contract that allowed a billposting company to sue without having the landowner or tenant join the proceeding; or the conceptual basis of damages to hoardings: was it actual bills ruined, or an abstract economic value? The rent system emerged through scrutiny of such questions, to the point that it became the grounds of argument against flyposting: billposting companies asserted that flyposting was unfair competition because legitimate business 'had to pay large rents'.[18]

In addition to rights in stations, rights in bills were established, and delegitimized pasting-over practices even where a space was not under a rent contract.[19] Cases of malicious damage to property, in which bills were damaged by competitors, coalesced with two other, ideologically contradictory practices. On the one hand, damage by protesters angered by particular posters, shabby appearance, or outdoor advertising per se. This was joined by petty, usually youthful, violence of boys who tore, threw stones, or adorned posters with their own additions. On the other hand were poster collectors and their helpers in the age of the poster craze, more on which below. The billposting trade pursued all attacks on its bills in courts, and often summoned young boys on principle; the educating effect was uniform, disparate motivations notwithstanding. Companies published their law suits for maximum effect. Their success was evident in a circulating joke about a

---

[17] On steps taken by the trade see Sheldon, *History of Poster Advertising*, 1937, chs 5, 7; *Billposter*, November 1900, 48; *Billposter*, November 1890, 274.

Civil cases: for example, *Robbins* (1888) (breach of rent contract by letting it to another); *Boyle* (1889) (flyposter sued for rent for using a wall); *Walter Hill & Co.* (1892) (trespass and damage for posting on Hill's hoarding at St George's Circus. Walter Hill, former president of the national association, was particularly active in courts); *Rockley's Ltd.* (1908) (damages and injunction to restrain from posting on Rockley's stations. The *Billposter* recommended actions for injunction in addition to damages). Claims for damage to property were known after frenzied election postings. *Globe*, 31 March 1880. 3.

Criminal cases: for example *Coleman* (1890), in which Willing and Co. billposters brought a case against a boy who flyposted, so that 'this sort of thing... be put a stop to'. Alderman Gray limited the order to costs under the circumstances. In Nottingham, a flyposter who refused to pay a fine and damages was sent to prison for fourteen days with hard labour, *Willing and Co.* (1893). At Fenton, a man summoned for posting on a gatepost defended that he had posted on that gate for twenty years, but was told he could not do so without permission, *Billposter*, April 1908, 112. At Liversedge, an elderly man defended by arguing there was nothing wrong with the bills he posted, but was answered: 'People must not post bills of any kind now without permission.' He was fined. Often, the employer was in court to pay the fine, *Billposter*, February 1901, 77.

Private property owners' defence of their property was experienced as a new thing. As one defendant summoned for damage to a private fence said, he saw bills on the fence, and thought he might do the same, *Billposter*, March 1912, 117. Another defendant argued that the fence he used had been a billposting station for three hundred years, and that the public could not be robbed of a site 'where announcements regarding important coming events could be read amidst ideal surroundings'. He was fined, *Billposter*, July 1914, 9–10.

Courts held both employers and employees, or in some cases agents and principals, liable, for example, *Billposter*, October 1901, 46. Judges could be lenient with fines, and preferred to flag the decision as a warning for the future, for example, *Ramsay*, 1910. But see Feltham Police Court, where a Post Office attempt to prosecute the advertiser as well as billposter was rejected, apparently on the argument that criminal liability could not be based on agency, *Billposter*, December 1911, 82.

[18] *Roberts* (1909) (emphasis added). [19] For example, *Guildford* (1892).

hunter reluctant to shoot a charging elephant, because the animal was covered with adverts and the fine could be high. Flyposters begged for mercy, but were met with disdain: 'tears in his voice as well as his eyes, and coupled with the most abject apology...swears that he did not know he was doing wrong...He hasn't twopence...and amongst his excuses...an invalid mother, a bedridden grandmother, and others to keep (and these don't die...)'.[20]

The cultural gap between flyposting and billposting was repeatedly iterated. The industry described flyposting as premodern, 'a relic of an obsolete period when the first comer had the prior claim to a vacant space...The bitterest animosities which still exist...between rival billposters are the legacy of the old billposting Vendettas, when every knight of the brush felt it to be a point of honour to cover up...the bills his rival had posted.' In *Longman v Pascall*, litigated in the High Court in 1892, a plaintiff claimed damages for slander, which consisted in a statement that he 'had only six stations, the rest were simply flyposting stations'. Longman argued that he was injured in his credit and reputation. Anthony Trollope's *The Struggles of Brown, Jones and Robinson*, 1862, represented mid-Victorian advertising as a cultural shift that victimized the flyposter. The novel traces the life of a failing haberdashery firm, which Trollope intended as a satire on trade. Yet, as Trollope said, no one saw the fun in it; the novel itself failed, like the firm. One source of ambivalence in the novel, which leaves it undecided between satire and sentimental romance, is that Robinson, who embodies the shift from old billsticking to modern advertising, is a complex character. He is the advertising partner of the firm and operationalizes advertising extravagances by writing fantastic lies and running expensive publicity stunts. Yet, his character is a mismatch: Robinson is a touchingly honest lover and guileless businessman cheated by his partners. His integrity is closely aligned with his flyposting beginnings. Although 'bill-sticker' is a term of abuse, his past is the origin of his literacy and impels his attraction to advertising as a literary mode. His faith in advertising, far from cunning to match his actions, reflects a misdirected idea of moral duty in trade that has to be discarded for a cynical outlook. In this way, the flyposter was implicitly romanticized by Trollope.[21]

Yet flyposting was not just small economies and class difference, and was not in fact a historical relic to be denigrated or romanticized. In 1900 some three hundred 'pirate bill-stickers' operated in London alone according to one estimate—and cities were the centre of capitalist firms' efforts to drive them out. Into the twentieth century, flyposters were still surprised to discover that circumstances were changing.[22] The endurance of flyposting was tied to its notable

---

[20] *Advertisers' Review*, 1 October 1900, 5; *Billposter*, May 1908, 122–3.
[21] *Billposter*, October 1893, 61; *Longman* (1892); Trollope, *Struggles of Brown, Jones and Robinson*, 1862; Trollope, *Autobiography*, 1883, ch. 9.
[22] 'Stalking the Pirate Bill-Sticker', 1902.

cultural contexts. One was the travelling theatres and circuses, which partook in a transitory moment of modernity and were a diehard phenomenon.[23] Another was political posters that peaked near elections; flyposting belonged in the struggle for control of public space as a feature of electoral culture. Thus, stories of night adventures not only continued, but took on a new cast: companies engaged ex-detectives to watch over the hoardings, and spun new and exciting mythologies. Disguised 'trackers' risked their safety amid the weapons of brushes and pots: 'I have been covered with paste before now, and had bills posted over me while rolling over and over in the gutter among overturned paste-pots and scattered bills.'[24] Reliable numbers and their economic significance cannot be verified, but flyposting was enough of a threat for billposting companies to invest in ongoing legal action.

However, the efforts of capitalist firms were in trouble almost as soon as they began in earnest, as the visual landscapes they created met with a vociferous aesthetic criticism.

Aesthetic Criticism

Many contemporaries viewed the spread of industrialism and the democratization of consumption as the interrelated drivers of aesthetic degeneration that required urgent responses. As John Steegman said, the nineteenth century was afflicted with doubts about its taste, and set out to reform it in ways that never occurred to its predecessors. Efforts to improve tastes enjoyed a wide cultural purchase, from private homes, through indoor spaces of display—museums, galleries, exhibitions, and shops—to outdoor life.[25] Yet, the aesthetic criticism of outdoor advertising had a particular bite: the problem was an absence of art in a genre that claimed to circulate images in the public sphere as never before, and unlike newspapers that left readers some choice, tyrannically 'violate[d] the wayfarer's mind'.[26]

Aesthetic criticism assumed dominance in the last three decades of the century, and overshadowed earlier criticisms of outdoor advertising, which, as Greenhalgh

---

[23] Scholarship debates whether they were remnants of an old carnivalesque tradition, or, at the other extreme, the lubricating mechanisms of capitalism and a consumerist engine. For a review and analysis of the circus as a repackaging of controversial traditions for widespread consumption, see Kwint 'Legitimization of the Circus'.

[24] Thompson, 'Pictorial Lies?' 203; 'Stalking the Pirate Bill-Sticker', 1902.

[25] Steegman, *Victorian Taste*. And see for example, Cohen, *Household Gods*; Nead, *Victorian Babylon*; Kriegel, *Grand Designs*; Maltz, *British Aestheticism*; Waterfield, *People's Galleries*. These themes informed well-known movements, like the Arts and Crafts Movement from the 1880s, the Town Planning Movement from the 1890s, artists' and preservation societies.

[26] H.R. Haxton, 'Advertisement', in *Encyclopaedia Britannica*, 1902, 96. This might seem like a newspaper-biased account, yet billposting representatives agreed in substance if not in form. As Sheldon said, 'No one is able to evade the message of a good poster.' Sheldon, *Billposting*, 1910, 8.

observes, treated it physically in terms of nuisance and obstruction, within a broader preoccupation with managing crowded city streets. In the closing decades of the century, discussions of advertising turned increasingly to aesthetics. Eyesores, disfigurement, desecration, defacement, vulgarization, horrors, hideousness, and ugliness became widespread currencies, reaching a pitch in the 1890s. In 1890, an Art Congress announced that advertising was a national disgrace. William Morris wrote in 1893 that although adverts disgusted him, he rejoiced at the 'spectacle of the middle classes so annoyed and so helpless before the results of the idiotic tyranny which they themselves have created'. The *Billposter* carefully collected criticisms, which were accepted by supporters no less than 'enemies'. The *World*, for example, published an article supportive of outdoor advertising, yet reflected, 'the whole billposting fraternity continues to display ... a truly shocking indifference to schemes of colour ...'[27]

Timothy Hyde argues that judgements of ugliness should usually give us pause. Far from secluded questions of taste, they are instrumental in the invigoration of social processes. An affective response of disgust, which Morris's comment exemplified, often came with these judgements. Disgust was bound up with an entire public language that recommended aesthetic revulsion, as Zachary Samalin shows. And indeed, aesthetic criticism became a civil organization. SCAPA was established in 1893; the architect and Royal Academician Alfred Waterhouse was president, the Irish barrister Richardson Evans its active secretary. SCAPA numbered over seven hundred members in 1894, an elite but politically diverse and gender-mixed group that enjoyed broad support. Its aims were 'checking the abuse of the practice of spectacular advertising, and ... protecting and promoting the picturesque simplicity of rural and river scenes, and the dignity and propriety of our towns'. To these it added in later years a general aesthetic goal of 'asserting generally the importance, as a great public interest, of maintaining the elements of interest and beauty in out-of-door life'.[28] SCAPA's journal, *A Beautiful World*, recorded its legal work vis-à-vis the billposting trade, local governments, parliament, and civil society.

Why were advertising aesthetics important? Commentators reflected diverse perspectives rather than any unified theory, but arguments that tied aesthetics with ethical education and ideals of national progress dominated.[29] Especially important was national morality, often discussed with a competitive eye to the advances of other countries. The 'topsyturvydom of commercial morals', as

---

[27] Greenhalgh, *Injurious Vistas*, ch. 1; *Billposter*, December 1890, 295; Morris, 1893; *Billposter*, March 1896, 147. Also *Billposter*, March 1896, 148; *Billposter*, June 1890, 189; *Billposter*, February 1906, 338.
[28] Hyde, *Ugliness and Judgment*; Samalin, *Masses Are Revolting*. Samalin does not address advertising; Readman, 'Landscape Preservation'; *BW*, November 1893, appendix A, 26; *BW*, May 1903, 121.
[29] On diversity in aesthetic thought and its relation to consumer culture, see Gagnier, *Insatiability of Human Wants*. The hedonism that Gagnier finds on the rise in the 1890s did not dominate critical responses, but was possibly implicit in the support for advertising aesthetics discussed in the third section in this chapter.

SCAPA called it, had to be reined in by higher purposes. The threat was a corruption of civilization. As the critic and SCAPA member William Lecky argued, '[f]ew greater misfortunes can befall a people than the decay of their sense of beauty, and it is impossible to vulgarise national taste without, at the same time, lowering national character.' Speaking in a 1901 SCAPA meeting, the jurist and former Liberal MP James Bryce described the hoardings as a decline to barbarism: 'Those crude colours which are employed are the revival of the vivid tints with which our ancestors dyed their skins, and produced very much the same satisfaction.' Critics complained that it was inconsistent to invest in museums, galleries, and art education, but undermine their values by adverts.[30] The religious undertones of quests for moral progress, and any non-rational aura art carried, were channelled into an educational civilizing project bent on rationalizing tastes.

Criticisms might seem close to what Tony Bennett describes as governance through culture, but the cause was actually more diffuse. The complex relations of aesthetic critics to class clarify the point. On the one hand, classed discourses were prominent, for critics treated the lower classes as both agents of change who would learn to reject ugly adverts, and beneficiaries of any aesthetic improvement. SCAPA wanted to teach ideals of sobriety, neatness, and order to 'the common folk' and 'the multitude'. As Peter Gurney observes, SCAPA's leaders were isolated from radical organizations. On the other hand, aesthetic criticism fed on a convergence of class interests. SCAPA speakers argued: 'the tastes which we seek to develop and protect exist in all classes', and brought to the aid socialist criticisms of 'ugly placards'. It was at least true that the cleansing project that wanted to save the poor from being 'condemned to vulgarity' in streets, resonated not only with aesthetic elitists but also with socialist critics of capitalist advertising. Charges against advertising aesthetics were therefore irreducible to a high-brow governance project.[31]

Beyond national morality, aesthetic criticism received additional rationales as critics tried to enlist broad support. Particularly important were economic

---

[30] Evans, *Account of the SCAPA Society*, 1926, 136. The argument that 'our artists' and 'our advertisers' have much to learn was often repeated. For example, *Globe*, 14 August 1913, 2. William E.H. Lecky, *New Review*, November 1893, 467; *BW*, May 1903, 84, 88; The artist Arthur Severn, *Billposter*, March 1889, 127; Architect, in *Billposter*, January 1890, 103; *St James' Gazette*, 28 May 1891; SCAPA speakers, *BW*, February 1898, appendix II; *BW*, September 1909, 224–7. See also architects' letter to the London County Council, *BW*, September 1909, 89.

[31] Bennett, *Birth of the Museum*, ch. 1; *BW*, December 1894, 114–15; *BW*, November 1893, 8; *BW*, November 1893, 9; Gurney, *Making of Consumer Culture*, 81; *BW*, May 1903, 130–1 (referring to the *Co-operator's Year Book*, 1901). On the complexity of SCAPA's position, see also Greenhalgh, *Injurious Vistas*, 75–7; Spielmann, 'Streets as Art-Galleries', 1881. On the paradoxes of aesthetic democracy in Ruskin and Morris and the aristocratic sentiment at its heart, see Dowling, *Vulgarization of Art*. On politically diverse support for cultural instruction more broadly, see Waterfield, *People's Galleries*, ch. 1. On assumptions about public space as a locus of instruction, shared by advertisers and their critics in the USA, see Baker, 'Public Sites'. For the interpretation of the process as a governance project in the USA and Canada, see Valverde, *Everyday Law*, ch. 3.

arguments against advertising display, which included strict economic interests such as the touristic income from beautiful sceneries, and more complex ideas like a concept of private property in one's sight that competed with the economic assets of billposting companies.[32]

With criticism came calls for legislative oversight. In his book *Democracy and Liberty*, Lecky called on the legislature to free the public from 'gigantic advertisements... [which] destroy the beauty both of town and country...'[33] Parliamentary work was high on SCAPA's agenda. Yet, legal responses to aesthetic criticism began before legislation and beyond public authorities. Advertisers realized that the capture of space through the rent system depended on an attendant aesthetic definition, and were committed to its elaboration.

Private Law and Advertising Aesthetics

Rent: Display Aesthetics

The trade argued that new rent practices were really an assumption of responsibility over aesthetic display, in order to overcome the travesties of flyposting. On a common argument, flyposters' indifference to aesthetic effects entailed a loss of meaning. One reader claimed to have read this advertising collage:

> *Pigs fattened in six weeks on the Englishman, edited by Dr. Kennedy. Price 2d weekly, and kills fleas, beetles, insects and all kinds of vermin. Perry Davis' pain killer cures smoky chimneys, and notice to mothers, feed your infants on Bond's marking Ink, 6d. per bottle.*[34]

Visual examples were also familiar. Figure 3.4 is one of the earliest photographs of street advertising, taken by William Henry Fox Talbot during the construction of Nelson's Column in Trafalgar Square, 1844, hinting, as Elizabeth Guffey puts it, at a vast urban terrain newly discovered for the picking.[35] Display was characterized by discontinuous pasting and random and often overlapping accumulations. The old advertising station in Figure 3.5 was a drawing in an advertising professional's publication, which emphasized messy display and overlap as a problem of flyposting. Probably the most famous representation of this theme remains *A London Street Scene* by John Orlando Parry, 1835, in Figure 3.6. The painting has been interpreted as a commentary on advertising's power to overtake cities, and on the

---

[32] For example, *BW*, May 1903, 124; *BW*, September 1909, 31; *BW*, September 1909, 55; *BW*, May 1903, 25–8. On similar justifications for the promotion of art within the museum movement, see Waterfield, *People's Galleries*, chs 2, 6.
[33] Lecky, *Democracy and Liberty*, vol. 2, 1896, 139.   [34] *Billposter*, April 1890, 149.
[35] Guffey, *Posters*, 55.

Figure 3.4 William Henry Fox Talbot, Nelson's Column under construction, Trafalgar Square, first week of April 1844.

fascination and terror its accumulation aroused. What needs emphasis is that this display style represented the 'chaotic result of the fly-posting era', as a *Times* retrospective put it. As Sadiah Qureshi observes, Parry's painting captured how reading was made difficult by the overlaying of bills, their boundaries hard to discern.[36]

Already in 1863 William Smith advised a shift to orderly presentation with aesthetic commitments: 'have painted boards with neat mouldings and in bright colour; get them of as near one size as possible. This will give them an air of respectability...' Drawings accompanied the advice (Figure 3.7). The new rent system was hailed for achieving the rational order of Smith's dreams.[37] Billposting companies advocated a rational aesthetic as the *raison d'être* of their hoardings, dubbed galleries of the people, and so wedded property power

---

[36] *Times*, 30 October 1961; Qureshi, *Peoples on Parade*, 51–2. For a discussion of Parry and the taking over of city life, see Thornton, *Advertising, Subjectivity*, 21–2.

[37] Smith, *Advertise*, 1863, 119; Sheldon, *History of Poster Advertising*, chs 5, 7.

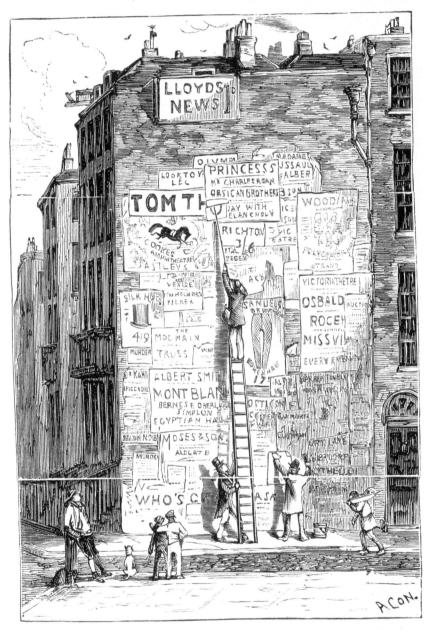

Figure 3.5 An old bill-posting station. Clarence Moran, *The Business of Advertising* (London: Methuen & Co., 1905).

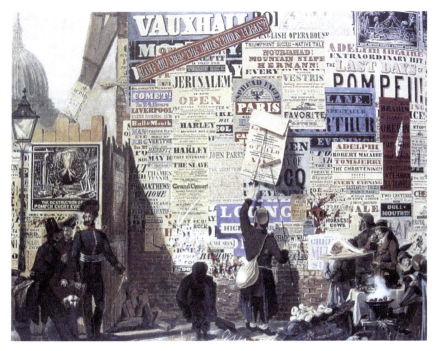

Figure 3.6 John Orlando Parry, *A London Street Scene*, 1835.

with aesthetic responsibility. Their advocacy drew on the goals of public museums as non-exclusionary spaces with a national civilizing mission.

A rational aesthetic was streamlined into the contractual infrastructure of billposting on a trade-wide basis. The trade wanted hoardings 'smartened up, kept clean, well ordered, all out of date posters covered immediately'. Bordering and symmetry became standard requirements of professional billposting. 'Good repair' eventually became a standard contract term.[38] These aesthetic aspirations resonated with the nineteenth-century museum as a rational alternative to the disorder of competing exhibitionary institutions and historical cabinets of curiosities. The narrative was a similar one of chaos to order.[39] Of course, the hoarding could never embody all the cultural assumptions associated with museums. Billposting companies did not control content, where broadly political questions like representativeness, intellectual synthesis, social power, and history began to inform museum exhibitions, nor could they choose creators, specific combinations, or the scope and length of exhibition. As we will see, companies also had no

---

[38] *Billposter*, February 1896, 124–5; *Billposter*, December 1896, 95; Sheldon, *History of Poster Advertising*, 23–4.

[39] The narrative is described in Bennett, *Birth of the Museum*.

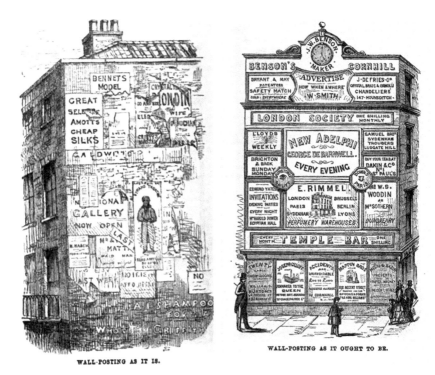

Figure 3.7 R.T. Powney, Wall-posting as it is and as it should be. William Smith, *Advertise: How? When? Where?* (London: Routledge, Warne and Routledge, 1863).

interest in sacrificing paying contracts for overarching aesthetic agendas. However, similar challenges were also true for mushrooming galleries and museums, most of which were built between 1870 and 1914. Therefore, within the nascent terms of Victorian art exhibitions, advocacy for the hoarding was not as remote from the art museum as it can ring today. In the shifting context of exhibitions, questions of arrangement, picture crowding, and background colours, all of which were taken up by the billposting trade, were regularly aired and criticized as institutions like the National Gallery fell short of ideals of clean hangings, proportion, and order.[40] The trade's arguments that its displays served the advancement of knowledge, and that it was alert to its civic mission, therefore made sense. With the materials under its hands, within a new legal structure, there

[40] As Giles Waterfield showed, museums grew out of the mixture of instruction with commerce and entertainment that typified international exhibitions of the industrial age. Concepts of exhibition and educational strategies were all emergent and unstable, collections depended on private donors and were haphazard rather than preplanned policies, and challenges of consistency or even identifiable logic were typical. Waterfield, *People's Galleries*, chs 5–8.

was room for discretion absent from flyposting, and the trade claimed a progressive change.

As with legal rights to rent, so with display on rented hoardings—the lessons needed hammering in. In its second issue, the *Billposter* announced that it was engaging an inspector to report on the condition of stations and encourage trade members to 'improve their style'. Inspectors were also employed by billposting companies and advertising agents to oversee the quality of pasting and observance of clients' instructions, and to guard against flyposters. These contractual concomitants served the same cleansing act. We thus see mundane contractual practices between billposters and end-advertisers, and between an organized trade and its members, deployed to establish and defend an aesthetic meaning for advertising.[41]

In 1897 the *Billposter* began a run of object lessons of 'artistic billposting'. For example, it advised that the hoarding in Figure 3.8, although 'neat and attractive', could be improved by more bordering and less bills. The chastening of exhibition style became a major preoccupation. The hoarding in Figure 3.9 was congratulated for 'artistic posting', exhibiting good spacing.

Rhymes for 'The Billposting Station's Appeal' also circulated:

> ... Back well my sheets and in a twinkle
> You'll find there's neither crease nor wrinkle.
> ... Always make my sheets to blend
> If you would taste and neatness lend.
> If to your work you would add weight
> Be sure and keep the lines quite straight.
> Large posters should be placed on high
> But small ones in the line of eye...[42]

The formal rationality recommended in these rhymes was not easy to internalize in the trade. Sheldon contrasted the hoarding in Figure 3.10, viewed as irregular and uneven, with the one in Figure 3.11, showing standard sizes and achieving 'really presentable appearances'. Bad aesthetics, he argued, were mistakes of small and inexperienced contractors, while professionals knew how to give effect to adverts.[43] Figure 3.10 often strikes twenty-first-century observers as more attractive; this highlights the historical emphases on straight lines, consistent filling of space, and symmetry, which informed the display seen in Figure 3.11 (the symmetrical treatment of the top right and bottom left is particularly striking). The same emphases informed many art galleries.

---

[41] *Billposter*, August 1886, 11; 'Why There Is Bill-Posting', 1902.
[42] J.O. Rogers, c.1900, in Allen, *David Allen's*, 128.
[43] *Placard*, April 1912, 5. The magazine started in April 1912, sponsored by Sheldon's Ltd.

156 THE RISE OF MASS ADVERTISING

Figure 3.8 Keighley hoarding. *Billposter*, April 1897.

In 1899, the first advertisers' exhibition of their methods opened at Niagara Hall (Figure 3.12). The capitalist hoarding's aesthetic actually moved into the gallery. As James Taylor observes, the spate of advertising exhibitions that followed broke with the 'chaotic-exotic' style in favour of a rational aesthetic. These efforts reiterated the rationale claimed for the hoarding-as-exhibition.[44]

[44] *Billposter*, May 1899, 117; *Billposter*, June 1899, 13; Taylor, 'Fascinating Show'.

Figure 3.9 Horwich hoarding. *Billposter*, July 1897.

Display efforts attracted approving commentary:

> at Kensington a hoarding... had been treated as if it were a wall in an art gallery. First of all, a background has been prepared by covering the wooden hoarding with a dark brown paper, round which runs a scroll border. Then on this wall the coloured posters, which are mainly pictorial, have been affixed, with black spaces intervening and with due regard to the individual characteristics. The principle followed is indeed that which our more advanced artistic societies have adopted when hanging their works. As each painting is as far as need be isolated, so each poster stands alone, and the eyesore which is caused by jumbling and overdoing is avoided.[45]

The artist Walter Crane reportedly praised billposting: 'the billposter does not do his hanging badly; quite as well, in fact, as the committee of the Academy...' Clients too appreciated the new display style. C. Bliss, director of Mellin's Food, who were a prominent advertisers, explained that location, colour relations between posters, preservation of posters from paste, and bordering within a square, were necessary to bring out the art of their valuable posters. As one advertising professional put it, '[t]he value of the thing itself, and the importance of the space and situation... are very closely entwined...' David Henkin notes

---

[45] 'Art of the Wall Advertiser', 1893. Of course, there is no telling whence commendations originated.

Figure 3.10 Hoarding, *Placard*, April 1912.

that the collage of overlapping bills radically severed adverts from their author's control and intentions. There was a greater sense of control in bounded bills, which coalesced with the new aesthetic. The *News Agent and Booksellers Review* noted pedestrians' and bus riders' interest in hoardings, and recommended similar reforms in shop windows.[46]

In a lecture at the Bradford Club, a member noted additional strengths of the hoarding. Not only were notions of beauty conveyed to the masses, with proportions of good to bad pictures as in any gallery, but also '[s]moking was not prohibited, and one might point with stick or umbrella'.[47] This comment reveals the challenges of sustaining boundaries for the hoarding while attracting audiences. As in other concerns that admitted an undifferentiated mass public, behaviour had to be controlled. For outdoor adverts the challenge was technically and conceptually more complex because legal and material boundaries depended

---

[46] *Billposter*, June 1905, 253; *Billposter*, April 1897, 152. On Mellin's advertising, see Chapter 4. *Progressive Advertising*, November 1906, 11; Henkin, *City Reading*, 70; 'Billsticking', 1900, 192. Richard Altick notes that the earlier galleries of the poor were the eighteenth-century printshop windows. Altick, *Shows of London*, ch. 8. Significant shop window reforms awaited the lead of Selfridge's. Outka, *Consuming Traditions*, ch. 5.

[47] *Billposter*, May 1907, 117–18.

Figure 3.11 Hoarding, *Placard*, April 1912.

on an attendant aesthetic appreciation. As the trade's efforts to protect bills from diverse political and social bents—admirers and opponents of posters, petty vandalists, entrepreneurs, and high-minded aristocrats—revealed, the problem was not restricted to lower-class habits. Public institutions often worried about an uninitiated mob, but advertisers' goal was equally to secure respect from the initiated, who could be more threatening. The balance was delicate; gentlemanly stick-pointing was a conduct to be managed without destroying, for it could mean a coveted sympathy.

In 1911 William H. Lever announced the 'Artistic Hoardings Competition'.[48] Figures 3.13 and 3.14 show the first- and third-prize winners, exhibiting the aesthetic ideals of the trade.

As other photos and ongoing educational efforts clarify, these ideals were not usually attained. The new aesthetic was expensive. Aspirations of consistent sizes, bordering, and smaller numbers needed reconciling with profitability.[49] On any single hoarding this practically meant, in the lingua franca of the trade, running as

---

[48] *Billposter*, January 1911, 207.
[49] On the rise in advertising rates due to bordering, see Sheldon, *History of Poster Advertising*, 1937, 99; Nevett, *History of Advertising*, 91.

160   THE RISE OF MASS ADVERTISING

Figure 3.12 Stall at the Advertisers Exhibition, Niagara Hall, London, 1899. *Billposter*, April 1899.

Figure 3.13 Redhill hoarding, first place winner in Lever's Artistic Hoarding Competition. *Billposter*, August 1911.

ADVERTISING AND ART 161

Figure 3.14 East Sheen hoarding, third place in Lever's Artistic Hoarding Competition. *Billposter*, August 1911.

many contracts as possible at any given time. Ornamentation was minimal given space considerations, but was nonetheless advocated as something of a watered-down ideal of museum elegance. Architectural gestures appeared sometimes, as in Figure 3.15, although more typically ornamentation dealt with the borders of a given structure. Materials had to be cost effective. Paper (Figure 3.16, bottom example) rather than wood (top example) was both cheaper and easier to change. The cheap appearance of these economic choices did not seem to raise anxieties.

The trick was to economize on materials and get in a maximum number of bills, without violating minimal aesthetics. Economic success literally hung in the balance between too little and too much aesthetic commitment. Here were two cases: Figure 3.17, a station noted for the bordering of every bill without waste of space; Figure 3.18, evaluated as not elegant, but remunerative.

Despite compromises, and although to future advertisers the display aesthetics of these years would seem crude, billposting companies led a popular aesthetic change. The new aesthetic allowed them to create the hoarding as a bounded space. Its limits were understood in contrast to the emergent inaccessibility of spaces *not* contractually rendered as hoardings, on the one hand, and the limits of access to contractually rendered ones by anyone except rights holders, on the other hand. The legal consciousness of limits turned a rapid economic capture into its opposite: a clearing. The space also assumed an internal coherence defined by the legal control of the entire surface, which translated into the aesthetic management of construction materials, ornamentation, and display. This creation wedded competitive goals with responsiveness to aesthetic criticism. Sheldon summarized the trade's historical outlook: critics

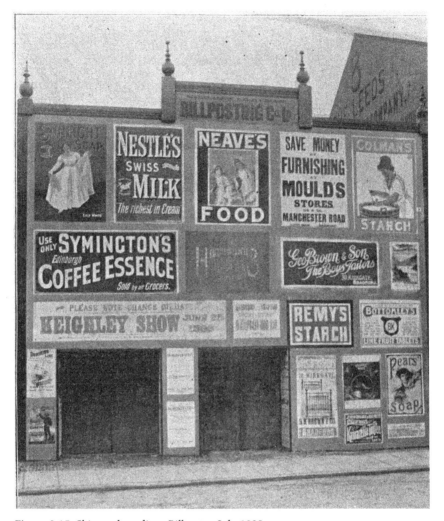

Figure 3.15 Skipton hoarding. *Billposter*, July 1898.

complaining about vulgarity and disfigurement after the turn of the century really had in mind the situation of a generation ago and not the new orderly world.[50]

Trade investments in the hoarding also transformed individual adverts. As I now turn to show, contractual commissions and copyright purchases were key to this transformation.

---

[50] Sheldon, *History of Poster Advertising*, chs 5, 7.

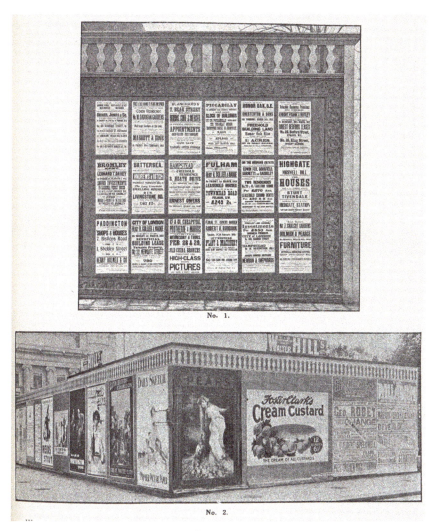

Figure 3.16 Hoarding adornment. *Billposter*, June 1912.

164 THE RISE OF MASS ADVERTISING

Figure 3.17 Nottingham hoarding. *Billposter*, September 1897.

Figure 3.18 Grimsby hoarding. *Billposter*, August 1898.

Contract and Copyright: Poster Aesthetics

'Artistic posters' were outdoor graphic posters understood in opposition to commercial ones, although both types were adverts. As Ruth Iskin explains, they were characterized by sophisticated colour, composition, and line, by replacement of realism and melodrama with decorative sensibilities, and in art history have been associated with modernist styles that embrace flatness, abolished shading, and often brilliant colours and bold lines, under a variety of artistic influences.[51] In popular discourse, artistic posters were often associated simply with the work of trained artists. The artistic poster has been the subject of extensive scholarship; this section changes perspective by placing it within the history of the hoarding. It briefly recalls developments, and then highlights their symbolic function within the transformation of space, while shining further light on the tensions of an aesthetically imbued economic space.

Two events are widely considered to have inaugurated the introduction of art to posters in Britain. One is Frederick Walker's poster, *The Woman in White*, 1871, created for the Olympic Theatre's adaptation of Wilkie Collins's novel (Figure 3.19).[52] The second is the 1886 use of a painting by John Everett Millais, *Bubbles* (originally titled *A Child's World*), for an advert of Pears Soap (Figure 3.20).[53] The two events were different from each other, and more interestingly given their status in advertising history, from what would become the widespread form of engaging artists in advertising in the next two decades, namely, contracts with printers who added artistic designs to their stocks.[54]

Walker anticipated the practice of commissioning artists to design posters that became widespread from the late 1880s, but *The Woman in White* was commissioned directly by Collins, an artist-to-artist engagement that set the case apart. With Millais, the artist did not anticipate advertising when he created the original. *Bubbles* was an oil painting, its copyright first bought by the *London Illustrated News* for reproduction in a Christmas supplement. Thomas J. Barratt, the managing partner of Pears, acquired it from the

---

[51] Iskin, *Poster*, introduction. See also Barnicoat, *Posters*.

[52] On Walker's motivations, see Haill, 'Posters for Performance'. Walker's design was the first image-centred poster by a Royal Academician; as Iskin explains, it was innovative in privileging image over typography, and, as Marion Spielmann noted in 1895, in using a single symbolic image rather than a realist illustration. Iskin, *Poster*, ch. 7; M.H. Spielmann, *Graphic*, 9 February 1895. It also marked the end of an era: a woodcut, when lithography was becoming the standard method. Nevett, *Advertising in Britain*, 87; Rickards, *Rise and Fall*, 15.

[53] Commentators sometimes pointed to earlier designs that failed to attract the same attention. See, for example, 'Art on the Hoardings', 1908 (referring to an 1874 poster by Walter Crane, and 1881 by Hubert Herkomer).

[54] Hewitt, 'Designing the Poster'. Advertising agencies superseded printers only in the 1920s to 1930s.

Figure 3.19 Frederick Walker, *The Woman in White*, 1871.

newspaper for £2,200, and then asked Millais's permission to add his firm's name and a bar of soap. A controversy endures about Millais's response: was he helpless, or satisfied?[55] Contentiousness only served the campaign. As Barratt himself said, the cultural focus on the original purchase missed the fact that most of the company's efforts went to reproduction. *Bubbles* was not the only case of adaptation of artworks, but the practice remained marginal in posters.[56] At its best, it was a subversive move that countered what George Wallis, the first Keeper of Fine Art Collection at South Kensington Museum (later the Victoria & Albert), called the fetishistic worship of original works.[57] But harnessing a work of this kind for advertising, and running copies by the millions, popularized a possibility that could not but summon a Benjaminian set of concerns about the status of art in capitalism. Complaints about the prostitution of art

---

[55] Respectively: Millais, *Life and Letters*, ch. 18; Barratt's Letter to the *Times*, 17 November, 1899. The controversy continued in letters to the *Times* during November 1899. See also Bingham, 'Commercial Advertising', 172; Dempsey, *Bubbles*.

[56] *Bubbles* was viewed as an 'incalculable service' for the industry. *Billposter*, October 1892, 57; Barratt, 'How Nearly £3,000,000 Were Spent', 1908. Another famous case was Lever's purchase of *The New Frock* by William Powell Frith. On the debate, see Cooper, *Art and Modern Copyright*, ch. 6.

[57] Wallis, 'Economical Formation', 1888.

Figure 3.20 John Everett Millais, (artist), A. & F. Pears Ltd (publisher), *Bubbles*, c.1888 or 1889.

were forthcoming. We might view Barratt's copyright purchase as a forced connection in an atmosphere in which artists risked shaming if they cooperated with advertisers.

The atmospheree was hard to overcome, despite encouragement. For example, the *Magazine of Art* that the author and critic Marion Spielmann edited, wanted to see artists driving 'hideousness' out of the streets. This was part of the artist Hubert Herkomer's reformist agenda for advertising posters. However, artists were uncomfortable, often refusing to sign designs, and adopting pseudonyms for poster work. As John Hewitt observes, poster designers trained in art maintained a distance from advertisers even as they worked for them, for example by working in private studios rather than the printing workshop (Figure 3.21), and by creating speculative designs that were not explicitly tailored to particular products.[58]

---

[58] Spielmann, 'Streets as Art-Galleries', 1881; Korda, 'Streets as Art Galleries'; *Billposter*, November 1886, 71; 'Triumph of the Art Poster', 1905; Hewitt, 'Designing the Poster'.

Figure 3.21 The studio at Benson's advertising agency. S.H. Benson, *Force in Advertising* (1904).

The author and journalist William Courtney turned the tension between art and advertising on hoardings into a comedic *Romance of the People's Picture Gallery*. In his animist rendering, poster characters gathered for a Christmas party after their 'heads had been turned in consequence of the notice paid to them as the main factors in the artistic education of the democracy'. A conversation ensued between artistic and commercial posters:

> 'Are you artistic?' asked the Geisha, timidly, looking with some wonder at Sister Mary Jane's Top Note.
>
> 'No, my dear, I am not, and I don't want to be,' was the answer. 'My object in life is to appear as if my legs had been cut off and my mouth turned permanently awry. But you are, my dear. I suppose you are one of the London results of Chéret's pictorial activities in Paris. You do your creator credit, though you have no backbone.'
>
> 'Is it a necessity of High Art to be backboneless?' asked the Geisha, innocently.
>
> 'Well, it is not a bad definition of it, at all events,' laughed Charley's Aunt, whom no one accused of being artistic... But if there was one thing of which she was intolerant... it was the introduction of aestheticism into a

Figure 3.22 Dudley Hardy, *The Geisha*, Daly's Theatre, 1896, Waterlow & Sons Printers.

Figure 3.23 Chadwick Rymer, *Charley's Aunt*, c.1892.

poster. 'You might as well place the Poet Laureate on a motor-car,' she remarked, indignantly, 'or bring Ruskin into the Kaffir Circus, or put a moral into a roaring farce...'[59]

Despite the prevalent view that art and advertising were in tension, the Barratts of the world were not deterred. Barratt himself argued that he was spreading art and culture more than the Royal Academy and 'endless galleries', a claim repeatedly echoed in celebrations of *Bubbles*, and of posters generally:

> 'Tis welcomed by Poverty's children, for
> Pleasant they find it.

---

[59] Courtney, 'Romance', 1896. The V&A reference for Figure 3.23 does not include the artist, who is identified by Catherine Haill. *Charlie's Aunt* play premiered in the Globe in 1893 and was extremely popular. Edward VII believed that the Aunt was a caricature of his mother, Queen Victoria, and refused to see the play. Haill, *Fun Without Vulgarity*, plate 22. On the successful Geisha opera and Hardy's poster for it (Figure 3.22), see Haill, *Fun Without Vulgarity*, plate 10.

> Poverty stays with them always, the
>   poster is changed.
> How can you fathom you light-hearted
>   man who designed it,
> All the appeal of the colours and forms
>   you arranged?[60]

These arguments attempted a radicalization of pubic museums' access mission, and often gained a hearing. An inspector of Poor Law Schools could praise in 1899 the headmistress of the Dover Union Girls' School for decorating school walls with 'pictures used as advertisements' by 'well known firms as Pears, Nestlé, etc.' Success led to thefts, which in turn allowed poster effects to resonate widely, with public cautionary notices and legal proceedings. At the Bolton Borough Police Court, two billposters were charged with stealing *Bubbles* pictures. One defendant fit it into a frame and hung it up. The assistant prosecutor J.H. Hall appeared on behalf of the advertising agents and described the pictures as beautiful. He asked the court not to be severe, the purpose was merely 'to demonstrate that these valuable pictures cannot be removed with impunity'. Alderman Nicholson was resistant, 'You cannot use the Court for your own purposes', but he levied a fine. In the Hammersmith Police Court, another billposter was sent to prison for stealing two copies of *Bubbles* that he had resold.[61]

By the mid-1890s the industry was self-congratulatory amid an international poster movement. Comments on the popularity of posters and on the collecting spree were widespread.[62] The movement gained a place in art and design histories, a success due to the international character of works that created a cross-border artistic language. British designers quickly rejected the academic tradition in favour of French influences. The quality of creations as art was bolstered by a dedicated literature that sprang to study posters; periodical reports on new works on the hoardings; exhibitions; galleries; design competitions; and collecting, which in turn encouraged a market in poster prints. These satellites of posters, however motivated, provided forms of instruction and intellectualization absent from hoardings-as-galleries; they functioned as symbolic compensation for shortfalls in museum-like aspirations. The billposting trade embraced these trends, albeit selectively: in line with its sources of inspiration in the public museum movement,

---

[60] Urwick, 'Verses for a Poster', 1910.

[61] Local Government Board Nineteenth Report, 1889–90, 155; *Billposter*, October 1888, 39; *Billposter*, July 1889, 13 (publication by Pears' advertising agents).

[62] See, for example, Edinburgh billposters conference, *Billposter*, May 1896, 181; Marion H. Spielmann, *Graphic*, 9 February 1895. See also Rickards, *Rise and Fall*.

it did not flag the modernist challenge of many posters to the academic tradition and to narrative-art collections in galleries and museums.

And yet, even as the industry managed to bring artists within its routine operations, artistic posters did not overtake advertising, as photos of hoardings in the previous section clarify. The majority of posters remained anonymous designs outside the poster movement, while recognized artists remained a minority. The limited purchase of artistic posters, even at their golden age, is instructive. For one, it clarifies the aesthetic outlook of the advertising industry. Advertisers were never fully converted to aesthetic goals, which they found hard to reconcile with commercial ones. This was particularly clear on the level of individual posters, where advertisers were repeatedly embarrassed by modernist art. Despite French influences, British tastes for narrative remained significant in this period. Most advertisers did not take the advice of the poster designer and collector W.S. Rogers, who argued that only skilled artists could impress the crowd and give posters their 'carrying force'. Distance from art was a recurrent sentiment: 'The great bulk of us are simple citizens without any special technical training, we know what combinations of colour and form please us and what offend us...'[63]

Furthermore, the limits of artistic posters reveal the focal point of the billposting trade's aesthetic outlook, which was the hoarding, not individual adverts, and highlight the role of symbolic investments in capturing space. The focus of art and design histories on posters and artists has left this connection under-examined, yet it shaped the history of the poster no less than artistic dialogue across borders, or artists' conflicts between legitimacy and income. Artistic posters, which required high capital investments, never became widespread, yet had a formative effect on the status of the hoarding, which the billposting trade actively bolstered. The symbolic function is attested by *The Woman in White* and *Bubbles*, which continued to be celebrated and remain famously associated with the poster in Britain, while being in fact atypical of the genre. By bringing established artists into the fold, advertisers short-circuited aesthetic criticism, which was unable to deny 'progress'. The billposting trade cooperated in marking an aesthetic-cum-price distance from the world of flyposting. Even reluctant voices in SCAPA gave something up: 'It would be perilous to express an opinion as to how far the new varieties deserve to be called in the higher sense "artistic"; but many of the wall

---

[63] On the limits of artistic posters see Iskin, *Poster*, introduction. This was also true for other countries. For comments on artistic posters as outliers, see, for example, *Billposter*, March 1911, 229; Sheldon, *History of Poster Advertising*, 76. On narrative art see Thompson, 'Poster'. See also Tickner, *Modern Life*, ch. 1 (referencing the work of Pamela Fletcher). Rogers, *Book of the Poster*, 1901, 8–9; *Billposter*, October 1892, 57; *Billposter*, March 1911, 224.

pictures of today are...entertaining and pleasing...' The organized voice of aesthetic criticism was converted to the possibility that adverts *could* be artistic. This was a significant achievement for the project of defining the hoarding.[64]

Advertisers bounded off spaces and imbued them with aesthetic meaning. Ironically, their success only accentuated the sense that advertising threatened the domain of art, and they clearly had no interest in bounding the process itself: why not turn any rentable surface into a hoarding? Set against this dynamic, aesthetic criticism pitched just at the golden age of the poster, and put increasing pressure on the dilemma of where, within a broader imagination of national landscape, it was appropriate to display adverts. The next section examines the public laws enlisted to answer this question.

Public Law and Advertising Aesthetics

Aesthetic Hierarchy

The aesthetic outlook that informed legislative and administrative reforms shifted from formal improvements in adverts and display on hoardings, to their contextual assessment within space conceived on an axis between two ideals: nature and commerce.

The regulatory route focused on licensing powers for local governments. Initially, the strategy was private parliamentary acts obtained by discrete municipalities. In 1907 SCAPA succeeded in creating an easier procedure through a general act that authorized municipalities to pass bylaws: The Advertisements Regulation Act, 1907. The act adopted a new aesthetic language, but drew on earlier developments in which aesthetic considerations already loomed large.[65] Under both private acts and bylaws enacted under the 1907 general act, local governments were given aesthetic discretion in line with SCAPA's position that the appropriate level for advertising oversight was municipal. It was a decentralized view premised on the democratic argument that local governments were best positioned to cater to their communities. However, discretion was framed by state oversight, encouraged by the billposting trade's apprehensions about 'faddists' and its objection to variations in practice. Parliamentary committees that heard petitions against private bills, and the Home Office that reviewed and approved all bylaws under the 1907 act, imposed state models on municipalities. This section draws on their records to examine the national and local regulatory

---

[64] *BW*, December 1896, 6–7.

[65] Pragmatically, the act was a compromise between the advertising industry and promoters of legislation. Its parliamentary promoter, Lord Balfour of Burleigh, and SCAPA in the background, negotiated acceptable terms to secure its passage. The final vote was 207 to 12, Commons Sitting, 14 June 1907.

policies on outdoor advertising. Ultimately, public laws created an aesthetic hierarchy premised on the relative distance of environments from the visual transformations of commerce. Landscapes revealing natural beauty were at the high end of aesthetic ideals; landscapes artificially preserved for non-commercial activity and those containing historical and cultural heritage were next; at the lower end of the aesthetic scale was advertising on hoardings in urban environments; and finally, on the verge of complete exclusion, various other forms of outdoor advertising: the historical antagonist—flyposting—but also newer forms of competition, such as sky-signs, field-boards, and flashing projections. The hierarchy accepted the hoarding's superior aesthetics over competitors in line with the private law initiatives that framed the hoarding as aesthetic property. At the same time, the hoarding's beauty was relegated to a low position in the total scale of aesthetics. Its doubtful qualities fitted environments considered already aesthetically troubled, namely, urban landscapes.

At this stage we can see the subtleties of legal boundary work. Binary oppositions attributed to the nineteenth century have been revisited in recent years by scholarship that challenges narratives of separation and distinction between art and industry, or culture and commerce.[66] As we saw in the previous section, hybridity and co-dependence, rather than separation, were true for the binaries of art and advertising. Yet that section also showed that mixtures were uneasy. The advertising industry struggled with aesthetic values at the same time that it claimed them, while its critics attacked advertising even as they had to acknowledge aesthetic improvements. How were both mixtures and binarism maintained? Aesthetic hierarchy in legislation and its implementation turned relative distance from commerce into an aesthetic concern and formalized it. This logic allowed different phenomena to be aesthetically graded while still being defined as commercial. In this way, aesthetics and commerce were entangled and yet distanced. For the hoarding, the very name of which brought forth imagery of greed and thus evoked the negative associations of profit seeking, the implications were palpable.[67] By turning commerce into a (low) aesthetic marker, the hoarding's locations in space—particularly its urban appropriateness—were defined, and its concurrent elevation and degradation as a visual experience established. The following discussion unpacks the aesthetic hierarchy of public laws and the ways of seeing advertising that they embedded.

---

[66] The literature is expansive. Reviews and discussion of art/industry can be found, for example, in Nichols et al., *Art versus Industry?* On culture/commerce, particularly the debate sparked by Wiener's *English Culture and the Decline of the Industrial Spirit*, see, for example, Readman, *Storied Ground*. On modernism as hybrid, see, for example, Outka, *Consuming Traditions*. On culture/commerce in relation to advertising, see, for example, Strachan and Nally, *Advertising, Literature*. See discussion of mixed attitudes to urbanity below.

[67] While the meaning of 'hoarding' as an advertising medium was relatively new (note 2), a centuries-old meaning was tied with money: 'the action of the verb hoard; especially the accumulation and hiding of money', and also 'that which is hoarded; money laid up'. 'Hoarding, n.' *OED Online*.

Nature and Culture: Beauty and Amenity

The 1907 act established two routes for local authorities' bylaw-making, which implied two types of environments: one was natural, semi-natural, and heritage-containing environments; the other was environments transformed by industry and commerce. State, municipal, and industry interpretation and implementation tended to associate these environments with the country and city, despite their more complex basis.

In one route, municipalities were allowed to regulate, restrict, or prevent the exhibition of adverts in places, manner, or means 'as to effect injuriously the amenities of a public park or pleasure promenade, or to disfigure the natural beauty of the landscape' (s. 2(2)). Both beauty and amenity were innovative language in this context; they created a public aesthetic interest not otherwise recognized in law.[68] As the Liberal MP Herbert Samuel observed, the British parliament protected beauty for the first time. Aesthetic motivations had informed legislation about advertising before the 1907 act. For example, sections in acts passed by Edinburgh (1899) and Dover (1901) were motivated by outrage about adverts that covered treasured natural and historic sites: the Dover cliffs, and a view of the Edinburgh castle. However, before 1907, legislation was based on private acts and typically resorted to technical language or otherwise to safety and health considerations.[69] SCAPA therefore complained about legal fictions. In a 1904 memorandum to the Home Office, it pointed to the 'want of the means of giving precise political point to the desire' to protect aesthetic interests. Advertising supporters could not agree more; for them, the problem was that faddists were using legal fictions to promote their veiled aesthetic preferences. The issue, however, exceeded legal fictions: existing frameworks could not be stretched far enough despite all creativity. Outdoor advertising could easily be made innocent in terms of nuisance, obstruction, physical danger, or public health threats. Indecency regulation had limited reach given its content-based approach.[70] In 1907, for the first time, aesthetic motivations were forefront.

---

[68] Amenity was familiar in limited contexts, particularly land law. In terms of public interest, it was familiar as a legitimate improvement goal. See also Greenhalgh, *Injurious Vistas*, ch. 3.

[69] The same tendency informed the American regulation of billboards. The open endorsement of aesthetics as a regulatory goal in Britain, and the organization of aesthetic criticism that impacted trade practice, were significantly early in comparison. See Burnett, 'Judging the Aesthetics of Billboards'. On the international flow of ideas about advertising regulation, see Greenhalgh, *Injurious Vistas*, 90–3.

[70] Evans, *Memorandum*, 1904; *BW*, September 1909, 27; *Billposter*, March 1891, 349. As the *Daily Telegraph* said, posters are 'rarely indecent, but ... are too frequently horrible and, in nine cases out of ten, devoid of artistic merit'. *Daily Telegraph*, 21 January 1888. I return to indecency in Chapter 6.

Beauty and amenity were both in dialogue with idealizations of landscape.[71] The terminology of beauty as a natural condition of landscape envisioned areas unspoiled by industrialization, typically found in the countryside. Amenity envisioned mixed environments. Public parks were a formal category: they were managed by public authorities for the recognized goals of recreation and exercise. This was the achievement of the Parks Movement that advocated open spaces in towns to promote well-being and health. The less formal category to which amenity applied, that of pleasure promenades, was conceived as a contrast to business and work. These landscapes typically included green environments and those containing cultural and historical heritage.[72] Implicitly, an aesthetic hierarchy already operated within the clause, which idealized connections with nature, recalling the eighteenth-century tradition that took appreciation of nature for the purest form of disinterested aesthetic attention. Amenity, while lower down the scale than the beauty of nature, was also an aesthetic category, which tied aesthetic pleasures with utilitarian goals of well-being as well as higher ideals of civic and national identities. It was a rising value in the same years in urban planning (itself a new idea).[73] All of these environments, which shared an assumed distance from the functions, temporality, and physical conditions of commerce, were placed in contrast to advertisement display, in line with an accepted sense of threat.

Protected environments were clearly exceptional for large parts of urban landscapes. Administrative oversight in turn confined beauty and amenity to the countryside even more than the act itself implied. Bylaws required the approval of the Secretary of State or parallel authorities in Scotland and Ireland; therefore, state officials effectively determined the forms of local regulation. It quickly transpired that the Home Office treated municipal discretion with suspicion, and would not sanction bylaws viewed as uncertain; it repeatedly iterated, 'byelaws must be of the nature of definite requirements'. Its approach revealed a continuing resistance to abstract aesthetic concepts, as the following discussion demonstrates.[74]

The Home Office found itself dealing with creative drafting that included, for example, protection of 'views from the sea', which it saw as imprecise.[75] In its model bylaws, the operative principle was that municipalities would give details of

---

[71] On the relation of these visions to national identity, see, generally, Readman, *Storied Ground*, and on SCAPA specifically, Readman, 'Landscape Preservation'.

[72] Metropolitan Open Spaces Act 1877, and its later amendments; Jordan, 'Public Parks, 1885–1914'; Waterfield, *People's Galleries*, ch. 4; Greenhalgh, *Injurious Vistas*, ch. 3. On amenity as heritage value, see Readman, *Storied Ground*, ch. 4. The original inclusion of residential districts under the clause was omitted because of 'vagueness'. Advertisement Regulation Bill, Amendments, 1905.

[73] See, generally, Graham, *Philosophy of the Arts*. On Victorian thinkers' privileging of Nature particularly as a contrast to the city, see Levine, 'From "Know-not-Where" to "Nowhere"'. The Housing, Town Planning, &c. Act, 1909, encoded amenity as a planning goal.

[74] Home Office to Borough of Newark, 1911. See also *BW*, September 1909, 126–7.

[75] Home Office to Borough of Folkestone, 1912. In some cases, municipalities succeeded nonetheless.

specific landscapes that contained natural beauty, and would replace the abstract language of amenity with a list of protected locations. Boroughs and urban districts were advised to list the areas to which licensing requirements applied if they wanted their bylaws approved. Municipalities had to add maps that highlighted protected locations, which revealed vividly the limitations implied. The shaded areas in Figure 3.24, for example, were those covering protected aesthetic interests.[76]

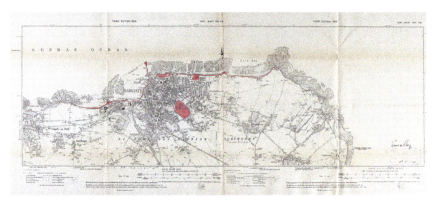

Figure 3.24 Map filed by the Borough of Margate, 1908.

Parks and promenades also required justifications, or, as it was put, 'full information' on the character of districts and landscapes. For example, the Borough of Bromley described to the Home Office the Queens Gardens (shaded patch on the left in Figure 3.25), referring to details like flower beds and 'quiet reading'. A generalized language of natural beauty in bylaws required strong reasons.[77]

Resistance to the conceptual language of beauty received visual form in recommendations for Newark's bylaws, presented by a Commissioner for the Secretary of State (Figure 3.26). Not only did he find no amenity in any of the listed locations, he resolutely deleted with red ink the preamble that began with a conceptual goal: 'to prevent the appearance of the town being spoilt by hoardings for advertisements, and if possible to increase rather than diminish the beauty of the Borough'.

Amenity was a particularly susceptible category: it applied to mixed environments, typically in towns, where a race to the bottom of the aesthetic scale was always an option. Where lists replaced aesthetic categories, as per the Home Office's demand, their contents were individually fought over. Mixtures were assessed by seeking signs of commerce that would rule out aesthetics. For example, the Newark Billposting Company opposed the list of locations in Newark's draft

[76] Home Office model bylaws, 1908.
[77] Borough of Bromley letter, 1909; Home Office to Southborough Urban District Council, 1911.

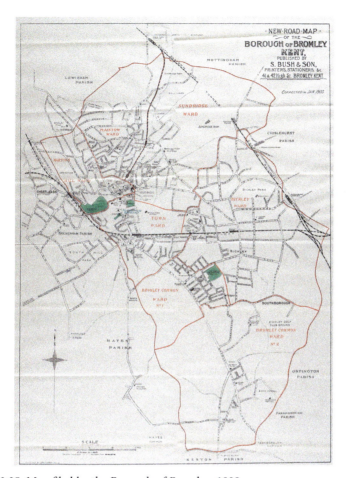

Figure 3.25 Map filed by the Borough of Bromley, 1909.

bylaws. It argued that a location described as 'Footpaths in Beacon Hill Road' (Figure 3.27) could not be a pleasure promenade having amenity, because it was part of a highway leading to the 'works of... Ransome & Co. employing about 700 men' and other businesses; nor could another footpath next to a farm in which 'the refuse of Newark' was deposited. The council disagreed, yet it negotiated with the trade and cut down the list.

Even as the Home Office approved the compromise, it was 'by no means certain that the validity of this byelaw may not be challenged in a Court of Law...'[78] Judges and legislators who heard advertisers' appeals against municipal refusals of licenses revealed a similar tendency to seek signs of commerce: they assessed the

---

[78] Home Office to Town Council of Newark, 1911. Following an inquiry, the Home Office recommended deletion of the location from the list.

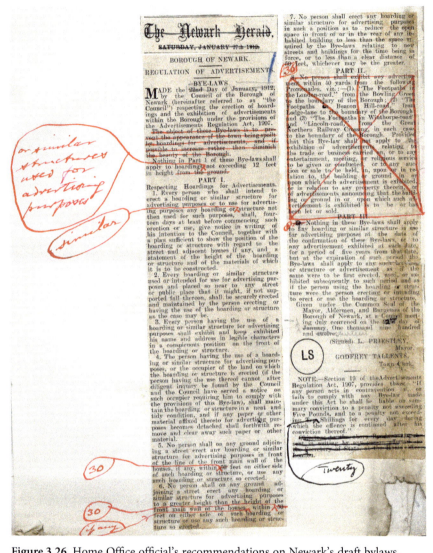

Figure 3.26 Home Office official's recommendations on Newark's draft bylaws, 11 January 1913.

Figure 3.27 Beacon Hill photo submitted by the Council of Newark in justification of proposed bylaws.

'amount of amenity' in specific locations. Every new hoarding became an established fact enabling the next one.[79]

Ironically, in order to overcome fears of aesthetic discretion Home Office officials themselves engaged in detailed aesthetic evaluations. For example, in examining Evesham's proposals for protected areas, an official agreed that a hoarding with a church in background, was 'no doubt' a thing worth preventing (Figure 3.28). It bears noting here the literal competition between advertising and spirituality and the effort to avoid it. However, he was 'a little doubtful' if the other cases (like Figure 3.29) were aesthetically valuable since the Midland Railway station was situated there and was 'an unsightly object.' Objections from a billposting company degraded the surroundings further in order to legitimize

---

[79] For example, appeal against Edinburgh Corporation, *Billposter,* April 1909, 108. The same logic informed billposting trade's petitions against private bills, which were regularly made before the 1907 Act:

> Having regard to the amenities of the towns [Gateshead, Middlesbrough, Merthyr Tydfil, and Hull] ... we do not see why [they] should not cheerfully accept as sufficient for all their purposes the model clause [twelve-foot limitation] ... especially as it has been held to be sufficient for such popular seaside places and health resorts as Colwyn Bay ... Buxton ... Swansea .... &c, and also for such towns as Birkenhead, Leeds, &c ....
>
> (*Billposter*, March 1903, 88)

Figure 3.28 Evesham hoarding between Bengeworth Church and Bench Hill, 1904.

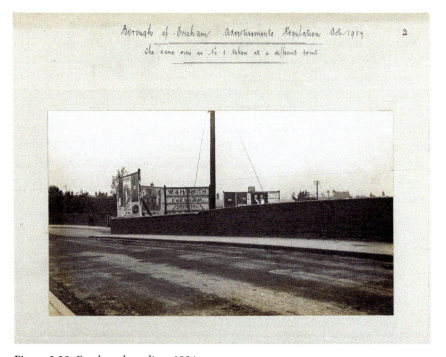

Figure 3.29 Evesham hoarding, 1904.

Figure 3.30 Evesham view, 1904.

itself: what view is there to protect in this case?, the company asked while filing a different photo of the same area (Figure 3.30).

Resistance to aesthetic categories decreased with the distance from urban environments. The Home Office sanctioned abstract aesthetic concepts in bylaws of counties 'with large areas of picturesque scenery', where a list of identified spaces could be deemed unnecessary. The result was that in municipal legislation, aesthetic concepts were applied to types of municipalities (counties), more readily than to complexities within them.[80]

Urbanity: A Loss of Conceptual Language

The second route in the 1907 act authorized local governments to regulate and control 'hoardings and similar structures used for the purpose of advertising when

---

[80] The first successful case of abstract language in bylaws, which roused anxiety among professional advertisers, was the 1911 bylaws of Hampshire County Council, *AW*, October 1911, 577–8. Even here the Home Office had doubts whether generalized bylaws were valid. In 1926, the High Court confirmed the validity. It rejected the argument that bylaws applying to a whole county were void. Shearman J's closing opinion interestingly criticized the administrative logic favoured by the Home Office: '"Natural beauty" is a thing which cannot be defined by specific instances, and the only complaint of the appellants really is that the county council have not attempted to define the indefinable.' *United Billposting Co.* [1926], 901.

they exceed twelve feet in height' (s. 2(1)). Hoardings up to twelve feet, that is, more than double the average adult pedestrian eye level, were exempt in the greater parts of urban landscapes—those that were not landscapes of natural beauty and did not consist of public parks and pleasure promenades.

The formulation drew on height limitations established previously in private bills, known as the Farnsworth model, which both the billposting trade and parliament encouraged as default. The height limitation played between safety and aesthetics; on the former, it catered to arguments that high structures were dangerous; on the latter, it treated extreme height as 'unsightly' and aimed to clear skyscape views. Skies were implicitly part of the protection of natural beauty beyond the reach of commerce on the ground, and as Taylor notes, invoked spiritual sensibilities. The association of advertising with spirituality was once again avoided.[81]

On its face, the height provision sounded a negative aesthetic judgement about urban environments. Even above twelve feet the approach was less demanding for advertisers: the terminology of prevention and restriction was absent—regulation and control replaced it. Furthermore, the technical language of height stood in contrast to the conceptual language of injury to amenity and disfigurement of beauty. However, the *relativity* of negative judgement requires emphasis. Urbanity did not lack aesthetic values; the era saw a search for terms that would capture them. In the context of advertising, we see a duality that is worth exploring. On the one hand was a concession that advertising was a commercial phenomenon corrosive of the highest ideals of natural beauty. Advertising therefore belonged in urban environments as aesthetically compromised locales. On the other hand was an elevation of hoardings over other commercial artefacts, which revealed a search for relative aesthetic merit within the commercial, and for some, an unreserved embrace of commercial aesthetics. Interpretations of legislation of this kind as strictly critical and imposed on behalf of bourgeoisie values against the masses might miss this complexity. In what follows I briefly examine the elements of reserve as well as those of celebration, which we find legislated in this clause.

To begin with aesthetic reserve, the acceptance of hoardings in urban landscapes drew on assumptions of tension between art and commerce. The place of nature at the top of the aesthetic hierarchy gave the continuum of artefacts below it a Ruskinian feel, which implied that adverts, as part of commerce, could not be good art. As we have already seen, reserve was part of the popular binarist complaint that commerce threatened beauty. It was propounded by critics who

---

[81] Farnsworth Urban District Council Act 1900, 63 & 64 Vict. ch. 233, s. 67. The alternative, threatening for the trade, was modelled on the Edinburgh Corporation Act 1899, which limited all advertising to licensed hoardings, all licenses to four years, and placed no height limitation on licensing powers. The twelve-foot limit was reached in agreement with the trade. Commons Sitting, 14 June 1907 (Herbert Samuel); Committee, Lords Sitting, 11 July 1907. Taylor, 'Written in the Skies'.

argued that it was 'war...in which the worshippers of beauty and order...are arrayed against the worshippers of ugliness and Mammon', but also by optimists of applied art. In the context of advertising, binarism retained resonance despite all aesthetic investments. Two reasons for its enduring power bear noting. First, binarism was culturally useful in suppressing the market entanglements of art. As Susan Sontag commented in discussing the history of the poster, views of the artwork as intrinsically valuable were simplistic and unhistorical. Well-known artists had worked with advertisers before, while in the nineteenth century, art was part of a viable and rapidly growing market. Projecting the realities of marketization to advertising as a contrast to art rescued the latter by implication.[82]

Rescuing art by contrasting it with advertising could be self-defeating. As the advertising contractor Charles Vernon noted, critics of advertising undermined their own cause, because advertisers would only consider art if they could be persuaded that it served their purposes. And indeed, a second reason for binarism was that advertisers often accepted it. The advertising industry developed an opposition between advertising and art on two fronts. Contra aspiring regulators, it resisted encroachments on profit in the name of aesthetics. When the 1907 act was debated in parliament, objectors claimed interference with business on 'sentimental grounds'. Similarly, as debates about municipal bylaws reveal, the industry implicitly conceded the low aesthetic value of its productions in its incessant search for signs of commerce to protect them. Put simply, when regulation was imminent, industry representatives emphasized the commercial necessity of renouncing aesthetic commitments, rather than congruities between economics and aesthetics.[83]

The advertising industry also subscribed to binarism within its own practices. Many worried that art in posters could undermine commercial 'effectiveness'. The *Advertisers' Review*, for example, ran a regular commentary on the hoardings, and reminded its readers: 'The first essential in a poster is to advertise'; art came second, if it did not interfere.[84] Advertising professionals often asserted their self-worth by doubting the abilities of artists. Even Thomas Brook Browne, owner of one of Britain's largest advertising agencies, who proudly stated that his studio artists often did not know what advert they were working on, implied only a

---

[82] W.B. Richmond, *New Review*, November 1893, 476; 'Art on the Hoardings', 1908; Sontag, 'Posters'; Presbrey, *History and Development of Advertising*, 1929, 29–32; Nichols et al., 'Art versus Industry?' introduction; Waterfield, *People's Galleries*. The second half of the century was the first era of an impersonal market in art. Figes, *Europeans*. Nineteenth-century views of art as a separate realm arguably built on the eighteenth-century placement of aesthetics, the theory of beauty, on par with epistemology (truth) and ethics (goodness), and the consolidation of what Paul Kristeller called the modern system of the arts. Kristeller, 'Modern System of the Arts'.

[83] Charles Vernon, *Profitable Advertising*, March 1901, 76–7; Commons Sitting, 14 June 1907. See also legislative negotiations, Lords Sitting, 4 July 1905; Committee, Lords Sitting, 11 July 1907 (contrasting pleasure with advertising). As we have seen, the same position was iterated to explain compromises in display aesthetics.

[84] *Advertisers' Review*, 13 August 1900, 4.

184   THE RISE OF MASS ADVERTISING

residual independence, subject to his control: artists worked 'upon the various new and attractive pictorial ideas which are evolved by the head of the establishment'. Commenting on a private exhibition of the poster artist Louis Rhead, the *Billposter* complained that 'Weird, strange-looking creatures in quaint, flowing costumes abound, but of effective, clear-speaking posters which tell their tale at a glance there are only a very few...'[85] An 1896 poster by the Beggarstaffs (James Pryde and William Nicholson) for Rowntree cocoa attracted attention, but observers did not know what it meant. Rowntree turned the problem into an opportunity: they offered prizes to those who found a story in their poster. No one got close to the Beggarstaffs' idea of representing 'three generations of sturdy British types of men, the latest comer enjoying a privilege denied to his ancestors' of Rowntree's cocoa, and so prizes were awarded to the most ingenious wrong guesses. The story itself then became an advert (Figure 3.31). Here was the problem: 'When an artist, in

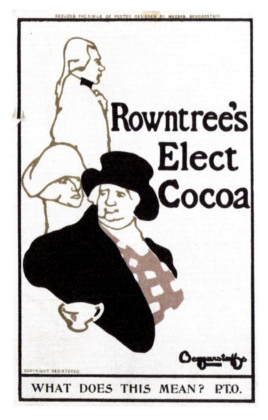

Figure 3.31 The Beggarstaffs, Rowntree advertisement, playing on the problem of meaning in the Beggarstaffs' poster, c.1896.

[85] *Advertiser's ABC*, 1892, x; *Billposter*, June 1897, 184.

a spasm of professional *esprit*, soars into the upper stratas, he loses sight of the commercial aspect of his work.'[86]

As advertisers' comments suggest, the limits of aesthetic commitment came to light when they faced the modernist formal rejection of realism. Ideas of salesmanship demanded control over interpretations of advertising messages, with a referential anchor. Of course, referential art too was open to interpretation, but the industry took a position that opposed narrative and the modern, and was therefore often uncomfortable with artistic posters. Sheldon summarized: 'Strong individual designs of distinction and distinctiveness produced by such artists as the Beggarstaff Brothers...Aubrey Beardsley...Dudley Hardy...Julius Price... gave an immense impetus to the appetite for beauty on the hoardings. Many of these...were pretty bad as advertisements. They...did not drive the message home...' Historians have argued that the uniqueness of artistic posters depended precisely on their commercial context, yet industrial actors appeared to grow wary in proportion to the emergence of a distinct genre.[87]

The logic of competition itself was contrasted with art. Competition made advertisers, on their own arguments, slaves to popular demand, not its manipulators. They told critics that 'they are forced to neutralise the effect of their competitors' eyesores by erecting more numerous and more incisive eyesores of their own.' Not everyone was willing to let the industry off so easily: 'it was discovered that to make a placard "telling", it had far better be grotesque and horrible than a thing of beauty.'[88] Something of this spirit came across in the curt language and impatient tone of a letter from an advertising agent to a sketch artist:

> Will you please knock me off a couple of small sketches immediately. The point is, I want to get an advt... that will stand out, better, bolder, and more up to date in every way... Do not take great pains with them; merely an idea is wanted.[89]

Whether as victims or propagators, advertisers saw a distance between adverts and art. These attitudes fed into public laws.

Overall, the idea that there was something aesthetically irredeemable about commerce enjoyed a wide cultural purchase. From this perspective, adverts belonged in urban surroundings, where commercial needs governed, hence the

---

[86] *Penny Illustrated Paper*, 5 March 1898, 151; Sparrow, *Advertising and British Art*, 1924, 13; *Billposter*, April 1898, 101.

[87] Sheldon, *Billposting*, 1910, 71. Advertisers' reluctance to adopt designs by artists like the Beggarstaff Brothers remained a mystery to the *Poster* contributors. Hewitt, '"The Poster"', 43. Iskin argues for a formative effect of the poster on modernist aesthetics, while Sontag argues that artistic posters drew on elitist art conventions rather than led them; their uniqueness came from the context. Iskin, *Poster*; Sontag, 'Posters'. And see Hiatt, *Picture Posters*, 1895, ch. 7, on the importance of artists who prioritized the 'primary purpose' of advertising.

[88] *Billposter*, October 1903, 32–3; *BW*, May 1903, 17; *London Evening Standard*, 5 May 1890. The industry's complicity in a race to the aesthetic bottom was confirmed in the annual trade conference, *Billposter*, October 1903, 32–3.

[89] Samson, Clark and Co. to Percy Cotton, 1896.

186   THE RISE OF MASS ADVERTISING

twelve-foot exemption from licensing powers. 'We do not agree with [SCAPA] that wall-posters in town should be regulated by aesthetic considerations. Street advertisements exist for commercial purposes among more or less commercial surroundings.'[90] As Vernon warned, to give legislative expression to the binarist opposition between advertising and art was a Pyrrhic victory. Once the appropriate environmental contexts were reified and entrenched in legislation, their future aesthetic development could only issue from the trade's own ideas of what best served its goals, but the goals were now conceived in constitutive tension with aesthetics. Put otherwise, legislation effectively entrenched an otherwise uncertain opposition between commerce and beauty and therefore did not encourage additional aesthetic investments in advertising display and content. Instead, it perpetuated the visual culture that it was criticizing. Urban centres led economic progress, and were expected to pay an aesthetic price:

> It may be that London will suffer-
> Not *too* picturesque as it is-
> But he's an aesthetical duffer
> Who'd venture to cavil and quiz.
> It doesn't require an oration
> To prove to the open of mind
> That, if we're to thrive as a nation,
> The cog-wheels of Commerce *must* grind.[91]

Urban temporality supported the same view. Adverts fitted in cities because they were characterized by rapid pace and ephemerality, unlike art, which denoted a longue durée and required slow contemplation. As the history discussed so far should make clear, advertising's ephemerality was a legal construct, which supported the logic of novelty. Requirements to keep posters new and up to date were included in commercial contracts and in municipal bylaws. Ephemerality was also built into the hoarding as structure. Thus, the London hoarding in Figure 3.32 had to be removed after a judge decided that it had 'a certain degree of permeance about it' and was therefore a structure within the meaning of the London Building Act, 1894. *Im*permanence was requisite.[92]

On these views, the street was for adverts but not for art, therefore artistic improvements were necessarily short lived: '[A] crowded street is not the place in

---

[90] *Billposter*, March 1901, 90.
[91] 'Sky Signs Up to Date', 1892. This was a commentary on the so-called 'wheel in the sky'—a fifty-foot high windmill used to advertise flour. It was eventually brought down in court as a sky-sign. *London City Council* [1892]. As the next section explains, hoardings were the favoured form selected for perpetuation.
[92] Thornton, *Advertising, Subjectivity*, ch. 1. See also Henkin, *City Reading*, 80. On the contemplative mode of viewing art, encouraged by the Aesthetic Movement in contrast to distracted viewing, see Korda, 'Streets as Art Galleries'. *London County Council* (1901).

Figure 3.32 Walter Hill & Co., London hoarding. *Billposter*, April 1901.

which to study an artistic production to advantage... The poster is essentially an ephemeral production intent upon driving its point home with a mallet.'[93]

These rampant forms of aesthetic reserve about advertising, however, were relative. As historians have shown in recent years, responses to urbanization were not all negative, and involved pleasure, fascination, and civic pride. In the case of advertising, the relativity of aesthetic degradation manifested when the hoarding was compared to other forms of advertising—a point we will see in the next section—and also when it was compared to other urban artefacts. In urban environments, many numbered hoardings among the better manifestations of commerce: 'in our manufacturing towns—enveloped in smoke and begrimed with dirt—the existence of colour, as represented in the modern art poster, conveys a "refreshing sensation" to those who have few opportunities of viewing the varying phases of Nature herself.' Supporters praised 'brilliant colouring and really artistic merit... which hide the bareness of dead walls, and cover the huge hoardings which without them would be objects of unredeemed ugliness.' Posters gained in beauty contextually. As the poster artist Joseph Simpson put it, large advertisements were eyesores in the country, however good they were; '[b]ut they were all right in the town and suburbs'.[94]

---

[93] *Globe*, 15 March 1901.
[94] Layton-Jones, *Beyond the Metropolis*; Readman, *Storied Ground*, pt 3. SCAPA itself encouraged the emergence of city planning based on urban aesthetic values. Roberts, *Picture Poster*, c.1900s; 'Picture Galleries of the Streets', 1889; *Daily Graphic*, 13 September, 1913, 6.

Some reactions revealed an absolute embrace of commercial aesthetics, not just a relative preference. This was obvious in celebrations of the industry's private law initiatives that many viewed as an incontestable aesthetic victory. The so-called poster craze similarly spoke to the popular appeal of advertising aesthetics. As the *Poster Fiend* rhymes had it, it was a taste more contagious than learned, an irresistible appeal, which hinted at enchantment: 'But I chanced to get one, then two, then three—Its catching, like measles, sir, you see—And now—ah, I never laugh or sneer; But gather in posters far and near!' These were something of a popular equivalent to avant-garde views of the lyricism of urban scenery. A report about London crowds engrossed 'all day long' by a 'splendid thing'—a huge soap poster—spoke to the same fascination. The *Irish Times* acknowledged the limits of regulation given that 'glaring broadsheets' gave joy. The late nineteenth and early twentieth centuries also saw rising numbers of posters in exhibitions that celebrated their artistic value. The year 1899 marked the start of dedicated advertising exhibitions that became popular spectacles (see Figure 3.12). Flocks of visitors, who as Taylor observes, likely represented a social mix, revealed a taste for commercial aesthetics.[95]

SCAPA idealists thought that positive aesthetic positions revealed problematic constitutions. In one imaginary discourse, a man said: 'You know what a curious sense of enjoyment our race gets out of disagreeables...lots of people...do not get the pleasure that we do from nature and art: they do not, in fact, *see* what is fine and it follows that defacement inflicts on them no sense of loss or pain.' As Samalin observes, appetites for the rotten and grotesque troubled critics of modern industrialization. In democratic moments, SCAPA too acknowledged the importance of positive views of advertising aesthetics.[96] Yet, the strongest indication of the hoarding's popularity was actually what SCAPA saw as mass apathy. Failures to criticize advertising were neither apathetic nor ineffective. The hoarding's appeal manifested in the reluctance of local and national authorities to promote legal reforms premised on aesthetics in urban centres, and in the significant scope for advertising actually created when reforms passed. This implicit support did not employ explicit aesthetic arguments, and thus revealed the limits of the aesthetic debate as a whole, to which I will return in the Conclusion.

Overall, the twelve-foot clause partook in a framing of posters and hoardings as aesthetically questionable, and yet as a taken-for-granted urban scene, in fact a permanent one—comments on advertising's ephemerality have limits to be remembered. Incentives to build hoardings for advertising were put in place with this clause, which required neither licenses nor their renewal for hoardings

---

[95] *Billposter*, March 1897, 142; on the avant-garde, see Tickner, *Modern Life*; *AW*, May 1905, 358; *Irish Times*, 12 April 1902, 6; Hewitt, 'Designing the Poster'; Taylor, 'Fascinating Show'. Work on the circulation of popular print more broadly reveals fascination, evident for example in the sales of illustrated penny magazines. For example, Anderson, *Printed Image*.

[96] *BW*, September 1909, 67; Samalin, *Masses Are Revolting*; *BW*, May 1903, 36–7.

up to twelve feet, regardless of temporary building or safety needs. In this way, urbanity itself was legally structured. The point requires emphasis given widespread assumptions that urban advertising was a wild capture of space. Contemporaries sometimes spoke of 'surrender' and of advertising's aggressive agency. John Taylor indeed argues that by 1907 cities were given up as a lost cause to advertising. However, the process was far from a recapitulation before uncontrolled forces; legal shaping was part and parcel of their advance. The aesthetic scale created in law assumed a meaning of urbanity that brought it into being. If, as Lynda Nead argues, advertising was a perfect match of metropolitan visual experience characterized by movement and exchange, it is necessary to see that the match was created, not found.[97]

The Hoarding's Competitors

When Herbert Samuel celebrated the 1907 legislation, he went too far in asserting that it 'would not add sixpence to anyone's wealth but was simply one for suppressing ugliness'.[98] The billposting trade achieved a competitive advantage in the process through implied aesthetic gradations of outdoor advertising. If twelve-foot hoardings were contextually acceptable in urban settings, the last category on the aesthetic scale, and another layer in the hoarding's aesthetic elevation, was competing advertising forms excluded by implication.

The 1907 act undermined historical flyposting, on the one hand, and more recent advertising forms, on the other, which were at best subsidiary to the poster business, and at worst in competition with it. As SCAPA put it, its prime goals were 'sky-signs, gigantic letters, the devices in gas or electric light, which threaten to extinguish town architecture; the brutal monotony of enamel plaques; the fieldboards, which deprive the people of England of much of the pleasure which landscape affords.' By comparison, SCAPA was willing to encourage 'pictorial invention on paper'. The competitive edge was clear: 'poster display in suitable, or rather not violently unsuitable positions, is the most innocent form of publicity-hunting. (To many eyes and minds posters are interesting and attractive.)' The billposting trade could not agree more: it had long argued that alternative advertising forms were not the work of legitimate business. It gradually created a list of everything it was not: 'advertising enormities as the "Quaker Oats" vandalism in the erection on Dover Cliffs, flashlights, sky-signs, advertising on sailing boats and bathing machines, boards in fields and disfigurement of rural scenery.'[99]

---

[97] *BW*, June 1894, 95 (G.B. Stretton); *BW*, September 1909, 26; Taylor, 'Alphabetic Universe', 190–1. As Peter Mandler observes, too often processes of urban change are described as an inexorable consequence of impersonal processes. Mandler, 'Creative Destruction'. Nead, *Victorian Babylon*, ch. 3.

[98] Commons Sitting, 14 June 1907.

[99] *BW*, May 1903, 31; *BW*, December 1896, 6–7; Evans, *Memorandum*, 1904; *Billposter*, February 1900, 71; *Billposter*, April 1901, 92.

Figure 3.33 Illegitimate billposting on high-class architecture illustrated. *Billposter*, October 1888.

Maintaining this position depended on continuously chastising members whose practices lacked the subtleties of aesthetic discretion that could set the hoarding apart. For example, the *Billposter* decried posting on 'high class permanent buildings' (Figure 3.33) and a gable in Ipswich near the Great White Horse Hotel immortalized in Dickens's *Pickwick Papers* (Figure 3.34).

Figure 3.34 Advertising by the Great White Horse Hotel, Ipswich. *Billposter*, January 1913.

Many forms of competition with hoardings had been incrementally curtailed over the period in more tailored forms, like the London Sky-Signs Prohibition Act of 1891,[100] restrictions on advertising vehicles from mid-century,[101] limitations on

---

[100] On the longer history of sky advertising, see Taylor, 'Written in the Skies'.
[101] Hackney Carriage Act 1853. See also, for example, Doncaster Corporation Act 1904, s. 91.

flash lights,[102] and repeat prosecutions of outdoor advertising under a variety of headings, such as defacing pavements, obstructing thoroughfares, or littering.[103] In the 1907 act, these advertising forms were depressed further through the two available routes: both the height limitation, for many were high, of 'abnormal size and character' as a memorial by fifteen hundred Londoners complained about sky and flash signs; and the protection of beauty and amenity—the location of the hoarding's competitors was often in landscapes designated for protection.[104]

The 1907 act created a five-year grace period before its new restrictions came into force, which applied to 'hoardings and similar structures'—but not to other forms of advertisement exhibition.[105] The grace period not only implied that urban hoardings were more tolerable aesthetically than other modes of advertising but also was constitutive: it perpetuated environments that municipalities would later find hard to designate as public parks and pleasure promenades. As we have seen, amenity was vulnerable to claims of exiting use. The five-year clause recognized the long-term planning implied in the rent system that first established the hoarding's aesthetics, and now became the basis of legislation.

Conclusion

In a democracy concerned with beauty as part of its vision of progress, diverse legal means and structures were brought to bear on the question of advertising's aesthetic value. The hoarding's history began with the creation of a new legal system of rent that transformed advertising practices and perceptions of access to public spaces, and that required an aesthetic definition to create and maintain its property status. Long before legislative reform implicated the hoarding, the advertising industry relied on private law initiatives to promote a vision of aesthetic progress, which highlighted the rational aesthetic value of poster exhibitions on hoardings, and also drew on the symbolic power of relatively few investments in artistic posters. Public law reforms accepted this vision as a basis for an aesthetic imagination of advertising within national landscapes, which implied an aesthetic hierarchy based on the relative distance of environments from commerce. At the top of the hierarchy was the beauty of nature, at its

---

[102] London County Council passed bylaws under the Municipal Corporations Act, 1882, s. 23.

[103] For example, Metropolitan Streets Act 1867, s. 9, limited street advertising—sandwichmen and handbill distribution. Similarly, private acts like the Birmingham Corporation Act 1883, s. 123, authorized regulation of street advertising. Alternative advertising forms did not disappear. However, their centrality and desirability, both conceptual and practical, were depressed.

[104] BW, September 1909, 32.

[105] S. 3. The section also allowed grace for 'advertisements exhibited at the time'. The hoarding was thus protected as a medium. Presumably, advertisements other than business signs would not have such a long life. The grace period was a significant achievement of the trade's negotiations with the act's promoters.

bottom, outdoor advertising forms that competed with the hoarding. The hoarding was in between.

When the bottom of the hierarchy is read upwards and then backwards in time, the process of creation comes into view. Disparate positions about the possibilities of art and beauty in advertising, which operated through disparate legal powers, ultimately cooperated to mainstream the hoarding and manage the contentious boundaries between economic and aesthetic categories. The hoarding became a contained space manifesting borders, clear rights of use and norms of access, a logic within, and locatability within a broader conceptualization of landscape in the wake of industrialization and urbanization. It achieved a secure position between the extremes of the legally anchored aesthetic hierarchy. However, the process that entrenched the hoarding as a visual feature of outdoor life also implied a degradation. Aesthetic criticism posited art as a normative horizon for advertising, yet the process affirmed that, as horizon, art was always receding. A subtle legal management of cultural distance between art and advertising was at work around the hoarding, repeatedly asserted and elaborated. The reformist zeal that informed public laws cooperated with advertising interests to reify hoardings as aesthetically compromised but not lost causes, at once permissible and disparaged. Ironically, once the conceptual opposition between commerce and beauty was stabilized, pressures to improve advertising aesthetics lessened. Legal developments did not end there, but the conceptual scheme established in the formative years of the hoarding continued to hold and to inform the aesthetic evaluation of advertising.[106]

The terms of the debate about art and advertising were so absorbing and became so well established that you could lose sight of a glaring absence: the most sustained debate in the nineteenth century about advertising images, which commanded the serious attention of thinkers and practitioners of art, advertising, and law over an extended period of time, offered no conceptual tools with which to think about the enchanting effects of advertising images. Even the more limited question of visual persuasion was not a central theme or justification for demands for aesthetic change, and never became a regulatory concern. While critical views hinted at affective relations with adverts, and at alternative ontologies that informed their spread, those remained subdued. They had a limited outlet in the discussion of indecency I examine in Chapter 6, but no general place in the debate about advertising aesthetics, which remained focused on the progressive education of the nation. No wonder that the most significant support for the hoarding

---

[106] For a study of developments up to 1962, see Greenhalgh, 'Control of Outdoor Advertising'; Greenhalgh, *Injurious Vistas*. Greenhalgh reads this history within state conceptualizations of public space. He finds that significant changes in regulation occurred in the post-war era not due to a change in views of advertising but rather as a result of new philosophies of urban modernism that advocated greater uniformity. These philosophies reframed amenity as a generalized quality of everyday environments.

was silent on aesthetics. While SCAPA saw it as apathy, it bespoke a relationship with advertising images that the discourses of beauty, ugliness, and aesthetic education simply did not encompass. This disconnect is close to an absence that art historian David Freedberg observes in museums, apropos his criticism of art history's failure to explore the non-rational side of visual experience: 'The image that rouses us powerfully'—including the advertising image—'has no place in the museum.'[107] Analogically, the question of enchantment had no place in the debate that shaped outdoor advertising. As we saw in Chapter 2, the oversight was not limited to this debate alone. Freedberg's argument addresses an active suppression of enchantment with images, which he associates with art theory. Yet, the hoarding's history, as well as that of the press, show that the disavowal of enchantment was not limited to intellectuals but rather widespread, with numerous loci that drew on legal powers. I postpone further reflection for yet another chapter.

---

[107] Freedberg, *Power of Images*, 424. Freedberg emphasizes sensual arousal. I abstract from his insight, perhaps unfairly.

4

Advertising and Science

The Exaggerations of Quackery

Medical adverts were a significant and visible portion of advertising in the long nineteenth century, as we began to see in earlier chapters. These adverts were viewed by contemporaries, as by historians, as the functional and representational key to the era's huge market in unregulated medicines and treatments, often decried as quackery, which flourished alongside regular medicine. The adverts attracted serious attention in the second half of the century as concerns about quackery escalated.

The debate had a dual background. On the one hand, regular medicine was being consolidated as a profession and sought closer imbrications with science. Its key nineteenth-century achievement was the Medical Act of 1858, which created a register of qualified practitioners based on licensing bodies, extended privileges to registered doctors, and established the UK's General Council of Medical Education and Registration (GMC), an ethical and legal authority over regular medicine.[1] On the other hand, the market for quackery expanded and its imperatives for doctors and patients intensified and put pressure on regular medicine. Legislation did not prevent or regulate the market provision of preparations and treatments except at the margins, and market provision outside the purview of the GMC expanded and outpaced the rise in real wages and population growth. Estimated sales of proprietary medicines rose from half a million pounds in mid-century to four million at its end, and five million in 1914. Pills and tonics reached closer to homes than doctors: most could be purchased in outlets such as bookshops, stationery shops, barbers, tobacconists, groceries, and pharmacies and were more accessible economically

---

[1] This was the era in which medicine's long history of practice-orientation and status traditions began to change. For reviews, see Bowler and Morus, *Making Modern Science*; Bynum, *Science and the Practice of Medicine*; Digby, *Making a Medical Living*; Porter, *Cambridge Illustrated History of Medicine*; Porter, *The Greatest Benefit*; Brown, *Performing Medicine*. Additional references appear in the following sections.

The medical register consolidated a divided profession (historically: physicians, surgeons, and apothecaries, which morphed by mid-century into a division between general practitioners, and consulting physicians and surgeons). Registered doctors became exclusively eligible for public appointments, were exempted from duties like jury service, and were exclusively entitled to recover reasonable charges for medical advice, treatment, prescription, and supply.

than doctors. Consumer expenditure on medicines almost tripled, from 0.06 per cent to 0.16 per cent.[2] Medical advertising expanded in scope, media, and capital expenditure. Spending figures are not available, but an estimate of two million pounds annually (over £230 million in 2020) by members of the Proprietary Articles Section of the London Chamber of Commerce (PATA), which represented about three hundred proprietors, seemed reasonable. As one contemporary said, 'the money spent in advertising pills ought to be enough to cure earthquakes—not to mention the endowment of hospitals.'[3] Some historians estimate that quack advertising made up 20–30 per cent of all advertising by the late century. Advert numbers were on a rapid rise with the rising circulation of newspapers and expansions in outdoor and direct-to-consumer advertising.[4]

This chapter revisits the historical debate about medical quackery. While the last two chapters examined media-based debates, this one focuses on a particular sector and its advertising, which cut across media. Yet, here again the goal is to trace the history of cultural boundaries created in a debate about advertising, and to historicize a legally supported perception of advertising that has been treated axiomatically, namely, advertising as exaggeration. The analysis draws on an archive of litigation that the expansive historiography of British medicine has overlooked, to show how concerns about quackery gave rise to a cultural division of labour that carved differentiated roles for science and the market. Science was defined by ideals of restraint that typified scientific method, logic, and subjectivity, while their negation—leading to exaggeration—defined advertising and the consumer market.

I examine this history from three angles. The first section examines the conceptual relationship between medicine and quackery in a reality of mixed and incoherent practices of medical provision. Quackery was resented not simply

---

[2] On sale estimates based on tax returns, see Chapman, *Jesse Boot*, ch. 1 and appendix 1. For a slightly lower estimate, see Corley, *Beecham's*. Fraser argues that sales of medicines rose by 400 per cent between 1850 and 1914. Fraser, *Coming of the Mass Market*, 139. On outlets, see Stebbings, *Tax, Medicines*, 94–7; Loeb, 'Doctors and Patent Medicines', 409; Digby, *Making a Medical Living*, 62–8. On expenditure, see Corley, *Beecham's*, 38.

On legislators' reluctance, see Porter, *Greatest Benefit*; Stebbings, *Tax, Medicines*, 166–72. The legal tax regime was even perceived as an official guarantee of the quality of proprietary medicines. Stebbings, *Tax, Medicines*, ch. 4.

Pre-marketing approval of medicines awaited 1968. For regulatory developments after 1914, see Bodewitz et al., 'Regulatory Science'; Dunlop, 'Medicines, Governments'; Stebbings, *Tax, Medicines*, chs 4–5.

[3] Select Committee on Patent Medicines, 1914, qq. 6333–8; *Chamber's Journal*, 13 May 1895, 311. The total expenditure on advertising in Britain in 1912 has been estimated at £15 million.

[4] For estimates see Ueyama, *Health in the Marketplace*, 74; Loeb, 'Doctors and Patent Medicines', 409. Terry Nevett's press sample for 1810–55 found only 6.5 per cent of adverts to be medical ones. Nevett, *Advertising in Britain*, 31. BNA data cannot at present be analysed to assess the percentage of medical advertising within the general volume. However, in terms of relative change in percentage, the mid-century appears to have been the high point, and the turn of the twentieth century a start of decline. The salience of medical advertising could have been a function of additional media, coupled with cultural attention.

as competition but as an existential threat, in the sense that medicine could degenerate into quackery. It therefore endangered the status of medicine as science when that status was still in the making. The threat led to intensifying efforts in ethical codes to police doctors' attempts to advertise. The next two sections move to courts, which, unlike ethical codes, functioned as public forums for testing the boundaries between medicine and quackery. In courts we find a polyphony of voices—judges, juries, lawyers, litigants, witnesses, and audiences, who represented diverse perspectives. The second section examines the legal definition of quackery developed in libel litigation, where persons accused of quackery sued and led courts to examine the meaning of the term. The third section examines the status of consumer testimonials in libel and fraud litigation. Testimonials were the most important advertising strategy of quacks, which went to the heart of quackery's challenge to medical cosmology. Together, the three angles reveal that quackery's claims to scientific value lost in seriousness as advertising was associated with exaggeration. With the aid of law, quack adverts were construed less as frauds than jokes, the medicines they marketed less dangerous than useless, and the medical choices they encouraged more embarrassing to consumers than interesting for scientific knowledge.

From the perspective of medicine, this history is a classic case of Thomas Gieryn's boundary work in science. Medicine's association with scientific truth became stronger through comparison to market exaggerations, and medicine's epistemic authority was thus strengthened at a historical stage in which it was underdetermined by the practices of doctors themselves.[5] By contrast, advertising's association with exaggeration would appear strictly derogative and therefore questionable as a source of cultural power. Yet, there were gains for advertising and market activity that were not strategically intended but nonetheless accrued. Compared with the demands of science, exaggeration had a light and liberating implication. Adverts appeared unconstrained by methods and states of mind committed to formal objectivity, patience, and even just seriousness, which permitted expansion and encouraged an unbridled culture of health consumerism. Thus, both medicine and quackery were there to stay as practices of medical provision, but more importantly as ideal cultural types of restraint and exaggeration against which an array of mixed practical options could be understood.

Law's place in the history of medical quackery has been repeatedly conceptualized in terms of absence. The medical establishment, which failed to enlist legislators to the profession's control of medical services, propounded the view that the growing market for quackery was a result of legal inaction. This was confirmed by the parliamentary Select Committee on Patent Medicines, which found Britain's regulation of medical provision laxer than that of any other

---

[5] Gieryn, *Cultural Boundaries*; Gieryn, 'Boundary-Work'.

country and summarized the law in 1914 as abnormal and inadequate. It has since been accepted by historians who have highlighted the state's reluctance to regulate quackery. This view of the role of law implicitly supports assumptions that advertising was a free-market phenomenon and therefore distorts the ways in which it was encouraged and shaped with legal means. On a more theoretical level of jurisprudence, this view privileges the role of law as a regime of prohibitions and permissions studied for their direct effects on commercial activity and the distribution of economic capital, over law's role as a regime of meaning, which regulated by producing cultural content and distributing cultural capital. The two perspectives are not mutually exclusive, yet the latter has been overlooked in the historiography of quackery. As Chantal Stebbings argues in her study of the taxation of proprietary the medicines, these kinds of legal influences are too often ignored by the medical humanities. Law's support of the differentiation between science and the market was not quantifiable in terms of commercial effects, but it informed enduring cultural categories of modernity.[6]

Medicine and Quackery, Jekyll and Hyde

In the long nineteenth century, it was hard to know where medicine ended and quackery began. The dividing lines were murky as qualified doctors often worked with and for quacks, were directors and shareholders in their businesses, prescribed and recommended their medicines, and published their adverts in professional publications. The middle grounds of pharmacy were even murkier. Chemists and druggists occupied an obscure position between trade and professionalism and drew on both. Faced with doctors dispensing medicines, on the one hand, and consumers self-medicating with quack preparations, on the other, chemists joined proprietary-medicine businesses in the last decades of the century. Meanwhile, leading quack businesses transitioned to scientific, laboratory-based pharmacy. The *Pharmacopoeia* itself was periodically updated with established quack medicines. The difficulty of essentialism is as it should be, Roy Porter argued about the early modern era, for it is a useful index of how things really were.[7] However, in the nineteenth century this elusiveness of categories signified more than messy realties. Contemporaries began to think about it as the *meaning* of quackery—a relational concept that represented the loss of scientific restraints under the pressures of the profit motive. The cultural anxiety was not simply that quacks were competing with regular doctors (they certainly were), but that medicine itself could degenerate into quackery. In other words, quackery represented a

---

[6] Stebbings, *Tax, Medicines*, 4.
[7] Porter, *Quacks*, 11. For the role of pharmacy, see Stebbings, *Tax, Medicines*, ch. 3; Ueyama, *Health in the Marketplace*; Church, 'Trust'; Anderson, 'From "Bespoke" to "Off-the-Peg"'.

potentiality that existed also *in* medicine and therefore threatened medicine's association with science, not merely the economic success of practitioners. From this perspective, a quack was not an essentially different practitioner from a regular doctor, but an image of a fallen doctor, a cautionary figure. What we see emerging are relational ideal types. Restraint became a conceptual tool that explained how medicine and quackery differed, despite—or indeed because of—complexities in practice.

The market was construed as everything that scientifically aspiring medicine could not be, its cultural Mr Hyde. In rhetorical modes, hyperbole contrasted with positivistic minimalism. Quackery's promises of remarkable cures stood in contrast with medicine's focus on observable effects, and its emphasis on danger over hope. In modes of wanting, the interested presence of individual desire, particularly for money, contrasted with the self-effacing subject of objective science. Quackery's refusal to share knowledge of medical formulae and its reliance on advertising were therefore criticized in the name of the public good. In modes of thinking, impatience, imagination, and fantasy replaced careful observation and rational analysis. Quackery minimized contact with patients and circulated exotic stories of discovery, while medicine hailed the laborious accumulation of data. The principle of restraint functioned as medical science's mode of knowledge as Michel Foucault argued in *The Birth of the Clinic*, and indeed as its mode of being. Exaggeration signified its failure.[8]

The idea that quackery was a fall from science through failure of restraint underwrote Well's *Tono-Bungay*. The novel's protagonist, George Ponderevo, swings back and forth between science and quackery. He starts out with a passion for scientific knowledge, but the commercial metropolis and a pressing need for money to marry draw him out of the laboratory. George joins his uncle's business and helps develop the quack brand 'Tono-Bungay'. The business is an incredible success, a prototypical proprietary-medicine empire of the era that floods the environment with adverts.[9] To George, Tono-Bungay is also an incredible swindle. The pendulum shifts back to Science, capital S, when Tono-Bungay and George's marriage become unbearable. He then returns to his comfort zone: 'Science, with her order, her inhuman distance, yet steely certainties, saved me from despair.'[10] He is an aspiring aeronaut and concentrates on building a flying machine, yet the pull downwards of the profit motive is finally decisive. George is called back to save his uncle's business. He attempts to do so by digging

---

[8] As Foucault argued, the self-imposed modesty was highly ambitious. Foucault, *Birth of the Clinic*. Restraint had a broader resonance in Victorian ideals of character. See Collini, *Public Moralists*, ch. 3. On concepts of scientific objectivity in this period and the role of observation, see Daston and Galison, *Objectivity*.

[9] For an argument that Tono-Bungay was modelled on Burroughs Wellcome, see Kennedy, 'Tono-Bungay'.

[10] Wells, *Tono-Bungay*, 204.

radioactive 'quap' in Africa, which unleashes horrific colonial violence. At this point, the dangers of quackery and the horrors of imperialism come together.

Tono-Bungay has been repeatedly read as a critique of quackery and an idealization of science. Jackson Lears, for example, argues that Wells joined other thinkers who equated science and reality and longed for expertise that would present a kernel of actuality and penetrate market misrepresentations.[11] Wells did express these longings, yet his novel was equally important for showing the back-and-forth movement between science and quackery, that is, a pendulum structure that revealed how a shift from one to the other was always possible. In this structure, the profit motive could bring about a fall from the sky—where the machine of science flew, to the underground, where the 'quap' of quackery lurked. Indeed, the novel's mythic move between heaven and the underworld, science and quackery, resonated with the first British airship flown by Stanley Spencer just a few years earlier, in 1902. The airship was prepared as an advert for Mellin's Food—among the leaders of the health food industry that occupied the huge margins of the medical market. The advert covered the airship both literally and in the cultural imagination, and so exemplified the easy move from one to the other (Figure 4.1). As Gustav Mellin described the pioneering flight, 'we have a

Figure 4.1 Russell and Sons., the first British airship, flown as an advertisement for Mellin's Food. The photo was titled 'The Mellin Airship'. *Illustrated Sporting and Dramatic News*, 27 September 1902, 24.

---

[11] Lears, *Fables of Abundance*, ch. 11. See also Richards, *Commodity Culture*, ch. 4; Brantlinger and Higgins, 'Waste and Value'; Outka, *Consuming Traditions*, ch. 4.

sensational advertisement in preparation the shape of an airship. This, we expect, will be one of the best advertisements we have ever had.' In this phrasing, the leading force of innovation was not science but advertising.[12]

As anxieties intensified from mid-century, the relational view of quackery gained traction. It manifested in normative efforts to articulate the boundary line, so that elements banished from scientific medicine according to the rule of restraint, were the realm of advertising quacks.[13]

One area of normative development was medical ethical codes, a budding genre of the nineteenth century. Because advertising was viewed as the key enactment of quackery's lack of restraint, it received anxious attention in the era's codes. Reservations about advertising had early roots in Hippocratic ethics and in gentlemanly honour codes that distanced the professions from trade, yet elaboration awaited the Victorian era, when prohibitions expanded in proportion to market temptations. While codes were not adopted formally, the need for an ever-expanding normative instruction revealed that doctors reacted to competitive pressures by straining old ideals of honour as well as budding ones of science.[14]

Three central codes, Thomas Percival's *Medical Ethics*, 1803 (which followed his 1794 *Medical Jurisprudence*), Jukes Styrap's *Code of Medical Ethics*, 1878, and Robert Saundby's *Medical Ethics*, 1902, revealed a rising concern. Percival's, the first modern code, did not even address advertising. He discussed a duty to apprise patients of the fallacy of quack medicines while also agreeing to compromise with patient demands. The dominating concern of his time was intra-professional conflict.[15] Seventy-five years later, Styrap expanded on advertising as a threat to professional status:

> It is...derogatory to the profession to solicit practice by advertisement, circular, card, or placard; also, to offer, by public announcement, gratuitous advice to the poor, or to promise radical cures; to publish cases and operations in the daily

---

[12] Interview with Gustav Mellin, *AW*, June 1902, 24.

[13] As Digby notes, the Victorian age was distinctive in its efforts to draw demarcation lines between regular medicine and quackery. Digby, *Making a Medical Living*, 62–8. For a legally related analysis, see Bull, 'Managing the "Obscene M.D."'.

[14] For earlier views, see, for example, Gregory's influential Edinburgh lectures, 1772, which described 'a profession to be exercised by gentlemen of honour...the dignity of which can never be supported by means that...tend only to increase the pride and fill the pockets of a few individuals.' Gregory, *Lectures*, 1817, 41. See also McCullough, 'Discourses of Practitioners'. On the Edinburgh reformers' role in connecting gentlemanly ideals with science (and sympathy), see Baker, 'Discourses of Practitioners'. On the power of anti-trade gentry culture generally, see Wiener, *English Culture*. On the preference for jurisprudence over codification, see Crowther, 'Forensic Medicine'. On reluctance to codify or enforce ethical rules, see Baker, 'Discourses'.

[15] Percival, *Medical Ethics*, 1803, ch. 2, ss. XXI–XXII. One concern related to advertising was canvassing for positions. On intra-professional conflict, see Waddington, *Medical Profession*; McCullough, 'Discourses'. Generally, historical professions saw a tension between competition and courteous treatment among members.

press, or knowingly, to suffer such publications to be made; to advertise medical works in non-medical papers; to invite laymen to be present at operations; to boast of cures and remedies; to adduce testimonials of skill and success...[16]

As Peter Bartrip observes, Styrap showed a hardening of lines.[17]

Saundby, secretary of the British Medical Association (BMA),[18] was even more elaborate at the turn of the twentieth century. He addressed the innovations of doctor-advertisers and a flourishing celebrity culture, while responding to the argument that everyone advertised and that any public appearance was an advertisement. His code instructed that medical men should not advertise their studies and experience in the lay press. Even when employed by commercial firms, a medical man's name must not appear in lay newspaper adverts or other laudatory notices. Forbidden were testimonials in adverts; quotations from a medical man's professional literature in an advert; circulars about a change of address or practice beyond 'bona-fide patients only'; paragraphs in the press about a doctor in attendance of celebrities; and signed articles and letters on diseases and their treatment in the lay press. Any 'too favourable an opinion' of secret nostrums, even in conversation, was dangerous because it could be quoted in an advert. Popular lectures and adverts announcing them should not 'draw attention to the lecturer's ability to treat certain kinds of disease'. Medical men were warned that in interviews to newspapers, if unavoidable, they 'should confine themselves to giving such information as they possess'.[19]

In addition to codes, organizations such as the Royal Colleges of Physicians and of Surgeons, local practitioner unions, the BMA, and the GMC, exercised powers over members on ethical transgressions. Here too responses to advertising gathered momentum in late century. A dentist struck off the register for advertising appealed in 1887, claiming that there was no precedent to this disciplinary position. Amusingly, his problem was that patients thought he must have done something much worse, since so many registered dentists advertised.[20]

Internally, the profession could do little more than try to police its ranks. The task was uneasy as both economic and cultural arguments against advertising lost ground. On one front, free-market ideologies questioned professional organizations' control over the economic freedom of their members. Judges' ability to adjudicate disputes was also doubted because they submitted to the tyranny

---

[16] Styrap, 'Code of Medical Ethics', 1878. [17] Bartrip, 'Secret Remedies', 193.

[18] Founded in 1832 as the Provincial Medical and Surgical Association, it represented by 1912 over twenty-five thousand practitioners and saw itself as 'the voice and opinion of the medical profession as a whole'. Select Committee on Patent Medicines, 1914, q. 1529.

[19] Saundby, *Medical Ethics*, 1907, 3–8.

[20] For bylaws and resolutions regarding advertising, see Saundby, *Medical Ethics*, appendix. For GMC decisions on advertising, see Smith, 'Legal Precedent'. On the dentist case, see *Partridge* (1887–92). There were a number of hearings. The last two addressed the question of advertising as disgraceful conduct. See also Bull's discussion of disciplinary efforts. Bull, 'Managing the "Obscene M.D."'.

of their Bar.²¹ On another front, gentlemanly traditions appeared increasingly opaque in the age of advertisement: if the eminent Dickens placarded towns, why not doctors?²² Against these erosions, and as medical spokesmen sought a closer identification with science, the meaning of science itself was developed to justify prohibitions. An 1893 *Hospital* article titled '*Why Do Doctors Not Advertise?*' presented the modern logic. Advertising was not per se 'wicked' but rather deeply incompatible with medicine, which required discipline and 'self-crucifixion'. Medicine was committed to 'calmness and sobriety, patience and watchfulness'. It was 'forced down... upon the immovable bed-rock of reality' and therefore would not 'thrive "up in the air"' as advertisers did. This explanation acknowledged that objections to trade rooted in gentlemanly cultures were insufficient, and provided the alternative language of science. Michael Brown observes that changes in medicine's self-image were turning the market from an irritating financial competition into a moral affront, but arguments actually reached beyond morality, to ontology: advertising lacked restraint, where restraint was science's way of being.²³

Libel and fraud cases functioned as public arenas with leeway to examine and solidify the meaning of exaggeration vis-à-vis restraint beyond the internal conversations of the profession.

Defining Quackery: Libel

From Character Type to Action Type

The significance of libel for the history of quackery should be self-evident. If premoderns knew that quackery was a bad thing, as Porter said, and if the one certain thing about the uncertain term 'quack' was that it was a term of abuse, as Stebbings argues, then the legal field for grappling with abuse had to become a locus of conceptualization, yet it has been neglected by historians.²⁴ A few tens of suits by persons seeking redress against quackery accusations accumulated from the eighteenth century, with important discussions of the quack figure in the nineteenth century. The cases were part of a trend historians find in the nineteenth century, in which defamation suits were tried as civil cases of libel (written words or other expressions with some degree of permanence, as different from slander, a distinct tort for speech²⁵), against press publications, where no proof of

---

[21] *Times*, 24 March 1892, 9. Lord Esher indeed took for granted in *Partridge* that the competitive spirit of advertising was disgraceful to his profession as to medicine. However, the view was not universally shared. See, for example, Paterson, 'Professionalism', on solicitors; and Pue, *Lawyers' Empire*, ch. 4, on barristers.
[22] *Elgin Courier*, 7 December 866, 5.
[23] *Hospital*, 13 May 1893, 97–8; Brown, 'Medicine, Quackery'.
[24] Porter, *Quacks*, 15; Stebbings, *Tax, Medicines*, 15.
[25] See generally, Baker, *Introduction to English Legal History*, ch. 25.

special damage was required. This section demonstrates the role of libel in boundary work, focusing on key examples that operated within the broader run, which conceptualized quackery as loss of restraint. Most reported cases involved qualified doctors who sued because they were called quacks, rather than unqualified persons who tried to silence criticisms, reflecting the idea that quackery was a degeneration of medicine.[26] From a legal history perspective, this process, which focused on the medicine-science/quackery-market, relationality, muddied the dominance of class identities, which were otherwise a strong a determinant of outcomes in libel.[27]

What turned a physician into a quack? Libel litigation shifted the historical emphasis on quackery as character type, to an elaboration of action type that placed advertising at the centre. Quackery as a character type was dominant in popular culture. The genre of caricature was a familiar application: shouty, oversized, over-imposing on physical and legal space. Such, for example, was Linley Sambourne's engraving (Figure 4.2). Dr Dulcamara, referenced in the caricature, was a quack figure from Gaetano Donizetti's 1832 opera, *L'elisir d'amore* (the elixir of love); Sambourne brought it 'up to date' to complain about the weakness of law to stop quackery—hence the lifeless policeman and the jury quotation. This was in all likelihood a reference to the oculists' trial that ended a few days earlier, more on which later in this chapter.

While striking a familiar note, the itinerant showman caricature had a Georgian feel. It could not contend with Victorian businessmen and scientific aspirants, who were powerful and outdid their historical progenitors by propounding a philosophy that opposed regular medicine on principle. Victorian quacks accused regular medicine of complicating healthcare for its own aims and robbing patients of hope.[28] Libel cases shifted the emphasis for the age of big business. They retained the popular association of the quack with noisy attention-grubbing, but focused on action rather than character. Specifically, cases examined adverts as enactments of excess. Adverts exaggerated discoveries, curing abilities, and patients' and carers' satisfaction in an unbridled pursuit of profit. It bears emphasis that the *search* for the content of exaggeration was the crucial conceptual move here. By repeatedly asking about the presence, extent, and substance of exaggeration, quackery was framed as a breach of scientific restraints. Of course, the question of what exactly any specific advert exaggerated was important

---

[26] I have not found indications of a reversal of this trend in unreported cases, although it is possible.
[27] Historians observe a growing judicial impatience with the press, explained by the class difference between the judiciary and popular readership. For example, Cornish, 'Personal Reputation'. In the libel of quackery, we often find support for the press. We might have assumed, alternatively, that judges identified with the medical establishment and press publications supporting it given shared class and professional identities. This was occasionally so, but as we will see, the meaning of quackery developed in courts complicated class identities.
[28] Porter, *Bodies Politic*, ch. 10.

Figure 4.2 Linley Sambourne, quackery caricature. *Punch*, 11 November 1893, 218.

contextually for every case. However, for boundary work, posing the question was more important than the concrete answers provided.[29]

---

[29] Gieryn makes an analogous point about struggles for credibility among scientific experts: the routine appeal to science to settle the question is more important than the outcome of the particular dispute. Gieryn, *Cultural Boundaries*, 3–4.

A vivid presentation of this outlook appeared in the Irish High Court in 1845. A surgeon named Michael Larkin published an advert for pills in the *Nation*. He claimed to have shown the newspaper testimonials of successful recoveries from 'appalling stomach, liver, bowel, asthma, and consumptive diseases'. The newspaper's owner, Charles Gavan Duffy, discovered the advert too late and therefore printed his 'great regret that a quack advertisement...has crept in'. Larkin sued for £500.

In opening the defence, counsel for the *Nation*, O'Hagan—almost certainly Thomas O'Hagan who would become the Lord Chancellor of Ireland—explored the term 'quack'. His address is worth quoting at some length:

> It is one of those words which we can better understand than define...on looking to the dictionary of our great lexicographer [Samuel Johnson], I find...: 'To cry as a goose'; and, in its secondary meaning, 'to chatter boastingly-to brag loudly-to talk ostentatiously'. I find, also, that the term is used in Hudibras [seventeenth-century satirical poem by Samuel Butler], where persons are spoken of who
>
> > 'Believe mechanic virtuosi,
> > Can raise them mountains in Postosi –
> > Seek out for plants, with signatures
> > To quack of universal cures.'
>
> You will see, when I come to read the advertisement, how clearly it comes within the meaning of the word...how full it is of absurd boasting and incredible assertion, and how remarkably it bears the characteristic of all quackery of all ages...A quack advertisement is always distinguishable by offering some panacea to the public—some promise which cannot be realised—some mysterious mode of relief unknown to nature and rejected by science...These are the professions of quackery—universal cures-immediate cures-mystical cures-impossible cures; and all these professions are made in the most flagrant and preposterous way, by the advertisement of the plaintiff.

Having read the advert amid laughter, O'Hagan continued:

> It professes to announce a discovery which the wisdom of four thousand years had failed to accomplish...It has the true old quack quality of perfect disinterestedness...He is impelled by the purest charity...The wretched half-crowns he despises...diseases—all yield to its magic power...the simple reading of it should...abundantly demonstrate its character to every rational understanding...Is there a single quality of quackery wanting to it—mystery and ignorance, absurd boasting, ridiculous pretension, and extravagant assertion?[30]

---

[30] *Freeman's Journal*, 20 June 1845, 3.

O'Hagan discussed substantive elements of quackery, particularly promises of cure. However, his linguistic choices were no less crucial. He used the advertising techniques that he condemned and showed how linguistic colour could stand in inverse proportion to the reality it claimed to describe. The richness of his language represented the poverty of Larkin's cure, hence the flow of adjectives that made the point stylistically: absurd, incredible, impudent, flagrant, preposterous, extravagant, ridiculous. Contra ideals of scientific rationality, which explicated reality, quackery made it opaque and left one with words without a referent. References to languages of enchantment: mystery, mysticism, magic, a moving of mountains, were all in the service of this point. In relation to disenchanted medical science, quackery was a denial of its wisdom, but it was the *style* that made the content: no restraint. The argument reduced enchanted ontologies to a failure of rationality, which appeared as meaningless excess.

O'Hagan enjoyed only partial confirmation. His client's defence suffered from the seemingly unprincipled position of the *Nation*, which attacked Larkin but not other advertisers, and was up against testimonies of satisfied patients. Consequently, Duffy lost, albeit with damages of 40s. and 6d. costs (approximately £170 in 2020). Larkin had to bear his own costs, and did not receive the £500 he wanted. The jury's wide discretion on damages enabled a complex view, which cut both ways. Duffy was dismayed by the ambiguity.[31] The case was not formally reported and therefore could not be cited as a legal authority. Yet, it deserves attention within the history of legal boundary work, because it was a popular event and a harbinger of things to come. O'Hagan's approach to the analysis of quackery would be embraced and developed, with a growing focus on exaggeration as failure, and with little room left for non-rational ontologies. At the same time, the implication would not be to quash quackery, as the jury in this case seemed to recognize. Quackery would not be delegitimized, but rather differentiated from medicine. Its ideal type would be associated with market imperatives and allowed to thrive so long as the difference was acknowledged.

Hunter v Sharpe, 1866

In 1866, the same issues came to the fore with more judicial engagement. Robert Hunter, a doctor certified in New York and Canada, advertised his book on consumption and its cure by oxygen inhalation in a series of column publications. The first advert in the *Times*, for example, was an entire column of text, alongside

---

[31] Duffy's main burden was legal expenses; the Wexford Medical Association collected subscriptions for him. *Limerick Reporter*, 22 July 1845, 4. He obtained a conditional order to set the verdict aside, but no further development was recorded. *Banner of Ulster*, 11 November 1845, 4.

For the history of jury discretion, see Mitchell, *Making of the Modern Law of Defamation*, ch. 3.

a variety of reports and letters to the editor. Similar ones appeared in the *Standard*, *Morning Post*, *Telegraph*, *Star*, and other newspapers in Britain. The adverts avoided the familiar pitfalls of quackery, particularly cure-all promises and secret formulas. The first one included a 'Just Published' and price label at the top, but in others nothing appeared but 'Communicated'. As one commentator noted, even to the practised eye the adverts appeared like 'scientific contributions put in by the editor...'[32]

Contrary to the last comment, which assumed that Hunter tried to disguise the publications' status, he was actually comfortable with identifying these columns as adverts. He presented paid publicity as a public service in light of a failing medical response to fatality. Britain had seen a surge of tuberculosis with the spread of industrialization and urbanization. When Hunter arrived in 1864, tuberculosis was fatal and lacked a cure. The medical profession's dominant theories echoed romanticized views and it was groping in the dark against the foremost killer of the nineteenth century. Mortality rates are impossible to determine accurately, but estimates for Britain move between 300 and 600 deaths per 100,000. Between 1851 and 1910, nearly four million deaths were attributed to tuberculosis in England and Wales. The percentage out of total deaths for 1851–70 was 14.2–16.3, but for the vital age group of 15–34, it was 43.3–49.3 per cent; the threat was overwhelming. The search for a cure was an industry, with treatments, health tourism, ventilation solutions, medical books, and brochures in wide circulation. At this point, no one—including Hunter, had a cure.[33]

Hunter's work, *Practical Letters*, quickly went through six editions of one thousand copies each, on his account as a result of the adverts. He attacked the medical establishment for ignoring his treatment against rational explanation and facts of success, and denying the fallacy of its own practices. The profession's errors were hidden beneath a technical jargon of 'bad Latin and worse Greek... worthy only an age of ignorance'. Hunter attributed to medicine the opacity traditionally attributed to quackery, and touched a sensitive nerve. He argued that if the medium was not cheap and universal, the benefits would not reach the public, therefore the profession had breached its duty of instruction by shunning publicity. This policy 'may have added to the social status and dignity of the profession itself, but it undoubtedly has proved most fatal to mankind'. He presented himself as a world-historical paradigm breaker facing the wrath of orthodoxy, of the order of Galileo, Jenner, Harvey, and Newton. Things were exacerbated by Hunter's foreign qualifications, which clarified the limits of the

---

[32] *Times*, 6 September 1864, 10; *Morning Post*, 7 June 1865, 3; *Dublin Medical Press*, 12 December 1866, 597.

[33] Cronjé, 'Tuberculosis', 79. Lung disease represented 60–80 per cent of tuberculosis. Germ theory, an alternative to theories of inheritance, was on the rise from the 1860s; Robert Koch discovered the germ in 1882; vaccination awaited 1923, antibiotic 1944. See generally, Porter, 'Consumption'; Carpenter, *Health*, ch. 3; Byrne, *Tuberculosis*, ch. 1; Arnold, *Disease*.

Medical Act. He obtained legal advice that he was not barred from practising in the UK and decided to forgo a British qualification. Yet, an indefatigable man, he tried and failed to enter the register and soon proposed to the Home Office to amend the act and include practitioners from the colonies and foreign countries. Presumably building on his Canadian qualification, he complained about the injustice of allowing British practitioners to work in the colonies but limiting their colleagues in Britain.[34]

Hunter attracted criticism in medical journals.[35] The combination of medical content and mass advertising was particularly enraging:

> 'Dr. Hunter' has no British qualification... yet he has been permitted to do what we believe no British physician or surgeon was ever allowed... to publish his advertisements, not in the ordinary form known to Mr. Morrison and Professor Holloway, in which they would have been at once recognised by the public, but in that of scientific contributions inserted in the body of the newspaper... Hunter imported here a transatlantic system of 'doing medical business' which was painfully felt... to be highly derogatory to the position due to Medicine as a profession...[36]

This comment admitted that the difficulty of distinguishing a quack from a doctor was more problematic than the fact that quackery existed.

In late 1865 the *Pall Mall Gazette* attacked Hunter in an article titled 'Impostors and Dupes'. It began with an onslaught on the 'modern system of easy advertising' that enabled medical impostors. Admittedly, Hunter's adverts were 'free from the mysterious hints and suggestions... of the basest class of medical puffs'. However, he was a quack, for he advertised as no 'reputable physician' would, and capitalized on fears. Hunter sued the publisher. *Hunter v Sharpe*, 1866, was an expensive case with experts and patients brought into court to testify on certification, scientific theories, and medical practice. It was extensively covered by the general press, debated in legal and medical publications, and followed by Hunter's *The Great Libel Case*, a four-hundred-page verbatim account of the trial interspersed with repudiations of its injustices—for Hunter, as we will see, considered the outcome a loss. This was an event, one of the few *causes célèbres* of the year in the courts according to the *Law Times*.[37]

---

[34] Hunter, *Great Libel*, 1867, 353, 368; Hunter, *Practical Letters*, 1865, xxxviii–xxxix, xli–xlii; *Lancet*, 3 June 1865; *BMJ*, 10 June 1865, 598.

[35] See, for example, *Lancet*, 7 October 1865, 420. The *BMJ* was more reserved, probably because it profited from Hunter's adverts; for example, *BMJ*, 3 September 1864, 290. It did, however, join criticisms: for example, *BMJ*, 13 October 1866, 411–12, and after the trial: *BMJ*, 8 December 1866, 641–3, and was not shy of chastising the *Times* for its part in the affair: *BMJ*, 2 December 1865, 591.

[36] *Lancet*, 18 November 1865, 57–71 (quoting the *Daily News*, 7 November 1865).

[37] *Pall Mall Gazette*, 19 November 1865, 10; 'The Legal Year 1866', 42, *Law Times* (1867) 179.

The newspaper's defence was based on two grounds: the truth of its accusations, and fair comment. The latter became the case's main legal legacy. Within the doctrinal history of libel, *Hunter* was important because statements by Lord Chief Justice Alexander Cockburn clarified the scope of protected criticism. This was important for the press, which sought protections to balance the presumption of malice in defamatory publications.[38] However, it was the truth defence that led the court to examine the meaning of quackery, and where boundary work occurred.

Cockburn LCJ put the question to the jury:

> Is Dr. Hunter's system one which he has propounded to the public as an honest medical writer or practitioner, for the purpose of enlightening the profession or benefiting the public? Or is it a system of quackery, delusion, and dishonesty put forward – no matter at what cost to the victims... for the purpose of putting money into his own pocket?[39]

The instruction ideologically bifurcated scientific enlightenment and private profit. The decision was for the jury yet Cockburn instructed them, trusting, he said ironically, that they had 'a due supply of oxygen'. Medical witnesses led Cockburn to conclude that Hunter's work was so grossly erroneous that it could only exist to excite exaggerated hopes and fears for profit. The 'system' was illuminated by the advertising campaign. Cockburn exclaimed: 'Gentlemen, we are not in America; we are in England... Empirics advertise; professional men do not.' The *British Medical Journal (BMJ)*, the organ of the BMA, recommended that Cockburn's words be written in gold; the ethical rules of the great professions, it said, 'are only the applications of the general laws of morality and social order'.[40]

---

[38] Cockburn decided that a reaction to a matter already in the public domain by a writer exercising his vocation was protected even if the comment involved an error. On the legal questions, see Mitchell, *Making of the Modern Law of Defamation*, ch. 8. Cockburn's statements also became part of his judicial legacy. Veeder, 'Sir Alexander Cockburn', 94. For the case's presence in statements of the law, see, for example, Shortt, *Law Relating to Works of Literature and Art*, 1871, 446; Paterson, *Liberty of the Press*, 1880, 138; William E. Ball (ed.), *Leading Cases on the Law of Torts* (London: Stevens, 1884), 80; Kelly, *Law of Newspaper Libel*, 1889, 67; Odgers, *Digest of the Law of Libel*, 1911, 224.

Both Hunter and Cockburn were convinced that the writer was a medical man, but it was actually J.M. Capes—likely the Catholic author John Moore Capes. He wrote at the request of George Smith, owner of the *Pall Mall Gazette*, who was enraged by private encounters with Hunter. Smith, 'Lawful Pleasures', 1901, 193–4.

For the history of libel as applied to the media, see Mitchell, *History of Tort Law*, ch. 6. For legal debates about freedom of the press in the wake of the case, see, for example, 'The Law of Libel', *Cornhill Magazine*, January 1867, 36–46; 12 *Jurist* (1866), 465–9.

[39] *Hunter* (1866), 983.

[40] *Hunter, Great Libel*, 1867, 294, 355; *BMJ*, 8 December 1866, 642. The lead medical witness was Dr Williams, who was Cockburn's medical adviser, a point not raised at the time. The newspaper's owner enjoyed watching Cockburn's friendly questioning that, he admitted, exceeded what was relevant for the case. Smith, 'Lawful Pleasures', 1901, 190.

The jury decided for Hunter but with damages of one farthing, leaving each party to defray its own substantial costs. The decision bore striking similarities to *Larkin*: again the plaintiff won but was not compensated. While commentators pondered the ambiguity, the parties saw it as the newspaper's victory. Hunter's critics were concerned with his challenge to the boundary between medicine and quackery more than with the fact that he existed. Because the decision affirmed the conceptual boundary, it justified a celebration. In a ceremony presided over by the president of the Royal College of Physicians, the *Lancet* and the *BMJ* gave George Smith, the newspaper owner, a £250 silver vase with an address of 181 men. The lid represented 'The Flight of Genius', and the medallion showed the crowning of Wisdom and Science in the presence of the Virtues (Figure 4.3). Smith was praised for efforts 'to expose the social evil of barefaced systematic quackery, especially the degrading practice of self-laudation...' The turn to symbolism and ritual clarified just how profoundly scientific medicine depended on the public arenas of courts to articulate its sphere of authority.[41]

Figure 4.3 Vase presented to the owner of the *Pall Mall Gazette*. *Illustrated London News*, 17 August 1867, 12.

---

[41] The *Pall Mall Gazette*'s legal costs were £1,400. Smith, 'Lawful Pleasures', 1901, 190. On conflicting interpretations, see, for example, *Evening Standard*, 3 December 1866, 4; *Beverley and East Riding Recorder*, 26 January 1867; and a collection of opinions: *Pall Mall Gazette*, 3 December 1866, 2. On the parties' interpretation, see Smith, 'Lawful Pleasures', 1901, 193–4; Hunter, *Great Libel*, 1867. On the ceremony, see *Illustrated London News*, 17 August 1867, 12. See also Smith, 'Lawful Pleasures', 1901, 193.

The event framed advertising as the centre of quackery's excess. The *BMJ* argued that advertising was more crucial than Hunter's 'pure nonsense' theory: 'what deeply concerns us all is...the propriety of the method by which this...theory were [sic] forced upon public notice.'[42] The question of science became, simply, to advertise or not to advertise. It summarized:

> Once admit the propriety of a professional man seeking publicity by such forms of advertisements, let the long purse and the unblushing cheek become recognised elements in professional success, and the temptations to exaggeration, to excess in self-laudation, to an estimation of the means at the advertisers' command, will soon undermine the regard for truth. Where modesty and reserve are destroyed...the result will not be likely to be favourable to true scientific progress.[43]

Temptation, exaggeration, excess—associated with advertising, all driven by the profit motive, contrasted with modesty and reserve that stood for truth delivered by science.

The unrestrained Hunter was driven out of England. In his admonitions he unwittingly demonstrated the exaggerative bent. If what was done to him had been done to other discoverers, he wrote, 'the world might still have been a plain resting on the back of a turtle; the Archean spirit would certainly have reigned supreme in the arterial tubes; the smallpox have served to prune and keep down our redundant population; while Newton would never have been such a fool as to notice the "fall of the apple"...'[44]

The cases of *Larkin* and *Hunter* demonstrate how a focus on exaggeration allowed legal actors to engage in boundary work and develop the differences between science and the market one against the other. This perspective was incompatible with a formal definition that described quackery simply as lack of credentials. Such an option had been available before mid-century and was actually salient in slander suits, where credentials were important for procedural reasons.[45] From 1858 the Medical Act was in place and provided a *substantive* reason to focus on credentials in the definition of quackery. Despite this development, this way of distinguishing trade from professionalism was rejected in law, and the perspectives we see in *Larkin* and *Hunter* were adopted, as I now turn to show. This occurred at the turn of the twentieth century, when the campaign of the medical establishment against quackery was at its height.

---

[42] *BMJ*, 8 December 1866, 642. [43] *BMJ*, 8 December 1866, 643.
[44] Hunter, *Great Libel*, 1867, 368.
[45] Until the Common Law Procedure Act, 1852, a physician plaintiff who sued for slander had to prove under the general issue that he practised legally, which often depended on proof of medical certification. After 1852, the plaintiff's qualification was taken to be admitted by default. Folkard, *Law of Slander*, 1876, 412–13.

The Precedent of *Dakhyl v Labouchere*

The rejection of a credentials-based definition of quackery became a legal precedent following a series of decisions between 1904 and 1907, when the MP and owner of the journal *Truth*, Henry Labouchere, was sued for libel by Hanna Nassif Dakhyl. Labouchere's legal battles over *Truth* were widely publicized. This was the forty-fourth action against him; as his editor said, his court encounters had no parallel.[46] Of Dakhyl, who was a doctor of medicine, a bachelor of science, and a bachelor of arts from the University of Paris, he wrote:

> Possibly this gentleman may possess all the talents which his alleged foreign degrees denote, but, of course, he is not a qualified medical practitioner, and he happens to be the late 'physician' to the notorious Drouet Institute for the Deaf. In other words, he is a quack of the rankest species. I presume that he has left the Drouet gang in order to carry on a 'practice' of the same class on his own account...

The Drouet Institute's faults were diagnosis and treatment by correspondence, mostly for deafness.[47] It undermined medical authority by denying patients' need to see doctors, or indeed to be seen at all. This problem spoke to Foucault's productive concept of the medical gaze, that is, the objectifying position that scientific medicine assumed over bodies, which many consumers resisted by going to quacks. We also see here more basically the uncertain status of diagnosis in person, which the impersonality of advertising and print technologies more broadly threw into doubt.[48]

Dakhyl sued, Labouchere defended with both truth and fair comment. Alverstone LCJ instructed the jury to distinguish commentary on treatment by correspondence from a personal attack on Dakhyl. He thought that the latter was unjustified. A quack, according to a definition that Alverstone had found, was a 'boastful pretender to a medical skill he did not possess'.[49] Dakhyl was skilled, was allowed to practise in England although it was 'one of the grievances of the medical profession', and had satisfied patients. Alverstone was not willing to see every advertising medical provider as a quack. As he put it, 'because a man has

---

[46] Bennett, 1913, 506. By that point Labouchere had won nineteen cases, lost eight, in two the jury disagreed, five were settled, and ten abandoned by plaintiffs. *Edinburgh Evening News*, 12 March 1904, 8.

[47] A team of clerks sent over one hundred formulaic letters to patients every day. *Yorkshire Post and Leeds Intelligencer*, 9 November 1907, 12; *Bradford Daily Telegraph*, 5 November 1907, 6. The Institute closed by the end of Dakhyl's trials.

[48] Foucault, *Birth of the Clinic*. Recent celebrations of communication technologies that broaden access to healthcare, show how the wheel has turned; negative framings evident in *Dakhyl* have been nuanced.

[49] Probably from Noah Webster, *A Dictionary of the English Language* (London, 1828).

published an advertisement showing that he is not a gentleman...it does not show that he is a quack...' Following this instruction, the jury awarded Dakhyl £1,000.[50]

Alverstone's definition was formalist. Far from the ideological bifurcation between scientific enlightenment and self-interested profit, it limited the purview to acquired skill, and not even to the medical register at that. Worse still for ideologues of science, he failed to treat advertising as a problem for the *scientific* aspirations of medicine. By referring to gentlemanliness he instead associated objections to advertising with medicine's roots in status, from which medicine was seeking to disentangle itself. Unfortunately for Alverstone and Dakhyl, the adamant Labouchere was the losing party. He requested a retrial on grounds of jury misdirection. The Court of Appeal agreed, and the House of Lords affirmed that the definition of quackery must remain open. There are, Lord Loreburn said, other meanings to 'quack', such as a 'person who, however skilled, lends himself to a medical imposture'. With 'all respect to the learned Chief Justice', said Lord Atkinson, he had fallen into error.[51]

Definitional openness was a revealing move in terms of the legal commitment to boundary work, because opting for it was not an obvious choice. From a legal-institutional perspective, it required the appeal courts to overturn a decision of the Lord Chief Justice and order a new trial. More fundamentally, it implied a shift of power from judges to juries. Jury sovereignty was not usually palatable to judges. As William Cornish recounts, the era was characterized by judicial efforts to attain greater control over defamation verdicts. Therefore, judges could be expected to endorse formal limitations on the jury's discretion, such as a formalist test of credentials. However, when it came to quackery, courts endorsed a cultural perspective that preferred to define quackery as a breach of scientific ideals. This demanded a contextual examination of conduct, and judges supporting it therefore showed no formalizing urge.[52] This leads to a second point. Set against the Medical Act, the refusal to formalize quackery as credentials throws into relief the role of litigation in boundary work. While credentials were an easy guideline and the key anchor of modern professionalism, they were limited as a tool for defining *modes of being* in science and in the market. This more profound effort of cultural organization could not be satisfied with formal anchors.

A new trial was ordered, with Darling J presiding. While he too instructed the jury on the meaning of quackery, he shifted from dictionaries to literature to emphasize the excesses of advertising. The etymology of the word 'quack' was

---

[50] *Dakhyl* (1907), 365; *Times*, 11 March 1904, 13.   [51] *Dakhyl* [1908], 326, 328.
[52] Cornish, 'Personal Reputation', 870–2. Generally, it was the role of the jury to determine what meaning the insulting words conveyed to an ordinary reader. The jury's discretion in civil cases followed *Parmiter* (1840), which decided that Fox's Libel Act, 1792, which made the question of criminal libel a matter for jury determination, applied also to civil cases. Mitchell, *Defamation*, 37.

uncertain, he said, but it had long been in use. He then read a passage by Joseph Addison, one which O'Hagan read in *Larkin* over sixty years earlier: 'At the first appearance that a French quack made in Paris a boy walked before him, publishing with a shrill voice, "My father cures all sorts of distempers", to which the doctor added, in a grave manner, "The child says true."' Darling J continued: 'a quack may have great skill, but that would only make his trade the more disgraceful. Charlatans, or quacks in all professions had been castigated by writers of genius in all languages; for example, in Pope...and Molière.' On the facts of the case Darling had a clear stand: The Drouet system sent medicines that would do 'no earthly good', and no careful man, however skilled, would adopt it. This reasoning suggested metonymically rather than logically, that the style of exaggeration—a 'shrill voice'—also implied a substance of worthless practice and lack of care. After Darling's summation, it took the jury fifteen minutes to find for Labouchere.[53]

The case cost Dakhyl £3,184 and rendered him bankrupt. The *Lancet* celebrated: 'Fortunately, the meaning of the word quack is not very well established... The back waters of science are the natural lurking-places of imposture...'[54] In fact, the meaning of 'quack' was now well established in law, not as specifiable content but rather as a mode of thought and conduct marked by diminishing restraint, and hence by the erosion of science.

The Implications of Precedent

To clarify the historical significance of *Dakhyl* as a contribution to cultural meanings, we should appreciate its limits in terms of practical outcomes. First, despite the *Lancet*'s celebration, definitional openness did not necessarily serve the medical establishment. The division of labour between science and the market was a cultural process that established ideal types, and as such was not fully aligned with the aspirations of the real historical establishment to decide who was in and who was out of the boundaries of science. Second, definitional openness did not guarantee a correct assessment of curative value, because ideal types were, indeed, only ideals. The things that *Dakhyl* did not achieve suggest that it would be misleading to assess its impact in terms of direct case outcomes. Instead, it should be evaluated within emergent understandings of modern science and the modern consumer market. The cases that demonstrate this point have suffered from an undeserved obscurity, but at the time they occupied the medical community and were reported in the press. As we will see, one of them has continued to interest pharmaceutical and medical historians.

---

[53] *Nation*, 21 June 1845, 604; *Times*, 9 November 1907, 7; *BMJ*, 16 November 1907, 1469; *Daily News*, 9 November 1907, 2.
[54] *Lancashire General Advertiser*, 28 May 1908, 2; *Lancet*, 16 November 1907, 1401–2.

Shortly after *Dakhyl*, the *Lancet* itself was successfully sued for imputing quackery to a man who marketed an asthma inhaler by an American doctor, in the case of *Tucker v Wakley*. Thomas Wakley was the *Lancet*'s owner. Augustus Tucker was the doctor's brother and agent. The *Lancet* hired John Eldon Bankes, who represented Labouchere in *Dakhyl*, but lost. Tucker had no credentials and admitted that he had no idea how his inhaler worked, but in court the discussion turned on the treatment's scientific basis, and the *Lancet* was unable to establish a distance from science. Large numbers of patients, including aristocrats, lawyers and doctors, were on Tucker's side. Efficacy was not contested, at least on the level of asthmatic symptoms—but rather the reasons behind it. The *Lancet*'s main argument was that the treatment contained cocaine, but it turned out that many doctors prescribed medicines that contained it, and its dangerousness was contested. The jury awarded £1,000 damages with Ridley J's encouragement. His comments framed the controversy as a genuinely scientific one. The fact that Tucker did not advertise in the press, which Ridley conceded to be problematic, but rather distributed his brother's pamphlets, worked in his favour. Ridley also did not find quack exaggerations of the cure. More interestingly, however, he noted that doctors themselves regularly promised cures.[55]

As the *Lancet* learned, the definitional openness of quackery allowed judges to interpret the shifting lines of science and the meaning of exaggeration as a relational concept, in ways that did not always affirm established orthodoxies, not even those backed by the *Lancet*. Leslie E. Keeley, the world's best-known addiction cure doctor at the end of the nineteenth century, would have been surprised. As Timothy Hickman shows in a study of the medicalization of addiction, Keeley's immensely successful 'Gold Cure' for inebriety was marketed in the 1890s under a London franchise and enjoyed a high-class patronage, as Tucker soon would. Keeley filed a libel suit against the *Lancet* and Ireland's *Medical Press and Circular* for quackery accusations in 1892, but unlike Tucker he withdrew it, fearing that his Americanness and the *Lancet*'s status foretold a certain loss. The medical establishment celebrated its victory over Keeley. Like him, it did not perceive the complexity embedded in legal interpretations of quackery, which *Dakhyl* would eventually formalize.[56]

In 1912 the BMA paid heavily for its attack on Dr Robert Bell, who claimed to have found a cure for cancer. A *BMJ* article accused Bell of quackery and said he was 'one of the most advertised cancer curers of our time'. Bell sued. Alverstone LCJ presided and had learned his *Dakhyl* lesson: 'I once made a mistake on this matter, and therefore it is in my mind. All I say is, a qualified medical man may be guilty of "quackery"...' Yet Alverstone figured out how to let a man off the hook by moulding him into the image of the reticent hard-working scientist. He

[55] *Tucker* (1908).   [56] Hickman, 'We Belt the World'.

conveniently ignored the question of advertising, which would have brought forth a debate about exaggeration, and portrayed Bell's disagreement with prevalent medical opinion as a scientific controversy. He emphasized the long years of work that made Bell poorer. This apparent lack of interest in profit brought Bell closer to ideals of restraint. The jury awarded him £2,000, a decision received with 'great applause from the back of the court...continuing until ushers sternly cried "Silence"'.The frustrated *BMJ* described it as 'Applause...immediately suppressed'.[57]

The BMA won a different libel case that year, but one that history judged to have been wrong. In 1909 it published *Secret Remedies*, the first of two collections in which it analysed and criticized some 270 quack medicines.[58] Charles Henry Stevens, who was targeted in the book, sued. The case was unusual within the run of quack libel cases: unlike many plaintiffs, Stevens had no medical qualifications nor a partnership with doctors. Moreover, most of the advertisers attacked in *Secret Remedies* did not respond, as we will see later. Stevens decided otherwise.

Stevens claimed to have discovered a cure for consumption, still deadly more than fifty years after *Hunter*. Like Hunter, he argued that the medical establishment refused to consider his findings. He enraged the BMA with the 'effrontery' of sending patients to their doctors with questions and asking them to remain under their care so that doctors could observe his medicine's efficacy. He also challenged the Brompton Hospital for Consumptives to inoculate him with tuberculosis on the condition that if he cured himself, the hospital would adopt his medicine. His story was as exotic as such stories got. Sick with tuberculosis, he was sent by his doctor to South Africa, where a Dutchman offered to take him to a native healer. He camped in a tent at the outskirts of Maseru, Basutoland, where on the next evening a native appeared wearing a blanket and leopard skin, with little pouches hanging around him. The native cooked crushed roots on open fire while smoking a long pipe, and produced a liquid that caused violent vomiting. However, Stevens persevered until cured. He added insult to injury by revealing his formula and claiming to undo secrecy: eighty grains of umckaloabo root and 13.5 grains of chijitse to every ounce. The herbs were ridiculous to the BMA: 'The farce of revealing the formula by the employment of such fancy names as these is one of the oldest dodges of the quack medicine man...'[59]

---

[57] *BMJ*, 27 May 1911, 1230; *BMJ*, 22 June 1912, 1463; Bell (1912); *BMJ*, 22 June 1912, 1467.
[58] BMA, *Secret Remedies*, 1909. The volume sold between sixty thousand and one hundred thousand copies and was widely discussed. The higher estimate appeared in Select Committee on Patent Medicines, 1914, q. 1747. The lower is in Bartrip, 'Secret Remedies', 199. For a history of the BMA's campaign, see Hall, *Sale and Manufacture*.
[59] BMA, *Secret Remedies*, 1909, 22; C.H. Stevens to the Medical Experts of the Brompton Hospital, 1908; *Times*, 22 July 1914, 4.

As it turned out, umckaloabo not only existed but Stevens's cure was good for many cases of tuberculosis. The saving of the drug awaited experiments published in the late 1920s by a French–Swiss physician, Adrein Sechehaye—and Stevens was still active and able to celebrate. The plant was truly mysterious at the time; botanical origins were only confirmed in 1974.[60] Yet, in court Stevens lost. Historians of medicine and pharmacy have noted this historical mistake, but the case's relationship to the legal meaning of quackery can shed more light on its outcome. Stevens's working assumption was that if he could prove that the BMA's chemical analysis was wrong, he would win. He was able to challenge the analysis, but the chemical details did not replace the focus on exaggeration rooted in advertising, which remained the legal core of quackery. Two judges in two courts explained to juries that the evaluation of quackery was an exercise in recognizing excess, which was always a relative matter.

Pickford J presided over the first trial in the High Court. He read extensively from Stevens's adverts. As he explained, '[t]he foundation of the article is that Mr. Stevens is claiming for this [medicine] something which he knows that he cannot perform.' Stevens had testimonies from both patients and doctors, but indications of efficacy were not enough; Pickford insisted that the point was relative: 'I say you must consider "efficacy to what extent."' This statement clarified how style and substance were mutually supportive in the legal framing of quackery: stylistic exaggeration meant that even if there was a substantive merit to a medicine, the claims made were disproportionate. The jury could not agree, and Shearman J presided over a second trial two years later. Observing *Dakhyl*'s authority, Shearman told the jury that he would not comment: 'A case very much like this was tried...when the judge instructed the jury as to what is the meaning of the word "quack"...The higher court said that it is for the jury to decide...' He then went on to tell the jury what to think while prefacing every suggestion with the caveat that they were 'obviously the best people to judge'. Stevens represented himself and was disadvantaged. Shearman too read out adverts, and agreed: 'the gist of the libel' was the promise of infallible cure, and the question of fair comment was relative to the advertisements. The jury decided within a few minutes for the BMA, and Stevens sustained costs of £2,000. The Select Committee on Patent Medicines, reporting shortly after the decision, announced that Stevens's cure was a fraud.[61]

Stevens did not give up. He argued in the Court of Appeal that the question of therapeutic value was not properly put before the jury, to no avail. Bankes J, who had represented Labouchere and the *Lancet*, was now on the bench. He placed the

---

[60] Advertisement by Stevens in *Graphic*, 21 January 1928, 120; Helmstädter, 'Umckaloabo'; Newsom, 'Stevens' Cure'; Bladt and Wagner, 'From the Zulu'; Brendler and van Wyk, 'Historical, Scientific'; Footler, 'Umckaloabo'.

[61] *BMJ*, 9 November 1912, 1343, 1344; *BMJ*, 1 August 1914, 267, 272, 270; Select Committee on Patent Medicines, 1914, s. 43.

right to comment in proportion to marketization: it had to be free where 'large sums were made out of proprietary medicines'. For many years, Stevens continued to lobby medical authorities, continued to advertise, and continued to sell. His rehabilitated cure became a lucrative medicine that survived him. In 2006 it had a turnover of €80 million.[62]

When we read the big picture, it is clear that legal outcomes did not serve a single interest group, were open to criticism in terms of their ability to identify curative value, and anyway did not consistently determine the fate of medical providers, some of whom collapsed in the wake of legal battles while others continued to thrive. Their historical significance was their cultural impact as public forums for boundary work. They began with the profit motive and converged on advertising as the par excellence quack 'method'. In examining advertising, ideals of medical science came into play, which celebrated a philanthropic exercise characterized by methodological reticence, positivistic minimalism, and personal humility. These ideals enjoyed an expansive legal articulation precisely because they were always in danger of losing restraints and unleashing quackery. Quackery, in turn, was not delegitimized completely, but rather made to inhabit a differentiated role characterized by exaggeration. The next section examines the active preservation of quackery by turning to the legal differentiation between quack and medical cosmologies.

The Sick Man: Testimonials

Testimonials and Knowledge of the Body

Patient testimonials were the key advertising strategy of quacks, who filled adverts with cure narratives, grateful patients, and recuperated bodies. Figures 4.4–4.6 show testimonials from Carbolic Smoke Ball, Bile Bean, and Mellin's Food, all advertisers I revisit in Chapter 5.

Testimonials grounded quackery's knowledge in the voices and experiences of patients.[63] To see their significance we should place them within the debate about medical cosmology—or medical ways of knowing, which draws on Nicholas Jewson's famous argument. In an article that became a pillar of the medicalization narrative, which argues for the rising authority of medicine over lived experience, Jewson described a transformation in doctor–patient relations in Europe between 1770 and 1870. The mode of production of medical knowledge shifted from bedside medicine, to the hospital, and then to the laboratory. This implied a

---

[62] *BMJ*, 15 May 1915, 873; Brendler and van Wyk, 'Historical, Scientific', table 2. Stevens's success after the legal loss was not unusual. As Hickman shows, Keeley too continued to prosper despite the medical establishment's claims of victory. Hickman, 'We Belt the World'.

[63] On popular participation and the expansion of science's boundaries more generally, see Fyfe and Lightman, *Science in the Marketplace*.

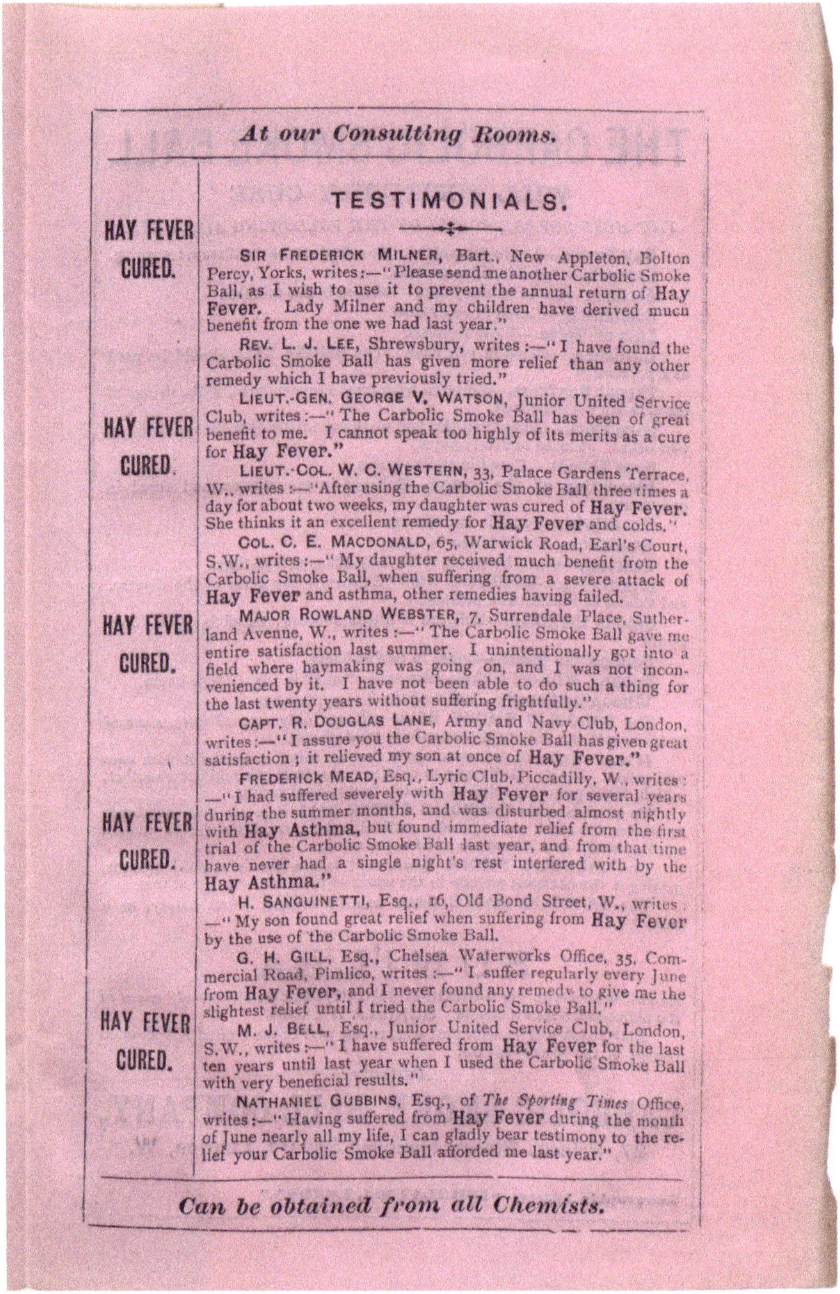

Figure 4.4 Carbolic Smoke Ball, testimonials in advertisement, 1890.

Figure 4.5 Bile Bean, testimonials in advertisement, 1902.

Figure 4.6 Mellin's Food, testimonials in advertisement, c.1890–1900.

shift from a person-oriented cosmology to an object-oriented one, in which the patient ultimately disappeared from the purview of science. Jewson called it the disappearance of the sick man [sic] from medical cosmology. The thesis has since been complicated and nuanced. Not all medical practice became disease-centred or impersonal, nor were either doctors or patients at any point entirely compliant or disempowered vis-à-vis the others; nor did the thesis do justice to variation across social groups and forms of treatment. Yet, as an account of the shifting loci of authoritative knowledge, Jewson's argument sheds light on quack advertising by pointing to historical modes of knowing.[64]

Testimonials signified a relatively levelled relationship between patient and medical provider as part of a consumerist model, in which demand was both cause and effect of advertised cures. In this model, knowledge flowed between mutually dependent advertisers and consumers: consumers reported their experiences to advertisers, who in turn reported back to them about the curative abilities of medicines. Admittedly, the patients of testimonials did not embody the holistic image that Jewson associated with bedside medicine whose patients were ruling-class patrons. Like the object-patients of Jewson's hospital medicine, patients in testimonials mattered in their recurring, quantitative characteristics, despite the occasional appearance of celebrities. The advertised representations of patients were broken-down bites, flashes of existence that signified by accumulation in efforts to compensate for the otherwise dispersed structure of quackery, its haphazard interactions with patients, and its reliance on secrecy. However, unlike object-patients, quack patients mattered more rather than less as the century progressed, and the recurring characteristic that mattered most was their subjective satisfaction, which stood for successful cure.

Set against the cosmology of testimonials, regular medicine highlighted its alternative knowledge base in the laboratory, as chemical analyses became the dominant tool in campaigns against quackery. If quackery claimed openness to patients' voices, medicine argued that what mattered was the openness of medical formulae, which quackery hid as trade secrets. Already in 1827, we can find the *Lancet* analysing and publishing the compositions of quack medicines. However, the late nineteenth century saw a growing emphasis on a particular finding of chemical analyses, namely, *emptiness*. The argument was that quack preparations were empty of active ingredients and therefore inert. This was an alternative emphasis to danger, which dominated attacks on quackery before the mid-nineteenth century. The shift was visible, for example, in medical ethics. In 1902, Saundby spoke of the 'absolute or relative worthlessness of most patent foods and medicines', where a century earlier Percival emphasized injury and danger to life.[65]

---

[64] Jewson, 'Disappearance of the Sick-Man'. For different models of the patient–doctor relationship, see Digby, *Making a Medical Living*, pt 4.
[65] Saundby, *Medical Ethics*, 1907, 5; Percival, *Medical Ethics*, 1803, ch. 2, s. XXI.

Emptiness was confirmed by the Select Committee on Patent Medicines, which concluded that dangerous ingredients in quack medicines were a small class.[66] This was a reiteration of the main argument in the BMA's *Secret Remedies*, which brought out the full implications of the emptiness argument. Where early in the century the *Lancet* published compositions without comment, the BMA's chemical analyses appeared next to adverts:

> The articles... have not been confined to a mere dry statement of the results of analysis. Care has been taken to reproduce the claims and exuberant boasts of the vendor, and the contrast between them and the list of banal ingredients which follow must strike every reader. This juxtaposition of analytical facts and advertising fancies is instructive and sometimes entertaining, the fancy is so free and the fact so simple.[67]

These accusations targeted the heart of quackery's business model, which treated the medical formula as a trade secret. Secrecy was more crucial for big business than the lone healers of earlier eras. And secrecy, the BMA asserted, enabled the sale of worthless things. *Secret Remedies* treated chemistry as an objective truth, a departure point against which the exaggerations of advertising could be measured: 'It is often, indeed, for inert preparations that the most extravagant and emphatic claims are made...' The distance between efficacy and advertising content was the extent of the profit motive: 'It is the victim's money that is wanted; therefore let the price be fixed high, and the advertisements be written up to it.' The money-grabbing scheme was sharpened by translating 'banal ingredients' to market cost, to show how worthlessness became gold. For example, the price of Beecham's Pills was 1s. 1½d. (almost £5 in 2020), they were famously advertised as 'worth a guinea a box' (some £85 in 2020) (Figure 4.7) and the BMA estimated that the ingredients cost half a farthing (next to nothing).[68]

Accusations of empty medicines, likened by the BMA to 'plain water', reverberated beyond the confines of interested parties. Here was James Matthew Barrie's *Peter Pan*: '"And now, Peter," Wendy said... "I am going to give you your medicine before you go." She loved to give them medicine, and undoubtedly gave them too much. Of course it was only water, but it was out of a bottle, and she always shook the bottle and counted the drops, which gave it a certain medicinal quality.' H.G. Wells too deployed the image in *Tono-Bungay*. The logic was simple: 'You turn water into Tono-Bungay.'[69]

Porter found it remarkable that the BMA's reports were 'revelations of the inertness of quack preparations rather than of their dangerousness'. He attributed

---

[66] Select Committee on Patent Medicines, 1914, ss. 34, 55. [67] BMA, *Secret Remedies*, 1909, vi.
[68] BMA, *Secret Remedies*, 1909, 20, 21, 118.
[69] BMA, *Secret Remedies*, 1909, 118; Barrie, *Peter Pan*, 1911, 100; Wells, *Tono-Bungay*, 1909, 160.

ADVERTISING AND SCIENCE 225

Figure 4.7 Canning & Co. Lancashire, Beecham, 'worth a guinea a box' advertising song sheet, c.1890–1910.

the findings to the downfall of quackery that lost its erstwhile lead in medical innovation.[70] However, given that the reports examined a small portion of a huge market and included many marginal preparations, and given the campaign's overt goal to undermine quackery, chemical emptiness should also be examined as a product of selection and emphasis.[71] Why did the BMA marginalize danger? One explanation could be the impression that there were effective laws against dangerous medicines. The Pharmacy Act, 1868, and the Poisons and Pharmacy Act, 1908, limited the sale of scheduled poisons, while criminal law could be deployed against bodily harm. However, this explanation is partial at best. The list of poisons was limited and acts under-enforced, while the use of scientific expertise to convict for harm by medication was fraught with difficulties, as Ian Burney has shown. Another explanation could be that doctors themselves prescribed poisons,

---

[70] Porter, *Quacks*, 206. Stebbings examines concerns with danger in quack medicines, but likewise notes findings of emptiness in the BMA reports. Stebbings, *Tax, Medicines*, ch. 4.

[71] Most preparations examined were unfamiliar to PATA, which argued that nearly half had no sales. Select Committee on Patent Medicines, 1914, qq. 6290–4, 8365, 10160–2.

therefore criticizing danger was self-defeating. While this may have motivated some arguments, it is too narrow.[72]

The deeper explanation, I propose, is that dealing with danger was simply not enough to depress quackery. As Kevin Morrison observes, despite numerous reports about deaths from quack medicines in an 1840s campaign in the *Lancet*, the trade flourished.[73] The benefits of quack medicines—the magical thinking they enabled and the dreams they encouraged—were experienced more readily than dangers. Thus, *Peter Pan* showed the power of magic even while it ridiculed bourgeoisie self-medication. In the plot, *rejecting* quack medicines was fraught with danger.[74] As Owen Davies observes, quackery also mixed with the more explicitly magical world of cunning folk and charmers; in a multifarious medical market, cultural expectations did not make clear distinctions. Medical spokesmen too knew they were facing a deep cultural drive: 'Count Mattei's "remedies" for cancer have been analyzed, and it has been proved that his bottles contained nothing but distilled water. What of that? cried the believers; shall electricity be weighed in scales and the vital force be measured by a galvanometer?'[75] The chemistry campaign highlighted emptiness to counteract the magic.

Quack businesses themselves recognized emptiness as the new frontier. A chemist argued on behalf of PATA: 'I say with the fullest sense of responsibility that this assumption is erroneous and untrue. The better known proprietary medicines contain highly active useful ingredients...' However, as Frederick Phillips, a chemist who published a rebuttal of *Secret Remedies* in 1910 discovered, most advertisers refused to engage with chemical analyses. Instead, they ignored them and counted on alternative evidence: quacks argued that market success proved medicinal value. Patient satisfaction was so significant, they argued, that no attack premised on chemistry would undermine their medicines. They insisted that the BMA's attempt to reveal formulas would only lead to exponential growth through a rise in imitations of quack medicines. Some analyses contained in *Secret Remedies* were already reproduced as recipes and sold on the streets to people who then asked chemists to prepare them, hoping to obtain the same popular medicine at a lower price.[76]

---

[72] The Pharmaceutical Society was reluctant to use its powers of prosecution. Parssinen, *Secret Passions*, ch. 6; Ueyama, *Health in the Marketplace*, ch. 1; Burney, *Bodies of Evidence*; Burney, *Poison*. See also the discussion of *Tucker* (1908), below.

[73] Morrison, 'Dr. Locock and His Quack'. Similarly, Michael Brown notes regarding Morrison's pills—the most famous quack medicine of the early nineteenth century—that prosecutions for manslaughter were contested as persecutions. Brown, 'Medicine, Quackery'.

[74] When Mr Darling rejects his medicine, the protection over the nursery is withdrawn (by the dog-nanny) in the fatal evening of his children's disappearance. Later, Peter too rejects his medicine, and so Captain Hook pours poison into his cup, which Tinker Bell must drink to save him. Only the magic of fairies can remedy the damage. On Barrie's biographical interest in 'doctoring', see Jack Zipes, 'Introduction' to Barrie, *Peter Pan*.

[75] Davies, 'Cunning-Folk'; *BMJ*, 30 July 1892, 269.

[76] For claims to medical efficacy see Select Committee on Patent Medicines, 1914, q. 11,245; protestations from Mother Seigel's Syrup, Beecham Pills, and Mrs. Johnson's American Soothing

Not only were testimonials grounded in deep needs and an entire cosmology, they were also not easy to dismiss in an age of empiricism. Some critics argued that they were fictitious, and there was certainly fiction—from complete invention, through forgery, extortion, purchase, or a taking out of context. However, many were genuine, sourced from satisfied patients.[77] In such cases, testimonials represented experience. The chemistry campaign was a more serious effort to undermine experience by scientific experiment. The distinction between experiment and experience was endlessly elaborated. For example, an 1862 article conceded to quackery that learning from experience was fundamental, but physicians were *enlightened* empirics. They confined their conclusions to observations and patiently waited until they gathered enough proof, whereas quacks generalized imprudently from isolated cases. Quack confidence was absolute, while the physician's was 'relative and tentative'. Quack testimonials were therefore '*no* evidence'. Admittedly, said the author, medicine of the past had been as ignorant as quack adverts, but it was now in pace with science.[78] George Bernard Shaw put it better in his satirical play, *The Doctor's Dilemma*, 1906:

Mere experience by itself is nothing. If I take my dog to the bedside with me...he learns nothing from it. Why? Because he's not a scientific dog.[79]

These tensions over curative knowledge came to a head in courts, which tested arguments about testimonials as evidence of cure. Two important contexts were libel cases already introduced, and fraud cases, in which an advertiser defended against an accusation of obtaining money by false pretences to cure. Testimonials were not admissible, they were hearsay, therefore to get them heard patients were brought into courts. Their stories were evaluated vis-à-vis scientific evidence from doctors and chemists who contested cure arguments. Cases revealed that the cosmology in which testimonials partook was maintained and even encouraged, on the condition that the knowledge generated be construed outside the realm of science, as part of consumer relations: it was not a *medical* cosmology. To see this, it is essential to read libel and fraud cases together. Libel cases typically evinced

---

Syrup, qq. 6452, 8976, 9113, 9128, 10168. On refusal to cooperate see Phillips, *Sequel*, 1910. For market success arguments see Select Committee on Patent Medicines, 1914, qq. 6203 (Umney), 6658 (Ratcliffe), 9378–9 (Beecham), q. 9595 (Woodward). On reproduction of formulas see testimony of Mother Seigel's Syrup's managing director. Beecham told a similar story. Boots's director argued that that publication of formulas would encourage people to try home preparations. Select Committee on Patent Medicines, 1914, qq. 6520–9, 9030–40, 8768–70.

[77] See, for example, the practices of medical providers discussed below: The Medical Battery Company in Loeb, 'Consumerism'; and the Indian Oculists in Mukherjee, 'Warning'. As the discussion below clarifies, with these advertisers too some patients were genuinely pleased.

Phillips contacted persons who provided testimonials and many were confirmed. He found cases of rebuttal and regret a minority. Phillips, *Sequel*, 1910, 15–18. See also the testimony of George Sidney Paternoster, *Truth*'s assistant editor, Select Committee on Patent Medicines, 1914.

[78] 'Physicians and Quacks', 1862, 170. On the age of empiricism and quacks' claims to factuality, see Porter, *Quacks*, chs 1, 7.

[79] Shaw, *Doctor's Dilemma*, 1906.

dismissals of patient testimonies, yet in fraud we can see that patient knowledge was not eliminated but rather confined to the realm of consumption. Health was not containable within science, but divided through boundary work between coexisting registers. The following discussion examines first the dismissals of patient testimonies found in libel, and next the preservation of patient perspectives in fraud.

Patients in Libel Proceedings

The encounter of patients with medical opinion in libel suits did not present easy choices for juries and judges, who were themselves medical consumers. As we saw in *Larkin* and *Hunter*, for example, a quack won but was not compensated. One way of reading the ambiguity is as an embarrassed response to the irreconcilability of patient and scientific evidence. Juries were unwilling to decide between them and sent mixed signals. Increasingly, however, libel cases tended to demean the role of patients in defending quack cures.

The most significant argument against patient testimonies was quantitative, reliant on statistical awareness.[80] On this argument, even if patients had been cured, their numbers were negligible and could be explained away as coincidence. This implied that patients only misled decision makers from the truth. Labouchere's counsel in *Dakhyl*, for example, argued: 'The way to judge of this treatment was what was the percentage of cures effected...it was absolutely infinitesimal...What proportion did 400 cures bear to the 15,000 cases?' In another case a counsel argued, 'Every quack could produce cases in which cure followed upon his treatment, but the cure was not in consequence of the quack treatment...but...chanced at the time of the treatment.' In *Stevens*, the defence attributed cures to Nature's work. When Shearman J summarized the evidence, he said he did not want to undervalue the twenty-nine patient testimonies that were 'a strong part' of Stevens's case and he imagined Stevens could bring 129, but he must have produced 'his best specimens' out of the thousands of people treated 'and one knows that some must die'. Quantitative arguments were intuitive rather than methodical. They gained a hearing because their premises were uncontested, as advertisers themselves relied on quantities and expected the impressive numbers of testimonies to convince, in and out of courts. They therefore also introduced contrary quantitative arguments, usually reliant on absences. Alverstone LCJ, for one, was impressed by the absence of patient complaints in *Dakhyl*'s first trial; Labouchere's lawyers countered in the second trial that failures were in the churchyard.[81]

---

[80] On its significance, see Digby, *Making a Medical Living*, ch. 3.
[81] *Times*, 9 November 1907, 7; *Cunningham* (1900); *BMJ*, 1 August 1914, 272; *Times*, 11 March 1904, 13; *Morning Post*, 8 November 1907, 3. On the relationship between lack of complaints and enchantment, see Chapter 1.

Quantitative intuitions contrasted with testimonies' narrative force. In *Tucker*, in which the *Lancet* lost, Ridley J invited the jury to read testimonials from people across Britain: 'Some of them are of the most touching character. I do not mind saying this much: I would rather have one of those testimonials put in the scale than I would have the adverse opinion of a doctor.'[82] However, Ridley's ability to elevate human stories was an outlier, conditioned by the admissible evidence in the case. A long line of eminent medical men testified to the success of Tucker's inhaler and thus eliminated the distance between doctors and patients. Things deteriorated for the *Lancet* when its position proved inconsistent with medical practice. Quantitative intuitions too worked against the *Lancet* because it could not produce significant evidence for cocaine addiction. Finally, as Ridley J complained, it presented an unfair account by ignoring the 30,000 people who had benefited from the treatment. However, in most cases the treatment of human stories was dismissive. Quantitative dismissals were accompanied by individual ones that countered the effectiveness of human faces in courts by doubting witnesses' state of health, however good they felt. This logic did not deny patient satisfaction, but instead suggested that it was no match to medical opinion on questions of bodily health.

Dismissals of patient stories took myriad forms. One was diagnoses performed in courts, which would startle aspiring scientists in any other context. Thus, in *Larkin*, the *Nation* brought to the stand an eminent physician who observed patients in court and concluded that, contrary to their testimonies, one was consumptive and another in 'hopeless asthma'. In *Hunter*, the *Pall Mall*'s lawyer demanded that a patient who testified that he recovered and gained weight be asked whether he was weighed with his 'great coat on', and Cockburn LCJ actually asked the question. In *Dakhyl*, Labouchere's counsel, Bankes, asked one Nettie Bishop, who testified she had been cured from deafness: 'Is it the fact that you cannot hear me unless you see my lips moving?' Bishop denied that she could read lips but that did not stop Labouchere's second lawyer from arguing to the jury that witnesses could not hear when Bankes turned his head. In *Stevens*, the BMA's counsel argued that the procession of poor people in the witness box who believed themselves cured was 'pathetic'. They were either uncured or wrongly diagnosed in the first place. In Shearman J's summary in *Stevens*, he countered the public suspicion that doctors were self-interested: 'if you ... say that because a doctor will only listen to professional men, you are to disregard what they say in favour of Tom, Dick, or Harry, who have never had the smallest medical experience from the beginning of their lives, we are getting perilously near a gross absurdity.' A scientific experiment had to count for more than the evidence of Stevens's patients, because a doctor isolated the tubercle bacillus and put it in Steven's

---

[82] *Lancet*, 1 February 1908, 381.

medicine, and 'there was the little beggar alive and kicking.' Without expert testimonies for Stevens, Shearman J thought there was little to refute the BMA's evidence that he was an exaggerating quack. Stevens had hundreds of testimonials from doctors too, but could not turn them into admissible testimonies, on his account because the BMA prevented them from testifying. Patients themselves were no counterweight to doctors on questions of drug efficacy.[83]

An informal but nonetheless significant dismissal was the laughter of the audience in courts. The ubiquity of informal reports from trials allowed the recording and dissemination of these responses, which would be otherwise lost on contemporaries and historians. For example, the audience in *Dakhyl* laughed when Colonel Mark Mayhew testified to an enchanting experience: Dakhyl cured his deafness and he 'felt his health like being resurrected'. Thomas Joyce, who thought that Larkin saved him from death, responded resentfully to the audience: 'you may laugh at it, but I know the story well.' In *Vaughan v Johnson*, 1892, Johnson was called a quack by Charles J because he had written a testimonial that an illiterate patient signed. The patient testified that he understood the words 'without prejudice' to mean that Johnson ought to have a testimonial, but this implicit confirmation of his satisfaction was dismissed amid laughter.[84]

Audience laughter was not necessarily spontaneous. It could be orchestrated by parties who peopled courtrooms with their supporters. The extent of this phenomenon was not reported and cannot be verified. Furthermore, we cannot assess the balance between laughter and other emotive responses to testimonies, such as identification and sympathy, which were not recorded. Laughter should therefore be read as a combination of occurrence—orchestrated or not—and the narrative choice of reporters who rendered it part of the normative scene. The meaning of laughter is itself complex. Its locations in texts seemed to move between two options. One was an expression of the embarrassment of people who could recognize themselves in the stories they heard and were therefore driven to self-deprecation. A second option was a direct dismissal of patients' perspectives—a kind of popular version of scientific critique that expressed superiority over the witness. Either way, the effect was to remove the context of quack cures from the seriousness of medical science. The dominant theories of laughter, whether as a failure of rational control in classical and modern philosophies and in the Christian tradition, as a mode of catharsis or release, or as a recognition of incongruity and failure of expectation, all provide cues as to why laughter was

---

[83] *Nation*, 21 June 1845, 601; Hunter, *Great Libel*, 1867, 87; *BMJ*, 16 November 1907, 1469; *Morning Post*, 8 November 1907, 3; *Sheffield Independent*, 24 July 1914, 1; *BMJ*, 1 August 1914, 271. A similar argument to that in *Stevens* appeared in Cockburn's instructions to the jury in *Hunter*. Hunter, *Great Libel*, 1867, 361. Complaints about doctors prevented from testifying were repeated in the select committee by other witnesses. Select Committee on Patent Medicines, 1914, qq. 9645-50.

[84] *Pall Mall Gazette*, 6 November 1907, 8; *Nation*, 21 June 1845, 601; *Cheshire Observer*, 2 April 1892, 6.

indeed foreign to science. It was possibly consumer-specific as well. Adorno and Horkheimer commented on laughter: 'It indicates a release...from the grip of logic...self-assertion which...dares to celebrate its liberation from scruple.' They saw laughter as a consumer reaction to the deprivations of desire in consumer culture. The audience appeared to confirm the deprivation, whether through identification or derision. At a minimum, there was an uncertainty about patients' perception of reality that led to laughing outbursts in courts.[85]

The discussion so far would seem to imply a triumph of science, but this picture should be qualified. First, in all cases, from quantitative claims, through participants' concrete criticisms of cure testimonies, to laughter, the direction was not towards scientific hermeticism. More than a rise of a strictly medical jurisprudence, what came to light was how deeply science depended for its own elevation on the cultural–legal dismissal of patients' perceptions. Even a judicial preference for scientific experiment, as in *Stevens*, did not simply reveal the power of demonstration of chemical evidence as Burney calls it, but the need to popularize it as a 'little beggar' who could kick 'Tom, Dick or Harry'.[86] The second reservation requires attention to fraud cases, where patient testimonies functioned differently.

Patients in Fraud Proceedings

In fraud cases, satisfied patients were effective evidence, which meant that the charge would be dismissed. A quack would not be held guilty of fraudulently advertising cures if patients said he had cured them, because criminal intent was not proved: he was deemed not to have 'guilty knowledge', that is, knowledge that his cure promise was untrue. There was nothing particularly logical about this legal position. It was equally logical to expect that medical evidence combined with failed cures would weigh enough to meet the criminal burden of proof, at least occasionally. The element that made patients' role in fraud an inversion of libel was conceptual: in libel, the stakes were between medicine and quackery. In fraud, they were between a quack and his patients, who were conceptually on the same consumerist side. It was entirely consistent with the role of patients in libel to allow a quack to be persuaded by satisfied patients, by levelling him down to their consumer perspective—scientifically worthless, but not criminal. Empty, really. This approach to patients had a chilling effect: very few cases of fraud for false cure promises were tried. However, two well-known ones are worth noting to complete the picture of patient testimonies.

In 1893, four oculists, Heere Shah, Karim Bakesh, Khair Deen, and Shahah Bedean, faced a private criminal prosecution for fraud at the Old Bailey, for falsely

---

[85] Horkheimer and Adorno, 'Culture Industry', 112. For a general introduction to theories of laughter, see Morreall, 'Philosophy of Humor'.
[86] Burney, *Poison*, ch. 3.

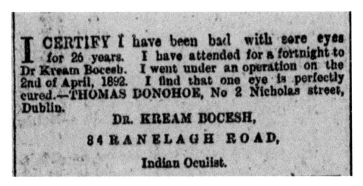

Figure 4.8 Testimonial advertisement by the oculists. *Freeman's Journal*, 7 April 1892, 8.

representing that they could cure diseases of the eye by operation.[87] They advertised in the press and by handbills distributed in the streets with testimonials of successful cures (Figure 4.8). The prosecutor presented the case as an effort to save the poor from fraud and direct them to free medical treatment in hospitals. The evidentiary structure was similar to that of libel: on the one side, a chemical analysis and medical experts supported by unhappy patients; on the other side, satisfied patients, here also with evidence on indigenous medical knowledge. Here too, doctors questioned patients' stories of cure. Here too, patient testimonies elicited laughter. One witness, for example, described the advice he received to rub his bandaged eye with a warm brick; the *Daily News*'s report of the short testimony was interspersed with laughter and 'renewed laughter' four times.[88]

Despite the similarities to libel, in this case patient testimonies did not lose meaning but rather supported acquittal, because they spoke to the oculists' belief in their capacity to cure, as did their Indian culture. Fulton J summarized: the question was 'purely as to bona fides of the prisoners'. He warned that a decision to acquit was not equivalent to approval. Indeed, he thought that the uselessness of the treatment had been proved. The oculists would never again be able to claim innocence after their own ignorance was revealed to them. The jury could not find criminal intent, but following the cue from Fulton it ensured the decision did not bespeak any esteem by adding a rider: it 'deeply deplored' that the law did not prevent ignorant practice. This construction ensured that patient testimonies did not interfere with the view of practitioners like the oculists as quacks, even as they escaped criminal liability. Sambourne's caricature of quackery followed (see Figure 4.2). Soon after the trial the oculists became destitute, entered the

---

[87] *Heere Shan and others* (1893). The prosecution was instituted by the London and County Medical Protection Society, which brought together individual patients. *Times*, 25 October, 3; see also Mukherjee, 'Warning'.

[88] See, for example, *Daily News*, 31 October 1893, 2; *Daily News*, 28 October 1893, 7.

Stepney workhouse, and finally asked to return to India. They abandoned ship in Egypt and disappeared.[89]

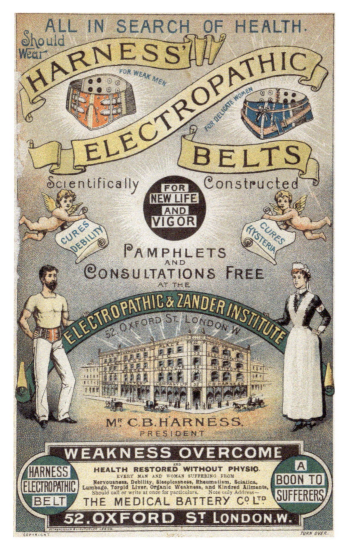

Figure 4.9 Electropathic & Zander Institute by Cornelius Bennett Harness, magazine insert advertisement, c.1890.

The Medical Battery Company's fraud case began before the oculists' trial ended. The company marketed electrical appliances with a sweeping advertising

---

[89] *Lloyd's Weekly*, 5 November 1893, 2; *Daily News*, 31 October 1893, 2; *Hants and Berks Gazette and Middlesex and Surrey Journal*, 27 January 1894, 7; Mukherjee, 'Warning', 88.

campaign. Its adverts contained elaborate testimonials and promised to cure multiple conditions (Figure 4.9). The owner and director of the company, Cornelius Bennett Harness, and three alleged co-conspirators—a physician, a salesman, and a masseur—were charged by displeased patients. The false representations concerned Harness's electrical and medical knowledge and the curing abilities of his appliances.

The case was part of Harness's growing entanglement in legal disputes that eventually led to winding up. They began with an attempt to force an unhappy consumer to pay his balance, which failed; the company had to pay and attracted hostile publicity. As Lori Loeb argues, ultimately, angry consumers brought the business down. The *BMJ* described the process as 'pricking the bubble'. And yet, against this background, the outcome of the fraud charges stood out. The prosecution never moved beyond the Marlborough Police Court. Testimonies of patients who stated that the belt cured them led Hannay J to decide that no jury would convict. Harness and his partners were all discharged to the applause of supporters. If laughter denied scientific seriousness, applause was a reminder of the market's independent power. The Public Prosecutor's refusal to take the case proved correct.[90]

As with the oculists, patient testimonies did not cast scientific worth on Harness's inventions, nor did he imagine it. An electrical engineer testified that Harness told him, 'Take my advice—science does not pay. If you will step down from your scientific pedestal to our level, and help to sell the goods, I will make your fortune.' The same hierarchical juxtaposition of science (up) and the profit motive (down), informed boundary work in the trial. Hannay J did give credit to patients and was willing to assume that the management believed in the value of appliances. However, he detached these market dynamics from science. During the trial he noted that 'scientific evidence had not so great a bearing on the case.' In conclusion he discharged the accused while criticizing the 'reprehensible' practice of exacting large sums of money from patients.[91]

Two outliers of successful prosecutions in 1906, in which the Public Prosecutor took the case, bear noting. William Henry Hawkins claimed that his medicines, Gloxiensis and Corassa Compound, could cure forty-seven diseases, some of

---

[90] *Medical Battery Company* (1892); Loeb, 'Consumerism'; *BMJ*, 11 November 1893, 1063; *Illustrated London News*, 10 February 1894, 27; *Irish News and Belfast Morning News*, 1 February 1894, 8. On the refusal of the Public Prosecutor, see Select Committee on Patent Medicines, 1914, q. 1056.

[91] *Reynolds's Newspaper*, 26 November 1893, 5; *Reynolds's Newspaper*, 31 December 1893, 3; *Buckingham Express*, 3 February 1894, 6; *Illustrated London News*, 10 February 1894, 27. A similar result obtained when fraud was argued in civil proceedings against Harness. One of the private prosecutors, Colonel Jeremiah Brasyer, sued Harness and McCully at the High Court for fraudulent misrepresentation of advertised cures. In summary, Charles J distinguished between the quackery that he thought was obvious from advertisements that promised 'to cure by a single specific every ill to which the flesh is heir', and the belief of Harness himself in the concern. The jury could not agree whether Harness had made misrepresentations. Quotation from *St James's Gazette*, 11 July 1894, 6. The proceedings were reported in detail in consecutive issues of the *Times*, 3–11 July 1894.

Figure 4.10 William Henry Hawkins, guaranteed cure advertisement. *Stonehaven Journal*, 28 November 1901, 4.

which can be seen in his advert in Figure 4.10, and was convicted of fraud. The exception, however, spoke to the rule: the charge did not rest on the efficacy of the medicine alone but on additional misrepresentations about exotic discoveries, starring a fictional Reverend Joseph Hope and fellow clergymen, and spanning two continents. Hawkins did not tender evidence of happy patients. After the Brighton magistrates committed the case to trial, he changed his plea to guilty, but only because his exotic story was false. As we saw in *Stevens* and the oculists, and will see again in Chapter 5, exoticism was being associated with quack exaggerations. In this way, the issue of efficacy was formally excluded from Hawkins's guilty outcome.[92]

Potentially more interesting was Albert Edward Richards, who advertised as Dr Edward Moross and promised myriad cures by his electric chair and battery. Although he had enthusiastic patients on his side, the jury decided against him on the spot. With few surviving reports the decision remains unclear. One explanation may be his failure to testify to his belief in the treatment. He apparently already had a global reputation as a swindler. Meanwhile, among his most enthusiastic upper-class patients were the Cranston couple, who neared perjury when it transpired that Richards invested £5,000 in their Tea Rooms business. The question of criminal intent was apparently not argued and Bingham J seemed unperturbed by it and eager to convict.[93]

---

[92] *Preston Herald*, 28 November 1906, 5; *Nottingham Evening Post*, 18 October 1906, 3; *Cheltenham Chronicle*, Ct. 13, 1906, 3; *West Somerset Free Press*, 1 December 1906, 3; *Derbyshire Courier*, 1 December 1906, 2; *Banbury Advertiser*, 29 November 1906, 3; *Faringdon Advertiser*, 1 December 1906, 2; Select Committee on Patent Medicines, 1914, qq. 432, 1050–6.

[93] Select Committee on Patent Medicines, 1914, q. 1058; *Belper News*, 3 August 1906, 3.

The most important indication of the exceptionality of convictions was the sparsity of charges. It was easier to find other grounds. For example, *Truth* and the Newspaper Society had long complained about John Nicholson who advertised ear drums and was involved with the Drouet Institute, but he finally got in fraud trouble over a prize competition.[94] More broadly, the formal position of the Public Prosecutor was that ineffective—or empty—treatments, as opposed to dangerous ones, did not raise public health concerns that needed intervention. Cases depended on private initiative and had slim chances of success.[95]

When the fortunes of patient stories are examined in fraud and libel together, we can see how legal proceedings enacted a cultural denial that patient satisfaction carried scientific meaning. And yet, set against the narrative of medicalization, what needs emphasis is that legal proceedings affirmed that satisfaction mattered. The sick man—and woman—were preserved within advertising's cosmology; indeed, the process set the terms on which they would continue to have a say despite the scientization of medicine. Within the field of exaggeration, advertised testimonials resonated as part of a consumerist dialogue that evoked less fear than mirth, and could therefore remain active.

Conclusion

The quackery debate led to a legal elaboration of advertising as an epistemologically doubtful but not illegal field of exaggeration. This view undergirded the boundary work that carved differentiated roles for science and the market, whereby science was defined by restraint and the market by its lack. The process was so successful that advertising's relationship to exaggeration has become axiomatic, its history almost forgotten. This chapter recovered it to show how advertising was mainstreamed and legitimized together with criticism, a duality that should now ring familiar. The conspicuous absence of a conceptualization of enchantment that came with this duality should also be familiar.

Views of advertising as exaggeration joined views of advertising as biased information and low aesthetics in their rationalist perspective, which dismissed the seriousness of enchanted viewpoints. As we have seen, quackery offered magic. Of all the enchantments of advertising, these are probably the most extensively discussed. Quacks were part of a culture in which health was not merely about treating diseased bodies, and adverts were not about the rational utility of medicines, but about dreams of youth and well-being that consumer markets offered.

---

[94] Nicholson pleaded guilty. *Nicholson and Richards* (1901). For earlier concerns with his medical adverts, see, for example, *NSC*, August 1897, 8, February 1899, 7. Prize competitions are discussed in Chapter 6.
[95] Select Committee on Patent Medicines, 1914, qq. 1098–100.

As Porter argued, consumers responded to adverts that promised them cures not because they took them for factual statements, but because they were the market's way of offering much more than cures. Consumers wanted a sense of wholeness, an explanation for their troubles, a key to the meaning of life. Digby observes that quacks were skilful popular psychologists who recognized the desire for reassurance and privacy. People bought medicines, as Takahiro Ueyama concludes, because they were therapeutic commodities inducing a fantasy of vitality. Health commodities were tied with imaginaries of balanced lives, dreams of beautiful bodies, and existential fears in the face of human mortality. These observations align with the broader phenomenon of enchantment. Medical advertising drew on the will to enchantment and fuelled imaginations of metamorphosis in the market. As we have seen, consumers were often described as dupes or victims of manipulation, yet these reductions could not do away with enchantment, which only gained in force in years in which therapeutic practice lagged behind theory and advances in diagnosis outstripped advances in curing.[96] It was not easy to break the spell of advertising, because information about chemistry and medical theory did not address these deeper questions and needs, nor indeed the imaginative levels on which they were experienced. Critics often understood that. For all his impatience with quackery, H.G. Wells had a character in *Tono-Bungay* explain the needs it served:

> The real trouble of life... isn't that we exist – that's a vulgar error; the real trouble is that we *don't* really exist and we want to. That's what this – in the highest sense – just stands for! The hunger to be – for once – really alive – to the fingertips![97]

To Wells, the capitalist satisfaction of existential hunger was an all-encompassing system: 'It was all a monstrous payment for courageous fiction, a gratuity in return for the one reality of human life – illusion.' He despised it, but understood its power.[98]

Considered in light of the cultural drives that propelled quackery, the legally grounded disavowal of enchantment is thrown into sharp relief. The soft laws of medical ethics as well as the public debates processed in courts, focused on a rationalist contrast between scientific restraint and market exaggeration, which left little room for non-rational ontologies. Those kept appearing, only to be subjected to rationalist reduction. What emerged was a view of advertising as an epistemologically suspect field that failed to observe the procedures and states of mind that grounded authoritative knowledge. This account disavowed the basis of the market that it was helping to create.

---

[96] Porter, *Quacks*; Digby, *Making a Medical Living*, chs. 2–3; Ueyama, *Health in the Marketplace*, ch. 1. See also Richards, *Commodity Culture*, ch. 4; Thornton, *Advertising, Subjectivity*, ch. 2; Haley, *Healthy Body*; Vincent, *Culture of Secrecy*, 114–15.
[97] Wells, *Tono-Bungay*, 158.   [98] Wells, *Tono-Bungay*, 221.

5
Puffery
Exaggeration as Doctrine

Exaggeration had a way of turning on itself: it gravitated not to more but rather to nothing. The more effort advertisers invested in promoting their product, it was argued, the less the effect. The argument rehearsed the dual logic of legitimation and critique, and attained a dedicated legal doctrine known the doctrine of puffery, which is the subject of this chapter. The doctrine identified futile speech, typically of a seller, which was presumably unconvincing, and for which the speaker therefore was not held responsible in law. The paradigmatic case would be a statement in an advert about the merits of a commodity, which consumers presumably did not believe, and for which the advertiser would not be held liable vis-à-vis consumers and competitors, whether or not anyone in fact responded to it.

Puffery was and still is usually invoked as a defence argument. The speaker claims that their speech was just a puff for which they cannot be sued. It operated, and still operates, in multiple legal fields including contracts, torts, criminal law, trademarks, and more. Its study in this chapter challenges the traditional view of the doctrine as a legal preference for sellers over buyers, and therefore as an instance of *caveat emptor* that supported advertising. Puffery was actually more complex, because alongside the protection of sellers the doctrine involved a legal inferiorization of adverts, viewed as the paradigmatic case of the sales pitch.[1] In effect, language intended to promote a sale was construed as legally meaningless, on the assumption (normative, of course) that such language was anyway futile and ineffective in the market. In this way, far from simply shielding advertisers from liability, courts also exacted a non-quantifiable but very real cultural price from them. This chapter argues that this was a legal mode of ridicule, which implied a markdown in the cultural capital of advertisers. Advertisers were therefore often uncomfortable with the puffery defence.

Given the scant literature on puffery, I begin with a brief account of developments based on primary sources. The history of the doctrine has been patchy,

---

[1] As we will see, cases typically involved speech intended to promote a sale, but speech could also be more remotely related to sales efforts, for example, by promoting the reputation of a business or a trader. Furthermore, as a matter of law, not all the cases examined sales, and could, for example, address a libel in which a sales pitch was involved. References to sales pitches should therefore be understood in this broader context.

mostly considered in American legal contexts, and generally bifurcated on two levels. First, it is typically discussed within specific areas of law rather than across them.[2] A field-crossing perspective is important in understanding puffery's emergence and import. Second, discussions tend to split between a long periodization that dissolves the doctrine into the history of *caveat emptor*, and a short one starting in 1892 with the case of *Carlill v Carbolic Smoke Ball*.[3] The first section proposes an alternative periodization that takes account of the historical circumstances in which puffery became important, in the first period of mass advertising in Britain. I trace beginnings from the 1820s, and their elaboration after mid-century. After providing the general historical picture of puffery's emergence and its doctrinal logic, in the second and third sections I examine key legal decisions on puffery that came from the history of quackery. These sections revert back to the concrete historical problem of the boundary between science and the market. In that context, puffery's role as a legal mode of ridicule was particularly clear.

Importantly, the ridicule effect did not emerge from the unenforceability of puffs in itself, but from the combined linguistic, market-historical, and legal circumstances of the doctrine. Linguistically, the term 'puff' carried insulting meanings that attained legal formalization in the doctrine. Historically, formalization occurred in the formative decades of mass advertising and in dialogue with the debates that previous chapters examined. Finally, the legal context is perhaps the most stunning of all. Cases of unenforceable speech in law were typically explained as occurring outside the market. However, the doctrine of puffery explicitly treated the puff as a market phenomenon, indeed the paradigmatic instance of *marketing*, yet denied that it carried legal implications. The doctrine therefore implied a hierarchization of statements within the market, in which the puff was low, in fact not serious enough to merit response. The treatment shines light on the normalization of advertising through critical treatment.[4]

By approaching the history of advertising in terms of a legal doctrine, this chapter takes a step back from the concreteness of historical debates, at least to begin with. I do so for two reasons. First, the doctrine of puffery demonstrates the conceptualization of advertising as a failure, legitimized precisely because it is so. I am unaware of another legal doctrine that mainstreamed a system of capitalism

---

[2] For examples of this bifurcation, sometimes viewed as doctrinal chaos, see Hoffman, 'Best Puffery Article'.

[3] *Carlill* [1892]; *Carlill* [1891–4] (CA). For the long periodization, see Preston, *Great American Blow-Up*. For the short one, see, for example, Colaizzi et al., 'Best Explanation'.

[4] Examples of unenforceable statements explained as non-market included promises between friends, viewed as part of a sphere of intimacy beyond the market. The intimacy/market context is discussed below, in reference to *Carlill*. Unenforceable statements also included gambling contracts, which were distinguished from legitimate market transactions and viewed as an illegitimate mode of pursuing profit. The Gaming Act of 1845, which rendered wagering contracts unenforceable, was a major milestone in the state's efforts to differentiate legitimate market speculation from gambling. I discuss this theme further in Chapter 6. Statements treated as only verging on the market, particularly expressions of intention, could also be deemed unenforceable for that reason.

by enacting ridicule as this one did. The doctrine thus provides a formal demonstration, perhaps an epitome, of a conceptualization of advertising I have so far examined in dispersed legal contexts. Second, the doctrinal approach to advertising and the market examined here is important for a further consideration of the disavowal of enchantment. The force of ridicule, which built tautologically on the view that consumers who responded to adverts exhibited failures of rationality, highlights the refusal to treat advertising's effects in terms of enchantment. Worlds of imagination, dream, adventure, wonder, and mystery that informed economic behaviour were reduced with this doctrine to exaggeration. We thus see disavowal enacted in a legal doctrine dedicated specifically to marketing.

Puffery

According to the *OED*, uses of 'puff' to denote idle boasting, an inflated praise or commendation, go back to the sixteenth century. In eighteenth- and nineteenth-century popular discourse, to puff was often to advertise, a use that connoted exaggeration that baselessly inflated reputations. Henry Fielding, for example, complained in 1740 about the 'Art of Puffing' by which bad authors were promoted. By the late eighteenth century, and throughout the nineteenth century, uses of 'puff' to refer to press endorsements of market services and products—books included—were widely familiar and continued to reverberate as we saw in Chapter 2. More broadly, as Neil McKendrick argued in *The Birth of Consumer Society*, an entire vocabulary had developed by 1800 to describe puff types, that is, the variety of advertising techniques and styles. However, in the eighteenth century the term 'puff' also took on another meaning, namely, the act of a person employed to bid at an auction in order to raise the price. That person was known as a puffer. This latter meaning became a formal legal term in the law of auctions. In 1776, Lord Mansfield undercut the use of puffers by defining it as fraud, a decision that led to almost a century of debates about the extent of the prohibition and its implications for the validity of auction sales.[5] Meanwhile, from the 1820s, and with increasing intensity after the mid-nineteenth century, the term 'puff,' with its noun, gerund, verb, and adjectival forms, was used in case law in its earlier meaning, and so with an inverse implication. Rather than a fraud that might undermine the validity of transactions, the puff came to stand for inertness or futility that could not influence anyone, and hence also for the opposite of legally serious speech. The process could be seen in a variety of legal fields.

---

[5] 'puff', *OED Online*; Fielding, 1740; McKendrick et al., *Birth of a Consumer Society*, 148–50; *Bexwell* (1776). The Sale of Land by Auction Act, 1867, clarified some of the contentious issues between equity and common law.

The language of puff began to be used to denote the opposite of a binding representation in sales[6]—an intuition not easily accepted.[7] After the landmark decision of *Carlill*—more on which below—a puff was also speech denoting the opposite of an intention to create legal relations in the law of contract. In criminal fraud, puffing emerged as an exception to a misrepresentation and therefore did not attract criminal liability.[8] In the law governing economic competition, puffery had a role to play in two contexts. One was the practice of disparaging another seller's goods. Here, a puff was an exception to a statement that could ground an action.[9] A second context was the practice of imitation, governed by trademark law and passing off doctrine. Here, on the one hand, marks that were based in puffing as opposed to a distinct value (contribution to commerce), were not protected against copying competitors who used them.[10] On the other hand, a plaintiff's involvement in misrepresentations, but not in 'mere puffing', could lead to a denial of legal protection against copying competitors.[11] In fiduciary contexts, trusting to puffery, which implied a failure of rational evaluation, could be a breach of duty.[12] In all of these fields and despite their widely diverse contexts, puffery coalesced consistently around the idea of futile speech. It was a speech that law refused to heed on the theory that it was anyway ineffective in the market.

As legal decisions formalized puffery and turned it into a legal concept, treatise writers could generalize it. Earlier cases about speech that did not give rise to liability, which never used the term 'puff' or its derivatives, could then be described under the puffing category or become associated with it, and so the doctrine was extended both backward in time, and in its conceptual reach within law.[13] By the late nineteenth century, therefore, puffery had become a familiar part of the legal landscape, and one that appeared to have been a long-recognized legal principle.[14]

The historical shift of emphasis in the legal use of puffery, from fraudulent speech—as applied in auctions, to idle speech—as it began to emerge in the 1820s,

---

[6] Including sales by auction and sales of shares based on prospectuses, where particular rules applied. *Beaumont* (1821); *Magennis* (1829); *Watson* (1848); *Higgins* (1862); *Dimmock* (1866); *Bellairs* (1884); *Paul & Co* (1900); *Romanes* (1912).
[7] In *Jones* (1829), Best CJ viewed a laudatory statement ('we will supply him well') as a trap for buyers that should be discouraged. However, the decision did not turn on this question.
[8] *Welman* (1853); *Bryan* (1857); *Ardley* (1871); *Lloyd* (1899); *Nathan and Harris* (1909).
[9] *Western Counties Manure Company* (1874); *White* [1895]; *Hubbuck* [1899]; *Lyne* (1906).
[10] *Braham* (1863). [11] *Bile Bean Manufacturing Co.* (1906).
[12] *Fry* (1884) (trustees who relied on puffery held liable); *Cochrane* [1896].
[13] For example, Bateman, *Practical Treatise*, 1882, 58, read decisions that did not use derivatives of 'puff,' such as *Scott* [1829], as referring to 'puffing statements'. Earlier editions of Bateman made no reference to puffing in this sense. Anson, *Principles*, 1893, 39, included puffery for the first time in a general summary of cases indicating what an offer is, following the decision in *Carlill*. Anson now discussed a statement that was an advertisement or puff that 'no reasonable person would take to be serious'.
[14] Processes of synthesis and explication suggest why puffery is usefully regarded as a doctrine. This approach to puffery is in line with existing scholarship, yet some readers may prefer 'legal principles' to 'doctrine'. I am comfortable with this option so long as the overriding historical logic and the normative

was more than a case of semantic complexity. Its context was the move to mass consumption on the basis of mass advertising. Advertisers were the paradigmatic examples for the application of the doctrine. Of course, not every legal case involved advertisements, and individuals therefore did not always have advertising in mind; likewise, not every historical actor, such as a judge or litigant, in every specific case, intended to belittle the utterer. The fact that advertisers were paradigmatic or even just dominant is sufficient for the argument. The growing recurrence of puffery language in various fields of law and, critically, its field-crossing logic that came into view despite and above all contextual complexity, spoke to the doctrine's embeddedness in the rise of mass advertising, which was replacing auctions as a cultural symbol of the market. For ordinary people and daily transactions, advertising was the new spectacle of exchange, to borrow a phrase that Desmond Fitz-Gibbon uses to describe the impact of the London auction mart from the eighteenth century.[15] One indication of the shift can be found in Graph 5.1. I have used data from the British Newspaper Archive (BNA) to examine the change in proportions of adverts containing the word 'auction' to all adverts containing the letter 'a'. There are significant limitations on results, but assuming a consistency of errors across all periods and newspapers, the graph reveals the diminishing part of auction adverts within a broader category of press adverts. Additional indications point in the same direction.[16]

As advertising captured the cultural imagination, an inversion in legal emphasis came into view. The puff's association with a dangerous influence on economic exchange values lessened in importance, while its association with efforts to raise value viewed as so ineffective as to merit no legal response, gained in importance. There was actually a consistency of logic in this change. The key quality of the puffer in auctions was that his identity as a representative of the seller was hidden.[17] In the new use of puffery, the key quality of the speaker or author was

and cultural implications are understood, and the complexity embedded in legal treatments of puffery above the local nuances of specific cases and legal fields, is clear.

On the meaning of doctrine, see generally, Smits, 'What is Legal Doctrine'; Schlag and Griffin, *How to Do Things with Legal Doctrine* (narrow and broad definitions of 'doctrine'). For a historical perspective on doctrinal analysis, see Getzler, 'Legal History as Doctrinal History'. For examples of treatments of puffery as a doctrine in scholarship in varying contexts see Hoffman, 'Best Puffery Article'; Yosifon, 'Resisting Deep Capture'; Sheff, 'Veblen Brands'.

[15] Fitz-Gibbon, *Marketable Values*, ch. 1.

[16] Advertisements containing 'a' were chosen so as to create a group inclusive of 'auctions' and as large as possible. The database does not allow a search of the category of 'advertisement' without an additional content qualifier. However, search results suffer from false positives and negatives; hence, actual numbers cannot be relied on as accurate. In addition, the database's guidelines for categorizations of publications as advertisements are not published, and are presumably debatable. Nevett addresses the dominance of auctions within advertising in the first half of the nineteenth century, and the rise in retail advertising thereafter. Nevett, *Advertising in Britain*, chs 4, 5.

[17] Thus, when Mansfield decided that puffery in auctions was fraudulent he reasoned: 'The basis of all dealings ought to be good faith...that could never be the case, if the owner might secretly and privately inhance the price, by a person employed for that purpose'. *Bexwell* (1776), 396.

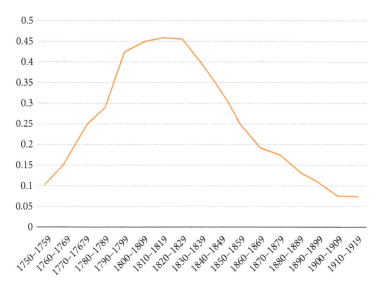

Graph 5.1 Proportion (in decimal fractions) of auction advertisements to advertisements containing the letter 'a' over time. BNA data as of April 2019.

that he spoke openly as a seller, or on the seller's behalf. Put otherwise, as sellers communicated directly with buyers in the mass consumer market and advertising came into view as a system of communication, puffery came to stand for futile speech. The position suggested that there was something inherently ineffective, rather than dangerous, about advertising. The emergent legal logic belittled the typical marketing utterance, that is, the advertisement, and formalized its cultural status as legitimate and yet inferior in the world of commerce. Here was a diminution of advertising as it was becoming society's main mode of sales-speech.

The doctrine's application was not logically rigorous. As various utterances were designated puffs (for example, a house described as fit for the residence of a respectable family; a statement that the directors 'confidently believe the profits of this company will be more than sufficient to pay dividends of at least 50 per cent. on the nominal capital'; a statement that the spoons were of silver quality equal to Elkington's A; a statement that 'it is quite evident that W.H. & Co.'s zinc has a slight advantage over Hubbuck's'[18]) and others determined not to be puffs (for example, a statement that the seller 'intended to make the lane wide and commodious'; a statement that the chain was 15-carat gold[19]), judges attempted to

---

[18] *Magennis* (1829); *Bellairs* (1884); *Bryan* (1857); *Hubbuck* [1899].
[19] *Beaumont* (1821); *Ardley* (1871).

provide analytic explanations, which often appeared strained. For example, some judges resorted to the difference between fact and opinion and argued that puffery was mere opinion rather than a factual statement, but the distinction was unconvincing and difficult to apply consistently. The difficulties were to be expected because the doctrine was not created to address a problem of analytic precision, but rather historical anxieties about advertising.[20]

The role of puffery as ridicule has been absent from scholarship, which has instead explained the doctrine as part of *caveat emptor*. True, in seller–buyer contexts, and particularly in advertiser–consumer relationships, puffery's immediate effect was to shield advertisers from liability. Consequently, criticisms and concerns that law had and continues to fail to protect consumers have been forthcoming. This premise has led policy-oriented scholarship of recent decades to conduct experiments designed to test how consumers respond to puffery. The goal is to determine whether there is cause for concern about the lack of legal protection. These assumptions echo historical ones, including some within the advertising industry itself. For example, Thomas Russell argued that courts gave immoral sanction to dishonesty in advertising through the doctrine. Concerns about the legal protection afforded to advertisers are valid, but their exclusivity in the discussion obscures the implications of the doctrine.[21]

A full understanding requires attention to puffery's dual effect, which demonstrates the historical processes that previous chapters have been unveiling: it mainstreamed advertising while demeaning it as a cultural form. On the side of mainstreaming, the doctrine encouraged advertising in two ways. Functionally, advertisers were not liable for puffs and therefore the scope of advertising was

---

[20] One well known example of analytic difficulties was the leading case of *Bryan*, in which twelve judges debated whether a misdescription of the silver quality of spoons to a pawnbroker was a fraud. The majority discharged the borrower with the explanation that the misleading description applied to a quality and not to the essence of the article, and was therefore a puff. Some of the judges explicitly tied this explanation to the idea that the statement was mere opinion. The minority rightly criticized the majority's logic as unconvincing.

[21] Preston has been influential for the *caveat emptor* interpretation. See also, for example, comments on legal permission to lie in Keeton, *Prosser and Keeton*, ch. 18; and on legal generosity to puffers in Diamond, 'Puffery'. Some of these interpretations are implied. For example, Patrick Atiyah does not discuss the concept of the puff in his classical history of contract law, but does view the protection afforded in *Carlill* as a retreat from caveat emptor. Atiyah, *Rise and Fall*, 771.

Even when ridicule has been observed, it has been marginalized. For example, Richard Leighton notes cynicism towards advertising in the application of puffery in trademark law, which goes some way towards acknowledging an element of ridicule, yet he ultimately subscribes to the *caveat emptor* interpretation rooted in English law history, and locates the policy problem in the under-protection of buyers. Leighton, 'Materiality and Puffing'.

On current scholarship see literature reviews in Assaf, 'Magical Thinking'; Richards, 'New and Improved'. For an economic theory perspective concerned with trust, see Offer, *Challenge of Affluence*, ch. 6.

Russell, *Commercial Advertising*, 23. See also the testimony of Guy Stephenson, Assistant Director of Public Prosecutions, Select Committee on Patent Medicines, 1914.

enlarged. The second encouragement, less well appreciated, was conceptual. The doctrine associated the concept of the puff with specific elements *within* adverts; therefore the larger category—advertising—was salvaged. This was part of broader change of terms. As the nineteenth century advanced, 'advertising' as a category no longer overlapped with puffery in the popular imagination as was more common in the eighteenth century. It is perhaps unsurprising that references in the press to 'the puffing system' dropped after the mid-nineteenth century, while 'the advertising system' picked up, as BNA data suggest in Graph 5.2. Database limitations warn against reliance on numbers; hence the point is the apparent trend.[22] The legal formalization of the puff as an element within an advert selected for special treatment, necessarily implied that not all advertising was puffery.

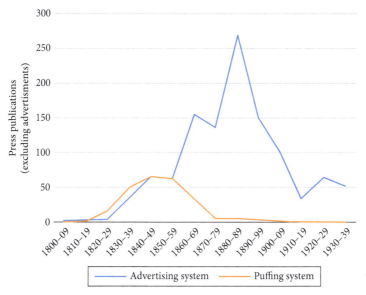

Graph 5.2 Trends of references in the press to the 'puffing system' and the 'advertising system'. BNA data as of May 2019.

Yet, alongside these encouragements of advertising, there was an element of ridicule. The doctrine of puffery demeaned adverts by giving legal form to the prevalent idea that they contained unserious puffs. As significant parts of advertising were treated as bereft of serious communication, the doctrine sent a message that degraded advertising as a field. The next section examines ridicule in cases concerned with quack adverts, which also became leading decisions on puffery.

---

[22] A similar picture obtains with Google Ngram.

Quackery and the Doctrine of Puffery

Rhetorical associations of quackery with puffery as empty boasting often surfaced in courts. For example, in *Jones v Bright*, 1829, a copper seller promised to supply 'well', and then supplied poor-quality copper. His counsel argued in his defence that if his client was held liable, soon 'the purchaser of a quack medicine [would] complain that he has been imposed on by an advertisement, which all the world recognises as a puff'. Similarly, as we saw in Chapter 4, the litigation of the libel of quackery was replete with puffery references.[23] Within this run of commentary, *Carlill* deserves special consideration because it formalized the association between advertised cure claims and puffery. Ironically, formalization occurred through an exception to the rule. The case has been extensively researched and even more extensively taught to law students, yet its precise relationship to puffery has remained underappreciated.

Carlill began when Louisa Elizabeth Carlill, self-described as a literary lady, saw an advert for an inhalation treatment (or, hard to resist: a puffing treatment!) in the *Pall Mall Gazette* (Figure 5.1). As Brian Simpson's study of the case showed, the Carbolic Smoke Ball Company, a one-man enterprise of Frederick Augustus Roe, began marketing the ball in the late 1880s. Sales benefited from an influenza epidemic that Britain had not seen for almost fifty years. Influenza was not usually lethal but it was incapacitating and well publicized in accumulating reports about the rapid spread of infection from late 1889, and again in 1891-2. The advert indeed stated that thousands of balls had been sold during the epidemic and there were no ascertained cases of contracted disease among users. Carlill bought a smoke ball, used it as instructed, but contracted influenza. She asked for the reward, a position familiar from cases of rewards for information or help, but not for failures of quack medicines. The case stood out also because a woman was at the forefront (albeit with her husband in backing, issuing demands to the company). As one writer jeered, the turn of events reflected 'no shame on the ball – it merely shows that matter must succumb in the struggle with mind, especially the female mind.' As his phrasing revealed, Carlill's position evoked deep anxieties about gender performance. Roe refused to pay and ended up losing at first instance and in the Court of Appeal. The latter's reasoning construed the advert as a binding offer, which, when accepted by Carlill through performance of its terms, became an enforceable contractual obligation.[24]

---

[23] *Jones* (1829), 1171; *Wells* (1862); *Hunter* (1866).
[24] Simpson, 'Quackery and Contract Law'; *Lancashire Evening Post*, 6 July 1892, 2. For examples of reward cases, see Jones, *Law Relating to Advertisements*, 1906, ch. 1.

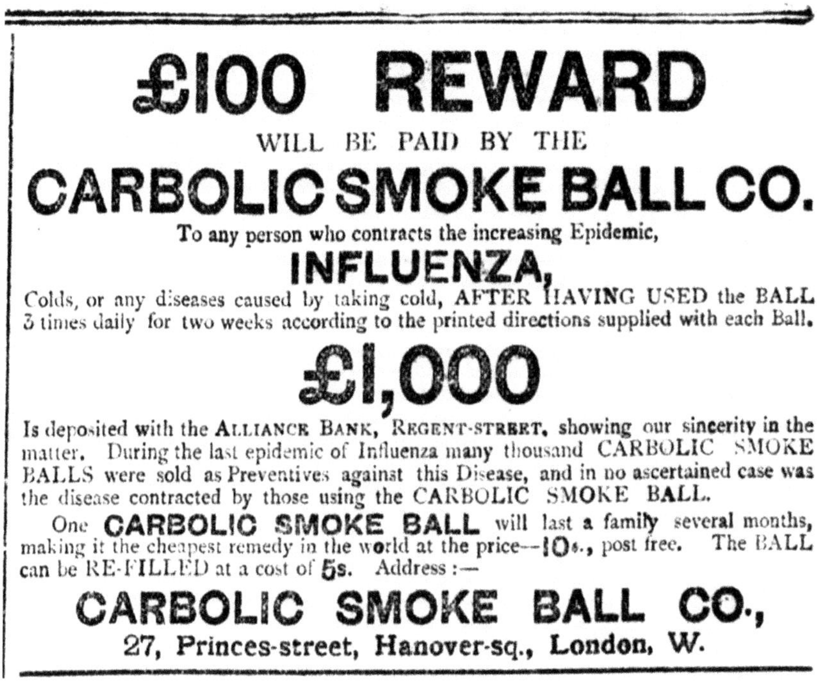

£100 REWARD

WILL BE PAID BY THE

CARBOLIC SMOKE BALL CO.

To any person who contracts the increasing Epidemic,

INFLUENZA,

Colds, or any diseases caused by taking cold, AFTER HAVING USED the BALL 3 times daily for two weeks according to the printed directions supplied with each Ball.

£1,000

Is deposited with the ALLIANCE BANK, REGENT-STREET, showing our sincerity in the matter. During the last epidemic of Influenza many thousand CARBOLIC SMOKE BALLS were sold as Preventives against this Disease, and in no ascertained case was the disease contracted by those using the CARBOLIC SMOKE BALL.

One **CARBOLIC SMOKE BALL** will last a family several months, making it the cheapest remedy in the world at the price—10s., post free. The BALL can be RE-FILLED at a cost of 5s. Address:—

CARBOLIC SMOKE BALL CO.,
27, Princes-street, Hanover-sq., London, W.

Figure 5.1 Carbolic Smoke Ball Co., advertisement. *Pall Mall Gazette*, 13 November 1891, 4.

Simpson noted two reasons for the case's legal significance. One was that the court forced a unilateral contract within the doctrinal terms of offer and acceptance—and became the standard way of teaching those contracts. Second, it was the first case to recognize the requirement of an intention to create legal relations, which exponents of the will theory of contract took from Continental jurisprudence.[25] These two elements were interrelated: intention to create legal relations was a precondition for an offer. Now, these legal innovations began with a particular defence argument of the Carbolic Smoke Ball Company, namely, that the advertised offer was a mere puff that could not ground a binding contract. On this argument, the offer of a reward was 'just a way to express the confidence they entertained in the efficacy of their remedy', as opposed to an offer intended to mature into a contract. The court dismissed the defence. To do so, each of the three judges fastened on the bold statement in the advert, which declared a deposit of £1,000 (about £130,000 in 2020) with the Alliance Bank to show the company's

---

[25] Simpson, 'Quackery and Contract Law'. For a confirmation of this view, see Ibbetson, *Historical Introduction*, ch. 12. The case of *Balfour* [1919] is sometimes considered the one that incorporated the doctrine of intent to create legal relations into English law. Atiyah, *Rise and Fall*, 690.

sincerity. The judges thought that the statement precluded the defence of puffery. As Lindley J wrote in the lead opinion, '[w]hat is that passage put in for, except to negative the suggestion that this is a mere puff, and means nothing at all?'[26]

The decision was celebrated. One commentator remarked, '[a] considerable limitation has now been put to the venerable doctrine that to puff one's goods, however falsely, is not to bring oneself within the four corners of the law of contract; a doctrine closely connected with the still more venerable maxim of *caveat emptor*...'[27] However, the crucial point about *Carlill* was actually what remained beyond its reach. The promise that the smoke ball would protect from influenza and all diseases caused 'by taking cold' needed no independent analysis under the court's construction, which isolated the offer and acceptance from the promise of medical effect. It could be argued that there was simply no promise of effectiveness in this case. The company's counsel initially did so in his efforts to present the advert as an illegal wager or insurance, by saying that his client did not make any promises concerning cure but only promised to pay to a person who contracted the disease under certain circumstances. However, Hawkins J in the High Court did not think so. He would not be pulled into linguistic finery, and read the advert as a guarantee of medical effect. Despite this explicit rejection, and despite the company's argument that explained the reward promise as an expression of trust in the medicine's efficacy, the cure promise remained marginal to the analysis, and the court sought a different anchor for the seriousness of an otherwise fantastic reward promise (in 2020 it would be about £13,000, the ball itself sold for £65). The mention of a large bank deposit rationalized the reward, while the only role of the cure promise was to assist the court in interpreting the timeframe within which consumers could claim the reward. In this way, while the court managed to hold the Carbolic Smoke Ball Company liable for the reward promise, it implicitly confirmed that the cure promise was not a serious matter in its own right. If consumers like Carlill were moved by epidemic anxiety to seek potent protections, the legal position that treated cure promises as puffery did not reflect the seriousness of such responses to adverts. The position was not strictly apathetic to cure promises, nor, therefore, strictly liberating for advertisers. Rather, it implied a derisive view of an advertiser's key claims about its business.[28]

A similar legal confirmation that cure claims were idle puffs was adopted for the passing off doctrine in the 1905–6 Scottish case, *Bile Bean Manufacturing Co., Limited v Davidson*, which drew on English precedents to replicate the same logic

---

[26] *Carlill* [1891–4] (CA), 129.

[27] *Globe*, 8 December 1892, 1. See also *Billposter*, September 1892, 56: 'most critics agree that this is a fair and proper sequel, and that it is likely to act as a fair and proper check on the issue of too literal advertisements.' Not only rewards, but also promises to reimburse payments were occasionally enforced after *Carlill*. For example, *Eagleton* (1912).

[28] The timeframe was at issue because the company argued for vagueness that undermined a binding contract. To address this defence required an interpretation of the implied term of the contract, which took account of the cure promise.

in a different legal field. The Bile Bean Company, an operation of Charles Edward Fulford and Ernest Albert Gilbert, started in Australia. Fulford was impressed with a quack medicine branded Pink Pills for Pale People and began his new venture by seeking a catchy alliteration. Inspiration struck him at 4 a.m. one morning: Bile Beans for Biliousness. He then decided it was time to create a formula. The company operated from Leeds from 1899 and expanded through agencies across the British Empire, marketing millions of pills for biliousness and other conditions, which were ordered from a manufacturer in Detroit. On Fulford's and Gilbert's account, the British advertising campaign cost a prodigious £300,000. It included eighty-three million pamphlets distributed door to door; publicity stunts such as the 'Bile Bean March' musical event and cookery books, as well as extensive press advertising. Having invested in branding, they claimed to have stopped several imitators. When they discovered that George Graham Davidson, a chemist in Edinburgh, was selling Bile Beans of his own and supplying them to customers who asked for Bile Beans (Figure 5.2), they took him to court.[29]

Figure 5.2 Bile Beans competing labels; one was yellow and black, the other chocolate and white. *Bile Bean Manufacturing Co. v. Davidson* (1906) 22 RPC 553.

Lord Ordinary Ardwall at the Outer House of the Court of Session, and after him the Second Division of the Inner House that heard the appeal, refused to help. The reason was that they saw the Bile Bean Company as a fraudulent trader. According to both courts, the 'foundation stone' of Bile Bean's success was a fictional story of origins. In this fiction, the pills were made in modern laboratories from a secret Australian herb, which had been long known to natives whose robust health was attested by none other than Captain Cook; the herb was allegedly discovered by an

---

[29] To get a sense of the expenditure it can be compared with other advertisers. W.H. Lever, among the era's largest advertisers, spent on average £100,000 a year, while Beecham had spent £120,000 in 1891. Nevett, 'Advertising and Editorial Integrity', 151.

250   THE RISE OF MASS ADVERTISING

'eminent scientist' named Charles Forde, who did not exist. (Figure 5.3). As the courts reasoned, this tale amounted to a fraudulent misrepresentation.

It was not clear, however, that the Australian tale was so central to the advertising campaign. Some adverts certainly contained stories and images that would not shame greater authors, and straddled the procedures of modern science and the excitements of imperial imaginaries. The one in Figure 5.3, read in court, was a

Figure 5.3 Bile Bean Manufacturing Co., pamphlet advertisement 1900s, read in court by Ardwall J.

textual and visual mix of symbols, with Big Ben among exotic trees, birds, and kangaroos.[30] However, multiple press adverts and pamphlets did not mention the Australian tale or only used the name Forde and abstract references to a discovery. Instead, all these adverts focused on promises and testimonials of cure.[31]

In the appeal, the company argued as much. If the tale was not central it was hard to construe Bile Bean as a fraudulent trader on its basis. However, the courts focused on what Ardwall described as the foundation fiction without which 'these beans would never have taken the hold of the public they have done'. He argued that the name Forde conveyed the entire fiction, and was itself inseparable from the tradename, Bile Beans. Therefore, even adverts that did not mention the Australian tale implicitly included it. As with *Carlill*, here too the important and interesting takeaway was the distinctions that the courts drew between different contents within adverts, and most crucially—the content left outside the definition of misrepresentation, within the scope of puffery. The statements in the tale, as the Lord Justice Clerk Kingsburgh put it, 'were not of the mere puffing order, not of the "never failing", the "incomparable", the "unique", or the "worth a guinea a

---

[30] Bile Bean pamphlet, 1900s.
[31] This is confirmed roughly by Gale's Topic Finder Tool. Keywords found most often in the text with the search term 'bile beans for biliousness' do not include Australia (Graph 5.3).

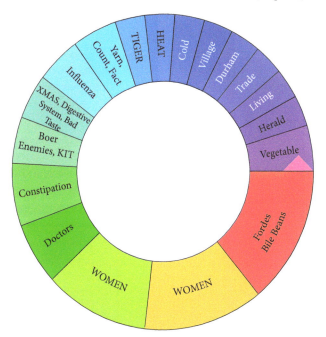

Graph 5.3 Gale's Topic Finder Tool, October 2017.

box" order'; they were factual misrepresentations that amounted to fraud, which the court examined in detail.[32] The one detail it did not cover was the extensive curing abilities claimed for the pills. Bile Beans were regularly advertised as good for a wide variety of conditions (Figure 5.4).

For the judges, the combined story of empire and science lent credibility to cure claims, while without it the adverts were ineffective and their promises meaningless. The decision relied on a strained interpretation of branding, whereby the brand name implied an entire exotic narrative more readily than it implied the cure promises that consistently appeared with it. In this way, the decision suggested that cure promises were not in themselves effective devices of persuasion. As Lord Stormonth-Darling put it, '[m]ere puffing will not do. Exaggeration, however gross, of the merits and virtues of a remedy will not do.' Only the fiction on which 'the whole superstructure rested' did.[33]

In 1914, the Select Committee on Patent Medicines complained that newspapers did not report the *Bile Bean* case, just as they did not report criticisms of secret remedies more generally. The remedy, the report said, 'still has a considerable sale'. The committee assumed that Bile Bean succeeded because the legal decision was hidden. However, as Simpson noted about *Carlill*, which was widely reported, neither Roe nor other medical advertisers were deterred, and consumers continued to buy. Bile Bean itself survived twentieth-century regulatory hurdles and continued to sell until the 1980s.[34] In both *Carlill* and *Bile Bean*, the important takeaway was not the limitation placed on medical advertising, but the implication that its core fell within the scope of the doctrine of puffery. *Carlill* confirmed puffery as a valid defence with a broad application. Were it not for the promise of reward backed by a deposit, the advert that claimed extensive medical effects would not have warranted a demand for compensation. *Bile Bean* confirmed that such advertising content would not invalidate brand protections. These legal positions encouraged advertising, with an attendant ridicule. In both cases, the point was that the content was not serious enough to raise concerns.

It is easy to see the ambivalent implications of puffery in these cases, which involved ridicule within a permissive logic. Advertisers and their lawyers were well aware of this complexity, as was demonstrated in the trial of Arthur Lewis Pointing and its aftermath. In Chapter 1, I discussed Pointing and the invisible elevators he advertised, which promised a miraculous bodily transformation to 'little people'. In 1897 he was charged with fraud by disappointed consumers who did not appear taller with the elevators and suffered pain while using them. One of the defence

---

[32] *Bile Bean* (1906) (OH), 563; *Bile Bean* (1906) (IH), 734.
[33] *Bile Bean* (1906) (IH), 736. Lord Stormonth-Darling also read *Holloway* (1850) as a decision confirming that cure-all promises were not misrepresentations. Lord Langdale did not actually decide that in *Holloway*, but he did not respond to that argument from the defence and said that he did not have 'any sort of respect for this sort of medicines'.
[34] Select Committee on Patent Medicines, 1914, s. 28; Rowe, 'Bile Beans'.

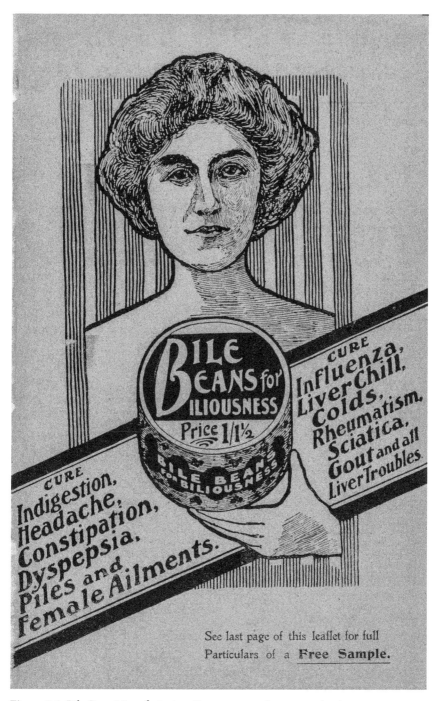

Figure 5.4 Bile Bean Manufacturing Co., cure promises, magazine insert advertisement, 1902.

arguments presented by Pointing's lawyer, Horace Avory, was that the advertised promises were mere puffery and did not amount to fraudulent misrepresentations.[35] At the Bow Street Police Court, he argued that the question was not 'whether the tricks or artifices by which business was carried on were commendable'. The argument explicitly demeaned his client's methods in order to acquit him. He continued to argue that adverts about four-inch elevators were but a 'trade device', and advertising the elevators as comfortable 'was no more criminally liable than the man who advertised that anyone could take his pills with comfort, although anyone who tried them experienced marked discomfort afterwards'. Avory drew loud laughter from the audience. This was an ingenious argument that built on a well-known problem of unpalatable remedies. Discomfort was a familiar element in the consumption of medicines. Thus, the inconvenience of using the smoke ball in *Carlill*'s case was viewed by the court as part of the contractual consideration. In *Peter Pan*, the narrative began with the family's father, Mr Darling, evading his medicine and causing a family row that ends in Peter taking the children with him that night. The BMA theorized that discomfort was part of the attraction, producing 'a glow of virtue' in those who overcame it. By invoking this familiar experience, Avory marginalized the problem of discomfort, which could be just a side issue in medicines, but completely negated the ability to use his client's elevators. Vaughan J was less amused than the audience. He rejected the defence and committed the case to trial. However, Pointing was discharged at the Old Bailey. Fulton J did not agree that there was more than puffing at stake. He complained about the legality of 'all manner of circulars, in the faith of which no person of common sense could believe'. However, it was no crime: 'all that had taken place was exaggeration.'[36]

The consequence of permissive derogations of adverts was that advertisers promised all kinds of effects while also engaging in reputation-maintenance in their dialogue with the public. Pointing, for one, did not like being acquitted on the basis of puffery, which undermined his business. His lawyers sent letters to the press stating that had the trial continued, he would have proved his bona fides with satisfied customers: 'a large number of medical gentlemen, actors, theatrical costumiers, bootmakers, and others from all classes...' He went on to become a successful vendor of quack medicines with a flair for bodily transformation, selling remedies to prevent inordinate blushing, getting too fat, and getting too lean.

---

[35] The other argument was that Pointing believed in the efficacy of the elevators. As we saw in Chapter 4, this was usually an effective argument in fraud cases, but Avory probably saw that he could not depend on it here because the simplicity of the cork pieces made it hard to accept that Pointing believed more than was possible to the naked eye.

[36] *Reynolds's Newspaper*, 20 June 1897, 4; *Daily News*, 18 June 1897, 9; *Times*, 18 June 1897, 16; *Carlill* [1891–4] (CA), 131, 135, 137; BMA, *Secret Remedies*, 1909, vi–vii; *Pointing* (1897); *Standard*, 3 June 1897, 3; *Standard*, 18 June 1897, 10; *Standard*, 1 July 1897, 2; *Illustrated Police News*, 10 July 1897, 9.

When he died in an asylum, his will (a significant $40,000–$80,000 (approximately £4.8–£9.6 million in 2020)) was fittingly contested by an advertising agent. His story demonstrated advertisers' efforts to have it both ways by arguing that their wonderful cure promises were unenforceable puffs, while maintaining reputations.[37]

A similar but more salient example was Lord Duncannon, chairman of Bovril, known for its branded meat extract. In 1905 he responded to criticisms against Bovril adverts that claimed miraculous effects on health. He invited some 1,300 doctors to visit his premises and showed them the 'spotless brightness and cleanliness', the 'advertising novelties', and the 'splendidly equipped laboratories'. The irony was that Duncannon tried to overcome derogatory views, but the visit he organized depended on them. Over a decade after *Carlill*, doctors could join the marketing visit unperturbed by Bovril's adverts that liberally promised to prevent influenza (Figure 5.5), because the doctrine of puffery confirmed that there was nothing serious in these adverts.[38]

Carlill merits one last comment. As noted above, it was the legal precedent that introduced the requirement of intention to create legal relations into contract law. The requirement was a doctrine of seriousness. As David Ibbetson argues, nineteenth-century British jurists picked up what the Natural lawyers saw as 'the feature that distinguished a genuine promise from a joke'.[39] The requirement was also market-oriented as it distinguished business from intimate relations. And yet, *Carlill* was also the era's most famous case to confirm that quack advertising should usually be regarded as puffery. And so, ironically, the most significant elements of an advert were excluded from the framework of market seriousness at the moment this framework was adopted in case law, and why? Because such elements were not serious. This exclusion was perhaps the bluntest expression of the role of ridicule in the doctrine.

The Logic of Ridicule

I have so far examined the importance of ridicule in the doctrine of puffery, and traced its relationship to the construct of exaggeration developed in the quackery debate. This section considers the 1895 case of *White v Mellin* that dealt with infant health food. *White* was important because it confirmed that puffery assumed normative significance in the context of the modern mass market, rather than abstractly in any sale context at any time in history. By explicitly explaining the doctrine with reference to nineteenth-century market circumstances, the case

---

[37] *Morning Post*, 2 July 1897, 7; Select Committee on Patent Medicines, 1914, q. 5412; *Daily News*, 5 May 1911, 5.
[38] *Whitby Gazette*, 1 December 1905, 7; *Evening Star*, 24 November 1905.
[39] Ibbetson, *Historical Introduction*, 233.

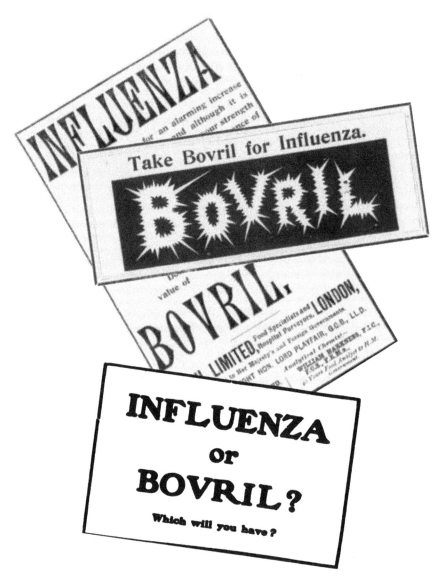

Figure 5.5 Bovril and influenza, advertisement cuttings. *Knaresborough Post*, 12 April 1902; *Speaker*, 26 February 1898, 279; *Judy*, 20 March 1901.

clarified the historical concreteness of a doctrine that was prone to universalist abstractions. Indeed, earlier judicial explanations of the legal insignificance of puffery tended to use naturalistic imagery: they suggested that all sellers had a natural tendency to exaggerate the good qualities of their wares. The logical implication was that no one should place much reliance on sellers' pitches and law may disregard them.⁴⁰ In *White*, competitive market dynamics were presented as the appropriate context for understanding sellers' behaviour and the mistrust that the doctrine recommended. It appeared to confirm the prescient John Stuart Mill, who argued in 1836 about 'puffing':

> nobody seems to have remarked, that these are the inevitable fruits of immense competition; of a state of society where any voice, not pitched in an exaggerated key, is lost in the hubbub ... For the first time, arts for attracting public attention form a necessary part of the qualifications even of the deserving ...⁴¹

White integrated this account with the doctrine of puffery.

As we saw in Chapter 4, Gustav Mellin was a manufacturer of health foods. He focused on infant food, which was a quickly growing business and an emergent scientific concern in the last decades of the nineteenth century. The business flourished as part of the rise of scientific childcare, set against growing concerns about infant mortality, a decline in breast feeding, and their relationship to national health. Originally a chemist, Mellin drew on the German chemist Justus Freiherr von Liebig's chemical principles to create an easy-to-use formula that became a successful global business. His adverts regularly promised disease prevention and circulated images of healthy babies, such as that in Figure 5.6.⁴²

Timothy White was a retailer and owner of Dr Vance's Prepared Food. He sold Mellin's product in his chemist shops without removing the brand name or wrapper, but he added labels with the following statement:

> *Notice: the public are recommended to try Dr. Vance's prepared food for infants and invalids, it being far more nutritious and healthful than any other preparation yet offered.*⁴³

When Mellin discovered what White was doing, he went to court for an injunction. The claim's basis was the economic tort of slander of goods, or injurious falsehood. The tort addressed disparagements of a person's goods, rather than the person himself. Its origins were in statements about title to land, from which it was gradually extended to falsehoods concerning goods and to features other than title.⁴⁴ From the perspective of puffery, the dilemma was how to distinguish puffs from statements serious enough to be actionable. The

---

⁴⁰ Bryan (1857); *Dimmock* (1866).   ⁴¹ Mill, 'Civilization', 1836, 133.

⁴² Apple, *Mothers and Medicine*; Gurjeva, 'Child Health'. On the rising significance of infant foods within the business of proprietary medicines, see Report as to the Practice of Medicine and Surgery by Unqualified Persons in the UK, 1910.

⁴³ *White* (1895) (HL).

⁴⁴ As late as 1862 it was not clear that an action based in comparative advertising existed beyond the confines of claims to title. *Young* (1862) (Cockburn LCJ). The disparaging statement in that case was

Figure 5.6 Mellin's Food, magazine insert advertisement, 1900s.

dilemma surfaced occasionally before this case arose, but it awaited *Mellin* for a dedicated judicial commentary.[45]

---

that Macrae's paraffin oil was better than Young's in measures such as colour and light output. While unfamiliar, Cockburn was willing to entertain an action but decided that a statement of comparative superiority was not enough: a false description of qualities of the commodity was needed.

[45] See *Western Counties Manure* (1874); *Thorley's Cattle Food Company* (1880).

In the Chancery Division, Romer J saw White's advert as a mere puff that no consumer would take seriously. Mellin appealed. In the Court of Appeal, Lindley J turned evidentiary logic upside down to allow a new trial. His formal reasoning was that Romer heard only Mellin's evidence. Of course, this could only work for Mellin's benefit, but Lindley hung on the procedural problem to allow a new trial because he was outraged by the 'new idea' of selling a tradesman's goods with labels that disparaged them. This time White appealed, repeating the argument that his label was a mere puff. The case came before the House of Lords, which restored Romer's decision.

Herschell LC, who wrote the lead opinion, gave two reasons for dismissing Mellin's suit. One was that the advert was a puff. Herschell showed this by conflating the futility of puffery with the requirement of special damages that applied to trade libels. As he explained, Mellin did not prove loss of clientele—the typical case of special damage. This was no surprise because no consumer would believe an anonymous puffing description 'merely because a person who obviously was seeking to push a rival article said that his article was better…'[46] A second reason, more widely repeated but that was actually obiter, was that Herschell doubted that comparative advertising was actionable at all, because it could drag courts into the endless dynamics of competition:

> That this sort of puffing advertisement is in use is notorious… The Court would then be bound to inquire… whether this ointment or this pill better cured the disease which it was alleged to cure… Courts of law would be turned into a machinery for advertising rival productions by obtaining a judicial determination which of the two was the better…[47]

Herschell's second reason for dismissal vividly illustrated what he meant by a person 'seeking to push' an article. In his reasoning, puffs in comparative advertising could not give rise to legal liability, because in the context of competition with a continual stream of adverts, every statement cast in comparative terms was geared to outdo competitors, and was therefore by its very logic prone to claim too much. Comparative adverts were logically overreaching, and therefore they were categorically unconvincing. They were factual statements (a point worth emphasizing, because puffs were sometimes explained as non-factual), but their facts concerned comparisons of competing commodities and only existed relationally,

---

[46] *White* (1895) (HL), 160. This conflation made it easy for Herschell to decide that special damages were part of the wrong, not just the remedy; since a wrong had not materialized, no injunction could be granted. This part of the decision was the important one from a tort law perspective. See, for example, Cornish, 'Personal Reputation', 856.

[47] *White* (1895) (HL), 164, 165. Herschell drew on *Evans* (1844), in which the court denied that a disparagement of goods was actionable. Lord Denham commented there that to 'decide so would open a very wide door to litigation, and might expose every man who said his goods were better than another's to the risk of an action'. *Evans* (1844), 631.

260 THE RISE OF MASS ADVERTISING

in the space of asserted difference. In this way, Herschell showed that the structural conditions of market competition, rather than the general wish of all sellers to sell, was the reason to mistrust them.

Herschell's emphasis on competition overcame an inherent weakness in the way courts distinguished puffs from actionable claims in comparative advertising. Earlier cases hinged on a little-elaborated difference between praise for one's own commodity and disparagement of another's. Three judges in *White*, Watson, Morris, and Shand, adopted the same emphasis. However, it was clear to all that the difference hung on a thread. Obviously, self-praise implied disparagement of others. The case illustrated the point with inescapable literality, when White's self-praise was glued to Mellin's competing product. It did not require an imaginative spirit to see the disparaging reference. Herschell's conceptual framework overcame this problem when he distinguished between economic competition in which an advertiser engaged in self-promotion, and other contexts in which a person wanted to injure another.[48] The market context, rather than choice between a eulogistic and a critical vocabulary, explained what counted as puffery, and excluded White's labels from liability. The futility of both eulogistic and critical claims, so long as they were comparative, became an accepted position for trade adverts.[49]

Herschell's view of competition also allowed him to incorporate assumptions about consumers, who would presumably make nothing of comparative claims given the conditions of competition that led to the 'notorious' use of 'puffing advertisement.' Of course, this assumption was normative. Scholarship on legal constructions of consumers usually focuses on the gap between the ideal and the real consumer. In discussions of the doctrine of puffery the focus translates into studies of consumers' actual responses to adverts, as already noted. However, the effect of this legal construct on the inferiorization of advertising deserves emphasis. Herschell's picture of the consumer was also a normative construction of advertising itself, which advised against taking adverts seriously. This permissive ridicule, which simultaneously licensed and derogated advertising, was not unusual in itself. However, the reasoning in *White* turned the competitive market into a formal part of legal logic in the doctrine of puffery, and implicitly confirmed the historical connection between the rise of mass advertising and the emergence of a doctrine that performs ridicule.

Due to the competitive context in which *White* was set, advertisers could easily perceive that the puffery defence was not strictly to their benefit. *Advertising*

---

[48] *White* (1895) (HL), 164.
[49] As Lindley J put it three years later, 'If the defendants had made untrue statements concerning the plaintiffs' goods beyond saying that they were inferior to, or, at all events, not better than, those of the defendants, *or if the defendants were not rivals in trade* and had no lawful excuse for what they said, it would not have been right summarily to strike out the statement of claim...' But since they were, there was no actionable claim. *Hubbuck* [1899] (emphasis added).

published an opinion that described the decision as 'startling' because it allowed a state of affairs that could confuse consumers and undermine the legitimate advertising investments of manufacturers like Mellin. Mellin himself could not have been happy. Early in the proceedings, White made an offer to Mellin to stop attaching competing labels if Mellin dropped the suit, each side bearing his own expenses, but Mellin refused. He must have regretted that obstinacy, which made him the historical agent who secured the status of comparative adverts as puffs, and demeaned his own business methods. After all, his career was devoted to blurring the lines between his trade and science, and he certainly took his adverts very seriously.[50]

Conclusion

The doctrine of puffery was a legal construct that demeaned sales pitches—as paradigmatically found in adverts—while also acknowledging them to be a structural element of the mass market, and indeed licensing them in practice. The virtually exclusive focus of scholarship on the benefits that advertisers obtained from the doctrine has obscured its role as legal ridicule. An explicit doctrine performing ridicule was and remains an unusual legal phenomenon. While legal responses to advertising were replete with disparagement and critique, the doctrine of puffery was surely an epitome in its explicit incorporation of exaggeration as a legal concept, and in its scope, which exceeded particular advertising media, contexts, and contents. The doctrine of puffery was thus a concentrated instance of a much broader and diffuse drive rehearsed and consolidated in the same years in multiple cultural legal sites engaged in boundary work. It became part of law, assuming an independent standing in analyses of adverts.

The pitch of ridicule in the doctrine leads me back to perceptions of modernity, and specifically to fears of enchantment. By licensing advertising and yet treating it as unserious, and construing consumers' reason as defective if they responded to adverts, the doctrine of puffery joined other realms of law and legality in a disavowal of enchantment. Telling consumers that they lacked common sense, or assuming that they were irrational, ignorant, or weak was simply beside the point for those actively seeking transformative miracles in the market and inhabiting imaginary worlds as a matter of course. The doctrine that licensed the proliferation of adverts was perhaps the clearest effort to disavow a phenomenon that revealed that reason was not the systemic basis of economic relationships, and

---

[50] *Advertising*, May 1895, 1014; *Chemist and Druggist*, 16 February 1895, 245.

that undermined hopes that capitalism was both an agent and manifestation of historical disenchantment.

In the next chapter I return to thematic historical controversies about advertising, to examine boundary work in debates about gambling and indecency. These were the two areas in which legal responses to advertising came closest to conceptualizing enchantment, and they therefore provide more insight into historical disavowal and its limits.

6
Gambling, Indecency, and the Bounded Realms of Enchantment

Theories of enchantment in legally inflected discussions of advertising have so far been conspicuous by their absence, but they were not entirely missing. The closest cases I have been able to find occurred in two debates, concerned with gambling and indecent print consumption. As these practices reached a mass scale in the second half of the nineteenth century, they generated alarmist accounts of their implications for British culture and the British economy, which can be described as theories—or more loosely discourses—of enchantment. The theory of gambling highlighted gamblers' defiance of reason and failure to follow rationalist approaches to time, money, and labour, all replaced with quasi-mystical views and ecstatic behaviours. The theory of indecency placed primacy on concepts of influence. It conceptualized the power of print to interact with receptive minds, ignite desires, and draw affective responses beyond reason's control. Gambling and indecency were in many ways separate worlds, but in public debate they often came together under the banner of moral reform, not least in the 1908 parliamentary Select Committee on Lotteries and Indecent Advertisements. Occasionally, gambling was even viewed as a subcategory of indecency. However, my interest in examining these histories together is not a necessary connection, but rather their common concern with consumers' non-rational responses to mass culture. It is unsurprising to find religious organizations at the centre of legal action in both cases, for their sensibilities not only encouraged so-called moral campaigns but also were tuned to spectres of mass enchantment. In both cases, the unstable boundary between popular culture and enchantment was explicitly crossed, and both provided conceptual languages that could open up a broader debate about advertising in terms of enchantment.

This chapter has a dual goal. First, it highlights the presence of theories of enchantment. While previous chapters have shown how debates about advertising gravitated towards its legitimation *and* criticism within rationalist paradigms, this one demonstrates a different focus. As various legal powers were mobilized to respond to mushrooming loci of activity in gambling and indecent print, discourses of enchantment received legal articulations that went further than other debates of the same years, and therefore deserve attention. Yet, the potential of theories of enchantment to reconceive advertising was checked, and they ended on a weak and even banal note. This was a dog that did not bark, and as Sherlock Holmes would have it, '*that* was the curious incident'.[1] The second goal of this chapter is to explore this dynamic, which meant that legal logic and practice effectively shielded the better part of advertising from a developed discussion of enchanting appeals. We see here how censorious theories, by presuming to recognize and curb enchantment, actually had affirmative effects on the bulk of advertising. Thus, despite a different initial focus, in these debates too law affirmed that advertising was compatible with a disenchanted culture.

Admittedly, from the perspective of advertising the theories of enchantment were limited to begin with. They were tied with topical concerns that intersected with advertising but were not strictly *about* it. Efforts to censor and prohibit gambling and indecent adverts were offshoots of debates that were not focused on advertising as a distinct problem nor intended to explain its powers of enchantment as an independent question. Advertising was conceived as just one of many loci in which problems arose, therefore aspiring censors took a content-based approach that tried to eradicate specific advertising content and was not well placed to theorize enchantment in advertising more broadly. Moreover, when applied to advertising's enchantments, the theories were limited by their premises. A central premise was the loss of reason and volition, which was misaligned with the continuum between disenchanted and enchanted ontologies explored in Chapter 1. While consumers' experience of mundane magic, animation, metamorphosis, mystery and much else, blended easily with their sense of realism and reason, and involved diverse emotive and cognitive positions, the theories explored here denied such complexities. Instead, they represented enchantment as a total alternative to reason and as strictly dangerous. Couched in fear, the goal was suppression. Another limited premise was the theoretical understanding of enchantment as a product of individual adverts rather than their accumulation, which was crucial as Chapter 1 showed. Yet, despite limitations, the theories examined in this chapter had an expansive potential for advertising in general. They therefore deserve attention for their presence and for their curtailment.[2]

Given this chapter's too broad a scope, I proceed through select loci. In gambling, I examine the litigation of prize competition advertising, which challenged the distinction between gambling—usually conceived as a commodity, and advertising—usually conceived as the marketing tool of commodities. In this case the gamble was—or appeared to be—also the advert and therefore the extension of enchantment theory to advertising lurked close to the surface. Private and public

---

[1] Doyle, *Adventure of Silver Blaze*, 1892.
[2] Content-based approaches did not *necessarily* preclude expansive theories. As we saw in Chapter 4, an approach focused on the content of adverts—in that case adverts for medicines—could be premised on a generalized theory of advertising—in that case as a field of exaggeration.

litigants came to courts with these competitions and led to decisions about their status as prohibited gambling. Viewed as a whole, decisions cut the knot between advertising and gambling. On the one hand, courts confirmed that the advertising culture of competitions was not the same as gambling and therefore was not enchanted—it was just low culture. On the other hand, they confirmed that when competitions amounted to gambling and therefore involved enchantment, they need not be seen as adverts at all.

While courts had a theory on the boundaries of gambling as enchanted culture, they did not have one for indecency. To the contrary, legal theory focused on concepts of influence by print that had no theoretical endpoint. Therefore, the possibility that enchantment theory could extend to much of advertising seemed even more likely. Yet, censorship strategies checked this possibility, as I show in two contexts: one in the poster industry, and the other in the campaign against adverts for abortions. For different and in fact ideologically opposed reasons—the one supportive of advertising and the other critical—censors in both contexts treated enchanting effects as isolated and identifiable occurrences rather than a generalized characteristic of mass advertising.

The case studies I examine differed in their subject matter, social tensions, institutional locations, legal frameworks, dominant ideological viewpoints, and scope, reflecting incidentally the era's decentralized approach to action on public morals.[3] The discussion inevitably has something of wandering quality, travelling disparate routes in forests of censorship and prohibition. Yet that is also the reason that commonalities tell us something that rises above local histories. From differing directions and with no unified perspective, legal engagements reveal that enchantment in advertising was being disavowed. It inevitably intruded again and again only to be recast as low culture or reduced to discrete occurrences. Disavowing the systemic quality of enchantment and its proliferation allowed British culture to live with its capitalism, where avowal would have transformed capitalism's very image.

Gambling and Advertising

The formative years of mass advertising were also those in which gambling commercialized and drew all social classes in locations that crossed work and leisure, from clubs, through pitches and racecourses, to streets, pubs, shops, and the press that carried gambling beyond urban centres and freed it from dedicated physical environments.

---

[3] Hilliard, *Matter of Obscenity*, 8.

As Gerda Reith recounts, all basic forms of gambling—cards, dice, and lots—originated in the ancient practice of divination and were inseparable from religious ritual, but the courting of chance had become a distinct problem in modernity, which extricated it from divine will and imagined it as an independent ontological presence. The nineteenth century drew on the Enlightenment legacy that viewed games of chance as failures of reason, and emphasized the gambler's rejection of the imperatives of the Protestant ethic: the importance of time, money, and disciplined labour. Those were substituted with a mystical world view in which concepts of the gambler's own magical efficacy, and quasi-religious ideas of fate and destiny, reigned supreme. These views also received medicalized versions of nervous excitement, which described gambling as the suppression of reason, will, conscience, and affections in favour of an overloading of the emotions.[4]

As an economic activity, gambling troubled contemporaries. It was viewed, David Dixon explains, as an organized rejection of all reason and therefore contrary to the civilizing process itself, at the heart of which was the minimization of chance and risk, the taming of animal instincts that made for emotional anarchy of conduct, and the increased capacity of rational conduct. From this perspective, gambling was an illegitimate method of dealing with property that undermined justifications for capitalism.[5] While gamblers themselves, particularly of the lower classes, often saw their pursuit as no less rational than saving, their critics saw a threat to rational capital accumulation.[6] Historians have studied nineteenth-century legal policies against gambling as a process that defined economic rationality and legitimized capitalist activity by what Dixon describes as the purification of capital, and Ann Fabian as the creation of the 'negative analogue' to the accepted pursuit of profit. The prohibitive working paradigm asserted that the state could only legitimately eliminate commercial gambling, not regulate it. Of course, every new capitalist invention required new and subtle distinctions that set capitalism apart from the dreams of gamblers. Prohibition was never wholeheartedly enacted or enforced and would finally give way to regulation in the second half of the twentieth century.[7] However, what concerns me here is the dominating presence of a theory of enchantment that impacted advertising.

---

[4] Reith, *Age of Chance*.

[5] Dixon, *From Prohibition to Regulation*, 48–60. See also Clapson, *Bit of a Flutter*, 20–2.

[6] On gamblers' views, see Dixon, *Bit of a Flutter*, 49; McKibbin, 'Working-Class Gambling', 147–78, 162–5; Itzkowitz, 'Fair Enterprise'; Huggins, *Vice and the Victorians*, 106; Holt, *Sport and the British*, 183.

[7] Dixon, *From Prohibition to Regulation*; Fabian, *Card Sharps*; Huggins, *Vice and the Victorians*; Clapson, *Bit of a Flutter*; Miers, *Regulating Commercial Gambling*; Itzkowitz, 'Fair Enterprise'.

Within the broader debate about gambling, the status of advertising sometimes seemed to partake in its bewitchments, which halted regular time and invited consumers to seek transformative treasures in states of frenzy. Languages of temptation multiplied and cast advertisers as professional tempters.[8] A London magistrate demonstrated the way advertising sparked deep-seated passions even in banal circumstances:

> I was coming along the street... and I saw a most tempting thing just outside a news shop – 'Three £5 notes for a penny.' I was sorely tempted to buy one, but I really had no time... I only mention that as one of thousands of instances... of the tendency of modern days: everybody wishes to get rich.[9]

The National Anti-Gambling League (NAGL), a coalition of Nonconformist Protestant Churches supported by middle-class reformers and labour leaders, established in 1890, called on legislators to stop the 'avalanche of temptation which is pouring over the land', and regularly drafted new bills to limit advertising.[10] However, because gambling was conceived as a (bad) commodity that advertising marketed, gambling and advertising remained conceptually distinct. In attacks on gambling adverts, advertising was treated as a neutral system of communication that should not be harnessed to bad ends. Advertising's effects were dramatic because of the mass exposure it produced to a problematic commodity, but not because it had, in itself, anything to do with enchantment.[11] This view was reflected in legislative provisions that outlawed adverts for lotteries and betting houses.[12]

Games known as prize or coupon competitions became a popular feature in advertising in the last decade of the nineteenth century. Newspapers relied heavily on games, but so did marketers of tea, flour, tobacco, bicycles, medicines, entertainment, and other commodities. Competitions included predictions of future events like sport matches, horseraces, business sales, state revenues, or demographic change; estimating data like the Bank of England's gold coinage; games like picture-puzzles, missing words, rhymes, or story-telling; and straightforward draws. In one of many attacks, the liberal social commentator Charles Frederick Gurney Masterman accused the popular press of directing readers 'away from

---

[8] For example, Select Committee of the House of Lords on Betting, 1902, ss. 5, 9; *NAGL Bulletin*, November 1902, 8–9.

[9] Select Committee of the House of Lords on Betting, 1902, q. 497 (Sir Albert de Rutzen).

[10] *NAGL Bulletin*, November 1912, front page. Attempted legislation included a Bill to Render Penal the Inciting Persons to Betting and Wagering in 1901, a Gambling Advertisements Bill in 1907, and a few versions of a Betting Inducements Bill between 1912 and 1914.

[11] See, for example, the Archbishop of Canterbury's comment about dangerous misuse of communication systems, Lords Sitting, 12 December 1912.

[12] For example, the Lotteries Act, 1836, criminalized adverts for foreign and illegal lotteries; the Betting Houses Act, 1853, the Prevention of Gaming (Scotland) Act, 1869; and the Betting Act, 1874, criminalized adverts for betting houses and surrounding activities.

consideration of any rational or serious universe'. They have been 'nourished...in this unreal world of impudence, nonsense, vicarious sport and gambling', starting with guessing competitions in boys' papers, and going on 'insensibly' to missing words or limerick games. The religious press was no better, only 'smeared with a grease of piety'. Eventually, Masterman warned, persons were so engrossed in alternative worlds that they were unfit to face reality.[13]

In prize competitions, the game was also an advertising strategy and therefore undermined the neutral view of advertising and brought it closer to gambling and its enchantments. Once this threshold was crossed, it was easy to cross with regard to other adverts too. As we saw in Chapter 1, adventure, play, and affective investments in dreams of gold were not confined to formal games. Prize competitions were thus a cultural site for thinking about enchantment by advertising, in which courts found themselves regularly concerned. The adverts could violate either betting or lottery prohibitions, but the problem of gambling as an advertising strategy usually became apparent under lotteries legislation.[14]

By the mid-nineteenth century almost all lotteries were outlawed; therefore, the main question in courts was whether the game was a lottery.[15] The accepted interpretation of legislation required three conditions to establish a lottery: a prize; its distribution by chance rather than skill; and a payment for participation by a significant portion of competitors. The legal niceties of interpretation were trying even for ardent lovers of legal nuance. As Vaughan Williams J commented in one case, 'these questions beat any of those which were discussed by schoolmen in medieval times.'[16] However, as a matter of cultural logic, the effect was straight forward: case law differentiated advertising from the enchantments of gambling. This was ultimately a rescue project of commercial culture. It was not a rescue of the high ideals of capitalist rationality—most commentators viewed advertising as an embarrassingly low culture, yet over the period courts moved from resistance to confirmation of that culture by distinguishing it from the enchanted world of the gambler.

---

[13] Masterman, *Condition of England*, 1909, 91–4.

[14] Betting legislation was mainly applied to adverts of sport competitions. Usually, these were not considered a strategy for marketing the events themselves. It was widely acknowledged that the sport industry depended on gambling, but the chain of dependencies down to the advertiser was a knot of contracts that tied bettors and race organizers via the mediation of betting houses. In consequence, betting adverts did not appear to present the dilemma of gambling as an advertising strategy, they seemed simply to market gambles. In the situations examined in this chapter, the advertiser of the competition was also the direct interest-holder in another commodity.

[15] The Lotteries Act, 1823, which ended the public lottery for the next century and a half, essentially pronounced that rational progress—to which funds from public lotteries were supposedly directed—could not be promoted with means that contradicted it. In 1846, lottery distributions of art works by art unions were exempted from prohibitions as part of the movement for public education. Other exceptions were created in practice through enforcement policy, as David Miers shows. Miers, *Regulating Commercial Gambling*, ch. 6.

[16] Smith and Monkcom, *Law of Betting*, ch. 14; Miers, *Regulating Commercial Gambling*, ch. 6; *Torquay Times*, 26 June 1908, 9 (comment in the hearing of *Blyth* (1908)).

Chance v Skill

The distinction between chance and skill, a key feature of the legal approach to gambling, was an application of the tension between enchantment and reason. As Reith explains, in games of chance mystical beliefs govern, while skill requires rational mastery through the application of knowledge.[17] In theory, a lottery was and remains paradigmatic of the enchantments of gambling because it is a game based strictly on chance. As the 1808 Select Committee on Lotteries commented, no 'species of adventure' was known 'where the infatuation is more powerful, lasting, and destructive'.[18] In practice, however, identifying a lottery required courts to decide whether chance or skill predominated, and decisions were difficult. By 1915, Charles Darling J was exasperated by arguments that chance and skill could not be disentangled, which he perceived as an attack on the very concept of free will:

> there are persons who are accepted as people of great wisdom who maintain, that there is no such thing as choice, and that there is no such thing as chance, but in these courts we are persuaded that there is such a thing as chance and there is such a thing as volition...we cannot ask merely, was there choice, or was it all chance...We think this is a lottery, although it fails to satisfy some philosophic definition of chance or choice.[19]

Deciding whether a competition was based on chance was an effort to discern the so-called 'spirit of gambling'.[20] This was almost literally a ghost chase. Between 1912 and 1914 the Home Office considered and despaired of legislation against prize competitions because distinctions between chance and skill were impossible to implement so as to target only cases considered problematic.[21] What interests me is how courts explained *skill* as they struggled to articulate defensible positions. Gradually and grudgingly, minimal objective standards of skill as well as fully subjective ones—all of which could be easily ridiculed as substandard culture—were accepted as sufficient to save an advert from association with the spirit of gambling. Eventually, *any* skill, minimal and unimpressive as it may have been, was enough to drive out enchantment. If the chance/skill distinction seemed a strained analytic position as Darling J recognized, as a cultural performance its

---

[17] Reith, *Age of Chance*, 93. The significance of this distinction was emphasized in the Gaming Act of 1845, which was a landmark in the state's efforts to differentiate legitimate and illegitimate capital accumulation. Dixon, *From Prohibition to Regulation*, ch. 2. See also Coldridge and Swords, *Law of Gambling*, 1913, 267.
[18] Second Report from the Committee on the Law Relating to Lotteries, 1808, 12.
[19] *Minty* (1915), 167.   [20] A common reference was Cresswell J in *Allport* (1845), 830.
[21] Miers, *Regulating Commercial Gambling*, 184.

adjudication iterated a boundary between advertising culture and enchantment. What follows is a closer look at this process.

In December 1892, the newspaper magnate-to-be Arthur Pearson found himself at the centre of litigation. He began his career in journalism in *Tit Bits* in 1884, where he suitably got the job as a prize for winning a *Tit Bits* 130-question competition.[22] In 1890 he established his own paper, *Pearson's Weekly*, and in 1891 started missing-word competitions that soon became an economic storm. The idea was simple: the newspaper published a paragraph with a missing word, which was deposited in advance with an accountant. Readers could cut out the coupon in the paper, write the word and send it with a 1s. postal order to the newspaper (Figures 6.1 and 6.2). The money collected became the prize and was distributed to winners. In this model, the mass supported itself, raising its dreams of riches by participating. Readers could submit multiple coupons and the newspaper profited from the rise in sales.

The competitions took time to catch on. Not before the eleventh week did the newspaper reach two thousand entries. In number 17 it had five thousand, in number 41 over ten thousand. Rapid growth continued, so that in number 52 there were 316,508, and in 53 over 470,000 entries. By the close of 1892 Pearson claimed to have given—or, more fairly, redistributed, £175,000 in prizes (over £22.5 million in 2020). Other newspapers soon followed suit. Newspapers otherwise busy distinguishing news from advertising, as we saw in Chapter 2, were trying to meet demand by printing their issues one to three weeks before the publication date, foregoing the supply of any *new* news for the sake of their advertising.[23]

Challenges to Pearson's snowballing success began with a criminal charge against a different newspaper, the pictorial weekly penny paper *Pick-Me-Up*. It published similar competitions except that the word was not selected in advance but rather drawn from a hat or bag containing a number of possibilities. *Pick-Me-Up* also held art competitions in which readers ranked the best eight pictures in every issue. The result was decided by popular vote, with a pre-set prize (Figure 6.3). Entries were in the few thousands but this was a test case. *Pick-Me-Up*'s owner, Henry Reichert, and his printers were charged with holding illegal lotteries before John Bridge in the Bow Street Police Court. Pearson joined the defence, while the Public Prosecutor, Augustus K. Stephenson, attended. As one paper reported, the case drew attention 'as would a great battle'.[24]

---

[22] Dark, *Life of Sir Arthur Pearson*, 1922, ch. 2.
[23] *Western Times*, 29 December 1892, 4; *Manchester Courier*, 7 December 1900, 3; *Newcastle Daily Chronicle*, 16 December 1892, 5.
[24] *Yorkshire Evening Post*, 14 December 1892, 2.

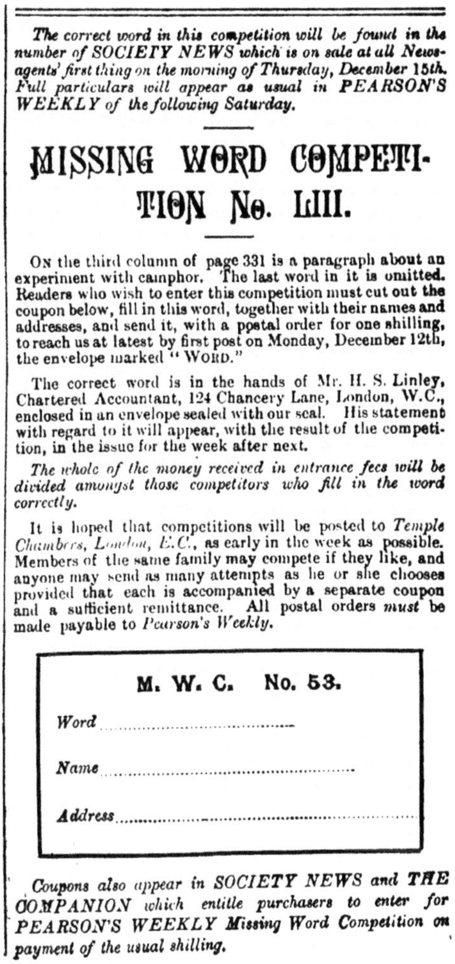

The correct word in this competition will be found in the number of SOCIETY NEWS which is on sale at all News-agents' first thing on the morning of Thursday, December 15th. Full particulars will appear as usual in PEARSON'S WEEKLY of the following Saturday.

MISSING WORD COMPETITION No. LIII.

ON the third column of page 331 is a paragraph about an experiment with camphor. The last word in it is omitted. Readers who wish to enter this competition must cut out the coupon below, fill in this word, together with their names and addresses, and send it, with a postal order for one shilling, to reach us at latest by first post on Monday, December 12th, the envelope marked "WORD."

The correct word is in the hands of Mr. H. S. Linley, Chartered Accountant, 124 Chancery Lane, London, W.C., enclosed in an envelope sealed with our seal. His statement with regard to it will appear, with the result of the competition, in the issue for the week after next.

The whole of the money received in entrance fees will be divided amongst those competitors who fill in the word correctly.

It is hoped that competitions will be posted to *Temple Chambers, London, E.C.,* as early in the week as possible. Members of the same family may compete if they like, and anyone may send as many attempts as he or she chooses provided that each is accompanied by a separate coupon and a sufficient remittance. All postal orders *must* be made payable to *Pearson's Weekly.*

M. W. C.   No. 53.

Word ....

Name ....

Address ....

Coupons also appear in SOCIETY NEWS and THE COMPANION which entitle purchasers to enter for PEARSON'S WEEKLY Missing Word Competition on payment of the usual shilling.

Figure 6.1 *Pearson's Weekly*'s missing-word competition no. 53, which became the subject of litigation. *Pearson's Weekly*, 10 December 1892, 323.

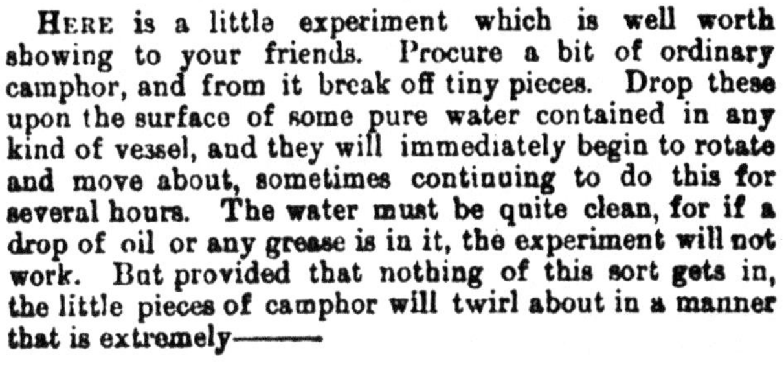

HERE is a little experiment which is well worth showing to your friends. Procure a bit of ordinary camphor, and from it break off tiny pieces. Drop these upon the surface of some pure water contained in any kind of vessel, and they will immediately begin to rotate and move about, sometimes continuing to do this for several hours. The water must be quite clean, for if a drop of oil or any grease is in it, the experiment will not work. But provided that nothing of this sort gets in, the little pieces of camphor will twirl about in a manner that is extremely———

Figure 6.2 *Pearson's Weekly*'s missing word paragraph appeared in a column titled 'facts', and invited experimental play. The missing word was 'unaccountable'. *Pearson's Weekly*, 10 December 1892, 331.

£120 IN CASH.

(And Forty Volumes of PICK-ME-UP.)

Write on a slip of paper the eight pictures in this number of "PICK-ME-UP" which you like best. Put the picture which you think will be the most popular first, and so on in the order of merit. Attach to the top of the slip of paper, as a coupon, that portion of the front green cover of this issue containing the date, and situated underneath the "ME" in the title "PICK-ME-UP." Enclose this slip in an envelope marked on the outside "Art Competition," and forward the letter, which must reach us not later than the first post on Monday next, to "PICK-ME-UP" Offices, 11 and 12, Southampton Buildings, London, W.C.

The competitor each week who selects the whole of the eight pictures, and places each of the eight in its proper order, will receive

£100 IN CASH.

The senders of the forty-seven lists which come nearest to the list decided by the popular vote, will receive respectively :—

1st Prize, £10 in Cash.
2nd Prize, £5 in Cash. 5th Prize, £1 in Cash.
3rd Prize, £1 in Cash. 6th Prize, £1 in Cash.
4th Prize, £1 in Cash. 7th Prize, £1 in Cash.

Prizes 8 to 47, forty elegantly-bound Vols. of " Pick-Me-Up " (3/6 each).

₀*₀ Each series of Drawings counts as one picture.
₀*₀ Each person can send as many lists as he or she likes, provided that each list is accompanied by the aforesaid coupon.

Figure 6.3 *Pick-Me-Up* art competition, 22 October 1892, 55.

Did chance decide the competitions? The Treasury argued it did because nothing else could: 'It is not as though a particular paragraph is given from the works of some great writer, and the competitors invited to exercise their skill and judgement, either from their knowledge of the author's works or their acquaintance with his style...' The defence argued that courting chance was not the point: 'A great deal of skill and judgement was required...when people set their wits to work to find a suitable word...they generally went to a great deal of trouble. They referred to books...' As for the art competition, 'since it had been started the public had been so educated in artistic matters that their judgment was almost equal to that of the Royal Academy.' The audience was amused, apparently finding the argument strained, and so did Bridge who sided with the Treasury. On the whole, he said, 'persons were induced' to stake their money on chance. There was no standard of literary merit that determined the result as there were many appropriate words. In the art competitions, the popular decision on artistic merit was apparently no indication of merit at all.[25] *Punch* was quick to echo

[25] *Times*, 30 November 1892, 13; *Times*, 14 December 1892, 13; *Dublin Daily Express*, 14 December 1892, 3.

the point when it ridiculed the argument that the mass could have a cultural authority on art:

> Oh, rejoice, Academicians!
> Learned Bridge knew what to do;
> Artisans or mechanicians
> Might have grown as wise as you.[26]

The different positions in fact accepted a single assumption: 'skill' required an objective standard of merit that could be identified and adjudicated by the advertiser. The prosecution and the defence referenced a standard of high culture. Reichert even associated himself with the highest goals of public education.[27] The audience's laughter pointed to a less ambitious possibility, hinted by *Punch* and many other commentators, in which competition adverts involved skill of a lower order. At this point, however, the low-culture possibility was rejected.

Following the decision, Pearson held back the money collected in his competitions and waited for a High Court instruction. A number of civil suits were filed by competitors and one was stated for the Chancery Division. This was the case of *Barclay v Pearson*, which examined the latest Pearson competition, with £23,628 14s. awaiting distribution (over £3 million in 2020). Stirling J decided that missing-word competitions were lotteries. In his view, there had to be a clear standard and it had to be actually applied in the process of selection. However, there was more than one appropriate word and no instruction on choosing it; therefore the selection was 'perfectly arbitrary'—based on chance. It did not matter that there was no draw because 'the use of a physical lot is form, not substance'. Stirling's emphasis on substance recognized that courting chance was a cultural imaginary and that courts were in search of a ghost. The ghost dominated minds if you could not identify and apply an indisputable standard of merit.[28]

The decision seemed to settle the legal position, but Pearson was not one to give up. His weather-forecasting competition of 1893 invited readers to prove that they were 'prophets' of rain and sunshine, gave them data on previous months, and promised that according to legal advice the competition was based on skill. Stephenson was not convinced. Bridge was again the judge and had to work hard to explain why this was a lottery. The weather, he said, was not an

---

[26] *Punch*, 24 December 1892, 289.

[27] Reichert and other advertisers may have hoped to draw support from the art unions exception (see note 15), which tolerated even straightforward prize draws in the name of art. On the challenges this created, see Smith, 'Art Unions', 97.

[28] *Barclay* [1893], 164. See also Stirling's similar decision about a competition in *Answers*, *Rayner* (1893); *Yorkshire Post and Leeds Intelligencer*, 19 June 1893, 4.

established science and 'was governed by a law absolutely unknown to man'. Bridge thought that the forecast for the day was a case in point, as the day was supposed to be showery. To the audience's glee, Pearson's counsel observed that the day was not over. Again, the analysis built on the absence of an objective standard—in this case a 'real science'. It also emphasized the relationship between the absence of standard and the enchanted behaviour of consumers. Forecasting and future-telling were close anyway. Bridge explained what an imagined mass was doing in predicting the weather: 'to the ordinary run of mankind it would be a matter of chance and not of skill'. As the *Law Times* confirmed, 'few of us can claim to be masters of meteorological knowledge.' Bridge concluded that Pearson would not have invented the game had he not wanted it taken up 'by the million', people who were revelling in incalculable forces. For him, those who did not have access to high culture, whether of literature, art, or science, were enchanted.[29]

The search for objective standards of merit could legitimize the popular culture of advertising games by accepting that it contained remote resonances or remnants of high culture, and that those sufficed. This option informed the High Court's position on a competition by Bingham Cox in the *Rocket* for predicting the births and deaths in London in one week of 1897. Cox's advert adopted the vocabulary of enchantment: 'your golden chance in life has come to win a fortune easily without working for it . . . You only have to answer a simple question . . .' Yet, like Pearson's weather competition, it also provided data for calculation, thus mixing enchantment with reason. The *Rocket*'s weekly sales jumped from four thousand to fifty thousand. The case was a civil suit by Henry Hall who had studied London statistics, submitted 252 coupons, and claimed that one of them was correct and entitled him to the $1,000 prize. Lawrance J at the Leeds assizes decided that the game was a lottery, but on appeal Smith LJ rejected the argument. He explained that predictions involved 'statistical investigations' and that even a small role for skill meant the competition was not a lottery. Hall got his prize.[30]

The rhetoric of minimal skill opened the door to more subjective accounts of merit. For example, a judge at the Westham Police Court in 1905 did not know what to do with an advertising campaign for soap. The Cook company placed shining discs in some of its soap packets and advertised prizes (Figure 6.4). If a consumer found a disc, she was asked to send a postcard showing her 'skill in praising or criticizing one of [the] soaps', in return for a prize. The competition increased sales by 47 per cent in two months. Consumers appeared enchanted by

---

[29] Pietruska, 'Forecasting'; 95 *Law Times* (1893) 445; *Standard*, 7 September 1893, 7; *Cheltenham Chronicle*, 9 September 1893, 8; *Manchester Courier*, 9 September 1893, 15; *St James's Gazette*, 7 September 1893, 11; *Lakes Chronicle*, 1 September 1893, 3; *Times*, 26 August 1893, 9.

[30] *Derbyshire Times*, 26 March 1898, 8; *Hall* [1899]. The lottery argument was raised by Cox because he had already been fined for running a lottery.

LIGHTNING SOAP

Whitens and sweetens the clothes and does not injure the hands. Look out for the Shining Discs.

Thousands of Prizes given.

Edward Cook & Co., Ltd. The Soap Specialists, London, E.

Figure 6.4 Edward Cook & Co., soap competition advertisement. *Ampthill & District News*, 29 July 1905, 3.

the glitters of discs and yet they also used their critical faculties in writing reviews. Horace Avory argued in Cook's defence that the prize depended on 'mental effort' and the judge finally agreed.[31]

Advertisers kept inventing games, as the *Law Times* reported with frustration:

> The latest insanity, unremittingly exploited by a class of newspapers, is the limerick. Edward Lear [poet, 1812–1888], the genius of nonsense... would have blushed at the imitations and parodies of him that have won prizes within the last few months... sheer imbecility has usually carried the day... 'The dice of Zeus,' says the Greek poet, 'fall ever luckily.' They do; but Zeus is the bookmaker, the tipster, and the newspaper owner.[32]

In limerick competitions, readers were invited to write the last line, pay for submitting it, and win fixed prizes. The Post Office reported a dramatic jump in 1907 in sales of sixpenny postal orders, usually used for limericks, from under one million in the first half of the year to almost eleven million in its second half. Shortly Oliver Onions would describe this as an 'advertising orgy'.[33] NAGL thought that competitions were 'cunningly devised disguised Lotteries', as nothing else could explain the 'craze'. NAGL's honorary secretary, John Hawke, complained that the twenty winners in one competition, each of whom won £80, were paid 'four times as much as Milton received for "Paradise Lost"'. The implication

---

[31] Cook, 'Newspaper Advertising', 1908; *Daily News*, 10 August 1905, 9.
[32] 124 *Law Times* (1908), 410.
[33] Select Committee on Lotteries and Indecent Advertisements, qq. 909–10; Onions, *Good Boy Seldom*, 1911, 150.

was that competitions could not be considered within the logic of acculturation; rather, the gambling spirit dominated. Henry Labouchere commented in *Truth* on a 'gem' from *Pearson's Weekly*:

> There was a young lady called May,
> Whose tresses commenced to grow grey;
> So she went to a quack,
> But alas! And alack!

———

The winning line was, *No testimonials she'll give him they say*. Labouchere wrote: 'An ordinary commonplace poet would have held himself more or less bound by the law of metre...but this original genius...has actually introduced *three* extra syllables into his lines.' The fact that the line won confirmed that there was no examination of merit. These comments rehearsed the search for objective standards of culture.[34]

In 1907 the Court of Appeal examined a limerick competition advert in *Ideas*. The paper belonged to the Hulton family, another dominant name in the history of competition adverts. Its newspaper empire also included the *Sporting Chronicle*, the *Sunday Chronicle*, and the *Athletic News*. The limerick was this:

> He wished her a happy new year
> And endeavoured to make it quite clear
> That her happiness lay
> In her naming the day

———

The advert weaved enchantment with reason. On the one hand, it announced that the prize, £300 (almost £37,000 in 2020), was 'a year's income for a minute's work'. On the other hand, it promised that lines would be carefully examined by a competent staff and judged on their merits. The winning line among some sixty thousand submitted was '*When the ring and the book shall appear.*' Arthur Blyth, a commercial traveller from Old Trafford, sent this line but to his dismay someone else had sent the same line and was the sole winner. Blyth sued Hulton for a prize. At the Manchester assizes Pickford J rejected the suit because competitors agreed to accept the editor's decision as final. Hulton won again on appeal, but only because the court decided that this was an unenforceable game of chance, where Hulton's lawyers expressly said he did not want to win on that ground.

---

[34] *NAGL Bulletin*, May 1908, 205; Select Committee on Lotteries and Indecent Advertisements, 1908, q. 571; *Truth*, 5 February 1908, 308.

In construing the advert as a lottery, Lord Buckley amused the audience by asking whether the editor could choose the following line, which neither scanned nor rhymed: *'But she replied: "You had better go home and ask my mother."'* The question hinted at the editor's unfettered discretion, which lacked objective standards of the genre of limerick. It led to the conclusion that the game was a lottery; therefore, the contract based on the advert was unenforceable.[35] Lord Vaughan Williams read the big picture of mass enchantment:

> Although the words were carefully chosen to make it look like a trial of skill... everyone must have known that...there would be a very large number of competitors...the winner would be selected not according to merit, but according to fancy or to some temporary rule which the editor might choose to adopt.[36]

Of course, it was not clear that 'everyone must have known' this was all chance. The reality was a circulation of popular culture. A market in advice books like the *Rapid Rhymester* developed to help competitors. Testimonials from winners posited a continuity between concepts of skill and chance: 'Your excellent little book has been in my hands since I first began to try my luck in competitions, and the new edition seems to me to be more useful than ever.' As this testimonial suggested, luck could always be aided by knowledge.[37]

Low culture was again rejected in another civil case, this time between Leeds Laboratory, a quack advertiser who promoted medicines with limerick- and missing-word adverts, and their advertising agents—Smith's Advertising Agency. The agents found they could not enforce payment for their services because the contract was for advertising a lottery. Lord Vaughan Williams read the various adverts by Leeds Laboratory together, and dismissed their express language, which promised that entries would be examined by an expert literary staff (Figure 6.5).

On Vaughan Williams's analysis, this was an illegal contract 'dressed up with passages which were not intended to be acted on'. The language was 'loose' and did not commit anyone to a literary merit, nor did the mass expect it: 'Taking the advertisements as a whole... He could only arrive at the negative conclusion that it was not anticipated that the decision would be made according to any literary merit or any other standard than mere chance.' Kennedy LJ added: 'it was impossible seriously to contend that any reasonable person could read these advertisements as indicating that any real competition was to take place.' Objective standards of high culture were construed as the only ones available; therefore, their absence implied succumbing to the spirit of gambling. Yet, poor

---

[35] *Torquay Times*, 26 June 1908, 9.   [36] Blyth (1908), 719.
[37] *Pearson's Weekly*, 2 December 1909, 23.

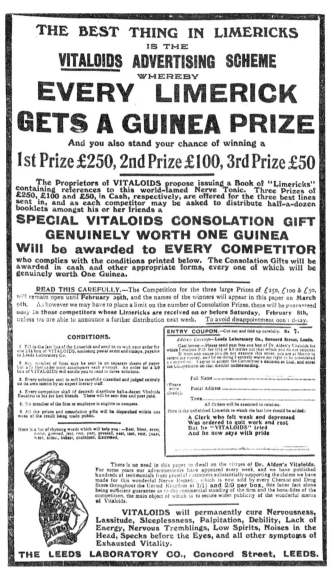

Figure 6.5 Leeds Laboratory Co., limerick advertisement. 'Every solution sent will be carefully classified and judged entirely on its own merits by an expert literary staff.' *Hull Daily Mail*, 31 January 1908, 8.

literary merit was an option lurking in the decision's reference to reasonable persons.[38]

The 1908 select committee was aware that poor skills complicated the chance/skill distinction. It was impatient with subjects of 'little or no literary, artistic or

[38] *Smith's Advertising Agency* (1910), 336–7.

scientific interest'. The skills they involved seemed unworthy to the committee, which wanted them suppressed whether or not they fell within the legal theory of chance. The *Law Times* agreed that the spirit of gambling was there. However, the recommendations were not adopted. Instead, the settled legal authority on word games became the 1914 case of *Scott v Director of Public Prosecutions*, which expressly admitted popular culture into the concept of skill.[39]

At issue was a Hulton word game called 'Bounties'. Lush J set a dual test, which considered both the adverts and their broader background. In interpreting an advert, the question was whether 'on the face of it' it was a lottery. There was no sign of that. The advert did not mention skill but Channell J thought that was a fair reading: 'looking at it as a whole, it does bear the interpretation that the prize is to be given to the most witty or epigrammatic sentence.' This was a generous reading, willing to indulge the culture of games. If the advert did not suggest a lottery, then it could still conceivably be 'a mere blind or cloak to cover up the true nature of the scheme'. Here, 'extraneous evidence' was needed to prove that the parties contemplated distributing money by chance. However, the interpretive stance was again generous. The low quality of literary merit did not prove anything because—and here was a novel point in the adjudication of lotteries—the editor's (or other judge's) decision was a matter of taste. Taste could be low or poor but as long as it was honest, it was not chance. Criticizing the decision against limericks in *Blyth*, Lush continued:

> I cannot see how the absence or presence of a 'standard' can convert an adjudication into a lottery or not a lottery according as the merit is of a low or high order. It appears to me that a decision according to honest taste or fancy is not a decision by chance and nothing else, however justly one may belittle the class or degree of merit.

As his language suggested, Lush was going for the familiar disparagements of popular culture. On the facts of the case, he did not see how assumptions that there was not sufficient time to check submissions could lead to a conclusion that this was a lottery. On the contrary, most consumers were surely ignorant enough to be dismissed upfront:

> It is a much more probable assumption that a large number of the answers would be rejected either through not complying with the conditions or through their being so pointless in comparison with the others...But one must take the published answers into consideration, and, poor as the degree of literary merit may be...they show that mere chance was not...the only determining factor.

[39] Select Committee on Lotteries and Indecent Advertisements, 1908, s. 12; 125 *Law Times* (1908), 462; *Scott* (1914). On the case's authority, see Miers, *Regulating Commercial Gambling*, 174.

Atkin J went even further. He did not think literary skill was relevant. Rather, '[a]ny kind of skill or dexterity, whether bodily or mental, in which persons can compete would prevent a scheme from being a lottery.'

Lush thought that as popular culture descended low it came close to the enchantment boundary. As he put it, the effects of this world of poor taste and big money were 'mischievous', and 'in many cases the real incentive to the readers of the newspapers to take part in them is something not far removed from the spirit of gambling.' Indeed, he acknowledged that chance and skill mixed and thought that this phenomenon required a conceptualization of its own, which old laws simply did not foresee. In this way, Lush acknowledged that adverts falling outside the conceptual scheme of a lottery could in substance involve enchantment. However, having no legal framework for addressing them, he resorted to the language of bad taste and poor judgement. With this decision, the idea of merit became fully subjectivized. Taste replaced objective standards of culture, and popular advertising culture was legitimized as distinct from, rather than part of, worlds of enchantment.[40]

Scott could be used either to allow or prohibit advertising games in practice, depending on the evidence. Moreover, it was not viewed as a refutation of earlier decisions because the entire field was typically explained in terms of factual complexities. However, as a matter of cultural perspective, the idea that low culture was *not* enchanted culture became an established, if begrudged, legal position. A few months later, when Darling J adjudicated a word competition by a medical advertiser, he had to accept a competitor's claim to a prize, regretting 'very much that is should be possible to allow this kind of competition ... It was no advantage to education, but simply led to a great waste of time ...' What started out as a potential reorientation of views of advertising in terms of enchantment, became its opposite: not an alternative ontological experience, but part of a disenchanted world that could be both derided and tolerated.[41]

Prize and Money

Assuming a competition *was* found to be a game of chance, it would seem that the advert and the gamble were one and the same. At least in those cases, an advert seemed to correspond to a theory of enchantment. However, the two other conditions of lottery: a prize, and payment for the chance of winning it, essentially recreated the gamble as a commodity rather than advertising strategy, and so

---

[40] *Scott* (1914). See also *Minty* (1915). The decision suggested that not every exercise of discretion would be considered as precluding the rule of chance, only that of honest judgement rather than pretence to volition.

[41] *von Sachs* (1914). The Court of Appeal later allowed an appeal on grounds of excessive damages. *Birmingham Daily Post*, 5 May 1915, 10; *Times*, 4 May 1915, 3.

maintained a distance between advertising and enchantment even here. In what follows I briefly demonstrate how adjudication differentiated advertising from gambling. If the chance/skill condition construed legitimate advertising as low but not enchanted culture, the money-for-a-prize condition implied that illegitimate gambling was not an advertisement. In this way, case law secured a double distancing of advertising from enchantment.

A leading decision was the 1883 case of *Taylor v Smetten*. Taylor was an itinerant seller who travelled from town to town with two caravans. On arrival, he would build a tent and start a sale. His advertising was traditional: men announced that packets of tea contained prize coupons. The tea was sold at a market price and consumers were reportedly happy with it. However, Taylor was convicted of holding an illegal lottery. Hawkins J reasoned:

> There can be no doubt that the appellant in enclosing and announcing the enclosure of the coupon in the packet of tea, did so with a view to induce persons to become purchasers... it is impossible to suppose that the aggregate prices charged... did not include the aggregate prices of the tea and the prizes. Nor can it be doubted that in buying a package, the purchaser... bought the tea coupled with the chance of getting something of value by way of a prize.[42]

Hawkins was correct about the elasticity of demand, and correctly argued that the value of any commodity included the benefits and meanings associated with it through its advertising campaign. Commodities were being sold together with dreams of riches, and consumers were paying for the whole package. However, his legal analysis was not geared to explain the real market price of tea in a situation of rising demand, but rather to unbundle the advertising campaign and show that there was a price element attributable specifically to the prize competition as a distinct experiential commodity, *in isolation* from the tea and its marketing process. As he explicitly stated: 'To us it seems utterly immaterial whether a specific article was or was not conjoined with the chance, and as the subject-matter of the sale.' The legal analysis was training the cultural eye to *see* lotteries—and treated commodity (tea) advertising as obscuring the real object.[43]

The alternative theory could be glimpsed in the case of John Simpson, a grocer prosecuted in Lincoln for selling Una tea with competition tickets in 1888. The London Tea Supply Association defended Simpson, arguing that this was not a lottery but an advertisement. On its economic analysis, prizes were not funded by rising demand but rather by saving on alternative advertising costs:

[42] *Taylor* (1883), 210. See also *Harris* (1866), 353.   [43] *Taylor* (1883), 212.

> Advertising had become a fine art, and a great variety of means had been adopted... of pushing goods. As the Magistrates were aware very large sums of money were spent in advertising in newspapers and in bill-posting, and instead of spending... the Association advertised it by giving those persons who purchased their tea a portion of the profits... It was their method of advertising.[44]

The defence continued to argue that there was 'full value for money in the tea itself'. As these efforts suggest, traders recognized that the conceptual question was whether the gamble was an advertising strategy or a commodity. They attempted an alternative analysis in which unbundling a distinct economic value for gambling as commodity was impossible. They failed, as the court refused to see an advert and a gamble as one and the same thing.

Advertisers repeatedly tested the extent of the theory. The *Weekly Telegraph* tried to create an environment in which there was no payment for participation in the game. Medals—the equivalent of a coupon—were distributed freely, the newspaper issue that announced winners could be read at the offices without charge, and the prize could be had without buying the newspaper. Nonetheless, Alverstone LCJ saw a lottery and would not be confused. He clarified that the theory of payment was based on a collective analysis of consumers:

> this Court would be stultifying itself were it to give any effect to the ingenious argument... we must ask ourselves how many of the recipients of these medals, who are unable to go into the office and inspect the paper for nothing, would pay a penny for the paper, not for the purpose of reading it in the ordinary way, but in order to see whether the number of their medal is the lucky one... The persons who receive the medals therefore contribute collectively (though each individual may not contribute) sums of money which constitute the fund from which the profits of the newspaper, and also the money for the prize winners in this competition, come.[45]

Alverstone struggled to unbundle the advertising campaign and attribute to consumers only one of two motivations for spending, which related to two separate commodities: the newspaper and the game. Consumers were either reading 'in the ordinary way', or courting luck. Competition adverts actually worked by tying these motivations together and using one to market the other. Consumers experienced the newspaper commodity through the games that advertised it. In 1912 the High Court clarified its position for advertisers who thought that courts cared how they financed their prizes: what mattered was not the income side of the advertiser, but the expenditure side of consumers who were

---

[44] *Simpson and another*, 1888.   [45] *Willis* [1907], 453–5.

driven to pay for hope. Courts exhibited sophistication by seeing the gambling spirit behind 'ingenuous' arguments. Yet, as they did so they also engaged in a cleansing project of advertising, by returning gambling to its status as a commodity.[46]

The legal theory of gambling as commodity was not a function of lottery law alone. As noted earlier, games were also examined under betting legislation—typically in cases of sport competitions. Here it was easier to see the gamble as a commodity because nothing else was being sold. However, occasionally courts stumbled on an additional commodity that put strain on legal assumptions. Such cases help us see the assumptions more clearly.

A series of High Court cases that dealt with the question of prize competitions under betting law began with a horseracing competition in the Hulton press. The coupons were sold in a weekly book called the *Racing Record*, and the winners were announced in the *Sporting Chronicle*. Edward Hulton had been warned by the Public Prosecutor but had legal advice that supported him, and agreed to obtain a court decision. In 1891, a competition with some twenty-seven thousand entries was examined in a case known as *Caminada v Hulton*. Day and Lawrance JJ decided that a bet required money lost or won over a contested question, but there was nothing lost by competitors because they paid their shilling for the book. The 'scheme', as Day called it, was at most a device for attracting people to buy the books—or more simply, an advert. Without money attributable to the game alone, it reverted back from the status of commodity to that of advertisement 'attracting' buyers.[47]

In 1895 *Caminada* was virtually replicated in a case against Stoddart—also a large sport publisher, which published titles like the *Athletic Journal, Turf Life*, and *Sporting Luck*. However, Wright J said he would be open to consider that horserace coupon competitions were bets in disguise when appropriate facts were proved. Within a few years, Wright's suggestion materialized. NAGL secured High Court decisions against both Stoddart and Hulton, which suggested that they were accepting money in consideration for a promise to pay on a contingency.[48] Again, the important point was not deciding either way. Instead, the important point was that to find a gamble, the legal logic required money to be conceptually distinguishable and attributable to the gambling transaction. Gambling was conceived as a commodity and detached from the broader advertising scene in which it was in fact taking place. The language of judges reflected

---

[46] Bartlett [1912]. In this case concert tickets were advertised with a promise that one of them would be selected and win a bicycle. Accused of holding a lottery, the organizers argued that the prize was contributed by the manufactures as an advertisement, and not funded by the ticket entries, but their argument was rejected.

[47] Formally it was *R. v Hulton*. Caminada was a police inspector.

[48] *Stoddart* [1895]; *Times*, 3 August 1895, 13; *Stoddart* [1900]; *Hawke* (1905). These decisions, and a number of others, did away with the need to define bets and focused instead on statutory language which referred to money received.

the separation, as for example in this statement from Darling J: 'in this paper the appellant issued far more than a mere advertisement: he issued a series of coupons.' By distinguishing coupons from adverts, Darling denied that the games were part of holistic advertising schemes for commodities.[49]

Overall, the commodity theory of the gamble implied that paying for dreams of a windfall was a distinct occurrence associated with a forbidden commodity, rather than a characteristic of consumer responses to adverts of all kinds. Added to the theory that embarrassing tastes and low culture were part of a disenchanted culture of skill, this legal perspective ensured that the discourses of enchantment, which regularly applied to gambling, did not implicate views of advertising more broadly.

In the next section I turn to indecency to examine how very different contexts of censorship evinced similar disavowals of the place of enchantment in advertising.

Indecency and Advertising

The theory of indecent adverts came from the regulation of obscene and indecent print, which the state managed in close cooperation with religiously based anti-vice societies. Objections to indecency were deeply political, permeated by fears of expropriation and revolution that picked up in the late eighteenth century, and ridden with visions of collapsing sexual hierarchies.[50] Legal routes to suppress indecency had a variety of formal bases, including the often-used Vagrancy Acts of 1824 and 1838. However, the second half of the century and the early twentieth century saw dedicated legislation and an elaborate account of the influence of print suited for a commercial age. With mass commercial print it became clear that capitalism did not tame the sexual passions with the profit interest, as Albert Hirschman described early hopes for it, but to the contrary unleashed them in daily life. In the rising tide of reformist efforts, disorder was explained as a product of the permeability and suggestibility of minds.[51]

An important milestone was the Obscene Publications Act, 1857, the first legislation dedicated to obscenity. As Lynda Nead argues, the act reflected a new regulatory approach that recognized print culture as a problem distinct from general street disorder.[52] Lord Campbell, who promoted the act, originally

---

[49] *Mackenzie* [1902]. Separations of coupons from adverts were also reiterated when courts decided whether the business operated in the UK or abroad. *Hart* (1900).

[50] On the role of religious societies, see Bristow, *Vice and Vigilance*; Hilliard, *Matter of Obscenity*. As Hilliard observes, social order was a more palatable theory than the moral censorship of free speech.

[51] Hirschman, *The Passions and the Interests*. For a discussion of psychological theories of mind in this period, see Chapter 7.

[52] Nead, *Victorian Babylon*, 192. See also Manchester, 'Changing Rationale'; Cox et al., *Public Indecency*, introduction. Formally, the act merely eased common law procedure against obscene prints

explained its goals in terms of an authorial theory of intent. In his words, the target was 'works *written for the single purpose* of corrupting the morals of youth, and of a nature calculated to shock the common feelings of decency in any well regulated mind'. Nonetheless, his explanations also featured theories of reception, which became entrenched a decade later, in *R. v Hicklin*, when authorial intent became redundant. The case famously examined *The Confessional Unmasked*, an exposé of sexual confessions that the Protestant Electoral Union circulated in an anti-Catholic campaign. The material reached the courts following a confiscation of copies in Wolverhampton. The test set in *Hicklin* was an object–subject dialectical theory, which acknowledged the agency of print matter (object), dependent on the openness of the mind of the reader (subject) to influence. In the famous words of Cockburn CJ: 'the test of obscenity is this, whether the tendency of the matter charged as obscenity is to deprave and corrupt those whose minds are open to such immoral influences, and into whose hands a publication of this sort may fall.' As he continued to explain, reader–print interaction occurred regardless of authorial motive. The author may have had a legitimate motive, but revealing libidinous thoughts and acts to a mass public in print would 'do mischief to the minds ... by suggesting ... desires which would not have occurred to their minds'. This perspective, often inflected with imagery of poison, intoxication, and non-cognitive impulses, was of a non-rational ilk and offered a version of enchantment theory. Of course, not all sexual or embodied affect amounted to enchantment. However, the theory cast a wide net over the fantasy worlds that could flourish in reader–print interaction driven by the profit motive. While both Campbell in parliament and Cockburn in court assumed distinctions between print for the upper classes and the masses those were never stable, particularly not in advertising.[53]

By theorizing the enchanting effects of mass print, *Hicklin* provided justification for oversight, even as the scope of prohibitions remained vague and inconsistently applied.[54] When it came to advertising, the common argument about

---

by giving magistrates the power to issue search and seizure warrants (excepting Scotland). No one was ever charged under it, Christopher Hilliard stresses; it was instead used to destroy obscene matter distributed for gain. Hilliard, *Matter of Obscenity*, 7.

[53] Lords Sitting, 25 June 1857; *Hicklin* (1868), 371. On the imagery of poison, see Brantlinger, 'Case of the Poisonous Book'; Nead, *Victorian Babylon*; Stern, 'Wilde's Obscenity Effect'; Samalin, *Masses Are Revolting*, ch. 5. Samalin observes the animism involved.

A high/low distinction based on differences in audience, treated mass culture as more dangerous than exposures to indecency in art and science. Nead, 'Bodies of Judgement'; Hilliard, *Matter of Obscenity*, ch. 1; Bull, 'Managing the "Obscene M.D."'; Mullin, 'Poison More Deadly'.

[54] The relationship between obscenity and indecency itself was unclear. Indecency was a malleable concept, which referenced religious ideas of virtue and secular ones of social order. In legislation, indecency and obscenity sometimes appeared together and exchangeably, for example, in the Indecent Advertisements Act, 1889, but indecency was viewed as more expansive. On disagreements about the scope of indecency and its relationship to obscenity, see Cox et al., *Public Indecency*, introduction, chs 3–4. The 1908 committee noted disagreements in its report.

indecent adverts drew on *Hicklin*'s theory: calls for censorship began with the premise that adverts put receptive readers on the path to sexual promiscuity and antisocial behaviour, as the intoxication of minds led to dangerous action. The theory was potentially coextensive with advertising in general because of its focus on readers' response rather than specific themes. It could bring non-rational communication and influence to the forefront and tip debates about bias, exaggeration, and aesthetic compromise in advertising, which we saw in previous chapters, towards a fuller discussion of the place of enchantment.

However, the potential for discussion was not realized, because practices of censorship evaded it. One mode of evasion was reductionist: discrete facts replaced the idea of non-rational influence as a general theory. A typical reductionist strategy was to treat adverts as if they were codes capable of being decoded, and so shift from affect and influence to object interpretation. From this perspective, certain words or images, for example a nude body, stood for indecency by force of convention, with the consequence that nothing more had to be said about influence. If a code appeared, indecency could be assumed and censored. Otherwise, the implicit assumption was that enchantment was not at issue. In another reductionist strategy, the decision about indecency was deflected to concrete historical readers. Censors pointed to readers who saw an advert as indecent and based their censorship on those readers. In this case too, censors did not need to discuss influence in the abstract; they merely had to observe someone being influenced. Reductions helped censors overcome accusations that indecency was a product of their own imagination or, as it was often put, dirty minds.[55] By reducing indecency to conventional codes or to specific instances of influence, censors could claim to see and eradicate it while avoiding self-implication.[56] For the cultural status of advertising, the important impact of reductions was that they cut the idea of enchantment at the bud.

Alongside reductionism was also a second evasion, in which censors argued that recognizing and preventing influence was a professional expertise. This evasion was unique to industry censors, who argued that experts prevented influence. In so doing, they contained the discussion of enchantment by advertising from the production rather than reception end. Combined with reductionist approaches, little was left of the expansive potential of *Hicklin* for advertising.

---

[55] This was a staple response to censors. For example, the artist James Affleck responded to attacks on his poster by saying, 'The eye artistic sees that which is beautiful in nature, while...the ecclesiastical optic pictures only that which is vile.' Rickards, *Banned Posters*, 52. Most famous was Oscar Wilde, who in 1890 replied to a critic: 'What Dorian Gray's sins are no one knows. He who finds them has brought them.' Mason, *Oscar Wilde*.

[56] On expectations from censors to be beyond influence, see Crawley, 'The Chastity of our Records'; Nead, 'Bodies of Judgement'.

In what follows I demonstrate these evasions, while moving between two different worlds of late nineteenth-century advertising censorship. First, the poster censorship committee (PCC), established in 1890 in the wake of the so-called Zaeo scandal.

The London Royal Aquarium advertised gymnastic shows with a poster of its performer dressed in leotard and tights that apparently looked like skin, which outraged the National Vigilance Association (NVA) (Figure 6.6).[57] The NVA was founded in 1885 to enforce and improve laws to repress vice and immorality. It initially focused on the sexual exploitation of women, but expanded the scope to indecency in multiple contexts under the energetic hands of its Puritan secretary William Coote.

Figure 6.6 Zaeo the 'moral marionette, and the vigilantes on their way to the London City Council.' *St Stephen's Review* presentation cartoon.

The NVA tried to obtain a judgement against the Aquarium under the new Indecent Advertisements Act of 1889, which targeted primarily medical advertising as we will see. However, John Bridge J was not cooperative. He thought that the police had sufficient authority to act and did not want to interpret the new legislation for the NVA, although in a letter to the Aquarium he proposed that

---

[57] For an image of the original poster, which many historians assumed to have been destroyed without traces, see Davis, 'Sex in Public Places'.

Zaeo's tights be coloured blue and her cheerful expression solemnized. The Aquarium was defiant, because the heat became capital; the sensation put it back on its financial feet. The NVA turned its pressure to the London City Council Theatres and Music Hall Committee, which eventually conditioned the Aquarium's license on a withdrawal of Zaeo's adverts.[58]

The Zaeo episode was set within the broader debate about outdoor advertising that we saw in Chapter 3, which encouraged local governments to regulate it. Following Zaeo, the idea of subjecting poster contents to review beyond the reach of licensing committees gained traction. Attacks on indecent posters were directed to the billposting trade, in recognition of its power to shape outdoor visuals. It was already managing a critical atmosphere on the aesthetic front and decided to establish the PCC to contain the threat, as it explained: 'We are living in precarious times...unless we can secure popular support we shall certainly lose...' The move from the question of indecency to the broader question of taste was slippery as critics often conflated ugliness, vulgarity, and indecency. However, from a trade perspective, indecency seemed manageable in terms of specific content, and the PCC indeed separated it from the problem of advertising aesthetics. Culturally, this was the same approach that courts exhibited in gambling when they placed bad taste within the logic of disenchantment. As we saw in Chapter 3, the ambitious attack on advertising aesthetics continued unabated. However, the PCC operated throughout the period, and so kept the aesthetic theme separate from the problem of non-rational influence.[59]

The PCC's power built on the tight organization of the trade. Billposters had discretion to submit bills for review and were encouraged to be conservative. The PCC examined every submission and decided to permit, mandate corrections, or ban. Small prints of every banned poster were sent to all registered billposters with instructions to refrain from posting, backed by a threat of sanctions. The implication was that billposting companies would not contract with the advertiser and discontinue outstanding contracts. The association committed to hold members harmless against breach-of-contract claims, and subjected them to a constant stream of reminders and warnings about committee positions.

---

[58] *Era*, 24 May 1890, 15. In referring to police authority, Bridge probably had in mind the Metropolitan Police Act of 1839, which prohibited the distribution or exhibition of profane, indecent, or obscene print. On Bridge's proposal, see Davis, 'Sex in Public Places', 4. On the turn of events see *Billposter*, October 1890, 258; *Billposter*, November 1890, 278–9; Rickards, *Banned Posters*, 28; Allen, *David Allen's*, 141–2; *Standard*, 3 October 1890, 2. For additional discussion, see Hewitt, 'Poster Nasties'.

[59] Executive Committee of the United Billposter Association, *Billposter*, November 1889, 263. On criticisms directed to the trade see Hewitt, 'Poster Nasties', 164.

Censorship was initially based on the London association and then on a joint committee of the London and national associations. Printers and theatre representatives joined billposters in 1901, in a joint committee that reviewed stock posters, and from 1902 also as minority representatives (7:2:2) on the PCC. The London association objected to the change and continued a separate committee for the metropolis. Allen, *David Allen's*, ch. 6. Theatres rarely sent representatives to the meetings. *Billposter*, February 1904, 72.

Zaeo was a harbinger of things to come, as popular entertainment posters for theatres, music halls, and touring companies remained the centre of censorship. These posters, used for short advertising spans and aimed at an immediate arrest of attention, depicted scenes and performers with a sensational bent. The PCC's secretary followed travelling theatres and warned billposting companies in advance against banned posters. The committee's power was acute for these advertisers because the implication of censorship, which started rolling when a bill landed with a billposting company that did not like it, could be financially significant: it turned print into waste and could undermine ticket sales. Theatres felt 'under the thumb of bill-posters'. Eventually, many began to submit designs ahead of print to reduce the financial exposure, but the problem of printed stock nonetheless remained significant, because printers offered advertisers a choice from existing stocks and were financially vulnerable to censorship.[60]

When theatres were invited to join the PCC, the *Stage* cautioned against investing a private body with a judicial capacity and acknowledging its absolute authority. This was all too true: a formally voluntary body assumed significant powers because in addition to trade organization, it short-circuited bureaucratic and judicial hurdles. It was cheaper and more efficient to contact the PCC than go through courts under available legislation. Consequently, local watch committees as well as police officials regularly did. For example, when the Birmingham Chief Constable received complaints about posters he went to the committee, which promised to keep a closer eye on Birmingham to the frustration of the theatre and touring management who were not even contacted.[61] The PCC also tried to expand its jurisdiction beyond registered billposting companies. Many theatres managed their own hoardings and resorted to flyposting. This situation frustrated the organized trade because the public did not make the distinction and aberrant posting sabotaged its efforts to contain hostility. When the Oldham council decided in 1904 to subject all theatre licenses to its vetting of adverts, the *Billposter* warned darkly that theatres encouraged this trend because they published adverts that the PCC censored. It reminded theatres that cooperating with the committee was less drastic than having their license revoked.[62] It also participated in licensing

---

[60] *Stage*, 7 January 1904, 21. Concerns about compromise of property were forthcoming; for example, *Stage*, 7 December 1911, 20. On the growth of the entertainment industry in this period, see Daly, *Sensation and Modernity*, introduction; Haill, *Fun Without Vulgarity*. Advertising heralded performances with posters printed and sent in advance for billposting, which was overseen by the host theatre, the visiting company, or both.

[61] *Stage*, 11 April 1901, 12; *Stage*, 17 January 1901, 13. Similarly, when the Oldham Chief Constable saw a poster 'highly suggestive of indecency' he prompted the PCC into action. *Billposter*, May 1904, 110.

[62] *Billposter*, October 1904, 138–9. By the end of 1905, fourteen councils included the requirement in their licenses. *Billposter*, December 1905, 319.

hearings to put pressure on recalcitrant managers. In 1905, for example, a controversy erupted with William Morton, manager of the Alexandra Theatre in Hull who used two stock posters banned by the PCC. The committee petitioned the local government to condition the theatre's license on cooperation with it, which led to threats of legal action and finally to a compromise. In short, the PCC presented a model of self-regulation that gathered powers verging on public ones. It had become, as the trade leader Walter Hill put it, 'a public institution wielding a very considerable power and involving far-reaching consequences to very large interests outside the Billposters' trade.' In rejecting some advertisers who wanted a voice on the PCC, but accepting that printers and theatre managers had a legitimate claim to join it if they paid, the national association managed a fine line between its claims to guard the public psyche, and the demands of capital.[63]

A different censorship context emerged around adverts for abortifacients, also viewed as indecent. Here, legal action was part of the medical establishment's campaign against quackery that we saw in Chapter 4, drew on patriarchal traditions, but perhaps most critically belonged in the debate about national demography and British imperial power. Between the mid-1870s and 1914, Britain saw a dramatic fall in birth rates, with married women's fertility down by 30 per cent. Many suspected that birth control, which became more accessible with mass advertising, was part of the problem. In 1914, the *Malthusian* estimated that one hundred thousand women a year took drugs to induce miscarriage. If indecency was a driver of degeneration, in the eyes of critics abortions proved the causal connection by revealing how imperial potency was lost. As the Earl of Meath said when he promoted a bill to regulate advertising more closely: 'We own one fifth of the earth's surface, a great mass of which is quite capable of being filled up by people of the Anglo-Saxon race, and unless we are prepared to accept that duty and to fill those lands the British Empire cannot last.' Whether abortifacients were causally important for demographic change remains a contested question, but for the history of advertising, the fear that they were was critical.[64]

In the late nineteenth century, there were two main legal bases to stop abortion adverts. One was the general concept of incitement to crime. Abortion by medication at any stage of a pregnancy was criminalized under the Offences Against the Person Act of 1861; therefore, advertising abortifacients could be considered incitement. A second was the Indecent Advertisements Act, 1889, the only legislation on indecency dedicated to advertising. The act criminalized the public

---

[63] *Stage*, 2 February 1905, 11, 13; *Stage*, 30 March 1905, 18; *Stage*, 6 April 1905, 14; *Billposter*, March 1905, 209–10; *Billposter*, February 1902, 81. For opposition to a theatre in Yorkshire, see *Billposter*, January 1905, 197–8.

[64] Lords Sitting, 12 July 1910; McLaren, *Birth Control*, 248 and n. 44 (referencing *Malthusian*, June 1914, 42). See also Kilday and Nash, *Shame and Modernity*, ch. 5. On the controversy about the use of birth control, and an argument that sexual abstinence was the norm, see Cook, *Long Sexual Revolution*. On indecency and degeneration generally, see Cox et al., *Public Indecency*, ch. 3.

exhibition of indecent or obscene prints—but not their publication in newspapers or direct-to-consumer pamphlets.[65] Its immediate goal was quack adverts for sex-related conditions, on which medical and purist reformers converged. In promising to liberate sex from unwanted consequences, quack medicines were viewed by critics as leading 'to what may be called free love'. As Judith Walkowitz observes, moral crusaders and vigilance groups attacked a broad range of publications on the single premise that they all finally led to sexual degeneracy.[66] The NVA, which promoted the act with the Earl of Meath, included a definition of indecent adverts in section 5: 'any advertisement relating to syphilis, gonorrhea, nervous debility, or other complaint or infirmity arising from or relating to sexual intercourse'. Potentially, pregnancy was one 'complaint' arising from intercourse.

Between available legal routes, an active advertising scene for abortifacients, or more precisely for women's dreams of abortions, nonetheless flourished in Britain. Because the legal environment was prohibitive, advertisers sharpened their capacities for suggestion and consumers exhibited enhanced suggestibility. 'Suggestibility' was explained in nineteenth-century psychology as a person's degree of openness to accept implied propositions without critical deliberation. As Daniel Pick recounts, the discourse of suggestibility addressed a dizzying array of social phenomena that threatened to lead to mental anarchy rather than education. The 'shadowy world of social communication and mutual psychic entanglement' beyond conscious relationships was at the heart of all this. Yet psychology did not ponder the *legal* conditions of suggestion. Clearly, illegality exacerbated whatever capacities for layered meaning advertisers otherwise developed, and whatever will to enchantment consumers otherwise possessed, because clear facts were not forthcoming. Imaginative work in which assumptions, associations, and fantasy mixed was unavoidable because adverts never referred to abortion. As the *Lancet* confessed, in many adverts 'there is no direct reference to anything at all'. The adverts in Figure 6.7 were typical examples: their referent was couched in mystique.[67]

The legal environment of uncertainty could deteriorate to fraud, which was in fact encouraged, because selling useless rather than effective drugs was legally

---

[65] The patchiness of prohibitions clarifies that Britain was never committed to eradicating sex-related advertising. This casts doubt on the repressive hypothesis, as Michel Foucault called it, which describes the nineteenth century as a culture that repressed sexuality and persecuted its representations, but also on the alternative hypothesis of incitement to discourse, in which a proliferation of representations of sex was overseen by modern fields of expertise about the body. Neither repression nor disciplinary management of discourses about sex are convincing accounts as far advertising history goes. Foucault, *History of Sexuality*.

[66] Select Committee on Patent Medicines, 1914, q. 4673; Walkowitz, *City of Dreadful Delight*, 125. Religious spokesmen saw the power of adverts as a direct competition with religious organizations, which could not distribute tracts as effectively. The Archbishop of Canterbury, Lords Sitting, 8 April 1889.

[67] McDougall, 'Suggestion', 1911; Pick, *Svengali's Web*, ch. 4; *Lancet*, 24 December 1898, 1723–4.

TO LADIES.

The experience of over 140 years has established the character of these Pills as a safe, efficacious, and truly invaluable medicine. Beware of deleterious compounds. The name of Dr. John Hooper, in white letters, on the special Government stamp, is a proof of genuineness. Apply to Chemists and Patent Medicine Vendors at home or abroad.

IMPORTANT TO LADIES.

ESPECIALLY to those who require an ABSOLUTELY CERTAIN and speedy remedy; a remedy which in thousands of cases has never failed to afford COMPLETE RELIEF, generally in a few hours, as Mrs. W. writes—

"By adopting your treatment, my anxiety and misery was over Within Twenty-four Hours, although for three months I had been daily taking pills and other things in vain. Half the quantity you sent me proved effective."

Full particulars will be forwarded to any lady on receipt of addressed envelope. The medicine is not expensive, as one bottle at 4s. 6d. is generally amply sufficient.

A SWORN GUARANTEE accompanies all Testimonials.

WRITE AT ONCE TO
Mrs. B. B. F. ALLEN, 145, Stockwell Road, London, S.W.

Figure 6.7 Adverts for abortifacients? Top: *Illustrated London News*, 27 November 1886, 596; Bottom: *Jackson's Oxford Journal*, 28 December 1895, 2.

safer. Thus, Darling J opined in an Old Bailey case that a seller who knowingly sold useless drugs was not inciting to abortion. He thought that the advertiser could be convicted of fraud, but this option was sterile. As the Assistant Director of Public Prosecutions Guy Stephenson explained, the sole witness in a fraud case would be the woman, but since she was considered a partner in crime her testimony would require corroboration. And anyway, what public department would put an advertiser on trial for fraud when *not* defrauding was a crime?[68] Women were caught between public and private persecutors, could be defrauded with impunity, and were. In a case I now turn to discuss, advertisers actually obtained a certificate from a chemist confirming that their medicine would not induce abortion, because some newspapers demanded it before printing the adverts. Put simply, there were commercially powered and legally backed lies organized along the advertising chain.[69] Overall, in conditions of illegality and legal license to lie to women, their space of uncertainty as drug consumers was huge. Abortion adverts thus provided an extreme case of the role of imagination and magical thinking in advertising. Women engaged in them for lack of choice and arguably rationally, as a matter of risk-management. Nonetheless, their responses revealed how suggestion and leaps of faith operated in the advertising environment and underwrote an entire economic industry. They motivated an equally extreme drive to eradicate these spaces of dream and incalculability. Abortion adverts were thus a symptomatic if intense case of a dilemma that appeared elsewhere in advertising.

Towards the turn of the twentieth century, legal and medical authorities concentrated efforts on penetrating and censoring this advertising environment. The immediate cause was an outrageous blackmail by three brothers. Edward, Richard, and Leonard Chrimes marketed 'Lady Montrose Pills' in adverts promising to remove the 'most obstinate obstructions, irregularities, etc. of the female system' and to be stronger than any medicine on earth (Figure 6.8). They spent two years collecting over ten thousand names of women who responded, and then began to blackmail them (Figure 6.9).

Kate Clifford's husband opened her blackmail letter and went to the police, and so the brothers were convicted of extortion in 1898. The drugs were useless, but the case revealed the scale of women's desires to control their bodies. Fire was turned to newspapers for advertising and brought to the fore the status of the adverts. Critics claimed that they were unambiguously indecent. The Newspaper Society's solicitor warned that anyone but a child would know what the adverts were about. The jury commented that the 'vile plot...could only have been

---

[68] Darling's comment was in *Brown* (1899), discussed in the next section. Darling made the same suggestions in *Owen* (1898). For Stephenson's remarks, see Select Committee on Patent Medicines, 1914, qq. 1061, 1266.

[69] *Belfast News*, 3 December 1898; *Daily News*, 3 December 1898; Digby J, *Chrimes* case presentation, 1899.

Figure 6.8 The Chrimes brothers, advertisement for miraculous female tabules. *Royal Cornwall Gazette*, 7 July 1898, 2.

possible by the acceptance of such immoral advertisements by a section of the Press'. Alderman Newton saw the adverts as 'an ugly blot' on the press, and Hawkins J at the Old Bailey promised to pass the matter to the Home Secretary. The prosecutor, Richard Muir, notified newspapers that they were liable for incitement to crime if they did not stop advertising when warned. However, on another view there was no way to read indecency into the adverts. Henry Whorlow, the secretary of the Newspaper Society, worried that by the same rule censors could taboo 'Stock Exchange advertisement, lodgings to let, financial and various other classes of public announcements, all of which are open to abuse.' He located the problem in criminal motivations rather than adverts themselves.[70] Questioned in parliament in the wake of the case, the Secretary of State Matthew

---

[70] Joseph Soames, solicitor to the Newspaper Society, *NSC*, December 1898, 7–8; *Daily News*, 3 December 1898, 9; *Standard*, 22 November 1898, 7; *Reynolds's Newspaper*, 27 November 1898, 5; *Illustrated Police News*, 31 December 1898, 2; Chrimes (1898); *NSC*, January 1899, 4–5.

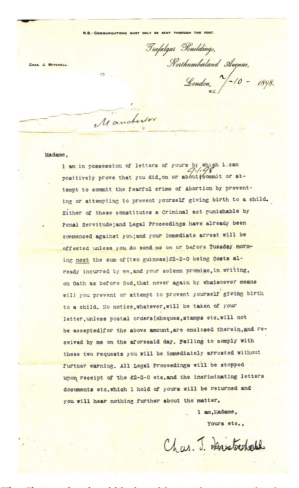

Figure 6.9 The Chrimes brothers' blackmail letter, threatening legal proceedings unless £2 2s. (approximately £265 in 2020) were paid with a written promise to never again attempt abortion.

Ridley did not have a clear response. He could only say that an amendment of the Indecent Advertisements Act deserved serious consideration.[71]

The moment was apt for the *Lancet*, which launched a series of articles about abortion adverts. Its ambitious goal was the whole trade in sex medicines, yet abortion was the horse expected to pull the cart. The gaps in the Indecent Advertisements Act, which allowed press and direct-to-consumer advertising, made abortion the only promising route, based on the construct of incitement to crime.[72] The trouble was that abortion adverts had never been a legal focus of criminal prosecutions. Authorities typically prosecuted for the abortive treatment

---

[71] Commons Sitting, 16 February 1899.
[72] On frustration with the act, which also led to the Select Committee on Lotteries and Indecent Advertisements, 1908, see Cox et al., *Public Indecency*, ch. 4.

itself, especially when women were harmed or died, or when another crime was committed, like the Chrimes' blackmail. Courts occasionally sent warnings, but the Home Office seemed indifferent and the *Lancet* decided to prompt it into action. In the next sections I examine its efforts to interpret indecency in adverts alongside those of the billposters' committee. Despite their different contexts, censors shared a need to concretize the idea of non-rational influence, with the consequence that its expansive potential was lost.

The PCC and the anti-abortion campaign addressed different types of advertising matter—image and text, different levels of abstraction—the one a generalized case, the other dealing with a specific commodity, and reflected different institutional loci and ideological views of advertising. Industry self-regulation was based on a trade committee and motivated by efforts to legitimize advertising. The medico-legal campaign involved state institutions, was set in contexts of gender, medical, and imperial history, and was generally oppositional to advertising. These differences allow us to see commonalities and divergences in the strategies they adopted.

Indecency as Coded Convention

Censors could evade a general account of advertising as enchanting, by treating adverts as if they were codes capable of being decoded. Whenever a conventional code of indecency appeared it was censored, with the implication that absent the code adverts were innocent of non-rational interaction.

Reliance on codes informed PCC policy. As G.W. Goodall explained in a 1914 study, it applied three categories of censorship: first, posters 'impure in suggestion'; second, posters that were 'ultra-sensational – scenes of blood, murder, and horror, for instance'; and third, posters 'likely to offend religious susceptibilities'.[73] The first two, sex ('impure suggestion') and sensationalism, dominated. Both were closely tied with affect and non-cognitive excitement, yet the accepted view was that censoring sensationalism extended the meaning of indecency beyond the reach of legislation. While sex was almost coterminous with indecency, sensationalism was a broad tent, which invoked an expansive concept of the technologically manufactured audience response.[74]

By the 1880s, Jonathan Crary explains, classical ideas of sensation as an interior faculty were replaced by a model of technologically produced effects that could be measured or observed externally. As a product of industrial mass culture, 'sensationalism' became associated with fears of crowds and was highly controversial. It was an aesthetically, morally, and politically loaded term used to dismiss both

---

[73] Goodall, *Advertising*, 1914, 29–30. This study was part of a seminar with Sidney Webb at the London School of Economics. Goodall interviewed advertisers, but may have also drawn on Moran, *Business of Advertising*, 1905, 125, where a similar taxonomy appeared.

[74] On the dominance of sex in understandings of indecency, see Cox et al., *Public Indecency*, ch. 2. Yet, as the authors observe, indecency easily encompassed a broader set of concerns.

particular kinds of representations, and the affective responses they produced, as Ann Cvetkovich observes. Nicholas Daly explains the conceptualization of the audience of sensationalism as a physiologically based theory of viewer response, which appeared in the 1860s in counterpoint to the growth of the mass market as industrial technologies, urbanization, and consumer culture transformed the nature of sensory experience, and the concurrent rise of mass democracy that sparked fears about crowds.[75]

Mass culture was soaked in sensational products like the sensation novel, penny-dreadfuls, and the cheap press, and was therefore well conditioned to both expect and seek sensationalism in adverts too. Contemporary comments on posters referred to advertisers' efforts 'to make the flesh creep...and more adversely affect the nervous system of highly-strung persons than even a visit to the chamber of horrors'.[76] Well before the PCC came into being, *Punch* showed sensational posters wreaking havoc in a street enfolded in their gestures (Figure 6.10).

Figure 6.10 Posters wreaking havoc. *Punch*, 3 December 1887, 262.

---

[75] Crary, *Suspensions of Perception*, ch. 1; Cvetkovich, *Mixed Feelings*, 14; Daly, *Sensation and Modernity*, introduction.

[76] *Billposter*, May 1904, 113 (quoting the *Yorkshire Telegraph and Star*). On the familiarity of both the working and lower-middle classes with sensation as the background for advertising spectacle, see Church, 'Advertising Consumer Goods', 630. And see, for example, the contemporary commentary in 'Sensational Advertising', 1862.

In *Good Boy Seldom*, 1911, Onions demonstrated the automated affective response to sensational print. He depicted a boy lost in contemplation of a theatrical poster in which only the 'gnarled and taloned hands of the terrible Apache could be seen... encircling the neck of an already moribund victim'. The boy reacts physically and psychologically, 'copying in involuntary sympathy' the victim's expression while reading the title aloud.[77]

The era's familiarity with the concept of sensationalism meant that advertising's enchantments could be easily conceptualized in terms even wider than *Hicklin*. However, in practice the PCC reduced both sex and sensationalism to conventional codes, and veered away from a general theory of enchantment by print.

The most prevalent PCC decision was to amend posters so that they were 'rendered innocuous'. The tendency to amend rather than ban was more pronounced with printed posters as opposed to preprint designs, when economic pressure was significant, but in any case, the PCC felt justified and able to intervene. The printer or advertiser was asked to eliminate the 'objectionable part' either with additional printing or by covering it with slips.[78] The logic of these decisions reduced indecency to discrete objects and words taken as conventional meaning. For example, in a 'Face at the Window' poster, a dagger was removed from the hand of one figure, a scar from the hand of another, and an 'objectionable lettering at foot'; in 'Mysteries of the Thames', a broken bottle, blood, and the motto were all removed; covering the dagger in a 'Brave Hearts' poster with a slip bearing the word 'matinee' was not enough: a new print without dagger was required; in 'What a Woman did', a bed was painted out of a bedroom scene; in 'Queen of the Night', the 'red-hot end' of tongs was obliterated with instructions not to reprint; in 'Transit of Venus', the right breast of the 'recumbent female figure' was obscured; in 'Rogues and Vagabonds', two men holding pistols close to each other's heads were left without weapons.[79] The committee treated objects and words like codes for sex and sensation. The working assumption was that removing the code overcame the problem of viewer arousal. Amended results

---

[77] Onions, *Good Boy Seldom*, 1911, 42.

[78] United Billposters' Association, *Posters Condemned*, 1904. Between 1902 and 1909, the PCC examined 174 posters, approved seventy (roughly 40 per cent), amended eighty-one (47 per cent), and banned twenty-three (13 per cent). It also examined seventy-three sketches, approved sixteen (roughly 22 per cent), amended twenty-nine (39 per cent), and banned twenty-nine (39 per cent). It occasionally allowed amendments in an outstanding stock of posters with the additional request not to reprint. Reportedly, decisions to amend became even more dominant over time. By 1909 the PCC mostly recommended corrections. *AW*, September 1909, 387–8.

Pressure to approve printed posters was also evident in the joint committee on stock posters (see note 59). It examined 113 posters between 1901 and 1904, approved fifty-four (roughly 48 per cent), amended twenty-three (20 per cent), and banned thirty-six (32 per cent). The joint committee worked by banning but then allowing printers to propose changes. Banned posters were those that printers did not choose to resubmit. Some posters approved in the joint committee were later banned by the PCC. *Billposter*, January 1904, 63; *Billposter*, February 1904, 71; *Yorkshire Evening Post*, 4 September 1902, 3.

[79] *Billposter*, January 1904, 63; *Billposter*, December 1904, 131; *Billposter*, April 1905, 226.

seemed ridiculous to critics, but the regulative cultural massage was serious and was actually reinforced by criticism. Both censors and critics agreed that the devil was in the details and channelled the heat away from a generalized theory of influence.

Banned posters needed a more complex analysis, yet here too the censoring mind worked by reduction to codes. In a 1909 article about the PCC's work, Cyril Sheldon described some banned posters with graphic detail. One was 'a poster titled "Lady Satan," showing a woman strung up by her wrists to a frame, stripped to the waist, and having weals on her back, her naked feet extending towards a brazier, with another woman at the left of the picture with a cat-o'-nine tails in her right hand.' He did not show the image but this would appear to be a stock design censored already in 1902 (Figure 6.11). It is easy to see the eroticized violence that led to censorship. In Sheldon's rendering, it was a list of discrete things. He implied that there were too many of them to start amending, but refrained from providing a general account of the poster's presumed effect.[80] Of course, eroticism did not necessarily involve enchantment, nor should we assume generally that every affective reaction to adverts meant enchantment. The point is simply the expansive potential to conceptualize advertising's subliminal appeals and consumers' imaginative and sensual responses. The search for conventional codes evaded any discussion.

Because the PCC worked through discrete objects, it often left advertisers in the dark. They were not given general guidelines and had 'no appeal from Caesar'. One theatre manager was dismayed to find two of his 'best pictorials' censored without explanation. He could not understand what was offensive because he followed the code method: 'All daggers, revolvers and blood have been religiously kept out, though the play is a drama.' Another advertiser prepared to meet the code if required: he published a poster in which 'a military officer is taking a farewell embrace of his wife, who has a child in her arms.' As self-insurance he prepared 'the marriage and birth certificates of mother and daughter... ready to affix to the pictorial on the first sign of danger...' These advertisers were perhaps feigning naiveté, but certainly both the committee and its critics shared the comfort of discussing trees rather than forests.[81]

In 1900 the *Poster* raged about the committee's censorship of an advert by Mosnar Yendis (Sidney Lewis Ransom) in Figure 6.12. As the journal put it, the statue was undraped but 'we have occasionally seen undraped figures in our museums and art galleries, and we may yet see the authorities personally supervising the hanging of flannel petticoats on figures at the Academy.'[82] Attacks on

[80] *AW*, September 1909, 388.
[81] Marriott Watson, *Stage*, 31 December 1903, 27; Frank Denman-Wood, *Stage*, 14 January 1904, 10; William Bourne, *Stage*, 9 February 1905, 11; *Stage*, 14 January 1904, 12; *Billposter*, December 1904, 183; *Stage*, 9 February 1905, 11.
[82] *Poster*, January 1900, 226–7.

Figure 6.11 Censored poster, 1902. Maurice Rickards, *Banned Posters* (London: Evelyn, Adams & Mackay, 1969), 14 (text removed, AR).

the high/low distinction in censorship were standard, with easy gains for self-proclaimed liberals who wrote against 'prudes'.[83] The PCC did not object. Instead, it assumed the apparently conservative position that 'the hoardings of

[83] Rogers, *Book of the Poster*, 1901, 47. Rogers was a poster designer, advertiser, and collector. He also complained about Yendis's censorship.

the street have infinitely greater influence than the walls of the gallery.' The galleries of the people had to take account of a 'miscellaneous view', which included youth and people that were not 'sound, healthy-minded', and was involuntary; therefore, nudity was out of the question. The PCC purposely self-branded as overcautious and censored even the occasional Royal Academician. It was a sign of its success that the NVA saw it as a satisfying result of the Zaeo campaign, and regularly contacted it with censorship requests.[84] For the broader cultural framing of advertising, this conservatism checked the discussion of influence, particularly the role of affect and imagination in advertising. The cheeky humour in Yendis's work, which played with advertising's license to blend high and low, needed no analysis given the PCC's focus on nudity as code. Yendis had a gentleman, possibly—but not certainly—staring at the forward-thrusted fig-leaved genitals of a classical figure, in an advert for a 'home trainer for physical culture', with rigid male guards in background. The homo-erotic reference and the complexity of potential encounters with the advert on hoardings were left without comment while the *Poster* and the PCC disputed the basic objection to the nude body.

Even as the committee failed to satisfy critics on the liberal end—who were anyway less of a problem because they did not tend to acknowledge the agency of print objects[85]—its reliance on codes successfully contained the debate. Meanwhile, active imaginations were never limited to lists of objects and words, hence, for example, the excited response to a Nestlé poster (Figure 6.13), which staged a different kind of erotic encounter and reportedly 'hit the public taste very much'. Sexual imaginations could easily find routes for proliferation.[86] How arousal occurred in encounters with adverts, what kinds of arousal were possible, and what they implied for the way an advertising economy and culture worked, were not explained but rather replaced with conventional codes.

The third category of censorship, of offences to religious sensibilities, essentially recast historical prohibitions on blasphemy. PCC records suggest that it was marginal, but the occasional demon in church or horrors of the cross for sale (Figure 6.14) were censored.[87] Here too a search for conventional symbols of religiosity was clear. This reduction avoided the broader phenomenon we have seen in previous chapters: whether or not adverts included religious symbols, they

---

[84] *Pall Mall Gazette*, 3 October 1890, 1; *Billposter*, May 1903, 118–19. When the PCC censored a John Hassall poster for the Whitney Theatre showing an officer strangling a man, one newspaper thought it could focus on someone other than 'one of the cleverest artists of the day'. *Gloucester Citizen*, 11 May 1912, 3. On the PCC-NVA cooperation, see *Times*, 16 May 1906, 5; Coote, *Romance of Philanthropy*, 1916, 70; Green and Karolides, *Encyclopedia of Censorship*, 378.
[85] Samalin, *Masses Are Revolting*, ch. 5.
[86] *AW*, March 1905, 358; Foucault, *History of Sexuality*, 78.
[87] *Billposter*, December 1909, 70; *Billposter*, May 1903, 122.

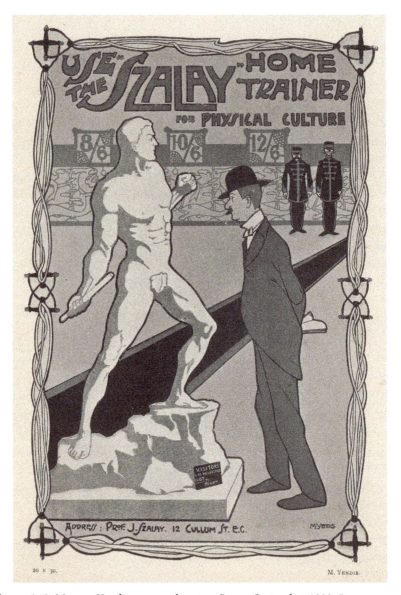

Figure 6.12 Mosnar Yendis, censored poster. *Poster*, September 1899, 5.

Figure 6.13 G. Lackeray, Nestlé poster. Erotic encounters did not need nude, nor, necessarily, human figures. The advert played on a nursery rhyme that circulated in multiple versions:

>Where are you going, my pretty maid?
>I'm going a milking, sir, she said.
>May I go with you, my pretty maid?
>You're kindly welcome, sir, she said.
>What is your fortune, my pretty maid?
>My face is my fortune, sir, she said.
>Then I won't marry you, my pretty maid.
>Nobody asked you, sir, she said.

presented a competing source of enchantment to religion. In PCC practice, images and texts of worship were admittedly problematic because of their express link between enchantment and commercial entertainment, but everything else was salvaged by implication.

Figure 6.14 The horrors of the cross. United Billposters' Association, *Posters Condemned by Censorship Committee of the United Billposters Association* (London: Burton, c.1904).

* * *

Efforts to treat adverts as conventional codes were even more urgent for censors of abortion advertising, who searched for facts that satisfied standards of criminality. Here the focus was not images but text, and the trouble was that texts seemed innocent. The Post Office, for example, refused to suppress adverts that passed under its hands because it did not hold them indecent 'apart from the language in which they are couched'. Censors assumed that there was a clear truth to be unearthed. Their approach narrowed the idea of influence by print to a concept of criminally coded language.[88] Just as the PCC searched for conventional images, here a search for the conventional meaning of words was underway in what amounted to a detective mission.

In 1898, shortly before the Chrimes scandal, Darling J presided over the breach-of-contract case of *Owen v Greenberg*. This was a suit against the advertising agent of *Pick-Me-Up*. Like many other newspapers, *Pick-Me-Up* published adverts for Allen's cure (see Figure 6.7, bottom). The advertiser, whose real name was Edward Owen, paid in advance, but when the journal changed hands the new owners argued that the adverts marketed abortifacients and were therefore immoral and illegal. Owen sued the agent, who defended that although he did not realize it in advance, the contract between them was unenforceable because the adverts were immoral. What were the adverts about? Darling J was not surprised to see that they did not mention abortion, because if you advertised something illegal you would use 'very guarded terms'. There was, however, a hidden truth. The next step was to search for clues. Darling noted a statement that appeared in some of Owen's adverts that every hour was of importance, which 'pointed to pregnancy'. The jury took up the clue and decided that Owen was advertising abortifacients, and so he lost.[89]

Owen became useful for the *Lancet*'s campaign launched at the end of that year with the same commitment to decoding, but its utility was paradoxical. The *Lancet* relied on the case to tell newspapers that they could stop advertising female pills without being exposed to breach of contract claims. However, the exposure only arose because it was *not* clear that the adverts were about abortion. Aware of the interpretive conundrum, the *Lancet* set out to show that the relationship of female-pills adverts to abortions was a verifiable fact. It was going to 'ascertain with certainty whether the business of selling these nostrums was of the nature which in our view the advertisements suggested...or whether the business was correctly indicated by that...which [is]...rather a thin veil designed to protect it from too curious observation'. The phrasing had a wish-fulfilling character because both interpretive options led to a single answer: abortion adverts. The task was to show how the code worked.[90]

How would you 'ascertain with certainty' the uncertain? Like the Chrimes' adverts, many referred to the mysterious code of obstructions and irregularities (Figure 6.15).

---

[88] Select Committee on Lotteries and Indecent Advertisements, 1908, Appendix B, paper by Post Office solicitor Robert Hunter.
[89] *Owen* (1898). [90] *Lancet*, 10 December 1898, 1570–1.

SPECIAL TO LADIES.

A GENUINE REMEDY
to all who wish for a
SAFE AND CERTAIN
means of removing all
OBSTRUCTIONS & IRREGULARITIES.

Thousands of cases in which relief has been obtained in a few hours. No case hopeless, as Mrs. W. writes: "BY ADOPTING YOUR TREATMENT MY TROUBLE AND ANXIETY WAS AT AN END WITHIN TWENTY-FOUR HOURS, AFTER FOUR MONTHS OF HOPELESS WRETCHEDNESS AND CONTINUAL DISAPPOINTMENT, to my intense joy and surprise."
A sworn guarantee is enclosed with all testimonials and medicine

A GRAND OFFER.

For the next few weeks the 4s. 9d. bottle, which is usually sufficient for any case, will be sent post free from observation for

2s. 6d.

This special offer should induce all sufferers to give it a trial.
Write privately at once to—

Mrs. W. P.,
145. Stockwell Rd., London. S.W.

Figure 6.15 Advertisement for remedy to remove all obstructions and irregularities. *Illustrated Police News*, 2 October 1897, 10.

Presumably, the language referred to female sexual regularity, that is, the monthly period. Could fixing irregularity mean getting back your period? Could 'obstructions' mean foetuses obstructing the period? Possibly. The *Lancet* argued that the context for interpretation was sex generally. There was a frequent relation, it posited, between adverts concerning irregularities and everything sexual: impotence, venereal diseases, indecent photos, and indecent literature. But there was also an alternative interpretive context for female adverts, in the field of household remedies that had long promised to remove irregularities, from 'lowness of spirits' to 'weakness of the solids'. Advertisers consciously played on the ambiguity between quackery's promises of good health and references to irregularities.[91]

Even if you won the argument that irregularities were a code for menstruation, still medicines for regular menstruation could mean two diametrically opposed things: abortion, or reproduction. In efforts to penetrate this projection of a thing and its opposite, the *Lancet* advocated an 'inference from the circumstances of sale and from the interpretation of the advertisement or of the documentary matter

[91] *Lancet*, 8 July 1899, 11; *Lancet*, 17 December 1898, 1651; Widow Welch's Female Pill advert, *Hull Packet*, 28 November 1841, 2. Ambiguity was exemplified by Beecham: his adverts often referred to 'irregularity', which he insisted meant primarily constipation. Joseph Beecham's testimony, Select Committee on Patent Medicines, 1914.

accompanying it when sold'. The medical elite decided to obtain more information from advertisers. Male medical professionals adopted advertising practices of conjured identities and became female characters in the name of scientific progress. If advertisers posed as 'Lady Montrose' and 'Widow Welch', doctors pretended to be unmarried maidservants in trouble and 'plump' married women with a morning sickness. In response they were showered with pills, testimonials, and advice booklets. Some advertisers revealed clear intentions to assist with abortion, but not everyone. Others sent texts about menstruation stimulants that could be innocent. Even worse, many advertisers warned that the medicine must not be used by pregnant women because it could cause abortion. This only confirmed the suspicions of some commentators. Why would you warn someone not to use a medicine if they were pregnant, unless you clearly wanted them to use it in that case? Yet the *Lancet* saw that ambiguity remained.[92]

Other clues were forthcoming. For example, some advertisers recommended rigorous sport while taking the medicines. Sport was thought to induce miscarriage but of course it was also good for frail women who needed a health boost. When an exasperated *Lancet* writer had enough of smokescreens, he asked an advertiser explicitly for an abortifacient. Alas, he was referred to 'consult a medical man'. The journal commented, '[it] seems to us a fairly impudent suggestion'. However, the only way to have a legal abortion was for a doctor to find that it was medically necessary. Not very impudent after all.[93]

Another source of evidence was the testimonials in adverts. The *Lancet* offered two contradictory readings. One was that the testimonials were true and revealed an illegal trade. It provided an interesting explanation: according to medical data, few women suffered from irregular periods for any reason except pregnancy. As it was put to the 1908 committee, the trade in cures for irregular menstruation (amenorrhoea) 'does not exist and never has existed but has been conjured into imaginary existence'; therefore, the large numbers of testimonials must have spoken to an industry of abortion. Alas, here too a reversal of meaning was at the tips of your fingers. In a state of illegality, women seeking abortions were vulnerable consumers and easily pressured into signing fake testimonials. The *Lancet* itself also had an interest in arguing that testimonials were fake as part of its argument that quack medicines were useless. We have seen suspicions of testimonials in Chapter 4, but in this case another supportive argument was particularly interesting. The *Lancet* noted that testimonials expressed too much gratitude, which was suspicious because doctors never received such grateful

---

[92] *Lancet*, 17 December 1898, 1652; *Lancet*, 10 December 1898, 1571. An ironic interpretation of warnings against the use of pills during pregnancy was prevalent; for example, Courtenay, *Revelations of Quacks*, 1877, 107. Courtenay was a member of the Royal College of Surgeons. See also P. Bryne, Assistant Under-Secretary of State, Select Committee on Lotteries and Indecent Advertisements, 1908, q. 252.

[93] *Lancet*, 24 December 1898, 1724.

letters. The interpretation was equivocal as it also revealed the estrangement of doctors from women whom they refused to help. Conceivably, women *were* deeply grateful to traders in abortifacients.[94] Overall, interpretations of testimonials did not clear the picture any more than the advertising discourse of 'irregularities' did.

Assuming that you read female medicine adverts as references to abortion, another ambiguity was forthcoming: were the commodities in fact abortifacients? As we saw in Chapter 4, the scientific answer turned to chemical analyses. The *Lancet* showed that many pills were empty of active ingredients, as was also the case with the Chrimes brothers. Yet, some medicines contained active ingredients or could produce abortion by acting on neighbouring organs or through poisonous doses. The *Lancet* had an interest in highlighting those too. As Angus McLaren observes, successes upset doctors as much as failures.[95] For desperate consumers, the expanses of the unknown were worth exploring.

In any case, this all left the question still hanging: were the circulating adverts in fact marketing abortifacients? To borrow a phrase from Bruno Latour, female medicine adverts functioned as a chamber for the avoidance of certainty. Latour applies the metaphor to a legal functionary who kept producing objections to propositions so as ultimately to produce objectivity.[96] However, in this case the opposite occurred: uncertainty did not serve objectivity, it was endemic. The *Lancet* was committed to the assumption of the code, but with no code forthcoming it sought women readers who would confirm what the adverts meant for them.

Indecency as Historical Reader Response

The *Lancet*'s efforts of interpretation revealed the challenges of a decoding approach to adverts. An alternative reductionist route was to deflect the meaning of indecency to actual historical readers. If you could not prove that the advert referred to abortion, you could alternatively prove that it meant abortion for specific consumers. Following *Chrimes*, the *Lancet* pointed to readers' response as proof of indecency. It argued that the fact that hundreds of women succumbed to blackmail proved that consumers of medicines for irregularities bought them in the hope of procuring abortion. Again, there was an alternative interpretation: innocent women could be blackmailed simply because they knew it would be difficult to refute the accusation. The *Lancet* dismissed this alternative, but it was still in the dark.[97] A momentary success finally came when women were simply asked.

---

[94] *Lancet*, 11 March 1899, 718; *Lancet*, 24 June 1899, 1739; *Lancet*, 31 October 1908, 1308; *Lancet*, 10 December 1898, 1571.
[95] *Lancet*, 30 December 1899, 1845; McLaren, *Birth Control*, 240–1.
[96] Latour, 'Scientific Objects and Legal Objectivity'. [97] *Lancet*, 31 December 1898, 1807.

Under the *Lancet*'s pressure, the Public Prosecution charged William Brown and four accomplices with inciting women to abortion by advertising Madame Frain's Female Pills. The business had a notorious history with the law as deaths of women were connected with its medicines, but until that point there were no convictions.[98] At the Worship Street Police Court, the prosecutor linked advertising 'suggestion' with what consumers believed, clearly perceiving that success depended on showing print–reader interaction. The adverts again showed suspicious clues: they contained 'bold' suggestions about strong, extra strong, and special pills. They also contained testimonials that were all from married women. The prosecutor then called two single and four married women to testify to using the medicine when pregnant. Apparently, one child was stillborn. In another case a husband gave a testimonial about success. The evidence is hard to interpret because reports were partial and women were speaking obliquely under advice to avoid self-incrimination. However, the theory of adverts as codes was clearly insufficient; therefore, the analysis of indecent adverts shifted to real consumers whose responses provided concrete manifestations of indecency.[99]

The magistrate dismissed the charges because the pills were harmless, but the Attorney General wanted a decision from an upper court and took the case to the Old Bailey.[100] The legal dilemma reverted to the criminal knowledge of Brown and his partners on drug efficacy. Darling J thought that if the defendants knew that an overdose could be effective and recommended high doses, that was enough to convict. He warned newspapers that if they did not stop publishing 'advertisements of this kind' they would soon occupy the accused chair. The Newspaper Society Circular noted the 'significant warning'.[101] For some time, a decline in female medicine adverts was noticeable despite the fact that no newspaper had been charged, but the effect was short-lived.[102] The 1908 committee therefore

---

[98] The most recent event was only a few months earlier, in March 1899, when the business was criticized at an inquest of a woman who died after an attempted abortion, but nothing could be proved. *Lancet*, 24 June 1899, 1739.

[99] *Illustrated Police Budget*, 8 July 1899, 6 and 15 July 1899, 10; *Nottinghamshire Guardian*, 15 July 1899, 5; *People*, 9 July 1899, 5.

[100] He used a procedure under the Vexatious Indictments Act, 1859, which allowed him to continue to trial despite a magistrate's refusal. See House of Commons Returns, Prosecution of Offences Acts, 1900, 14–15. *Brown and others* (1899).

[101] *Times*, 24 November 1899, 15; *Times*, 23 November 1899, 15; *Lloyd's Weekly*, 26 November 1899, 3; *Pall Mall Gazette*, 27 November 1899, 2; *Dundee Courier*, 28 November 1899, 3; *NSC*, January 1900, 7. Darling repeated the warning some months later in a breach of promise case in which a pregnant woman became ill after taking pills that her fiancé bought from an advertiser. *Lancet*, 31 March 1900, 950.

[102] The fall was reported to the 1908 committee, Select Committee on Lotteries and Indecent Advertisements, 1908, q. 449. Graph 6.1 confirms it. It compares the category of adverts containing the terms 'female' and 'remedy' in the British Newspaper Archive, with the category of adverts containing the term 'remedy'. There are many limitations to results, but for our purposes it is enough that the limitations are equally applicable in both categories. As the graph shows, the categories generally reflected the same trends, but there is an interesting difference: in 1900 and just after, the decline in female remedy adverts in relation to the average correlation between the categories (Pearson

recommended new legislation on indecent adverts to forbid 'advertisement and sale of drugs or articles which might reasonably be considered as designed for promoting miscarriage or for procuring abortion'. Bills that added this category to the definition of indecent adverts were promoted over the next decade but did not pass. As McLaren notes, increased reportage on abortion had the opposite effect. It led social observers to address working women's attitudes to maternity and fuelled family-planning movements. The definition of female-pill adverts as indecent had become even more controversial and was never settled.[103]

For the question of enchantment by advertising, the importance of this historical episode was the potential theorization of consumer interactions with adverts. While comments routinely assumed that enticing language was effective, and that desperation made women indiscriminate, the assumption remained in background. The *Lancet* and the public prosecution turned to women only to support the rationalist proposition that the adverts were a conventional code that consumers understood. When *Brown* reached the Old Bailey, the meaning of the adverts was already taken for granted. In other words, the turn to women did not become an opportunity for a discussion of influence, suggestion, or imagination.

correlation coefficient) is significant, and the downward trajectory afterwards remains less well correlated than before, as the 'diff' line suggests.

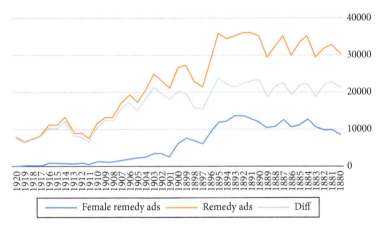

Graph 6.1 Relative change in the occurrence of advertisements with 'female' + 'remedy' compared with advertisements with 'remedy'. BNA data as of June 2019.

[103] Select Committee on Lotteries and Indecent Advertisements, 1908, s. 44; McLaren, *Birth Control*, 234. For legislative attempts, see, for example, Morality Bill H.C. 179, 1910; Criminal Law Amendment Bill H.C. 7, 1917. On controversy, see, for example, the Earl of Onslow, Lords Sitting, 9 March 1921.

It was another face of the same reductionist evasion. Even the process of incitement, which was the formal legal category at stake, was not argued as far as records reveal. How persuasion worked, what role dreams had, what it meant to 'capture' a consumer by an advert as the *Lancet* put it, all these did not receive attention while the role of adverts as codes remained the main preoccupation.[104]

A similar phenomenon was apparent in poster censorship, where we can observe it on a more systemic scale.

* * *

Consumer response was a useful justification for censorship when conventional codes were not enough to explain indecency. Codes were insufficient because advertising's effects were a combination of form and content, and because neither form nor content were reducible to discrete objects. The large size of posters, their colourful presence outdoors, and their accumulation were immersive, a point we can grasp, for example, in the proportions revealed in Figure 6.16 between persons and posters (similarly, Figure 0.2, top). Hoardings immersed viewers in experiences that the commodities advertised did not provide. This was true even in the case of theatres and music halls. As one county court judge put it, 'everyone knew how unlike the actual incidents the posters outside a theatre or other places of entertainment were.' Ironically, he explained the imaginative spectacle in a theatre as a step down from its advertisement: when you went inside you were 'disillusioned'.[105] For the manager of the Theatre Royal, 'sensational drama...is practically useless without sensational posters.' Adverts supplied excitement beyond the confines of walls and the limits of show time, in the advert-ridden public sphere. The trade was aware of these effects, yet the PCC did not censor adverts on the basis of size, colour, location, or broader visual context.[106] Matters of exhibition remained an accepted background while the committee focused on content, a point reinforced in the distribution of small versions of banned posters within the trade. These miniatures shifted attention away from the sensationalism of posters as form, to the specificity of content, reducing it to discrete occurrences.

Even on the level of content, the committee clearly perceived effects it did not articulate as it refused to explain decisions. The opening line of *Posters Condemned* clarified the point: 'The illustrations in this volume may safely be

---

[104] *Lancet*, 2 December 1899, 1540.
[105] *Moore* (1907), 5, Woolfall J. The comment explained why he rejected the defence of a performer who refused to pay for posters because they were unlike him. This was a widespread view. For example, one commentator thought that the disillusion must make adverts ineffective, *Globe*, 9 August 1905, while another described posters as going 'beyond actual stage-presentment', *Sheffield Daily Telegraph*, 2 April 1904, 8.
[106] *Yorkshire Evening Post*, 4 September 1902, 3. A reported exception was women's tights, which the PCC wanted in colours that could not be mistaken for skin. Zaeo continued to loom large. *Billposter*, May 1903, 122. The suspect colours were pink, pale green, and mauve. The writer recommended black, blue, crimson, orange, dark green, purple, or plain white to pass muster.

Figure 6.16 Frank H. Roberts, hoarding, revealing proportions of humans to posters. c.1900s.

left to speak for themselves.' Difficult cases were characterized, the *Billposter* explained, not by what was displayed 'but rather in that they suppress and yet suggest'.[107] Particularly revealing were three of the 'least objectionable' cases of censorship that Sheldon showed (Figure 6.17). The censored images played on the enchanting power of the gaze. Anxieties about the hypnotic gaze assumed a pitch in the last decade of the nineteenth century, with concerns about influence leading to over-passionate and impulsive publics. As Pamela Thurschwell observes, the hypnotizing villain became a staple of fin-de-siècle culture. Professional advice to advertisers confirmed that there was 'no device for arresting attention...more certain...than...the human eye looking straight at you...These eyes...catch the eye and impress the mind.' With no recorded explanation the committee refused these images of arresting heads and Gothic references, which did not depict a scene of violence nor relied on conventional eroticism, but rather invoked directly and boldly the potential of enchantment by posters through object–subject interaction.[108] Indeed, the uncanny generally attracted opposition, as other censored images reveal (Figure 6.18).

The PCC recognized enchantment but evaded a detailed analysis of its workings. When discrete objects like knives and nudes were not enough to justify a censorship decision, the strategy of referencing 'public opinion' kicked in. Just as anti-abortionists asked women what they saw in adverts, so here 'the public' became a touchstone of indecency, with the result that no one had to actually theorize enchantment in advertising. Far from a systemic presence, it was reduced to observed responses to discrete posters.

The *Billposter* was obsessive with monitoring public responses and getting a feel of the critical environment, which in turn became an independent reason for censorship. The PCC defined its standard as 'the healthy mean of public opinion', avoiding demands of 'extremists' and taking a stand 'at the side of the preponderance of right-minded persons'. As Goodall put it, the PCC's principles of censorship were capable of various interpretations but 'the bill-posters have used their best judgment as citizens of the world...' The committee self-represented as accommodating the public mood. To be sure, it *was* interested in appeasing the public, but the deeper effect of this position was to keep advertising clear of the debate about enchantment in popular culture.[109] Just as the *Lancet* and the *Brown*

---

[107] United Billposters' Association, *Posters Condemned*, 1904, 2; *Billposter*, May 1903, 119.
[108] Winter, *Mesmerized*, ch. 12; Thurschwell, *Literature, Technology*, 8; Pick, *Svengali's Web*; *AW*, July 1908, 184. As Winter notes, these visions replaced a more benign view of mesmerists in mid-century.
[109] United Billposters' Association, *Posters Condemned*, 1904, 3; Goodall, *Advertising*, 1914, 29–30. See also, for example, *Billposter*, February 1904, 70–2. Censors' deflection of decisions to public opinion was a prevalent tactic more broadly. Allison Wee's study of Home Office censorship of indecency finds that it did not necessarily examine the censored texts, but rather tracked public opinion about them. Wee, *Trials and Eros*, 75, 69.

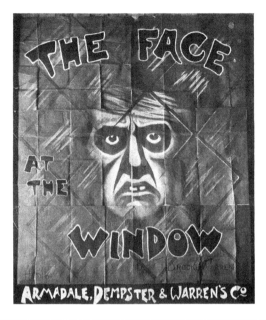
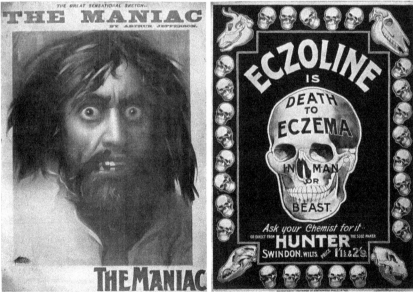

Figure 6.17 Three of 'the least objectionable' posters censored by the Billposters Censorship Committee according to Cyril Sheldon, *Advertising World*, September 1909, 386. United Billposters' Association, *Posters Condemned by Censorship Committee of the United Billposters Association* (London: Burton, c.1904).

GAMBLING, INDECENCY, AND THE BOUNDED REALMS OF ENCHANTMENT 315

Figure 6.18 Censored posters. The censorship of 'Because I Love You' posters led to heated controversy. United Billposters' Association, *Posters Condemned by Censorship Committee of the United Billposters Association* (London: Burton, c.1904).

prosecution staged pregnant consumers when faced with the imaginative complexities of adverts, so here observations of 'public sentiment' replaced the complexities of poster influence.

Overall, reductions that treated adverts as codes or deflected the meaning of influence to historical readers, trod a fine line between accepting the theory that popular print could enchant, and evading the implications for advertising as a system.

Enchantment as Expertise

I have been examining reductionist practices that limited the conceptual reach of theories of enchantment. This section observes a different approach, peculiar to professionalizing advertisers, in which enchantment was treated as planned and controlled by experts. From this perspective, you did not have to examine reception, because you could recognize enchanting power as a professional. As Daly observes, the other side of the spectre of excited masses was the fantasy of engineering their responses.[110] Chapter 7 is dedicated to this theory of professional advertising and explains its emergence. This section only examines one aspect, which was rooted specifically in poster censorship. From the perspective of this chapter, the claim of expertise was yet another way of preventing the theory of print influence from applying to advertising at large. Experts claimed they could recognize and prevent it, and demanded cultural trust that they succeeded. Their claim rested on the legal structure of poster censorship as private ordering.

The idea of expertise gained much of its power from the fact that censorship occurred beyond the public purview. The trade was self-congratulatory about removing 'objectionable posters' without public attention, and was considered more effective than other censors such as licensing committees. The universal problem of public censors was and remains that they undermine their own goals by making their targets more alluring. The heightened popularity of Zaeo's pictures was just one example of this problem, which judicial bodies and legislators struggled with. A regular solution in law was not to exhibit or repeat obscene and indecent content. For this reason, for example, the Old Bailey report of the Chrimes case was technical and merely noted: 'The particulars of this case are unfit for publication.'[111] However, these strategies only invited attention to the missing centres of conversations, and often sent sales spiralling up. Private legal power did not have this problem because there was no public scrutiny. Billposters

---

[110] Daly, *Sensation and Modernity*, 8.
[111] *Bradford Daily Telegraph*, 5 September 1902, 4; *Chrimes* (1898). For a discussion of the dilemma, see, for example, Blumberg, 'Obscenity and Marginality'.

therefore presented their committee as an organization that overcame the paradigmatic trap of censorship. The other side of the same coin was that the PCC demanded a blind trust in its discretion. The dissemination of banned posters within the trade created a visual counter-imagination to the decent accessible only to insiders, which appeared to shock outside observers. One amazed journalist described 'a mass of sensational designs', and another 'a chamber of horrors'. The accumulating stock reinforced itself as billposters developed a consciousness of expertise on enchanting posters. Vis-à-vis the public, the trade claimed an exclusive understanding and an ability to control influence, shielding 'humanity from the consequences of its own frailty'.[112]

Censorship was there to control all types of imaginative digressions by advert viewers and claimed to keep hoardings free from suggestiveness, yet even on the level of individual adverts—to say nothing about the level of accumulation—this assumption of mastery was precarious. Complaints about posters often revealed that enchantment was not controllable. While the trade was comfortable with complaints that it was over-zealous, it lost equanimity with critics who still found faults with posters. In those cases, the *Billposter* gave up all sophistication in understanding suggestiveness, forgot its commitment to cater to 'varied' sensibilities, and reverted to the traditional impatience of advertisers with their field's ever-digressing cultural status:

> perhaps there is no representation – be it animal, vegetable or mineral – that would fail to convey an insinuation of evil to some over-anxious, morbid mind... It is none of our business to discover how this niggling over nonsensical details comes about. We cannot get into the brain pans and nerve-sheaths of these fantastically sensitive people and decide how they came into this lamentable condition... for after all this world is designed for the use and enjoyment of healthy people...[113]

Similarly, there was no end to the trade's frustration when Ada Ballin, scholar, editor, and dress reformer known for her championship of rational child-rearing, sent a letter to the press criticizing posters. Ballin argued that images of 'deformities and other objects calculated to injure the unborn' led to births of deformed babies by 'impressing the sensitive nerves' of pregnant women. A nation concerned with reducing infant mortality should be more careful, she warned in an effort to tie her censorship proposal with the demographic problem. Although the *Billposter* returned the attack, it also dedicated the lead article of February 1905 to refuting the argument that the hoardings could have any 'seriously prejudicial

---

[112] *St. James's Gazette*, 13 February 1904, 16; *Daily News*, 20 May 1904, 12; *Billposter*, May 1903, 118–19.
[113] *Billposter*, August 1909, 13.

effect' on minds. The heat of its response to an outlandish accusation revealed the need to check the influence debate and claim exclusive expertise in knowing where it endured, and how it worked.[114]

As we will see in Chapter 7, in the same years professional advertisers were developing theories of expertise that increasingly centred on consumers and adopted the psychological vocabularies of the mind. In this context, enchantment was theorized as inherent to the work of advertising. The idea of a responsible expertise on non-rational influence, theorized as inseparable from reason rather than oppositional to it, was taking off. Meanwhile, in the debate about indecency, the PCC argued that dangerous enchantment was off the table, and gained a cultural hearing.

Conclusion

Previous chapters demonstrated a persistent focus of cultural legal debates on advertising's rationalizing effects. The consequence was criticisms and anxieties about the shortfalls of advertising as a rationalizing force. The other side of the same coin was a persistent failure to account for the role of enchantment. Without the histories of gambling and indecency, this could be explained away simply by the contingencies of historical development. Because advertising was conceptualized through boundary work—both legitimized and criticized in its relationships to the fields of news, art, and science—the evaluative criteria applied were those promoted by the dominant voices in each debate. The values of information, beauty, and scientific knowledge, as promoted in contemporary debates, were part of discourses of modern disenchantment. As a result, so the argument would go, enchantment was predictably under-conceptualized. Yet this explanation is unsatisfying. Common patterns across otherwise divergent debates cast doubt on its validity. This chapter puts it to rest, for here were two topical cultural concerns in which theories of enchantment were forefront and informed public and private legal responses to advertising. If enchantment remained marginal here, this could not have been the result of the contingencies of debate. If that dog still did not bark, the silence merits attention.

Admittedly, the theories of enchantment developed for gambling and indecency were limited as accounts of advertising for reasons discussed at the beginning of this chapter, yet they had an expansive potential. Their close dialogue with the rise of commercial mass culture and its perception as dangerous, as well as their abstract logic, *could* be extended to explain important elements in advertising's appeals and its cultural effects. The legal definition of gambling trod an unstable line between

[114] *Daily News*, 11 January 1905, 3; *Billposter*, February 1905, 199–200.

disenchantment and enchantment in the distinction between chance and skill, and between commodities and advertisements, while that of indecency had an expansive potential because its theory of influence by print was easy to apply to multiple content-types. Yet, legal analyses of advertising ultimately shielded it from a systemic association with enchantment.

The concrete motivations of public and private actors for delimiting the reach of enchantment theory were local and varied, determined by their institutional and ideological contexts. Actors who examined prize-competitions, posters, and abortion adverts had no unifying goals, and their institutional characteristics as wielders of legal power corresponded to different levels of organization. Judicial decisions on gambling were a broad legal scene set within pressures on courts to define legitimate capitalist activity and the limits of the mass market. Industry censorship of posters was a tight trade-controlled organization aiming to protect advertising from aspiring regulators and win public approval. Anti-abortionism was a diffuse phenomenon that linked medical and legal professionals and administrators who wanted to unearth the truth of women's reproduction, informed by a host of concerns about religion, gender, medicine, and imperialism. Yet all actors justified their decisions by aligning themselves with rationalist viewpoints on ideal economic and cultural life. In the context of advertising, they all contributed to a focus on its rational elements—low, banal, or reprehensible though they may have been, over a discussion of enchantment as a characteristic of this system. Enchantment was either domesticated within rationalist perspectives, as when courts described popular advertising-games in terms of poor skills, or its manifestations were prohibited. When prohibition kicked in, the analysis evaded a principled discussion of the ways in which advertising could enchant, and preferred to reduce it to discrete occurrences, such as the conventional symbols of indecency in posters, or evidence of actual attempts to abort pregnancies. The result was that permitted adverts were not examined through the lens of enchantment. The theories of non-rationalism that the era explored for gambling and indecency remained inapplicable to the bulk of advertising.

Read with previous chapters, the histories examined here clarify the extent of cultural commitment to modernity-as-disenchantment. While disenchantment was not a historical reality, it was an active normative enterprise made up of diverse legal investments across British culture. The normative disavowal of enchantment finally became an opportunity for a new definition of expertise in advertising that the next chapter examines. Like a Freudian return of the repressed, enchantment found a place in contained form at the heart of advertising, precisely because legal disavowals left it unaddressed.

7

The Market Enchanters

Professional Advertisers' Self-Branding

By the close of the nineteenth century, advertising professionals were facing a formidable challenge of self-definition.[1] The market for advertising was expanding yet their own significance as service providers, especially the most familiar function of advertising agencies today—planning and creating campaign content—was not obvious to potential clients, or as one put it 'the advertising-man has no real status.'[2] To carve a place for themselves practitioners had to forge the need for their services. They attempted to do so in advertising literature, a genre spanning books, essays, pamphlets, course offerings, and periodical publications dedicated to advertising, which expanded from the mid-1880s and became salient in the early twentieth century. This literature facilitated processes of professionalization, yet more critically and less well appreciated, it was a form of advertising. The genre was speaking not only within the profession but outward to clients, articulating the logic of the industry's existence.[3] Practitioners were partly motivated by internal competition, but more important were shared themes and assumptions. Collectively, they branded advertising in terms of expertise in the human mind. They staged consumers as tough nuts to crack, and the expert as the sorcerer capable of cracking by working magic across the distance between producers and consumers, capturing consumers' attention and altering their desires. This theory of expertise centralized the non-rational mind and in so doing endorsed a psychologized version of enchantment. The process put pressure on ideals of

---

[1] I use 'professionals' and 'practitioners' interchangeably, both as distinguished from end-advertisers. The concept of advertising as a profession was just emerging. Practitioners changed titles: contractors, consultants, canvassers, experts, agents, and more, and were running agencies alongside positions within businesses and other work such as printing and posting. Their scope of work varied dramatically from full-service to nothing but 'farming' a couple of theatre programmes. See generally Nevett, *Advertising in Britain*, chs 4–5. For an example of variations in Glasgow, see *Advertisers' Review*, 15 July 1901, 1.

[2] Fred A. Hunt, *Progressive Advertising*, June 1906, 12.

[3] This is not to say that all literature was intended as advertisement. In particular, the important trade journal, the *Advertising World* founded in 1901 by the Welsh journalist and later newspaper publisher William Berry, declared its independence from advertising agents, printers, newspapers, and engravers. It was nonetheless a prominent voice for professional advertising and a medium for practitioners who addressed a readership of end-advertisers.

volition for it cast doubt on consumer reason and deliberation in everyday economic lives. Practitioners therefore made serious efforts to retain rational consumer capacities as part of their accounts, even as they brought enchantment into the fold. The process also cast doubt on descriptions of the advertising industry itself as a progressive profession, given that it trafficked in the non-rational. Practitioners therefore sought ways of claiming rational mastery even as they self-branded as modern magicians. These efforts, which shaped the image of professional advertisers as market enchanters, are the subject of this chapter.

Advertising literature attempted to reshape an environment that curbed expansions of professional services. Until the close of the nineteenth century, the dominant view of expertise in advertising centred on media placement. Commissions were usually paid by media owners, therefore it was not clear that practitioners really served end-advertisers and identified with their goals, despite their efforts to assure clients.[4] Meanwhile, some businesses were resistant to advertising, and others handled their own advertising without so much as a professional department, and only turned to professionals for discrete services. Many businesses did not believe that a third party could represent their products better than them. If that was not enough, for all end-advertisers, including those who hired agencies or established advertising departments, the meaning of advertising suffered from a contested legitimacy. Practitioners faced the weight of criticisms that were attaining legalized forms, which made it hard to rely on accepted venues of cultural authority. They could not assume a seamless integration of advertising with concepts of knowledge, information, aesthetic progress, and even common morality, and could not draw easily on them to enter and expand markets. While debates were still raging, practitioners saw that they could not win with denials. Their goal was to overcome the field's inferior status: 'the advertiser is often a modern Ishmaelite, every man's hand is against him. The Advertising Agent must devise methods by which he can overcome this feeling of repulsion.'[5]

The starting point was to accept the major criticisms. As we have seen, explanations of why and how advertising 'worked' appeared as negations of worth: it worked by exaggeration, vulgarity, sensation, bias verging on lies. Far

---

[4] The Incorporated Society of Advertisement Consultants, established in 1909 with Thomas Russell as president, tried to change the structural relationship by keeping professionals 'free of [space] brokerage and finance' and charging consultancy fees from clients. This kept many prominent professionals outside the society, including, for example, Charles Frederick Higham, *AW*, November 1911, 648–9, although he apparently succumbed, *Advertiser's Weekly*, 2 August 1913, 71. For a theorization of a double role for agents, as insurers for publishers and advisers for end-advertisers, see *Advertisers' Review*, 3 February 1902, 9–10. On early practitioners' identification with clients despite dependence on newspapers, see Nevett, 'London's Early Advertising Agents'.

[5] Stead, *Art of Advertising*, 1899, 45.

322 THE RISE OF MASS ADVERTISING

from questioning these negations, practitioners recast them as expert advice. They became spokespersons for ideals of truth, factuality, restraint, and aesthetic awareness in advertising. Rhymes printed in 1899 in the transatlantic *Advertising* were typical in their call to avoid exaggeration, be aesthetically gentle, factually accurate, and accept the boundaries of news:

> Once I thought I'd write my ad
> Myself, and make it fine;
> Adjectives superlative,
> Stuck in every line...
> 'Twould draw like a magnet, sure,
> I had not a doubt;
> When I ran a beautiful
> Border roundabout...
> And I straight inserted it,
> So that all could see;
> Top of column, next to where
> Reading matter'd be...
> Though I waited hopefully
> For the biz to hum –
> Not a single customer
> To my store did come...[6]

Businesses were warned not to 'poison the wells of public information' by using editorial columns for advertising, nor antagonize the pubic by using art 'venerated by thousands of cultivated people' in adverts. Proposals circulated for professional action against frauds. A recipe was in the making: 'Take the Good English, Concise Expression, Business Knowledge, and stir... over the fire of human experience until quite hot. Take off carefully any abundance of expression which will have arisen to the top. Sprinkle in crumbs of Originality, and whip the whole together with Attractiveness... Allow the whole to cool in the mould of Truth and Reason, and serve with Brevity.'[7]

Previous chapters have shown practitioners joining the chorus of criticism: the billposting trade led aesthetic reforms and censorship initiatives, and advertising agents defended the independence of the press. Accepting criticisms was not just a defensive battle, but more radically an attempted reversal of their logic. The imaginary counterfactual of criticisms was a world without advertising; therefore, advertising appeared as an interference and perversion of rational progress. By contrast, practitioners accepted criticisms while promoting an opposite imaginary: in their vision, by responding to criticisms advertising would expand. They suggested that the problem was clients' failure to consult professionals. The rhymes in *Advertising* were a dream of the professional's victory:

---

[6] *Advertising*, September 1899, 595.
[7] *Profitable Advertising*, January 1900, 4; Jones, *Handbook on Advertising*, 1912, 25; *AW*, May 1914, 713–15; *AW*, July 1908, 186; *Advertisers' Review*, 4 June 1900, 4 (quoting the *Caterer*).

> But a happy moment brought
> The solution plain;
> Swift I sought a good ad-smith
> To write that ad again.
> ...
> He told in a simple tale
> What I had to sell,
> With a clever cut just to
> Make the thing look well.
> Did it bring me good results?
> Well, now, I should grin;
> Watch the goods a-going out,
> Money coming it.[8]

Having insisted that advertising had no reason to breach the boundaries of other cultural fields and should not violate the values they represented, professional literature had to say what advertising *was*. Good taste, adequate English, truthfulness, moderateness, respectability, these were all necessary, but they were treated across the cultural-legal board at best as inferior simulations of values promoted elsewhere. This only underlined the conceptual vacuum: what *was* expertise in advertising? Moody's advertising agency in Birmingham recognized already in the 1880s: 'we want a new method, which is more difficult to discover than improvements upon old ones.' The author frankly admitted he had no idea. What was, to quote an advert for 'ad specialists', 'advertising *that advertises*'? By the late 1890s professionals were filling the vacuum by claiming a unique knowledge of consumers, which they would come to celebrate as 'the study of that wonderful subject, the human mind.' Expertise in minds became the field's philosopher's stone.[9]

The study of mind was attaining in the same years a disciplinary status that requires a brief introduction, for histories of psychology clarify the close connection between the modern study of mind and enchantment.

As an independent discipline, psychology emerged in the late decades of the nineteenth century. Its history is generally described as a struggle to create a distinct intellectual and institutional identity vis-à-vis philosophy and physiology, in which the non-rational assumed centre stage. As Alex Owen explains, the psychologized self of the nineteenth century marked a break with an earlier Enlightenment legacy focused on the conscious thinking 'I'. The latter, detached from the non-rational spiritual dimension—the soul—was the hallmark of post-Enlightenment culture. In the model of the new self, theological formulations remained subdued, but the soul was exchanged for a secularized non-rational—the unconscious—as integral to the process of self-constitution. The study of the non-rational was not new, but it attained a new diffusion and began to be accommodated rather than suppressed. Investigations of the nature of consciousness, memory, experience, and sensation led to an explosion of interest in questions of psychic subjectivity, for which the

---

[8] *Advertising*, September 1899, 595.
[9] *Advertiser's Guide to Publicity*, 1887, 4; Advertisement by Selkirk-Minns, *Progressive Advertising*, 20 December 1901. 258 (emphasis added); *Advertisers' Pocketbook*, 1913, 1; *Advertisers' Review*, 6 September 1901, 16–17.

concept of a single, stable consciousness seemed inadequate. The 'I' was now a fragmented or multiple creature.[10]

Charles Taylor argues that locating enchantment in the mind, and the mind of humans only, was a disenchanting move in the sense that it removed the possibility of mystery, nonhuman agency, and magic from the world, into the bounded or buffered self. As this chapter shows, for professional advertisers this move was indeed a way to contain unruly manifestations of consumer enchantment. For their culture, it was certainly less alarming than ideas of incalculable forces in the world outside the mind—particularly in the economy. However, locating enchantment in the mind was still ambivalent and not strictly disenchanting, because it turned the mind itself into a supernatural space, in Terry Castle's words.[11]

Some psychological topics appeared to pull towards enchantment more than others. Psychological investigations of paranormal and psychic phenomena were obvious candidates for casting doubt on disenchantment. Freudian psychoanalysis was perhaps the most haunted of all, as Jason Josephson-Storm describes it. Hypnotism too was ambivalent; it essentially recast the mesmerism of old in a scientific garb and demonstrated the precariousness of consciousness. But even topics at the conventional end, such as memory and attention, could not be rid of notions of transcendence and mystery, which they attempted to rationalize. For example, Ian Hacking explains psychological studies of memory—which were central to nascent theories of advertising as we will see—as efforts to scientize the soul. Knowledge about memory came into being as the public forum that addressed that last bastion of thought free from scientific scrutiny. Publications in applied psychology, including the psychology of advertising, were part of this trend. For example, the American psychologist Walter Dill Scott described human sense organs as windows of the soul. He promoted the idea that human economic behaviour was based on emotion or sentiments rather than rationality or logic, and urged the application of psychology to problems of business. In studying consumer motivation, he examined the role of non-rational elements such as impulse and habits as routes to access and influence consumers. Scott was among the most influential early writers on advertising. His articles appeared in the *Advertising World* and his *Psychology of Advertising* was published in Britain in 1909.[12]

If scientizing transcendence was not enough, the models adopted by psychologists were ambivalent also because of their materialism. Because they drew on the

---

[10] Owen, *Place of Enchantment*, 115–20. In addition to the histories referenced later in this chapter, I have drawn on the following: Hearnshaw, *Short History of British Psychology*; Bowler and Morus, *Making Modern Science*; Baker, *Oxford Handbook of the History of Psychology*.

[11] Taylor, *Secular Age*; Castle, 'Phantasmagoria'.

[12] Castle, 'Phantasmagoria'; Josephson-Storm, *Myth of Disenchantment*; Crary, *Suspensions of Perception*, 65–71; Hacking, *Rewriting the Soul*; Scott, *Theory of Advertising*, 1903, 226; Friedman, *Birth of a Salesman*; Schultz and Schultz, *History of Modern Psychology*, ch. 8.

natural sciences, they overturned the two-tiered ontology that separated mind from matter: the active powers of the will no longer transcended material phenomena. The new psychology was therefore plagued with anxieties about volition, which stood on the brink of overdetermination.[13] Psychologists attempted to reconcile their ideas with an ethically meaningful concept of volition that was, as Lorraine Daston puts it, the salvageable part of Christian teaching. For example, some of the heroes of the new psychology, like James Sully, theorized voluntarism as a choice to attend certain mental representations in preference to others. The will was not radically free, but rather free to choose among elements available within the field of consciousness.[14] Thus, both the primacy of matter and the focus on the non-rational challenged ideals of free will.

The resonances of psychology appeared in the language and assumptions of advertising professionals, who began to address psychological topics like instincts, habits, suggestibility, susceptibly to command, and unconscious association. It is tempting to treat the process teleologically as a growing impact of psychology on advertising, especially given later developments in the industry: the interwar rise of consumer research and post-war motivation research, a systemic role of academic psychology in advertising agencies, and a view of advertising in terms of social engineering.[15] However, this reading would mischaracterize the historical role of psychology before 1914. The causal relationship was not a unidirectional transformation of advertising by psychology. Practical insight often preceded theory as we will see.[16] Professionals also drew on a cross-border flow of industrial ideas. (American advice and cooperation were the most recurrent, but the flow was multidirectional between Britain, Europe and the USA, rather than a process of Americanization.[17]) Psychology itself was part of the broader vogue for the non-rational as Albert Hirschman called it, as contemporaries discussed the instinctual-intuitive, the habitual, the unconscious, the ideologically and neurotically driven.[18]

But even granted an influence of psychology, we should ask why professional advertisers centralized it given that it threatened modernity-as-disenchantment and had an ambivalent status. A retrospective evaluation might wrongly assume

---

[13] On the significance of this question for the status of psychology, see Woodward and Ash, *Problematic Science*.

[14] Daston, 'British Responses to Psycho-Physiology'.

[15] On these developments, see Schwartzkopf, 'What Was Advertising?'

[16] In the American context, Merle Curti describes psychology in advertising as an after-the-fact appearance. Curti, 'Changing Concept'. For psychology's dependence on marketing more generally see Bowlby, *Shopping with Freud*.

[17] American salesmanship itself had sources of inspiration outside the USA. Friedman, for example, examines the influence of the German psychologist Wilhelm Wundt, who founded the first laboratory for psychological experiment in Leipzig in 1879. Friedman, *Birth of a Salesman*, 168-71.

[18] Hirschman, *Essential Hirschman*, 209.

that psychology was just an irresistible boon. Historians often assume that it was inevitable that advertisers should adapt psychology to their purposes once it attained a disciplinary status, because vocabularies of the non-rational simply suited their proclivities, or were a necessary response to market pressures that required them to create and accelerate consumer demand.[19] However, if natural fit had been the case, the non-rational would not have appeared so late and uneasily. It is also irreducible to the counterpart of economic competition, else we would find arguments tailored to specific commodity markets, rather than cast as the new theory of advertising. Although market conditions have some explanatory power as we will see, the industry's embrace of the non-rational was ultimately an effect of mounting criticisms governed by rationalist values, on which advertising seemed to fall short. Criticisms created a conceptual vacuum that needed filling, while the disavowals of enchantment with legal means made it available as a filler, free from legal attention. In other words, the embrace of enchantment in psychological terms was yet another attempt—a strikingly successful one in retrospect, to attain cultural authority, this time by claiming mastery over the scene of enchantment left otherwise unattended. The turn to psychology was a product of the longer-term dynamics explored in this book, which drove a profession without a cultural home to embrace a language with which to domesticate the already widespread phenomenon of market enchantment, which lacked a conceptual home.

To trace these developments, the following discussion examines interrelated tensions in conceptualizations of advertising. On the one hand, the effects of advertising on consumers: what were they, and how should they be analysed? On the other hand, the status of the industry: what social domain did expertise in advertising occupy? We can consider the tensions schematically along an axis moving between concepts of disenchantment and enchantment.

---

[19] For example, Rappaport points to surplus production handled by creating more consumers through advertising, rather than new uses for products. Rappaport, *Thirst for Empire*, 39. As a general explanation for the rise of national and international advertising, the argument about surplus goods is contested. For a critique of different versions of the argument in Nevett, *Advertising in Britain*, and in Richards, *Commodity Culture*, see Church, 'Advertising Consumer Goods'. Historians also point to pressures on advertising to cater to the oligopolistic market that emerged after two decades of depression from the mid-1870s, which was dominated by large firms that sought market control through branding. For a discussion, see Gurney, *Making of Consumer Culture*, ch. 4; Williams, 'Advertising'. Advertisers themselves spoke to the competitive interest of manufacturers to differentiate their products, and to compel retailers to stock their brands by creating demand. For example, *AW*, April 1911, 389. On the novel need to force demand for a higher standard of living in the twentieth century, as opposed to earlier periods, see Thompson, *Voice of Civilisation*, ch. 3. For accounts of psychology as a ready opportunity for advertisers elsewhere see for example, Beale, *Modernist Enterprise*, ch. 1 (France); Friedman, *Birth of a Salesman* (the USA).

	disenchantment	↔	enchantment
Effects on consumers	Calculable, predictable measurable	Incalculable, long term—but certain (goodwill, consumer loyalty to the brand)	Mysterious, unpredictable
	The analysis focuses on sales generated by advertising investment	The analysis focuses on consumers, effects are associated with specific campaigns	The analysis focuses on culture and on materiality; effects are associated with advertising as a cultural system and an immersive material environment with which consumers interact
Social domains of the industry	Science; cliché man	Art, psychology (the contested science); modern wo/man	Chance, luck, fantasy, magic; cliché woman

With many hues and inconsistencies, professionals coalesced around the middle, where enchantment mixed easily with reason and where ideals of science cast in masculine vocabularies were complicated so as to endorse the psyche's mysteries and become more feminized. Professionals engaged in a precarious balancing act of endorsing enchantment without feeding into their culture's fears. They were mindful of circulating representations of danger, like Oliver Onions's *Good Boy Seldom*, whose advertising agent says: 'I offer you—my power of making people think what I want 'em to think.' This was an expression of anxieties about psychological regression and perverse influence.[20] Old and new knowledges were packaged and deployed so as to turn enchantment to novel account that mythologized practitioners as the key to capitalism's fundamental uncertainty—how to succeed?—while evading visions of danger.

Effects

From the Sales Paradigm to Psychological Effects

Until the close of the nineteenth century, advertising literature rarely discussed the psychological appeal of advertisements. Consumers were typically categorized according to formal class data based on geographical locations, income and occupational patterns, and those were linked directly with types of commodities and services presumably appropriate for each group. Where psychological appeal

---

[20] Onions, *Good Boy Seldom*, 1911, 156. Pick describes those fears as a recasting of older eighteenth-century debates about capitalism. Pick, *Svengali's Web*, ch. 4.

was mentioned, it was likely to apply a rigid partition in which minds were reducible to a single overarching power of either rationality or its absence, predetermined by social type. In this view, for example, social elites were typically logical, and the masses emotional or superstitious. By the early twentieth century the reflex was changing: 'one realises the incompleteness of this view'. The reason was not a democratic sentiment, although professionals certainly had good reasons to expand consumer circles. Instead, new languages of psychological complexities had much to offer to a profession in search of a definition. All minds were increasingly represented as complex compounds of rational and non-rational elements. Views diverged on fundamental questions like the place of metaphysics in the theory of consciousness, yet the idea that in advertising 'the operations of thought...will be looked upon as the most vital' gained ground. In 1882 the advertising agent and publisher of press directories Henry Sell confessed himself 'incompetent to discuss or analyse the exact manner in which the mind is influenced by Advertisements'; thirty years later professionals already insisted the advert creator must 'know a good deal of the psychology of the customer...' In the interim, having a deep knowledge of human nature began to be seen as a set of psychological problems.[21]

The turn to the mind involved a subtle but profound recasting of the goals of advertising. Until the last years of the nineteenth century, comments on 'effective' advertising typically meant sales, and occasionally a more tailored consumer response to an advert, for example a follow-up request for information or samples. In other words, advertisers were looking for an observable response. On professionals' own accounts, the sales framework—today known as a modelling approach that measures effects on an aggregate level of inputs (expenditure) to outputs (sales)—created difficult tensions. Sales do not occur in a linear correlation to advertising investment; therefore, traders complained that advertising did not work and were reluctant to pay for services. As Onions expressed the anxiety: 'you never know how much you owe to it [advertising].'[22] Yet, when clients did pay, they expected measurable results. Professionals' turn to mind-management displaced sales as the paradigm of effectiveness. They suggested that advertising 'worked' and was not a wild guess, but its effects should be analysed in terms of the mind. Creating interest, impressing the brand name on memories, encouraging a structure of feeling in favour of commodities, these became new terms of art for effects. They complicated and extended the space between advert and sale, and therefore also facilitated concepts of creativity for its own sake, which are familiar in contemporary discussions of advertising. Client expectations would for a long

---

[21] *Practical Advertising*, 1909, 12; F.W. Pettit, *Progressive Advertising*, April 1904, 24–5; Sell, *Philosophy of Advertising*, 1882, vi; *AW*, September 1912, 259; *Advertising*, October 1899, 9.

[22] Onions, *Good Boy Seldom*, 1911, 112. For late twentieth-century anxieties, see, for example, Nava, 'Framing Advertising'. As Nava observes, investigations have demonstrated little correlation between sales and the money spent on advertising.

time be hard to adjust to these concepts, which required faith in the power of adverts rather than sober calculation. Today this is known as a behavioural model, yet long before academics formalized models, professionals began to develop them.[23]

It is worth emphasizing the non-obvious gap we see here: in the years in which an audit culture was coming into its own and could abstract from persons to calculation on the basis of data, professional advertisers turned from the apparent objectivity of numbers to the complexities of minds. Advertising's effects were repositioned between the rationalist concept of observable sales, which was downplayed but not dismissed, and an enchanted culture of the imagination. Even someone like Thomas Russell, who theorized 'scientific advertising' in terms of sales, accepted that they were not a necessary goal. He recognized the alternative of creating 'some sort of public belief'.[24] The avalanche of advice that informed this shift is worth examining in detail to see how the non-rational assumed its now familiar place as the very logic of professional advertising, and the challenges involved in this process.

Resistant Minds

Most commentators were clear that advertising was not limited to the communication of wants but rather had to create them. The idea was to forge 'a wish for things which the public never knew or imagined it wanted... while previous to the days of modern advertising methods the supply only followed a manifestation of the desire for its presence.' As the advertisement manager of the *Morning Leader* announced in a collection of essays from the era's leading advertisers, success depended on organizing the sources of supply and then creating the demand.[25] These ideas were developed without addressing their contradiction with the paradigm of the communication of wants, and more interestingly, with little sense that they were outrageous or politically explosive, as they would become, for example, in the hands of Ken Galbraith when he argued half a century later that the creation of wants pulled the rug from under the justification of production.[26] Of course, doubt was close to the surface. We see it, for example, in a

---

[23] For a review of the modelling and behavioural approaches, see Fennis and Stroebe, *Psychology of Advertising*, ch. 1.
[24] *AW*, May 1911, 537–9; *AW*, October 1911, 420. Russell remained more comfortable than other commentators with letting clients define the goal of their adverts rather than reframe it for them, but like others he was advocating the concept of entire campaign policy.
[25] *Advertisers' Pocketbook*, 1913, 1; *Advertising*, August 1899, 593; Simonis, *Success in Advertising*, 1908, 2.
[26] Galbraith, *Affluent Society*. The Cambridge Marxist economist Maurice Dobb argued as much in 1937 when he charged the capitalist system with raising itself indefinitely 'by its own bootlaces'. As he explained, consumers' desires were constituted as the starting-point for a theory of value and at the same time admitted to be dependent variables. Dobb, *Political Economy*, ch. 6.

front-page denial in the *Advertiser's Weekly* that advertising persuaded people to buy things they did not want.[27] Yet, practitioners subdued ideological doubt and focused, like economists, only on the assumption that wants (a vague term between needs and desires) were theoretically infinite.[28]

Creating wants was no mean feat. It meant shaping minds, which were theorized in advertising literature as resistant things: they failed to pay attention, and they were hard to persuade. The dominant account of consumer psychology in advertising literature was a dynamic one that theorized overcoming resistance as consecutive stages attained by a mix of rational and non-rational appeals. The sequence was generally in keeping with the hierarchy-of-effects model penned by the American advertising practitioner E. St. Elmo Lewis, known as AIDA: Attention, Interest, Desire, Action.[29] The model did not assume a direct link between the advertised message and consumer response, but rather intermediate steps. In its first, cognitive stage, consumers directed conscious attention to an advert's content. The subsequent stage, desire, was affective, as thinking gave way to emotional responses and the formation of preferences for the brand. Finally, a conative stage included behaviour, such as purchasing or reusing a product. The hierarchy was both temporal and substantive, in the sense that each stage not only followed the previous one but also depended on it to occur.[30] Already in the mid-1880s practitioners articulated an early version of this model:

> The first time a man looks at an advertisement he does not see it. The second time he does not notice it. The third time he is conscious of its existence. The fourth time he faintly remembers having seen it before. The fifth time he reads it. The sixth time he turns up his nose at it. The seventh time he reads it through and says, 'Oh! Bother!' The eighth time he says, 'Here's that confounded thing again!' The ninth time he wonders 'if it amounts to anything'. The tenth time he thinks he will ask his neighbour if he has tried it. The eleventh time he wonders how the advertiser makes it pay. The twelfth time he thinks perhaps it may be worth something. The thirteenth time he thinks it must be a good thing. The fourteenth time he remembers that he has wanted such a thing for a long time. The fifteenth time he thinks he will buy it some day. The sixteenth time he makes a memorandum of it. The seventeenth time he is tantalised because he cannot afford to buy it. The eighteenth time he swears at his poverty. The nineteenth

---

[27] *Advertiser's Weekly*, 12 September, 1913, 309. See also the discussion of wants-creation below, by note cues 55–56.

[28] On this assumption in marginal utility theory, see Gagnier, *Insatiability of Human Wants*.

[29] Lewis provided the blueprint for the majority of sales books in 1910s and 1920s America. Friedman, *Birth of a Salesman*, 158.

[30] Fennis and Stroebe, *Psychology of Advertising*, 27–34.

time he counts his money carefully; and the twentieth time he sees it, he buys the article, or instructs his wife to do so!³¹

The account of gradual response was intended to persuade advertisers to persevere despite seeing no immediate results. However, at this point it did not yet work from a theory of the mind but to the contrary from experience that would be theorized around the turn of the twentieth century.

Research has since cast doubt on the validity of think-feel-do models given variations in levels of consumer involvement and the diversity of influences that interact with discrete adverts.³² The early models, which were neither formal nor complete, are important because they reveal professional efforts to theorize a prominent role for consumer agency and reason while the non-rational was being embraced. In the majority of comments, the consumer mind was present in its own making, to borrow from Mathew Thomson's account of the psychological subject in the early twentieth century. Thomson describes the fundamental idea of the era's psychology, according to which 'a vast area of human consciousness and associated potential lay hidden in the normal waking mind, both in the force of instinct and in the unconscious.' The challenge became to access, mobilize, and channel this hidden power to attain self-realization.³³ In the hands of early professional advertisers, consumers were not strictly products of determinism but mixtures of rational and non-rational, deliberative reason and agency, as well as vulnerability to manipulation. These all had a role to play in advertising's dreams of victory. In preserving concepts of free will while introducing the non-rational, practitioners paralleled concerns within psychology itself about the meaning of volition, but they also protected a capitalist ideology of the consumer market.

Resistance Theorized and Overcome

The problem of attention was typically explained in terms of the overloaded modern environment, where every advert competed with a rush of stimuli: 'the panorama of daily incidents diverts the mind... happenings increase in number and importance, and the public mind is ever being conducted to a new channel of thought and consideration.' One commentator observed, as Georg Simmel would soon argue, '[h]uman beings collectively are... not unlike a blasé child.' The audience was 'already bored or distracted', another commentator warned. People

---

[31] Smith, *Successful Advertising*, 1884, 18. Smith is still cited in contemporary scholarship and teaching on the effects of repetition on consumer behaviour.
[32] Fennis and Stroebe, *Psychology of Advertising*, ch. 1. On the factors interacting with adverts, see also, for example, Schudson, *Advertising, the Uneasy Persuasion*; Church, 'Advertising Consumer Goods'.
[33] Thomson, *Psychological Subjects*, 8 and *passim*.

went through different modes of receptivity; they might even sleep, say on a train, therefore you had to be ready when they opened their eyes again, as W.H. Smith advised railway advertisers. While readers were conditioned to passive resistance by overload, antagonism to advertising also motivated conscious refusals of attention. One writer chastised advertisers who 'seem to forget that... [t]he majority turn over the page rapidly when they come to the commercial columns...' Advertising was in the worst position of all print because it had 'to extort reluctant attention, whereas every other writer addresses eager attention'. Unless compelled, '[t]he average man never reads an advertisement.' Even if not resistant, practitioners theorized, consumers were not eager: 'even the woman at home, with plenty of leisure, when she is not looking for a particular article, does not... search through her journal for hidden advertisements.'[34] Professionals therefore theorized how attention could be gained.

Procedures of stimulation and technologies of attraction preoccupied advertising literature. We find the preoccupation, for example, in professionals' clamour to theorize the old common wisdom of 'striking' the eye in the languages of attention-management, which gave images a key role. As commentators advised, the love of pictures was a universal human weakness that could be harnessed to profit-making. This was a line of thought that Jonathan Crary describes as the model of the attentive human observer that emerged in the 1880s. There was a troubling tension between induced stimulation and concepts of consumers' free will, but professionals smoothed it by arguing that stimulating the senses supported rational agency. The logic was that the arrest of attention made consumers more rather than less alert, because matter activated mind: advertising stimulation was 'like a succession of gentle knocks at the door of popular intelligence'. The goal was to nudge the public to exercise judgement. It was the 'awakened citizen' who would respond to the 'hypnotic influence' of poster images and exclaim: 'the blessed thing is everywhere!' The rational and non-rational thus worked in tandem.[35]

Persuasion was a separate problem, since attentive readers were not yet committed consumers. As Stuart Hirst, Advertising Director of E.C. Fulford Ltd which owned the famous Bile Beans and other successful patent medicines, observed, 'you can get the people here to read your advertising much more readily than you can get them to buy.'[36] Resistance to persuasion was theorized in a pincer movement, from two directions: on the one hand, in terms of historical cultural

---

[34] *Profitable Advertising*, September 1901, 47; C. Manners Smith, *Advertising*, March 1898, 259; Collins, *Advertisers' Guardian*, 1891, 85; *AW*, June 1908, 48; W.H. Smith Railway Advertising Offices; *AW*, August 1908, 282–3; Thomas Russell, *AW*, March 1912, 265; Shore, 'Craft of the Advertiser', 1907, 303; Annie Meerloo, *AW*, January 1914, 106–8.

[35] *Practical Advertising*, 1903, 10; *Advertising*, May 1895, front page; Crary, *Suspensions of Perception*, ch. 1; *Modern Advertising*, June 1900, 5; C. Manners Smith, *Advertising*, March 1898, 259; *AW*, October 1902, 295; *Advertising*, July 1898, 484–6; Sheldon, *Billposting*, 1910, 8–10.

[36] Hirst, 'Art of Understanding the Public', 1908, 38.

types that presented concrete resistances, and on the other hand, in terms of universal psychological traits that applied across concrete cases, and were the key to overcoming resistance. In this dialectic we see the move from character to personality that psychological languages brought forth.

Cultural types included nationality, religiosity, occupation, gender, and more complex if often stereotyped formulations, which presented specific kinds of resistance. For example, Britishness was discussed in terms of its reticence, which troubled practitioners. Unlike Americans, one commentator said, Brits were neither rush nor fashionable buyers, hard to attract 'merely for excitement or the novelty...or because an article...is loudly or broadly talked about...' The British consumer, Hirst warned, 'comes of a most discerning and discriminating stock...a strong strain of conservatism...An article has got to be a good deal more meritorious than catchy for it to show up creditably in the eyes of our democracy.' Women were another key consumer type, recognized as the managers of the household purse. 'Nine-tenths of all the articles on the markets of the world today are bought by women,' argued Annie Meerloo, Incorporated Advertising Consultant. Male practitioners saw women as 'the dominating factor' and were concerned with understanding their views and tastes, for as Clarence Moran put it, '[i]t is their peculiar function to spend'. They too were viewed as careful and discerning, indeed no less than the stereotyped Brit.[37]

Curiously, cultures of the colonies were not usually discussed in terms of distinct psychological traits. Large agencies claimed reach into the colonies but their commentary focused on access to media and knowledge of market conditions. If colonial subjects were not psychologized, this also meant that their otherness was not thematized to the extent that historians find in actual adverts, in imperial trade policies, and in the structures of exchange. For example, Anne McClintock argues that soap advertising created a commodity racism in which the values of domesticity were marketed as a civilizing mission. Anandi Ramamurthy suggests that colonial traders promoted an image of African underdevelopment and willing subordination. Rappaport's history of tea points to planters' view of advertising as a gospel spreading the blessings of tea among the heathen. While planters treated the British and Americans as rational consumers who would be conquered by facts, they viewed those in colonial India as passive and ignorant consumers who had to be forced to have new wants. Yet, British advertising literature did not typically recommend a trade on primitivism, just as it did not celebrate only the rationality of Brits. The occasional comment on colonial

---

[37] *Practical Advertising* 1903, 13–14; Hirst, 'Art of Understanding the Public', 1908, 38; *AW*, January 1914, 106; *Advertisers' Review*, 8 April 1901, 2; Moran, *Business of Advertising*, 1905, 15–16; C. Manners Smith, *Advertising*, February 1899, 268; Leslie Perry, *Progressive Advertising*, February 1909, 35. As Lori Loeb argues, women were perceived as careful critics. Loeb, *Consuming Angels*, 9. On their treatment as subjects in Selfridge's see Nava, 'Cosmopolitanism of Commerce.'

consumers was more likely to claim similarity.[38] For example, Mather and Crowther encouraged clients to advertise in colonies by arguing that '[t]he native Indian continues to grow in his taste for things European.' Indian advertising therefore presumably appealed alike to Europeans and natives. Of course, racial difference was implied in the suggestion that natives were learning to desire European goods and in the reiteration of commodities' civilizing impact, but the emphasis on homogeneous desire meant that consumers in colonies could be influenced similarly to those in Britain.[39] In practice, Rappaport observes, promotional efforts applied the same strategies in India as they did in Great Britain, Australia, or the USA despite the orientalist assumptions of tea promoters.[40]

Alongside specific cultural types was the abstract category of 'the public', an elusive entity that was hard to hold under powers of persuasion. Professionals warned that the public was capricious, disloyal, in need of surveillance. As one commentator had it, 'The public are not as a body philanthropic, and they are certainly a bit sluggish... There are rooted prejudices to overcome.' It had 'a hard head'. This entity needed constant managing: 'those moods must... be anticipated and punctually ministered by the expert.' The public was an amalgam of types; therefore, for some commentators, the locus of expertise was the ability to address diverse audiences together, a typical problem of national and international advertising. J.R. Charter, who edited the *Advertising World*, distinguished the professional advertiser from the traditional salesman. The latter could adapt to the person before him, while the former operated in an unprecedented environment that addressed millions of people at once. As *Advertising* had it, 'Human beings are, as a body... to be forcibly appealed to by a man who has made the taste and methods of collective mankind subjects of special study.'[41]

All consumer categories were treated with generalized psychological concepts, which could mystify social divisions. As Erik Linstrum observes about imperial psychology, it had an unstable political valance because it was not only a means of control but also a vehicle to undermine racial difference and problematize distinctions between the primitive and the modern.[42] In advertising, psychological generalization served the positionality of professionals and of advertising itself as trans-social. It also supplied theories of persuasion as all consumers were

---

[38] Of course, there were also comments about difference. For example, an agent in South Africa expected to gain from the 'fickle-mindedness' of local consumers, *Advertisers' Review*, 14 May 1900, 2–3. McClintock, *Imperial Leather*, ch. 5; Ramamurthy, *Imperial Persuaders*; Rappaport, *Thirst for Empire*, ch. 6.

[39] *Practical Advertising*, 1903–4, xv. For a discussion of Egyptian demand for the 'comforts' of 'modern civilisation', see A.I. Shedden, *Progressive Advertising*, June 1906, 36.

[40] Rappaport, *Thirst for Empire*, 211. On commercial orientalism as erasing distance and anti-insular see Nava, 'Cosmopolitanism of Commerce.'

[41] Morgan, 'Get Outside Yourself', 1908, 219. Morgan worked for W.H. Smith. *Advertisers' Review*, 12 February 1900, 2 (quoting the *Anglo-Saxon*); *Practical Advertising*, 1905–6, 20; *Practical Advertising*, 1903, 9; Charter, 'What Advertising Means to the Public', 1908, 238–9; *Advertising*, May 1898, 369.

[42] Linstrum, *Ruling Minds*.

described as more or less responsive to rational and non-rational appeals under circumstances that could be broken down to workable units. Here again, the non-rational became increasingly important, albeit never exclusive.

One recurrent advice of a non-rational ilk was to imprint messages on memories. Professionals liked to quote William Gladstone on iteration. In an 1876 speech he commented on advertising apropos his complaint that even important publications would not be read if they were not advertised: 'Its power is enormous... It depends wholly on producing an impression upon the public mind by iteration or by constant repetition of the same thing...' When Gladstone started his second premiership, his statements became adverts for advertising. The wisdom was to '[k]eep on hammering away at the public, and do it so persistently that they cannot overlook you...' The impression should become 'irremovable'. The image of iteration as hammer was a popular visualization of an otherwise elusive form of control.[43] Towards the turn of the twentieth century, ideas became more sophisticated as psychology was brought into the fold:

> Authorities on what has been called psychology of publicity, a science which examines the operations caused in the public mind by advertising, assert that if a fact is kept constantly and vividly before the world, the world in time grows to accept it, and albeit unconsciously, associates it with certain things and circumstances.[44]

The subliminal appeals of adverts translated into a set of responses: 'the person will reason something like this: "Oh, that 'Sypno." Where did I read about it? I can't remember, but, never mind, they sell it here. I'll try it!'[45] The 'child as a factor in advertising' was conceptualized as an agent of iteration. A rhyme book containing brand names demonstrated the process:

> the transcendent merits of Diploma Milk are kept well to the fore... the mother is continually hearing the words 'Diploma Milk' prattled in artless innocence by her unsuspecting infant. She can never forget them... It is not long – such is the inevitable effect of familiarity – before she says to herself: 'I might as well try a tin...'[46]

Professionals' efforts to penetrate minds thus moved back and forth between local experience and new theory.

---

[43] *Daily Gazette for Middlesbrough*, 24 April 1876, 8; *Daily Gazette for Middlesbrough*, 27 September 1881, 2; *Profitable Advertising*, May 1903, 45; *Progressive Advertising*, October 1908, 42. For references to Gladstone, see, for example, *Advertiser's Guide to Publicity*, 1887, 16.
[44] *Practical Advertising*, 1905–6, 20.   [45] *AW*, June 1911, 677.
[46] T. Michael Pope, *AW*, June 1912, 659–60.

The search for methods to shape brand memories was demonstrated in a Pears advert, which invited viewers to test whether they were colour blind by staring at the brand name and experiencing the power of optical illusions (Figure 7.1). While Pears highlighted the scientific basis of the test, it was equally interested in the enchanting effects of mindless staring amid a crowd. The advert invited viewers to join advertising characters around the spectacle, collapsing distinctions between real and imagined audiences. Physical proximity among readers and images was intended as a mind-altering process.

Figure 7.1 Pears optical illusion advert. Pears scrapbook, source unknown.

Psychological experiments on the effects of repetition by Scott and by the German-American psychologist Hugo Münsterberg, gained professional attention in Britain. Even earlier, professionals were interested in academic references to their practice and flattered by them. For example, Sully's popular *Outlines of Psychology* explained that single impressions were insufficient because images grew faint in memories. The 1892 edition (but not earlier ones that appeared from 1884) noted advertisements as 'not very interesting' impressions that nonetheless 'manage by their importunity to stamp themselves on the memory'.[47]

Sully was among the promoters of associationism in Britain, a concept with origins in mental philosophy that was widely discussed by advertising professionals. The theory maintained that knowledge was acquired and ordered through the linking of ideas, so that simple elements combine into complex mental experiences; it received physiological formulations in the new psychology. Professionals applied local understandings of associationism to a variety of cases. For example, the *Advertising World* celebrated a Kodak campaign that associated cameras with 'some absorbing interest present in the minds of those appealed to', like the charm of childhood and the pleasure of holidays. In emergent branding theory, more on which later, advertisers' work with associationism was akin to a conjuror's method of forcing a card: 'you have to link a necessity with a nonentity', the latter being an impersonal brand. The concept of business identity was based on associations created by advertising with desirable qualities. As Dixon's advertising course manual explained, like a badly dressed person, so a badly dressed business covered with substandard adverts suggested a suspect identity. By contrast, a 'dignified' advert would make it 'almost impossible to imagine that [the] firm...would stock "shoddy" goods, or deal in any way dishonestly...' Gordon Selfridge similarly explained that an advert 'should be a reflection of the...personality of the house'. This is what historians have called the corporate soul, or as Eugene McCarraher describes it, a pecuniary metaphysics of corporate enchantment achieved through advertising animation.[48]

Suggestion was another term of art, concerned, as we saw in Chapter 6, with a non-deliberative assimilation of ideas. Images of crowds, for example, were theorized as a suggestion that activated emulative instincts. Cultural celebrities too had a suggestive function, which short-circuited deliberation by linking elite ideas with consumer products, as the *Advertiser's Weekly* demonstrated in a campaign of a furnishing business. The advertiser quoted personas like Goethe, John Ruskin, and William Morris ('Have nothing in your homes that you do not know to be useful and believe to be beautiful'). Suggestion and atmosphere,

---

[47] *Advertiser's Weekly*, 3 May 1913, 84. Sully was noted in Moran, *Business of Advertising*, 1905, 10–11. Sully, *Outlines of Psychology*, 1892, 190.
[48] Schultz and Schultz, *History of Modern Psychology*, ch. 2; Collins, 'England'; Winter, *Pleasures of Memory*, ch. 1; *AW*, August 1911, 139–41; Clarence Rook, *Advertising News*, 26 August 1904, 26; Dixon, *Advertising Course*, 1909, 19; *AW*, February 1911, 132; McCarraher, *Enchantments of Mammon*, ch. 10.

the author wrote, were key in this appeal to the imagination and call on spirituality. At the other extreme of suggestion was direct advertising command. The mysterious effect, which one author explained as 'almost "hypnotic" suggestion', overcame the inaction caused by overload, and produced mechanical compliance.[49]

As occurred in discussions of attention, so in discussions of persuasion practitioners were alert to fears that professional advertising worked by suppressing the intellect with 'blood and passion', and were careful to draw on reason and tie it with the expertise in the non-rational mind. For example, the advertising manager of the famous Colman's Mustard opened an essay on advertising by stating that a remarkable advertiser necessarily 'believes in the outstanding intelligence of the people', and ended by insisting that you had to advertise 'until the very name of the product is unconsciously associated with that of the manufacturer'. Others recommended diversity in adverts so that they appeal first to 'the visual sense, and through that sense to the reason'. Charles Vernon saw this as the very definition of advertising: 'an appeal to man's understanding through his senses.' Vernon exalted facts and logic, yet explored their relationship to the unconscious. He was convinced, for example, that 'the Hebrew' had the 'quality of hypnotism or magnetism... in an ordinary form', which allowed him to influence customers' minds. The anti-Semitic trope drove Vernon to recommend turning adverts into magnets. Practitioners theorized 'magnetic features' as techniques for focusing restless minds on their rational needs.[50]

Alongside theories of consumer response, professionals discussed diversity in style as a strategy that combined the non-rational with the rational. Rational appeals were commonly viewed as the effect of text, and therefore of press and pamphlet advertising. As one advertising handbook put it, '"All letterpress" advertisements are generally favoured by advertisers having a definite proposition to put before the public, capable of being argued out and proved logically and conclusively...' Text could also be turned from 'education' to non-rational influence with 'great reiterativness', which some advertisers adopted. Meanwhile, images worked on a subliminal level.[51] Mather & Crowther's agency applied the advice of combining styles in its self-advertising (Figure 7.2).

---

[49] *Advertiser's Weekly*, 19 April 1913, 9; *Progressive Advertising*, May 1903, 24.

[50] Onions, *Good Boy Seldom*, 1911, 242 (narrating the philosophy of Good Boy Seldom: 'Did they think that people's deeper passions... were going to be stirred by such academic appeals to the mere intellect...? everybody... had feelings – could be moved by the dramatic instinct...'); Carmichael, 'Methods and Moments for Advertising', 1908, 34; C. Manners Smith, *Advertising*, March 1898, 258; *Profitable Advertising*, July 1900, 132; *Profitable Advertising*, September 1900, 54; *Advertisers' Review*, 5 December 1903, 8–9.

[51] Jones, *Handbook on Advertising*, 1912, 28–30 and *passim*. See also *Practical Advertising*, 1904–5, 6–7; *AW*, May 1911, 534–5.

Figure 7.2 Mather & Crowther, advertisement for agency services. *Practical Advertising* (London: Mather & Crowther, 1905–6).

The advert identified the role of visual imagery in 'holding the eye' and 'compelling the mind' to consider the argument, and proposed a 'perfect' combination of 'terse' text and good visuals. The vocabulary of power—'strength', 'hold', 'compel'—and the appeal to a sensual response governed by sight, mixed with rational argument. The agency told readers that it created all the adverts in the picture and could make theirs too. In this way, it performed the sequence it advocated, from holding the eye, to compelling the mind, to presenting a logical argument (experience of success).

The conditions of the market facing advertisers were occasionally used to motivate specific appeals, which suggests that market dynamics can explain concrete choices in campaigns. On a common assumption, when introducing a new product, a rational appeal or 'educational advertising' was required to explain to consumers why they wanted what they did not know. By contrast, in a saturated market, advertisers managed competition with equivalent products. In this case, the goal was branding, and reasons were less important than brand loyalty that depended on penetrating memories. Some commentators argued conversely. For example, the *Advertisers' Review* quoted the American author Joel Benton, who explained the role of mystery in introducing new things, when the mind was ready for wonder.[52] Either way, the professional was a student of human faith under differing market conditions. The governing question was how to mix appeals. No practitioner seemed content to leave the non-rational out, just as none would let go of consumer reason.

Social Domain

Magic?

The uncomfortable position between enchantment and rationalism needed careful management not only in the stories told about consumers, but equally about advertising professionals themselves. Practitioners craved the respectability of rational experts, yet introduced the forbidden element of enchantment, supposedly rejected in capitalism, into the heart of the system. In bringing the non-rational into the fold they claimed something approaching magical powers, as one aspiring philosopher of advertising put it: 'the successful advertiser and the successful conjuror are one and the same.' They had to claim such powers to convince businesses that they could re-present commodities in ways that those who invented and manufactured them could not, could in fact *make* commodities by imbuing things with accelerating movement. As Smith's advertising agency put

---

[52] Sheldon, *Billposting*, 1910, 8–10; *Advertisers' Review*, 1 October 1900, 1; *Advertisers' Review*, 6 September 1902, 11.

it, they knew how to 'make it go!' Such powers manifested in effective words and images—practically the definition of magic.[53]

Practitioners worried about their close relationship to enchantment, and therefore rejected associations that pulled towards anti-rationalism. As one advice book argued, to be considered 'a serious business force' advertising had to disentangle from loci of traditional enchantment: 'quackery, magic, the circus or the theatre'. All concepts of chance, gamble, and mystery as the basis of success were vehemently denied. In 1914, the advertising agent Edward Sidney Hole asked: 'What is the essential secret of advertising?... is it, as was said... "white magic"?' How did it lead to 'voluntary purchases of the same known product' and culminated 'in the *habit* of buying and recommending it... producing... crescendo of demand...'? In a joint treatise with a fellow agent, Hole charged economic theory with the 'Great Omission' of failing to explain the utility of advertising. At first glance, the theme appeared thoroughly disenchanted, since Hole seemed to provide an economic account to replace 'white magic'. However, his style was saturated with religious imagery and revealed enchantment lurking close to the surface. In his excited vision, the Twelve Apostles were 'the most successful advertising men of the Christian era' and the Bible was 'the most successfully advertised book of all time.' In the early twentieth century, the apostles were advertising agents and the disciples were the ranks of employés. The power of advertising was 'mighty in its influence upon the destinies of the race'. In this discourse, the economic logic of advertising came close to religious ecstasy.[54]

The 'Great Omission' that Hole condemned began to be rectified only after the war. As Denys Thompson put it, economists seemed for a long time to agree in ignoring advertising. The first major economist to theorize it was Alfred Marshall, in his 1919 *Industry and Trade*. The analysis was not all that Hole desired, because Marshall criticized subliminal appeals that bypassed reason in a distinction he made between constructive and combative advertising. The former drew attention to opportunities for buying and selling that people may wish to take. The latter was the obtruding force of mere capital found in 'incessant iteration of the name of a product, coupled perhaps with a claim that it is of excellent quality...' The main influence of combative advertising was not an appeal to reason but the blind force of habit drawing on the human inclination to prefer the familiar, and it was therefore wasteful. Even constructive

---

[53] Clarence Rook, *Advertising News*, 26 August 1904, 26; Advertisement by Smith's Advertising Agency, in Simonis, *Success in Advertising*, 1908.
[54] *Twelve Months Advertising*, 1910, 14; *Profitable Advertising*, June 1902, front page; Smith, *Successful Advertising*, 1884, 13–14; *Advertising*, June 1900, 450; Hole, *Advertising and Progress*, 1914, 161–3, 27, 37–47, 179–80.

advertising could be overdone and cause social waste by raising prices without adequate return.[55]

Marshall's concern with bypassing reason circulated in earlier economic debates, for example when a Cambridge University lecturer and reverend, Canon Masterman, argued in 1910 that advertising was wasteful because it persuaded people to buy things they were not conscious of wanting. The *Billposter* responded by invoking Marshall's comments on the dynamism of wants in his 1890 *Principles of Economics*, in an effort to connect non-rational persuasion with progress. 'It is not for the good of society,' the *Billposter* argued, 'to leave the consumer undisturbed in his sloth.' A developed economy in which wealth and comforts circulated depended on tuning consumers to more than 'elementary conscious wants'. It quickly connected this argument with informational appeals: 'the modern world, besides being highly developed, is a large and even crowded place, and some sort of advertising is required to let the individual know that the article he wants exists...' The *Billposter*'s response thus treated the question of non-rational appeals together with rational ones, and argued that both supported rational progress.[56] (While the argument relied on Marshall, he actually envisioned the possibility of a stationary state in which no new 'important wants' would exist, although he did not see it on the horizon.[57] The *Billposter* evaded the dangerous question whether all wants were equally legitimate and important.) In any event, unlike Marshall, Hole and his fellows refused to set apart the rational and non-rational. They realized that the separation led to visions of dangerous enchantment. Therefore, just as they claimed to engage consumers' logical capacities and non-rational minds together, so they described themselves by combining concepts of science as well as art, with vocabularies of enchantment thrown into the mix.

Science, Art, and Magic on Top

Scientific tropes were a broad tent in the quest for rational expertise. They included 'laws' of advertising to be discovered and applied; professional training based on streamlined knowledge; practical experience cast as empirical investigation; and the occasional academic reference. Psychology was identified as a scientific ally. Do not sneer at the word psychology as mere theory, was one advice: 'When we say a man "knows human nature"... it is only another way of saying that he is a practical psychologist.'[58] Scientific aspirations were also

---

[55] Thompson, *Voice of Civilisation*, 31; Marshall, *Industry and Trade*, 1920, ch. 7.
[56] *Billposter*, September 1910, 151–2.
[57] Marshall, *Principles of Economics*, 1890, bk 3 ch. 4, bk 4 ch. 7.
[58] *Advertisers' Pocketbook*, 1913, 8–9.

expressed visually in the images of the modern agency, a material environment that enforced logical process. Rationalization inhered in the specialization of departments and in visions of carefully calculated practice, architecture, and movement (Figures 7.3 and 7.4).

Figure 7.3 T.B. Browne's agency, checking department and newspaper filing room. Images of straight lines bespoke rational order and calculable movement. William Stead, *The Art of Advertising: Its Theory and Practice Fully Described* (London: T.B. Browne, Ltd, 1899), 67, 69.

Figure 7.4 Mather and Crowther's agency, images of specialized departments, divided in space and labour, each exhibiting an internal rationality and all an unwavering work ethic. *Practical Advertising*, January 1903, ix.

Timothy de Waal Malefyt argues that divisions in contemporary agencies are essential to magic, which depends on managing tensions between creative and commercial imperatives, or sacred and mundane elements of advertising work. His emphasis on the creative department as the locus of magic helps us see the specificity of early perspectives. They did not locate magic only in functions we would today associate with creatives, but rather dispersed it among functions, each of which exhibited superpowers, while all were bound together by the authority of rationality. For example, T.C. Bench's agency marketed its 'essential seven' to clients: the 'idea producer'; the 'supplier of scientific facts'; the 'finder of weak spots'; the 'keenest of keen space buyers'; the man '[t]horoughly conversant with every important town in the British Isles'; the 'writer of strong appeals'; finally also a woman professional 'whose experience in appealing to the millions of readers of the *Daily Mail*, *Daily Graphic* and *Daily Chronicle* is now concentrated on advertising'. As Brian Moeran comments, the 'motley crew' requires different magicians to negotiate the best way of getting audiences to believe in their efficacy.[59]

There was a fundamental tension between the powers claimed for advertising and the disenchanted image of science; therefore, science was rejected as often as it was invoked. On a common view, expertise in human nature lacked 'hard and fast rules'. Many commentators thought that no protocols could apply to a field in which intuition was pivotal. Hirst rejected without hesitation arguments that advertising was a science with discoverable laws:

> The problem how to make advertising pay, has... produced more grey hairs than any other perplexity of modern commerce. Laws in advertising, notwithstanding all that your young experts in psychology may say, are chiefly conspicuous for their exceptions. Advertising men... are men with a subtle sensitiveness to the public pulse... It is the very willfulness and elusiveness of successful advertising that makes it the most fascinating pursuit in the world.[60]

His employers at Bile Bean certainly knew all about fascination, as we saw in Chapter 5. Hirst went on to describe the advertising industry as full of 'mental monstrosities'. Professionals in agencies did not share the wild insults, but many resisted reductions of their expertise to laws. There was no 'exact science'. Advertising was done 'by arts unteachable... by methods inscrutable he must kindle the flame of desire'. As one advertising consultant put it, 'If all were a matter of reason, of logic, of calculation, of experience, then... all... would reap gold. The born advertiser must have insight; he must be endowed with... imagination...' Knowing how to 'rivet the attraction' was a gift.[61] Concepts of art could assist these arguments, and therefore appeared in the imagery of agencies. The images in Figure 7.3 appeared in a book titled *The Art of Advertising*, while in Figure 7.4 flowers and symbols of gift decorated Mather & Crowther's images of the rational agency and complicated their message.

---

[59] Malefyt, 'Magic of Paradox'; *AW*, February 1914, 249; Moeran, 'Business, Anthropology'.
[60] Hirst, 'Art of Understanding the Public', 1908, 40.
[61] Hirst, 'Art of Understanding the Public', 1908, 43; *Profitable Advertising*, May 1901, front page; *Practical Advertising* 1909, 12; Shore, 'Craft of the Advertiser', 1907, 302; *Advertising*, November 1900, 65; Spiers, *Art of Publicity*, 1910, 18.

The dilemma of domain was clearest when professionals discussed the mushrooming schools of advertising, which implied an objectifiable craft. Their rise was necessary for the idea of a profession, but appeared too straightforward for experts on minds. In 1911 the Thirty Club, which included leading lights of the industry, addressed schools in a debate titled 'Do Advertising Schools Make for the Good of Advertising?' Most commentators argued that schools were good on technicalities such as type, layout, and media, but could not teach a man 'who had not got it in him' to become a professional. This view retained an aura of mystery around advertising, which was smoothed with the argument that the same was true of every wise profession.[62]

Many commentators settled the dilemma of domain by representing advertising as both science and art.[63] This perspective resonates with what Lorraine Daston and Peter Galison describe as trained judgement, a view that emerged in the scientific disciplines of the early twentieth century. It supplemented mid-nineteenth-century ideals of objective science that devalued subjectivity, with judgement that brought the interpretive position of the expert to the fore, and in which intuition was key to scientific knowledge. The emergent paradigm, informed by the efflorescence of psychologies of the unconscious, moved away from contrasts between science and art by combining patience and industry with intuitive and instinctual thinking.[64]

The most important and theoretically developed mode in which commentators combined art and science was the idea that facts required expert treatment, which turned them from neutral things into powerful effects on minds. The professional advertiser was described as a sorcerer of facts who could make the commodity come to life. A favourite one-liner of postmodern quality put the advertising wisdom succinctly: 'A rose is not a rose, if improperly described.' As Daston and Galison describe the twentieth-century scientific episteme, only the trained eye of the scientist could make objects transcend the silent obscurity of the mechanical form and bring out significant structures from the morass of uninteresting artefact and background. To be sure, advertisers' goal was to show uniqueness in the products they represented while scientists sought common patterns in natural phenomena, but the dialectical relationship between the unusual and the regular meant that problems of representation troubled both.[65]

The 'work of a master' with facts was repeatedly exemplified in advertising literature. Only a professional could make, say, coffee, yield facts that showed it

---

[62] *AW*, November 1911, 644–8.

[63] For example, advertising contractor Ernest H. Miers, *Advertisers' Review*, 5 March 1900, 5; *AW*, November 1911, 649.

[64] Daston and Galison, *Objectivity*, ch. 6. See also my discussion of Carlo Ginzburg and conjectural knowledge in the human sciences, examined in Chapter 1 in the context of advert-readers' approach to clues in adverts. Ginzburg, 'Clues and Scientific Method'.

[65] *Advertising*, June 1900, front page; Daston and Galison, *Objectivity*, 328. On representation in advertising and in the era's aestheticism see Bowlby, *Shopping with Freud*, ch. 1.

unlike any other coffee on the market, and only he could find 'unanswerable reasons why... books, calculated to work enthralling charm upon a certain class of people, should be bought'. Onions had his fictional advertising agent similarly explain the sorcery of facts, yet in his hands the magic was aggressive in its apathy to real value: 'There was, for example... Beer. In capable hands, what could not be made of the subject of Beer?... If one thing could be forced on the Public so could another.'[66]

The fear that advertising representation was an abuse of power also appeared in *Tono-Bungay*:

> Advertisement has revolutionised trade and industry; it is going to revolutionise the world. He takes mustard that is just like anybody else's mustard, and he goes about saying, shouting, singing, chalking on walls, writing inside people's books, putting it everywhere, 'Smith's Mustard is the Best.' And behold it is the best![67]

Wells appreciated the power of advertising, but he missed the professional way of thinking about it, perhaps rightly so, as his fictional advertiser was not a professional. 'The best' and other superlatives were explicitly rejected as professionals accepted criticisms about exaggeration. Onions's agent was more sophisticated, but in his case, adverts displace products until he eventually sees material things as disturbances: 'the materia of business... so many unimportant and rather cumbersome counters, designed merely to give a stiffening of actuality to... other things that really mattered.' Advertising thus detached from matter and reality. Meanwhile, early professionals' ideas of fact-sorcery sought midways in which they represented themselves not as gods but as servants of products. In their idealized accounts, their powers, while unusual, bolstered rather than displaced realism. They reimagined adverts in terms of ever more careful work with facts, so much so that like microscopic detail unavailable to the naked eye, they would be experienced as a revelation. On this theory, adverts did not displace products by eluding their objective qualities, as many contemporaries feared; they worked by expert exposure. Truth itself was seductive in the right hands. Consequently, advertising could be explained ever more openly, in a process that only enhanced its powers: 'In the bad old days the less the public knew about advertising, the more the advertiser profited; now it is all to the advantage of the majority of advertisers that the public should learn as much as possible of their aims and methods.'[68]

---

[66] *Practical Advertising*, 1905–6, 18; *Practical Advertising*, 1906–7, 12. See also advertisement by T.C. Bench, *AW*, February 1914, 249; *Profitable Advertising*, June 1902, 137; Charles Frederick Higham, *AW*, April 1912, 391; Thomas Russell, *AW* June 1911, 671–2; *Advertising*, January 1898, 184; Onions, *Good Boy Seldom*, 1911, 242. Onions's agent moves here from commercial to political campaigns. On concerns with manipulation in political advertising, see Thompson, 'Pictorial Lies?'.

[67] Wells, *Tono-Bungay*, 1909, 158–9.

[68] Onions, *Good Boy Seldom*, 1911, 274–5; *AW*, January 1914, 16. As James Taylor recounts, towards the mid-twentieth century there were rising concerns in the industry about revealing too much. Taylor, 'Fascinating Show'.

Much like science, the distinguishing ideal that marked professional advertising apart from sorcery was public openness.[69]

Insecurity

Try as they might to reconcile powers over minds with reason, professionals were insecure about their own arguments and never sure how their magic really worked. As one advised, advertisers needed 'nerve' because '[i]t is hard to project the imagination into a million homes...The advertiser doesn't pay for type and ink and paper. He pays for an effect in people's minds. It is as intangible as air, and as permanent as steel beams.'[70] Recurrent languages of nerve, courage, and grit spoke to the vast expanses of the unknown. They were intended for clients and agents, encouraging them all to overcome a wavering resolve. The more commentators tied their cultural capital with the mind, the more courage became a version of faith. Vocabularies of force recurred to the point of obsession:

> The showcard should be effective, and so strong; the iron plate should be aggressive; the poster must be striking; but it is particularly in the Newspaper and Magazine advertising that an Agent has an opportunity to introduce force of some kind which directly or indirectly will constrain the public to read his advertisement and to purchase the advertised article...whether it be in the working, in the illustrations, or in the type, the one essential to success is 'strength'.[71]

The languages were gendered and were forthcoming in proportion to the rising emphasis on the non-rational mind, which had feminine resonance. Despite the modern reference to scientific psychology, concepts of the non-rational, of intuition, feeling, temptation, and influence, were associated with femininity. Here, for example, was Eleanor M. Clark, who had been on the advertising staff of the Wanamaker New York-based department store, recasting her sex as the future of advertising for a British audience:

> Temperamentally, a woman is fitted to be an advertiser...a woman has more intuition and is a quicker reader of character than a man – two assets more valuable in advertising than in perhaps any other profession. As the subtler sex she can more often get 'right there' with less striving after effect than a man, and as the 'appealing' sex her writing will...carry an appeal which cannot be resisted.[72]

---

[69] On openness in psychology-as-science, see Danziger, *Constructing the Subject*, 27. On openness in science generally, see Chapter 4.
[70] *Advertiser's Review*, 19 March, 1904, 21.   [71] Hole, *Advertising and Progress*, 1914, 36–7.
[72] *AW*, January 1914, 116–18.

Clark introduced clichéd femininity as a new power in the era of the mind. Professionals also highlighted women's dominance as consumers. Surely, some argued, a woman could appeal to her sisters better than men. These perspectives informed calls for a greater place for women in the male-dominated advertising industry, in which female management and ownership were rare. G.E. Worrall, who successfully managed the advertising department of the Palmer Tyre Company, complained about her loneliness.[73]

Female power was threatening. In 1901 the *Advertising World* opposed an American commentator who championed women. Advertising, it argued, 'demands business ability of the highest order and great discrimination. The average woman is not qualified by nature.' At the same time, it conceded that women could be good advert-writers under male management. A decade later there was more openness and a growing conviction of women's importance, yet some firms still did not make public 'the fact that the spending of a large sum of money [advertising budget] is in the hands of a female'. Women's advertising work was often credited to men, and the term 'advertising *man*' for professional advertisers remained the standard linguistic gesture and cultural assumption. A commentator emphasized the timidity of the first Association of Advertising Women, established in 1910, and hoped members would acquire the 'pushfulness' they lacked. Meanwhile, women were excluded from male associations, including the new National Advertising Society.[74] Continuing discomfort points not only to obvious concerns with preserving male power, but more profoundly to the problematic status of expertise in the human mind: even as practitioners saw benefits in involving women, they were uneasy about the distance of their emerging expertise from the traditional masculinity of the rational. The problem was the *conceptual* feminization of their field. The continual flow of masculine vocabularies, and the continual resistance to women, implicitly counteracted feminization.

The balancing act between the feminine undertones of mind-management and masculine authority was obvious when women asserted their own worth. They implicitly responded to fears about their place in advertising with masculine languages of productivity, rationality, and energy. Meerloo, for one, argued that her insight into the female mind ensured paying rather than 'non-productive' adverts. Florence A. Degen's article on the 'industrial emancipation of woman' tapped categories usually invoked by male professionals. She argued that many women now had 'the qualities necessary for a successful advertiser – an appreciation of the "fitness of thing," tact, energy, enterprise, adaptiveness, the ability to

---

[73] *AW*, May 1912, 590. One manageress of an agency was noted in *Progressive Advertising*, May 1903, 28.
[74] *AW*, December 1901, 24–6; *AW*, May 1912, 577; *Advertiser's Weekly*, 19 April 1913, 24; *Advertiser's Weekly*, 19 July 1913, 23.

organize, and the gift of expression... An advertisement ought to read like an item of interesting business news told by one intelligent buyer to another...' To these images of rational entrepreneurship, Degen added the powers of femininity that could activate the non-rational mind: 'Read the average railway advertisements; they are as dry as dust... Surely a woman... would see the situation from a sentimental standpoint, and write something alluring...' Of course, a woman would do so without forgetting practicalities, Degen said, ever careful not to argue one side too exclusively.[75]

Raymond Williams interpreted the languages of force and attack in professionals' discourse as hostility. Like Onions, whose narrator saw forces of commerce 'brandish their weapons at the passer-by' so was Williams terrified. Attack, he said, is the structure of feeling in which impact has become the normal description of successful communication. He thought it was monstrous that advances in psychology, sociology, and communication were used against people.[76] However, in the pre-war years, the majority of writers in the advertising literature were not confrontational in their imagined relationship to consumers, as Onions and Williams both assumed. The typical approach treated consumers as forces to be reckoned with, not subjugated or outmanoeuvred. After all, professionals were performing the double task of speaking to clients not only as advertisers (to the public) but also as consumers (of advertising services), and could not afford to attract hostility or tap cultural anxieties. Instead, vocabularies of aggression compensated for the insecurity of a profession claiming a modern and rational expertise on the elusive concept of the mind, which was encouraging itself and its clients to persevere.

Contained Enchantment

Enchantment was being embraced in contained form: in the scientific garb of the psychological mind, in languages that upheld the rational while introducing the non-rational, in terms that asserted calculability while claiming incredible influence. All this was appeasing for a culture wary of enchantment in its economy. For advertising professionals, it was also a way of reclaiming an otherwise embarrassingly messy picture. As we saw in Chapter 1, fascination with adverts was more varied and imaginative than marketing goals. This was a phenomenon that professionals were reluctant to acknowledge, because it was beyond even their most ambitious powers of control, did not consistently serve

---

[75] *AW*, January 1914, 106–8; *AW*, January 1909, 220–2. Degen's efforts continued, see *Advertiser's Weekly*, 2 August 1913, 68.

[76] Williams, 'Advertising'; Onions, *Good Boy Seldom*, 1911, 191. For a similar criticism of the 'dictator-mind' of advertising experts, see Thompson, *Voice of Civilisation*, 99.

commerce, and—worst of all—fed into criticisms as advertising infiltrated lives beyond utilitarian exchange and aroused people in unpredictable ways.

Previous chapters have shown professionals' mobilization of legal power such as censorship, which minimized the role of enchantment in advertising and claimed control over it. A vivid illustration of their reluctance to acknowledge the proliferation of enchantment, even among their own crowd, could be seen in a 1905 meeting of the Sphinx Club, an advertising dining club established the previous year. Its president, the British-domiciled American John Morgan Richards, brought what he called 'a genuine specimen of "the Man in the Street"'. This was Fred Sumner, a London bus driver who came attired in his working clothes and badge. Sumner congratulated his hosts on the improvement in posters and related their popular reception in vivid detail. Recorded carefully in his working-class dialect, Sumner proved conversant in theories of mind. As he explained colour posters: 'When you can get the people to notice a thing like that it impresses itself upon the public mind.' The most striking element in the verbatim report was the repeated outbreak of laughter among club members. They were obviously jovial, but the places of laughter revealed an incredulous disbelief toward Sumner's unabashed enthusiasm and literal experience of advertising characters. Here, for example, we see the reaction to his story about a theatre poster I discussed in Chapter 1 (see Figure 1.16). Sumner explained passengers' interest by their identification with an imaginary lifeworld rather than detached curiosity, and provided an enlivened account of advert characters:

'The Beauty and the Barge' poster caught their eye – you know the one I mean, with the old boy leaning over the bar and chucking the fat barmaid under the chin. (Loud laughter). That pleased them very much, as the old boys were seafaring chaps, and they said they would go and see that piece. (Laughter). That gives you an idea.

Sumner continued with his animated experience of Sunny Jim, a transatlantic brand character for Force cereals:

A little time ago there was a poster out with Force – (laughter) – a chap called 'Sunny Jim.' (Renewed laughter.) That took the public eye very much, and old Sunny Jim got all round and became a by-word.[77]

Before saying more on the club's laughter, its broader context of advertising animation should be recalled. Sumner's comments were an early example of the power of brand mascots.[78] Sunny Jim was not the only one. In Chapter 3 we saw

---

[77] *AW*, March 1905, 358.
[78] On the interwar theorization of mascots, see Hornsey, 'The Penguins Are Coming'.

William Courtney's *Romance of the People's Picture Gallery*, which featured animated poster characters. Another case, for example, was Nestlé's cats, which one commentator described as the 'never too familiar White Cat and Brown Cat, who discuss their feline gastronomy in every station', and who alleviate your misery when you miss the train (Figure 7.5).[79]

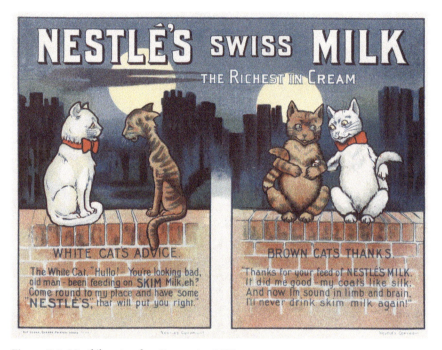

Figure 7.5 Nestlé's cats advertisement, *c*.1890s.

Professionals were interested in the animistic power of brands, which they saw as the key to goodwill. By the early twentieth century, the theory of goodwill, traditionally known as 'the probability that the old customers will resort to the old place',[80] was being recast in psychological terms as 'the inherent human tendency to habituate in the mode of expenditure... in place of the previous picking and choosing the consumer simply asks for a monosyllabic or bisyllabic product for a specific need.' The fact that goodwill was sometimes the only asset of a business, it was argued, proved the value of advertising.[81] Goodwill was built on brands, which facilitated habituation. Stefan Schwarzkopf argues that the idea that advertising had to build up the total value of the brand in the mind of consumers, rather

---

[79] *Billposter*, March 1901, 90 (quoting the *Daily News*).
[80] Lord Eldon in *Cruttwell* [1810]. Eldon's definition circulated in advertising literature, for example, *Practical Advertising*, 1905–6, x.
[81] Hole, *Advertising and Progress*, 1914, 80; *Profitable Advertising*, January 1902, 67.

than simply put a trademark in front of them, was first developed tacitly in agency practices and only later conceptualized. He therefore argues that the beginning of branding, usually a post-First World War story, was in fact earlier and located in practices of leading agencies. However, the commentary sprinkled in advertising literature suggests not only an earlier practice but also an earlier conceptualization that already focused on consumer minds as the loci of brands.[82]

Brand theory drew on developments in trademark law between 1860 and 1910. As Lionel Bently recounts, in this period law created property rights in marks and recognized a dual system of protection, one based on a central registry established according to the Trade Marks Registration Act, 1875, and the other based on marketplace use. The system relied on a denotative theory in which trademarks were indications of trade origin. Registration implied a decontextualized understanding of marks, because in order to obtain protection traders had to identify the meaning of the mark in advance and as a self-contained thing, outside communicative contexts. Meanwhile, as Megan Richardson and Julian Thomas observe, from the early stages of the new system, businesses did not view trademarks as mnemonic devices for sharing information, but rather invested them with symbolic meanings. Within trademark law, acknowledging the imaginative expanses of brands and the animism they involved appeared only gradually, reluctantly, and never fully.[83] The role of advertising in turning marks into brands was not a central theme in discussions of law, but it was central to practitioners who turned it into a professional undertaking.[84] They regularly recommended that clients register marks rather than rely on common law protections, which was

---

[82] Schwarzkopf, 'Turning Trademarks into Brands'; see also Jobling, *Man Appeal*, ch. 1.

[83] Bently, 'Making of Modern Trade Marks Law'; Richardson and Thomas, *Fashioning Intellectual Property*, ch. 8. On the development of trademark law, see also Mercer, 'Mark of Distinction'; Higgins, 'Trademarks and Infringement'.

Scholarship on late twentieth- and twenty-first-century law shows more conceptual room for enchantment, albeit mainly in the legal approach to competition between businesses, where brands receive significant protection beyond informational paradigms, particularly protection against brand dilution by association with a competing business even if there is no confusion as to trade origin. The legal approach to consumer–advertiser relationships remains governed by a rationalist paradigm. Assaf, 'Brand Fetishism'; Assaf, 'Magical Thinking'; Lury, *Brands*, ch. 5. However, a case could be made for the imaginative meaning of trade origins in terms of nationalism. I am grateful to Jennifer Davis for this suggestion.

[84] Discussions of advertising in parliamentary committees on trademark law were marginal. Legal treatise writers examined advertising with questions such as whether the text of an advert could be a trademark, whether adverts were relevant for establishing market use, whether adverts could constitute a trademark infringement, and whether advertised misrepresentations could undermine trademark protection. See, for example, Sebastian, *Law of Trade Marks*, 1890; Kerly and Underhay, *Law of Trade-Marks*, 1901. Thus, even as they paid some attention to advertising, legal treatises did not address significant parts of expanses between trademarks and brands.

Professionals operated in an unstable regime in other ways too. Legal policymakers were conflicted about turning language into a subject of property rights; therefore, permissible marks were a contested and changing category. Between the passage of the 1875 Trade Marks Act and the early twentieth century, policy moved from accepting only invented, non-referential words, to accepting also extant words, and then also oblique references.

indeed happening on a large scale. Advice then explained how marks built brands. The name should be registrable, one professional advised, but legal registrability was just a beginning, to be followed by mind-penetrating practices. In one advice, the physical gesture of pronunciation was key; therefore, a mark had to be 'short, euphonious, and easily pronounced'. The word, said another, had to convey a hint of meaning, which it was for the expert to expand: 'the advertising expert's task... is... to weave fancy round such appellation, and develop its meaning in an endless variety of ways.'[85] The result was dramatic:

> The best asset of a business is a well-known trade-mark. Do you realise what that means? It means that in the convolutions of thousands or millions of human brains that trade-mark is indelibly impressed. You can't see it, but it is there and it is property – you can capitalise it.[86]

Commentary was still haphazard, yet the shift in the discourse revealed the rise of modern branding theory.

Against this background, we can return to the laughing professionals in the Sphinx Club. Their laughter revealed the uncertain status of brand penetration that might spin out of control. Some advertisers met the unexpected effects of adverts by trying to reclaim them. For example, the British Vacuum Cleaner Company created new adverts from political adaptations of its 'Help' campaign featuring John Hassall's vital machine (Figure 7.6). Reclaiming effects was a way of acknowledging their unexpected nature, which the Sphinx Club seemed unsure how to fathom. The overflowing effects of poster characters embarrassed members; their laughter bespoke a preference for professional control over brand proliferation. Professionals supported a contained image of their role as market enchanters, in which they initiated processes that led to market action—not free imaginations.

By seeking control, professionals retained a rationalist framework for consumer enchantment.[87] They kept clear of the wilder and incalculable enchantments of the advert-saturated environment itself. When Sumner showed a fascinated dwelling in animistic worlds, the Sphinx Club members were amused rather than certain that they were witnessing a serious impact of their work. In retrospect, Sunny Jim confirmed their embarrassment. He certainly 'got all around' as Sumner said, became a household name and even James Joyce's nickname, but as Jackson Lears recounts, the company failed and Sunny Jim turned into a cautionary figure for

---

[85] Benson, *Force in Advertising*, 1904, 13–14; C. Manners Smith, *Advertising*, January 1898, 177–8.
[86] *Advertiser's Review*, 19 March 1904, 21.
[87] They thus re-placed production behind the steering wheel of capitalism. Mapping disenchantment and enchantment onto production and consumption has since become familiar. See, for example, Gellner, *Spectacles & Predicaments*, ch. 2.

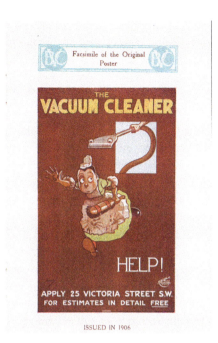

Figure 7.6 British Vacuum Cleaner Company booklet of poster adaptations, 1906–9.

creativity overwhelming the business sense.[88] Enchantment was to be endorsed but carefully contained, professionals knew.

Conclusion

Advertising professionals engaged in their own branding from the late nineteenth century. They jostled for terms of art that would describe their unique and necessary role in economic and cultural life, and found those in concepts of expert access to minds. Stuart Ewen describes American advertising as an attempted change in the psychic economy, which could only be achieved if advertisers began to talk about readers rather than products. In Britain, it was by talking about readers that professional advertisers persuaded clients to let them talk about their products.[89] In professionals' accounts, minds were susceptible to both rational and non-rational appeals and most crucially to their expert combination, which would overcome conscious and unconscious consumer resistance. In doing so, commentators incorporated the non-rational into their professional definition. They had new languages for it with the rising prestige of psychology, which provided a venue for authority when other venues led to disparagement and inferiorization. No less critically, the manifold legal powers that were being mobilized to deal with advertising disavowed its enchantments to such an extent that enchantment became an attractive field of action, free from direct legal attention. Advertisers stood a greater risk of cultural legal backlash when they ventured into rationalist terrains. In yet another ironic twist of advertising's turbulent history, criticisms of its rationalist shortfalls, which were driven by fears of enchantment, ended up encouraging professional advertisers to explore its potential.

In their theories of contained enchantment, in which the incalculable was confined to minds and in turn described as both explicable and controllable by rational commercial calculation, a strictly disenchanted enchantment, early professionals laid the foundations of a myth that would become incredibly powerful over the twentieth century, of advertisers as the sorcerers of capitalism.[90] In 1911 the *Advertising World* celebrated a new series of lectures on advertising: 'Perhaps at some not too distant day,' the writer dreamt, 'the giants of the advertising world will be hall-marked by the degrees...'[91] He was not too far off the mark, but the

---

[88] On Joyce, see Leonard, *Advertising and Commodity Culture*, 1 (citing Stanislaus Joyce). Leonard speculates on the impact of nicknaming on Joyce's art in ch. 1; Lears, *Fables of Abundance*, 309–10.

[89] Ewen, *Captains of Consciousness*. Ewen discusses the 1920s.

[90] For 'disenchanted enchantment' see Ritzer, *Enchanting a Disenchanted World*. Saler, *As If*, also develops this concept, but he does not refer to rationally planned enchantment but rather to a duality in which something enchants and disenchants simultaneously, so that the enchanted remain aware that they are embracing an illusion or engaging in an imaginary exercise, and are not deluded.

[91] *AW*, January 1911, 46. The lectures were given at the Regent Street Polytechnic by Thomas Russell.

academic attention that future decades would accord the industry involved much more critique than he anticipated. Twentieth-century critical theories and histories have suspiciously explored the enchanting powers of advertising. At the same time, they have also repeated the central myth that advertising professionals started building. As we saw in the Introduction, that advertising enchants by design has become a familiar argument. Thus, Thompson wrote urgently in 1843 that the aim of most adverts was 'to influence the thoughts and actions of a large number of people by inducing them to suspend individual and rational judgement'. They were selling illusions, influencing masses of people by 'irrational appeals'. And so, while early criticisms disavowed enchantment, twentieth-century intellectuals reversed them as they already responded to the myth of the market enchanters with the assumption that they succeeded all too well. Those who doubted advertisers' power, like Michael Schudson, now had the work cut out for them.[92]

As we saw in Chapter 1, advertising made enchantment integral to everyday life, but its force was not a product of advertisers' rational planning or control. The myth represented professionals as authors when they were in fact participants in a structural phenomenon that depended on the advertising environment as a whole, and on consumers' own will to enchantment, which exceeded individual plans and products. Jennifer Wicke reminds us that advertising's endurance comes from its plenitude, its historical association with multiple cultural fields, its basis not only in individual makers but also in diverse institutional settings, collective aspirations and values, adoption and creative uses by publics, and place in the overall political economy. We should add to these the materiality of environments with which it operated, the form it gave to technological innovation, the shapes it bestowed on everyday surroundings, and the transformative powers it implied. Yet the myth took hold. Today, argues Moeran, the creatives of the advertising industry possess magical powers because of the way society regards them as able to accomplish things beyond the power of normal human beings.[93]

In its most recent version, an avalanche of work on the attention economy repeats the early myth. For example, legal and media scholar Tim Wu argues that '[f]rom the 1890s through the 1920s, there arose the first means for harvesting attention on a mass scale and directing it for commercial effect ... advertising was

---

[92] Thompson, *Voice of Civilisation*, 11, 190, and *passim*. Schudson was among the better-known efforts to debunk the myth as he argued that advertisers were stabbing in the dark much more than practising precision microsurgery on the public consciousness. Instead of marketing effects, he analysed advertising as a cultural force preaching, without consistent success, individualist consumer values. Echoing the concept of socialist realism in art, he termed it capitalist realism. Schudson, *Advertising, the Uneasy Persuasion*.

In a close context, Schwarzkopf charges advertising historians with writing a Hegelian narrative of modernity. As he puts it, historians 'failed to notice that their narratives merely promoted the self-created professional identity of the early advertising industry, which tried to make the world believe that the logic of history had taken it into an "Advertising Age"'. Schwartzkopf, 'Subsidizing Sizzle', 529.

[93] Wicke, *Advertising Fictions*, 15–16; Moeran, 'Business, Anthropology'.

the conversion engine that, with astonishing efficiency, turned the cash crop of attention into an industrial commodity.'[94] Professionals certainly tried, but mostly against an urgent need to provide a resonant account of a nascent industry. While the efficiency of advertising remains contested, the myth that advertising experts could enchant to rational ends was certainly efficient. In the mythical form of a unidirectional force deployed by experts on minds, enchantment was enlisted to give advertising meaning and reason, and perhaps most crucially for the industry's early actors, a powerful cultural role.

[94] Wu, *Attention Merchants*, pt 1.

Conclusion

Oliver Onions wondered about the significance of his fictional advertising agent, Good Boy Seldom:

> What was he – the visionary, the seer, the poet even of commerce? Who can say?[1]

These evocations of mystical figures were appropriate for advertising, which introduced to commercial life 'afflatus, sound, air, the unknown, metaphysical quantities', or what I have been investigating as enchantment. The impalpable became economic value, and imagination ran, as Onions put it, 'consumingly free'. When contemporaries had to account for their historical moment, many enlisted law to disavow this constitutive experience of market culture. Legally imbued debates enacted obsessively what we today know as the Weberian thesis of modernity. Time and again, the cultural boundaries of celebrated fields, which promoted rationalist values, were guarded against encroachments by advertising. In the process, advertising was criticized for its rationalist shortfalls as it did not live up to the highest ideals of aesthetic appreciation, objective knowledge, and impartial information. It was instead the preserve of vulgarity, exaggeration, bias, or just the ridiculous. These views have become so familiar that their history has been forgotten. As Jonah Siegel says, the most successful lessons are those we forget having learned.[2] Their effects, however, went deep. Languages of rationality and its failures disavowed the significance of enchantment by advertising, and so affirmed modernity-as-disenchantment, denying modern visionaries, seers, and indeed their enabling crowds and communities. As Onions put it, the country 'shuts her eyes to their larger significance'.[3] Placing legal powers, forms, and logics behind disenchantment turned a wavering ideology into a formal normative enterprise.

The cultural legal efforts invested in disenchantment were precarious and analytically weak, but they nonetheless became common sense. Modernity-as-disenchantment, with the host of perspectives it entailed in terms of the rationalities of cultural fields and the dispassionate mentality of economic life itself, were and remain dominant and popular despite everything: despite the porousness of boundaries; despite all fields operating under the pressures of the profit motive

---

[1] Onions, *Good Boy Seldom*, 1911, 186. [2] Siegel, *Desire and Excess*, preface.
[3] Onions, *Good Boy Seldom*, 380.

that was more often a heated passion than a sober interest; despite the prevalence of enchantment. The commonsensical status of disenchantment can only be fully understood once law is brought into the picture, because it turned this world view into practical daily outcomes. We find its impact in legally imbued responses to advertising, for example in contracts entered or refused, regulations of the place and material qualities of adverts, evaluations of consumer responses to them by censors, or the management of competition between advertisers through courts. By attending law and legality we can trace the many implications of the normative project of disenchantment.

Why was law so central? It bears repeating that 'law' here refers to myriad legal investments by private and public actors who mobilized legal powers, procedures, and concepts available to them in attempts to negotiate the challenges of advertising; 'law' does not imply only a state apparatus or professional pursuit. This has not been an account of law as a coherent field or institution, but of historical actors who concurrently found that legal means were useful for preserving modernity-as-disenchantment. To be sure, there was much in formal state law and in professional legal discourses that aligned with this worldview, and so actors enlisted them to the task. However, if legal professionals or formal institutions of law alone had been committed to disenchantment, they would have failed. It was a broader picture of a culture, which included the advertising industry, commercial advertisers, media owners, civil society organizations of many hues, social critics, and diverse consumers and readers. They all wanted to conceive their public life and economic order as disenchanted and to find a place for advertising on those terms. Even as they preserved their will to enchantment, they mobilized law and preformed legality in creative ways to uphold a disenchanted account of their common lives.

Of course, the normative enterprise of disenchantment did not preclude enchantment. Onions speculated that efforts to embattle it were doomed:

> That essential spark that burns clear in the breast of the seer and visionary is denied many opportunities in these our days; yet that same spark is the sole unquenchable, imperishable thing in the world. Can it then be that, refused its proper altar, it burns up with its immortal fire the very dampers cast upon it to extinguish it? For it is certainly not extinguished. An age that can turn a mere work, a song... an appearance, an impalpable impression, the unseizable stuff of Thought itself, to hard, quotable, saleable values, is not deserted of Imaginativeness.[4]

---

[4] Onions, *Good Boy Seldom*, 186.

Refused a 'proper altar', enchantment came to occupy the very centre of capitalism. We have evidence enough of this process in reception evidence from readers and viewers of adverts; in the deep anxieties that mass advertising provoked, which led to expansive public debates; and finally in the self-branding of advertisers themselves. At the same time, due to disavowal, consumers were deprived of normative conceptual languages to account for their experiences and were often belittled. Onions saw that too, and recognized a cultural imperative to dismiss and scapegoat advertising:

> Marvels of Advertising were passed with scarcely a glance, or pushed aside with a 'Pish, Pish!'... The very loafer at the street-corner was sophisticated... He characterized anything he did not immediately understand as 'some advertising dodge.'... even had his imagination been touched, he would not have dared to say so.[5]

Yet, even so, there was room for manoeuvre. The criticisms and ridicule cast on advertising ultimately had ironic outcomes. They supplied the disenchanted languages with which Britain actually mainstreamed and legitimized this enchanting system. Meanwhile, because disenchanted languages construed advertising as an inferior element of modernity, they unwittingly liberated it from rationalist inhibitions and encouraged its non-rational 'spark'. All this finally drove professional advertisers to adopt a theory that celebrated enchantment.

Of course, a backlash would follow. The struggle of disenchantment continued, and continues still. Advertising remains contested; theory continues to argue about its Janus face as a rationalizing and enchanting system; it remains trivialized and yet awed; and many of us continue to nurture a love–hate, attraction–repulsion relationship with this inescapable environment. This book has sought the roots of these responses, their legal basis, their cultural logic. Advertising energized an entire culture to examine and articulate the terms on which it lived. Rather than treat those terms as true or false, we should appreciate their world-generating power for late capitalism in terms of aesthetics, epistemology, and ontology. It is on those terms that the full impact of advertising becomes clear.

---

[5] Onions, *Good Boy Seldom*, 208.

Bibliography

1. Primary Sources

(i) Archives (undigitized sources)

Bodleian Library, University of Oxford, John Johnson Collection (JJ)
British Library (BL)
History of Advertising Trust (HAT)
Manchester Met University Special Collections, Sir Harry Page Collection of Scrap Albums and Common Place Books
Museum of London (ML)
National Gallery of Canada (NGC)
National Railway Museum, York
Royal Danish Library (RDL)
St Bride Foundation (SBF)
The National Archives, UK)TNA(
University of Cambridge Library (CL)
Victoria and Albert Museum
Wellcome Collection (WC)

(ii) Cases

Unreported cases are listed if at least one party was named in the source.

Allport v Nutt (1845) 135 ER 826.
Ardley (1871) LR 1 CCR 301.
Balfour v Balfour [1919] 2 KB 571.
Barclay v Pearson [1893] 2 Ch 154.
Bartlett v Parker [1912] 2 KB 497.
Bays and others, 1862, Old Bailey Proceedings Online (t18621027-1095).
Beaumont v Dukes (1821) 37 ER 910.
Bell v Bashford and British Medical Association, *Northern Whig*, 15 June 1912, 9.
Bellairs v Tucker (1884) 13 QBD 562.
Bexwell v Christie (1776) 98 ER 1150.
Bile Bean Manufacturing Co. v Davidson (1906) 23 RPC 725 (Inner House).
Bile Bean Manufacturing Co. v Davidson (1906), 22 RPC 553 (Outer House).
Bile Bean Manufacturing Co., Limited v Davidson (1906) 8 F 1181.
Binet, 1893, Old Bailey Proceedings Online (t18930724-680).
Blyth v Hulton & Co. Ltd. (1908), 24 TLR 719.
Boyle v Turner, Barnstaple County Court, *Billposter*, March 1889, 127.
Braham v Bustard (1863) 71 ER 195.
Brown and others, 1899, Old Bailey Proceedings Online (t18991120-1).
Bryan (1857) 169 ER 1002.
Carlill v Carbolic Smoke Ball Co [1891–4] All ER 127 (CA).
Carlill v Carbolic Smoke Ball Co [1892] 2 QB 484.
Carpenter, 1911, Old Bailey Proceedings Online (t19111205-56).

Charles Pool & Co. v J. Lemesle, Co., *AW*, May 1914, 848–50.
Chrimes and others, 1898, Old Bailey Proceedings Online (t18981212-90).
Cochrane v MacNish and Son [1896] AC 225.
Coleman, Billposter, May 1890, 175.
Cooke and others, 1895, Old Bailey Proceedings Online (t18951118-59).
Cruttwell v Lye [1810] All ER Rep 189.
Cunningham v Daily Express, *Times*, 21 December 1900, 9.
Dakhyl v Labouchere (1907) 23 TLR 364.
Dakhyl v Labouchere [1908] 2 KB 325 (HL)
Dann v Curzon (1911) 27 TLR 163, 55 Solic. J. & Wkly. Rep. 189, 104 LT (1910) 66.
Davenport and Moyle, 1906, Old Bailey Proceedings Online (t19060205-242).
Dimmock v Hallett (1866) LR 2 Ch App 21.
Eagleton v Shirley, Clerkenwell County Court, *Sevenoaks Chronicle and Kentish Advertiser*, 18 October 1912.
Edgar, 1910, Old Bailey Proceedings Online (t19100426-40).
Evans v Harlow (1844) 5 QB 622.
Fry v Tapson (1884) 28 Ch 268.
Fryer, 1892, Old Bailey Proceedings Online (t18920307-312).
Gabriel and others, 1899, Old Bailey Proceedings Online (t18990626-478).
Goudie and Burge, 1902, Old Bailey Proceedings Online (t19020210-198).
Guildford v Smith, Billposter, November 1892, 88.
Hall v Cox [1899] 1 QB 198.
Halley, 1886, Old Bailey Proceedings Online (t18860503-547).
Harris (1866) 10 Cox CC 352.
Hart v Nisbet & Co. (1900) SCJC 39.
Hawke v Hulton, *Times*, 19 December 1905, 3.
Hicklin (1868) LR 3 QB 360.
Higgins v Samels (1862) 70 ER 1139.
Holloway v Holloway (1850) 13 Beav 209.
Hooley and Lawson, 1904, Old Bailey Proceedings Online (t19041114-51).
Howard, 1885, Old Bailey Proceedings Online (t18850518-371).
Hubbuck and Sons v Wilkinson [1899] 1 QB 86.
Humphries, 1884, Old Bailey Proceedings Online (t18841229-216).
Hunter v Sharpe (1866) 4 F & F 983, 176 ER 875.
Illife, Sona and Strumey Ltd. v Lombards Ltd., City of London Court, *Coventry Evening Telegraph*, 10 August 1900 3.
Jones v Bright (1829) 130 ER 1167.
Jones, 1891, Old Bailey Proceedings Online (t18911214-104);
Krahn and others, 1897, Old Bailey Proceedings Online (t18971122-42).
Labouchere, *Northampton Mercury*, 26 March 1881, 13.
Leverson, 1868, Old Bailey Proceedings Online (t18680817-721).
Lloyd v H.M. Advocate (1899) 1 F (J) 31.
London City Council v Carwardine [1892], 68 LT 761.
London County Council v Walter Hill & Co., *Billposter*, April 1901.
Longman v Pascall, 1892, *Billposter*, March 1892, 145–146.
Lupton and others, 1898, Old Bailey Proceedings Online (t18980725-526).
Lyne v Nicholls (1906) 23 TLR 86.
Mackenzie v Hawke [1902] 2 KB 216.
Magennis v Fallon (1829) 2 Mol 561.

Manchester Billposting Co. Ltd. v Sidney Prince, Manchester County Court, *Billposter*, February 1909, 78–81.
Medical Battery Company v Jeffery (1892), Bloomsbury County Court, *Lancet*, 23 July 1892, 224–6; *BMJ*, 23 July 1892, 205; *Pall Mall Gazette*, 20 October 1893, 1–2.
Milson, 1851, Old Bailey Proceedings Online (t18511215-122).
Minty v Sylvester (1915) 114 LT 164.
Moore v Goldin, Westminster County Court, *Daily Telegraph*, 14 June 1907, 5.
Morris v Brinsmead, 1892, *Lancaster Gazette*, 3 February 1892, 2; *Lloyd's Weekly*, 7 February 1892, 4; *Sheffield Independent*, 3 February 1892, 4; *Blackburn Standard and Weekly Express*, 6 February 1892, 5; *Morning Post*, 3 February 1892, 8.
Nathan and Harris (1909) 2 Cr App R. 35.
Nicholson and Richards, 1901, Old Bailey Proceedings Online (t19011021-728).
Northern Whig v Northern Union Coursing Club, Belfast Quarter Sessions, *NSC*, June 1904, 7.
Owen v Greenberg, *Times*, 10 March 1898, 13.
Parmiter v *Coupland* (1840) 6 M & W 105.
Partridge v GMC, *Times*, 23 March 1892, 3; (1892) 8 TLR 311; (1890) 25 QBD 90; (1887) 19 QBD 467.
Paul & Co v Corporation of Glasgow (1900) 3 F 119.
Paynter, 1908, Old Bailey Proceedings Online (t19081110-43).
Pointing, 1897, Old Bailey Proceedings Online (t18970628-461).
Ramsay, Belfast, *Billposter*, June 1910, 126.
Rayner v The 'Answers' Company Ltd., *Leigh Chronicle*, 23 June 1893, 7.
Reeves,1880, Old Bailey Proceedings Online (t18800112-171).
Riches, 1877, Old Bailey Proceedings Online (t18770205-247).
Robbins v Cooper, Clerkenwell County Court, *Billposter*, May 1888, 211.
Roberts, Leeds Police Court, *AW*, November 1909, 744.
Rockley's Ltd. v Holmes, Nottingham County Court, *Billposter*, May 1908, 122.
Romanes v Garman (1912) 2 SLT 104.
Salmon, 1886, Old Bailey Proceedings Online (t18860111-210).
Scott v Director of Public Prosecutions (1914), 111 LT 59.
Scott v Hanson [1829] 1 Russ & M 127.
Shan and others, 1893, Old Bailey Proceedings Online (t18931016-946).
Simpson and another, Lindsey petty sessions, *Lincoln, Rutland and Stamford Mercury*, 20 July 1888, 6.
Smith's Advertising Agency v Leeds Laboratory (1910) 26 TLR 335.
Stanley, 1882, Old Bailey Proceedings Online (t18820227-330).
Stoddart [1900] 1 QB 177 (CA).
Stoddart v Sagar [1895] 2 QB 474.
Symons and others, 1907, Old Bailey Proceedings Online (t19070128-43).
Tarrant and Fry, 1897, Old Bailey Proceedings Online (t18971025-709a).
Taylor v Smetten (1883) 11 QBD 207.
Thompson, 1878, Old Bailey Proceedings Online (t18780506-533).
Thorley's Cattle Food Company v Massam (1880) 14 Ch 763.
Tucker v Wakley (1908), KB, *Daily News*, 21 January 1908, 6; *Lancet*, 1 February 1908, 301–83; *Times*, 21 January 1908, 10.
United Billposting Co. v Somerset County Council [1926], Law J Rep (n.s.) 899.
von Sachs v Ashton and Parson Ltd., KB, *Birmingham Daily Post*, 24 October 1914, 4.
Walker and Carter, 1879, Old Bailey Proceedings Online (t18791202-137).
Walter Hill & Co. v J.W. Currans, Bloomsbury County Court, *Billposter*, January 1892, 111.
Walter Hill & Co. v Jacobs and Wright of "Wonderland", Bloomsbury County Court, *Billposter*, April 1903, 114–15.

Walter Judd, Ltd. v Longstreths, Ltd., City of London Court, NSC, April 1904, 10.
Ward, 1844, Old Bailey Proceedings Online (t18441021-2384).
Watson v Earl of Charlemont (1848) 116 ER 1091.
Wells v Webber (1862) 175 ER 1253.
Wells, 1893, Old Bailey Proceedings Online (t18930306-349).
Welman (1853) 169 ER 690.
Western Counties Manure Company v Lawes Chemical Manure Company (1874) LR 9 Ex 218.
White v Mellin (1895) HL 155.
White v Mellin [1895] AC 154.
Willing and Co. prosecutors, Billposter, June 1893, 13.
Willis v Young [1907] 1 KB 448.
Woodman, 1899, Old Bailey Proceedings Online (t18990109-126).
Young v Macrae (1862) 122 ER 100.

(iii) Legislation

Advertisements Regulation Act, 1907, 7 Edw. 7, c. 27.
Advertisements Regulation Bill, Amendments, Home Office, 28 February 1905 (TNA, HO45/10507–126729/4).
Advertising Stations (Rating) Act, 1889, 52 & 53 Vict., c. 27.
Betting Act, 1874, 27 & 38 Vict. c. 15.
Betting Houses Act, 1853, 16 & 17 Vict. c. 119.
Betting Inducements HL Bill, 361, 1912–13.
Betting Inducements HL Bill, 159, 1913.
Betting Inducements HL Bill, 147, 1914.
Birmingham Corporation Act, 1883, 46 & 47 Vict. c. 70.
Criminal Law Amendment HC Bill, 7, 1917.
Doncaster Corporation Act, 1904, 4 Edw. 7 c. 103.
Edinburgh Corporation Act, 1899, 62 & 63 Vict. c. 71.
Farnworth Urban District Council Act 1900, 63 & 64 Vict. c. 233.
Gaming Act, 1845, 8 & 9 Vict. c. 109.
Hackney Carriage Act, 1853, 16 &17 Vict. c. 33.
Housing, Town Planning, &c. Act, 1909, 9 Edw. 7 c. 44.
Indecent Advertisements Act, 1889, 52 & 53 Vict. c. 18.
London Building Act, 1894, 57 & 58 Vict. c. 213.
London Sky-Signs Prohibition Act, 1891, 54 & 55 Vict. c. 78.
Lotteries Act, 1823, 4 Geo. 4, c. 60.
Lotteries Act, 1836, 6 & 7 Will. 4, c. 66.
Medical Act, 1858, 21 & 22 Vict. c. 90.
Metropolis Management Amendment Act, 1862, 25 & 26 Vict. c. 102.
Metropolitan Open Spaces Act, 1877, 40 & 41 Vict. c. 35.
Metropolitan Police Act, 1839, 2 & 3 Vict. c. 47.
Metropolitan Streets Act 1867, 30 & 31 Vict. c. 134.
Morality HC Bill, 179, 1910.
Municipal Corporations Act, 1882, 45 & 46 Vict. c. 50.
Obscene Publications Act, 1857, 20 & 21 Vict. c. 83.
Offences Against the Person Act, 1861, 24 and 25 Vict. c. 100.
Pharmacy Act, 1868, 31 & 32 Vict. c. 121.
Poisons and Pharmacy Act, 1908, 8 Edw. 7 c. 55.

Prevention of Gaming (Scotland) Act, 1869, 32 & 33 Vict. c. 87.
Repeal of Certain Stamp Duties Act, 1853, 16 & 17 Vict. c. 63.
Sale of Land by Auction Act, 1867, 30 & 31 Vict. c. 48.
Trade Marks Act, 1905, 5 Edw. 7 c. 15.
Trade Marks Registration Act, 1875, 38 & 39 Vict. c. 91.
Vagrancy Act, 1824 (5 Geo. 4 c. 83).
Vagrancy Act, 1838, 1 & 2 Vict. c. 38.
Vexatious Indictments Act, 1859, 22 & 23 Vict. c. 17.

(iv) Newspapers and Periodicals

Aberdeen Journal
Advertiser's Weekly (BL)
Advertisers' Review (BL)
Advertising: A Monthly Journal for Every Advertiser (BL and HAT)
Advertising News (BL)
Advertising World (AW) (HAT)
Age
All the Year Round
Ampthill & District News
Athenaeum
Banbury Advertiser
Banner of Ulster
Bath Chronicle
Beautiful World: The journal of the Society for Checking the Abuses of Public Advertising (BW) (CL)
Bedfordshire Times and Independent
Belfast News
Belper News
Beverley and East Riding Recorder
Bexhill-on-Sea Observer
Billposter (earlier: *Bill Poster and Advertising Agent*) (BL)
Birmingham Daily Post
Blackburn Standard and Weekly Express
Blackwood's Magazine
Bradford Daily Telegraph
Bradford Observer
Bristol Mercury
British Medical Journal (BMJ)
Buckingham Express
Bury and Norwich Post, and Suffolk Herald
Chambers' Edinburgh Journal
Chamber's Journal
Cheltenham Chronicle
Chemist and Druggist
Cheshire Observer
Cornhill Magazine
Coventry Evening Telegraph
Coventry Herald
Daily Express

Daily Gazette for Middlesbrough
Daily Graphic
Daily News
Daily Telegraph
Dart
Derby Mercury
Derbyshire Courier
Derbyshire Times
Dublin Daily Express
Dublin Medical Press
Dundee Courier
Dundee Evening Telegraph
Edinburgh Evening News
Edinburgh Review
Elgin Courier
Era
Evening News
Evening Star
Examiner
Exeter and Plymouth Gazette
Faringdon Advertiser
Fortnightly Review
Frazer's Magazine
Freeman's Journal
Funny Folks
Globe
Gloucester Citizen
Graphic
Hants and Berks Gazette and Middlesex and Surrey Journal
Henley Advertiser
Hospital
Household Words
Hull Daily Mail
Hull Packet
Illustrated Chips
Illustrated London News
Illustrated Police Budget
Illustrated Police News
Illustrated Sporting and Dramatic News
Irish News and Belfast Morning News
Irish Times
Judy
Jurist
Knaresborough Post
Lady's Newspaper & Pictorial Times
Lakes Chronicle
Lancashire Evening Post
Lancashire General Advertiser
Lancaster Gazette and General Advertiser for Lancashire, Westmorland, and Yorkshire

Lancet
Law Times
Leader and Saturday Analyst
Leeds Mercury
Leicester Chronicle
Leigh Chronicle
Leisure Hour
Limerick Reporter
Lincoln, Rutland and Stamford Mercury
Liverpool Mercury
Lloyd's Weekly
Long Eaton Advertiser
Luton Times and Advertiser
Magazine of Art
Manchester Courier
Mansfield Reporter
Modern Advertising (supplement to the *Poster*)
Morning Post
Nation
New Review
Newcastle Daily Chronicle
Newcastle Guardian
News Agent and Bookseller's Review
Newspaper Society Circular (NSC) (SBF)
Nineteenth Century
Norfolk News
Northern Whig
Nottingham Evening Post
Nottinghamshire Guardian
Observer
Pall Mall Gazette
Pearson's Weekly
Penny Illustrated Paper
People
Pick-Me-Up
Placard
Poster
Practical Advertising (HAT)
Preston Herald,
Profitable Advertising (BL)
Progressive Advertising (later: *Progressive Advertising and Outdoor Publicity*) (BL)
Punch
Quarterly Review
Reasoner
Reynolds's Newspaper
Royal Cornwall Gazette
Saturday Review
Sevenoaks Chronicle and Kentish Advertiser
Sheffield Daily Telegraph

Sheffield Evening Telegraph
Sheffield Independent
Shields Daily Gazette
Speaker
St James's Gazette
Standard
Stonehaven Journal
Times
Torquay Times
Truth
Weekly Dispatch (BL)
West Somerset Free Press
Western Daily Press
Western Mail
Western Times
Whitby Gazette
York Herald
Yorkshire Evening Post
Yorkshire Post and Leeds Intelligencer

(v) Reports

Board of Trade Committee on the Duties, Organization and Arrangement of the Patent Office under the Patents, Designs and Trade Marks Act, 1875, as relates to Trade Marks and Designs, 1888.
Committee on the Law Relating to Lotteries, Second Report, 1808.
House of Commons Returns, Prosecution of Offences Acts, 1879 and 1884, June 29, 1900.
Local Government Board: Nineteenth Report, C.6141 3, 1889–90.
Select Committee of the House of Lords on Betting, 1902.
Select Committee on Lotteries and Indecent Advertisements, 1908.
Select Committee on Newspaper Stamps, 1851.
Select Committee on Patent Medicines, 1914.
Select Committee on the Trade Marks Bill, 1905.
Select Committee on Trade Marks Bill and Merchandize Marks Bill, 1862.
The Practice of Medicine and Surgery by Unqualified Persons in the UK, Cd. 5422, 1910.

(vi) Other

The Advertiser's Guide to Publicity: A Practical Treatise on the Principles of Successful Advertising, 2nd edn (Birmingham: Moody's Printing Company, 1887) (CL).
Advertisers' Pocketbook (London: International Correspondence Schools, 1913) (HAT).
'The Advertising System'. *Edinburgh Review*, February 1843, 1–2.
'The Age of Veneer'. *Fraser's Magazine*, January 1852, 92.
Advertiser's ABC of Official Scales and Advertisement Press Directory (London: T.B. Browne, 1892) (HAT).
Allen, W.E.D. *David Allen's: The History of a Family Firm, 1857–1957* (London: John Murray, 1957).
Anderson, Robert. *The Lighter Side of My Official Life* (London: Hodder and Stoughton, 1910).
Anson, William Reynell. *Principles of the English Law of Contract and of Agency in Its Relation to Contract*, 7th edn (Oxford, 1893).

'The Art of the Wall Advertiser'. *Pall Mall Gazette*, 19 September 1893, 1–2.
'Art on the Hoardings'. *Morning Post*, 31 August 1908.
Barratt, Thomas J. 'How Nearly £3,000,000 Were Spent in Advertising by One Firm'. In *Success in Advertising*, edited by H. Simonis (London: Morning Leader, 1908) (RDL).
Barrie, J.M. *Peter Pan* (Penguin, 2013) (1911).
Bateman, Joseph. *A Practical Treatise on the Law of Auctions*, 6th edn (London: Maxwell, 1882).
Bennett, R. In Algar Labouchere Thorold, *The Life of Henry Labouchere*, (G.P. Putnam's Sons, 1913).
Benson, S.H. *Force in Advertising* (London, 1904) (private collection).
Bentham, Jeremy. 'Of Publicity'. In *The Works of Jeremy Bentham*, vol. 2 (Edinburgh: William Tait, 1838–43).
Besant, Walter and Dorothy Wallis. *Dorothy Wallis: An Autobiography* (Longmans, Green & Co., 1892).
Bile Bean advertisement, 1902 (WC, Drug advertising ephemera, box 18).
Bile Bean pamphlet, 1900s, (JJ, Patent Medicines 8 (24)).
'Billsticking'. *News Agent and Bookseller's Review*, 8 September 1900, 192.
Borough of Bromley, letter, 18 December 1909 (TNA, HO45/10565.173.473/5).
British Medical Association. *Secret Remedies: What They Cost and What They Contain, Based on Analyses made for the British Medical Association* (London: British Medical Association, 1909).
Brontë, Charlotte. *Jane Eyre* (Vintage Classics, 2007) (1847).
Burn, James Dawson. *The Language of the Walls: And a Voice from the Shop Windows, or the Mirror of Commercial Roguery* (Manchester: Heywood, 1855).
Carlyle, Thomas. *Past and Present* (Project Gutenberg, 2004) (1843).
Carmichael, R.C. 'Methods and Moments for Advertising'. In *Success in Advertising*, edited by H. Simonis (London: Morning Leader, 1908) (RDL).
Charter, J.R. 'What Advertising Means to the Public'. In *Success in Advertising*, edited by H. Simonis (London: Morning Leader, 1908) (RDL).
Clarke, Tom. *My Northcliffe Diary* (London: Victor, Gollancz, 1931).
Coldridge, Ward, Cyril V. Hawksford and William F. Swords. *The Law of Gambling, Civil and Criminal*, 2nd edn (London: Stevens and Sons, 1913).
Collet, Dobson Collet. *The History of the Taxes on Knowledge: Their Origin and Repeal*, vol. 1 (London: T.F. Unwin, 1899).
Collins, Louis. *The Advertisers' Guardian* (1891) (HAT).
Cook, T.A. 'Newspaper Advertising and Selling Schemes'. In *Success in Advertising*, edited by H. Simonis (London: Morning Leader, 1908) (RDL).
Coote, William Alexander. *A Romance of Philanthropy: being a record of some of the principal incidents connected with the exceptionally successful thirty years' work of the National Vigilance Association* (London: National Vigilance Association, 1916).
Courtenay, Francis B. *Revelations of Quacks and Quackery* (London: Bailliere, Tindall and Cox, 1877).
Courtney, William 'Romance of the People's Picture Gallery'. *Daily Telegraph*, 21 December 1896, 5.
Dark, Sidney. *The Life of Sir Arthur Pearson* (London: Hodder and Stoughton, 1922),
Dickens, Charles. 'Bill-Sticking'. *Household Words* 52, 22 March 1851, 601.
Dickens, Charles. Letter to W.C. Macready, 31 January 1852. In *Life, Letters, and Speeches of Charles Dickens*, vol. 1, edited by Pierce, Gilbert Ashville (Boston and New York: Houghton, Mifflin & Co. 1891).

Digby, Kenlem, Judge. *Chrimes* case presentation, 3 March 1899 (TNA, HO144/562/A60716B).
Doyle, Arthur Conan. *The Adventure of Silver Blaze* (1892).
Dixon, Thomas. *The Advertising Course of the Dixon Institute* (London, 1909) (JJ, Publicity box 4).
Encyclopaedia Britannica. 7th edn, vol. 2 (Edinburgh: Adam and Charles Black, 1842).
Encyclopaedia Britannica. 8th edn, vol. 2 (Edinburgh: Adam and Charles Black, 1853).
Encyclopaedia Britannica. 9th edn, vol. 1 (Edinburgh: Adam and Charles Black, 1878).
Encyclopaedia Britannica.10th edn, vol. 25 (Edinburgh and London: Adam and Charles Black, 1902).
Encyclopaedia Britannica. 11th edn, vol. 1 (New York: Encyclopaedia Britannica Company, 1910).
Evans, Richardson. *An Account of the SCAPA Society* (London: Constable & co., 1926) (HAT).
Evans, Richardson. *Memorandum on the Legislative Aspect of the Work of Scapa*, 28 January 1904 (TNA, HO45/10507–126729).
Fielding, Henry. *Champion*, 1 March 1740, 321.
Folkard, Henry Coleman. *The Law of Slander and Libel* (London: Butterworths, 1876).
Gilzean-Reid, H. 'Mr. Harold Cox on Journalism,' *Times*, 29 March, 1910, 9.
Gissing, George. *In the Year of Jubilee* (London: Lawrence and Bullen, 1894).
Goodall, G.W. *Advertising: A Study of a Modern Business Power* (London: Constable & Co., 1914).
'The Grand Force!'. *Frazer's Magazine*, March 1869.
'The Great Advertisers of the World'. *Pall Mall Gazette*, 14 June 1884, 19.
Gregory, John. *Lectures on the Duties and Qualifications of a Physician* (Philadelphia: M. Carey and Son, 1817).
Hewitson, Anthony. Diary (Lancashire Archives, DP512/1/5).
Hiatt, Charles. *Picture Posters: A Short History of the Illustrated Placard with Many Reproductions of the Most Artistic Examples in all Countries*, 2nd edn (London: G. Bell and Sons, 1895).
Hirst, Stuart A. 'The Art of Understanding the Public'. In *Success in Advertising*, edited by H. Simonis (London: Morning Leader, 1908) (RDL).
Hole, E.S. *Advertising and Progress: A Defence by E.S. Hole and a Challenge by John Hart* (London: Review of Reviews, 1914).
Home Office model bylaws, 1908 (TNA, HO45/10383–168.425).
Home Office to Borough of Folkestone, draft letter 17 February 1912. (TNA, HO45/10557.165.650).
Home Office to Borough of Newark, draft letter 3 July 1911 (TNA, HO45/10640.205.460)
Home Office to Southborough Urban District Council, letter 7 July 1911 (TNA, HO45/10643.207.774/2).
Home Office to the Walton-on-Thames Urban District Council, draft letter August 1912 (TNA, HO45/10574–177032/4).
Home Office to Town Council of Newark, letter 18 October 1911 (TNA, HO45/10640.205.460/2).
Hunter, Robert. *Practical Letters on the Nature, Causes and Cure of Catarrh, Sore Throat, Bronchitis, Asthma, and Consumption*, 5th edn (London: C. Mitchell, 1865).
Hunter, Robert. *The Great Libel Case: Dr Hunter versus Pall Mall Gazette* (London: Mitchell, 1867).
Jones, T. Artemus. *The Law Relating to Advertisements* (London: Butterworth, 1906).
Jones, Christopher. *A Handbook on Advertising* (London: Sir Isaac Pitman, 1912) (HAT).
Jones, Kennedy. *Fleet Street and Downing Street* (London: Hutchinson & Co., 1920).

Kelly, Richard J. *The Law of Newspaper Libel* (London: W. Clowes, 1889).
Kerly, Duncan Mackenzie and Frank George Underhay. *The Law of Trade-Marks, Trade-Name, and Merchandise Marks* (London: Sweet & Maxwell, 1901).
Kingsley, Charles. *Alton Lock, Tailor and Poet: An Autobiography* (London: Routledge, 1892) (1850).
Larwood, Jacob and John Camden Hotten. *The History of Signboards: From the Earliest Times to the Present Day* (London: John Camden Hotten, 1866) (JJ).
Lecky, William E.H. *Democracy and Liberty* (London: Longmans, Green & Co., 1896).
McDougall, William. 'Suggestion'. *Encyclopaedia Britannica*, 11th edn, vol. 26 (New York: Encyclopaedia Britannica Company, 1911).
Maltwood, John. 'How Advertising Grows'. In *Success in Advertising*, edited by H. Simonis (London: Morning Leader, 1908) (RDL).
Malvery, Olive Christian. *The Soul Market* (London: Hutchinson, 1907).
Marshall, Alfred. *Industry and Trade: A Study of Industrial Technique and Business Organization; and of Their Influences on the Condition of Various Classes and Nations*, 2nd edn (London, 1920).
Marshall, Alfred. *Principles of Economics* (London: Macmillan and Co., 1890).
Martineau, Harriet. *Harriet Martineau's Autobiography* (Boston, J.R. Osgood & Co., 1877).
Marx, Karl. *Capital: A Critique of Political Economy*, vol. 1, trans. Samuel Moore (Electric Book, 2001) (1867).
Masterman, Charles Frederick Gurney. *The Condition of England* (London: Methuen & Co., 1909).
May, Thomas Erskine. *The Constitutional History of England*, 2nd edn, vol. 2 (London: Longman, Green & Co., 1865).
Mill, John Stuart. 'Civilization'. In *Collected Works of John Stuart Mill*, vol. 18, edited by John M. Robson (University of Toronto Press, 1963) (1836).
Millais, John Guille. *The Life and Letters of Sir John Everett Millais: President of the Royal Academy*, vol. 2 (New York: Frederick A. Stokes Company, 1899).
Mitchell's Newspaper Press Directory, 1851. In John Plunkett and Andrew King, *Victorian Print Media: A Reader* (Oxford University Press, 2005).
Moran, Clarence. *The Business of Advertising* (London: Methuen & Co., 1905).
Morgan, H.E. 'Get Outside Yourself'. In *Success in Advertising*, edited by H. Simonis (London: Morning Leader, 1908) (RDL).
Morris, William to E.T. Lowater, letter, 1893. *BW*, September 1909, 94.
Morton, J.F. 'How the Manufacturer Advertises for the Retailer'. In *Success in Advertising*, edited by H. Simonis (London: Morning Leader, 1908) (RDL).
National Anti-Gambling League Bulletin (BL).
'Next-of-Kin Agencies'. *Cornhill Magazine*, June 1885, 619–35.
Odgers, William Blake, et al. *A Digest of the Law of Libel and Slander* (London: Stevens, 1911).
Onions, Oliver. *Good Boy Seldom: A Romance of Advertisement* (London: Methuen, 1911).
Palmer, H. James. 'The March of the Advertiser'. *Nineteenth Century*, January 1897, 135–41.
Paterson, James. *The Liberty of the Press, Speech, and Public Worship* (London: Macmillan, 1880).
Percival, Thomas. *Medical Ethics* (Cambridge University Press, 2014) (1803).
Phillips, Frederick. *A Sequel to 'Secret Remedies'* (s.l. 1910) (CL).
'Physicians and Quacks'. *Blackwood's Magazine*, February 1862, 165–78 (WC).
'The Picture Galleries of the Streets'. *Birmingham Daily Post*, 24 January 1889, 7.

Presbrey, Frank. *The History and Development of Advertising* (Greenwood Press, 1968) (1929).
'The Puffing System'. *Times*, 11 January 1894.
Purcell, John S. 'Billposters and Posters: Interview with Mr. Walter Hill'. *Poster*, January 1900, 206-8.
Roberts, Frank H. *The Picture Poster as an Influence for Good*, c.1900s (JJ, Publicity box 5).
Rogers, W.S. *A Book of the Poster* (London: Greening & Co., 1901).
Russell, Thomas. *Commercial Advertising* (London: G.P. Putnam's Sons, 1919).
'Sammy Slap the Bill Sticker'. 1830 (NLS, collection of broadside ballads).
Sampson, Henry. *A History of Advertising from the Earliest Times* (London: Chatto and Windus, 1874).
Samson Clark and Co. (advertising agents) to Dr. H.S. Lunn (client), letter, 16 December 1897 (no. 238) (HAT).
Samson, Clark and Co. (advertising agents) to Percy Cotton, letter, 18 November 1896 (no. 305) (HAT).
Saundby, Robert. *Medical Ethics* (London: Charles Griffin, 1907).
Schlesinger, Max. *Saunterings In and About London* (London: Otto Wenckstern, 1853).
Scott, Walter Dill. *The Theory of Advertising: A Simple Exposition of the Principles of Psychology in Their Relation to Successful Advertising* (Boston: Fort Hill Press, 1904).
Sebastian, Lewis Boyd. *The Law of Trade Marks and Their Registration* (London: Stevens, 1890).
Sell, Henry. *Sell's Dictionary of the World's Press* (London: Sell's Advertising Agency, 1887).
Sell, Henry. *The Philosophy of Advertising* (London: Sell's Advertising Office, 1882).
'Sensational Advertising'. *Leisure Hour*, 13 February 1862, 102-3.
Shaw, George Bernard. *Pygmalion* (1912).
Shaw, George Bernard. *The Doctor's Dilemma* (1906).
Sheldon, Cyril. *A History of Poster Advertising* (London: Chapman & Hall, 1937).
Sheldon, Cyril. *Billposting Up-to-Date* (Leeds: Sheldon Limited, 1910).
Shore, W. Teignmouth. 'The Craft of the Advertiser'. *Fortnightly Review* 81 (1907): 301-10.
Shortt, John. *The Law Relating to Works of Literature and Art* (London: H. Cox, 1871).
Simmel, Georg. 'The Metropolis and Mental Life'. In *Classic Essays on the Culture of Cities*, edited by Richard Sennett (Appleton-Century-Crofts, 1969) (1903).
Simonis, H., ed. *Success in Advertising* (London: Morning Leader, 1908) (RDL).
'Sky Signs Up to Date'. *Funny Folks*, 2 April 1892, 106.
Smith, Charles Manby. *Curiosities of London Life: Or, Phases, Physiological and Social, of the Great Metropolis* (London: Cash, 1857).
Smith, Elizabeth. *George Smith: A Memoir, With Some Pages of Autobiography* (London: [s.n.], 1902).
Smith, George M. 'Lawful Pleasures'. *Cornhill Magazine*, February 1901, 188-201.
Smith, Philip Vernon. *History of the English Institutions* (Philadelphia: J.B. Lippincott, 1874).
Smith, Thomas. *Successful Advertising: Its Secret Explained*, 6th edn (1884) (HAT).
Smith, William. *Advertise: How? When? Where?* (London: Routledge & Co., 1863).
Sparrow, Walter Shaw. *Advertising and British Art: An Introduction to a Vast Subject* (London: Lane the Head, 1924).
Spielmann, Marion. 'The Streets as Art-Galleries'. *Magazine of Art* 4 (1881): 298-302.
Spiers, Ernest A. *The Art of Publicity: And Its Applications to Business* (London: Unwin, 1910).
'Stalking the Pirate Bill-Sticker'. *Billposter*, January 1902, 79.

Stead, William, Jr. *The Art of Advertising: Its Theory and Practice Fully Described* (London: T.B. Browne. 1899).
Stevens, C.H. to the Medical Experts of the Brompton Hospital, letter, 16 July 1908. In *Medical evidence given in the consumption cure libel action: Stevens v The British Medical Association*, The Royal College of Surgeons of England (WC).
Styrap, Jukes. 'A Code of Medical Ethics'. In *The Codification of Medical Morality*, vol. 2, edited by Robert B. Baker (Kluwer, 1995).
Sully, James. *Outlines of Psychology, with Special Reference to the Theory of Education* (New York: D. Appleton, 1892).
Taylor, Henry A. *Robert Donald* (London: Stanley Paul & Co., 1934).
Thackeray, William Makepeace. 'Ogres'. In William Makepeace Thackeray, *Roundabout Papers*, August 1861.
Thomson, John and Adolphe Smith. *Victorian London Street Life in Historic Photographs* vol. 1 (London: Sampson Low, Marston, Searle and Rivington,1877).
'Triumph of the Art Poster'. *Daily Express*, 28 December 1905.
Trollope, Anthony. *An Autobiography*, ed. David Skilton (Penguin, 1996) (1883).
Trollope, Anthony. *The Struggles of Brown, Jones and Robinson* (1862).
Twelve Months Advertising for a Jeweller (London: Carlton Service, 1910) (HAT).
United Billposters' Association. *Posters Condemned by Censorship Committee of the United Billposters Association* (London: Burton, c.1904) (NGC).
Urwick, E. 'Verses for a Poster'. *AW*, May 1910, 594.
Veeder, Van Vechten. 'Sir Alexander Cockburn'. *Harvard Law Review* 14 (1900–1): 79–97.
W.H. Smith. Railway Advertising Offices (JJ, Publicity box 15).
'Why There Is Bill-Posting'. *Pearson's Weekly*, 6 March 1902, 570.
Wallis, George. 'The Economical Formation of Art Museums for the People'. In *Transactions of the National Association for the Advancement of Art and Its Application to Industry, Liverpool Meeting* (London, 1888).
Webb, Sidney, Introduction to G.W. Goodall, *Advertising: A Study of a Modern Business Power* (London: Constable & Co., 1914).
Wells, H.G. *Tono-Bungay* (Penguin, 2005) (1909).
Williams, J.B. 'The Early History of London Advertising'. *Nineteenth Century*, November 1907, 793–800.

2. Secondary Sources

Alsdorf, Bridget. *Gawkers: Art and Audience in Late Nineteenth-Century France* (Princeton University Press, 2022).
Altick, Richard D. *The English Common Reader: A Social History of the Mass Reading Public, 1800–1900*, 2nd edn (Cambridge University Press, 1998).
Altick, Richard D. *The Shows of London* (Harvard University Press, 1978).
Anderson, Patricia. *The Printed Image and the Transformation of Popular Culture 1790–1860* (Oxford University Press, 1991).
Anderson, Stuart. 'From "Bespoke" to "Off-the-Peg": Community Pharmacists and the Retailing of Medicines in Great Britain 1900 to 1970'. *Pharmacy in History* 50 (2008): 43–69.
Appadurai, Arjun. *Modernity at Large: Cultural Dimensions of Globalization* (University of Minnesota Press, 1996).

Appadurai, Arjurn. Foreword. In *Magical Capitalism: Enchantment, Spells, and Occult Practices in Contemporary Economies*, edited by Brian Moeran and Timothy de Waal Malefyt (Palgrave Macmillan, 2018).
Apple, Rima D. *Mothers and Medicine: A Social History of Infant Feeding, 1890–1950* (University of Wisconsin Press, 1987).
Arnold, Marc. *Disease, Class and Social Change: Tuberculosis in Folkstone and Sandgate, 1880–1930* (Cambridge Scholars, 2012).
Asprem, Egil. *The Problem of Disenchantment: Scientific Naturalism and Esoteric Discourse, 1900–1939* (Brill, 2014).
Assaf, Katya. 'Magical Thinking in Trademark Law'. *Law & Social Inquiry* 37 (2012): 595–626.
Assaf, Katya. 'Brand Fetishism'. *Connecticut Law Review* 43 (2010): 83–148.
Atiyah, Patrick S. *The Rise and Fall of Freedom of Contract* (Clarendon, 2003).
Baker, David B., ed. *The Oxford Handbook of the History of Psychology: Global Perspectives* (Oxford University Press, 2012).
Baker, John. *Introduction to English Legal History*, 5th edn (Oxford University Press, 2019).
Baker, Laura E. 'Public Sites versus Public Sights: The Progressive Response to Outdoor Advertising and the Commercialization of Public Space'. *American Quarterly* 59 (2007): 1187–213.
Baker, Robert B. 'The Discourses of Practitioners in Nineteenth- and Twentieth-Century Britain and the United States'. In *The Cambridge World History of Medical Ethics*, edited by Robert B. Baker and Laurence B. McCullough (Cambridge University Press, 2008).
Baker, Robert B., ed. *The Codification of Medical Morality: Historical and Philosophical Studies of the Formalization of Western Medical Morality in the Eighteenth and Nineteenth Centuries*, vol. 2 (Kluwer, 1995).
Barker, Hannah. 'Medical Advertising and Trust in Late Georgian England'. *Urban History* 36 (2009): 380–98.
Barnicoat, John. *Posters: A Concise History* (Thames & Hudson, 2003).
Barstow, Susan Torrey. '"Hedda Is All of Us": Late-Victorian Women at the Matinee'. *Victorian Studies* 43 (2001): 387–411.
Barthes, Roland. 'The Advertising Message'. In Roland Barthes, *The Semiotic Challenge*, trans. Richard Howard (University of California Press, 1994).
Barthes, Roland. *Mythologies*, trans. Annette Lavers (Hill and Wang, 1972).
Bartrip, Peter. 'Secret Remedies, Medical Ethics, and the Finances of the British Medical Journal'. In *The Codification of Medical Morality*, edited by Robert B. Baker (Kluwer, 1995).
Baudrillard, Jean. *The Consumer Society: Myths and Structures* (Sage, 1998).
Beale, Marjorie A. *The Modernist Enterprise: French Elites and the Threat of Modernity, 1900–1940* (Stanford University Press, 1999).
Beard, Fred K. 'A History of Advertising and Sales Promotion'. In *The Routledge Companion to Marketing History*, edited by Brian Jones and Mark Tadajewski (Routledge, 2016).
Beckert, Jens. *Imagined Futures: Fictional Expectations and Capitalist Dynamics* (Harvard University Press, 2016).
Begg, Paul. *Jack the Ripper: The Definitive History* (Routledge, 2005).
Belk, Russell, Henri Weijo, and Robert V. Kozinets. 'Enchantment and Perpetual Desire: Theorizing Disenchanted Enchantment and Technology Adoption'. *Marketing Theory* 21 (2021): 25–52.
Bell, Karl. *The Magical Imagination: Magic and Modernity in Urban England 1780–1914* (Cambridge University Press, 2012).

Benjamin, Walter. *The Arcades Project*, trans. Howard Eiland (Harvard University Press, 2002).
Bennett, Jane. *The Enchantment of Modern Life: Attachments, Crossings, and Ethics* (Princeton University Press, 2001).
Bennett, Tony. *The Birth of the Museum: History, Theory, Politics* (Routledge, 1995).
Benson, John. *The Rise of Consumer Society in Britain, 1880-1980* (Longman, 1994).
Bently, Lionel. 'The Making of Modern Trade Mark Law: The Construction of the Legal Concept of Trade Mark (1860-1880)'. In *Trade Marks and Brands: An Interdisciplinary Critique*, edited by Lionel Bently, Jennifer Davis, and Jane C. Ginsburg (Cambridge University Press, 2011).
Berg, Maxine and Helen Clifford. 'Selling Consumption in the Eighteenth Century: Advertising and the Trade Card in Britain and France'. *Cultural and Social History* 4 (2007): 145-70.
Berger, John. *Ways of Seeing* (Penguin, 1972).
Bingham, Julia. 'Commercial Advertising and the Poster from the 1880s to the Present'. In *The Power of the Poster*, edited by Margaret Timmers (V&A, 1998).
Bladt, Sabine and Hildebert Wagner. 'From the Zulu Medicine to the European Phytomedicine Umckaloabo'. *Phytomedicine* 14 (2007): 2-4.
Blair, Ann, Paul Duguid, Anja-Silvia Goeing, and Anthony Grafton, eds. *Information: A Historical Companion* (Princeton University Press, 2021).
Blank, Yishai. 'The Reenchantment of Law'. *Cornell Law Review* 96 (2011): 633-70.
Blumberg, F.L. 'Obscenity and Marginality'. *Law and Humanities* 11 (2017): 7-23.
Bodewitz, Henk J.H.W., Henk Buurma, and Gerard H. de Vries, 'Regulatory Science and the Social Management of Trust in Medicine'. In *The Social Construction of Technological Systems: New Directions in the Sociology and History of Technology*, edited by Wiebe E. Bijker et al. (MIT, 2012).
Boorstin, Daniel J. *The Mysterious Science of the Law: An Essay on Blackstone's Commentaries* (Beacon Press, 1941).
Bowlby, Rachel. *Just Looking: Consumer Culture in Dreiser, Gissing, and Zola* (Methuen, 1985).
Bowlby, Rachel. *Shopping with Freud* (Routledge, 1993).
Bowler, Peter J. and Iwan Rhys Morus. *Making Modern Science: A Historical Survey* (University of Chicago Press, 2005).
Boyer, George. 'Living Standards, 1860-1939'. In *The Cambridge Economic History of Modern Britain*, edited by Roderick Floud and Paul Johnson (Cambridge University Press, 2004).
Brady, Maureen E. 'Property and Projection'. *Harvard Law Review* 133 (2020): 1143-214.
Brantlinger, Patrick. 'The Case of the Poisonous Book: Mass Literacy as Threat in Nineteenth-Century British Fiction'. *Victorian Review* 20 (1994): 117-33.
Brantlinger, Patrick and Richard Higgins. 'Waste and Value: Thorstein Veblen and H.G. Wells'. *Criticism* 48 (2006): 453-75.
Brendler, T. and B.E. van Wyk. 'A Historical, Scientific and Commercial Perspective on the Medicinal Use of Pelargonium Sidoides (Geraniaceae)'. *Journal of Ethnopharmacology* 119 (2008): 420-33.
Brewer, John and Roy Porter, eds. *Consumption and the World of Goods* (Routledge, 1994).
Bristow, Edward J. *Vice and Vigilance: Purity Movements in Britain since 1700* (Gill and Macmillan 1977).
Brown, Michael. 'Medicine, Quackery and the Free Market: The "War" against Morison's Pills and the Construction of the Medical Profession, c.1830-c.1850'. In *Medicine and*

the Market in England and Its Colonies, c.1450–c.1850, edited by Mark S.R. Jenner and Patrick Wallis (Palgrave Macmillan, 2007).

Brown, Michael. *Performing Medicine: Medical Culture and Identity in Provincial England, c.1760–1850* (Manchester University Press, 2011).

Bull, Sarah. 'Managing the "Obscene M.D.": Medical Publishing, the Medical Profession, and the Changing Definition of Obscenity in Mid-Victorian England'. *Bulletin of the History of Medicine* 91 (2017): 713–43.

Burnett, David. 'Judging the Aesthetics of Billboards'. *Journal of Law and Politics* 23 (2007): 171–231.

Burney, Ian A. *Bodies of Evidence: Medicine and the Politics of the English Inquest, 1830–1926* (Johns Hopkins University Press, 2000).

Burney, Ian A. *Poison, Detection, and the Victorian Imagination* (Manchester University Press, 2006).

Bynum, W.F. *Science and the Practice of Medicine in the Nineteenth Century* (Cambridge University Press, 1994).

Byrne, Katherine. *Tuberculosis and the Victorian Literary Imagination* (Cambridge University Press, 2011).

Campbell, Colin. *The Romantic Ethic and the Spirit of Modern Consumerism* (Blackwell, 1987).

Carpenter, Mary Wilson. *Health, Medicine, and Society in Victorian England* (Praeger, 2010).

Castle, Terry. 'Phantasmagoria: Spectral Technology and the Metaphorics of Modern Reverie'. *Critical Inquiry* 15 (1988): 26–61.

Castoriadis, Cornelius. *The Imaginary Institution of Society*, trans. Kathleen Blamey (MIT, 1998).

Chalaby, Jean K. *The Invention of Journalism* (Palgrave Macmillan, 1998).

Chapman, Stanley D. *Jesse Boot of Boots the Chemists: A Study in Business History* (Hodder and Stoughton, 1974).

Church, Roy. 'Advertising Consumer Goods in Nineteenth-Century Britain: Reinterpretations'. *Economic History Review* 53 (2000): 621–45.

Church, Roy. 'Trust, Burroughs Wellcome & Co. and the Foundation of a Modern Pharmaceutical Industry in Britain, 1880–1914'. *Business History* 48 (2006): 376–98.

Clapson, Mark. *A Bit of a Flutter: Popular Gambling and English Society, c.1823–1961* (Manchester University Press, 1992).

Cohen, Deborah. *Household Gods: The British and Their Possessions* (Yale University Press, 2009).

Colaizzi, Roger, Chris Crook, Claire Wheeler, and Taylor Sachs, 'The Best Explanation and Update on Puffery You Will Ever Read'. *Antitrust* 31 (2017): 86–90.

Collini, Stefan. *Public Moralists: Political Thought and Intellectual Life in Britain 1850–1930* (Clarendon Press, 1991).

Collins, Alan F. 'England'. In *The Oxford Handbook of the History of Psychology: Global Perspectives*, edited by David B. Baker (Oxford University Press, 2012).

Comaroff, Jean and John L. Comaroff, 'Millennial Capitalism: First Thoughts on a Second Coming'. *Public Culture* 12 (2000): 291–343.

Comaroff, Jean and John L. Comaroff, 'Occult Economies, Revisited'. In *Magical Capitalism: Enchantment, Spells, and Occult Practices in Contemporary Economies*, edited by Brian Moeran and Timothy de Waal Malefyt (Palgrave Macmillan, 2018).

Conboy, Martin. *The Press and Popular Culture* (Sage, 2002).

Cook, Hera. *The Long Sexual Revolution: English Women, Sex, and Contraception, 1800–1975* (Oxford University Press, 2005).

Cooper, Elena. *Art and Modern Copyright: The Contested Image* (Cambridge University Press, 2018).
Corley, T.A.B. *Beecham's, 1848-2000: From Pills to Pharmaceuticals* (Crucible Books, 2011).
Cornish, William R. 'Personal Reputation, Privacy and Intellectual Creativity'. In *The Oxford History of the Laws of England*, vol. XIII, edited by Cornish et al. (Oxford University Press, 2010).
Cox, David J., Kim Stevenson, Candida Harris, and Judith Rowbotham, *Public Indecency in England 1857-1960: 'A Serious and Growing Evil'* (Routledge, 2015).
Crary, Jonathan. *24/7: Late Capitalism and the Ends of Sleep* (Verso, 2014).
Crary, Jonathan. *Suspensions of Perception: Attention, Spectacle, and Modern Culture* (MIT, 2001).
Crawford, Jason. 'The Trouble with Re-Enchantment'. *L.A. Review of Books*, September 2020.
Crawley, Karen. '"The Chastity of Our Records": Reading and Judging Obscenity in Nineteenth-Century Courts'. In *Censorship and the Limits of the Literary: A Global View*, edited by Nicole Moore (Bloomsbury, 2015).
Cronjé, Gillian. 'Tuberculosis and Mortality Decline in England and Wales, 1851-1910'. In *Urban Diseases and Mortality in Nineteenth-Century England*, edited by Robert Woods and John Woodward (Batsford Academic and Educational, 1984).
Crowther, M. Anne. 'Forensic Medicine and Medical Ethics in Nineteenth-Century Britain'. In *The Codification of Medical Morality*, edited by Robert B. Baker (Kluwer, 1995).
Curran, James. 'The Impact of Advertising on the British Mass Media'. *Media, Culture and Society* 3 (1981): 43-69.
Curran, James and Jean Seaton. *Power Without Responsibility: The Press, Broadcasting, and New Media in Britain*, 6th edn (Routledge, 2003).
Curti, Merle. 'The Changing Concept of "Human Nature" in the Literature of American Advertising'. *Business History Review* 41 (1967): 335-57.
Cvetkovich, Ann. *Mixed Feelings: Feminism, Mass Culture, and Victorian Sensationalism* (Rutgers University Press, 1992).
Daly, Nicholas. *Sensation and Modernity in the 1860s* (Cambridge University Press, 2009).
Damkjær, Maria. *Time, Domesticity and Print Culture in Nineteenth-Century Britain* (Palgrave Macmillan, 2016).
Danziger, Kurt. *Constructing the Subject: Historical Origins of Psychological Research* (Cambridge University Press, 1994).
Daston, Lorraine. 'British Responses to Psycho-Physiology, 1860-1900'. *Isis* 69 (1978): 192-208.
Daston, Lorraine and Peter Galison. *Objectivity* (Zone Books, 2007).
Davies, Owen. 'Cunning-Folk in the Medical Market-Place During the Nineteenth Century'. *Medical History* 43 (1999): 55-73.
Davies, Owen. *Magic: A Very Short Introduction* (Oxford University Press, 2012).
Davis, Tracy C. 'Sex in Public Places: The Zaeo Aquarium Scandal and the Victorian Moral Majority'. *Theatre History Studies* 10 (1990): 1-13.
Debord, Guy. *Society of the Spectacle* (Black & Red, 1983).
Deighton, John and Kent Grayson. 'Marketing and Seduction: Building Exchange Relationships by Managing Social Consensus'. *Journal of Consumer Research* 21 (1995): 660-76.
Dempsey, Mike, ed. *Bubbles: Early Advertising Art from A & F Pears Ltd* (Collins, 1978).

Diamond, Aubrey L. 'Puffery'. *Poly Law Review* 1 (1975): 12–14.
Di Bello, Patrizia. *Women's Albums and Photography in Victorian England: Ladies, Mothers and Flirts* (Routledge, 2007).
Digby, Anne. *Making a Medical Living: Doctors and Patients in the English Market for Medicine, 1720–1911* (Cambridge University Press, 1994).
Dixon, David. *From Prohibition to Regulation: Bookmaking, Anti-Gambling, and the Law* (Clarendon, 1991).
Dobb, Maurice. *Political Economy and Capitalism: Some Essays in Economic Tradition* (Routledge, 2012) (1937).
Douglas, Mary and Baron Isherwood. *The World of Goods: Towards an Anthropology of Consumption* (Routledge, 1996).
Dowling, Linda. *The Vulgarization of Art: The Victorians and Aesthetic Democracy* (University Press of Virginia, 1996).
Dunlop, Derrick. 'Medicines, Governments and Doctors'. *Drugs* 3 (1972): 305–513.
Easley, Alexis. 'The Resistant Consumer: Scrapbooking and Satire at the Fin de siècle'. *Nineteenth-Century Studies* 30 (2018): 89–111.
Eliot, Simon. 'The Reading Experience Database; or, what are we to do about the history of reading?' http://www.open.ac.uk/Arts/RED/redback.htm.
Elliott, Blanche B. *A History of English Advertising* (London Business Publications & B.T. Batsford, 1962).
Ewen, Stuart. *Captains of Consciousness: Advertising and the Social Roots of the Consumer Culture* (McGraw-Hill, 1976).
Ewick, Patricia and Susan S. Silbey. *The Common Place of Law: Stories from Everyday Life* (University of Chicago Press, 1998).
Fabian, Ann. *Card Sharps and Bucket Shops: Gambling in Nineteenth-Century America* (Routledge, 1999).
Faulkner, Alex, Bettina Lange, and Christopher Lawless. 'Introduction: Material Worlds: Intersections of Law, Science, Technology, and Society'. *Journal of Law and Society* 39 (2012): 1–19.
Fennis, Bob M. and Wolfgang Stroebe. *The Psychology of Advertising* (Psychology Press, 2010).
Figes, Orlando. *The Europeans: Three Lives and the Making of a Cosmopolitan Culture* (Penguin, 2019).
Fitzgerald, Robert. *Rowntree and the Marketing Revolution, 1862–1969* (Cambridge University Press, 1995).
Fitz-Gibbon, Desmond. *Marketable Values: Inventing the Property Market in Modern Britain* (University of Chicago Press, 2018).
Footler, P.J. 'Umckaloabo, Secret Remedy'. *Pharmaceutical Journal* (7 November 2012).
Foucault, Michel. *The Birth of the Clinic: An Archaeology of Medical Perception*, trans. A. M. Sheridan (Routledge, 1973).
Foucault, Michel. *The History of Sexuality*, vol. 1, trans. Robert Hurley (Pantheon Books, 1978).
Fox, Stephen. *The Mirror Makers: A History of American Advertising and Its Creators* (William Morrow, 1984).
Fraser, W. Hamish. *The Coming of the Mass Market, 1850–1914* (Macmillan, 1981).
Freedberg, David. *The Power of Images: Studies in the History and Theory of Response* (University of Chicago Press, 1989).
Friedman, Walter A. *Birth of a Salesman: The Transformation of Selling in America* (Harvard University Press, 2004).

Fritzsche, Peter. *Reading Berlin 1900* (Harvard University Press, 1996).
Frye, Northrop. *The Modern Century* (Oxford University Press, 1967).
Fyfe, Aileen and Bernard Lightman, eds. *Science in the Marketplace: Nineteenth-Century Sites and Experiences* (University of Chicago Press, 2007).
Gagnier, Regenia. *The Insatiability of Human Wants: Economics and Aesthetics in Market Society* (University of Chicago Press, 2000).
Galbraith, John Kenneth. *The Affluent Society* (Houghton Mifflin, 1998) (1958).
Galinou, Mireille and John T. Hayes. *London in Paint: Oil Paintings in the Collection at the Museum of London* (Museum of London, 1996).
Garvey, Ellen Gruber. *The Adman in the Parlor: Magazines and the Gendering of Consumer Culture, 1880s to 1910s* (Oxford University Press, 1996).
Gellner, Ernest. *Spectacles & Predicaments: Essays in Social Theory* (Cambridge University Press, 1979).
Getzler, Joshua. 'Legal History as Doctrinal History'. In *The Oxford Handbook of Legal History*, edited by Markus D. Dubber and Christopher Tomlins (Oxford University Press, 2018).
Gieryn, Thomas F. 'Boundary-Work and the Demarcation of Science from Non-Science: Strains and Interests in Professional Ideologies of Scientists'. *American Sociological Review* 48 (1983): 781–95.
Gieryn, Thomas F. *Cultural Boundaries of Science: Credibility on the Line* (University of Chicago Press, 1999).
Ginzburg, Carlo. 'Morelli, Freud and Sherlock Holmes: Clues and Scientific Method'. *History Workshop* 9 (1980): 5–36.
Graham, Gordon. *Philosophy of the Arts: An Introduction to Aesthetics*, 3rd edn (Routledge, 2005).
Green, Johnathon and Nicholas J. Karolides. *Encyclopedia of Censorship* (Facts on File Inc., 2005).
Greenberg, Clement. 'Avant-Garde and Kitsch'. In Clement Greenberg, *Art and Culture: Critical Essays* (Beacon Press, 1961).
Greenhalgh, James. 'The Control of Outdoor Advertising, Amenity, and Urban Governance in Britain, 1893–1962'. *The Historical Journal* 64 (2020): 1–26.
Greenhalgh, James. *Injurious Vistas: The Control of Outdoor Advertising, Governance and the Shaping of Urban Experience in Britain, 1817–1962* (Palgrave Macmillan, 2021).
Guffey, Elizabeth E. *Posters: A Global History* (Reaktion Books, 2015).
Gurjeva, Lyubov G. 'Child Health, Commerce and Family Values: The Domestic Production of the Middle Class in Late-Nineteenth and Early-Twentieth Century Britain'. In *Cultures of Child Health in Britain and the Netherlands in the Twentieth Century*, edited by Marijke Gijswijt-Hofstra and Hilary Marland (Rodopi, 2016).
Gurney, Peter. *The Making of Consumer Culture in Modern Britain* (Bloomsbury, 2017).
Habermas, Jürgen. *The Structural Transformation of the Public Sphere: An Inquiry into a Category of Bourgeois Society*, trans. Thomas Burger (MIT, 1991).
Hacking, Ian. *Rewriting the Soul: Multiple Personality and the Sciences of Memory* (Princeton University Press, 1998).
Hahn, Hazel. *Scenes of Parisian Modernity: Culture and Consumption in the Nineteenth Century* (Palgrave Macmillan, 2009).
Haill, Catherine. *Fun Without Vulgarity: Victorian and Edwardian Popular Entertainment Posters* (Public Record Office, 1996).
Haill, Catherine. 'Posters for Performance'. In *The Power of the Poster*, edited by Margaret Timmers (V&A, 1998).

Haley, Bruce. *The Healthy Body and Victorian Culture* (Harvard University Press, 1978).
Hall, Elsje J. 'The Sale and Manufacture of Proprietary Medicines and the Campaign by the B.M.A. Against "Secret Remedies"' (PhD diss., Wellcome Institute, 1995) (WC).
Hampton, Mark. 'Defining Journalists in Late-Nineteenth Century Britain'. *Critical Studies in Media Communication* 22 (2005): 138–55.
Hampton, Mark. 'Journalists and the "Professional Ideal" in Britain: The Institute of Journalists, 1884–1907'. *Historical Research* 72 (1999): 183–201.
Hampton, Mark. 'Newspapers in Victorian Britain'. *History Compass* 2 (2004): 1–8.
Hampton, Mark. *Visions of the Press in Britain, 1850–1950* (University of Illinois Press, 2004).
Haug, Wolfgang Fritz. *Critique of Commodity Aesthetics: Appearance, Sexuality and Advertising in Capitalist Society*, trans. Robert Bock (Polity Press, 1986).
Hawkins, Richard A. 'Marketing History in Britain from the Ancient to Internet Eras'. In *The Routledge Companion to Marketing History*, edited by Brian Jones and Mark Tadajewski (Routledge, 2016).
Hearnshaw, Leslie Spencer. *A Short History of British Psychology, 1840–1940* (Methuen, 1964).
Helmstädter, Axel. '"Umckaloabo": Late Vindication of a Secret Remedy'. *Pharmaceutical Historian* 26 (1996): 2–4.
Henkin, David M. *City Reading: Written Words and Public Spaces in Antebellum New York* (Columbia University Press, 1998).
Hewitt, John. 'Designing the Poster in England, 1890–1914'. *Early Popular Visual Culture* 5 (2007): 57–70.
Hewitt, John. '"The Poster" and the Poster in England in the 1890s'. *Victorian Periodicals Review* 35 (2002): 37–62.
Hewitt, John. 'Poster Nasties: Censorship and the Victorian Theatre Poster'. In *Visual Delights: Essays on the Popular and Projected Image in the Nineteenth Century*, edited by Vanessa Toulmin and Simon Popple (Flicks Books, 2000).
Hewitt, Martin. *The Dawn of the Cheap Press in Victorian Britain: The End of the 'Taxes on Knowledge', 1849–1869* (Bloomsbury, 2014).
Hickman, Timothy A. '"We Belt the World": Dr. Leslie E. Keeley's "Gold Cure" and the Medicalization of Addiction in 1890s London'. *Bulletin of the History of Medicine* 95 (2021): 198–226.
Higgins, David M. 'Trademarks and Infringement in Britain, c.1875–c.1900'. In *Trademarks, Brands and Competitiveness*, edited by Teresa da Silva Lopes and Paul Duguid (Routledge, 2010).
Hilliard, Christopher. *A Matter of Obscenity: The Politics of Censorship in Modern England* (Princeton University Press, 2021).
Hilton, Boyd. *The Age of Atonement—the Influence of Evangelicalism on Social and Economic Thought, 1795–1865* (Clarendon, 1988).
Hirschman, Albert O. *The Essential Hirschman*, edited by Jeremy Adelman (Princeton University Press, 2013).
Hirschman, Albert O. *The Passions and the Interests: Political Arguments for Capitalism Before Its Triumph* (Princeton University Press, 1977).
Hobbs, Andrew. *A Fleet Street in Every Town: The Provincial Press in England, 1855–1900* (Open Book, 2018).
Hoffman, David A. 'The Best Puffery Article Ever'. *Iowa Law Review* 91 (2006): 1395–448.
Holt, Richard. *Sport and the British: A Modern History* (Clarendon, 1989).

Horkheimer, Max and Theodor W. Adorno. 'The Culture Industry: Enlightenment as Mass Deception'. In *Dialectic of Enlightenment* (Stanford University Press, 2002).
Hornsey, Richard. '"The Penguins Are Coming": Brand Mascots and Utopian Mass Consumption in Interwar Britain'. *Journal of British Studies* 57 (2018): 812–39.
Horrell, Sara. 'Consumption, 1700–1870'. In *The Cambridge Economic History of Modern Britain: Volume 1: Industrialisation, 1700–1870*, edited by Roderick Floud, Jane Humphries, and Paul Johnson (Cambridge University Press, 2014).
Huggins, Mike. *Vice and the Victorians* (Bloomsbury Academic, 2016).
Hyde, Timothy. *Ugliness and Judgment: On Architecture in the Public Eye* (Princeton University Press, 2019).
Ibbetson, David. *A Historical Introduction to the Law of Obligations* (Oxford University Press, 2010).
Inflation calculator, Bank of England, https://www.bankofengland.co.uk/monetary-policy/inflation/inflation-calculator.
Inglis, Fred. *The Imagery of Power: A Critique of Advertising* (Heinemann, 1972).
Iskin, Ruth E. *The Poster: Art, Advertising, Design, and Collecting, 1860s–1900s* (Dartmouth College Press, 2014).
Itzkowitz, David C. 'Fair Enterprise or Extravagant Speculation: Investment, Speculation, and Gambling in Victorian England'. *Victorian Studies* 45 (2002): 121–47.
Jenkins, Richard. 'Disenchantment, Enchantment and Re-Enchantment: Max Weber at the Millennium'. *Max Weber Studies* 1 (2000): 11–32.
Jervis, John. *Sensational Subjects: The Dramatization of Experience in the Modern World* (Bloomsbury Academic, 2015).
Jewson, Nicholas D. 'The Disappearance of the Sick-Man from Medical Cosmology, 1770–1870'. *Sociology* 10 (1976): 225–44.
Jobling, Paul. *Man Appeal: Advertising, Modernism and Menswear* (Berg, 2005).
Johnson, Tom. 'Legal History and the Material Turn'. In *The Oxford Handbook of Legal History*, edited by Markus D. Dubber and Christopher Tomlins (Oxford University Press, 2018).
Jones, Aled. *Powers of the Press: Newspapers, Power and the Public in Nineteenth-Century England* (Routledge, 1996).
Jordan, Harriet. 'Public Parks, 1885–1914'. *Garden Society* 22 (1994): 85–113.
Josephson-Storm, Jason Ānanda. *The Myth of Disenchantment: Magic, Modernity, and the Birth of the Human Sciences* (University of Chicago Press, 2017).
Kang, Hyo Yoon and Sara Kendall. 'Legal Materiality'. In *The Oxford Handbook of Law and Humanities*, edited by Simon Stern, Maksymilian Del Mar, and Bernadette Meyler (Oxford University Press, 2020).
Keeton, W. Page, Dan B. Dobbs, Robert E. Keeton and David G. Owen, eds. *Prosser and Keeton on the Law of Torts*, 5th edn (West Publishing, 1984).
Kelley, Victoria. *Soap and Water: Cleanliness, Dirt and the Working Classes in Victorian and Edwardian Britain* (I.B. Tauris, 2010).
Kennedy, Meegan. '*Tono-Bungay* and Burroughs Wellcome: Branding Imperial Popular Medicine'. *Victorian Literature and Culture* 45 (2017): 137–62.
Kilday, Anne-Marie and David S. Nash. *Shame and Modernity in Britain: 1890 to the Present* (Palgrave Macmillan, 2017).
Korda, Andrea. '"The Streets as Art Galleries": Hubert Herkomer, William Powell Frith, and the Artistic Advertisement'. *Nineteenth-Century Art Worldwide* 11 (2012): 55–72.
Kriegel, Lara. *Grand Designs: Labor, Empire, and the Museum in Victorian Culture* (Duke University Press, 2008).

Kristeller, Paul Oskar. 'The Modern System of the Arts: A Study in the History of Aesthetics'. *Journal of the History of Ideas* 13 (1952): 17–46.

Kwint, Marius. 'The Legitimization of the Circus in Late Georgian England'. *Past & Present* 174 (2002): 72–115.

Landy, Joshua and Michael Saler, eds. *The Re-Enchantment of the World: Secular Magic in a Rational Age* (Stanford University Press, 2009).

Lanning, Katie. 'Tessellating Texts: Reading *The Moonstone* in *All the Year Round*'. *Victorian Periodicals Review* 45 (2012): 1–22.

Latour, Bruno. *On the Modern Cult of the Factish Gods*, trans. Catherine Porter and Heather MacLean (Duke University Press, 2010).

Latour, Bruno. 'Scientific Objects and Legal Objectivity', trans. Alain Pottage. In *Law, Anthropology, and the Constitution of the Social: Making Persons and Things*, edited by Alain Pottage, Martha Mundy, and Chris Arup (Cambridge University Press, 2004).

Latour, Bruno. *We Have Never Been Modern* (Harvard University Press, 1993).

Layton-Jones, Katy. *Beyond the Metropolis: The Changing Image of Urban Britain, 1780–1880* (Manchester University Press, 2016).

Lears, Jackson. *Fables of Abundance: A Cultural History of Advertising in America* (Basic Books, 1994).

Leavis, F.R. and Denys Thompson. *Culture and Environment: The Training of Critical Awareness* (Chatto & Windus, 1959).

Lee, Alan J. *The Origins of the Popular Press in England, 1855–1914* (Croom Helm, 1976).

Leighton, Richard J. 'Materiality and Puffing in Lanham Act False Advertising Cases: The Proofs, Presumptions, and Pretexts'. *Trademark Reporter* 94 (2004): 585–633.

Leiss, William, Stephen Kline, Sut Jhally, and Jacqueline Botterill, *Social Communication in Advertising: Consumption in the Mediated Marketplace*, 3rd edn (Routledge, 2005).

Leonard, Garry M. *Advertising and Commodity Culture in Joyce* (University Press of Florida, 1998).

LePore, Jill. 'Privacy in an Age of Publicity'. *New Yorker*, 17 June 2013.

Levine, George. 'From "Know-not-Where" to "Nowhere": The City in Carlyle, Ruskin and Morris'. In *The Victorian City: Image and Realities*, vol. 2, edited by Jim Dyos and Michael Wolff (Routledge, 1999).

Lewis, Brian. *So Clean: Lord Leverhulme, Soap and Civilisation* (Manchester University Press, 2008).

Linstrum, Erik. *Ruling Minds: Psychology in the British Empire* (Harvard University Press, 2016).

Litman, Jessica. 'Breakfast with Batman: The Public Interest in the Advertising Age'. *Yale Law Journal* 108 (1999): 1717–35.

Loeb, Lori A. 'Consumerism and Commercial Electrotherapy: The Medical Battery Company in Nineteenth-Century London'. *Journal of Victorian Culture* 4 (2010): 252–75.

Loeb, Lori A. *Consuming Angels: Advertising and Victorian Women* (Oxford University Press, 1994).

Loeb, Lori A. 'Doctors and Patent Medicines in Modern Britain: Professionalism and Consumerism'. *Albion* 33 (2001): 404–25.

Logan, Peter Melville. *Victorian Fetishism: Intellectuals and Primitives* (SUNY Press, 2009).

Lury, Celia. *Brands: The Logos of the Global Economy* (Routledge, 2004).

McCarraher, Eugene. *The Enchantments of Mammon: How Capitalism Became the Religion of Modernity* (Belknap Press, 2019).

McClintock, Anne. *Imperial Leather: Race, Gender and Sexuality in the Colonial Contest* (Routledge, 1995).

McCreery, John. 'Malinowski, Magic and Advertising'. In *Contemporary Marketing and Consumer Behavior: An Anthropological Sourcebook*, edited by John F. Sherry (Sage, 1995).
McCullough, Laurence B. 'The Discourses of Practitioners in Eighteenth-Century Britain'. In *The Cambridge World History of Medical Ethics*, edited by Robert B. Baker and Laurence B. McCullough (Cambridge University Press, 2008).
McEwen, John M. 'The National Press during the First World War: Ownership and Circulation'. *Journal of Contemporary History* 17 (1982): 459–86.
McFall, Liz. *Advertising: A Cultural Economy* (Sage, 2004).
McKendrick, Neil, John Brewer, and J.H. Plumb. *The Birth of a Consumer Society: The Commercialization of Eighteenth-Century England* (Europa, 1982).
McKibbin, Ross. 'Working-Class Gambling in Britain 1880–1939'. *Past & Present* 82 (1979): 147–78.
McLaren, Angus. *Birth Control in Nineteenth-Century England* (Croom Helm, 1978).
McLuhan, Herbert Marshall. *The Mechanical Bride: Folklore of Industrial Man* (Gingko Press, 2001).
Malefyt, Timothy de Waal. 'The Magic of Paradox: How Advertising Ideas Transform Art into Business and the Ordinary into the Extraordinary'. In *Magical Capitalism: Enchantment, Spells, and Occult Practices in Contemporary Economies*, edited by Brian Moeran and Timothy de Waal Malefyt (Palgrave Macmillan, 2018).
Maltz, Diana. *British Aestheticism and the Urban Working Classes, 1870–1900: Beauty for the People* (Palgrave Macmillan, 2006).
Manchester, Colin. 'The Changing Rationale of England's Obscenity Laws'. *Law & Justice: The Christian Law Review* 66 (1980): 64–76.
Mandler, Peter. *Aristocratic Government in the Age of Reform: Whigs and Liberals, 1830–1852* (Oxford University Press, 1990).
Mandler, Peter. 'The Creative Destruction of the Victorian City' (2018, on file with author).
Mannheim, Karl, *From Karl Mannheim*, edited by Kurt H. Wolff (Oxford University Press, 1971).
Marcus, Sharon. 'The Profession of the Author: Abstraction, Advertising, and *Jane Eyre*'. *PMLA* 110 (1995): 206–19.
Mason, Stuart, ed. *Oscar Wilde: Art and Morality* (Project Gutenberg, 2010).
Matthew, Henry C.G. 'Disraeli, Gladstone, and the Politics of Mid-Victorian Budgets'. *The Historical Journal* 22 (1979): 615–43.
Mazzarella, William. *The Mana of Mass Society* (University of Chicago Press, 2017).
Mercer, John. 'A Mark of Distinction: Branding and Trade Mark Law in the UK from the 1860s'. *Business History* 52 (2010): 17–42.
Miers, David. *Regulating Commercial Gambling: Past, Present, and Future* (Oxford University Press, 2004).
Mitchell, Paul. *A History of Tort Law 1900–1950* (Cambridge University Press, 2015).
Mitchell, Paul. *The Making of the Modern Law of Defamation* (Hart, 2005).
Moeran, Brian. 'Business, Anthropology, and Magical Systems: The Case of Advertising'. *Ethnographic Praxis in Industry Conference Proceedings* 1 (2014): 119–32.
Moeran, Brian and Timothy de Waal Malefyt, eds. *Magical Capitalism: Enchantment, Spells, and Occult Practices in Contemporary Economies* (Palgrave Macmillan, 2018).
Mokyr, Joel. *The Enlightened Economy: An Economic History of Britain, 1700–1850* (Yale University Press, 2009).
Moretti, Franco. *The Modern Epic: The World System from Goethe to García Márquez* (Verso, 1996).

Morgan, David. *Images at Work: The Material Culture of Enchantment* (Oxford University Press, 2018).
Morreall, John. 'Philosophy of Humor'. In *Stanford Encyclopedia of Philosophy*, edited by Edward N. Zalta. Revised 2020, https://plato.stanford.edu/entries/humor/.
Morrison, Kevin A. '"Dr. Locock and His Quack": Professionalizing Medicine, Textualizing Identity in the 1840s'. In *Victorian Medicine and Popular Culture*, edited by Louise Penner and Tabitha Sparks (Routledge, 2015).
Mukherjee, Sumita. '"A Warning Against Quack Doctors": The Old Bailey Trial of Indian Oculists, 1893'. *Historical Research* 86 (2012): 76–91.
Mullin, Katherine. 'Poison More Deadly than Prussic Acid: Defining Obscenity After the 1857 Obscene Publications Act (1850–1885)'. In *Prudes on the Prowl: Fiction and Obscenity in England, 1850 to the Present Day*, edited by David Bradshaw and Rachel Potter (Oxford University Press, 2013).
Mussell, James E.P. 'Elemental Forms: The Newspaper as Popular Genre in the Nineteenth Century'. *Media History* 20 (2014): 4–20.
Nava, Mica. 'The Cosmopolitanism of Commerce and the Allure of Difference: Selfridges, the Russian Ballet and the Tango 1911–1914'. *International Journal of Cultural Studies* 1 (1998): 163–96.
Nava, Mica. 'Framing Advertising: Cultural Analysis and the Incrimination of Visual Texts'. In *Buy This Book: Studies in Advertising and Consumption*, edited by Mica Nava, Andrew Blake, Iain MacRury, and Barry Richards (Routledge, 1997).
Nead, Lynda. 'Bodies of Judgement: Art, Obscenity, and the Connoisseur'. In *Law and the Image: The Authority of Art and the Aesthetics of Law*, edited by Costas Douzinas and Lynda Nead (University of Chicago Press, 1999).
Nead, Lynda. *Victorian Babylon: People, Streets and Images in Nineteenth-Century London* (Yale University Press, 2000).
Nevett, Terrence R. 'Advertising and Editorial Integrity in the Nineteenth Century'. In *The Press in English Society from the Seventeenth to the Nineteenth Centuries*, edited by Michael Harris and Alan Lee (Fairleigh Dickinson University Press, 1986).
Nevett, Terence R. *Advertising in Britain: A History* (Heinemann, 1982).
Nevett, Terence R. 'London's Early Advertising Agents'. *Journal of Advertising History* 1 (1977): 15–18.
Newsom, S.W.B. 'Stevens' Cure: A Secret Remedy'. *Journal of the Royal Society of Medicine* 95 (2002): 463–7.
Nichols, Kate, Rebecca Wade, and Gabriel Williams, eds. *Art versus Industry? New Perspectives on Visual and Industrial Cultures in Nineteenth-Century Britain* (Manchester University Press, 2016).
Nightingale, Andrea. 'Broken Knowledge'. In *The Re-Enchantment of the World: Secular Magic in a Rational Age*, edited by Joshua Landy and Michael Saler (Stanford University Press, 2009).
Nini, Andrea. 'An Authorship Analysis of the Jack the Ripper Letters'. *Digital Scholarship in the Humanities* (2018), https://doi-org.ezp.lib.cam.ac.uk/10.1093/llc/fqx065.
Oats, Lynne. 'The Abolition of the Taxes on Knowledge'. In *Studies in the History of Tax Law*, vol. 2, edited by John Tiley (Hart, 2007).
Offer, Avner. *The Challenge of Affluence: Self-Control and Well-Being in the United States and Britain since 1950* (Oxford University Press, 2006).
Ostergaard, Per, James A. Fitchett and Christian Jantzen. 'A Critique of the Ontology of Consumer Enchantment'. *Journal of Consumer Behaviour* 12 (2013): 337–44.
Otter, Chris. *The Victorian Eye: A Political History of Light and Vision in Britain, 1800–1910* (University of Chicago Press, 2008).

Outka, Elizabeth. *Consuming Traditions: Modernity, Modernism, and the Commodified Authentic* (Oxford University Press, 2009).
Owen, Alex. *The Place of Enchantment: British Occultism and the Culture of the Modern* (University of Chicago Press, 2004).
Packard, Vance. *The Hidden Persuaders* (Ig, 2007).
Parry, Jonathan. *The Rise and Fall of Liberal Government in Victorian Britain* (Yale University Press, 1993).
Parssinen, Terry M. *Secret Passions, Secret Remedies: Narcotic Drugs in British Society 1820-1930* (Manchester University Press, 1983).
Paterson, Alan A. 'Professionalism and the Legal Services Market'. *International Journal of the Legal Profession* 3 (1996): 137-68.
Pick, Daniel. *Svengali's Web: The Alien Enchanter in Modern Culture* (Yale University Press, 2000).
Pietruska, Jamie L. 'Forecasting'. In *Information: A Historical Companion*, edited by Ann Blair, Paul Duguid, Anja-Silvia Goeing, and Anthony Grafton (Princeton University Press, 2021).
Pietz, William. 'Fetishism and Materialism: The Limits of Theory in Marx'. In *Fetishism as Cultural Discourse*, edited by Emily Apter and William Pietz (Cornell University Press, 1993).
Plunkett, John and Andrew King. *Victorian Print Media: A Reader* (Oxford University Press, 2005).
Polanyi, Karl. *The Great Transformation: The Political and Economic Origins of Our Time* (Farrar & Rinehart, 1944).
Pomian, Krzysztof. *Collectors and Curiosities: Paris and Venice 1500-1800*, trans. Elizabeth Wildes-Portier (Polity Press, 1990).
Porten, Lili. 'The Metamorphosis of Commodities in Shaw's *Pygmalion*'. *Differences* 17 (2006): 69-86.
Porter, Roy. *Bodies Politic: Disease, Death and Doctors in Britain, 1650-1900* (Cornell University Press, 2001).
Porter, Roy, ed. *The Cambridge Illustrated History of Medicine* (Cambridge University Press, 1996).
Porter, Roy. 'Consumption: Disease of the Consumer Society'. In *Consumption and the World of Goods*, edited by John Brewer and Roy Porter (Routledge, 1994).
Porter, Roy. *The Greatest Benefit to Mankind: A Medical History of Humanity from Antiquity to the Present* (HarperCollins, 1997).
Porter, Roy. *Quacks: Fakers & Charlatans in English Medicine* (Tempus Publishing, 2000).
Potter, Simon J. *News and the British World: The Emergence of an Imperial Press System, 1876-1922* (Clarendon, 2003).
Preston, Ivan L. *The Great American Blow-Up: Puffery in Advertising and Selling* (University of Wisconsin Press, 1996).
Pue, W. Wesley. *Lawyers' Empire: Legal Professions and Cultural Authority, 1780-1950* (UBC Press, 2016).
Qureshi, Sadiah. *Peoples on Parade: Exhibitions, Empire, and Anthropology in Nineteenth-Century Britain* (University of Chicago Press, 2011).
Ramamurthy, Anandi. *Imperial Persuaders: Images of Africa and Asia in British Advertising* (Manchester University Press, 2003).
Rappaport, Erika. *A Thirst for Empire: How Tea Shaped the Modern World* (Princeton University Press, 2017).

Readman, Paul. 'Landscape Preservation, "Advertising Disfigurement", and English National Identity c.1890-1914'. *Rural History* 12 (2001): 61-83.
Readman, Paul. *Storied Ground: Landscape and the Shaping of English National Identity* (Cambridge University Press, 2018).
Reith, Gerda. *The Age of Chance: Gambling in Western Culture* (Routledge, 1999).
Richards, Jef I. 'A "New and Improved" View of Puffery'. *Journal of Public Policy & Marketing* 9 (1990): 73-84.
Richards, Thomas. *The Commodity Culture of Victorian England: Advertising and Spectacle, 1851-1914* (Stanford University Press, 1991).
Richardson, Megan and Julian Thomas. *Fashioning Intellectual Property: Exhibition, Advertising and the Press, 1789-1918* (Cambridge University Press, 2012).
Rickards, Maurice. *Banned Posters* (Evelyn, Adams & Mackay, 1969).
Rickards, Maurice. *The Rise and Fall of the Poster* (David and Charles, 1971).
Ritzer, George. *Enchanting a Disenchanted World: Revolutionizing the Means of Consumption*, 2nd edn (Sage, 2005).
Rose, Jonathan. *The Intellectual Life of the British Working Classes*, 2nd edn (Yale University Press, 2010).
Ross, Michael L. *Designing Fictions: Literature Confronts Advertising* (McGill-Queen's University Press, 2015).
Rowe, Raymond C. 'Bile Beans'. *International Journal of Pharmaceutical Medicine* 17 (2003): 137-40.
Ryan, James. 'Images and Impressions: Printing, Reproduction and Photography'. In *The Victorian Vision: Inventing Modern Britain*, edited by John M. Mackenzie (V&A, 2001).
Saler, Michael T. *As If: Modern Enchantment and the Literary Prehistory of Virtual Reality* (Oxford University Press, 2012).
Saler, Michael T. 'Modernity and Enchantment: A Historiographic Review'. *American Historical Review* 111 (2006): 692-716.
Samalin, Zachary. *The Masses Are Revolting: Victorian Culture and the Political Aesthetics of Disgust* (Cornell University Press, 2021).
Saunders, Robert. *Democracy and the Vote in British Politics, 1848-1867: The Making of the Second Reform Act* (Ashgate, 2011).
Schlag, Pierre. *The Enchantment of Reason* (Duke University Press, 1998).
Schlag, Pierre and Amy J. Griffin. *How to Do Things with Legal Doctrine* (University of Chicago Press, 2020).
Schneider, Mark A. *Culture and Enchantment* (University of Chicago Press, 1993).
Schudson, Michael. *Advertising, the Uneasy Persuasion: Its Dubious Impact on American Society* (Routledge, 1993).
Schultz, Duane P. and Sydney Ellen Schultz. *A History of Modern Psychology*, 10th edn (Wadsworth, 2011).
Schwarzkopf, Stefan. 'Sacred Excess: Organizational Ignorance in an Age of Toxic Data'. *Organization Studies* 41 (2020): 197-217.
Schwarzkopf, Stefan. 'The Subsiding Sizzle of Advertising History: Methodological and Theoretical Challenges in the Post Advertising Age'. *Journal of Historical Research in Marketing* 3 (2011): 528-48.
Schwarzkopf, Stefan. 'Turning Trademarks into Brands: How Advertising Agencies Practiced and Conceptualized Branding 1890-1930'. In *Trademarks, Brands and Competitiveness*, edited by Teresa da Silva Lopes and Paul Duguid (Routledge, 2010).

Schwartzkopf, Stefan. 'What Was Advertising? The Invention, Rise, Demise, and Disappearance of Advertising Concepts in Nineteenth- and Twentieth-Century Europe and America'. Business History Conference, 2009.

Searle, G.R. *Morality and the Market in Victorian Britain* (Oxford University Press, 1998).

Sheff, Jeremy N. 'Veblen Brands'. *Minnesota Law Review* 96 (2012): 769–832.

Sherryl, John F. Jr. 'Foreword: A Word from our Sponsor—Anthropology'. In *Advertising Cultures*, edited by Timothy deWaal Malefyt and Brian Moeran (Berg, 2003).

Siegel, Jonah. *Desire and Excess: The Nineteenth-Century Culture of Art* (Princeton University Press, 2000).

Simpson, A.W.B. 'Quackery and Contract Law: The Case of the Carbolic Smoke Ball'. *Journal of Legal Studies* 14 (1985): 345–89.

Slauter, Will. 'Periodicals and the Commercialization of Information in the Early Modern Era'. In *Information: A Historical Companion*, edited by Ann Blair, Paul Duguid, Anja-Silvia Goeing, and Anthony Grafton (Princeton University Press, 2021).

Slauter, Will. *Who Owns the News? A History of Copyright* (Stanford University Press, 2019).

Smith, Colin Milner and Stephen Philip Monkcom. *The Law of Betting, Gaming and Lotteries* (Butterworth, 1987).

Smith, Cordelia. 'Art Unions and the Changing Face of Victorian Gambling'. In *Culture and Money in the Nineteenth Century: Abstracting Economics*, edited by Daniel Bivona and Marlene Tromp (Ohio University Press, 2016).

Smith, Russell G. 'Legal Precedent and Medical Ethics: Some Problems Encountered by the General Medical Council in Relying upon Precedent when Declaring Acceptable Standards of Professional Conduct'. In *The Codification of Medical Morality*, edited by Robert B. Baker (Kluwer, 1995).

Smits, Jan M. 'What is Legal Doctrine?' In *Rethinking Legal Scholarship: A Transatlantic Dialogue*, edited by Rob van Gestel, Hans-W. Micklitz, and Edward L. Rubin (Cambridge University Press, 2017).

Sontag, Susan. 'Posters: Advertisement, Art, Political Artifact, Commodity'. In *The Art of Revolution: 96 Posters from Castro's Cuba, 1959–1970*, edited by Donald Stermer (Pall Mall Press, 1970).

Stebbings, Chantal. *Tax, Medicines and the Law: From Quackery to Pharmacy* (Cambridge University Press, 2018).

Steegman, John. *Victorian Taste: A Study of the Arts and Architecture from 1830 to 1870* (Century and the National Trust, 1987).

Stern, Simon. 'Wilde's Obscenity Effect: Influence and Immorality in *The Picture of Dorian Gray*'. *Review of English Studies* 68 (2017): 756–72.

Strachan, John. *Advertising and Satirical Culture in the Romantic Period* (Cambridge University Press, 2007).

Strachan, John and Claire Nally. *Advertising, Literature, and Print Culture in Ireland, 1891–1922* (Palgrave Macmillan, 2012).

Styles, John. 'Manufacturing, Consumption and Design in Eighteenth-Century England'. In *Consumption and the World of Goods*, edited by John Brewer and Roy Porter (Routledge, 1994).

Taylor, Charles. *Modern Social Imaginaries* (Duke University Press, 2004).

Taylor, Charles. *A Secular Age* (Harvard University Press, 2007).

Taylor, James. ''A Fascinating Show for John Citizen and his Wife': Advertising Exhibitions in Early Twentieth-Century London'. *Journal of Social History* 51 (2018): 899–927.

Taylor, James. 'Written in the Skies: Advertising, Technology, and Modernity in Britain Since 1885'. *Journal of British Studies* 55 (2016): 750–80.

Taylor, John. 'The Alphabetic Universe: Photography and the Picturesque Landscape'. In *Reading Landscape: Country, City, Capital*, edited by Simon Pugh (Manchester University Press, 1990).

Thompson, Craig J. 'Marketplace Mythology and Discourses of Power'. *Journal of Consumer Research* 31 (2004): 162–80.

Thompson, Denys. *Voice of Civilisation: An Enquiry into Advertising* (Frederick Muller, 1943).

Thompson, James. '"Pictorial Lies"? Posters and Politics in Britain c.1880–1914'. *Past & Present* 197 (2007): 177–210.

Thompson, James. 'The Poster: Art, Advertising, Design and Collecting, 1860s–1900 (review)'. *Journal of the History of Collections* 29 (2017): 527–8.

Thomson, Mathew. *Psychological Subjects: Identity, Culture, and Health in Twentieth-Century Britain* (Oxford University Press, 2006).

Thornton, Sara. *Advertising, Subjectivity and the Nineteenth-Century Novel: Dickens, Balzac and the Language of the Walls* (Palgrave Macmillan, 2009).

Thurschwell, Pamela. *Literature, Technology, and Magical Thinking, 1880–1920* (Cambridge University Press, 2001).

Tickner, Lisa. *Modern Life and Modern Subjects: British Art in the Early Twentieth Century* (Yale University Press, 2000).

Timmers, Margaret, ed. *The Power of the Poster* (V&A, 1998).

Tolkien, J.R.R. *Tolkien on Fairy-stories*, edited by Verlyn Flieger and Douglas A. Anderson (HarperCollins, 2008).

Trentmann, Frank. *Empire of Things: How We Became a World of Consumers, from the Fifteenth Century to the Twenty-First* (Penguin, 2016).

Tungate, Mark. *Adland: A Global History of Advertising* (Kogan Page, 2013).

Turner, E.S. *The Shocking History of Advertising* (Penguin, 2012) (1952).

Twyman, Michael. *A History of Chromolithography: Printed Colour for All* (Oak Knoll Press, 2013).

Ueyama, Takahiro. *Health in the Marketplace: Professionalism, Therapeutic Desires, and Medical Commodification in Late-Victorian London* (The Society for the Promotion of Science and Scholarship, 2010).

Valverde, Mariana. *Everyday Law on the Street: City Governance in an Age of Diversity* (University of Chicago Press, 2012).

Vernon, James. *Distant Strangers: How Britain Became Modern* (University of California Press, 2014).

Vincent, David. *The Culture of Secrecy: Britain, 1832–1998* (Oxford University Press, 1999).

Vincent, David. *The Rise of Mass Literacy: Reading and Writing in Modern Europe* (Polity Press, 2000).

Waddington, Ivan. *The Medical Profession in the Industrial Revolution* (Gill and Macmillan, 1976).

Wadsworth, Alfred P. 'Newspaper Circulations 1800–1954'. In *Transactions of the Manchester Statistical Society 1954–1955* (1955).

Walkowitz, Judith R. *City of Dreadful Delight: Narratives of Sexual Danger in Late-Victorian London* (University of Chicago Press, 1992).

Waller, Philp. *Writers, Readers, and Reputations: Literary Life in Britain 1870–1918* (Oxford University Press, 2006).

Waterfield, Giles. *The People's Galleries: Art Museums and Exhibitions in Britain, 1800-1914* (Yale University Press, 2015).
Weber, Max. *From Max Weber: Essays in Sociology*, trans. and ed. H.H. Gerth and C. Wright Millis (n.p., 1946).
Wee, Allison. 'Trials and Eros: *The British Home Office v. Indecent Publications*, 1857-1932' (PhD diss., University of Minnesota, 2003).
Wicke, Jennifer A. *Advertising Fictions: Literature, Advertisement and Social Reading* (Columbia University Press, 1988).
Wiener, Joel H. *The Americanization of the British Press, 1830s-1914: Speed in the Age of Transatlantic Journalism* (Palgrave Macmillan, 2011).
Wiener, Martin J. *English Culture and the Decline of the Industrial Spirit, 1850-1980* (Penguin, 1985).
Williams, Raymond. 'Advertising: The Magic System'. In *Problems in Materialism and Culture* (Verso, 1980).
Williamson, Judith. *Decoding Advertisements: Ideology and Meaning in Advertising* (Marion Boyars, 1978).
Winter, Alison. *Mesmerized: Powers of Mind in Victorian Britain* (University of Chicago Press, 1998).
Winter, Sarah. *The Pleasures of Memory: Learning to Read with Charles Dickens* (Fordham University Press, 2011).
Wohlrab-Sahr, Monika. 'Disenchantment and Secularization: Narratives and Counter-Narratives'. In *Narratives of Disenchantment and Secularization: Critiquing Max Weber's Idea*, edited by Robert A. Yelle and Lorenz Trein (Bloomsbury Academic, 2020).
Woodward, William R. and Mitchell G. Ash. *The Problematic Science: Psychology in Nineteenth-Century Thought* (Praeger, 1982).
Wu, Tim. *The Attention Merchants: The Epic Struggle to Get Inside Our Heads* (Atlantic Books, 2017).
Yosifon, David G. 'Resisting Deep Capture: The Commercial Speech Doctrine and Junk-Food Advertising to Children'. *Loyola of Los Angeles Law Review* 39 (2006): 507-601.
Zieger, Susan. *The Mediated Mind: Affect, Ephemera, and Consumerism in the Nineteenth Century* (Fordham University Press, 2018).
Zipes, Jack. 'Introduction' to J.M. Barrie, *Peter Pan* (Penguin, 2013).

Index

Note: Figures are indicated by an italic '*f*' following the page number.

For the benefit of digital users, indexed terms that span two pages (e.g., 52–53) may, on occasion, appear on only one of those pages.

Indexed terms include references in the main text, and only occasionally textual discussion in footnotes.

Aberdeen, Lord 100
abortifacients 290–3, 292*f*, 305, 308
abortion 295–6, 295*f*, 306–10, 319
    anti-abortionists 296, 313, 319
abortion adverts 24, 265, 290–3, 292*f*, 295–6, 304–5, 308, 319
    and magical thinking in advertising 291–3
    campaign against 24, 265
    censors of 304–5
    Lancet series of articles about 295–6
    legal bases to stop 290–1
Addison, Joseph 214–15
Adorno, Theodor 14–15, 26, 48–9, 83, 88–90, 230–1
Advertise: How? When? Where? 154*f*
advertisements; *see* adverts.
Advertiser's Weekly 329–30, 337–8
Advertisers Exhibition 160*f*
Advertisers' Review 81*f*, 183–5, 340
advertising
    Advertising (journal) 260–1
    Advertising News 6*f*
    Advertising: The Magic System 13–14, 350
    Advertising World 82, 114–15, 125–6, 324, 334, 337, 349, 356–7
    aesthetics 150–92
    agencies 18–19, 108–9, 118–19, 125–6, 129–32, 140–3, 168*f*, 183–5, 260–1, 277, 320–1, 323, 325, 340–1
    American 17–18, 330, 356 (*see also* America)
    and attendant ridicule 10, 11, 24, 32, 238–45, 252–5, 260–2, 361
    (*see also* disparagement of, legal inferiorization of, degradation)
    and gambling 263–84
    and indecency 284–318
    Art of Advertising, Its Theory and Practice Fully Described 343*f*, 345
    Association of Advertising Women 349
    Business of Advertising 136*f*, 152*f*
    conceptualization of 11, 19, 95–8, 105–6, 108–10, 239–40, 326, 352–3
    disparagement of 10, 23, 25, 193, 261, 356
    (*see also* attendant ridicule, legal inferiorization of, inferiorization)
    ephemerality of 47, 68, 80, 83, 186–8
    literature 29, 113–14, 320–1, 327–8, 330, 332–4, 346–7, 350, 352–3
    mainstreaming of 10, 28, 32, 96, 138, 193, 236, 239, 244, 361 (*see also* legitimation)
    normalization of 25, 239 (*see also* legitimation)
    outdoor, and the legal transformation of space 139–50
    professional, theory of 316
    psychology of 324
    "system" 245*f*
adverts
    abortion 24, 265, 290–3, 292*f*, 295–6, 304–5, 308, 319
    "Advertisements Disguised as News" 109
    Advertisements Regulation Act (1907) 172–4, 181–2, 189–92
    Age of Advertisement 1, 42
    auction 241–2, 243*f*
    exhibition of 139, 156, 160*f*, 170–1, 174, 188, 192–3, 290–1, 311
    indecent, theory and analysis of 284, 309–10
    legal inferiorization of 11, 96, 238, 260, 356
    (*see also* disparagement of, attendant ridicule)
    Next-of-Kin advertisement 51*f*
    sex-related medical 9–10
    Zaeo 287–8, 287*f*
aesthetics
    advertising 150–92
    and commerce 173
    and economics, congruities between 183
    "bad" 155
    change 161–2
    commercial 182, 188
    concepts 181
    criticism 147–50

aesthetics (cont.)
  display 150–65
  hierarchy 23, 172–4
  hoardings 136
  motivations 174
  outlook 172
  poster 139, 165–72
  progress, concept of 321
  property 9, 22, 136–47, 150–64, 192–4, 289, 353–4
  public laws, hierarchy of 173
  rational 151–6
  reserve 182–3, 187
  responsibility 151–3
  values 182
  vulgar, vulgarity 148–9, 162, 288, 359
AIDA (Attention, Interest, Desire, Action) 330
Alexandra Theatre 289–90
Alverstone LCJ 213–14, 216–17, 228, 282–3
amenity 174–81
America, United States of 17–18, 33–4, 104, 210, 216, 238–9, 325, 330, 333–4, 356
Ampthill & District News 275f
Anderson, Benedict 45–6
Anti Corn Law League 98–9
anti-abortionists 296, 313, 319
Appadurai, Arjun 45–6
Arcades Project 17
Ardwall, Lord Ordinary 250f, 251–2
art 342–8
  and advertising 136
  and commerce, tension between 182–3
  exhibitions 153–5
Art Congress 147–8
Art of Advertising: Its Theory and Practice Fully Described 343f, 345
"Art of Puffing" 240
Artistic Hoardings Competition 159
Asprem, Egil 27–8
Association for the Promotion of the Repeal of the Taxes on Knowledge (APRTOK) 99
Association of Advertising Women 349
Athletic Journal 283–4
Athletic News 276
Atkinson, Lord 214
Australia 130, 248–51
Avory, Horace 63–4, 252–4, 274–5

Bakesh, Karim 231–2
Ballin, Ada 317–18
Bankes, John Eldon 216, 218–19
banned posters 288–9, 299, 300f, 311, 316–17
  (*see also* censorship)
Barclay v Pearson 273

Barratt, Thomas J. 165–7, 169
Barrie, James Matthew 224, 254
Bartrip, Peter 202
Basutoland 217
Bath Chronicle 59f, 67f
Baudrillard, Jean 14–15
Bayswater Omnibus 76–7, 76f
Beacon Hill 179f
Beardsley, Aubrey 185
Beautiful World 148
beauty 62, 69f, 74, 136–9, 148–50, 158–9, 172–83, 185–7, 191–4, 318, 351
  and amenity 174–81
  legislated ideals of 22, 137–8
  role in the nation's education 23
  social access to 22
Beckert, Jens 16–17
Bedean, Shahah 231–2
Beecham's Pills 224, 225f
Beggarstaffs, the 183–5
Belfast Morning News 55f
belief system, unified 35–6
Bell, Dr Robert 216–17
Bell, Karl 91–2
Benjamin, Walter 17, 40–1, 86–8
Bennett Harness, Cornelius 233f
Bennett, Jane 16–17, 46–9, 56, 66
Bennett, Tony 149
Benson, S.H. 168f
Benson's advertising agency 168f
Bently, Lionel 353–4
Benton, Joel 340
Bile Bean Manufacturing Co., Limited v Davidson case 248–52, 332
Bile Beans 219, 221f, 248–52, 249f, 250f, 253f, 332–3, 345
Billposter 136f, 155, 156f–164f, 183–5, 189–90, 187f–190f, 311–18, 342
Billposters Association 143
Billposters Censorship Committee 304f, 314f, 315f
billposting
  "artistic" 155
  companies 22, 137–8, 140, 146–7, 149–55, 161–2, 288–90
  fraternity 147–8
  illegal 144–5
  illegitimate 190f
  infrastructure of 153–5
  Newark Billposting Company 176–7
  professional 153–5
  trade and industry 22, 24, 136–8, 143–6, 148, 153–5, 157–8, 170–3, 182, 189–90, 288, 316–17, 322
  versus flyposting 139–47

INDEX 395

billstickers 136f, 139–40, 146–7, 156f–164f, 187f–190f
Binet, George 57–8, 59f
Birmingham 323
Birth of the Clinic 199
blackmail 293–6, 308
blasphemy 301–2
Blyth, Arthur 276–8
Boer War 114–15
Bolton Borough Police Court 170
boundary work 10–12, 20–2, 24–7, 30, 136–7, 173, 197, 203–5, 207, 210, 212, 214, 219, 227–8, 234, 236, 261–2, 318
"Bounties" (word game) 277–8
bourgeois 86–7, 182, 224–6
Bourneville 3–7
Bovril 140, 141f, 255, 256f
  Magic Lantern 140, 141f
Bow Street Police Court 252–4, 270
Bradford Club 158–9
Bradford Observer 102
brands and branding
  animistic power of 352–3
  brand memories 336
  brand names 3–7, 70, 87–8, 249–52, 255–7, 327–9, 335–6, 351–2
  endorsement of 114, 119, 127
  implications of 3–7, 39, 47–8
  loyalty to 220, 326, 327, 328, 336, 340
  scholarship on 37–8
  self-branding 320
  theory 337, 340, 353–4
Bridge, John 270–3, 287–8
Bright, John 98–9
Brinsmead (piano makers) 112–13, 115–19, 116f–117f
British Empire 248–9
British Medical Association (BMA) 202, 216–18, 224–6, 229–30
British Medical Journal (BMJ) 210–12, 234, 283–4
British Newspaper Archive (BNA) 7f, 241–2, 243f, 244–5, 245f, 310f
British Vacuum Cleaner Company 354, 355f
Bromley 176, 177f
Brompton Hospital for Consumptives 217
Brontë, Charlotte 49–50
Brown, Michael 202–3
Brown, William 309–11, 313–16
Browne, T.B. (Thomas Brook) 183–5, 343f
Bryce, James 148–9
Bubbles 76–7, 165–7, 167f, 169–72
Buckingham 114–15
Buckley, Lord 277
Burke, Thomas 46–7

Burn, James 49, 83
business identity, concept of 337
Business of Advertising 136f, 152f
bylaws 172–81, 178f–179f, 183, 186

Cambridge University 342
Caminada v Hulton 283–4
Campbell, Colin 13–17, 59–60, 90
Campbell, Lord 284–5
Canada 207–8
capitalism 12–18, 25–33, 44, 60–1, 65–6, 86–7, 92, 97, 106, 140, 146–7, 149, 156, 165–7, 237, 239–40, 261–2, 265–6, 268, 284, 319, 327, 331, 340–1, 356–7, 361
  advertisers as sorcerers of 29, 356–7
  advertising, socialist critics of 149
  and Marx's commodity fetishism 60–1
  as disenchanting force 12–13
  capitalist expansion 106
  capitalist experience and religion, competition between 44
  capitalist rationality, ideals of 268
  Protestant Ethic and the Spirit of Capitalism 12–13
consciousness 15–16, 66, 70, 82, 87, 291, 317, 323–5, 328, 330–1, 332, 342, 356
  legal (consciousness) 138, 161
  commercial press and the victory of 106
  consumer market, ideology of 331
  critical perspectives on 14–15
  culture of 11–12
Carbolic Smoke Ball Company 60, 219, 220f, 238–9, 246–8, 247f, 251–5
caricature 1–3, 8f, 71f, 121, 204–5, 205f, 232–3
Carlill v Carbolic Smoke Ball Company 60–1, 238–9, 241, 246–8, 251–5
Carlill, Louisa Elizabeth 246
Carlyle, Thomas 42–4, 74
Castle, Terry 78–9, 324
celebrities 202, 223, 337–8
censorship 9–10, 24, 98, 136–7, 265, 284–7, 289–90, 296, 299–302, 304f, 311, 313–19, 314f, 315f, 322, 351
  banned posters 288–9, 299, 300f, 311, 316–17
  Billposters Censorship Committee 314f, 315f
  censored posters 304f, 314f, 315f
  of abortion adverts, *see* abortifacients, abortion
  of gambling adverts, *see* gambling
  of indecent adverts, *see* indecency
  Poster Censorship Committee 289–90, 296–305, 311, 313–18
Central News Agency 124
chance, concept of 269–80, 341
Chancery Division 259, 273
Chancery, Court of 50

Charley's Aunt 169f
Charter, J.R. 334
Chartism 98–9
Chelsea Hospital for Women 114–15
Child's World 165
Chrimes brothers 293–6, 294f, 295f, 305, 308, 316–17
Chrimes, Edward 293
Chrimes, Leonard 293
Chrimes, Richard 293
Christian teaching 324–5
Churchill, Lady Randolph 58–9
Cinderella 104
Clancarty, Earl of 47–8, 105–6
Clarence Pier 121
Clark, Eleanor M. 348–9
class
 cross-class health consumers and market providers 32–3
 cross-class political agenda 98–9
 difference 146–7
 erasure of 55–6
 First Class (painting) 49
 governance 149
 identities, dominance of 203–4
 impact of 32–3
 interests, convergence of 149
 lower 1–3, 32–3, 49, 103, 149, 158–9, 266
 middle 1, 88, 96–7, 147–8, 267
 patronage 216, 223
 "poorer" 54–5
 prominence of 31
 ruling 223
 Second Class (painting) 49, 50f
 structures, traversing 49
 upper 35–6, 58–9, 235, 284–5
 working 351
Clay, William 104–5
Clifford, Kate 293–5
Cobden, Richard 98–9, 103
Cockburn, Alexander, LCJ 210, 229–30, 258–9, 284–5
Code of Medical Ethics 201
Collins, Wilkie 165–7
Colman's Mustard 338
Coming South 44–5
command, susceptibly to 325
commerce and art, tension between 182–3
commercial aesthetics 182, 188
commercial print, advances in 3–7
commercialization 3, 20–1, 25–6, 95–7, 108–10
commodity
 aesthetics 14–15
 culture 88

fetishism 14–15
communication media 96
competition 274
 law governing 241
competitions 41, 91, 170–1, 264–5, 267–73, 275–7, 283–4, 319
 limerick 275–6
 missing-word 270, 271f, 273, 277
Consumer Society, Birth of 240
consumerist model 223
consumption, mass 3, 241–2
contract
 and copyright, poster aesthetics 165–72
 breach of 9–10
 in courts 118, 123, 126, 144, 277, 305
 law of 9, 123, 238, 239, 241, 244, 246–8, 254, 255
 practice (contract in everyday life) 10, 22, 97, 107, 109, 115, 119, 134, 137–8, 143, 145, 153–5, 161–2, 165–72, 186, 268, 288, 360
Cook company 274–5
Coote, William 287
Corn Laws 99
Cornhill Magazine 87
Cornish, William 214
Court of Appeal 214, 218–19, 246, 259, 276, 280
Courtney, William 168, 351–2
Cox, Bingham 274
Crane, Walter 157–8
Crary, Jonathan 65–6, 90, 296, 332
cults, history of 14–15
cultural boundaries 20–7
 (see also boundary work)
cultural celebrities 337–8
culture
 British 263, 265, 319
 disenchanted 263–4
 enchanted, boundaries of gambling as 265
Curran, James 96–7
Curzon, Frank 121–2
Cvetkovich, Ann 296

Daily Chronicle 344–5
Daily Graphic 344–5
Daily Mail 56, 131–2, 344–5
Daily News 61–2, 98–9, 111, 118, 231
Daily Telegraph 107, 136–7, 207–8
Dakhyl v Labouchere 215–18, 228–30
Dakhyl, Hanna Nassif 213–15
Daley, Charlie 53
Daly, Nicholas 296
Daly's Theatre 169f
Dann, Thomas Lumley 123, 129

Darling, Charles, Judge 214–15, 269–70, 280, 283–4, 291–3, 305, 309–10
Daston, Lorraine 324–5, 346
Davidson, George Graham 248–9
Davies, Owen 16–17, 224–6
Day, Frederick 62–3
Debord, Guy 14–15
Deen, Khair 231–2
defamation 9–10, 203–4, 214
Degen, Florence A. 349–50
degradation 22, 173, 187, 193
Democracy and Liberty 150
Denmark, Princess of 114–15
dentists 202
Dickens, Charles 66, 104, 140, 189–90, 202–3
disenchantment 10–20, 25–8, 30, 33–4, 38–9, 46–7, 60–1, 78–9, 86, 261–2, 288, 318–19, 324–6, 359–61
 concept of 326
 modern, discourses of 318
 normative enterprise of 360
Dixon, David 266
Doctor's Dilemma (play) 227
Donizetti, Gaetano 204
Douglas, Mary 60–1
Dover 174
Dover Union Girls' School 170
Dr Vance's Prepared Food 257
Drouet Institute for the Deaf 213–15, 236
Drummond, Henry 105–6
Duffy, Charles Gavan 206–7
Duncannon, Lord 255

Eardley, Blanche 121–3
Earl, George 44–5, 45*f*, 45*f*
Easley, Alexis 68, 88
East Sheen 161*f*
economic competition, law governing 241
economics and aesthetics, congruities between 183
economy, British 263
Edinburgh Castle 174
Edinburgh Review 40–1
Edward Cook Company 121, 275*f*
Eiffel Tower Factory 114–15
Electropathic & Zander Institute 233*f*
Eliot, Simon 36
Elixir of Love (opera) 204
Emanuel, Alfred Borthwick 128–9
Empire, British 3, 33–4, 248–9, 252, 290
enchantment
 advertising, place in 284
 advertising, role in 24, 36
 and commercial entertainment, link between 301–2
 as daydreaming 59–60
 as expertise 316–18
 as professional brand 28–9
 attachments key to 56
 boundary 280
 bounded realms of 263
 by advertising 310–11
 conceptualization of 23, 236, 326
 contained 350–6
 disavowal of 11–12, 24, 27–30, 40, 93, 134–5, 193–4, 237, 239–40, 261–2, 284, 319, 325–6, 361
 discourses of 284
 enchanted culture, boundaries of gambling as 265
 enchanters, market 320, 358
 enchanting events 121
 enchanting system 361
 experiences of 77
 in poetic Romanticism 78–9
 legal conceptualization of 23
 locus of 45–6
 market, phenomenon of 325–6
 mass 263, 277
 modern 38–9, 49–50, 78–9
 psychologized version of 320–1
 reason and realism in 88–90
 role of 24, 36, 39, 318, 351
 significance of 36
 systemic association with 318–19
 theories of 263–5, 318–19
 traditional 44, 74, 341
 vocabulary of 274
 will to 35–6, 46–7, 360
 worlds of 280
Encyclopaedia Britannica 2, 105–6
Enlightened Economy 25
Enlightenment legacy 266
entertainment 3–7, 21, 27–8, 37–8, 267–8, 289, 301–2, 311
ephemerality 46–7, 68, 80, 83, 186–9
Era 111–12, 117*f*
ethics 25–6, 52, 195, 324–5
 Code of Medical Ethics 201
 codes 9–10, 196–7, 201
 education 148–9
 medical 23, 196–7, 201, 210, 223, 237
 Protestant 266
Protestant Ethic and the Spirit of Capitalism 12–13
Romantic Ethic and the Spirit of Modern Consumerism 13–14

398 INDEX

ethics (cont.)
  transgressions 202
  work 344f
European revolutions 98–9
Evans, Richardson 148
Evening News 56, 94f
Evesham 179–81, 180f, 181f
Ewart, William 78, 105
Ewen, Stuart 15–16, 356
exaggeration 23, 32, 33 133, 195–237, 238-62
exaggeration as doctrine 238
Exeter and Plymouth Gazette 51f
exhibition of adverts 139, 156, 160f, 170–1, 174, 188, 192–3, 290–1, 311
exoticism 3, 52, 199, 217, 234–5, 251–2
expertise, idea and theory of 316–17, 320–58

Fabian, Ann 266
Fables of Abundance 17–18
"faddists" 172–3
fantasy 12–14, 22, 35–8, 50, 56, 59–64, 68–70, 78–9, 82, 84–5, 88–92, 199, 236–7, 284–5, 291, 316
Farnsworth model 182
female
  medicine 305, 308–10, 310f
  power 349
feminization 349–50
Fielding, Henry 240
First World War 20–1, 29, 34, 39, 95–6, 114–15, 352–3
Fitz-Gibbon, Desmond 241–2
flyposting 139–47, 150–1, 153–5, 171–2, 189–90, 289–90
Force in Advertising 168f
force, vocabularies of 348
Forde, Charles 249–50
forgery, patent medicine 95
Foucault, Michel 199, 231, 291
Fourth Estate 107
Fox Talbot, William Henry 150–1, 151f
France 129–30
fraud 58–60, 77–8, 95, 109, 123, 126–8, 133–4, 196–7, 218, 227–8, 231–6, 240–2, 249–54, 291–3, 322
  cases 9–10, 36–7, 58–60, 126–7, 203, 227–8, 231, 233–4
  litigation 23, 196–7
  proceedings, patients in 231–6
free will, ideals of 87, 269, 324–5, 331–2
Freedberg, David 193–4
Freeman's Journal 232f
free-market ideologies 202–3
Freud, Sigmund 15–16

Freudian psychoanalysis 324
Fritzsche, Peter 46–7
From Pentonville Road Looking West: Evening 42–4, 43f
Frye, Northrop 26
Fulford Ltd 332–3
Fulford, Charles Edward 248–9

Galbraith, Ken 329–30
Gale's Topic Finder 251f
Galison, Peter 346
gambling 7–10, 21, 263–319
  and advertising 264–84
  anti-gambling law 24
  as enchanted culture, boundaries of 265
  theory of 283–4
  concept of 341
  illegitimate 280–1
  legal definition of 318–19
  National Anti-Gambling League 275–6, 283–4
Geisha 169f
gender 16, 17, 31–3, 39–40, 48, 54–5, 61–2, 68–70, 91, 121, 148, 246, 296, 319, 333, 348–50
General Council of Medical Education and Registration (GMC) 195, 202
Gent, Stephen 63–4
George V 114–15
Gibson, Thomas Milner 98–9, 101–2
Gieryn, Thomas 10, 197
Gilbert, Ernest Albert 248–9
Ginzburg, Carlo 80
Gissing, George 42–4
Gladstone, William 100, 103, 335
Glasgow Herald 112
Gloxiensis and Corassa Compound 234–5
Goethe, Johann Wolfgang von 337–8
Going North 44–5, 45f
Good Boy Seldom: A Romance of Advertisement 41, 44, 275, 298, 327, 328, 338, 347, 350, 359–61
Goodall, G.W. 296, 313
Graphic 116f, 118
Great Libel Case 209
Great White Horse Hotel 191f
Greenberg, Clement 7–9
Greenhalgh, James 144, 147–8
Grimsby 164f
Guffey, Elizabeth 150–1
"guilty knowledge" 231
Gurney, Peter 149

Habermas, Jürgen 96–7
Hall, Henry 274

Halley, George 84–5, 84f
Hammersmith Police Court 170
Hanford, Charles 85f
Hannay J 234
Hardy, Dudley 169f, 185
Harmsworth, Alfred 131–2
Harness, Cornelius Bennett 234
Hassall, John 354
Haug, Wolfgang Fritz 14–15
Hawke, John 275–6
Hawkins, William Henry 235f, 248, 281, 293–5
health consumerism 23, 32–3, 197
Henkin, David 157–8
Herkomer, Hubert 167
Herschell 259–60
Hewitson, Anthony 128–9
Hewitt, Francis 120
Hewitt, Martin 98–9
Hicklin case 24, 284–6
Hickman, Timothy 216
High Court 146, 218, 248, 273–4, 282–4
Hill, Walter 289–90
Hirschman, Albert 284, 325
Hirst, Stuart 332–3, 345
hoardings
　acceptance in urban landscapes 182–3
　advocacy for 153–5
　aesthetics of 136–94
　Artistic Hoardings Competition 159
　as contained space manifesting borders 193
　as exhibition 156
　as "galleries of the people" 151–3
　competitors 189–92
　regulation of 181–2
Holyoake, George J. 103
Home Office 172–81, 178f, 208–9, 269–70, 295–6
Horkheimer, Max 14–15, 26, 48–9, 83, 88–90, 231
Horwich 157f
Hospital (periodical) 202–3
hospitals 54–5, 114–15, 195, 217, 219–23, 231
House of Lords 214, 259
Household Words 140
Hull 289–90
Hull Daily Mail 278f
Hulton press 283
Hulton, Edward 276–8, 283
Hume, Joseph 104
Hunter v Sharpe 207–13, 217, 228–30
Hyde, Timothy 148
hypnotism 313, 324, 332, 337–8

Ibbetson, David 255
iconography 70
Ideal Home exhibition 91
Ideas (newspaper) 276
identities, conjured 306–7
Illustrated Chips 62f
Illustrated London News 4f, 5f, 118, 211f, 292f
Illustrated Police News 85f, 306f
Illustrated Sporting and Dramatic News 200f
imagination 10–11, 13–15, 19, 22, 35–6, 40–1, 45–9, 52–3, 59–61, 63–5, 68–70, 77–83, 86–7, 90–2, 97, 104–5, 172, 192–3, 199–201, 236–7, 239–40, 242–5, 260, 286, 291–3, 299–301, 310–11, 313–17, 329, 337–8, 345, 348, 350–1, 353–4, 359–61
In the Year of Jubilee 42–4
Incorporated Society of Advertisement Consultants 112–13
indecency 7–10, 263, 284–318
Indecent Advertisements Act (1889) 287–8, 290–1, 293–6
indecent adverts, analysis of 309–10
individualism 22, 104, 357
　law, role in history of 29–30
industrial revolution 3
industrialization 175, 208
Industry and Trade 341–2
infant mortality 317–18
inferiorization 11–12, 96–7, 238, 260, 356
influenza 246–8, 255, 256f
information, concept of 22, 25, 39, 87, 95–135, 237, 318, 321–2, 342, 353, 359
Inland Revenue, Board of 99
insecurity 348–50
instincts 325
Institute of Advertising Professionals 74f
Institute, Drouet 236
intellectualization 86, 170–1
Invisible Elevators advertisement 62f
Ipswich 189–90, 191f
Ireland 175, 206, 216
Irish High Court 206
Irish News 55f
Irish Times 188
Isherwood, Baron 60–1
Iskin, Ruth 76–7, 165

Jack the Ripper 124
Jackson's Oxford Journal 292f
Jane Eyre 49–50, 64–5
Jekyll and Hyde 198–203
Jewson, Nicholas 219–23
John Bull 118
Jones v Bright case 246
Jones, Griffiths 82
Josephson-Storm, Jason 27–8, 324

journalism 67–8, 125, 127, 133–4, 270
  ideals of 125
  independence of 127
  journalists 8f, 48–9, 97, 124, 128–9, 168, 316–17
  New Journalism 108, 114, 123, 130
  values, place in 133–4
Joy, George William 76–7, 76f
Joyce, James 354–6
Judy 122f, 132–3
jurisprudence 197–8, 247–8
  Medical Jurisprudence 201, 231

Keeper of Fine Art Collection 165–7
Keighley 156f
Kensington 157
Kingsburgh, Lord Justice Clerk 251–2
Knaresborough Post 256f
knowledge
  concept of 321
  taxes on 21–2, 97–101, 111
Kodak 118–19, 337

Labouchere, Henry 107, 213–16, 228, 275–6
Lady Montrose Pills 293
Lady's Newspaper and Pictorial Times 101–2
Lamb, Charles 95
Lancet 211, 215–16, 218–19, 229, 293–6, 305–11, 313–16
Landy, Joshua 16–17, 28
Language of the Walls 49, 83
language, conceptual, loss of 181–9
languages, gendered 348
Larkin, Michael 206–7, 230
Larkin case 211–12, 214–15, 229–30
Latour, Bruno 61, 308
Law Times 93, 209, 275
law, -s 25–33 (*see also* consciousness (legal); legality; reforms; regulation)
  administrative 9–10, 172, 175–89
  aesthetic hierarchy of 173
  American legal contexts 238–9
  and advertising aesthetics 150–92
  anti-gambling 24
  bylaws 172–81, 178f–179f, 183, 186
  capitalism, role in history of 29–30
  centrality of 360
  competition 241
  contract 238, 241 (*see also* contract, contracts)
  Corn Laws 98–9
  criminal 9–10, 36–7, 48, 64, 93, 144–5, 225, 231–6, 238, 241, 267, 270–3, 290–1, 294–5, 304–10 (*see also* fraud)

  cultural theory of 30
  indencency, *see* indecency, regulation
  on lotteries 263–84 (*see also* gambling)
  Poor Law 170
  private, and advertising aesthetics 150–72
  property 9, 22, 136–47, 150–64, 192–4, 289, 353–4
  public 22, 137–8, 172–93
  tort, torts 9, 144, 203–31, 238, 248–52, 257–61 (*see also* libel)
  trademark, trademarks 20, 47, 238, 241, 244, 353–4
Lawson, Edward L. 107
Le Télémaque 52–3
Lear, Edward 275
Lears, Jackson 17–18, 45–6, 200–1, 354–6
Leavis, F.R. 14–15
Lecky, William 148–50
Leeds Laboratory Co. 277, 278f
legality 10, 31, 261, 360
legitimation 22–4, 31–2, 34, 132, 238, 263–4 (*see also* advertising- mainstreaming of, normalization of)
Leicester Daily Post 120
Leiss, William 39
leisure, commercialization of 3
Lemco 56, 91
Lever Brothers 114–15
Lever, William H. 159
Lewis, E. St. Elmo 330
libel 9–10, 23, 196–7, 203–19, 227–33, 236, 246, 259
liberalism 11, 22, 108, 111, 129
  secular religion of 15–18
  social aims of 27
  status of art in 165–7
Liebig 56
Liebig advertisement 58f
Liebig, Justus Freiherr von 257
limericks 277–8
Lincoln 281
Lindley, judge 247–8, 259
Linstrum, Erik 334–5
litigation 23, 109, 126, 196–7, 204, 214, 246, 264–5, 270, 271f
Liverpool Mercury 103
Loeb, Lori 234
London 1, 36–7, 44, 51f, 54–5, 68, 76–7, 82, 91–3, 103, 105–7, 109, 120, 129–30, 136–7, 140, 146–7, 160f, 168, 186, 187f, 188, 191–2, 216, 241–2, 267, 274, 287f, 351
  Aquarium 115, 287
  Building Act (1894) 186

INDEX 401

Proprietary Articles Section of the Chamber of Commerce (PATA) 195
City Council 287–8, 287f
City of 36–7, 125–6
Committee for Obtaining the Repeal of the Advertisement Duty 98–9
County Council 93
East End 124
Illustrated News 4f, 5f, 118, 165–7, 211f, 292f
Royal Aquarium 287–8
School of Economics 112–13
Sky-Signs Prohibition Act (1891) 191–2
Street Scene 150–1, 153f
Tea Supply Association 281–2
Victorian London Street Life in Historic Photographs 8f
Loreburn, Lord 214
lotteries 277, 279–81 (*see also* gambling)
  illegal 270, 281
  law on 263–84
  Select Committee on 269
Lush J, judge 277–8, 280
Luton Council 93

Madame Frain's Female Pills 309
Magazine of Art 167
magic, magical 10, 12–29, 37–93, 206–7, 226, 236, 264–6, 293, 320–7, 340–58
  element 90
  formulas 14–15
  imagination in modernity 91–2
  lantern 46, 48, 79, 140, 141f
  power of 224–6
  "system" 13, 39, 60–1
  systems 13–14, 17–18, 39, 60–1
  theories of 64–5
Malefyt, Timothy de Waal 17–18, 344–5
Malinowski, Bronislaw 64–5
Malvery, Olive 67–8
Manby Smith, Charles 140
Mansfield, Lord 240
Margate, map of 176f
marketing, legal doctrine dedicated to 239–40
marketization 182–3, 218–19
Markham, Joseph 53
Marlborough Police Court 234
Marshall, Alfred 341–2
Martineau, Harriet 66
Marx, Karl 14–15, 60–1
Masterman, Charles Frederick Gurney 267–8
Mather & Crowther 338, 339f, 344f, 345
Mazzarella, William 16–17
McCarraher, Eugene 12–13, 17, 78–9, 337
McClintock, Anne 333–4

McFall, Liz 39
McKendrick, Neil 240
McLaren, Angus 308–10
McLuhan, Marshall 42
Meath, Earl of 290–1
medical
  ethics 23, 196–7, 201, 210, 223, 237
  formula as trade secret 224
  Jurisprudence 201, 231
  Medical Act (1858) 195, 212, 214
  Medical Battery Company 233–4
  products 21, 195–237, 246–61
  provision, regulation of 197–8
  treatment, free 231
medicine
  and quackery 195–237, 246–61
  British, historiography of 196
  ethical and legal authority over 195
  female 305, 308–10, 310f
  empty 224–6, 236, 308
  proprietary 195, 197–8
Meerloo, Annie 333, 349–50
Mellin's Airship 200f
Mellin, Gustav 200–1, 257–61
Mellin's Food 157–8, 200f, 219, 222f, 258f
mesmerism 324
Metropolitan Police Act (1839) 139–40
Middlesex 36–7
Mill, John Stuart 255–7
Millais, John Everett 76–7, 165–7, 167f
mind, study of 320–58
mind, theory of 12, 29, 134, 263, 284–6, 313, 318, 320–58
miracles 24, 35–6, 64–5, 261–2
  mundane 35–6
  transformative 24, 261–2
misrepresented wares and services 9–10
missing-word competitions 270, 271f, 273, 277
modernity
  as disenchantment 10–12, 359–60
  capitalist, system of 11–12
  magical imagination in 91–2
  paradigms of 7–11
Moeran, Brian 17–18, 344–5
Mokyr, Joel 25
Monthly Journal for Every Advertiser 125–6
Moody's advertising agency 323
morality 7–11, 20–1, 24, 28–9, 148–50, 202–3, 210, 287, 321
Moran, Clarence 136f, 152f
Moretti, Franco 14–15
Morgan, David 16–17, 88–90
Morning Post 66, 118, 207–8
Moross, Dr Edward 235

Morris v Brinsmead 115–20
Morris, William 147–8, 337–8
Morrison, Kevin 224–6
Morton, William 289–90
Mowrer, Edgar 14–15
Muir, Richard 293–5
Münsterberg, Hugo 337
Music Hall Committee 287–8
mystery, mysterious 10, 12, 13, 15, 19, 35–6, 38, 46, 57–9, 80, 83, 86, 207, 209, 240, 324, 327, 338, 340, 341, 346

Nation (newspaper) 206–7, 229–30
National Advertising Society 349
National Anti-Gambling League (NAGL) 267, 275–6, 283–4
National Gallery 153–5
National Society for Checking the Abuses of Public Advertising (SCAPA) 136–7, 148–50, 171–4, 186, 188–90, 193–4
National Vigilance Association (NVA) 115, 287–8, 299–301
nature and culture, beauty and amenity 174–81
Nead, Lynda 188–9, 284–5
Nelson's Column 150–1, 151*f*
Nestlé 301, 303*f*, 351–2, 352*f*
Nevett, Terry 129, 196
New Journalism 108, 114, 123, 130
New York 207–8
Newark 176
　Billposting Company 176–7
　Council of 179*f*
　draft bylaws 178*f*, 179*f*
Newcastle Guardian 103
News Agent and Booksellers Review 157–8
news and advertising 94
newspapers
　circulations 106–7
　independence of 125, 127
　Newspaper Society 95–6, 109, 111–13, 125, 130–1, 236, 293–5, 309–10
　Newspaper Stamp Abolition Committee (NSAC) 98–9
　owners, financial interests and political aspirations of 107–8
　provincial 106–7
　taxes on 95–8, 100, 104, 106–7, 112
Newton, Alderman 293–5
Next-of-Kin agencies 51–2, 51*f*, 68
Niagara Hall 156, 160*f*
Nicholson, John 236
Nicholson, William 183–5
Nonconformist Protestant Churches 267
Norris, Arthur 8*f*

Nottingham 164*f*
novelty 46–7, 65–6, 186, 333

O'Connor, John 42–4, 43*f*, 74
O'Hagan, Thomas 206–7, 214–15
O'Reilly, Walter 35–6
Obscene Publications Act (1857) 284–5
occultism 27, 52, 54–5, 78–9
Offences Against the Person Act of (1861) 290–1
Old Bailey 36–7, 126, 231–2, 309–11, 316–17
Old Trafford 276
Oldham council 289–90
Olympic Theatre 165
Onions, Oliver 41–2, 44, 53–5, 74, 298, 327–9, 347–8, 350, 359–61
Osborne, J.H. 260–1
Owen v Greenberg 305
Owen, Alex 78–9, 323–4
Owen, Edward 305
Oxo 91

Packard, Vance 15–16
Pall Mall Gazette 87, 209, 211*f*, 229–30, 246, 247*f*
Palmer Tyre Company 349
Palmer, H. James 110, 129–30
Paris, University of 213
parks
　and promenades 176
　Movement 175
　public 175
Parry, John Orlando 150–1, 153*f*
Parry, Jonathan 99
patients
　and medical provider, relationship between 223
　in fraud proceedings 231–6
　in libel proceedings 228–31
　testimonies of 228
patriarchal traditions 290
Paynter, Frederick 55*f*, 55
Pears Ltd 73*f*, 165–7, 167*f*, 336*f*, 336
Pearson, Arthur 270, 273–4
Pearson's Weekly 271*f*, 275–6
Penny Illustrated Paper 64*f*, 84*f*, 123, 128*f*
Percival, Thomas 201
Peter Pan 224–6, 252–4
Pharmacopoeia 198–9
Pharmacy Act (1868) 224–6
Phillimore, Catherine 80
Phillips, Frederick 226
Pick, Daniel 291, 327
Pick-Me-Up (newspaper) 63*f*, 270, 305
Pickwick Papers 189–90
Pink Pills for Pale People 248–9

INDEX   403

Placard 158*f*, 159*f*
Pointing, Arthur Lewis 61–5, 62*f*–64*f*, 252–5
Poisons and Pharmacy Act (1908) 224–6
Poor Law Schools 170
population growth 3, 195
Port Sunlight 3–7
Porten, Lili 56
Porter, Roy 198–9, 203–4, 224–6, 236–7
Post Office 275–6
posters
   aesthetics, history of 139
   "artistic" 165, 171–2, 185, 192–3
   banned 288–9, 299, 300*f*, 311, 316–17
   censored 300*f*, 302*f*, 315*f*
   "craze" 188
   images, "hypnotic influence" of 332
   lithographic, image-centred 143
   Poster Censorship Committee 289–90,
      296–305, 311, 313–18
   Poster Fiend 188
   Poster, Age of 137–8
   Posters Condemned 304*f*, 311–13, 315*f*
Potter, Simon 120
Powney, R.T. 154*f*
Practical Advertising 339*f*, 344*f*
Press
   British, professionalization of 108–9
   commercial 94–135
   free 107–10
Preston Chronicle 128–9
Price, Julius 185
Prince of Wales theatre 121
prizes 3–7, 24, 29, 52, 78, 84–5, 84*f*, 91, 159,
   183–5, 236, 264–5, 267–70, 274–7,
   280–4, 319
professional ideal, in search of 124–34
professionalization 20, 29, 39, 108–10, 132, 137,
   320–1
Progressive Advertising 142*f*
prohibition, -s 9–10, 198–9, 201–3, 240, 265–6,
   268, 285–6, 301–2, 319
   London Sky-Signs Prohibition Act
      (1891) 191–2
Proprietary Articles Section of the London
   Chamber of Commerce (PATA) 195
Protestant Electoral Union 284–5
Protestant ethic 12–13, 266
Protestant Ethic and the Spirit of
   Capitalism 12–13
Pryde, James 183–5
psychology
   advances in 350
   as scientific ally 342–3
   emergence as independent discipline 323–4
   in advertising 29, 39, 237, 291, 298, 318,
      320–58
   influence of 325–6
   of publicity 335
   psychological effects 327–9
   psychological topics 325
   Psychology of Advertising 324
puffery
   and quackery 246–61
   "Art of Puffing" 240
   as legal concept 241, 261
   definition of 240
   doctrine of 23–4, 238, 240–6
   language of 241
   legal formalization of 245
   legal use of 241–2
   "paragraph" 117*f*
   ridicule in 244, 255–7
   "system" 244–5, 245*f*
Punch 8*f*, 102, 112*f*, 205*f*, 272–3, 296, 297*f*
Pygmalion 55

quacks and quackery 23, 195–237, 246–61,
   306
   advertisers 277
   adverts 245
   and the doctrine of puffery 246–55
   as term of abuse 203–4, 206
   business model 224
   campaign against 290
   caricature of 232–3
   etymology of 214–15
   in popular culture 204
   medicine 246, 248–9, 254–5
Quaker Oats 71*f*
Queens Gardens 176
Qureshi, Sadiah 150–1

Racing Record 283
Ransom, Sidney Lewis 299–301
rationalization 86, 342–3
Reading Experience Database 36
reading modes 38, 65–6
Reasoner (periodical) 103
Redhill 160*f*
reforms
   administrative 172
   aesthetic 322
   financial and electoral reform 98–9
   legal 188
   legislative 138–9, 172, 192–3
   moral 263
   rising tide of 284
   tax 9–10, 98–9, 104, 113, 134

regulation
    advertising 9–10
    of obscene and indecent print 284
    self regulation 10, 290, 296
Reichert, Henry 270–3
Reith, Gerda 266
religion, religious 1, 7, 13–16, 18, 20, 27–8, 42, 44, 46, 74, 92, 101, 149, 263, 266, 268, 284–5, 291, 296, 301–2, 319, 341
rent
    display aesthetics 150–65
    legal rights to 155
repetition, effects of 337
resistance 329–40
Reuter, Baron de 130–1
Reuters 130–1, 133–4
Revenue 111–13, 126–7
Rhead, Louis 183–5
Richards, Albert Edward 235
Richards, Thomas 17–18
Richardson, Megan 353–4
Rickards, Maurice 300*f*
ridicule 10–12, 24, 32, 104, 224–6, 238–40, 244–5, 252–7, 260–2, 269–70, 272–3, 361
    legal mode of 238–9
    logic of 255–61
Ridley J 216, 229, 293–5
Ritzer, George 15–18
Roberts, Frank H. 310*f*, 312*f*
Rocket 274
Roe, Frederick Augustus 246, 252
Rogers, W.S. 171
Romance of the People's Picture Gallery 168, 351–2
Romantic Ethic and the Spirit of Modern Consumerism 13–14
Romanticism 78–9
Rotary Illuminated Advertising 6*f*
Rowntree 91, 183–5, 184*f*
Royal Academy 169
Royal College of Physicians 202, 211
Royal Cornwall Gazette 294*f*
Royal George, wreck of 114–15
Ruskin, John 337–8
Russell and Sons 200*f*
Russell, John 98–9
Russell, Thomas 112–13, 133–4, 244, 329
Rymer, Chadwick 169*f*

Saler, Michael 16–17, 28, 57–9, 78–80
sales
    paradigm 327–9
    pitch 238
Samalin, Zachary 148, 188
Sambourne, Linley 204, 205*f*, 232–3

Sampson, Henry 55
Samuel, Herbert 189
satire and caricature 1–3
Saturday Review 119–20, 123
Saundby, Robert 201–2, 223
SCAPA, *see* National Society for Checking the Abuses of Public Advertising
Schlesinger, Max 1
Schudson, Michael 356–7
Schwarzkopf, Stefan 86–7, 352–3, 357
Schweppes 114–15
science 342–8
    and advertising 195–237
    relationship with advertising 23
scientific progress 11–12, 212, 306–7
Scotland 175
Scotland Yard 124
Scott v Director of Public Prosecutions 278–80
Scott, Walter Dill 324, 337
scrapbooks 68–70, 73*f*–76*f*, 74, 88, 89*f*
Seaton, Jean 96–7
Sechehaye, Adrein 218
Second Class—the parting 50*f*
secrecy as crucial for big business 224
Secret Remedies 217, 224, 226
Select Committee on Lotteries and Indecent Advertisements 263, 269
Select Committee on Patent Medicines 197–8, 218, 224, 252
self-branding 320–58, 361
Selfridge, Gordon, Selfridge's 127, 128*f*, 333, 337
Sell, Henry 113–14, 327–8
semiotics 15–16
sex and advertising 9, 71*f*, 284, 285–8, 290–1, 295–6, 298, 301, 306, 348
sexual promiscuity 285–6
sexualized images 71*f*
Shah, Heere 231–2
Shaw, George Bernard 55–6, 227
Shearman J 218, 228–30
Sheldon, Cyril 144, 155, 161–2, 185, 299, 311–13
Sheldon, Edward 144
Siegel, Jonah 359
Simmel, Georg 65–6, 331–2
Simpson, Brian 60, 246–8, 252
Simpson, John 281
Simpson, Joseph 187
Sinclair, Alexander 112
Singer Manufacturing Company 6*f*
skill (versus chance) 269–80
Skipton 162*f*
Smith, Adolphe 8*f*
Smith, George 87–8, 211
Smith, Thomas 260–1

Smith, W.H. 331–2
Smith, William 151–3, 154f
Smith's Advertising Agency 277
social
   debate 1–3
   domain 340–50
   engineering 325
   Social Communication in Advertising 39
Solomon, Abraham 49–50, 50f
Sontag, Susan 182–3, 185
South Africa 114–15, 217
South Kensington Museum 165–7
Southsea 121
Speaight, F. and R. 114–15
Spencer, Stanley 200–1
Sphinx Club 351, 354
Spielmann, Marion 165, 167
Sporting Chronicle 276, 283
Sporting Luck 283–4
St Stephen's Review 287f
Stage 289–90
Stamp Act (1712) 98
Standard 207–8
Star 115, 207–8
stationery shops 195
statistical awareness 228
Stead Jr, William 106–7
Stead, William 343f
Stebbings, Chantal 197–8, 203–4
Steegman, John 147
Stephenson, Augustus K. 270, 273–4
Stephenson, Guy 291–3
Stevens, Charles Henry 217–19
Stevens case 228–31, 234–5
Stonehaven Journal 235f
stories, fabricated 124–5
Stormonth-Darling, Lord 252
Strand Magazine 80, 81f
Struggles of Brown, Jones and Robinson 146
Styrap, Jukes 201–2
suggestibility 284, 291, 325
Sully, James 324–5, 337
Sumner, Fred 351–2, 354–6
Sunday Chronicle 276
Sunny Jim 351, 354–6
supernatural 10–11, 45–6, 48–9, 55, 70, 80, 92, 324
Sussex Drug Company 95

tax
   American system 104
   campaign against 97–8, 111, 113–14, 134
   indirect 100
   on advertising 21–2, 97–104, 111
   on editorials that endorsed brands 126–7

on "free speech" 102
on knowledge 21–2, 97–101, 111
on newspapers 95–8, 100, 104, 106–7, 112
on proprietary medicines 197–8
reform 113, 134
Taylor v Smetten 281
Taylor, Charles 324
Taylor, James 156, 182, 188
testimonials 219–36, 220f, 221f, 222f, 232f
   and knowledge of the body 219–28
   consumer 196–7
Thackeray, William 48
Thirty Club 346
Thomas, Julian 353–4
Thompson, Craig 68–70
Thompson, Denys 14–15
Thomson, John 8f
Thomson, Mathew 331
Thurschwell, Pamela 313
Tidy, Charlotte 80–2
Times 40–1, 52–3, 66, 105, 112–13, 115, 118–19, 130–4, 132f, 207–8
Tit Bits 270
Tolkien, J.R.R. 60
Tono-Bungay 77–8, 199–201, 224, 236–7, 347
Trade Marks Registration Act (1875) 353–4
tradenames 47–8, 91, 251–2
Trafalgar Square 150–1, 151f
transformation 3, 35–6, 52, 161–2
   achieved by advertisement 56
   in doctor–patient relations 219–23
   magical 19
   miraculous 45–6, 252–4
   of advertising by psychology 325
   of commerce 172–3
   of space 139–50, 165
   personal and environmental 49
   possibilities of 35–6
treasure hunts 52–6, 58–9, 78, 90–3, 123, 131–2
Trentmann, Frank 3, 13–14
Tribune 132–3
Trollope, Anthony 146
tropes, advertising 1–3
Truth (journal) 107, 213, 236
tuberculosis 208, 217–18
Tucker v Wakley 216
Tucker, Augustus 216
Tucker case 229
Turf Life 283–4

Ueyama, Takahiro 236–7
unconscious 34, 335, 338, 342, 346, 356
unconscious association 325

United Billposters Association, Censorship Committee of 304*f*, 314*f*–315*f*
urbanity 11–12, 137–8, 181–9
urbanization 40–1, 187, 193, 208, 296

Vagrancy Acts 284
values 21, 25–7, 182, 323, 357
   aesthetic 173, 182
   bourgeoisie 182
   economic-exchange 242–3
   educational 148–9
   imaginative 16–17
   journalism, relative place in 133–4
   of domesticity 333–4
   of information, beauty, and scientific knowledge 318
   of progressive modernity 25
   of the Industrial Enlightenment 25
   rationalist 10–11, 26, 325–6, 359
   saleable 360
   value systems 11–12
Vaughan v Johnson 230
Vernon, Charles 183, 185–6, 338
Vernon, James 40–1
Victoria & Albert Museum 165–7
Victorian era 98, 201
Victorian London Street Life in Historic Photographs 8*f*
volition 87–8, 264, 269, 320–1, 324–5, 331

Wakefield Herald 128–9
Wakley, Thomas 216
Wales 208
Walker, Frederick 165–7, 166*f*
Walkowitz, Judith 290–1
Wallis, Dorothy 42
Wallis, George 165–7
wants, communication of 100–7

Waterhouse, Alfred 148
Weber, Max 10–17, 27–8, 78–9, 86
Weekly Dispatch 52–3, 53*f*, 90, 57*f*, 123
   treasure hunt 52–3, 56, 123
Weekly Telegraph 282
Wells, Charles 80
Wells, H.G. 56, 77–8, 199–201, 236–7, 347–8
Welsford, Ernest 53
Westham Police Court 274–5
Westminster County Court 123
White v Mellin case 255–8
White, Timothy 257, 259
White, Watson, Morris, and Shand 260
Whorlow, Henry 109, 112–15, 118, 120–1, 126–7, 129–32, 293–5
Wicke, Jennifer 357
William Henry Hawkins 234–5
Williams, Lord Vaughan 268, 277–8
Williams, Raymond 13–15, 39, 60–1, 350
Williamson, Judith 15–16
William-Stubbs, Frederick 95
Wolverhampton 284–5
Woman in White 165–7, 166*f*, 171–2
women's advertising work 349–50
word games 278–9
Worrall, G.E. 349
Worship Street Police Court 309
Wu, Tim 357–8

Yendis, Mosnar 299–301, 302*f*
York Herald 111
Yorkshire Post 110

Zaeo 287–8, 316–17
   adverts 287–8, 287*f*
   scandal 287–9
Zieger, Susan 42